TAALGIDSEN VAN BERLITZ

Internationaal bekende taalgidsen met een schat aan woorden en zinnen, een grote woordenlijst en nuttige wenken en een fonetische spelling. Gemakkelijk in het gebruik.

De volgende titels zijn verkrijgbaar:

Engels
Amerikaans-Engels
Frans
Grieks

Russisch
Portugees
Russisch
Spaans

CASSETTES VAN BERLITZ

De meeste hierboven genoemde titels zijn eveneens verkrijgbaar in combinatie met tweetalige cassettes die u aan een goede uitspraak zullen helpen. Bij de cassettes ingesloten vindt u de complete tekst in twee talen van alle opgenomen woorden en zinnen.

Berlitz Dictionaries

Dansk
Engelsk, Fransk, Italiensk, Portugisisk, Serbo-Kroatisk, Spansk, Tysk

Deutsch
Dänisch, Englisch, Finnisch, Französisch, Italienisch, Niederländisch, Norwegisch, Portugiesisch, Schwedisch, Serbokroatisch, Spanisch

English
Danish, Dutch, Finnish, French, German, Italian, Norwegian, Portuguese, Serbo-Croatian, Spanish, Swedish

Español
Alemán, Danés, Finlandés, Francés, Holandés, Inglés, Noruego, Servocroata, Sueco

Français
Allemand, Anglais, Danois, Espagnol, Finnois, Italien, Néerlandais, Norvégien, Portugais, Serbo-Croate, Suédois

Italiano
Danese, Finlandese, Francese, Inglese, Norvegese, Olandese, Serbo-Croato, Svedese, Tedesco

Nederlands
Duits, Engels, Frans, Italiaans, Joegoslavisch, Portugees, Spaans

Norsk
Engelsk, Fransk, Italiensk, Portugisisk, Serbokroatisk, Spansk, Tysk

Português
Alemão, Danês, Finlandês, Francês, Holandês, Inglês, Norueguês, Servo-Croata, Sueco

Srpskohrvatski
Danski, Engleski, Finski, Francuski, Holandski, Italijanski, Njemački, Norveški, Portugalski, Španski, Švedski

Suomi
Englanti, Espanja, Italia, Portugali, Ranska, Ruotsi, Saksa, Serbokroaatti

Svenska
Engelska, Finska, Franska, Italienska, Portugisiska, Serbokroatiska, Spanska, Tyska

BERLITZ®

engels-nederlands
nederlands-engels
woordenboek

english-dutch
dutch-english
dictionary

By the Staff of Editions Berlitz

Revised edition 1979
Library of Congress Catalog Card Number: 78-78084

2nd printing 1981
Printed in Switzerland

Inhoud

Contents

Voorwoord

Toen wij enkele jaren geleden deze serie zakwoordenboeken begonnen, hebben wij ons tot doel gesteld elke uitgave zo praktisch en doelmatig mogelijk te maken voor het gebruik door toeristen, studenten en zaken-lieden. Dit is ook nu nog ons streven.

Gewoonlijk is het bijwerken van woordenboeken een moeizame en kostbare aangelegenheid, zodat er zelden herziene uitgaven verschijnen. Dit is niet het geval bij Berlitz. Onze woordenboeken worden samenge-steld met behulp van een computer, hetgeen snelle en regelmatige herzie-ning mogelijk maakt. Dank zij de computertechniek kon deze nieuwste uitgave van dit woordenboek op betrekkelijk eenvoudige wijze geheel worden herzien en de woordenschat met bijna 40 procent worden uitgebreid.

Tevreden gebruikers van de 36 oorspronkelijke uitgaven in tien ver-schillende talen kunnen twee nieuwe talen tegemoetzien – Portugees en Joegoslavisch – waardoor het totaal van onze edities op 54 komt.

In de onderhavige uitgebreide uitgave vindt u een meer overzichtelijke presentatie van de inhoud, meer betekenissen per woord en een beter leesbare drukletter. Behalve wat men altijd wel in woordenboeken vindt, biedt Berlitz nog de volgende extra's:

● een volledige fonetische transcriptie van elk grondwoord
● een aparte woordenlijst van culinaire begrippen om te gebruiken bij het lezen van een menu, zodat u in een buitenlands restaurant van tevoren kunt opzoeken wat u precies bestelt
● nuttige informatie over tijdsaanduiding, getallen, de vervoeging van onregelmatige werkwoorden, veelgebruikte afkortingen en een lijst van veelvoorkomende uitdrukkingen

Bij de selectie van de ongeveer 12 500 begrippen in elk van beide talen heeft de redactie uiteraard de behoeften van de moderne reiziger voor ogen gehad. Tegelijkertijd biedt het de student de basis-woordenschat, die hij nodig heeft.

Evenals onze succesvolle taal- en reisgidsen past het gemakkelijk in uw zak of tas.

Tenslotte nog dit: als u op reis een woord tegenkomt, waarvan u vindt dat het wel in een woordenboek van Berlitz thuishoort, laat het ons dan even weten. Een briefkaartje is al voldoende.

Preface

Having created this pocket-dictionary series some years ago, Berlitz aimed, then as now, to make each edition highly practical for the tourist and student as well as the businessman.

Ordinarily, updating a dictionary is a tedious and costly operation, making revision infrequent. Not so with Berlitz as these dictionaries are created with the aid of a computer-data bank, facilitating rapid and regular revision. Thus, thanks to computer technology, the current edition of the dictionary has been expanded—with nearly 40 per cent more vocabulary—and completely revised with relative ease.

Satisfied users of some of the 36 editions of our successful series in ten languages will welcome two additional languages—Portuguese and Serbo-Croatian—bringing the total number of editions programmed to 54.

This enlarged edition has an improved, clearer arrangement of word entries, additional definitions per word and a more easily read print. Besides just about everything you normally find in dictionaries, there are these Berlitz bonuses:

- imitated pronunciation next to each foreign-word entry making it as easy to read as your own language
- a unique, practical glossary to simplify reading a foreign restaurant menu and let you know what's in the soup and under the sauce
- useful information on telling time, numbers, conjugating irregular verbs, commonly seen abbreviations and converting to the metric system in addition to some handy phrases.

In selecting the approximately 12,500 word concepts in each language for this dictionary, it's obvious that the editors have had the traveller's needs foremost in mind. Thus, this book—which like our successful phrase-book and travel-guide series is designed to slip into your pocket or purse easily—should prove valuable in the jumbo-jet age we live in. By the same token, it also offers a student the basic vocabulary he is most likely to encounter and use. And if you run across a word on your trip which you feel belongs in a Berlitz dictionary, tell us. Just write the word on a postcard and mail it to the editors.

engels-nederlands

---

english-dutch

Afkortingen

adj	bijvoeglijk naamwoord	*p*	verleden tijd
adv	bijwoord	*pl*	meervoud
Am	Amerikaans	*plAm*	meervoud (Amerikaans)
art	lidwoord	*pp*	voltooid deelwoord
c	gemeenslachtig	*pr*	tegenwoordige tijd
conj	voegwoord	*pref*	voorvoegsel
n	zelfstandig naamwoord	*prep*	voorzetsel
nAm	zelfstandig naamwoord	*pron*	voornaamwoord
	(Amerikaans)	*v*	werkwoord
nt	onzijdig	*vAm*	werkwoord
num	telwoord		(Amerikaans)

Inleiding

Het woordenboek is zodanig opgezet, dat het zoveel mogelijk beantwoordt aan de eisen van de praktijk. Onnodige taalkundige aanduidingen zijn achterwege gelaten. De volgorde van de woorden is strikt alfabetisch, ook als het samengestelde woorden of woorden met een koppelteken betreft. Als enige uitzondering op deze regel zijn enkele idiomatische uitdrukkingen opgenomen als een afzonderlijk artikel, waarbij het meest toonaangevende woord van de uitdrukking bepalend is voor de alfabetische rangschikking. Wanneer bij een grondwoord nog daarvan afgeleide samenstellingen of uitdrukkingen zijn gegeven, staan ook deze weer in alfabetische volgorde.

Achter elk grondwoord vindt u een fonetische transcriptie (zie de Gids voor de uitspraak) en vervolgens, wanneer van toepassing, de woordsoort. Wanneer bij hetzelfde grondwoord meerdere woordsoorten behoren, zijn de vertalingen telkens naar de woordsoort gegroepeerd.

Het meervoud van zelfstandige naamwoorden is altijd opgenomen, wanneer dat onregelmatig is; tevens is het meervoud gegeven van bepaalde woorden waarover de gebruiker in twijfel zou kunnen verkeren.

Wanneer in onregelmatige meervoudsvormen of in afgeleide samenstellingen en uitdrukkingen het teken ∼ wordt gebruikt, duidt dit een herhaling aan van het grondwoord als geheel.

In onregelmatige meervoudsvormen van samengestelde woorden wordt alleen het gedeelte, dat verandert, voluit geschreven en het onveranderde deel aangegeven door een liggend streepje (-).

Een sterretje (*) voor een werkwoord geeft aan, dat dit werkwoord onregelmatig is. Voor nadere bijzonderheden kunt u de lijst van onregelmatige werkwoorden raadplegen.

Dit woordenboek is gebaseerd op de Britse spelling. Alle woorden en woordbetekenissen die overwegend Amerikaans zijn, zijn als zodanig aangegeven (zie lijst van gebezigde afkortingen).

Uitspraak

Elk trefwoord in dit deel van het woordenboek wordt gevolgd door een transcriptie in het internationale fonetische alfabet (IPA). In dit alfabet vertegenwoordigt elk teken altijd dezelfde klank. Letters die hieronder niet beschreven zijn worden min of meer op dezelfde wijze uitgesproken als in het Nederlands.

Medeklinkers

b	nooit scherp zoals in he**b**
d	nooit scherp zoals in raa**d**
ð	als de **z** in **z**ee, maar lispend uitgesproken
g	als een zachte **k**, zoals in het Franse **g**arçon
ŋ	als de **ng** in ba**ng**
r	plaats de tong eerst als voor de **ʒ** (zie beneden), open dan de mond enigszins en beweeg de tong daarbij naar beneden
∫	als de **sj** in **sj**ofel
θ	als de **s** in **s**amen, maar lispend uitgesproken
v	als de **w** in **w**aar
w	een korte, zwakke **oe**-klank
ʒ	als de **g** in eta**g**e

N. B. De lettergroep **sj** moet worden uitgesproken als een **s** gevolgd door een **j**-klank, maar *niet* als in **sj**ofel.

Klinkers

α:	als de **aa** in m**aa**t
æ	een klank tussen de **a** in **a**ls en de **e** in b**e**st
ʌ	min of meer als de **a** in **a**ls
e	als in b**e**st
ε	als de **e** in b**e**st, maar met de tong wat lager
ə	als de **e** in acht**e**r
ɔ	min of meer als de **o** in p**o**t
u	als de **oe** in g**oe**d, maar korter

1) Een dubbele punt (:) geeft aan dat de voorafgaande klinker lang is.

2) Enkele aan het Frans ontleende Engelse woorden bevatten neusklanken, die aangegeven worden d.m.v. een tilde boven de klinker (b.v. ã). Deze worden door de neus en de mond tegelijkertijd uitgesproken.

Tweeklanken

Een tweeklank bestaat uit twee klinkers, waarvan er één sterk is (beklemtoond) en de andere zwak (niet beklemtoond) en die samen als één klinker worden uitgesproken, zoals **ei** in het Nederlands. In het Engels is de tweede klinker altijd zwak. Een tweeklank kan soms gevolgd worden door een [ə]. In dergelijke gevallen heeft de tweede klinker van de tweeklank de neiging zeer zwak te worden.

Klemtoon

Het teken (') geeft aan dat de klemtoon op de volgende lettergreep valt. Als in een woord meer dan één lettergreep wordt beklemtoond, wordt het teken (ˌ) geplaatst vóór de lettergreep, waarop de bijklemtoon valt.

Amerikaanse uitspraak

Onze transcriptie geeft de gebruikelijke Engelse uitspraak aan. De Amerikaanse uitspraak verschilt in enkele opzichten van het Britse Engels en kent daarbij nog belangrijke regionale verschillen. Hier volgen enkele van de meest opvallende afwijkingen:

1) In tegenstelling tot in het Britse Engels wordt de **r** ook uitgesproken voor een medeklinker en aan het einde van een woord.

2) In vele woorden (b.v. *ask*, *castle*, *laugh* enz.) wordt [ɑ:] uitgesproken als [æ:].

3) De [ɔ]-klank wordt in het Amerikaans uitgesproken als [ɑ], vaak ook als [ɔ:].

4) In woorden als *duty*, *tune*, *new* enz. valt in het Amerikaans de [j]-klank voor de [u:] vaak weg.

5) Bovendien wordt bij een aantal woorden in het Amerikaans de klemtoon anders gelegd.

A

a [ei,ə] *art* (an) een *art*

abbey ['æbi] *n* abdij *c*

abbreviation [ə,bri:vi'eiʃən] *n* afkorting *c*

aberration [,æbə'reiʃən] *n* afwijking *c*

ability [ə'biləti] *n* bekwaamheid *c*; vermogen *nt*

able ['eibəl] *adj* in staat; capabel, bekwaam; *be ~ to* in staat *zijn om; *kunnen

abnormal [æb'nɔ:məl] *adj* abnormaal

aboard [ə'bɔ:d] *adv* aan boord

abolish [ə'bɔliʃ] *v* afschaffen

abortion [ə'bɔ:ʃən] *n* abortus *c*

about [ə'baut] *prep* over; betreffende, omtrent; om; *adv* omstreeks, ongeveer; omheen

above [ə'bʌv] *prep* boven; *adv* boven

abroad [ə'brɔ:d] *adv* naar het buitenland, in het buitenland

abscess ['æbses] *n* abces *nt*

absence ['æbsəns] *n* afwezigheid *c*

absent ['æbsənt] *adj* afwezig

absolutely ['æbsəlu:tli] *adv* absoluut

abstain from [əb'stein] zich *onthouden van

abstract ['æbstrækt] *adj* abstract

absurd [əb'sə:d] *adj* absurd, ongerijmd

abundance [ə'bʌndəns] *n* overvloed *c*

abundant [ə'bʌndənt] *adj* overvloedig

abuse [ə'bju:s] *n* misbruik *nt*

abyss [ə'bis] *n* afgrond *c*

academy [ə'kædəmi] *n* academie *c*

accelerate [ək'seləreit] *v* versnellen

accelerator [ək'seləreitə] *n* gaspedaal *nt*

accent ['æksənt] *n* accent *nt*; nadruk *c*

accept [ək'sept] *v* aanvaarden, *aannemen; accepteren

access ['ækses] *n* toegang *c*

accessary [ək'sesəri] *n* medeplichtige *c*

accessible [ək'sesəbəl] *adj* toegankelijk

accessories [ək'sesəriz] *pl* toebehoren *pl*, accessoires *pl*

accident ['æksidənt] *n* ongeluk *nt*, ongeval *nt*

accidental [,æksi'dentəl] *adj* toevallig

accommodate [ə'kɔmədeit] *v* *onderbrengen

accommodation [ə,kɔmə'deiʃən] *n* accommodatie *c*, logies *nt*, onderdak *nt*

accompany [ə'kʌmpəni] *v* vergezellen; begeleiden

accomplish [ə'kʌmpliʃ] *v* *volbrengen; bereiken

in accordance with [in ə'kɔ:dəns wið] ingevolge

according to [ə'kɔ:diŋ tu:] volgens; overeenkomstig

account [ə'kaunt] *n* rekening *c*; verslag nt; ~ for verantwoorden; on ~ of vanwege

accountable [əˈkauntəbəl] adj verklaarbaar

accurate [ˈækjurət] adj nauwkeurig

accuse [əˈkjuːz] v beschuldigen; aanklagen

accused [əˈkjuːzd] n verdachte c

accustom [əˈkʌstəm] v wennen; **accustomed** gewoon, gewend

ache [eik] v pijn *doen; n pijn c

achieve [əˈtʃiːv] v bereiken; presteren

achievement [əˈtʃiːvmənt] n prestatie c

acid [ˈæsid] n zuur nt

acknowledge [əkˈnɔlidʒ] v erkennen; *toegeven; bevestigen

acne [ˈækni] n acne c

acorn [ˈeikɔːn] n eikel c

acquaintance [əˈkweintəns] n bekende c, kennis c

acquire [əˈkwaiə] v *verwerven

acquisition [ˌækwiˈziʃən] n acquisitie c

acquittal [əˈkwitəl] n vrijspraak c

across [əˈkrɔs] prep over; aan de andere kant van; adv aan de overkant

act [ækt] n daad c; bedrijf nt, akte c; nummer nt, v *optreden, handelen; zich *gedragen; toneelspelen

action [ˈækʃən] n actie c, handeling c

active [ˈæktiv] adj actief; bedrijvig

activity [ækˈtivəti] n activiteit c

actor [ˈæktə] n acteur c, toneelspeler c

actress [ˈæktris] n actrice c, toneelspeelster c

actual [ˈæktʃuəl] adj eigenlijk, werkelijk

actually [ˈæktʃuəli] adv feitelijk

acute [əˈkjuːt] adj acuut

adapt [əˈdæpt] v aanpassen

add [æd] v optellen; toevoegen

adding-machine [ˈædiŋməˌʃiːn] n telmachine c

addition [əˈdiʃən] n optelling c; toe-

voeging c

additional [əˈdiʃənəl] adj extra; bijkomend; bijkomstig

address [əˈdres] n adres nt; v adresseren; *aanspreken

addressee [ˌædreˈsiː] n geadresseerde c

adequate [ˈædikwət] adj toereikend; adequaat, passend

adjective [ˈædʒiktiv] n bijvoeglijk naamwoord

adjourn [əˈdʒəːn] v uitstellen

adjust [əˈdʒʌst] v afstellen; aanpassen

administer [ədˈministə] v toedienen

administration [ədˌminiˈstreiʃən] n administratie c; beheer nt

administrative [ədˈministrətiv] adj administratief; bestuurlijk; ~ **law** bestuursrecht nt

admiral [ˈædmərəl] n admiraal c

admiration [ˌædməˈreiʃən] n bewondering c

admire [ədˈmaiə] v bewonderen

admission [ədˈmiʃən] n toegang c; toelating c

admit [ədˈmit] v *toelaten; *toegeven; bekennen

admittance [ədˈmitəns] n toegang c; **no** ~ verboden toegang

adopt [əˈdɔpt] v adopteren; *aannemen

adult [ˈædʌlt] n volwassene c; adj volwassen

advance [ədˈvaːns] n vooruitgang c; voorschot nt; v *vooruitgaan; *voorschieten; **in** ~ vooruit, van tevoren

advanced [ədˈvaːnst] adj gevorderd

advantage [ədˈvaːntidʒ] n voordeel nt

advantageous [ˌædvənˈteidʒəs] adj voordelig

adventure [ədˈventʃə] n avontuur nt

adverb [ˈædvəːb] n bijwoord nt

advertisement [ədˈvəːtismənt] n advertentie c; annonce c

advertising ['ædvətaiziŋ] n reclame c

advice [əd'vais] n advies nt, raad c

advise [əd'vaiz] v adviseren, *aanraden

advocate ['ædvəkət] n voorstander c

aerial ['ɛəriəl] n antenne c

aeroplane ['ɛərəplein] n vliegtuig nt

affair [ə'fɛə] n aangelegenheid c; verhouding c, affaire c

affect [ə'fekt] v beïnvloeden; *betreffen

affected [ə'fektid] adj geaffecteerd

affection [ə'fekʃən] n aandoening c; genegenheid c

affectionate [ə'fekʃənit] adj lief, aanhankelijk

affiliated [ə'filieitid] adj aangesloten

affirmative [ə'fə:mətiv] adj bevestigend

affliction [ə'flikʃən] n leed nt

afford [ə'fɔ:d] v zich veroorloven

afraid [ə'freid] adj angstig, bang; * be ~ bang *zijn

Africa ['æfrikə] Afrika

African ['æfrikən] adj Afrikaans; n Afrikaan c

after ['ɑ:ftə] prep na; achter; conj nadat

afternoon [,ɑ:ftə'nu:n] n middag c, namiddag c; **this** ~ vanmiddag

afterwards ['ɑ:ftəwədz] adv later; nadien, naderhand

again [ə'gen] adv weer; opnieuw; ~ **and again** telkens

against [ə'genst] prep tegen

age [eidʒ] n leeftijd c; ouderdom c; **of** ~ meerderjarig; **under** ~ minderjarig

aged ['eidʒid] adj bejaard; oud

agency ['eidʒənsi] n agentschap nt; bureau nt; vertegenwoordiging c

agenda [ə'dʒendə] n agenda c

agent ['eidʒənt] n vertegenwoordiger c, agent c

aggressive [ə'gresiv] adj agressief

ago [ə'gou] adv geleden

agrarian [ə'grɛəriən] adj agrarisch, landbouw-

agree [ə'gri:] v het eens *zijn; toestemmen; *overeenkomen

agreeable [ə'gri:əbəl] adj aangenaam

agreement [ə'gri:mənt] n contract nt; akkoord nt, overeenkomst c; overeenstemming c

agriculture ['ægrikʌltʃə] n landbouw c

ahead [ə'hed] adv vooruit; ~ **of** voor; * **go** ~ *doorgaan; **straight** ~ rechtuit

aid [eid] n hulp c; v *bijstaan, *helpen

ailment ['eilmənt] n kwaal c; ziekte c

aim [eim] n doel nt; ~ **at** richten op, mikken op; beogen, nastreven

air [ɛə] n lucht c; v luchten

air-conditioning ['ɛəkən,diʃəniŋ] n luchtverversing c; **air-conditioned** adj air conditioned

aircraft ['ɛəkrɑ:ft] n (pl ~) vliegtuig nt; toestel nt

airfield ['ɛəfi:ld] n vliegveld nt

air-filter ['ɛə,filtə] n luchtfilter nt

airline ['ɛəlain] n luchtvaartmaatschappij c

airmail ['ɛəmeil] n luchtpost c

airplane ['ɛəplein] nAm vliegtuig nt

airport ['ɛəpɔ:t] n luchthaven c

air-sickness ['ɛə,siknəs] n luchtziekte c

airtight ['ɛətait] adj luchtdicht

airy ['ɛəri] adj luchtig

aisle [ail] n zijbeuk c; gangpad nt

alarm [ə'lɑ:m] n alarm nt; v alarmeren

alarm-clock [ə'lɑ:mklɔk] n wekker c

album ['ælbəm] n album nt

alcohol ['ælkəhɔl] n alcohol c

alcoholic [,ælkə'hɔlik] adj alcoholisch

ale [eil] n bier nt

algebra ['ældʒibrə] *n* algebra *c*
Algeria [æl'dʒiəriə] Algerije
Algerian [æl'dʒiəriən] *adj* Algerijns; *n* Algerijn *c*
alien ['eiliən] *n* buitenlander *c*; vreemdeling *c*; *adj* buitenlands
alike [ə'laik] *adj* eender, gelijk
alimony ['æliməni] *n* alimentatie *c*
alive [ə'laiv] *adj* in leven, levend
all [ɔ:l] *adj* al; ~ **in** alles inbegrepen; ~ **right!** goed!; **at** ~ helemaal
allergy ['ælədʒi] *n* allergie *c*
alley ['æli] *n* steeg *c*
alliance [ə'laiəns] *n* bondgenootschap *nt*
Allies ['ælaiz] *pl* Geallieerden *pl*
allot [ə'lɔt] *v* *toewijzen
allow [ə'lau] *v* veroorloven, *toestaan; ~ **to** *laten; ***be allowed** *mogen; ***be allowed to** *mogen
allowance [ə'lauəns] *n* toelage *c*
all-round [,ɔ:l'raund] *adj* veelzijdig
almanac ['ɔ:lmənæk] *n* almanak *c*
almond ['ɑ:mənd] *n* amandel *c*
almost ['ɔ:lmoust] *adv* bijna; haast
alone [ə'loun] *adv* alleen
along [ə'lɔŋ] *prep* langs
aloud [ə'laud] *adv* hardop
alphabet ['ælfəbet] *n* alfabet *nt*
already [ɔ:l'redi] *adv* reeds, al
also ['ɔ:lsou] *adv* ook; tevens, eveneens
altar ['ɔ:ltə] *n* altaar *nt*
alter ['ɔ:ltə] *v* wijzigen, veranderen
alteration [,ɔ:ltə'reiʃən] *n* wijziging *c*, verandering *c*
alternate [ɔ:l'tə:nət] *adj* afwisselend
alternative [ɔ:l'tə:nətiv] *n* alternatief *nt*
although [ɔ:l'ðou] *conj* ofschoon, hoewel
altitude ['æltitju:d] *n* hoogte *c*
alto ['æltou] *n* (pl ~s) alt *c*
altogether [,ɔ:ltə'geðə] *adv* helemaal;

in totaal
always ['ɔ:lweiz] *adv* altijd
am [æm] *v* (pr be)
amaze [ə'meiz] *v* verwonderen, verbazen
amazement [ə'meizmənt] *n* verbazing *c*
ambassador [æm'bæsədə] *n* ambassadeur *c*
amber ['æmbə] *n* barnsteen *nt*
ambiguous [æm'bigjuəs] *adj* dubbelzinnig; onduidelijk
ambitious [æm'biʃəs] *adj* ambitieus; eerzuchtig
ambulance ['æmbjuləns] *n* ziekenauto *c*, ambulance *c*
ambush ['æmbuʃ] *n* hinderlaag *c*
America [ə'merikə] Amerika
American [ə'merikən] *adj* Amerikaans; *n* Amerikaan *c*
amethyst ['æmiθist] *n* amethist *c*
amid [ə'mid] *prep* onder; tussen, midden in, te midden van
ammonia [ə'mouniə] *n* ammonia *c*
amnesty ['æmnisti] *n* amnestie *c*
among [ə'mʌŋ] *prep* te midden van; tussen, onder; ~ **other things** onder andere
amount [ə'maunt] *n* hoeveelheid *c*; som *c*, bedrag *nt*; ~ **to** *bedragen
amuse [ə'mju:z] *v* amuseren, vermaken
amusement [ə'mju:zmənt] *n* amusement *nt*, vermaak *nt*
amusing [ə'mju:ziŋ] *adj* amusant
anaemia [ə'ni:miə] *n* bloedarmoede *c*
anaesthesia [,ænis'θi:ziə] *n* verdoving *c*
anaesthetic [,ænis'θetik] *n* pijnstillend middel
analyse ['ænəlaiz] *v* ontleden, analyseren
analysis [ə'næləsis] *n* (pl -ses) analyse *c*

analyst ['ænəlist] *n* analist *c*; analyticus *c*

anarchy ['ænəki] *n* anarchie *c*

anatomy [ə'nætəmi] *n* anatomie *c*

ancestor ['ænsestə] *n* voorvader *c*

anchor ['æŋkə] *n* anker *nt*

anchovy ['æntʃəvi] *n* ansjovis *c*

ancient ['einʃənt] *adj* oud; ouderwets,
verouderd; oeroud

and [ænd, ənd] *conj* en

angel ['eindʒəl] *n* engel *c*

anger ['æŋgə] *n* toorn *c*, boosheid *c*;
woede *c*

angle ['æŋgəl] *v* hengelen; *n* hoek *c*

angry ['æŋgri] *adj* kwaad

animal ['æniməl] *n* dier *nt*

ankle ['æŋkəl] *n* enkel *c*

annex[1] ['æneks] *n* bijgebouw *nt*; bijlage *c*

annex[2] [ə'neks] *v* annexeren

anniversary [,æni'və:səri] *n* verjaardag
c

announce [ə'nauns] *v* bekendmaken,
aankondigen

announcement [ə'naunsmənt] *n* aankondiging *c*, bekendmaking *c*

annoy [ə'nɔi] *v* irriteren, ergeren

annoyance [ə'nɔiəns] *n* ergernis *c*

annoying [ə'nɔiiŋ] *adj* vervelend, hinderlijk

annual ['ænjuəl] *adj* jaarlijks; *n* jaarboek *nt*

per annum [pər 'ænəm] jaarlijks

anonymous [ə'nɔniməs] *adj* anoniem

another [ə'nʌðə] *adj* nog een; een ander

answer ['ɑ:nsə] *v* antwoorden; beantwoorden; *n* antwoord *nt*

ant [ænt] *n* mier *c*

anthology [æn'θɔlədʒi] *n* bloemlezing
c

antibiotic [,æntibai'ɔtik] *n* antibioticum *nt*

anticipate [æn'tisipeit] *v* verwachten,

*voorzien; *voorkomen

antifreeze ['æntifri:z] *n* antivries *c*

antipathy [æn'tipəθi] *n* afkeer *c*

antique [æn'ti:k] *adj* antiek; *n* antiquiteit *c*; ~ **dealer** antiquair *c*

antiquity [æn'tikwəti] *n* Oudheid *c*;
antiquities *pl* oudheden *pl*

antiseptic [,ænti'septik] *n* antiseptisch
middel

antlers ['æntləz] *pl* gewei *nt*

anxiety [æŋ'zaiəti] *n* bezorgdheid *c*

anxious ['æŋkʃəs] *adj* verlangend; bezorgd

any ['eni] *adj* enig

anybody ['enibɔdi] *pron* wie dan ook

anyhow ['enihau] *adv* hoe dan ook

anyone ['eniwʌn] *pron* iedereen

anything ['eniθiŋ] *pron* wat dan ook

anyway ['eniwei] *adv* in elk geval

anywhere ['eniwɛə] *adv* waar dan
ook; overal

apart [ə'pɑ:t] *adv* apart, afzonderlijk;
~ **from** afgezien van

apartment [ə'pɑ:tmənt] *nAm* appartement *nt*, flat *c*; etage *c*; ~ **house**
Am flatgebouw *nt*

aperitif [ə'perətiv] *n* aperitief *nt/c*

apologize [ə'pɔlədʒaiz] *v* zich verontschuldigen

apology [ə'pɔlədʒi] *n* excuus *nt*, verontschuldiging *c*

apparatus [,æpə'reitəs] *n* apparaat *nt*,
toestel *nt*

apparent [ə'pærənt] *adj* schijnbaar;
duidelijk

apparently [ə'pærəntli] *adv* blijkbaar;
klaarblijkelijk

apparition [,æpə'riʃən] *n* verschijning
c

appeal [ə'pi:l] *n* beroep *nt*

appear [ə'piə] *v* *lijken, *schijnen;
*blijken; *verschijnen; *optreden

appearance [ə'piərəns] *n* voorkomen
nt; aanblik *c*; optreden *nt*

appendicitis [ə,pendi'saitis] *n* blindedarmontsteking *c*

appendix [ə'pendiks] *n* (pl -dices,
-dixes) blindedarm *c*

appetite ['æpətait] *n* trek *c*, eetlust *c*

appetizer ['æpətaizə] *n* borrelhapje *nt*

appetizing ['æpətaiziŋ] *adj* smakelijk

applause [ə'plɔːz] *n* applaus *nt*

apple ['æpəl] *n* appel *c*

appliance [ə'plaiəns] *n* toestel *nt*, apparaat *nt*

application [,æpli'keiʃən] *n* toepassing
c; aanvraag *c*; sollicitatie *c*

apply [ə'plai] *v* toepassen; gebruiken;
solliciteren; *gelden

appoint [ə'pɔint] *v* aanstellen, benoemen

appointment [ə'pɔintmənt] *n* afspraak
c; benoeming *c*

appreciate [ə'priːʃieit] *v* schatten;
waarderen, op prijs stellen

appreciation [ə,priːʃi'eiʃən] *n* schatting
c; waardering *c*

approach [ə'proutʃ] *v* naderen; *n* aanpak *c*; toegang *c*

appropriate [ə'proupriət] *adj* juist, geschikt, passend

approval [ə'pruːvəl] *n* goedkeuring *c*;
instemming *c*; **on** - op zicht

approve [ə'pruːv] *v* goedkeuren; ~ **of**
instemmen met

approximate [ə'prɔksimət] *adj* bij be-
nadering

approximately [ə'prɔksimətli] *adv* circa, ongeveer

apricot ['eiprikɔt] *n* abrikoos *c*

April ['eiprəl] april

apron ['eiprən] *n* schort *c*

Arab ['ærəb] *adj* Arabisch; *n* Arabier
c

arbitrary ['ɑːbitrəri] *adj* willekeurig

arcade [ɑː'keid] *n* zuilengang *c*, galerij
c

arch [ɑːtʃ] *n* boog *c*; gewelf *nt*

archaeologist [,ɑːki'ɔlədʒist] *n* archeoloog *c*

archaeology [,ɑːki'ɔlədʒi] *n* oudheidkunde *c*, archeologie *c*

archbishop [,ɑːtʃ'biʃəp] *n* aartsbisschop *c*

arched [ɑːtʃt] *adj* boogvormig

architect ['ɑːkitekt] *n* architect *c*

architecture ['ɑːkitektʃə] *n* bouwkunde *c*, architectuur *c*

archives ['ɑːkaivz] *pl* archief *nt*

are [ɑː] *v* (pr be)

area ['eəriə] *n* streek *c*; gebied *nt*; oppervlakte *c*; ~ **code** netnummer *nt*

Argentina [,ɑːdʒən'tiːnə] Argentinië

Argentinian [,ɑːdʒən'tiniən] *adj* Argentijns; *n* Argentijn *c*

argue ['ɑːgjuː] *v* argumenteren, debatteren, discussiëren; redetwisten

argument ['ɑːgjumənt] *n* argument *nt*;
discussie *c*; woordenwisseling *c*

arid ['ærid] *adj* dor

* **arise** [ə'raiz] *v* *oprijzen, *ontstaan

arithmetic [ə'riθmətik] *n* rekenkunde *c*

arm [ɑːm] *n* arm *c*; wapen *nt*; leuning *c*; *v* bewapenen

armchair ['ɑːmtʃeə] *n* fauteuil *c*, leunstoel *c*

armed [ɑːmd] *adj* gewapend; ~
forces strijdkrachten *pl*

armour ['ɑːmə] *n* harnas *nt*

army ['ɑːmi] *n* leger *nt*

aroma [ə'roumə] *n* aroma *nt*

around [ə'raund] *prep* om, rond; *adv*
rondom

arrange [ə'reindʒ] *v* rangschikken, ordenen; regelen

arrangement [ə'reindʒmənt] *n* regeling
c

arrest [ə'rest] *v* arresteren; *n* aanhouding *c*, arrestatie *c*

arrival [ə'raivəl] *n* aankomst *c*; komst
c

arrive [ə'raiv] *v* *aankomen

arrow ['ærou] *n* pijl *c*

art [ɑ:t] *n* kunst *c*; vaardigheid *c*; ~ **collection** kunstverzameling *c*; ~ **exhibition** kunsttentoonstelling *c*; ~ **gallery** kunstgalerij *c*; ~ **history** kunstgeschiedenis *c*; **arts and crafts** kunstnijverheid *c*; ~ **school** kunstacademie *c*

artery ['ɑ:təri] *n* slagader *c*

artichoke ['ɑ:titʃouk] *n* artisjok *c*

article ['ɑ:tikəl] *n* artikel *nt*; lidwoord *nt*

artifice ['ɑ:tifis] *n* list *c*

artificial [,ɑ:ti'fiʃəl] *adj* kunstmatig

artist ['ɑ:tist] *n* kunstenaar *c*; kunstenares *c*

artistic [ɑ:'tistik] *adj* artistiek, kunstzinnig

as [æz] *conj* als, zoals; even; aangezien, omdat; ~ **from** vanaf; met ingang van; ~ **if** alsof

asbestos [æz'bestɔs] *n* asbest *nt*

ascend [ə'send] *v* omhoog *gaan; *opstijgen; *beklimmen

ascent [ə'sent] *n* stijging *c*; beklimming *c*

ascertain [,æsə'tein] *v* constateren; zich vergewissen van, zich vergewissen van

ash [æʃ] *n* as *c*

ashamed [ə'ʃeimd] *adj* beschaamd; *be ~ zich schamen

ashore [ə'ʃɔ:] *adv* aan land

ashtray ['æʃtrei] *n* asbak *c*

Asia ['eiʃə] Azië

Asian ['eiʃən] *adj* Aziatisch; *n* Aziaat *c*

aside [ə'said] *adv* opzij, terzijde

ask [ɑ:sk] *v* *vragen; *verzoeken; uitnodigen

asleep [ə'sli:p] *adj* in slaap

asparagus [ə'spærəgəs] *n* asperge *c*

aspect ['æspekt] *n* aspect *nt*

asphalt ['æsfælt] *n* asfalt *nt*

aspire [ə'spaiə] *v* streven

aspirin ['æspərin] *n* aspirine *c*

ass [æs] *n* ezel *c*

assassination [ə,sæsi'neiʃən] *n* moord *c*

assault [ə'sɔ:lt] *v* *aanvallen; aanranden

assemble [ə'sembəl] *v* *bijeenbrengen; in elkaar zetten, monteren

assembly [ə'sembli] *n* vergadering *c*, bijeenkomst *c*

assignment [ə'sainmənt] *n* opdracht *c*

assign to [ə'sain] *opdragen aan; *toeschrijven aan

assist [ə'sist] *v* *bijstaan, *helpen; ~ **at** bijwonen

assistance [ə'sistəns] *n* hulp *c*; steun *c*, bijstand *c*

assistant [ə'sistənt] *n* assistent *c*

associate [ə'souʃiət] *n* partner *c*, vennoot *c*; bondgenoot *c*; lid *nt*; *v* associëren; ~ **with** *omgaan met

association [ə,sousi'eiʃən] *n* genootschap *nt*, vereniging *c*

assort [ə'sɔ:t] *v* sorteren

assortment [ə'sɔ:tmənt] *n* assortiment *nt*, sortering *c*

assume [ə'sju:m] *v* *aannemen, veronderstellen

assure [ə'ʃuə] *v* verzekeren

asthma ['æsmə] *n* astma *nt*

astonish [ə'stɔniʃ] *v* verbazen

astonishing [ə'stɔniʃiŋ] *adj* verbazend

astonishment [ə'stɔniʃmənt] *n* verbazing *c*

astronomy [ə'strɔnəmi] *n* sterrenkunde *c*

asylum [ə'sailəm] *n* asiel *nt*; gesticht *nt*, tehuis *nt*

at [æt] *prep* in, bij, op; naar

ate [et] *v* (p eat)

atheist ['eiθiist] *n* atheïst *c*

athlete ['æθli:t] *n* atleet *c*

athletics [æθ'letiks] *pl* atletiek *c*

Atlantic [ət'læntik] Atlantische Oceaan

atmosphere ['ætməsfiə] n atmosfeer c; sfeer c, stemming c

atom ['ætəm] n atoom nt

atomic [ə'tɔmik] adj atomisch; atoom-

atomizer ['ætəmaizə] n sproeier c; spuitbus c, verstuiver c

attach [ə'tætʃ] v hechten, vastmaken; aanhechten; bijvoegen; attached to gehecht aan

attack [ə'tæk] v *aanvallen; n aanval c

attain [ə'tein] v bereiken

attainable [ə'teinəbəl] adj haalbaar; bereikbaar

attempt [ə'tempt] v proberen, trachten; beproeven; n poging c

attend [ə'tend] v bijwonen; ~ on bedienen; ~ to passen op, zich *bezighouden met; letten op, aandacht besteden aan

attendance [ə'tendəns] n opkomst c

attendant [ə'tendənt] n oppasser c

attention [ə'tenʃən] n aandacht c; *pay ~ opletten

attentive [ə'tentiv] adj oplettend

attic ['ætik] n zolder c

attitude ['ætitjuːd] n houding c

attorney [ə'tɔːni] n advocaat c

attract [ə'trækt] v *aantrekken

attraction [ə'trækʃən] n attractie c; aantrekking c, bekoring c

attractive [ə'træktiv] adj aantrekkelijk

auburn ['ɔːbən] adj kastanjebruin

auction ['ɔːkʃən] n veiling c

audible ['ɔːdibəl] adj hoorbaar

audience ['ɔːdiəns] n publiek nt

auditor ['ɔːditə] n toehoorder c

auditorium [,ɔːdi'tɔːriəm] n aula c

August ['ɔːgəst] augustus

aunt [ɑːnt] n tante c

Australia [ɔ'streiliə] Australië

Australian [ɔ'streiliən] adj Australisch; n Australiër c

Austria ['ɔstriə] Oostenrijk

Austrian ['ɔstriən] adj Oostenrijks; n Oostenrijker c

authentic [ɔ'θentik] adj authentiek; echt

author ['ɔːθə] n auteur c, schrijver c

authoritarian [ɔ:,θɔri'teəriən] adj autoritair

authority [ɔ'θɔrəti] n gezag nt; macht c; authorities pl autoriteiten pl, overheid c

authorization [,ɔ:θərai'zeiʃən] n machtiging c; toestemming c

automatic [,ɔ:tə'mætik] adj automatisch

automation [,ɔ:tə'meiʃən] n automatisering c

automobile ['ɔ:təməbi:l] n auto c; ~ club automobielclub c

autonomous [ɔ:'tɔnəməs] adj autonoom

autopsy ['ɔːtɔpsi] n autopsie c

autumn ['ɔːtəm] n najaar nt, herfst c

available [ə'veiləbəl] adj verkrijgbaar, voorhanden, beschikbaar

avalanche ['ævəlɑːnʃ] n lawine c

avaricious [,ævə'riʃəs] adj gierig

avenue ['ævənjuː] n laan c

average ['ævəridʒ] adj gemiddeld; n gemiddelde nt; on the ~ gemiddeld

averse [ə'vəːs] adj afkerig

aversion [ə'vəːʃən] n tegenzin c

avert [ə'vəːt] v afwenden

avoid [ə'vɔid] v *vermijden; *ontwijken

await [ə'weit] v wachten op, afwachten

awake [ə'weik] adj wakker

*awake [ə'weik] v wekken

award [ə'wɔːd] n prijs c; v toekennen

aware [ə'wɛə] adj bewust

away [ə'wei] adv weg; *go ~ *weggaan

awful ['ɔːfəl] adj afschuwelijk, ver-

schrikkelijk
awkward ['ɔːkwəd] *adj* pijnlijk; onhandig
awning ['ɔːniŋ] *n* zonnescherm *nt*
axe [æks] *n* bijl *c*
axle ['æksəl] *n* as *c*

B

baby ['beibi] *n* baby *c*; ~ **carriage**
Am kinderwagen *c*
babysitter ['beibi,sitə] *n* babysitter *c*
bachelor ['bætʃələ] *n* vrijgezel *c*
back [bæk] *n* rug *c*; *adv* terug; *go* ~
*teruggaan
backache ['bækeik] *n* rugpijn *c*
backbone ['bækboun] *n* ruggegraat *c*
background ['bækɡraund] *n* achtergrond *c*; vorming *c*
backwards ['bækwədz] *adv* achteruit
bacon ['beikən] *n* spek *nt*
bacterium [bæk'tiːriəm] *n* (pl -ria) bacterie *c*
bad [bæd] *adj* slecht; ernstig, erg;
stout
bag [bæɡ] *n* zak *c*; tas *c*, handtas *c*;
koffer *c*
baggage ['bæɡidʒ] *n* bagage *c*; ~ **deposit office** *Am* bagagedepot *nt*;
hand ~ *Am* handbagage *c*
bail [beil] *n* borgsom *c*
bailiff ['beilif] *n* deurwaarder *c*
bait [beit] *n* aas *nt*
bake [beik] *v* *bakken
baker ['beikə] *n* bakker *c*
bakery ['beikəri] *n* bakkerij *c*
balance ['bæləns] *n* evenwicht *nt*; balans *c*; saldo *nt*
balcony ['bælkəni] *n* balkon *nt*
bald [bɔːld] *adj* kaal
ball [bɔːl] *n* bal *c*; bal *nt*
ballet ['bælei] *n* ballet *nt*

balloon [bə'luːn] *n* ballon *c*
ballpoint-pen ['bɔːlpɔintpen] *n* ballpoint *c*
ballroom ['bɔːlruːm] *n* danszaal *c*
bamboo [bæm'buː] *n* (pl ~s) bamboe
nt
banana [bə'nɑːnə] *n* banaan *c*
band [bænd] *n* orkest *nt*; band *c*
bandage ['bændidʒ] *n* verband *nt*
bandit ['bændit] *n* bandiet *c*
bangle ['bæŋɡəl] *n* armband *c*
banisters ['bænistəz] *pl* trapleuning *c*
bank [bæŋk] *n* oever *c*; bank *c*; *v* deponeren; ~ **account** bankrekening
c
banknote ['bæŋknout] *n* bankbiljet *nt*
bank-rate ['bæŋkreit] *n* disconto *nt*
bankrupt ['bæŋkrʌpt] *adj* failliet,
bankroet
banner ['bænə] *n* vaandel *nt*
banquet ['bæŋkwit] *n* banket *nt*
banqueting-hall ['bæŋkwitiŋhɔːl] *n*
banketzaal *c*
baptism ['bæptizəm] *n* doopsel *nt*,
doop *c*
baptize [bæp'taiz] *v* dopen
bar [bɑː] *n* bar *c*; stang *c*; tralie *c*
barber ['bɑːbə] *n* kapper *c*
bare [beə] *adj* naakt, bloot; kaal
barely ['beəli] *adv* nauwelijks
bargain ['bɑːɡin] *n* koopje *nt*; *v* *afdingen
baritone ['bæritoun] *n* bariton *c*
bark [bɑːk] *n* bast *c*; *v* blaffen
barley ['bɑːli] *n* gerst *c*
barmaid ['bɑːmeid] *n* barjuffrouw *c*
barman ['bɑːmən] *n* (pl -men) barman
c
barn [bɑːn] *n* schuur *c*
barometer [bə'rɔmitə] *n* barometer *c*
baroque [bə'rɔk] *adj* barok
barracks ['bærəks] *pl* kazerne *c*
barrel ['bærəl] *n* ton *c*, vat *nt*
barrier ['bæriə] *n* barrière *c*; slagboom

c

barrister ['bæristə] *n* advocaat *c*

bartender ['bɑː,tendə] *n* barman *c*

base [beis] *n* basis *c*; grondslag *c*; *v* baseren

baseball ['beisbɔːl] *n* honkbal *nt*

basement ['beismənt] *n* souterrain *nt*

basic ['beisik] *adj* fundamenteel

basilica [bə'zilikə] *n* basiliek *c*

basin ['beisən] *n* kom *c*, bekken *nt*

basis ['beisis] *n* (pl bases) grondslag *c*, basis *c*

basket ['bɑːskit] *n* mand *c*

bass¹ [beis] *n* bas *c*

bass² [bæs] *n* (pl ~) baars *c*

bastard ['bɑːstəd] *n* bastaard *c*; schoft *c*

batch [bætʃ] *n* partij *c*

bath [bɑːθ] *n* bad *nt*; ~ **salts** badzout *nt*; ~ **towel** badhanddoek *c*

bathe [beið] *v* baden, een bad *nemen

bathing-cap ['beiðiŋkæp] *n* badmuts *c*

bathing-suit ['beiðiŋsuːt] *n* badpak *nt*; zwembroek *c*

bathing-trunks ['beiðiŋtrʌŋks] *n* zwembroek *c*

bathrobe ['bɑːθroub] *n* badjas *c*

bathroom ['bɑːθruːm] *n* badkamer *c*; toilet *nt*

batter ['bætə] *n* beslag *nt*

battery ['bætəri] *n* batterij *c*; accu *c*

battle ['bætəl] *n* slag *c*; strijd *c*, gevecht *nt*; *v* *vechten

bay [bei] *n* baai *c*; *v* blaffen

*** be** [biː] *v* *zijn

beach [biːtʃ] *n* strand *nt*; **nudist** ~ naaktstrand *nt*

bead [biːd] *n* kraal *c*; **beads** *pl* kralensnoer *nt*; rozenkrans *c*

beak [biːk] *n* snavel *c*; bek *c*

beam [biːm] *n* straal *c*; balk *c*

bean [biːn] *n* boon *c*

bear [bɛə] *n* beer *c*

*** bear** [bɛə] *v* *dragen; dulden; *ver-

dragen

beard [biəd] *n* baard *c*

bearer ['bɛərə] *n* drager *c*

beast [biːst] *n* beest *nt*; ~ **of prey** roofdier *nt*

*** beat** [biːt] *v* *slaan; *verslaan

beautiful ['bjuːtifəl] *adj* mooi

beauty ['bjuːti] *n* schoonheid *c*; ~ **parlour** schoonheidssalon *c*; ~ **salon** schoonheidssalon *c*; ~ **treatment** schoonheidsbehandeling *c*

beaver ['biːvə] *n* bever *c*

because [bi'kɔz] *conj* omdat; aangezien; ~ **of** vanwege, wegens

*** become** [bi'kʌm] *v* *worden; goed *staan

bed [bed] *n* bed *nt*; ~ **and board** vol pension, kost en inwoning; ~ **and breakfast** logies en ontbijt

bedding ['bediŋ] *n* beddegoed *nt*

bedroom ['bedruːm] *n* slaapkamer *c*

bee [biː] *n* bij *c*

beech [biːtʃ] *n* beuk *c*

beef [biːf] *n* rundvlees *nt*

beehive ['biːhaiv] *n* bijenkorf *c*

been [biːn] *v* (pp be)

beer [biə] *n* bier *nt*; pils *c*

beet [biːt] *n* biet *c*

beetle ['biːtəl] *n* kever *c*

beetroot ['biːtruːt] *n* beetwortel *c*

before [bi'fɔː] *prep* voor; *conj* voordat; *adv* van tevoren; eerder, tevoren

beg [beg] *v* bedelen; smeken; *vragen

beggar ['begə] *n* bedelaar *c*

*** begin** [bi'gin] *v* *beginnen; *aanvangen

beginner [bi'ginə] *n* beginneling *c*

beginning [bi'giniŋ] *n* begin *nt*; aanvang *c*

on behalf of [ɔn bi'hɑːf ɔv] namens, in naam van; ten behoeve van

behave [bi'heiv] *v* zich *gedragen

behaviour [bi'heivjə] *n* gedrag *nt*

behind [bi'haind] *prep* achter; *adv* achteraan

beige [beiʒ] *adj* beige

being ['bi:iŋ] *n* wezen *nt*

Belgian ['beldʒən] *adj* Belgisch; *n* Belg *c*

Belgium ['beldʒəm] België

belief [bi'li:f] *n* geloof *nt*

believe [bi'li:v] *v* geloven

bell [bel] *n* klok *c*; bel *c*

bellboy ['belbɔi] *n* piccolo *c*

belly ['beli] *n* buik *c*

belong [bi'lɔŋ] *v* toebehoren

belongings [bi'lɔŋiŋz] *pl* bezittingen *pl*

beloved [bi'lʌvd] *adj* bemind

below [bi'lou] *prep* onder; beneden; *adv* onderaan, beneden

belt [belt] *n* riem *c*; **garter ~** *Am* jarretelgordel *c*

bench [bentʃ] *n* bank *c*

bend [bend] *n* bocht *c*; kromming *c*

*** bend** [bend] *v* *buigen; **~ down** zich bukken

beneath [bi'ni:θ] *prep* onder; *adv* beneden

benefit ['benifit] *n* winst *c*, baat *c*; voordeel *nt*; *v* profiteren

bent [bent] *adj* (pp bend) krom

beret ['berei] *n* baret *c*

berry ['beri] *n* bes *c*

berth [bə:θ] *n* couchette *c*; kooi *c*

beside [bi'said] *prep* naast

besides [bi'saidz] *adv* bovendien; trouwens; *prep* behalve

best [best] *adj* best

bet [bet] *n* weddenschap *c*; inzet *c*

*** bet** [bet] *v* wedden

betray [bi'trei] *v* *verraden

better ['betə] *adj* beter

between [bi'twi:n] *prep* tussen

beverage ['bevəridʒ] *n* drank *c*

beware [bi'wɛə] *v* zich hoeden, oppassen

bewitch [bi'witʃ] *v* beheksen, betove-

ren

beyond [bi'jɔnd] *prep* verder dan; voorbij; behalve; *adv* verder

bible ['baibəl] *n* bijbel *c*

bicycle ['baisikəl] *n* fiets *c*; rijwiel *nt*

big [big] *adj* groot; omvangrijk; dik; gewichtig

bile [bail] *n* gal *c*

bilingual [bai'liŋwəl] *adj* tweetalig

bill [bil] *n* rekening *c*; nota *c*; *v* factureren

billiards ['biljədz] *pl* biljart *nt*

*** bind** [baind] *v* *binden

binoculars [bi'nɔkjələz] *pl* verrekijker *c*; toneelkijker *c*

biology [bai'ɔlədʒi] *n* biologie *c*

birch [bə:tʃ] *n* berk *c*

bird [bə:d] *n* vogel *c*

Biro ['bairou] *n* ballpoint *c*

birth [bə:θ] *n* geboorte *c*

birthday ['bə:θdei] *n* verjaardag *c*

biscuit ['biskit] *n* koekje *nt*

bishop ['biʃəp] *n* bisschop *c*

bit [bit] *n* stukje *nt*; beetje *nt*

bitch [bitʃ] *n* teef *c*

bite [bait] *n* hap *c*; beet *c*; steek *c*

*** bite** [bait] *v* *bijten

bitter ['bitə] *adj* bitter

black [blæk] *adj* zwart; **~ market** zwarte markt

blackberry ['blækbəri] *n* braam *c*

blackbird ['blækbə:d] *n* merel *c*

blackboard ['blækbɔ:d] *n* schoolbord *nt*

black-currant [,blæk'kʌrənt] *n* zwarte bes

blackmail ['blækmeil] *n* chantage *c*; *v* chanteren

blacksmith ['blæksmiθ] *n* smid *c*

bladder ['blædə] *n* blaas *c*

blade [bleid] *n* lemmet *nt*; **~ of grass** grasspriet *c*

blame [bleim] *n* schuld *c*; verwijt *nt*; *v* de schuld *geven aan, beschuldi-

gen
blank [blæŋk] *adj* blanco
blanket ['blæŋkit] *n* deken *c*
blast [blɑːst] *n* explosie *c*
blazer ['bleizə] *n* sportjasje *nt*, blazer *c*
bleach [bliːtʃ] *v* bleken
bleak [bliːk] *adj* guur
*bleed [bliːd] *v* bloeden; *uitzuigen
bless [bles] *v* zegenen
blessing ['blesiŋ] *n* zegen *c*
blind [blaind] *n* rolgordijn *nt*, jaloezie *c*; *adj* blind; *v* verblinden
blister ['blistə] *n* blaar *c*, blaas *c*
blizzard ['blizəd] *n* sneeuwstorm *c*
block [blɔk] *v* versperren, blokkeren; *n* blok *nt*; ~ **of flats** flatgebouw *nt*
blonde [blɔnd] *n* blondine *c*
blood [blʌd] *n* bloed *nt*; ~ **pressure** bloeddruk *c*
blood-poisoning ['blʌd,pɔizəniŋ] *n* bloedvergiftiging *c*
blood-vessel ['blʌd,vesəl] *n* bloedvat *nt*
blot [blɔt] *n* vlek *c*; smet *c*; **blotting paper** vloeipapier *nt*
blouse [blauz] *n* blouse *c*
blow [blou] *n* klap *c*, slag *c*; windvlaag *c*
*blow [blou] *v* *blazen; *waaien
blow-out ['blouaut] *n* bandepech *c*
blue [bluː] *adj* blauw; neerslachtig
blunt [blʌnt] *adj* bot; stomp
blush [blʌʃ] *v* blozen
board [bɔːd] *n* plank *c*; bord *nt*; pension *nt*; bestuur *nt*; ~ **and lodging** vol pension, kost en inwoning
boarder ['bɔːdə] *n* kostganger *c*
boarding-house ['bɔːdiŋhaus] *n* pension *nt*
boarding-school ['bɔːdiŋskuːl] *n* internaat *nt*
boast [boust] *v* opscheppen
boat [bout] *n* schip *nt*, boot *c*
body ['bɔdi] *n* lichaam *nt*; lijf *nt*

bodyguard ['bɔdigɑːd] *n* lijfwacht *c*
bog [bɔg] *n* moeras *nt*
boil [bɔil] *v* koken; *n* steenpuist *c*
bold [bould] *adj* stoutmoedig; vrijpostig, brutaal
Bolivia [bə'liviə] Bolivië
Bolivian [bə'liviən] *adj* Boliviaans; *n* Boliviaan *c*
bolt [boult] *n* grendel *c*; bout *c*
bomb [bɔm] *n* bom *c*; *v* bombarderen
bond [bɔnd] *n* obligatie *c*
bone [boun] *n* been *nt*, bot *nt*; graat *c*; *v* uitbenen
bonnet ['bɔnit] *n* motorkap *c*
book [buk] *n* boek *nt*; *v* reserveren, boeken; *inschrijven
booking ['bukiŋ] *n* reservering *c*, bespreking *c*
bookseller ['buk,selə] *n* boekhandelaar *c*
bookstand ['bukstænd] *n* boekenstalletje *nt*
bookstore ['bukstɔː] *n* boekwinkel *c*, boekhandel *c*
boot [buːt] *n* laars *c*; bagageruimte *c*
booth [buːð] *n* kraam *c*; hokje *nt*
border ['bɔːdə] *n* grens *c*; rand *c*
bore¹ [bɔː] *v* vervelen; boren; *n* zeurpiet *c*
bore² [bɔː] *v* (p bear)
boring ['bɔːriŋ] *adj* vervelend, saai
born [bɔːn] *adj* geboren
borrow ['bɔrou] *v* lenen; ontlenen
bosom ['buzəm] *n* borst *c*
boss [bɔs] *n* chef *c*, baas *c*
botany ['bɔtəni] *n* plantkunde *c*
both [bouθ] *adj* beide; **both ... and** zowel ... als
bother ['bɔðə] *v* vervelen, hinderen; moeite *doen; *n* last *c*
bottle ['bɔtəl] *n* fles *c*; ~ **opener** flesopener *c*; **hot-water** ~ warmwaterkruik *c*
bottleneck ['bɔtəlnek] *n* flessehals *c*

bottom ['bɔtəm] n bodem c; achterwerk nt, zitvlak nt; adj onderst
bough [bau] n tak c
bought [bɔːt] v (p, pp buy)
boulder ['bouldə] n rotsblok nt
bound [baund] n grens c; *be ~ to *moeten; ~ for op weg naar
boundary ['baundəri] n grens c; landsgrens c
bouquet [bu'kei] n boeket nt
bourgeois ['buəʒwaː] adj burgerlijk
boutique [bu'tiːk] n boutique c
bow¹ [bau] v *buigen
bow² [bou] n boog c; ~ tie vlinderdasje nt, strikje nt
bowels [bauəlz] pl darmen, ingewanden pl
bowl [boul] n schaal c
bowling ['boulin] n bowling c, kegelspel nt; ~ alley kegelbaan c
box¹ [bɔks] v boksen; **boxing match** bokswedstrijd c
box² [bɔks] n doos c
box-office ['bɔks,ɔfis] n plaatskaartenbureau nt, kassa c
boy [bɔi] n jongen c; joch nt, knaap c; bediende c; ~ scout padvinder c
bra [braː] n beha c, bustehouder c
bracelet ['breislit] n armband c
braces ['breisiz] pl bretels pl
brain [brein] n hersenen pl; verstand nt
brain-wave ['breinweiv] n inval c
brake [breik] n rem c; ~ drum remtrommel c; ~ lights remlichten pl
branch [braːntʃ] n tak c; filiaal nt
brand [brænd] n merk nt; brandmerk nt
brand-new [,brænd'njuː] adj splinternieuw
brass [braːs] n messing nt; koper nt, geelkoper nt; ~ band n fanfarekorps nt

brassiere ['bræziə] n bustehouder c, beha c
brassware ['braːsweə] n koperwerk nt
brave [breiv] adj moedig, dapper; flink
Brazil [brə'zil] Brazilië
Brazilian [brə'ziljən] adj Braziliaans; n Braziliaan c
breach [briːtʃ] n bres c
bread [bred] n brood nt; **wholemeal** ~ volkorenbrood nt
breadth [bredθ] n breedte c
break [breik] n breuk c; pauze c
*break** [breik] v *breken; ~ down stuk *gaan; ontleden
breakdown ['breikdaun] n panne c, motorpech c
breakfast ['brekfəst] n ontbijt nt
bream [briːm] n (pl ~) brasem c
breast [brest] n borst c
breaststroke ['breststrouk] n schoolslag c
breath [breθ] n adem c; lucht c
breathe [briːð] v ademen
breathing ['briːðiŋ] n ademhaling c
breed [briːd] n ras nt; soort c/nt
*breed** [briːd] v fokken
breeze [briːz] n bries c
brew [bruː] v brouwen
brewery ['bruːəri] n brouwerij c
bribe [braib] v *omkopen
bribery ['braibəri] n omkoping c
brick [brik] n steen c, baksteen c
bricklayer ['brikleiə] n metselaar c
bride [braid] n bruid c
bridegroom ['braidgruːm] n bruidegom c
bridge [bridʒ] n brug c; bridge nt
brief [briːf] adj kort; beknopt
briefcase ['briːfkeis] n aktentas c
briefs [briːfs] pl slip c, onderbroek c
bright [brait] adj helder; blinkend; snugger, pienter
brill [bril] n griet c

brilliant ['briljənt] *adj* schitterend; briljant

brim [brim] *n* rand *c*

* **bring** [briŋ] *v* *brengen; *meebrengen; ~ **back** *terugbrengen; ~ **up** opvoeden, *grootbrengen; ter sprake *brengen

brisk [brisk] *adj* levendig

Britain ['britən] Engeland

British ['britiʃ] *adj* Brits; Engels

Briton ['britən] *n* Brit *c*; Engelsman *c*

broad [brɔːd] *adj* breed; ruim, wijd; globaal

broadcast ['brɔːdkɑːst] *n* uitzending *c*

* **broadcast** ['brɔːdkɑːst] *v* *uitzenden

brochure ['brouʃuə] *n* brochure *c*

broke¹ [brouk] *v* (p break)

broke² [brouk] *adj* platzak

broken ['broukən] *adj* (pp break) stuk, kapot

broker ['broukə] *n* makelaar *c*

bronchitis [brɔŋ'kaitis] *n* bronchitis *c*

bronze [brɔnz] *n* brons *nt*; *adj* bronzen

brooch [broutʃ] *n* broche *c*

brook [bruk] *n* beek *c*

broom [bruːm] *n* bezem *c*

brothel ['brɔθəl] *n* bordeel *nt*

brother ['brʌðə] *n* broer *c*; broeder *c*

brother-in-law ['brʌðərinlɔː] *n* (pl brothers-) zwager *c*

brought [brɔːt] *v* (p, pp bring)

brown [braun] *adj* bruin

bruise [bruːz] *n* blauwe plek, kneuzing *c*; *v* kneuzen

brunette [bruːˈnet] *n* brunette *c*

brush [brʌʃ] *n* borstel *c*; kwast *c*; *v* poetsen, borstelen

brutal ['bruːtəl] *adj* beestachtig

bubble ['bʌbəl] *n* bel *c*

bucket ['bʌkit] *n* emmer *c*

buckle ['bʌkəl] *n* gesp *c*

bud [bʌd] *n* knop *c*

budget ['bʌdʒit] *n* begroting *c*, budget

nt

buffet ['bufei] *n* buffet *nt*

bug [bʌg] *n* wandluis *c*; kever *c*; *nAm* insekt *nt*

* **build** [bild] *v* bouwen

building ['bildiŋ] *n* gebouw *nt*

bulb [bʌlb] *n* bol *c*; bloembol *c*; **light** ~ gloeilamp *c*

Bulgaria [bʌl'geəriə] Bulgarije

Bulgarian [bʌl'geəriən] *adj* Bulgaars; *n* Bulgaar *c*

bulk [bʌlk] *n* omvang *c*; massa *c*; meerderheid *c*

bulky ['bʌlki] *adj* lijvig, omvangrijk

bull [bul] *n* stier *c*

bullet ['bulit] *n* kogel *c*

bullfight ['bulfait] *n* stierengevecht *nt*

bullring ['bulriŋ] *n* arena *c*

bump [bʌmp] *v* *stoten; botsen; bonzen; *n* stoot *c*, bons *c*

bumper ['bʌmpə] *n* bumper *c*

bumpy ['bʌmpi] *adj* hobbelig

bun [bʌn] *n* broodje *nt*

bunch [bʌntʃ] *n* bos *c*; groep *c*

bundle ['bʌndəl] *n* bundel *c*; *v* *samenbinden, bundelen

bunk [bʌŋk] *n* kooi *c*

buoy [bɔi] *n* boei *c*

burden ['bəːdən] *n* last *c*

bureau ['bjuərou] *n* (pl ~x, ~s) bureau *nt*, schrijftafel *c*; *nAm* commode *c*

bureaucracy [bjuə'rɔkrəsi] *n* bureaucratie *c*

burglar ['bəːglə] *n* inbreker *c*

burgle ['bəːgəl] *v* *inbreken

burial ['beriəl] *n* teraardebestelling *c*, begrafenis *c*

burn [bəːn] *n* brandwond *c*

* **burn** [bəːn] *v* branden; verbranden; aanbranden

* **burst** [bəːst] *v* *barsten; *breken

bury ['beri] *v* *begraven; *bedelven

bus [bʌs] *n* bus *c*

bush [buʃ] *n* struik *c*

business ['biznəs] *n* zaken *pl*, handel *c*; bedrijf *nt*, zaak *c*; werk *nt*; aangelegenheid *c*; ~ **hours** openingstijden *pl*, kantooruren *pl*; ~ **trip** zakenreis *c*; **on** ~ voor zaken

business-like ['biznislaik] *adj* zakelijk

businessman ['biznəsmən] *n* (pl -men) zakenman *c*

bust [bʌst] *n* buste *c*

bustle ['bʌsəl] *n* drukte *c*

busy ['bizi] *adj* bezig; druk

but [bʌt] *conj* maar; doch; *prep* behalve

butcher ['butʃə] *n* slager *c*

butter ['bʌtə] *n* boter *c*

butterfly ['bʌtəflai] *n* vlinder *c*; ~ **stroke** vlinderslag *c*

buttock ['bʌtək] *n* bil *c*

button ['bʌtən] *n* knoop *c*; *v* knopen

buttonhole ['bʌtənhoul] *n* knoopsgat *nt*

*buy [bai] *v* *kopen; aanschaffen

buyer ['baiə] *n* koper *c*

by [bai] *prep* door; met, per; bij

by-pass ['baipɑːs] *n* ringweg *c*; *v* passeren

C

cab [kæb] *n* taxi *c*

cabaret ['kæbərei] *n* cabaret *nt*; nachtclub *c*

cabbage ['kæbidʒ] *n* kool *c*

cab-driver ['kæb,draivə] *n* taxichauffeur *c*

cabin ['kæbin] *n* cabine *c*; hut *c*; kleedhokje *nt*; kajuit *c*

cabinet ['kæbinət] *n* kabinet *nt*

cable ['keibəl] *n* kabel *c*; telegram *nt*; *v* telegraferen

cadre ['kɑːdə] *n* kader *nt*

café ['kæfei] *n* café *nt*

cafeteria [,kæfə'tiəriə] *n* cafetaria *c*

caffeine ['kæfiːn] *n* coffeïne *c*

cage [keidʒ] *n* kooi *c*

cake [keik] *n* cake *c*; gebak *nt*, taart *c*, koek *c*

calamity [kə'læməti] *n* onheil *nt*, ramp *c*

calcium ['kælsiəm] *n* calcium *nt*

calculate ['kælkjuleit] *v* uitrekenen, berekenen

calculation [,kælkju'leiʃən] *n* berekening *c*

calendar ['kæləndə] *n* kalender *c*

calf [kɑːf] *n* (pl calves) kalf *nt*; kuit *c*; ~ **skin** kalfsleer *nt*

call [kɔːl] *v* *roepen; noemen; opbellen; *n* roep *c*; visite *c*, bezoek *nt*; telefoontje *nt*; ***be called** *heten; ~ **names** *uitschelden; ~ **on** *bezoeken; ~ **up** *Am* opbellen

callus ['kæləs] *n* eelt *nt*

calm [kɑːm] *adj* rustig, kalm; ~ **down** kalmeren; bedaren

calorie ['kæləri] *n* calorie *c*

Calvinism ['kælvinizəm] *n* calvinisme *nt*

came [keim] *v* (p come)

camel ['kæməl] *n* kameel *c*

cameo ['kæmiou] *n* (pl ~s) camee *c*

camera ['kæmərə] *n* fototoestel *nt*; filmcamera *c*; ~ **shop** fotowinkel *c*

camp [kæmp] *n* kamp *nt*; *v* kamperen

campaign [kæm'pein] *n* campagne *c*

camp-bed [,kæmp'bed] *n* veldbed *nt*, stretcher *c*

camper ['kæmpə] *n* kampeerder *c*

camping ['kæmpiŋ] *n* camping *c*; ~ **site** camping *c*, kampeerterrein *nt*

camshaft ['kæmʃɑːft] *n* nokkenas *c*

can [kæn] *n* blik *nt*; ~ **opener** blikopener *c*

*can [kæn] *v* *kunnen

Canada ['kænədə] Canada

Canadian [kə'neidiən] *adj* Canadees;

n Canadees *c*

canal [kə'næl] *n* kanaal *nt*; gracht *c*, singel *c*

canary [kə'neəri] *n* kanarie *c*

cancel ['kænsəl] *v* annuleren; *afzeggen

cancellation [,kænsə'leiʃən] *n* annulering *c*

cancer ['kænsə] *n* kanker *c*

candelabrum [,kændə'la:brəm] *n* (pl -bra) kandelaber *c*

candidate ['kændidət] *n* kandidaat *c*, gegadigde *c*

candle ['kændəl] *n* kaars *c*

candy ['kændi] *nAm* snoepje *nt*; snoep *nt*, snoepgoed *nt*; ~ **store** *Am* snoepwinkel *c*

cane [kein] *n* riet *nt*; stok *c*

canister ['kænistə] *n* trommel *c*, bus *c*

canoe [kə'nu:] *n* kano *c*

canteen [kæn'ti:n] *n* kantine *c*

canvas ['kænvəs] *n* tentdoek *nt*

cap [kæp] *n* pet *c*, muts *c*

capable ['keipəbəl] *adj* kundig, bekwaam

capacity [kə'pæsəti] *n* capaciteit *c*; vermogen *nt*; bekwaamheid *c*

cape [keip] *n* cape *c*; kaap *c*

capital ['kæpitəl] *n* hoofdstad *c*; kapitaal *nt*; *adj* belangrijk, hoofd-; ~ **letter** hoofdletter *c*

capitalism ['kæpitəlizəm] *n* kapitalisme *nt*

capitulation [kə,pitju'leiʃən] *n* capitulatie *c*

capsule ['kæpsju:l] *n* capsule *c*

captain ['kæptin] *n* kapitein *c*; gezagvoerder *c*

capture ['kæptʃə] *v* gevangen *nemen, *vangen; *innemen; *n* vangst *c*; inneming *c*

car [ka:] *n* auto *c*; ~ **hire** autoverhuur *c*; ~ **park** parkeerplaats *c*; ~ **rental** *Am* autoverhuur *c*

carafe [kə'ræf] *n* karaf *c*

caramel ['kærəməl] *n* karamel *c*

carat ['kærət] *n* karaat *nt*

caravan ['kærəvæn] *n* caravan *c*; woonwagen *c*

carburettor [,ka:bju'retə] *n* carburateur *c*

card [ka:d] *n* kaart *c*; briefkaart *c*

cardboard ['ka:dbɔ:d] *n* karton *nt*; *adj* kartonnen

cardigan ['ka:digən] *n* vest *nt*

cardinal ['ka:dinəl] *n* kardinaal *c*; *adj* kardinaal, hoofd-

care [keə] *n* verzorging *c*; zorg *c*; ~ **about** zich bekommeren om; ~ **for** *houden van; *take ~ **of** zorgen voor, verzorgen

career [kə'riə] *n* loopbaan *c*, carrière *c*

carefree ['keəfri:] *adj* onbezorgd

careful ['keəfəl] *adj* voorzichtig; zorgvuldig, nauwkeurig

careless ['keələs] *adj* achteloos, slordig

caretaker ['keə,teikə] *n* concierge *c*

cargo ['ka:gou] *n* (pl ~es) lading *c*, vracht *c*

carnival ['ka:nivəl] *n* carnaval *nt*

carp [ka:p] *n* (pl ~) karper *c*

carpenter ['ka:pintə] *n* timmerman *c*

carpet ['ka:pit] *n* vloerkleed *nt*, tapijt *nt*

carriage ['kæridʒ] *n* wagon *c*; koets *c*, rijtuig *nt*

carriageway ['kæridʒwei] *n* rijbaan *c*

carrot ['kærət] *n* peen *c*, wortel *c*

carry ['kæri] *v* *dragen; voeren; ~ **on** voortzetten; *doorgaan; ~ **out** uitvoeren

carry-cot ['kærikɔt] *n* reiswieg *c*

cart [ka:t] *n* kar *c*, wagen *c*

cartilage ['ka:tilidʒ] *n* kraakbeen *nt*

carton ['ka:tən] *n* kartonnen doos; slof *c*

cartoon [ka:'tu:n] *n* tekenfilm *c*

cartridge ['ka:tridʒ] *n* patroon *c*

carve [ka:v] v *snijden; kerven, *houtsnijden

carving ['ka:viŋ] n houtsnijwerk nt

case [keis] n geval nt; zaak c; koffer c; etui nt; **attaché** ~ aktentas c; in ~ indien; in ~ of in geval van

cash [kæʃ] n contanten pl, contant geld; v verzilveren, incasseren, innen

cashier [kæ'ʃiə] n kassier c; caissière c

cashmere ['kæʃmiə] n kasjmier nt

casino [kə'si:nou] n (pl ~s) casino nt

cask [ka:sk] n ton c, vat nt

cast [ka:st] n worp c

*cast [ka:st] v gooien, *werpen; **cast iron** gietijzer nt

castle ['ka:səl] n slot nt, kasteel nt

casual ['kæʒuəl] adj ongedwongen; terloops, toevallig

casualty ['kæʒuəlti] n slachtoffer nt

cat [kæt] n kat c

catacomb ['kætəkoum] n catacombe c

catalogue ['kætələɡ] n catalogus c

catarrh [kə'ta:] n catarre c

catastrophe [kə'tæstrəfi] n catastrofe c

*catch [kætʃ] v *vangen; *grijpen; betrappen; *nemen, halen

category ['kætiɡəri] n categorie c

cathedral [kə'θi:drəl] n dom c, kathedraal c

catholic ['kæθəlik] adj katholiek

cattle ['kætəl] pl vee nt

caught [kɔ:t] v (p, pp catch)

cauliflower ['kɔliflauə] n bloemkool c

cause [kɔ:z] v veroorzaken; aanrichten; n oorzaak c; beweegreden c, aanleiding c; zaak c; ~ **to** *doen

causeway ['kɔ:zwei] n straatweg c

caution ['kɔ:ʃən] n voorzichtigheid c; v waarschuwen

cautious ['kɔ:ʃəs] adj bedachtzaam

cave [keiv] n grot c; spelonk c

cavern ['kævən] n hol nt

caviar ['kævia:] n kaviaar c

cavity ['kævəti] n holte c

cease [si:s] v *ophouden

ceiling ['si:liŋ] n plafond nt

celebrate ['selibreit] v vieren

celebration [,seli'breiʃən] n viering c

celebrity [si'lebrəti] n roem c

celery ['seləri] n selderij c

celibacy ['selibəsi] n celibaat nt

cell [sel] n cel c

cellar ['selə] n kelder c

cellophane ['seləfein] n cellofaan nt

cement [si'ment] n cement nt

cemetery ['semitri] n begraafplaats c, kerkhof nt

censorship ['sensəʃip] n censuur c

centigrade ['sentigreid] adj celsius

centimetre ['senti,mi:tə] n centimeter c

central ['sentrəl] adj centraal; ~ **heating** centrale verwarming; ~ **station** centraal station

centralize ['sentrəlaiz] v centraliseren

centre ['sentə] n centrum nt; middelpunt nt

century ['sentʃəri] n eeuw c

ceramics [si'ræmiks] pl aardewerk nt, ceramiek c

ceremony ['serəməni] n ceremonie c

certain ['sə:tən] adj zeker; bepaald

certificate [sə'tifikət] n certificaat nt; attest nt, akte c, diploma nt, getuigschrift nt

chain [tʃein] n keten c, ketting c

chair [tʃeə] n stoel c; zetel c

chairman ['tʃeəmən] n (pl -men) voorzitter c

chalet ['ʃælei] n chalet nt

chalk [tʃɔ:k] n krijt nt

challenge ['tʃæləndʒ] v uitdagen; n uitdaging c

chamber ['tʃeimbə] n kamer c

chambermaid ['tʃeimbəmeid] n kamermeisje nt

champagne [ʃæm'pein] n champagne

c

champion ['tʃæmpjən] n kampioen c; voorvechter c

chance [tʃa:ns] n toeval nt; kans c, gelegenheid c; risico nt; gok c; **by ~** toevallig

change [tʃeindʒ] v wijzigen, veranderen; wisselen; zich verkleden; overstappen; n wijziging c, verandering c; wisselgeld nt, kleingeld nt

channel ['tʃænəl] n kanaal nt; **English Channel** het Kanaal

chaos ['keiɔs] n chaos c

chaotic [kei'ɔtik] adj chaotisch

chap [tʃæp] n vent c

chapel ['tʃæpəl] n kerk c, kapel c

chaplain ['tʃæplin] n kapelaan c

character ['kærəktə] n karakter nt

characteristic [,kærəktə'ristik] adj kenmerkend, karakteristiek; n kenmerk nt; karaktertrek c

characterize ['kærəktəraiz] v kenmerken

charcoal ['tʃa:koul] n houtskool c

charge [tʃa:dʒ] v berekenen; belasten; aanklagen; *laden; n prijs c; belasting c, lading c, last c; aanklacht c; **~ plate** Am credit card; **free of ~** kosteloos, in **~ of** belast met; ***take ~ of** op zich *nemen

charity ['tʃærəti] n liefdadigheid c

charm [tʃa:m] n bekoring c, charme c; amulet c

charming ['tʃa:miŋ] adj charmant

chart [tʃa:t] n tabel c; grafiek c; zeekaart c; **conversion ~** omrekentabel c

chase [tʃeis] v *najagen; *verdrijven, *verjagen; n jacht c

chasm ['kæzəm] n kloof c

chassis ['ʃæsi] n (pl ~) chassis nt

chaste [tʃeist] adj kuis

chat [tʃæt] v kletsen, babbelen; n babbeltje nt, praatje nt, geklets nt

chatterbox ['tʃætəbɔks] n babbelkous c

chauffeur ['ʃoufə] n chauffeur c

cheap [tʃi:p] adj goedkoop; voordelig

cheat [tʃi:t] v *bedriegen; oplichten

check [tʃek] v controleren, *nakijken; n ruit c; nAm rekening c; cheque c; **check!** schaak!; **~ in** zich *inschrijven

check-book ['tʃekbuk] nAm chequeboekje nt

checkerboard ['tʃekəbɔ:d] nAm schaakbord nt

checkers ['tʃekəz] plAm damspel nt

checkroom ['tʃekru:m] nAm garderobe c

check-up ['tʃekʌp] n onderzoek nt

cheek [tʃi:k] n wang c

cheek-bone ['tʃi:kboun] n jukbeen nt

cheer [tʃiə] v juichen; **~ up** opvrolijken

cheerful ['tʃiəfəl] adj opgewekt, vrolijk

cheese [tʃi:z] n kaas c

chef [ʃef] n chef-kok c

chemical ['kemikəl] adj scheikundig, chemisch

chemist ['kemist] n apotheker c; **chemist's** apotheek c; drogisterij c

chemistry ['kemistri] n scheikunde c, chemie c

cheque [tʃek] n cheque c

cheque-book ['tʃekbuk] n chequeboekje nt

chequered ['tʃekəd] adj geruit, geblokt

cherry ['tʃeri] n kers c

chess [tʃes] n schaakspel nt

chest [tʃest] n borst c; borstkas c; kist c; **~ of drawers** ladenkast c

chestnut ['tʃesnʌt] n kastanje c

chew [tʃu:] v kauwen

chewing-gum ['tʃu:iŋgʌm] n kauwgom c/nt

chicken ['tʃikin] n kip c; kuiken nt

chickenpox ['tʃikinpɔks] n waterpokken *pl*

chief [tʃi:f] *n* chef *c*; *adj* hoofd-, voornaamst

chieftain ['tʃi:ftən] *n* opperhoofd *nt*

child [tʃaild] *n* (pl children) kind *nt*

childbirth ['tʃaildbə:θ] *n* bevalling *c*

childhood ['tʃaildhud] *n* jeugd *c*

Chile ['tʃili] Chili

Chilean ['tʃiliən] *adj* Chileens; *n* Chileen *c*

chill [tʃil] *n* rilling *c*

chilly ['tʃili] *adj* kil

chimes [tʃaimz] *pl* carillon *c*

chimney ['tʃimni] *n* schoorsteen *c*

chin [tʃin] *n* kin *c*

China ['tʃainə] China

china ['tʃainə] *n* porselein *nt*

Chinese [tʃai'ni:z] *adj* Chinees; *n* Chinees *c*

chink [tʃiŋk] *n* kier *c*

chip [tʃip] *n* schilfer *c*; fiche *c*; *v* *afsnijden, *afbreken; **chips** frites *pl*

chiropodist [ki'rɔpədist] *n* pedicure *c*

chisel ['tʃizəl] *n* beitel *c*

chives [tʃaivz] *pl* bieslook *nt*

chlorine ['klɔ:ri:n] *n* chloor *nt*

chock-full [tʃɔk'ful] *adj* afgeladen, stampvol

chocolate ['tʃɔklət] *n* chocola *c*; bonbon *c*; chocolademelk *c*

choice [tʃɔis] *n* keuze *c*; keus *c*

choir [kwaiə] *n* koor *nt*

choke [tʃouk] *v* stikken; wurgen; *n* choke *c*

* **choose** [tʃu:z] *v* *kiezen

chop [tʃɔp] *n* kotelet, karbonade *c*; *v* hakken

Christ [kraist] Christus

christen ['krisən] *v* dopen

christening ['krisəniŋ] *n* doop *c*

Christian ['kristʃən] *adj* christelijk; *n* christen *c*; ~ **name** voornaam *c*

Christmas ['krisməs] Kerstmis

chromium ['kroumiəm] *n* chroom *nt*

chronic ['krɔnik] *adj* chronisch

chronological [,krɔnə'lɔdʒikəl] *adj* chronologisch

chuckle ['tʃʌkəl] *v* grinniken

chunk [tʃʌŋk] *n* stuk *nt*

church [tʃə:tʃ] *n* kerk *c*

churchyard ['tʃə:tʃjɑ:d] *n* kerkhof *nt*

cigar [si'gɑ:] *n* sigaar *c*; ~ **shop** sigarenwinkel *c*

cigarette [,sigə'ret] *n* sigaret *c*; ~ **tobacco** shag *c*

cigarette-case [,sigə'retkeis] *n* sigarettenkoker *c*

cigarette-holder [,sigə'ret,houldə] *n* sigarettepijpje *nt*

cigarette-lighter [,sigə'ret,laitə] *n* aansteker *c*

cinema ['sinəmə] *n* bioscoop *c*

cinnamon ['sinəmən] *n* kaneel *c*

circle ['sə:kəl] *n* cirkel *c*; kring *c*; balkon *nt*; *v* omringen, *omgeven

circulation [,sə:kju'leiʃən] *n* circulatie *c*; bloedsomloop *c*; omloop *c*

circumstance ['sə:kəmstæns] *n* omstandigheid *c*

circus ['sə:kəs] *n* circus *nt*

citizen ['sitizən] *n* burger *c*

citizenship ['sitizənʃip] *n* staatsburgerschap *nt*

city ['siti] *n* stad *c*

civic ['sivik] *adj* burger-

civil ['sivəl] *adj* civiel; beleefd; ~ **law** burgerlijk recht; ~ **servant** ambtenaar *c*

civilian [si'viljən] *adj* burger-; *n* burger *c*

civilization [,sivəlai'zeiʃən] *n* beschaving *c*

civilized ['sivəlaizd] *adj* beschaafd

claim [kleim] *v* vorderen, opeisen; beweren; *n* eis *c*, aanspraak *c*

clamp [klæmp] *n* klem *c*; klemschroef *c*

clap [klæp] *v* applaudisseren, klappen

clarify ['klærifai] v ophelderen, verduidelijken

class [klɑ:s] n rang c, klasse c; klas c

classical ['klæsikəl] adj klassiek

classify ['klæsifai] v indelen

class-mate ['klɑ:smeit] n klasgenoot c

classroom ['klɑ:sru:m] n leslokaal nt

clause [klɔ:z] n clausule c

claw [klɔ:] n klauw c

clay [klei] n klei c

clean [kli:n] adj zuiver, schoon; v schoonmaken, reinigen

cleaning ['kli:niŋ] n schoonmaak c, reiniging c; ~ **fluid** reinigingsmiddel nt

clear [kliə] adj helder; duidelijk; v opruimen

clearing ['kliəriŋ] n open plaats

cleft [kleft] n kloof c

clergyman ['klə:dʒimən] n (pl -men) dominee c, predikant c; geestelijke c

clerk [klɑ:k] n kantoorbediende c, beambte c; klerk c; secretaris c

clever ['klevə] adj intelligent; slim, pienter, knap

client ['klaiənt] n klant c; cliënt c

cliff [klif] n rots c, klip c

climate ['klaimit] n klimaat nt

climb [klaim] v *klimmen; *stijgen; n stijging c

clinic ['klinik] n kliniek c

cloak [klouk] n mantel c

cloakroom ['kloukru:m] n garderobe c

clock [klɔk] n klok c; **at ... o'clock** om ... uur

cloister ['klɔistə] n klooster nt

close[1] [klouz] v *sluiten; **closed** adj toe, dicht, gesloten

close[2] [klous] adj nabij

closet ['klɔzit] n kast c; nAm kleerkast c

cloth [klɔθ] n stof c; doek c

clothes [klouðz] pl kleding c, kleren pl

clothes-brush ['klouðzbrʌʃ] n kleerborstel c

clothing ['klouðiŋ] n kleding c

cloud [klaud] n wolk c; **clouds** bewolking c

cloud-burst ['klaudbə:st] n wolkbreuk c

cloudy ['klaudi] adj betrokken, bewolkt

clover ['klouvə] n klaver c

clown [klaun] n clown c

club [klʌb] n club c; sociëteit c, vereniging c; knots c, knuppel c

clumsy ['klʌmzi] adj onhandig

clutch [klʌtʃ] n koppeling c; greep c

coach [koutʃ] n bus c; rijtuig nt; koets c; trainer c

coachwork ['koutʃwə:k] n carrosserie c

coagulate [kou'ægjuleit] v stollen

coal [koul] n kolen pl

coarse [kɔ:s] adj grof

coast [koust] n kust c

coat [kout] n mantel c, jas c

coat-hanger ['kout,hæŋə] n kleerhanger c

cobweb ['kɔbweb] n spinneweb nt

cocaine [kou'kein] n cocaïne c

cock [kɔk] n haan c

cocktail ['kɔkteil] n cocktail c

coconut ['koukənʌt] n kokosnoot c

cod [kɔd] n (pl ~) kabeljauw c

code [koud] n code c

coffee ['kɔfi] n koffie c

cognac ['kɔnjæk] n cognac c

coherence [kou'hiərəns] n samenhang c

coin [kɔin] n munt c; geldstuk nt, muntstuk nt

coincide [,kouin'said] v *samenvallen

cold [kould] adj koud; n kou c; verkoudheid c; **catch a** ~ kou vatten

collapse [kə'læps] v *bezwijken, instorten

collar ['kɔlə] n halsband c; boord nt/c, kraag c; ~ stud boordeknoopje nt

collarbone ['kɔləboun] n sleutelbeen nt

colleague ['kɔli:g] n collega c

collect [kə'lekt] v verzamelen; ophalen, afhalen; collecteren

collection [kə'lekʃən] n collectie c, verzameling c; lichting c

collective [kə'lektiv] adj collectief

collector [kə'lektə] n verzamelaar c; collectant c

college ['kɔlidʒ] n instelling voor hoger onderwijs; school c

collide [kə'laid] v botsen

collision [kə'liʒən] n aanrijding c, botsing c; aanvaring c

Colombia [kə'lɔmbiə] Colombia

Colombian [kə'lɔmbiən] adj Colombiaans; n Colombiaan c

colonel ['kɔ:nəl] n kolonel c

colony ['kɔləni] n kolonie c

colour ['kʌlə] n kleur c; v kleuren; ~ film kleurenfilm c

colourant ['kʌlərənt] n kleurstof c

colour-blind ['kʌləblaind] adj kleurenblind

coloured ['kʌləd] adj gekleurd

colourful ['kʌləfəl] adj bont, kleurrijk

column ['kɔləm] n pilaar c, zuil c; kolom c; rubriek c; kolonne c

coma ['koumə] n coma nt

comb [koum] v kammen; n kam c

combat ['kɔmbæt] n strijd c, gevecht nt; v *bestrijden, *vechten

combination [,kɔmbi'neiʃən] n combinatie c

combine [kəm'bain] v combineren; *samenbrengen

*come [kʌm] v *komen; ~ across *tegenkomen; *vinden

comedian [kə'mi:diən] n toneelspeler c; komiek c

comedy ['kɔmədi] n blijspel nt, komedie c; musical ~ musical c

comfort ['kʌmfət] n gemak nt, komfort nt, gerief nt; troost c; v troosten

comfortable ['kʌmfətəbəl] adj geriefelijk, comfortabel

comic ['kɔmik] adj komisch

comics ['kɔmiks] pl stripverhaal nt

coming ['kʌmiŋ] n komst c

comma ['kɔmə] n komma c

command [kə'mɑ:nd] v *bevelen; n bevel nt

commander [kə'mɑ:ndə] n bevelhebber c

commemoration [kə,memə'reiʃən] n herdenking c

commence [kə'mens] v *beginnen

comment ['kɔment] n commentaar nt; v aanmerken

commerce ['kɔmə:s] n handel c

commercial [kə'mə:ʃəl] adj handels-, commercieel; n reclamespot c; ~ law handelsrecht nt

commission [kə'miʃən] n commissie c

commit [kə'mit] v toevertrouwen; plegen, *begaan

committee [kə'miti] n commissie c, comité nt

common ['kɔmən] adj gemeenschappelijk; gebruikelijk, gewoon; ordinair

commune ['kɔmju:n] n commune c

communicate [kə'mju:nikeit] v meedelen, mededelen

communication [kə,mju:ni'keiʃən] n communicatie c; mededeling c

communiqué [kə'mju:nikei] n communiqué nt

communism ['kɔmjunizəm] n communisme nt

communist ['kɔmjunist] n communist c

community [kə'mju:nəti] n samenleving c, gemeenschap c

commuter [kə'mju:tə] n forens c

compact ['kɔmpækt] adj compact

companion [kəm'pænjən] n metgezel c

company ['kʌmpəni] n gezelschap nt; maatschappij c; firma c, onderneming c

comparative [kəm'pærətiv] adj relatief

compare [kəm'pɛə] v *vergelijken

comparison [kəm'pærisən] n vergelijking c

compartment [kəm'pa:tmənt] n coupé c

compass ['kʌmpəs] n kompas nt

compel [kəm'pel] v *dwingen

compensate ['kɔmpənseit] v compenseren

compensation [,kɔmpən'seifən] n compensatie c; schadevergoeding c

compete [kəm'pi:t] v wedijveren

competition [,kɔmpə'tifən] n wedstrijd c; concurrentie c

competitor [kəm'petitər] n concurrent c

compile [kəm'pail] v samenstellen

complain [kəm'plein] v klagen

complaint [kəm'pleint] n klacht c; **complaints book** klachtenboek nt

complete [kəm'pli:t] adj compleet, volledig; v voltooien

completely [kəm'pli:tli] adv helemaal, volkomen, geheel

complex ['kɔmpleks] n complex nt; adj ingewikkeld

complexion [kəm'plekfən] n teint c

complicated ['kɔmplikeitid] adj gecompliceerd, ingewikkeld

compliment ['kɔmplimənt] n compliment nt; v gelukwensen, feliciteren

compose [kəm'pouz] v samenstellen

composer [kəm'pouzə] n componist c

composition [,kɔmpə'zifən] n compositie c; samenstelling c

comprehensive [,kɔmpri'hensiv] adj uitgebreid

comprise [kəm'praiz] v omvatten

compromise ['kɔmprəmaiz] n compromis nt

compulsory [kəm'pʌlsəri] adj verplicht

comrade ['kɔmreid] n kameraad c

conceal [kən'si:l] v *verbergen

conceited [kən'si:tid] adj verwaand

conceive [kən'si:v] v opvatten; zich voorstellen

concentrate ['kɔnsəntreit] v concentreren

concentration [,kɔnsən'treifən] n concentratie c

conception [kən'sepfən] n begrip nt; conceptie c

concern [kən'sə:n] v *aangaan, *betreffen; n zorg c; aangelegenheid c; bedrijf nt, onderneming c

concerned [kən'sə:nd] adj bezorgd; betrokken

concerning [kən'sə:niŋ] prep omtrent, betreffende

concert ['kɔnsət] n concert nt; ~ **hall** concertzaal c

concession [kən'sefən] n concessie c; tegemoetkoming c

concierge [,kɔ̃si'ɛɔʒ] n concierge c

concise [kən'sais] adj beknopt, summier

conclusion [kəŋ'klu:ʒən] n gevolgtrekking c, conclusie c

concrete ['kɔŋkri:t] adj concreet; n beton nt

concurrence [kəŋ'kʌrəns] n samenloop c

concussion [kəŋ'kʌfən] n hersenschudding c

condition [kən'difən] n voorwaarde c; toestand c, conditie c; omstandigheid c

conditional [kən'difənəl] adj voorwaardelijk

conduct[1] ['kɔndʌkt] n gedrag nt

conduct[2] [kən'dʌkt] v leiden; begeleiden; dirigeren

conductor [kən'dʌktə] n conducteur c; dirigent c

confectioner [kən'fekʃənə] n banketbakker c

conference ['kɔnfərəns] n conferentie c

confess [kən'fes] v bekennen; biechten; *belijden

confession [kən'feʃən] n bekentenis c; biecht c

confidence ['kɔnfidəns] n vertrouwen nt

confident ['kɔnfidənt] adj gerust

confidential [,kɔnfi'denʃəl] adj vertrouwelijk

confirm [kən'fə:m] v bevestigen

confirmation [,kɔnfə'meiʃən] n bcvestiging c

confiscate ['kɔnfiskeit] v vorderen, beslag leggen op

conflict ['kɔnflikt] n conflict nt

confuse [kən'fju:z] v verwarren

confusion [kən'fju:ʒən] n verwarring c

congratulate [kən'grætʃuleit] v feliciteren, gelukwensen

congratulation [kən,grætʃu'leiʃən] n felicitatie c, gelukwens c

congregation [,kɔŋgri'geiʃən] n gemeente c; orde c, congregatie c

congress ['kɔŋgres] n congres nt; bijeenkomst c

connect [kə'nekt] v *verbinden; *aansluiten

connection [kə'nekʃən] n relatie c; verband nt; aansluiting c, verbinding c

connoisseur [,kɔnə'sə:] n kenner c

connotation [,kɔnə'teiʃən] n bijbetekenis c

conquer ['kɔŋkə] v veroveren; *overwinnen

conqueror ['kɔŋkərə] n veroveraar c

conquest ['kɔŋkwest] n verovering c

conscience ['kɔnʃəns] n geweten nt

conscious ['kɔnʃəs] adj bewust

consciousness ['kɔnʃəsnəs] n bewustzijn nt

conscript ['kɔnskript] n dienstplichtige c

consent [kən'sent] v toestemmen; instemmen; n instemming c, toestemming c

consequence ['kɔnsikwəns] n consequentie c, gevolg nt

consequently ['kɔnsikwəntli] adv bijgevolg

conservative [kən'sə:vətiv] adj behoudend, conservatief

consider [kən'sidə] v beschouwen; *overwegen; menen, *vinden

considerable [kən'sidərəbəl] adj aanzienlijk; flink, aanmerkelijk

considerate [kən'sidərət] adj attent

consideration [kən,sidə'reiʃən] n overweging c; consideratie c, aandacht c

considering [kən'sidəriŋ] prep gezien

consignment [kən'sainmənt] n zending c

consist of [kən'sist] *bestaan uit

conspire [kən'spaiə] v *samenzweren

constant ['kɔnstənt] adj aanhoudcnd

constipation [,kɔnsti'peiʃən] n obstipatie c, constipatie c

constituency [kən'stitʃuənsi] n kiesdistrict nt

constitution [,kɔnsti'tju:ʃən] n grondwet c

construct [kən'strʌkt] v bouwen; opbouwen, construeren

construction [kən'strʌkʃən] n constructie c; opbouw c; gebouw nt, bouw c

consul ['kɔnsəl] n consul c

consulate ['kɔnsjulət] n consulaat nt

consult [kən'sʌlt] v raadplegen

consultation [,kɔnsəl'teiʃən] n raadpleging *c*; consult *nt*; ~ **hours** *n* spreekuur *nt*

consumer [kən'sju:mə] *n* verbruiker *c*, consument *c*

contact ['kɔntækt] *n* contact *nt*; aanraking *c*; *v* zich in verbinding stellen met; ~ **lenses** contactlenzen *pl*

contagious [kən'teidʒəs] *adj* aansteke-lijk, besmettelijk

contain [kən'tein] *v* bevatten; *inhouden

container [kən'teinə] *n* reservoir *nt*; container *c*

contemporary [kən'tempərəri] *adj* eigentijds; toenmalig; hedendaags; *n* tijdgenoot *c*

contempt [kən'tempt] *n* verachting *c*, minachting *c*

content [kən'tent] *adj* tevreden

contents ['kɔntents] *pl* inhoud *c*

contest ['kɔntest] *n* strijd *c*; wedstrijd *c*

continent ['kɔntinənt] *n* continent *nt*, werelddeel *nt*; vasteland *nt*

continental [,kɔnti'nentəl] *adj* continentaal

continual [kən'tinjuəl] *adj* voortdurend; **continually** *adv* steeds

continue [kən'tinju:] *v* voortzetten, vervolgen; *voortgaan, *doorgaan

continuous [kən'tinjuəs] *adj* voortdurend, doorlopend, onafgebroken

contour ['kɔntuə] *n* omtrek *c*

contraceptive [,kɔntrə'septiv] *n* voorbehoedmiddel *nt*

contract[1] ['kɔntrækt] *n* contract *nt*

contract[2] [kən'trækt] *v* *oplopen

contractor [kən'træktə] *n* aannemer *c*

contradict [,kɔntrə'dikt] *v* *tegenspreken

contradictory [,kɔntrə'diktəri] *adj* tegenstrijdig

contrary ['kɔntrəri] *n* tegendeel *nt*; *adj* tegengesteld; **on the** ~ integen-deel

contrast ['kɔntrɑ:st] *n* contrast *nt*; verschil *nt*, tegenstelling *c*

contribution [,kɔntri'bju:ʃən] *n* bijdrage *c*

control [kən'troul] *n* controle *c*; *v* controleren

controversial [,kɔntrə'və:ʃəl] *adj* controversieel, omstreden

convenience [kən'vi:njəns] *n* gemak *nt*

convenient [kən'vi:njənt] *adj* geriefe-lijk; geschikt, passend, gemakkelijk

convent ['kɔnvənt] *n* klooster *nt*

conversation [,kɔnvə'seiʃən] *n* conversatie *c*, gesprek *nt*

convert [kən'və:t] *v* bekeren; omrekenen

convict[1] [kən'vikt] *v* schuldig *bevinden

convict[2] ['kɔnvikt] *n* veroordeelde *c*

conviction [kən'vikʃən] *n* overtuiging *c*; veroordeling *c*

convince [kən'vins] *v* overtuigen

convulsion [kən'vʌlʃən] *n* kramp *c*

cook [kuk] *n* kok *c*; *v* koken; bereiden, klaarmaken

cookbook ['kukbuk] *nAm* kookboek *nt*

cooker ['kukə] *n* fornuis *nt*; **gas** ~ gasfornuis *nt*

cookery-book ['kukəribuk] *n* kookboek *nt*

cookie ['kuki] *nAm* biscuit *nt*

cool [ku:l] *adj* koel; **cooling system** koelsysteem *nt*

co-operation [kou,ɔpə'reiʃən] *n* samenwerking *c*; medewerking *c*

co-operative [kou'ɔpərətiv] *adj* coöperatief; gewillig, bereidwillig; *n* coöperatie *c*

co-ordinate [kou'ɔ:dineit] *v* coördineren

co-ordination [kou,ɔ:di'neiʃən] *n* coördinatie *c*

copper ['kɔpə] n roodkoper nt, koper nt

copy ['kɔpi] n kopie c; afschrift nt; exemplaar nt; v kopiëren; namaken; **carbon** ~ doorslag c

coral ['kɔrəl] n koraal c

cord [kɔ:d] n koord nt; snoer nt

cordial ['kɔ:diəl] adj hartelijk

corduroy ['kɔ:dərɔi] n ribfluweel nt

core [kɔ:] n kern c; klokhuis nt

cork [kɔ:k] n kurk c; stop c

corkscrew ['kɔ:kskru:] n kurketrekker c

corn [kɔ:n] n korrel c; graan nt, koren nt; eksteroog nt, likdoorn c; ~ **on the cob** maïskolf c

corner ['kɔ:nə] n hoek c

cornfield ['kɔ:nfi:ld] n korenveld nt

corpse [kɔ:ps] n lijk nt

corpulent ['kɔ:pjulənt] adj corpulent; gezet, dik

correct [kə'rekt] adj goed, correct, juist; v corrigeren, verbeteren

correction [kə'rekʃən] n correctie c; verbetering c

correctness [kə'rektnəs] n juistheid c

correspond [,kɔri'spɔnd] v corresponderen; *overeenkomen

correspondence [,kɔri'spɔndəns] n briefwisseling c, correspondentie c

correspondent [,kɔri'spɔndənt] n correspondent c

corridor ['kɔridɔ:] n gang c

corrupt [kə'rʌpt] adj corrupt; v *omkopen

corruption [kə'rʌpʃən] n omkoping c

corset ['kɔ:sit] n korset nt

cosmetics [kɔz'metiks] pl kosmetica pl, schoonheidsmiddelen pl

cost [kɔst] n kosten pl; prijs c

***cost** [kɔst] v kosten

cosy ['kouzi] adj knus, gezellig

cot [kɔt] nAm stretcher c

cottage ['kɔtidʒ] n buitenhuis nt

cotton ['kɔtən] n katoen nt/c; katoenen

cotton-wool ['kɔtənwul] n watten pl

couch [kautʃ] n divan c

cough [kɔf] n hoest c; v hoesten

could [kud] v (p can)

council ['kaunsəl] n raad c

councillor ['kaunsələ] n raadslid nt

counsel ['kaunsəl] n raad c

counsellor ['kaunsələ] n raadsman c

count [kaunt] v tellen; optellen; meetellen; achten; n graaf c

counter ['kauntə] n toonbank c; balie c

counterfeit ['kauntəfi:t] v vervalsen

counterfoil ['kauntəfɔil] n controlestrook c

counterpane ['kauntəpein] n sprei c

countess ['kauntis] n gravin c

country ['kʌntri] n land nt; platteland nt; streek c; ~ **house** landhuis nt

countryman ['kʌntrimən] n (pl -men) landgenoot c

countryside ['kʌntrisaid] n platteland nt

county ['kaunti] n graafschap nt

couple ['kʌpəl] n paar nt

coupon ['ku:pɔn] n coupon c, bon c

courage ['kʌridʒ] n dapperheid c, moed c

courageous [kə'reidʒəs] adj dapper, moedig

course [kɔ:s] n koers c; gang c; loop c; cursus c; **intensive** ~ spoedcursus c; **of** ~ uiteraard, natuurlijk

court [kɔ:t] n rechtbank c; hof nt

courteous ['kɔ:tiəs] adj hoffelijk

cousin ['kʌzən] n nicht c, neef c

cover ['kʌvə] v bedekken; n schuilplaats c, beschutting c; deksel nt; omslag c/nt

cow [kau] n koe c

coward ['kauəd] n lafaard c

cowardly ['kauədli] adj laf

cow-hide ['kauhaid] n koeiehuid c

crab [kræb] n krab c

crack [kræk] n gekraak nt; barst c; v kraken; *breken, barsten

cracker ['krækə] nAm koekje nt

cradle ['kreidəl] n wieg c; bakermat c

cramp [kræmp] n kramp c

crane [krein] n hijskraan c

crankcase ['kræŋkkeis] n carter nt

crankshaft ['kræŋkʃɑ:ft] n krukas c

crash [kræʃ] n botsing c; v botsen; neerstorten; ~ barrier vangrail c

crate [kreit] n krat nt

crater ['kreitə] n krater c

crawl [krɔ:l] v *kruipen; n crawl c

craze [kreiz] n rage c

crazy ['kreizi] adj gek; dwaas, krankzinnig

creak [kri:k] v kraken

cream [kri:m] n crème c; room c; adj roomkleurig

creamy ['kri:mi] adj romig

crease [kri:s] v kreuken; n vouw c; plooi c

create [kri'eit] v *scheppen; creëren

creature ['kri:tʃə] n schepsel nt; wezen nt

credible ['kredibəl] adj geloofwaardig

credit ['kredit] n krediet nt, v crediteren; ~ card credit card

creditor ['kreditə] n schuldeiser c

credulous ['kredjuləs] adj goedgelovig

creek [kri:k] n inham c, kreek c

*creep [kri:p] v *kruipen

creepy ['kri:pi] adj eng, griezelig

cremate [kri'meit] v cremeren

cremation [kri'meiʃən] n crematie c

crew [kru:] n bemanning c

cricket ['krikit] n cricket nt; krekel c

crime [kraim] n misdaad c

criminal ['kriminəl] n delinquent c, misdadiger c; adj crimineel, misdadig; ~ law strafrecht nt

criminality [,krimi'næləti] n criminali-

teit c

crimson ['krimzən] adj vuurrood

crippled ['kripəld] adj kreupel

crisis ['kraisis] n (pl crises) crisis c

crisp [krisp] adj croquant, knappend

critic ['kritik] n criticus c

critical ['kritikəl] adj kritisch; kritiek, hachelijk, zorgwekkend

criticism ['kritisizəm] n kritiek c

criticize ['kritisaiz] v bekritiseren

crochet ['krouʃei] v haken

crockery ['krɔkəri] n aardewerk nt, vaatwerk nt

crocodile ['krɔkədail] n krokodil c

crooked ['krukid] adj verdraaid, krom; oneerlijk

crop [krɔp] n oogst c

cross [krɔs] v *oversteken; adj kwaad, boos; n kruis nt

cross-eyed ['krɔsaid] adj scheel

crossing ['krɔsiŋ] n overtocht c; kruising c; oversteekplaats c; overweg c

crossroads ['krɔsroudz] n kruispunt nt

crosswalk ['krɔswɔ:k] nAm zebrapad nt

crow [krou] n kraai c

crowbar ['kroubɑ:] n breekijzer c

crowd [kraud] n massa c, menigte c

crowded ['kraudid] adj druk; overvol

crown [kraun] n kroon c; v kronen; bekronen

crucifix ['kru:sifiks] n kruisbeeld nt

crucifixion [,kru:si'fikʃən] n kruisiging c

crucify ['kru:sifai] v kruisigen

cruel [kruəl] adj wreed

cruise [kru:z] n boottocht c, cruise c

crumb [krʌm] n kruimel c

crusade [kru:'seid] n kruistocht c

crust [krʌst] n korst c

crutch [krʌtʃ] n kruk c

cry [krai] v huilen; schreeuwen; *roepen; n kreet c, schreeuw c; roep c crystal ['kristəl] n kristal nt; adj kristallen

Cuba ['kju:bə] Cuba

Cuban ['kju:bən] adj Cubaans; n Cubaan c

cube [kju:b] n kubus c; blokje nt

cuckoo ['kuku:] n koekoek c

cucumber ['kju:kəmbə] n komkommer c

cuddle ['kʌdəl] v knuffelen

cudgel ['kʌdʒəl] n knuppel c

cuff [kʌf] n manchet c

cuff-links ['kʌfliŋks] pl manchetknopen pl

cul-de-sac ['kʌldəsæk] n doodlopende weg

cultivate ['kʌltiveit] v bebouwen; verbouwen, kweken

culture ['kʌltʃə] n cultuur c; beschaving c

cultured ['kʌltʃəd] adj beschaafd

cunning ['kʌniŋ] adj sluw

cup [kʌp] n kopje nt; beker c

cupboard ['kʌbəd] n kast c

curb [kə:b] n trottoirband c; v beteugelen

cure [kjuə] v *genezen; n kuur c; genezing c

curio ['kjuəriou] n (pl ~s) rariteit c

curiosity [,kjuəri'ɔsəti] n nieuwsgierigheid c

curious ['kjuəriəs] adj benieuwd, nieuwsgierig; raar

curl [kə:l] v krullen; n krul c

curler ['kə:lə] n krulspeld c

curling-tongs ['kə:liŋtɔnz] pl krultang c

curly ['kə:li] adj krullend

currant ['kʌrənt] n krent c; bes c

currency ['kʌrənsi] n valuta c; foreign ~ buitenlands geld

current ['kʌrənt] n stroming c; stroom c; adj gangbaar, huidig; alternating ~ wisselstroom c; direct ~ gelijkstroom c

curry ['kʌri] n kerrie c

curse [kə:s] v vloeken; vervloeken; n vloek c

curtain ['kə:tən] n gordijn nt; doek nt

curve [kə:v] n kromming c; bocht c

curved [kə:vd] adj krom, gebogen

cushion ['kuʃən] n kussen nt

custodian [kʌ'stoudiən] n suppoost c

custody ['kʌstədi] n hechtenis c; hoede c; voogdij c

custom ['kʌstəm] n gewoonte c; gebruik nt

customary ['kʌstəməri] adj gebruikelijk, gewoon, gewoonlijk

customer ['kʌstəmə] n klant c; cliënt c

Customs ['kʌstəmz] pl douane c; ~ duty accijns c; ~ officer douanebeambte c

cut [kʌt] n snee c; snijwond c

*cut [kʌt] v *snijden; knippen; verlagen; ~ off *afsnijden; afknippen; *afsluiten

cutlery ['kʌtləri] n bestek nt

cutlet ['kʌtlət] n karbonade c

cycle ['saikəl] n fiets c; rijwiel nt; kringloop c, cyclus c

cyclist ['saiklist] n fietser c; wielrijder c

cylinder ['silində] n cilinder c; ~ head cilinderkop c

cystitis [si'staitis] n blaasontsteking c

Czech [tʃek] adj Tsjechisch; n Tsjech c

Czechoslovakia [,tʃekəslə'va:kiə] Tsjechoslowakije

D

dad [dæd] n vader c

daddy ['dædi] n papa c

daffodil ['dæfədil] *n* narcis *c*

daily ['deili] *adj* dagelijks; *n* dagblad *nt*

dairy ['dɛəri] *n* zuivelwinkel *c*

dam [dæm] *n* dam *c*; dijk *c*

damage ['dæmidʒ] *n* schade *c*; *v* beschadigen

damp [dæmp] *adj* vochtig; nat; *n* vocht *nt*; *v* bevochtigen

dance [dɑːns] *v* dansen; *n* dans *c*

dandelion ['dændilaiən] *n* paardebloem *c*

dandruff ['dændrəf] *n* roos *c*

Dane [dein] *n* Deen *c*

danger ['deindʒə] *n* gevaar *nt*

dangerous ['deindʒərəs] *adj* gevaarlijk

Danish ['deiniʃ] *adj* Deens

dare [dɛə] *v* wagen, durven; uitdagen

daring ['dɛəriŋ] *adj* gedurfd

dark [dɑːk] *adj* duister, donker; *n* duisternis *c*

darling ['dɑːliŋ] *n* schat *c*, lieveling *c*

darn [dɑːn] *v* stoppen

dash [dæʃ] *v* snellen; *n* gedachtenstreepje *nt*

dashboard ['dæʃbɔːd] *n* dashboard *nt*

data ['deitə] *pl* gegeven *nt*

date[1] [deit] *n* datum *c*; afspraak *c*; *v* dateren; **out of ~** ouderwets

date[2] [deit] *n* dadel *c*

daughter ['dɔːtə] *n* dochter *c*

dawn [dɔːn] *n* ochtendschemering *c*; dageraad *c*

day [dei] *n* dag *c*; **by ~** overdag; **~ trip** excursie *c*; **per ~** per dag; **the ~ before yesterday** eergisteren

daybreak ['deibreik] *n* dageraad *c*

daylight ['deilait] *n* daglicht *nt*

dead [ded] *adj* dood; gestorven

deaf [def] *adj* doof

deal [diːl] *n* transactie *c*, affaire *c*

*** deal** [diːl] *v* uitdelen; **~ with** *v* te maken *hebben met; zaken *doen met

dealer ['diːlə] *n* koopman *c*, handelaar *c*

dear [diə] *adj* lief; duur; dierbaar

death [deθ] *n* dood *c*; **~ penalty** doodstraf *c*

debate [di'beit] *n* debat *nt*

debit ['debit] *n* debet *nt*

debt [det] *n* schuld *c*

decaffeinated [diː'kæfineitid] *adj* coffeïnevrij

deceit [di'siːt] *n* bedrog *nt*

deceive [di'siːv] *v* *bedriegen

December [di'sembə] december

decency ['diːsənsi] *n* fatsoen *nt*

decent ['diːsənt] *adj* fatsoenlijk

decide [di'said] *v* beslissen, *besluiten

decision [di'siʒən] *n* beslissing *c*, besluit *nt*

deck [dek] *n* dek *nt*; **~ cabin** dekhut *c*; **~ chair** ligstoel *c*

declaration [,deklə'reiʃən] *n* verklaring *c*; aangifte *c*

declare [di'klɛə] *v* verklaren; *opgeven; *aangeven

decoration [,dekə'reiʃən] *n* versiering *c*

decrease [diː'kriːs] *v* verminderen; *afnemen; *n* vermindering *c*

dedicate ['dedikeit] *v* toewijden

deduce [di'djuːs] *v* afleiden

deduct [di'dʌkt] *v* *aftrekken

deed [diːd] *n* handeling *c*, daad *c*

deep [diːp] *adj* diep

deep-freeze [,diːp'friːz] *n* diepvrieskast *c*

deer [diə] *n* (pl ~) hert *nt*

defeat [di'fiːt] *v* *verslaan; *n* nederlaag *c*

defective [di'fektiv] *adj* gebrekkig, defect

defence [di'fens] *n* verdediging *c*; defensie *c*

defend [di'fend] *v* verdedigen

deficiency [di'fiʃənsi] *n* gebrek *nt*

deficit ['defisit] *n* tekort *nt*

define [di'fain] v *omschrijven, bepalen, definiëren

definite ['definit] adj bepaald; vastomlijnd

definition [,defi'niʃən] n bepaling c, definitie c

deformed [di'fɔ:md] adj misvormd, mismaakt

degree [di'gri:] n graad c; titel c

delay [di'lei] v vertragen; uitstellen; n oponthoud nt, vertraging c; uitstel nt

delegate ['deligət] n gedelegeerde c

delegation [,deli'geiʃən] n delegatie c, afvaardiging c

deliberate[1] [di'libəreit] v beraadslagen, overleggen

deliberate[2] [di'libərət] adj opzettelijk

deliberation [di,libə'reiʃən] n beraad nt, overleg nt

delicacy ['delikəsi] n lekkernij c

delicate ['delikət] adj fijn; teder; delikaat

delicatessen [,delikə'tesən] n delicatessen pl; delicatessenwinkel c

delicious [di'liʃəs] adj lekker, heerlijk

delight [di'lait] n genot nt, verrukking c; v in verrukking *brengen; **delighted** opgetogen

delightful [di'laitfəl] adj heerlijk, verrukkelijk

deliver [di'livə] v afleveren, bezorgen; verlossen

delivery [di'livəri] n levering c, bezorging c; bevalling c; verlossing c; ~ **van** bestelauto c

demand [di'ma:nd] v vereisen, eisen; n eis c; navraag c

democracy [di'mɔkrəsi] n democratie c

democratic [,demə'krætik] adj democratisch

demolish [di'mɔliʃ] v slopen

demolition [,demə'liʃən] n afbraak c

demonstrate ['demənstreit] v aantonen; demonstreren, betogen

demonstration [,demən'streiʃən] n demonstratie c; betoging c

den [den] n hol nt

Denmark ['denma:k] Denemarken

denomination [di,nɔmi'neiʃən] n benaming c

dense [dens] adj dicht

dent [dent] n deuk c

dentist ['dentist] n tandarts c

denture ['dentʃə] n kunstgebit nt

deny [di'nai] v ontkennen; *onthouden, weigeren, *ontzeggen

deodorant [di:'oudərənt] n deodorant c

depart [di'pa:t] v *heengaan, *vertrekken; *overlijden

department [di'pa:tmənt] n departement nt, afdeling c; ~ **store** warenhuis nt

departure [di'pa:tʃə] n vertrek nt

dependant [di'pendənt] adj afhankelijk

depend on [di'pend] *afhangen van

deposit [di'pɔzit] n storting c; statiegeld nt; bezinksel nt, afzetting c; v storten

depository [di'pɔzitəri] n bergplaats c

depot ['depou] n opslagplaats c; nAm station nt

depress [di'pres] v deprimeren

depressed [di'prest] adj neerslachtig

depressing [di'presiŋ] adj triest

depression [di'preʃən] n neerslachtigheid c; depressie c; teruggang c

deprive of [di'praiv] *ontnemen

depth [depθ] n diepte c

deputy ['depjuti] n afgevaardigde c; plaatsvervanger c

descend [di'send] v dalen

descendant [di'sendənt] n afstammeling c

descent [di'sent] n afdaling c

describe [di'skraib] v *beschrijven

description [di'skripʃən] n beschrijving

c; signalement *nt*

desert[1] ['dezət] *n* woestijn *c*; *adj* woest, verlaten

desert[2] [di'zə:t] *v* deserteren; *verlaten

deserve [di'zə:v] *v* verdienen

design [di'zain] *v* *ontwerpen; *n* ontwerp *nt*; doel *nt*

designate ['dezigneit] *v* *aanwijzen

desirable [di'zaiərəbəl] *adj* begeerlijk, wenselijk

desire [di'zaiə] *n* wens *c*; zin *c*, begeerte *c*; *v* begeren, verlangen, wensen

desk [desk] *n* bureau *nt*; lessenaar *c*; schoolbank *c*

despair [di'speə] *n* wanhoop *c*; *v* wanhopen

despatch [di'spætʃ] *v* *verzenden

desperate ['despərət] *adj* wanhopig

despise [di'spaiz] *v* verachten

despite [di'spait] *prep* ondanks

dessert [di'zə:t] *n* dessert *nt*

destination [,desti'neiʃən] *n* bestemming *c*

destine ['destin] *v* bestemmen

destiny ['destini] *n* noodlot *nt*, lot *nt*

destroy [di'strɔi] *v* vernielen, vernietigen

destruction [di'strʌkʃən] *n* vernietiging *c*; ondergang *c*

detach [di'tætʃ] *v* losmaken

detail ['di:teil] *n* bijzonderheid *c*, detail *nt*

detailed ['di:teild] *adj* uitvoerig, gedetailleerd

detect [di'tekt] *v* ontdekken

detective [di'tektiv] *n* detective *c*; ~ **story** detectiveroman *c*

detergent [di'tə:dʒənt] *n* wasmiddel *nt*

determine [di'tə:min] *v* vaststellen, bepalen

determined [di'tə:mind] *adj* vastbesloten

detour ['di:tuə] *n* omweg *c*; omleiding *c*

devaluation [,di:vælju'eiʃən] *n* devaluatie *c*

devalue [,di:'vælju:] *v* devalueren

develop [di'veləp] *v* ontwikkelen

development [di'veləpmənt] *n* ontwikkeling *c*

deviate ['di:vieit] *v* *afwijken

devil ['devəl] *n* duivel *c*

devise [di'vaiz] *v* beramen

devote [di'vout] *v* wijden

dew [dju:] *n* dauw *c*

diabetes [,daiə'bi:ti:z] *n* diabetes *c*, suikerziekte *c*

diabetic [,daiə'betik] *n* suikerzieke *c*, diabeticus *c*

diagnose [,daiəg'nouz] *v* een diagnose stellen; constateren

diagnosis [,daiəg'nousis] *n* (pl -ses) diagnose *c*

diagonal [dai'ægənəl] *n* diagonaal *c*; *adj* diagonaal

diagram ['daiəgræm] *n* schema *nt*; figuur *c*, grafiek *c*

dialect ['daiəlekt] *n* dialect *nt*

diamond ['daiəmənd] *n* diamant *c*

diaper ['daiəpə] *nAm* luier *c*

diaphragm ['daiəfræm] *n* tussenschot *nt*

diarrhoea [daiə'riə] *n* diarree *c*

diary ['daiəri] *n* agenda *c*; dagboek *nt*

dictaphone ['diktəfoun] *n* dictafoon *c*

dictate [dik'teit] *v* dicteren

dictation [dik'teiʃən] *n* dictaat *nt*; dictee *nt*

dictator [dik'teitə] *n* dictator *c*

dictionary ['dikʃənəri] *n* woordenboek *nt*

did [did] *v* (p do)

die [dai] *v* *sterven; *overlijden

diesel ['di:zəl] *n* diesel *c*

diet ['daiət] *n* dieet *nt*

differ ['difə] *v* verschillen

difference ['difərəns] n verschil nt; onderscheid nt

different ['difərənt] adj verschillend; ander

difficult ['difikəlt] adj moeilijk; lastig

difficulty ['difikəlti] n moeilijkheid c; moeite c

* **dig** [dig] v *graven; *delven

digest [di'dʒest] v verteren

digestible [di'dʒestəbəl] adj verteerbaar

digestion [di'dʒestʃən] n spijsvertering c

digit ['didʒit] n cijfer nt

dignified ['dignifaid] adj waardig

dike [daik] n dijk c; dam c

dilapidated [di'læpideitid] adj bouwvallig

diligence ['dilidʒəns] n vlijt c, ijver c

diligent ['dilidʒənt] adj vlijtig, ijverig

dilute [dai'lju:t] v aanlengen, verdunnen

dim [dim] adj dof, mat; donker, zwak, vaag

dine [dain] v warm *eten

dinghy ['diŋgi] n bootje nt

dining-car ['dainiŋka:] n restauratiewagen c

dining-room ['dainiŋru:m] n eetkamer c; eetzaal c

dinner ['dinə] n warme maaltijd; avondeten nt, middageten nt

dinner-jacket ['dinə,dʒækit] n smoking c

dinner-service ['dinə,sə:vis] n eetservies nt

diphtheria [dif'θiəriə] n difterie c

diploma [di'ploumə] n diploma nt

diplomat ['dipləmæt] n diplomaat c

direct [di'rekt] adj rechtstreeks, direct; v richten; *wijzen; leiden; regisseren

direction [di'rekʃən] n richting c; instructie c; regie c; bestuur nt; di-

rectional signal Am richtingaanwijzer c; **directions for use** gebruiksaanwijzing c

directive [di'rektiv] n richtlijn c

director [di'rektə] n directeur c; regisseur c

dirt [də:t] n vuil nt

dirty ['də:ti] adj smerig, vies, vuil

disabled [di'seibəld] adj gehandicapt, invalide

disadvantage [,disəd'va:ntidʒ] n nadeel nt

disagree [,disə'gri:] v het oneens *zijn, van mening verschillen

disagreeable [,disə'gri:əbəl] adj onaangenaam

disappear [,disə'piə] v *verdwijnen

disappoint [,disə'pɔint] v teleurstellen; * **be disappointing** *tegenvallen

disappointment [,disə'pɔintmənt] n teleurstelling c

disapprove [,disə'pru:v] v afkeuren

disaster [di'za:stə] n ramp c; catastrofe c, onheil nt

disastrous [di'za:strəs] adj rampzalig

disc [disk] n schijf c; grammofoonplaat c; **slipped ~** hernia c

discard [di'ska:d] v afdanken

discharge [dis'tʃa:dʒ] v lossen, *uitladen; ~ **of** *ontheffen van

discipline ['disiplin] n discipline c

discolour [di'skʌlə] v verkleuren

disconnect [,diskə'nekt] v ontkoppelen; uitschakelen

discontented [,diskən'tentid] adj ontevreden

discontinue [,diskən'tinju:] v *opheffen, staken

discount ['diskaunt] n korting c, reductie c

discover [di'skʌvə] v ontdekken

discovery [di'skʌvəri] n ontdekking c

discuss [di'skʌs] v *bespreken; discussiëren

discussion [di'skʌʃən] *n* discussie *c*; gesprek *nt*, bespreking *c*, debat *nt*

disease [di'zi:z] *n* ziekte *c*

disembark [‚disim'ba:k] *v* van boord *gaan, ontschepen

disgrace [dis'greis] *n* schande *c*

disguise [dis'gaiz] *v* zich vermommen; *n* vermomming *c*

disgusting [dis'gʌstiŋ] *adj* misselijk, walgelijk

dish [diʃ] *n* bord *nt*; schotel *c*, schaal *c*; gerecht *nt*

dishonest [di'sɔnist] *adj* oneerlijk

disinfect [‚disin'fekt] *v* ontsmetten

disinfectant [‚disin'fektənt] *n* ontsmettingsmiddel *nt*

dislike [di'slaik] *v* een hekel *hebben aan, niet *houden van; *n* afkeer *c*, hekel *c*, antipathie *c*

dislocated ['disləkeitid] *adj* ontwricht

dismiss [dis'mis] *v* *wegzenden; *ontslaan

disorder [di'sɔ:də] *n* wanorde *c*

dispatch [di'spætʃ] *v* versturen, *verzenden

display [di'splei] *v* vertonen; tonen; *n* tentoonstelling *c*, expositie *c*

displease [di'spli:z] *v* ontstemmen, mishagen

disposable [di'spouzəbəl] *adj* wegwerp-

disposal [di'spouzəl] *n* beschikking *c*

dispose of [di'spouz] beschikken over

dispute [di'spju:t] *n* onenigheid *c*; ruzie *c*, geschil *nt*; *v* twisten, betwisten

dissatisfied [di'sætisfaid] *adj* ontevreden

dissolve [di'zɔlv] *v* oplossen; *ontbinden

dissuade from [di'sweid] *afraden

distance ['distəns] *n* afstand *c*; ~ **in kilometres** kilometertal *nt*

distant ['distənt] *adj* ver

distinct [di'stiŋkt] *adj* duidelijk; verschillend

distinction [di'stiŋkʃən] *n* onderscheid *nt*, verschil *nt*

distinguish [di'stiŋwiʃ] *v* onderscheid maken, *onderscheiden

distinguished [di'stiŋwiʃt] *adj* voornaam

distress [di'stres] *n* nood *c*; ~ **signal** noodsein *nt*

distribute [di'stribju:t] *v* uitdelen

distributor [di'stribjutə] *n* agent *c*; stroomverdeler *c*

district ['distrikt] *n* district *nt*; streek *c*; wijk *c*

disturb [di'stə:b] *v* storen, verstoren

disturbance [di'stə:bəns] *n* storing *c*; verwarring *c*

ditch [ditʃ] *n* greppel *c*, sloot *c*

dive [daiv] *v* *duiken

diversion [dai'və:ʃən] *n* wegomlegging *c*; afleiding *c*

divide [di'vaid] *v* delen; verdelen; *scheiden

divine [di'vain] *adj* goddelijk

division [di'viʒən] *n* deling *c*; scheiding *c*; afdeling *c*

divorce [di'vɔ:s] *n* echtscheiding *c*; *v* *scheiden

dizziness ['dizinəs] *n* duizeligheid *c*

dizzy ['dizi] *adj* duizelig

*** do** [du:] *v* *doen; voldoende *zijn

dock [dɔk] *n* dok *nt*; kade *c*; *v* aanleggen

docker ['dɔkə] *n* havenarbeider *c*

doctor ['dɔktə] *n* arts *c*, dokter *c*; doctor *c*

document ['dɔkjumənt] *n* document *nt*

dog [dɔg] *n* hond *c*

dogged ['dɔgid] *adj* hardnekkig

doll [dɔl] *n* pop *c*

dome [doum] *n* koepel *c*

domestic [də'mestik] *adj* huiselijk; binnenlands; *n* bediende *c*

domicile ['dɔmisail] *n* woonplaats *c*

domination [,dɔmi'neiʃən] *n* overheersing *c*

dominion [də'minjən] *n* heerschappij *c*

donate [dou'neit] *v* *schenken

donation [dou'neiʃən] *n* schenking *c*, gift *c*

done [dʌn] *v* (pp do)

donkey ['dɔŋki] *n* ezel *c*

donor ['dounə] *n* donateur *c*

door [dɔ:] *n* deur *c*; **revolving** ~ draaideur *c*; **sliding** ~ schuifdeur *c*

doorbell ['dɔ:bel] *n* deurbel *c*

door-keeper ['dɔ:,ki:pə] *n* portier *c*

doorman ['dɔ:mən] *n* (pl -men) portier *c*

dormitory ['dɔ:mitri] *n* slaapzaal *c*

dose [dous] *n* dosis *c*

dot [dɔt] *n* punt *c*

double ['dʌbəl] *adj* dubbel

doubt [daut] *v* betwijfelen, twijfelen; *n* twijfel *c*; **without** ~ zonder twijfel

doubtful ['dautfəl] *adj* twijfelachtig; onzeker

dough [dou] *n* deeg *nt*

down[1] [daun] *adv* neer; omlaag, naar beneden, omver; *adj* neerslachtig; *prep* langs, van ... af; ~ **payment** aanbetaling *c*

down[2] [daun] *n* dons *nt*

downpour ['daunpɔ:] *n* stortbui *c*

downstairs [,daun'steəz] *adv* naar beneden, beneden

downstream [,daun'stri:m] *adv* stroomafwaarts

down-to-earth [,dauntu'ə:θ] *adj* nuchter

downwards ['daunwədz] *adv* neer, naar beneden

dozen ['dʌzən] *n* (pl ~, ~s) dozijn *nt*

draft [drɑ:ft] *n* wissel *c*

drag [dræg] *v* slepen

dragon ['drægən] *n* draak *c*

drain [drein] *v* droogleggen; afwateren; *n* afvoer *c*

drama ['drɑ:mə] *n* drama *nt*; treurspel *nt*; toneel *nt*

dramatic [drə'mætik] *adj* dramatisch

dramatist ['dræmətist] *n* toneelschrijver *c*

drank [dræŋk] *v* (p drink)

draper ['dreipə] *n* manufacturier *c*

drapery ['dreipəri] *n* stoffen

draught [drɑ:ft] *n* tocht *c*; **draughts** damspel *nt*

draught-board ['drɑ:ftbɔ:d] *n* dambord *nt*

draw [drɔ:] *n* trekking *c*

*draw [drɔ:] *v* tekenen; *trekken; *opnemen; ~ **up** opstellen

drawbridge ['drɔ:bridʒ] *n* ophaalbrug *c*

drawer ['drɔ:ə] *n* la *c*, lade *c*; **drawers** onderbroek *c*

drawing ['drɔ:iŋ] *n* tekening *c*

drawing-pin ['drɔ:iŋpin] *n* punaise *c*

drawing-room ['drɔ:iŋru:m] *n* salon *c*

dread [dred] *v* vrezen; *n* vrees *c*

dreadful ['dredfəl] *adj* vreselijk, ontzettend

dream [dri:m] *n* droom *c*

*dream [dri:m] *v* dromen

dress [dres] *v* aankleden; zich kleden, zich aankleden; *verbinden; *n* japon *c*, jurk *c*

dressing-gown ['dresiŋgaun] *n* kamerjas *c*

dressing-room ['dresiŋru:m] *n* kleedkamer *c*

dressing-table ['dresiŋ,teibəl] *n* toilettafel *c*

dressmaker ['dres,meikə] *n* naaister *c*

drill [dril] *v* boren; trainen; *n* boor *c*

drink [driŋk] *n* borrel *c*, drank *c*

*drink [driŋk] *v* *drinken

drinking-water ['driŋkiŋ,wɔ:tə] *n* drinkwater *nt*

drip-dry [,drip'drai] *adj* zelfstrijkend,

no-iron
drive [draiv] *n* rijweg *c*; autorit *c*
*drive [draiv] *v* *rijden; besturen
driver ['draivə] *n* chauffeur *c*
drizzle ['drizəl] *n* motregen *c*
drop [drɔp] *v* *laten vallen; *n* druppel *c*
drought [draut] *n* droogte *c*
drown [draun] *v* *verdrinken; ***be drowned** *verdrinken
drug [drʌg] *n* verdovend middel; geneesmiddel *nt*
drugstore ['drʌgstɔ:] *nAm* drogisterij *c*, apotheek *c*; warenhuis *nt*
drum [drʌm] *n* trommel *c*
drunk [drʌŋk] *adj* (pp drink) dronken
dry [drai] *adj* droog; *v* drogen; afdrogen
dry-clean [,drai'kli:n] *v* chemisch reinigen
dry-cleaner's [,drai'kli:nəz] *n* stomerij *c*
dryer ['draiə] *n* centrifuge *c*
duchess [dʌtʃis] *n* hertogin *c*
duck [dʌk] *n* eend *c*
due [dju:] *adj* verwacht; verschuldigd; vervallen
dues [dju:z] *pl* schulden *pl*
dug [dʌg] *v* (p, pp dig)
duke [dju:k] *n* hertog *c*
dull [dʌl] *adj* vervelend, saai; flets, mat; bot
dumb [dʌm] *adj* stom; suf, dom
dune [dju:n] *n* duin *nt*
dung [dʌŋ] *n* mest *c*
dunghill ['dʌŋhil] *n* mesthoop *c*
duration [dju'reiʃən] *n* duur *c*
during ['djuəriŋ] *prep* gedurende, tijdens
dusk [dʌsk] *n* avondschemering *c*
dust [dʌst] *n* stof *nt*
dustbin ['dʌstbin] *n* vuilnisbak *c*
dusty ['dʌsti] *adj* stoffig
Dutch [dʌtʃ] *adj* Nederlands, Hollands

Dutchman ['dʌtʃmən] *n* (pl -men) Nederlander *c*, Hollander *c*
dutiable ['dju:tiəbəl] *adj* belastbaar
duty ['dju:ti] *n* plicht *c*; taak *c*; invoerrecht *nt*; **Customs** ~ accijns *c*
duty-free [,dju:ti'fri:] *adj* belastingvrij
dwarf [dwɔ:f] *n* dwerg *c*
dye [dai] *v* verven; *n* verf *c*
dynamo ['dainəmou] *n* (pl ~s) dynamo *c*
dysentery ['disəntri] *n* dysenterie *c*

E

each [i:tʃ] *adj* elk, ieder; ~ **other** elkaar
eager ['i:gə] *adj* verlangend, ongeduldig
eagle ['i:gəl] *n* arend *c*
ear [iə] *n* oor *nt*
earache ['iəreik] *n* oorpijn *c*
ear-drum ['iədrʌm] *n* trommelvlies *nt*
earl [ə:l] *n* graaf *c*
early ['ə:li] *adj* vroeg
earn [ə:n] *v* verdienen
earnest ['ə:nist] *n* ernst *c*
earnings ['ə:niŋz] *pl* inkomsten *pl*, verdiensten *pl*
earring ['iəriŋ] *n* oorbel *c*
earth [ə:θ] *n* aarde *c*; grond *c*
earthenware ['ə:θənwɛə] *n* aardewerk *nt*
earthquake ['ə:θkweik] *n* aardbeving *c*
ease [i:z] *n* ongedwongenheid *c*, gemak *nt*
east [i:st] *n* oost *c*, oosten *c*
Easter ['i:stə] Pasen
easterly ['i:stəli] *adj* oostelijk
eastern ['i:stən] *adj* oost-, oostelijk
easy ['i:zi] *adj* gemakkelijk; geriefelijk; ~ **chair** leunstoel *c*

easy-going ['i:zi,gouiŋ] *adj* ontspannen

*eat [i:t] *v* *eten

eavesdrop ['i:vzdrɔp] *v* afluisteren

ebony ['ebəni] *n* ebbehout *nt*

eccentric [ik'sentrik] *adj* excentriek

echo ['ekou] *n* (pl ~es) weerklank *c*, echo *c*

eclipse [i'klips] *n* verduistering *c*

economic [,i:kə'nɔmik] *adj* economisch

economical [,i:kə'nɔmikəl] *adj* spaarzaam, zuinig

economist [i'kɔnəmist] *n* econoom *c*

economize [i'kɔnəmaiz] *v* sparen

economy [i'kɔnəmi] *n* economie *c*

ecstasy ['ekstəzi] *n* extase *c*

Ecuador ['ekwədɔ:] Ecuador

Ecuadorian [,ekwə'dɔ:riən] *n* Ecuadoriaan *c*

eczema ['eksimə] *n* eczeem *nt*

edge [edʒ] *n* kant *c*, rand *c*

edible ['edibəl] *adj* eetbaar

edition [i'diʃən] *n* editie *c*, uitgave *c*; **morning** ~ ochtendeditie *c*

editor ['editə] *n* redakteur *c*

educate ['edʒukeit] *v* opleiden, opvoeden

education [,edʒu'keiʃən] *n* onderwijs *nt*; opvoeding *c*

eel [i:l] *n* aal *c*, paling *c*

effect [i'fekt] *n* gevolg *nt*, effect *nt*; *v* *teweegbrengen; **in** ~ feitelijk

effective [i'fektiv] *adj* doeltreffend, effectief

efficient [i'fiʃənt] *adj* efficiënt, doelmatig

effort ['efət] *n* inspanning *c*; poging *c*

egg [eg] *n* ei *nt*

egg-cup ['egkʌp] *n* eierdopje *nt*

eggplant ['eglɑ:nt] *n* aubergine *c*

egg-yolk ['egjouk] *n* eierdooier *c*

egoistic [,egou'istik] *adj* zelfzuchtig

Egypt ['i:dʒipt] Egypte

Egyptian [i'dʒipʃən] *adj* Egyptisch; *n* Egyptenaar *c*

eiderdown ['aidədaun] *n* donzen dekbed

eight [eit] *num* acht

eighteen [,ei'ti:n] *num* achttien

eighteenth [,ei'ti:nθ] *num* achttiende

eighth [eitθ] *num* achtste

eighty ['eiti] *num* tachtig

either ['aiðə] *pron* een van beide; **either ... or** hetzij ... hetzij, of ... of

elaborate [i'læbəreit] *v* uitwerken

elastic [i'læstik] *adj* elastisch; rekbaar; elastiek *nt*

elasticity [,elæ'stisəti] *n* rek *c*

elbow ['elbou] *n* elleboog *c*

elder ['eldə] *adj* ouder

elderly ['eldəli] *adj* bejaard

eldest ['eldist] *adj* oudst

elect [i'lekt] *v* *kiezen, *verkiezen

election [i'lekʃən] *n* verkiezing *c*

electric [i'lektrik] *adj* elektrisch; ~ **razor** scheerapparaat *nt*; ~ **cord** snoer *nt*

electrician [,ilek'triʃən] *n* elektricien *c*

electricity [,ilek'trisəti] *n* elektriciteit *c*

electronic [ilek'trɔnik] *adj* elektronisch

elegance ['eligəns] *n* elegantie *c*

elegant ['eligənt] *adj* elegant

element ['elimənt] *n* bestanddeel *nt*, element *nt*

elephant ['elifənt] *n* olifant *c*

elevator ['eliveitə] *nAm* lift *c*

eleven [i'levən] *num* elf

eleventh [i'levənθ] *num* elfde

elf [elf] *n* (pl elves) elf *c*

eliminate [i'limineit] *v* elimineren

elm [elm] *n* iep *c*

else [els] *adv* anders

elsewhere [,el'sweə] *adv* elders

elucidate [i'lu:sideit] *v* toelichten

emancipation [i,mænsi'peiʃən] *n* emancipatie *c*

embankment [im'bæŋkmənt] *n* kade *c*

embargo [em'bɑ:gou] *n* (pl ~es) embargo *nt*

embark [im'ba:k] v inschepen; instappen

embarkation [,embɑ:'keiʃən] n inscheping c

embarrass [im'bærəs] v in verwarring brengen; in verlegenheid *brengen; hinderen; embarrassed verlegen, gegeneerd; embarrassing pijnlijk

embassy ['embəsi] n ambassade c

emblem ['embləm] n embleem nt

embrace [im'breis] v omhelzen; n omhelzing c

embroider [im'brɔidə] v borduren

embroidery [im'brɔidəri] n borduurwerk nt

emerald ['emərəld] n smaragd nt

emergency [i'mə:dʒənsi] n spoedgeval nt, noodgeval nt; noodtoestand c; ~ exit nooduitgang c

emigrant ['emigrənt] n emigrant c

emigrate ['emigreit] v emigreren

emigration [,emi'greiʃən] n emigratie c

emotion [i'mouʃən] n ontroering c, emotie c

emperor ['empərə] n keizer c

emphasize ['emfəsaiz] v benadrukken

empire ['empaiə] n keizerrijk nt, rijk nt

employ [im'plɔi] v tewerkstellen; gebruiken

employee [,emplɔi'i:] n werknemer c, employé c

employer [im'plɔiə] n werkgever c

employment [im'plɔimənt] n tewerkstelling c, werk nt; ~ exchange arbeidsbureau nt

empress ['empris] n keizerin c

empty ['empti] adj leeg; v ledigen

enable [i'neibəl] v in staat stellen

enamel [i'næməl] n email nt

enamelled [i'næməld] adj geëmailleerd

enchanting [in'tʃɑ:ntiŋ] adj prachtig, betoverend

encircle [in'sə:kəl] v omcirkelen, omringen; *insluiten

enclose [iŋ'klouz] v *bijsluiten, *insluiten

enclosure [iŋ'klouʒə] n bijlage c

encounter [iŋ'kauntə] v ontmoeten; n ontmoeting c

encourage [iŋ'kʌridʒ] v aanmoedigen

encyclopaedia [en,saiklə'pi:diə] n encyclopedie c

end [end] n einde nt; slot nt; v beëindigen; *aflopen

ending ['endiŋ] n einde nt

endless ['endləs] adj oneindig

endorse [in'dɔ:s] v aftekenen, endosseren

endure [in'djuə] v *verdragen

enemy ['enəmi] n vijand c

energetic [,enə'dʒetik] adj energiek

energy ['enədʒi] n energie c; kracht c

engage [iŋ'geidʒ] v in dienst *nemen; *bespreken; zich *verbinden; engaged verloofd; bezig, bezet

engagement [iŋ'geidʒmənt] n verloving c; verplichting c; afspraak c; ~ ring verlovingsring c

engine ['endʒin] n machine c, motor c; locomotief c

engineer [,endʒi'niə] n ingenieur c

England ['iŋglənd] Engeland

English ['iŋgliʃ] adj Engels

Englishman ['iŋgliʃmən] n (pl -men) Engelsman c

engrave [iŋ'greiv] v graveren

engraver [iŋ'greivə] n graveur c

engraving [iŋ'greiviŋ] n prent c; gravure c

enigma [i'nigmə] n raadsel nt

enjoy [in'dʒɔi] v *genieten van

enjoyable [in'dʒɔiəbəl] adj fijn, prettig, leuk; lekker

enjoyment [in'dʒɔimənt] n genot nt

enlarge [in'lɑ:dʒ] v vergroten; uitbreiden

enlargement [in'lɑ:dʒmənt] n vergroting *c*

enormous [i'nɔ:məs] *adj* reusachtig, enorm

enough [i'nʌf] *adv* genoeg; *adj* voldoende

enquire [in'kwaiə] *v* informeren; *onderzoeken

enquiry [in'kwaiəri] *n* informatie *c*; onderzoek *nt*; enquête *c*

enter ['entə] *v* *betreden, *binnengaan; *inschrijven

enterprise ['entəpraiz] *n* onderneming *c*

entertain [,entə'tein] *v* vermaken, *onderhouden; *ontvangen

entertainer [,entə'teinə] *n* conferencier *c*

entertaining [,entə'teiniŋ] *adj* vermakelijk, amusant

entertainment [,entə'teinmənt] *n* vermaak *nt*, amusement *nt*

enthusiasm [in'θju:ziæzəm] *n* enthousiasme *nt*

enthusiastic [in,θju:zi'æstik] *adj* enthousiast

entire [in'taiə] *adj* heel, geheel

entirely [in'taiəli] *adv* helemaal

entrance ['entrəns] *n* ingang *c*; toegang *c*; binnenkomst *c*

entrance-fee ['entrənsfi:] *n* entree *c*

entry ['entri] *n* ingang *c*, entree *c*; toegang *c*; post *c*; **no** ~ verboden toegang

envelope ['envəloup] *n* envelop *c*

envious ['enviəs] *adj* afgunstig, jaloers

environment [in'vaiərənmənt] *n* milieu *nt*; omgeving *c*

envoy ['envɔi] *n* gezant *c*

envy ['envi] *n* afgunst *c*; *v* benijden

epic ['epik] *n* epos *nt*; *adj* episch

epidemic [,epi'demik] *n* epidemie *c*

epilepsy ['epilepsi] *n* epilepsie *c*

epilogue ['epilɔg] *n* epiloog *c*

episode ['episoud] *n* episode *c*

equal ['i:kwəl] *adj* gelijk; *v* evenaren

equality [i'kwɔləti] *n* gelijkheid *c*

equalize ['i:kwəlaiz] *v* gelijk maken

equally ['i:kwəli] *adv* even

equator [i'kweitə] *n* evenaar *c*

equip [i'kwip] *v* uitrusten

equipment [i'kwipmənt] *n* uitrusting *c*

equivalent [i'kwivələnt] *adj* equivalent, gelijkwaardig

eraser [i'reizə] *n* gom *c/nt*

erect [i'rekt] *v* opbouwen, oprichten; *adj* overeind, rechtopstaand

err [ə:] *v* zich vergissen; dwalen

errand ['erənd] *n* boodschap *c*

error ['erə] *n* fout *c*, vergissing *c*

escalator ['eskəleitə] *n* roltrap *c*

escape [i'skeip] *v* ontsnappen; vluchten, ontvluchten, *ontgaan; *n* ontsnapping *c*

escort[1] ['eskɔ:t] *n* escorte *nt*

escort[2] [i'skɔ:t] *v* escorteren

especially [i'speʃəli] *adv* voornamelijk, vooral

esplanade [,esplə'neid] *n* promenade *c*

essay ['esei] *n* essay *nt*; verhandeling *c*, opstel *nt*

essence ['esəns] *n* essentie *c*; kern *c*, wezen *nt*

essential [i'senʃəl] *adj* onontbeerlijk; wezenlijk, essentieel

essentially [i'senʃəli] *adv* vooral

establish [i'stæbliʃ] *v* vestigen; vaststellen

estate [i'steit] *n* landgoed *nt*

esteem [i'sti:m] *n* respect *nt*, achting *c*; *v* achten

estimate[1] ['estimeit] *v* taxeren, schatten

estimate[2] ['estimət] *n* schatting *c*

estuary ['estʃuəri] *n* riviermonding *c*

etcetera [et'setərə] enzovoort

etching ['etʃiŋ] *n* ets *c*

eternal [i'tə:nəl] *adj* eeuwig

eternity [i'tə:nəti] *n* eeuwigheid *c*

ether ['iːθə] *n* ether *c*

Ethiopia [iθi'oupiə] Ethiopië

Ethiopian [iθi'oupiən] *adj* Ethiopisch; *n* Ethiopiër *c*

Europe ['juərəp] Europa

European [,juərə'piːən] *adj* Europees; *n* Europeaan *c*

evacuate [i'vækjueit] *v* evacueren

evaluate [i'væljueit] *v* schatten

evaporate [i'væpəreit] *v* verdampen

even ['iːvən] *adj* effen, plat, gelijk; constant; even; *adv* zelfs

evening ['iːvniŋ] *n* avond *c*; ~ **dress** avondkleding *c*

event [i'vent] *n* gebeurtenis *c*; geval *nt*

eventual [i'ventʃuəl] *adj* eventueel; uiteindelijk

ever ['evə] *adv* ooit; altijd

every ['evri] *adj* ieder, elk

everybody ['evri,bɔdi] *pron* iedereen

everyday ['evridei] *adj* alledaags

everyone ['evriwʌn] *pron* ieder, iedereen

everything ['evriθiŋ] *pron* alles

everywhere ['evriwɛə] *adv* overal

evidence ['evidəns] *n* bewijs *nt*

evident ['evidənt] *adj* duidelijk

evil ['iːvəl] *n* kwaad *nt*; *adj* slecht

evolution [,iːvə'luːʃən] *n* evolutie *c*

exact [ig'zækt] *adj* nauwkeurig, precies

exactly [ig'zæktli] *adv* precies

exaggerate [ig'zædʒəreit] *v* *overdrijven

examination [ig,zæmi'neiʃən] *n* examen *nt*; onderzoek *nt*; verhoor *nt*

examine [ig'zæmin] *v* *onderzoeken

example [ig'zaːmpəl] *n* voorbeeld *nt*; **for** ~ bijvoorbeeld

excavation [,ekskə'veiʃən] *n* opgraving *c*

exceed [ik'siːd] *v* *overschrijden; *overtreffen

excel [ik'sel] *v* *uitblinken

excellent ['eksələnt] *adj* voortreffelijk, uitstekend

except [ik'sept] *prep* uitgezonderd, behalve

exception [ik'sepʃən] *n* uitzondering *c*

exceptional [ik'sepʃənəl] *adj* buitengewoon, uitzonderlijk

excerpt ['eksəːpt] *n* passage *c*

excess [ik'ses] *n* exces *nt*

excessive [ik'sesiv] *adj* buitensporig

exchange [iks'tʃeindʒ] *v* uitwisselen, wisselen, ruilen; *n* ruil *c*; beurs *c*; ~ **office** wisselkantoor *nt*; ~ **rate** koers *c*

excite [ik'sait] *v* *opwinden

excitement [ik'saitmənt] *n* drukte *c*, opwinding *c*

exciting [ik'saitiŋ] *adj* spannend

exclaim [ik'skleim] *v* *uitroepen

exclamation [,eksklə'meiʃən] *n* uitroep *c*

exclude [ik'skluːd] *v* *uitsluiten

exclusive [ik'skluːsiv] *adj* exclusief

exclusively [ik'skluːsivli] *adv* uitsluitend

excursion [ik'skəːʃən] *n* uitstapje *nt*, excursie *c*

excuse[1] [ik'skjuːs] *n* excuus *c*

excuse[2] [ik'skjuːz] *v* verontschuldigen, excuseren

execute ['eksikjuːt] *v* uitvoeren

execution [,eksi'kjuːʃən] *n* terechtstelling *c*

executioner [,eksi'kjuːʃənə] *n* beul *c*

executive [ig'zekjutiv] *adj* uitvoerend; *n* uitvoerende macht; directeur *c*

exempt [ig'zempt] *v* *ontheffen, vrijstellen; *adj* vrijgesteld

exemption [ig'zempʃən] *n* vrijstelling *c*

exercise ['eksəsaiz] *n* oefening *c*; thema *nt*; *v* oefenen; uitoefenen

exhale [eks'heil] *v* uitademen

exhaust [ig'zɔːst] *n* uitlaatpijp *c*, uitlaat *c*; *v* uitputten; ~ **gases** uit-

exhibit 53 extraordinary

laatgassen *pl*
exhibit [ig'zibit] *v* tentoonstellen; vertonen
exhibition [,eksi'biʃən] *n* expositie *c*, tentoonstelling *c*
exile ['eksail] *n* ballingschap *c*; balling *c*
exist [ig'zist] *v* *bestaan
existence [ig'zistəns] *n* bestaan *nt*
exit ['eksit] *n* uitgang *c*; uitrit *c*
exotic [ig'zɔtik] *adj* exotisch
expand [ik'spænd] *v* uitbreiden; uitspreiden; ontplooien
expect [ik'spekt] *v* verwachten
expectation [,ekspek'teiʃən] *n* verwachting *c*
expedition [,ekspə'diʃən] *n* verzending *c*; expeditie *c*
expel [ik'spel] *v* *uitwijzen
expenditure [ik'spenditʃə] *n* kosten *pl*, uitgave *c*
expense [ik'spens] *n* uitgave *c*; **expenses** *pl* onkosten *pl*
expensive [ik'spensiv] *adj* prijzig, duur; kostbaar
experience [ik'spiəriəns] *n* ervaring *c*; *v* *ervaren, *ondervinden, beleven; **experienced** ervaren
experiment [ik'sperimənt] *n* proef *c*, experiment *nt*; *v* experimenteren
expert ['ekspə:t] *n* deskundige *c*, vakman *c*, expert *c*; *adj* deskundig
expire [ik'spaiə] *v* *vervallen, *aflopen, *verstrijken; uitademen; **expired** vervallen
expiry [ik'spaiəri] *n* vervaldag *c*, afloop *c*
explain [ik'splein] *v* verklaren, uitleggen
explanation [,eksplə'neiʃən] *n* toelichting *c*, uitleg *c*, verklaring *c*
explicit [ik'splisit] *adj* uitdrukkelijk, expliciet
explode [ik'sploud] *v* ontploffen

exploit [ik'splɔit] *v* uitbuiten, exploiteren
explore [ik'splɔ:] *v* verkennen, *onderzoeken
explosion [ik'splouʒən] *n* explosie *c*
explosive [ik'splousiv] *adj* explosief; *n* springstof *c*
export[1] [ik'spɔ:t] *v* uitvoeren, exporteren
export[2] ['ekspɔ:t] *n* export *c*
exportation [,ekspɔ:'teiʃən] *n* uitvoer *c*
exports ['ekspɔ:ts] *pl* export *c*
exposition [,ekspə'ziʃən] *n* tentoonstelling *c*
exposure [ik'spouʒə] *n* blootstelling *c*; belichting *c*; ~ **meter** belichtingsmeter *c*
express [ik'spres] *v* uitdrukken; betuigen, uiten; *adj* expresse-; uitdrukkelijk; ~ **train** sneltrein *c*
expression [ik'spreʃən] *n* uitdrukking *c*; uiting *c*
exquisite [ik'skwizit] *adj* voortreffelijk
extend [ik'stend] *v* verlengen; uitbreiden; verlenen
extension [ik'stenʃən] *n* verlenging *c*; uitbreiding *c*; toestel *nt*; ~ **cord** verlengsnoer *nt*
extensive [ik'stensiv] *adj* omvangrijk; veelomvattend, uitgebreid
extent [ik'stent] *n* omvang *c*
exterior [ek'stiəriə] *adj* uiterlijk; *n* buitenkant *c*
external [ek'stə:nəl] *adj* uiterlijk
extinguish [ik'stingwiʃ] *v* blussen, doven
extort [ik'stɔ:t] *v* *afdwingen
extortion [ik'stɔ:ʃən] *n* afpersing *c*
extra ['ekstrə] *adj* extra
extract[1] [ik'strækt] *v* *uittrekken, *trekken
extract[2] ['ekstrækt] *n* fragment *nt*
extradite ['ekstrədait] *v* uitleveren
extraordinary [ik'strɔ:dənri] *adj* bui-

tengewoon

extravagant [ik'strævəgənt] *adj* overdreven, extravagant

extreme [ik'stri:m] *adj* extreem;
hoogst, uiterst; *n* uiterste *nt*

exuberant [ig'zju:bərənt] *adj* uitbundig

eye [ai] *n* oog *nt*

eyebrow ['aibrau] *n* wenkbrauw *c*

eyelash ['ailæʃ] *n* wimper *c*

eyelid ['ailid] *n* ooglid *nt*

eye-pencil ['ai,pensəl] *n* wenkbrauwstift *c*

eye-shadow ['ai,ʃædou] *n* ogenschaduw *c*

eye-witness ['ai,witnəs] *n* ooggetuige *c*

F

fable ['feibəl] *n* fabel *c*

fabric ['fæbrik] *n* stof *c*; structuur *c*

façade [fə'sɑ:d] *n* gevel *c*

face [feis] *n* gezicht *nt*; *v* het hoofd
*bieden aan; ~ **massage** gezichtsmassage *c*; **facing** tegenover

face-cream ['feiskri:m] *n* gezichtscrème *c*

face-pack ['feispæk] *n* schoonheidsmasker *nt*

face-powder ['feis,paudə] *n* gezichtspoeder *nt/c*

facility [fə'siləti] *n* faciliteit *c*

fact [fækt] *n* feit *nt*; **in** ~ in feite

factor ['fæktə] *n* factor *c*

factory ['fæktəri] *n* fabriek *c*

factual ['fæktʃuəl] *adj* feitelijk

faculty ['fækəlti] *n* vermogen *nt*; gave
c, talent *nt*, bekwaamheid *c*; faculteit *c*

fad [fæd] *n* gril *c*

fade [feid] *v* verkleuren, *verschieten

faience [fai'ɑ:s] *n* aardewerk *nt*, faience *c*

fail [feil] *v* falen; tekort *schieten;
*ontbreken; *nalaten; zakken;
without ~ beslist

failure ['feiljə] *n* mislukking *c*; fiasco
nt

faint [feint] *v* *flauwvallen; *adj* zwak,
vaag, flauw

fair [feə] *n* kermis *c*; beurs *c*; *adj* billijk, eerlijk; blond; mooi

fairly ['feəli] *adv* vrij, nogal, tamelijk

fairy ['feəri] *n* fee *c*

fairytale ['feəriteil] *n* sprookje *nt*

faith [feiθ] *n* geloof *nt*; vertrouwen *nt*

faithful ['feiθful] *adj* trouw

fake [feik] *n* vervalsing *c*

fall [fɔ:l] *n* val *c*; *nAm* herfst *c*

***fall** [fɔ:l] *v* *vallen

false [fɔ:ls] *adj* vals; verkeerd, onwaar, onecht; ~ **teeth** kunstgebit
nt

falter ['fɔ:ltə] *v* wankelen; stamelen

fame [feim] *n* faam *c*, roem *c*; reputatie *c*

familiar [fə'miljə] *adj* vertrouwd; familiaar

family ['fæməli] *n* gezin *nt*; familie *c*;
~ **name** achternaam *c*

famous ['feiməs] *adj* beroemd

fan [fæn] *n* ventilator *c*; waaier *c*; fan
c; ~ **belt** ventilatorriem *c*

fanatical [fə'nætikəl] *adj* fanatiek

fancy ['fænsi] *v* lusten, zin *hebben
in; zich verbeelden, zich voorstellen; *n* gril *c*; fantasie *c*

fantastic [fæn'tæstik] *adj* fantastisch

fantasy ['fæntəzi] *n* fantasie *c*

far [fɑ:] *adj* ver; *adv* veel; **by** ~ verreweg; **so** ~ tot nu toe

far-away ['fɑ:rəwei] *adj* ver

farce [fɑ:s] *n* klucht *c*, farce *c*

fare [feə] *n* reiskosten *pl*, tarief *nt*;
kost *c*, voedsel *nt*

farm [fɑ:m] *n* boerderij *c*

farmer ['fɑ:mə] *n* boer *c*; **farmer's**

wife boerin *c*

farmhouse ['fɑ:mhaus] *n* boerderij *c*

far-off ['fɑ:rɔf] *adj* afgelegen

fascinate ['fæsineit] *v* boeien

fascism ['fæʃizəm] *n* fascisme *nt*

fascist ['fæʃist] *adj* fascistisch; *n* fascist *c*

fashion ['fæʃən] *n* mode *c*; manier *c*

fashionable ['fæʃənəbəl] *adj* modieus

fast [fɑ:st] *adj* vlug, snel; vast

fast-dyed [,fɑ:st'daid] *adj* wasecht, kleurecht

fasten ['fɑ:sən] *v* vastmaken, bevestigen; *sluiten

fastener ['fɑ:sənə] *n* sluiting *c*

fat [fæt] *adj* vet, dik; *n* vet *nt*

fatal ['feitəl] *adj* fataal, dodelijk, noodlottig

fate [feit] *n* lot *nt*, noodlot *nt*

father ['fɑ:ðə] *n* vader *c*; pater *c*

father-in-law ['fɑ:ðərinlɔ:] *n* (pl fathers-) schoonvader *c*

fatherland ['fɑ:ðələnd] *n* vaderland *nt*

fatness ['fætnəs] *n* dikte *c*

fatty ['fæti] *adj* vettig

faucet ['fɔ:sit] *nAm* kraan *c*

fault [fɔ:lt] *n* schuld *c*; fout *c*, defect *nt*, gebrek *nt*

faultless ['fɔ:ltləs] *adj* foutloos; feilloos

faulty ['fɔ:lti] *adj* gebrekkig, defect

favour ['feivə] *n* gunst *c*; *v* begunstigen, bevoorrechten

favourable ['feivərəbəl] *adj* gunstig

favourite ['feivərit] *n* lieveling *c*, favoriet *c*; *adj* lievelings-

fawn [fɔ:n] *adj* lichtbruin; *n* reekalf *nt*

fear [fiə] *n* vrees *c*, angst *c*; *v* vrezen

feasible ['fi:zəbəl] *adj* uitvoerbaar

feast [fi:st] *n* feest *nt*

feat [fi:t] *n* prestatie *c*

feather ['feðə] *n* veer *c*

feature ['fi:tʃə] *n* kenmerk *nt*; gelaats-

trek *c*

February ['februəri] februari

federal ['fedərəl] *adj* federaal

federation [,fedə'reiʃən] *n* federatie *c*; bond *c*

fee [fi:] *n* honorarium *nt*

feeble ['fi:bəl] *adj* zwak

*****feed** [fi:d] *v* voeden; **fed up with** beu

*****feel** [fi:l] *v* voelen; betasten; ~ **like** zin *hebben in

feeling ['fi:liŋ] *n* gevoel *nt*

fell [fel] *v* (p fall)

fellow ['felou] *n* kerel *c*

felt[1] [felt] *n* vilt *nt*

felt[2] [felt] *v* (p, pp feel)

female ['fi:meil] *adj* vrouwelijk

feminine ['feminin] *adj* vrouwelijk

fence [fens] *n* omheining *c*; hek *nt*; *v* schermen

fender ['fendə] *n* bumper *c*

ferment [fə:'ment] *v* gisten

ferry-boat ['feribout] *n* veerboot *c*

fertile ['fə:tail] *adj* vruchtbaar

festival ['festivəl] *n* festival *nt*

festive ['festiv] *adj* feestelijk

fetch [fetʃ] *v* halen; afhalen

feudal ['fju:dəl] *adj* feodaal

fever ['fi:və] *n* koorts *c*

feverish ['fi:vəriʃ] *adj* koortsig

few [fju:] *adj* weinig

fiancé [fi'ã:sei] *n* verloofde *c*

fiancée [fi'ã:sei] *n* verloofde *c*

fibre ['faibə] *n* vezel *c*

fiction ['fikʃən] *n* fictie *c*, verzinsel *nt*

field [fi:ld] *n* akker *c*, veld *nt*; gebied *nt*; ~ **glasses** veldkijker *c*

fierce [fiəs] *adj* wild; woest, fel

fifteen [,fif'ti:n] *num* vijftien

fifteenth [,fif'ti:nθ] *num* vijftiende

fifth [fifθ] *num* vijfde

fifty ['fifti] *num* vijftig

fig [fig] *n* vijg *c*

fight [fait] *n* strijd *c*, gevecht *nt*

* **fight** [fait] v *strijden, *vechten
figure ['figə] n gestalte c, figuur c; cijfer nt
file [fail] n vijl c; dossier nt; rij c
Filipino [,fili'pi:nou] n Filippijn c
fill [fil] v vullen; ~ **in** invullen; **filling station** benzinestation nt; ~ **out** Am invullen; ~ **up** opvullen
filling ['filiŋ] n vulling c
film [film] n film c; v filmen
filter ['filtə] n filter nt
filthy ['filθi] adj smerig, vuil
final ['fainəl] adj laatst
finance [fai'næns] v financieren
finances [fai'nænsiz] pl financiën pl
financial [fai'nænʃəl] adj financieel
finch [fintʃ] n vink c
* **find** [faind] v *vinden
fine [fain] n boete c; adj fijn; mooi; uitstekend, prachtig; ~ **arts** schone kunsten
finger ['fiŋgə] n vinger c; **little** ~ pink c
fingerprint ['fiŋgəprint] n vingerafdruk c
finish ['finiʃ] v afmaken, beëindigen; eindigen; n einde nt; eindstreep c; **finished** af; op
Finland ['finlənd] Finland
Finn [fin] n Fin c
Finnish ['finiʃ] adj Fins
fire [faiə] n vuur nt; brand c; v *schieten; *ontslaan
fire-alarm ['faiərə,lɑ:m] n brandalarm nt
fire-brigade ['faiəbri,geid] n brandweer c
fire-escape ['faiəri,skeip] n brandtrap c
fire-extinguisher ['faiərik,stiŋgwiʃə] n brandblusapparaat nt
fireplace ['faiəpleis] n haard c
fireproof ['faiəpru:f] adj brandvrij; vuurvast
firm [fə:m] adj vast; stevig; n firma c

first [fə:st] num eerst; **at** ~ eerst; aanvankelijk; ~ **name** voornaam c
first-aid [,fə:st'eid] n eerste hulp; ~ **kit** verbandkist c; ~ **post** eerste hulppost
first-class [,fə:st'klɑ:s] adj eersteklas
first-rate [,fə:st'reit] adj eersterangs, prima
fir-tree ['fə:tri:] n denneboom c, den c
fish¹ [fiʃ] n (pl ~, ~es) vis c; ~ **shop** viswinkel c
fish² [fiʃ] v vissen; hengelen; **fishing gear** vistuig nt; **fishing hook** vishaak c; **fishing industry** visserij c; **fishing licence** visakte c; **fishing line** vislijn c; **fishing net** visnet nt; **fishing rod** hengel c; **fishing tackle** vistuig nt
fishbone ['fiʃboun] n graat c, visgraat c
fisherman ['fiʃəmən] n (pl -men) visser c
fist [fist] n vuist c
fit [fit] adj geschikt; n aanval c; v passen; **fitting room** paskamer c
five [faiv] num vijf
fix [fiks] v repareren
fixed [fikst] adj vast
fizz [fiz] n prik c
fjord [fjɔ:d] n fjord c
flag [flæg] n vlag c
flame [fleim] n vlam c
flamingo [flə'miŋgou] n (pl ~s, ~es) flamingo c
flannel ['flænəl] n flanel nt
flash [flæʃ] n flits c
flash-bulb ['flæʃbʌlb] n flitslampje nt
flash-light ['flæʃlait] n zaklantaarn c
flask [flɑ:sk] n flacon c; **thermos** ~ thermosfles c
flat [flæt] adj vlak, plat; n flat c; ~ **tyre** lekke band
flavour ['fleivə] n smaak c; v kruiden
fleet [fli:t] n vloot c

flesh [fleʃ] n vlees nt

flew [flu:] v (p fly)

flex [fleks] n snoer nt

flexible ['fleksibəl] adj buigbaar; soepel

flight [flait] n vlucht c; **charter ~** chartervlucht c

flint [flint] n vuursteen c

float [flout] v *drijven; n vlotter c

flock [flɔk] n kudde c

flood [flʌd] n overstroming c; vloed c

floor [flɔ:] n vloer c; etage c, verdieping c; **~ show** floor-show c

florist ['flɔrist] n bloemist c

flour [flauə] n bloem c, meel nt

flow [flou] v vloeien, stromen

flower [flauə] n bloem c

flowerbed ['flauəbed] n bloemperk nt

flower-shop ['flauəʃɔp] n bloemenwinkel c

flown [floun] v (pp fly)

flu [flu:] n griep c

fluent ['flu:ənt] adj vloeiend

fluid ['flu:id] adj vloeibaar; n vloeistof c

flute [flu:t] n fluit c

fly [flai] n vlieg c; gulp c

*****fly** [flai] v *vliegen

foam [foum] n schuim nt; v schuimen

foam-rubber ['foum,rʌbə] n schuimrubber nt

focus ['foukəs] n brandpunt nt

fog [fɔg] n mist c

foggy ['fɔgi] adj mistig

foglamp ['fɔglæmp] n mistlamp c

fold [fould] v *vouwen; *opvouwen; n vouw c

folk [fouk] n volk nt; **~ song** volkslied nt

folk-dance ['foukdɑ:ns] n volksdans c

folklore ['fouklɔ:] n folklore c

follow ['fɔlou] v volgen; **following** adj eerstvolgend, volgend

*****be fond of** [bi: fɔnd ɔv] *houden van

food [fu:d] n voedsel nt; eten nt, kost c; **~ poisoning** voedselvergiftiging c

foodstuffs ['fu:dstʌfs] pl levensmiddelen pl

fool [fu:l] n gek c, dwaas c; v foppen

foolish ['fu:liʃ] adj mal, dwaas

foot [fut] n (pl feet) voet c; **~ powder** voetpoeder nt/c; **on ~** te voet

football ['futbɔ:l] n voetbal c; **~ match** voetbalwedstrijd c

foot-brake ['futbreik] n voetrem c

footpath ['futpɑ:θ] n voetpad nt

footwear ['futweə] n schoeisel nt

for [fɔ:, fə] prep voor; gedurende; naar; vanwege, wegens, uit; conj want

*****forbid** [fə'bid] v *verbieden

force [fɔ:s] v noodzaken, *dwingen; forceren; n macht c, kracht c; geweld nt; **by ~** noodgedwongen; **driving ~** drijfkracht c

ford [fɔ:d] n doorwaadbare plaats c

forecast ['fɔ:kɑ:st] n voorspelling c; v voorspellen

foreground ['fɔ:graund] n voorgrond c

forehead ['fɔred] n voorhoofd nt

foreign ['fɔrin] adj buitenlands; vreemd

foreigner ['fɔrinə] n buitenlander c; vreemdeling c

foreman ['fɔ:mən] n (pl -men) voorman c

foremost ['fɔ:moust] adj hoogst

foresail ['fɔ:seil] n fok c

forest ['fɔrist] n woud nt, bos nt

forester ['fɔristə] n boswachter c

forge [fɔ:dʒ] v vervalsen

*****forget** [fə'get] v *vergeten

forgetful [fə'getfəl] adj vergeetachtig

*****forgive** [fə'giv] v *vergeven

fork [fɔ:k] n vork c; tweesprong c; v zich splitsen

form [fɔ:m] n vorm c; formulier nt;

klas *c*; *v* vormen

formal ['fɔːməl] *adj* formeel

formality [fɔːˈmæləti] *n* formaliteit *c*

former ['fɔːmə] *adj* voormalig; vroeger; **formerly** voorheen, vroeger

formula ['fɔːmjulə] *n* (pl ~e, ~s) formule *c*

fort [fɔːt] *n* fort *nt*

fortnight ['fɔːtnait] *n* veertien dagen

fortress ['fɔːtris] *n* vesting *c*

fortunate ['fɔːtʃənət] *adj* gelukkig

fortune ['fɔːtʃuːn] *n* fortuin *nt*; lot *nt*, geluk *nt*

forty ['fɔːti] *num* veertig

forward ['fɔːwəd] *adv* vooruit, voorwaarts; *v* *nazenden

foster-parents ['fɔstə,peərənts] *pl* pleegouders *pl*

fought [fɔːt] *v* (p, pp fight)

foul [faul] *adj* smerig; gemeen

found[1] [faund] *v* (p, pp find)

found[2] [faund] *v* oprichten, stichten

foundation [faunˈdeiʃən] *n* stichting *c*; ~ **cream** basiscrème *c*

fountain ['fauntin] *n* fontein *c*; bron *c*

fountain-pen ['fauntinpen] *n* vulpen *c*

four [fɔː] *num* vier

fourteen [,fɔːˈtiːn] *num* veertien

fourteenth [,fɔːˈtiːnθ] *num* veertiende

fourth [fɔːθ] *num* vierde

fowl [faul] *n* (pl ~s, ~) gevogelte *nt*

fox [fɔks] *n* vos *c*

foyer ['fɔiei] *n* foyer *c*

fraction ['frækʃən] *n* fractie *c*

fracture ['fræktʃə] *v* *breken; *n* breuk *c*

fragile ['frædʒail] *adj* breekbaar; broos

fragment ['frægmənt] *n* fragment *nt*; stuk *nt*

frame [freim] *n* lijst *c*; montuur *nt*

France [frɑːns] Frankrijk

franchise ['fræntʃaiz] *n* kiesrecht *nt*

fraternity [frəˈtəːnəti] *n* broederschap *c*

fraud [frɔːd] *n* fraude *c*, bedrog *nt*

fray [frei] *v* rafelen

free [friː] *adj* vrij; gratis; ~ **of charge** gratis; ~ **ticket** vrijkaart *c*

freedom ['friːdəm] *n* vrijheid *c*

*****freeze** [friːz] *v* *vriezen; *bevriezen

freezing ['friːziŋ] *adj* ijskoud

freezing-point ['friːziŋpɔint] *n* vriespunt *nt*

freight [freit] *n* lading *c*, vracht *c*

freight-train ['freittrein] *nAm* goederentrein *c*

French [frentʃ] *adj* Frans

Frenchman ['frentʃmən] *n* (pl -men) Fransman *c*

frequency ['friːkwənsi] *n* frequentie *c*

frequent ['friːkwənt] *adj* veelvuldig, frequent; **frequently** dikwijls

fresh [freʃ] *adj* vers, fris; ~ **water** zoet water

friction ['frikʃən] *n* wrijving *c*

Friday ['fraidi] vrijdag *c*

fridge [fridʒ] *n* koelkast *c*, ijskast *c*

friend [frend] *n* vriend *c*; vriendin *c*

friendly ['frendli] *adj* vriendelijk; amicaal, vriendschappelijk

friendship ['frendʃip] *n* vriendschap *c*

fright [frait] *n* angst *c*, schrik *c*

frighten ['fraitən] *v* *doen schrikken

frightened ['fraitənd] *adj* bang; *be ~ *schrikken

frightful ['fraitfəl] *adj* verschrikkelijk, vreselijk

fringe [frindʒ] *n* franje *c*

frock [frɔk] *n* jurk *c*

frog [frɔg] *n* kikker *c*

from [frɔm] *prep* van; uit; vanaf

front [frʌnt] *n* voorkant *c*; **in ~ of** voor

frontier ['frʌntiə] *n* grens *c*

frost [frɔst] *n* vorst *c*

froth [frɔθ] *n* schuim *nt*

frozen ['frouzən] *adj* bevroren; ~ **food** diepvries produkten

fruit [fru:t] *n* fruit *nt*; vrucht *c*
fry [frai] *v* *bakken; *braden
frying-pan ['fraiiŋpæn] *n* koekepan *c*
fuel ['fju:əl] *n* brandstof *c*; benzine *c*; ~ **pump** *Am* benzinepomp *c*
full [ful] *adj* vol; ~ **board** vol pension; ~ **stop** punt *c*; ~ **up** vol
fun [fʌn] *n* plezier *nt*, pret *c*; lol *c*
function ['fʌŋkʃən] *n* functie *c*
fund [fʌnd] *n* fonds *nt*
fundamental [,fʌndə'mentəl] *adj* fundamenteel
funeral ['fju:nərəl] *n* begrafenis *c*
funnel ['fʌnəl] *n* trechter *c*
funny ['fʌni] *adj* leuk, grappig; zonderling
fur [fə:] *n* pels *c*; ~ **coat** bontjas *c*; **furs** bont *nt*
furious ['fjuəriəs] *adj* razend, woedend
furnace ['fə:nis] *n* oven *c*
furnish ['fə:niʃ] *v* leveren, verschaffen; inrichten, meubileren; ~ **with** *voorzien van
furniture ['fə:nitʃə] *n* meubilair *nt*
furrier ['fʌriə] *n* bontwerker *c*
further ['fə:ðə] *adj* verder; nader
furthermore ['fə:ðəmɔ:] *adv* bovendien
furthest ['fə:ðist] *adj* verst
fuse [fju:z] *n* zekering *c*; lont *c*
fuss [fʌs] *n* drukte *c*; ophef *c*, herrie *c*
future ['fju:tʃə] *n* toekomst *c*; *adj* toekomstig

G

gable ['geibəl] *n* geveltop *c*
gadget ['gædʒit] *n* technisch snufje
gaiety ['geiəti] *n* vrolijkheid *c*, pret *c*
gain [gein] *v* *winnen; *n* winst *c*
gait [geit] *n* gang *c*, loop *c*
gale [geil] *n* storm *c*

gall [gɔ:l] *n* gal *c*; ~ **bladder** galblaas *c*
gallery ['gæləri] *n* galerij *c*
gallop ['gæləp] *n* galop *c*
gallows ['gælouz] *pl* galg *c*
gallstone ['gɔ:lstoun] *n* galsteen *c*
game [geim] *n* spel *nt*; wild *nt*; ~ **reserve** wildpark *nt*
gang [gæŋ] *n* bende *c*; ploeg *c*
gangway ['gæŋwei] *n* loopplank *c*
gaol [dʒeil] *n* gevangenis *c*
gap [gæp] *n* bres *c*
garage ['gæra:ʒ] *n* garage *c*; *v* stallen
garbage ['ga:bidʒ] *n* vuilnis *nt*, afval *nt*
garden ['ga:dən] *n* tuin *c*; **public** ~ plantsoen *nt*; **zoological gardens** dierentuin *c*
gardener ['ga:dənə] *n* tuinman *c*
gargle ['ga:gəl] *v* gorgelen
garlic ['ga:lik] *n* knoflook *nt/c*
gas [gæs] *n* gas *nt*; *nAm* benzine *c*; ~ **cooker** gasstel *nt*; ~ **pump** *Am* benzinepomp *c*; ~ **station** *Am* benzinestation *nt*; ~ **stove** gaskachel *c*
gasoline ['gæsəli:n] *nAm* benzine *c*
gastric ['gæstrik] *adj* maag-; ~ **ulcer** maagzweer *c*
gasworks ['gæswə:ks] *n* gasfabriek *c*
gate [geit] *n* poort *c*; hek *nt*
gather ['gæðə] *v* verzamelen; *bijeenkomen; oogsten
gauge [geidʒ] *n* meter *c*
gauze [gɔ:z] *n* gaas *nt*
gave [geiv] *v* (p give)
gay [gei] *adj* vrolijk; bont
gaze [geiz] *v* staren
gear [giə] *n* versnelling *c*; uitrusting *c*; **change** ~ schakelen; ~ **lever** versnellingspook *c*
gear-box ['giəbɔks] *n* versnellingsbak *c*
gem [dʒem] *n* juweel *nt*, edelsteen *c*; kleinood *nt*

gender ['dʒendə] n geslacht nt

general ['dʒenərəl] adj algemeen; n generaal c; ~ **practitioner** huisarts c; **in** ~ in het algemeen

generate ['dʒenəreit] v verwekken

generation [,dʒenə'reiʃən] n generatie c

generator ['dʒenəreitər] n generator c

generosity [,dʒenə'rɔsəti] n edelmoedigheid c

generous ['dʒenərəs] adj gul, royaal

genital ['dʒenitəl] adj geslachtelijk

genius ['dʒiːniəs] n genie nt

gentle ['dʒentəl] adj zacht; teer, licht; voorzichtig

gentleman ['dʒentəlmən] n (pl -men) heer c

genuine ['dʒenjuin] adj echt

geography [dʒi'ɔgrəfi] n aardrijkskunde c

geology [dʒi'ɔlədʒi] n geologie c

geometry [dʒi'ɔmətri] n meetkunde c

germ [dʒəːm] n bacil c; kiem c

German ['dʒəːmən] adj Duits; n Duitser c

Germany ['dʒəːməni] Duitsland

gesticulate [dʒi'stikjuleit] v gebaren

*get [get] v *krijgen; halen; *worden; ~ **back** *teruggaan; ~ **off** uitstappen; ~ **on** instappen; vorderen; ~ **up** *opstaan

ghost [goust] n spook nt; geest c

giant ['dʒaiənt] n reus c

giddiness ['gidinəs] n duizeligheid c

giddy ['gidi] adj duizelig

gift [gift] n geschenk nt, cadeau nt; gave c

gifted ['giftid] adj begaafd

gigantic [dʒai'gæntik] adj reusachtig

giggle ['gigəl] v giechelen

gill [gil] n kieuw c

gilt [gilt] adj verguld

ginger ['dʒindʒə] n gember c

gipsy ['dʒipsi] n zigeuner c

girdle ['gəːdəl] n step-in c

girl [gəːl] n meisje nt; ~ **guide** padvindster c

*give [giv] v *geven; *aangeven; ~ **away** verklappen; ~ **in** *toegeven; ~ **up** *opgeven

glacier ['glæsiə] n gletsjer c

glad [glæd] adj verheugd, blij; gladly graag, gaarne

gladness ['glædnəs] n vreugde c

glamorous ['glæmərəs] adj betoverend, fascinerend

glamour ['glæmə] n charme c

glance [glɑːns] n blik c; v een blik *werpen

gland [glænd] n klier c

glare [gleə] n scherp licht; schittering c

glaring ['gleəriŋ] adj verblindend

glass [glɑːs] n glas nt; glazen; glasses bril c; magnifying ~ vergrootglas nt

glaze [gleiz] v emailleren

glen [glen] n bergkloof c

glide [glaid] v *glijden

glider ['glaidə] n zweefvliegtuig nt

glimpse [glimps] n blik c; glimp c; v even *zien

global ['gloubəl] adj wereldomvattend

globe [gloub] n wereldbol c, aardbol c

gloom [gluːm] n duister nt

gloomy ['gluːmi] adj somber

glorious ['glɔːriəs] adj prachtig

glory ['glɔːri] n glorie c, roem c; eer c, lof c

gloss [glɔs] n glans c

glossy ['glɔsi] adj glanzend

glove [glʌv] n handschoen c

glow [glou] v gloeien; n gloed c

glue [gluː] n lijm c

*go [gou] v *gaan; *lopen; *worden; ~ **ahead** *doorgaan; ~ **away** *weggaan; ~ **back** *teruggaan; ~ **home** naar huis *gaan; ~ **in** *binnengaan;

~ **on** *doorgaan; ~ **out** *uitgaan;
~ **through** meemaken, doormaken
goal [goul] n doel nt; doelpunt nt
goalkeeper ['goul,ki:pə] n doelman c
goat [gout] n bok c, geit c
god [gɔd] n god c
goddess ['gɔdis] n godin c
godfather ['gɔd,fa:ðə] n peetvader c
goggles ['gɔgəlz] pl duikbril c
gold [gould] n goud nt; ~ **leaf** blad-goud nt
golden ['gouldən] adj gouden
goldmine ['gouldmain] n goudmijn c
goldsmith ['gouldsmiθ] n goudsmid c
golf [gɔlf] n golf nt
golf-club ['gɔlfklʌb] n golfclub c
golf-course ['gɔlfkɔ:s] n golfbaan c
golf-links ['gɔlfliŋks] n golfbaan c
gondola ['gɔndələ] n gondel c
gone [gɔn] adv (pp go) weg
good [gud] adj goed; lekker; zoet, braaf
good-bye! [,gud'bai] dag!
good-humoured [,gud'hju:məd] adj op-geruimd
good-looking [,gud'lukiŋ] adj knap
good-natured [,gud'neitʃəd] adj goed-hartig
goods [gudz] pl waren pl, goederen pl; ~ **train** goederentrein c
good-tempered [,gud'tempəd] adj goedgestemd
goodwill [,gud'wil] n welwillendheid c
goose [gu:s] n (pl geese) gans c
gooseberry ['guzbəri] n kruisbes c
goose-flesh ['gu:sfleʃ] n kippevel nt
gorge [gɔ:dʒ] n ravijn nt
gorgeous ['gɔ:dʒəs] adj prachtig
gospel ['gɔspəl] n evangelie nt
gossip ['gɔsip] n geroddel nt; v rodde-len
got [gɔt] v (p, pp get)
gourmet ['guəmei] n fijnproever c
gout [gaut] n jicht c

govern ['gʌvən] v regeren
governess ['gʌvənis] n gouvernante c
government ['gʌvənmənt] n bewind nt, regering c
governor ['gʌvənə] n gouverneur c
gown [gaun] n japon c
grace [greis] n gratie c; genade c
graceful ['greisfəl] adj bevallig
grade [greid] n graad c; v rangschik-ken
gradient ['greidiənt] n helling c
gradual ['grædʒuəl] adj geleidelijk; **gradually** adv langzamerhand
graduate ['grædʒueit] v een diploma behalen
grain [grein] n korrel c, graan nt, ko-ren nt
gram [græm] n gram nt
grammar ['græmə] n grammatica c
grammatical [grə'mætikəl] adj gram-maticaal
gramophone ['græməfoun] n grammo-foon c
grand [grænd] adj groots
granddad ['grændæd] n opa c
granddaughter ['græn,dɔ:tə] n klein-dochter c
grandfather ['græn,fa:ðə] n grootvader c; opa c
grandmother ['græn,mʌðə] n groot-moeder c; oma c
grandparents ['græn,peərənts] pl groot-ouders pl
grandson ['grænsʌn] n kleinzoon c
granite ['grænit] n graniet nt
grant [gra:nt] v gunnen, verlenen; in-willigen; n toelage c, beurs c
grapefruit ['greipfru:t] n pompelmoes c
grapes [greips] pl druiven pl
graph [græf] n grafiek c
graphic ['græfik] adj grafisch
grasp [gra:sp] v *grijpen; n greep c
grass [gra:s] n gras nt

grasshopper ['grɑːsˌhɒpə] *n* sprink-haan *c*

grate [greit] *n* rooster *nt*; *v* raspen

grateful ['greitfəl] *adj* erkentelijk, dankbaar

grater ['greitə] *n* rasp *c*

gratis ['grætis] *adj* gratis

gratitude ['grætitjuːd] *n* dankbaarheid *c*

gratuity [grə'tjuːəti] *n* fooi *c*

grave [greiv] *n* graf *nt*; *adj* ernstig

gravel ['grævəl] *n* kiezel *c*, grind *nt*

gravestone ['greivstoun] *n* grafsteen *c*

graveyard ['greivjɑːd] *n* kerkhof *nt*

gravity ['grævəti] *n* zwaartekracht *c*; ernst *c*

gravy ['greivi] *n* jus *c*

graze [greiz] *v* grazen; *n* schaafwond *c*

grease [griːs] *n* vet *nt*; *v* smeren

greasy ['griːsi] *adj* vet, vettig

great [greit] *adj* groot; **Great Britain** Groot-Brittannië

Greece [griːs] Griekenland

greed [griːd] *n* hebzucht *c*

greedy ['griːdi] *adj* hebzuchtig; gulzig

Greek [griːk] *adj* Grieks; *n* Griek *c*

green [griːn] *adj* groen; ~ **card** groene kaart

greengrocer ['griːnˌgrousə] *n* groente-boer *c*

greenhouse ['griːnhaus] *n* broeikas *c*, kas *c*

greens [griːnz] *pl* groente *c*

greet [griːt] *v* groeten

greeting ['griːtiŋ] *n* groet *c*

grey [grei] *adj* grijs; grauw

greyhound ['greihaund] *n* hazewind *c*

grief [griːf] *n* verdriet *nt*; bedroefdheid *c*, smart *c*

grieve [griːv] *v* treuren

grill [gril] *n* grill *c*; *v* roosteren

grill-room ['grilruːm] *n* grillroom *c*

grin [grin] *v* grijnzen; *n* grijns *c*

*****grind** [graind] *v* *malen; fijnmalen

grip [grip] *v* *grijpen; *n* houvast *nt*, greep *c*; *nAm* handkoffertje *nt*

grit [grit] *n* gruis *nt*

groan [groun] *v* kreunen

grocer ['grousə] *n* kruidenier *c*; **grocer's** kruidenierswinkel *c*

groceries ['grousəriz] *pl* kruideniers-waren *pl*

groin [grɔin] *n* lies *c*

groove [gruːv] *n* groef *c*

gross¹ [grous] *n* (pl ~) gros *nt*

gross² [grous] *adj* grof; bruto

grotto ['grɒtou] *n* (pl ~es, ~s) grot *c*

ground¹ [graund] *n* bodem *c*, grond *c*; ~ **floor** begane grond; **grounds** terrein *nt*

ground² [graund] *v* (p, pp grind)

group [gruːp] *n* groep *c*

grouse [graus] *n* (pl ~) korhoen *nt*

grove [grouv] *n* bosje *nt*

*****grow** [grou] *v* groeien; kweken; *worden

growl [graul] *v* grommen

grown-up ['grounʌp] *adj* volwassen; *n* volwassene *c*

growth [grouθ] *n* groei *c*; gezwel *nt*

grudge [grʌdʒ] *v* misgunnen

grumble ['grʌmbəl] *v* mopperen

guarantee [ˌgærən'tiː] *n* garantie *c*; waarborg *c*; *v* garanderen

guarantor [ˌgærən'tɔː] *n* borg *c*

guard [gɑːd] *n* bewaker *c*; *v* bewaken

guardian ['gɑːdiən] *n* voogd *c*

guess [ges] *v* *raden; *denken, gissen; *n* gissing *c*

guest [gest] *n* logé *c*, gast *c*

guest-house ['gesthaus] *n* pension *nt*

guest-room ['gestruːm] *n* logeerkamer *c*

guide [gaid] *n* gids *c*; *v* leiden

guidebook ['gaidbuk] *n* gids *c*

guide-dog ['gaiddɒg] *n* geleidehond *c*

guilt [gilt] *n* schuld *c*

guilty ['gilti] *adj* schuldig
guinea-pig ['ginipig] *n* cavia *c*
guitar [gi'tɑ:] *n* gitaar *c*
gulf [gʌlf] *n* golf *c*
gull [gʌl] *n* meeuw *c*
gum [gʌm] *n* tandvlees *nt* ; gom *c* ; lijm *c*
gun [gʌn] *n* geweer *nt*, revolver *c* ; kanon *nt*
gunpowder ['gʌn,paudə] *n* kruit *nt*
gust [gʌst] *n* windstoot *c*
gusty ['gʌsti] *adj* winderig
gut [gʌt] *n* darm *c* ; **guts** lef *nt*
gutter ['gʌtə] *n* goot *c*
guy [gai] *n* vent *c*
gymnasium [dʒim'neiziəm] *n* (pl ~s, -sia) gymnastiekzaal *c*
gymnast ['dʒimnæst] *n* gymnast *c*
gymnastics [dʒim'næstiks] *pl* gymnastiek *c*
gynaecologist [,gainə'kɔlədʒist] *n* gynaecoloog *c*, vrouwenarts *c*

H

haberdashery ['hæbədæʃəri] *n* garenen bandwinkel
habit ['hæbit] *n* gewoonte *c*
habitable ['hæbitəbəl] *adj* bewoonbaar
habitual [hə'bitʃuəl] *adj* gewoon
had [hæd] *v* (p, pp have)
haddock ['hædək] *n* (pl ~) schelvis *c*
haemorrhage ['heməridʒ] *n* bloeding *c*
haemorrhoids ['hemərɔidz] *pl* aambeien *pl*
hail [heil] *n* hagel *c*
hair [heə] *n* haar *nt* ; ~ **cream** haarcrème *c* ; ~ **piece** haarstukje *nt* ; ~ **tonic** haartonic *c*
hairbrush ['heəbrʌʃ] *n* haarborstel *c*
hair-do ['heədu:] *n* kapsel *nt*, coiffure *c*

hairdresser ['heə,dresə] *n* kapper *c*
hair-dryer ['heədraiə] *n* haardroger *c*
hair-grip ['heəgrip] *n* haarspeld *c*
hair-net ['heənet] *n* haarnetje *nt*
hair-oil ['heərɔil] *n* haarolie *c*
hairpin ['heəpin] *n* haarspeld *c*
hair-spray ['heəsprei] *n* haarlak *c*
hairy ['heəri] *adj* harig
half[1] [hɑ:f] *adj* half
half[2] [hɑ:f] *n* (pl halves) helft *c*
half-time [,hɑ:f'taim] *n* rust *c*
halfway [,hɑ:f'wei] *adv* halverwege
halibut ['hælibət] *n* (pl ~) heilbot *c*
hall [hɔ:l] *n* hal *c* ; zaal *c*
halt [hɔ:lt] *v* stoppen
halve [hɑ:v] *v* halveren
ham [hæm] *n* ham *c*
hamlet ['hæmlət] *n* gehucht *nt*
hammer ['hæmə] *n* hamer *c*
hammock ['hæmək] *n* hangmat *c*
hamper ['hæmpə] *n* mand *c*
hand [hænd] *n* hand *c* ; *v* *aangeven; ~ **cream** handcrème *c*
handbag ['hændbæg] *n* handtas *c*
handbook ['hændbuk] *n* handboek *nt*
hand-brake ['hændbreik] *n* handrem *c*
handcuffs ['hændkʌfs] *pl* handboeien *pl*
handful ['hændful] *n* handvol *c*
handicraft ['hændikrɑ:ft] *n* handenarbeid *c* ; handwerk *nt*
handkerchief ['hæŋkətʃif] *n* zakdoek *c*
handle ['hændəl] *n* steel *c*, handvat *nt* ; *v* hanteren; behandelen
hand-made [,hænd'meid] *adj* met de hand gemaakt
handshake ['hændʃeik] *n* handdruk *c*
handsome ['hænsəm] *adj* knap
handwork ['hændwə:k] *n* handwerk *nt*
handwriting ['hænd,raitiŋ] *n* handschrift *nt*
handy ['hændi] *adj* handig
***hang** [hæŋ] *v* *ophangen; *hangen
hanger ['hæŋə] *n* kleerhanger *c*

hangover ['hæŋ,ouvə] n kater c

happen ['hæpən] v *voorkomen, gebeuren

happening ['hæpəniŋ] n gebeurtenis c

happiness ['hæpinəs] n geluk nt

happy ['hæpi] adj blij, gelukkig

harbour ['haːbə] n haven c

hard [haːd] adj hard; moeilijk; **hardly** nauwelijks

hardware ['haːdwɛə] n ijzerwaren pl; ~ **store** handel in ijzerwaren

hare [hɛə] n haas c

harm [haːm] n schade c; kwaad nt; v schaden

harmful ['haːmfəl] adj nadelig, schadelijk

harmless ['haːmləs] adj onschadelijk

harmony ['haːməni] n harmonie c

harp [haːp] n harp c

harpsichord ['haːpsikɔːd] n clavecimbel c

harsh [haːʃ] adj ruw; streng; wreed

harvest ['haːvist] n oogst c

has [hæz] v (pr have)

haste [heist] n spoed c, haast c

hasten ['heisən] v zich haasten

hasty ['heisti] adj haastig

hat [hæt] n hoed c; ~ **rack** kapstok c

hatch [hætʃ] n luik nt

hate [heit] v een hekel *hebben aan; haten; n haat c

hatred ['heitrid] n haat c

haughty ['hɔːti] adj hooghartig

haul [hɔːl] v slepen

have [hæv] v *hebben; *laten; ~ **to** *moeten

haversack ['hævəsæk] n broodzak c

hawk [hɔːk] n havik c; valk c

hay [hei] n hooi nt; ~ **fever** hooikoorts c

hazard ['hæzəd] n risico nt

haze [heiz] n nevel c; waas nt

hazelnut ['heizəlnʌt] n hazelnoot c

hazy ['heizi] adj heiig; wazig

he [hiː] pron hij

head [hed] n hoofd nt; kop c; v leiden; ~ **of state** staatshoofd nt; ~ **teacher** schoolhoofd nt, hoofdonderwijzer c

headache ['hedeik] n hoofdpijn c

heading ['hediŋ] n titel c

headlamp ['hedlæmp] n koplamp c

headland ['hedlənd] n landtong c

headlight ['hedlait] n koplamp c

headline ['hedlain] n kop c

headmaster [,hed'maːstə] n schoolhoofd nt; rector c, directeur c

headquarters [,hed'kwɔːtəz] pl hoofdkwartier nt

head-strong ['hedstrɔŋ] adj koppig

head-waiter [,hed'weitə] n maître d'hôtel

heal [hiːl] v *genezen

health [helθ] n gezondheid c; ~ **centre** consultatiebureau nt; ~ **certificate** gezondheidsattest nt

healthy ['helθi] adj gezond

heap [hiːp] n stapel c, hoop c

hear [hiə] v horen

hearing ['hiəriŋ] n gehoor nt

heart [haːt] n hart nt; kern c; **by** ~ uit het hoofd; ~ **attack** hartaanval c

heartburn ['haːtbəːn] n maagzuur nt

hearth [haːθ] n haard c

heartless ['haːtləs] adj harteloos

hearty ['haːti] adj hartelijk

heat [hiːt] n warmte c, hitte c; v verwarmen; **heating pad** elektrisch kussen

heater ['hiːtə] n kachel c; **immersion** ~ dompelaar c

heath [hiːθ] n heide c

heathen ['hiːðən] n heiden c; heidens

heather ['heðə] n heide c

heating ['hiːtiŋ] n verwarming c

heaven ['hevən] n hemel c

heavy ['hevi] adj zwaar

Hebrew ['hi:bru:] n Hebreeuws nt
hedge [hedʒ] n heg c
hedgehog ['hedʒhɔg] n egel c
heel [hi:l] n hiel c; hak c
height [hait] n hoogte c; toppunt nt, hoogtepunt nt
hell [hel] n hel c
hello! [he'lou] hallo!; dag!
helm [helm] n roer nt
helmet ['helmit] n helm c
helmsman ['helmzmən] n stuurman c
help [help] v *helpen; n hulp c
helper ['helpə] n helper c
helpful ['helpfəl] adj hulpvaardig
helping ['helpiŋ] n portie c
hem [hem] n zoom c
hemp [hemp] n hennep c
hen [hen] n hen c; kip c
henceforth [,hens'fɔ:θ] adv voortaan
her [hə:] pron haar
herb [hə:b] n kruid nt
herd [hə:d] n kudde c
here [hiə] adv hier; ~ you are alstublieft
hereditary [hi'reditəri] adj erfelijk
hernia ['hə:niə] n breuk c
hero ['hiərou] n (pl ~es) held c
heron ['herən] n reiger c
herring ['heriŋ] n (pl ~, ~s) haring c
herself [hə:'self] pron zich; zelf
hesitate ['heziteit] v aarzelen
heterosexual [,hetərə'sekʃuəl] adj heteroseksueel
hiccup ['hikʌp] n hik c
hide [haid] n huid c
* hide [haid] v *verbergen; verstoppen
hideous ['hidiəs] adj afschuwelijk
hierarchy ['haiərɑ:ki] n hiërarchie c
high [hai] adj hoog
highway ['haiwei] n hoofdweg c; nAm autoweg c
hijack ['haidʒæk] v kapen
hijacker ['haidʒækə] n kaper c
hike [haik] v *trekken

hill [hil] n heuvel c
hillock ['hilək] n lage heuvel nt
hillside ['hilsaid] n helling c
hilltop ['hiltɔp] n heuveltop c
hilly ['hili] adj heuvelachtig
him [him] pron hem
himself [him'self] pron zich; zelf
hinder ['hində] v hinderen
hinge [hindʒ] n scharnier nt
hip [hip] n heup c
hire [haiə] v huren; for ~ te huur
hire-purchase [,haiə'pə:tʃəs] n huurkoop c
his [hiz] adj zijn
historian [hi'stɔ:riən] n geschiedkundige c
historic [hi'stɔrik] adj historisch
historical [hi'stɔrikəl] adj geschiedkundig
history ['histəri] n geschiedenis c
hit [hit] n hit c
* hit [hit] v *slaan; raken, *treffen
hitchhike ['hitʃhaik] v liften
hitchhiker ['hitʃ,haikə] n lifter c
hoarse [hɔ:s] adj schor, hees
hobby ['hɔbi] n liefhebberij c, hobby c
hobby-horse ['hɔbihɔ:s] n stokpaardje nt
hockey ['hɔki] n hockey nt
hoist [hɔist] v *hijsen
hold [hould] n ruim nt
* hold [hould] v *vasthouden, *houden; bewaren; ~ on zich *vasthouden; ~ up ondersteunen
hold-up ['houldʌp] n overval c
hole [houl] n kuil c, gat nt
holiday ['hɔlədi] n vakantie c; feestdag c; ~ camp vakantiekamp nt; ~ resort vakantieoord nt; on ~ met vakantie
Holland ['hɔlənd] Holland
hollow ['hɔlou] adj hol
holy ['houli] adj heilig
homage ['hɔmidʒ] n hulde c

home [houm] *n* thuis *nt*; tehuis *nt*, huis *nt*; *adv* thuis, naar huis; **at ~** thuis

home-made [,houm'meid] *adj* eigengemaakt

homesickness ['houm,siknəs] *n* heimwee *nt*

homosexual [,houmə'sekʃuəl] *adj* homoseksueel

honest ['ɔnist] *adj* eerlijk; oprecht

honesty ['ɔnisti] *n* eerlijkheid *c*

honey ['hʌni] *n* honing *c*

honeymoon ['hʌnimu:n] *n* huwelijksreis *c*, wittebroodsweken *pl*

honk [hʌŋk] *vAm* claxonneren

honour ['ɔnə] *n* eer *c*; *v* eren, huldigen

honourable ['ɔnərəbəl] *adj* eervol, eerzaam; rechtschapen

hood [hud] *n* kap *c*; *nAm* motorkap *c*

hoof [hu:f] *n* hoef *c*

hook [huk] *n* haak *c*

hoot [hu:t] *v* claxonneren

hooter ['hu:tə] *n* claxon *c*

hoover ['hu:və] *v* stofzuigen

hop[1] [hɔp] *v* huppelen; *n* sprong *c*

hop[2] [hɔp] *n* hop *c*

hope [houp] *n* hoop *c*; *v* hopen

hopeful ['houpfəl] *adj* hoopvol

hopeless ['houpləs] *adj* hopeloos

horizon [hə'raizən] *n* kim *c*, horizon *c*

horizontal [,hɔri'zɔntəl] *adj* horizontaal

horn [hɔ:n] *n* hoorn *c*; claxon *c*

horrible ['hɔribəl] *adj* vreselijk; verschrikkelijk, gruwelijk, afschuwelijk

horror ['hɔrə] *n* afgrijzen *nt*, afschuw *c*

hors-d'œuvre [ɔ:'də:vr] *n* hors d'œuvre *c*, voorgerecht *nt*

horse [hɔ:s] *n* paard *nt*

horseman ['hɔ:smən] *n* (pl -men) ruiter *c*

horsepower ['hɔ:s,pauə] *n* paardekracht *c*

horserace ['hɔ:sreis] *n* harddraverij *c*

horseradish ['hɔ:s,rædiʃ] *n* mierikswortel *c*

horseshoe ['hɔ:sʃu:] *n* hoefijzer *nt*

horticulture ['hɔ:tikʌltʃə] *n* tuinbouw *c*

hosiery ['houʒəri] *n* tricotgoederen *pl*

hospitable ['hɔspitəbəl] *adj* gastvrij

hospital ['hɔspitəl] *n* hospitaal *nt*, ziekenhuis *nt*

hospitality [,hɔspi'tæləti] *n* gastvrijheid *c*

host [houst] *n* gastheer *c*

hostage ['hɔstidʒ] *n* gijzelaar *c*

hostel ['hɔstəl] *n* herberg *c*

hostess ['houstis] *n* gastvrouw *c*

hostile ['hɔstail] *adj* vijandig

hot [hɔt] *adj* warm, heet

hotel [hou'tel] *n* hotel *nt*

hot-tempered [,hɔt'tempəd] *adj* driftig

hour [auə] *n* uur *nt*

hourly ['auəli] *adj* uur-

house [haus] *n* huis *nt*; woning *c*; pand *nt*; **~ agent** makelaar *c*; **~ block** *Am* huizenblok *nt*; **public ~** kroeg *c*

houseboat ['hausbout] *n* woonboot *c*

household ['haushould] *n* huishouden *nt*

housekeeper ['haus,ki:pə] *n* huishoudster *c*

housekeeping ['haus,ki:piŋ] *n* huishouden *nt*

housemaid ['hausmeid] *n* meid *c*

housewife ['hauswaif] *n* huisvrouw *c*

housework ['hauswə:k] *n* huishouden *nt*

how [hau] *adv* hoe; wat; **~ many** hoeveel; **~ much** hoeveel

however [hau'evə] *conj* evenwel, echter

hug [hʌg] *v* omhelzen; *n* omhelzing *c*

huge [hju:dʒ] *adj* geweldig, enorm, reusachtig

hum [hʌm] v neuriën
human ['hju:mən] adj menselijk; ~ being menselijk wezen
humanity [hju'mænəti] n mensheid c
humble ['hʌmbəl] adj nederig
humid ['hju:mid] adj vochtig
humidity [hju'midəti] n vochtigheid c
humorous ['hju:mərəs] adj grappig, geestig, humoristisch
humour ['hju:mə] n humor c
hundred ['hʌndrəd] n honderd
Hungarian [hʌŋ'gɛəriən] adj Hongaars; n Hongaar c
Hungary ['hʌŋgəri] Hongarije
hunger ['hʌŋgə] n honger c
hungry ['hʌŋgri] adj hongerig
hunt [hʌnt] v jagen; n jacht c; ~ for *zoeken
hunter ['hʌntə] n jager c
hurricane ['hʌrikən] n orkaan c; ~ lamp stormlamp c
hurry ['hʌri] v *opschieten, zich haasten; n haast c; in a ~ haastig
*hurt [hə:t] v pijn *doen, bezeren; kwetsen
hurtful ['hə:tfəl] adj schadelijk
husband ['hʌzbənd] n echtgenoot c, man c
hut [hʌt] n hut c
hydrogen ['haidrədʒən] n waterstof c
hygiene ['haidʒi:n] n hygiëne c
hygienic [hai'dʒi:nik] adj hygiënisch
hymn [him] n gezang nt
hyphen ['haifən] n koppelteken nt
hypocrisy [hi'pɔkrəsi] n huichelarij c
hypocrite ['hipəkrit] n huichelaar c
hypocritical [,hipə'kritikəl] adj huichelachtig, hypocriet, schijnheilig
hysterical [hi'sterikəl] adj hysterisch

I

I [ai] pron ik
ice [ais] n ijs nt
ice-bag ['aisbæg] n koeltas c
ice-cream ['aiskri:m] n ijs nt, ijsje nt
Iceland ['aislənd] IJsland
Icelander ['aisləndə] n IJslander c
Icelandic [ais'lændik] adj IJslands
icon ['aikɔn] n ikoon c
idea [ai'diə] n idee nt/c; inval c, gedachte c; denkbeeld nt, begrip nt
ideal [ai'diəl] adj ideaal; n ideaal nt
identical [ai'dentikəl] adj identiek
identification [ai,dentifi'keiʃən] n identificatie c
identify [ai'dentifai] v identificeren
identity [ai'dentəti] n identiteit c; ~ card identiteitskaart c
idiom ['idiəm] n idioom nt
idiomatic [,idiə'mætik] adj idiomatisch
idiot ['idiət] n idioot c
idiotic [,idi'ɔtik] adj idioot c
idle ['aidəl] adj werkeloos; lui; ijdel
idol ['aidəl] n afgod c; idool nt
if [if] conj als; indien
ignition [ig'niʃən] n ontsteking c; ~ coil ontsteking c
ignorant ['ignərənt] adj onwetend
ignore [ig'nɔ:] v negeren
ill [il] adj ziek; slecht; kwaad
illegal [i'li:gəl] adj illegaal, onwettig
illegible [i'ledʒəbəl] adj onleesbaar
illiterate [i'litərət] n analfabeet c
illness ['ilnəs] n ziekte c
illuminate [i'lu:mineit] v verlichten
illumination [i,lu:mi'neiʃən] n verlichting c
illusion [i'lu:ʒən] n illusie c; droombeeld nt
illustrate ['iləstreit] v illustreren
illustration [,ilə'streiʃən] n illustratie c
image ['imidʒ] n beeld nt

imaginary [i'mædʒinəri] *adj* denkbeeldig

imagination [i,mædʒi'neiʃən] *n* verbeelding *c*

imagine [i'mædʒin] *v* zich voorstellen;
zich verbeelden; zich *indenken

imitate ['imiteit] *v* nabootsen, imiteren

imitation [,imi'teiʃən] *n* namaak *c*, imitatie *c*

immediate [i'mi:djət] *adj* onmiddellijk

immediately [i'mi:djətli] *adv* meteen,
dadelijk, onmiddellijk

immense [i'mens] *adj* oneindig, reusachtig, onmetelijk

immigrant ['imigrənt] *n* immigrant *c*

immigrate ['imigreit] *v* immigreren

immigration [,imi'greiʃən] *n* immigratie *c*

immodest [i'mɔdist] *adj* onbescheiden

immunity [i'mju:nəti] *n* immuniteit *c*

immunize ['imjunaiz] *v* immuun maken

impartial [im'pa:ʃəl] *adj* onpartijdig

impassable [im'pa:səbəl] *adj* onbegaanbaar

impatient [im'peiʃənt] *adj* ongeduldig

impede [im'pi:d] *v* belemmeren

impediment [im'pedimənt] *n* beletsel
nt

imperfect [im'pə:fikt] *adj* onvolmaakt

imperial [im'piəriəl] *adj* keizerlijk;
rijks-

impersonal [im'pə:sənəl] *adj* onpersoonlijk

impertinence [im'pə:tinəns] *n* onbeschaamdheid *c*

impertinent [im'pə:tinənt] *adj* brutaal,
onbeschoft, onbeschaamd

implement[1] ['implimənt] *n* werktuig
nt, gereedschap *nt*

implement[2] ['impliment] *v* uitvoeren

imply [im'plai] *v* impliceren; *inhouden

impolite [,impə'lait] *adj* onbeleefd

import[1] [im'pɔ:t] *v* invoeren, importeren

import[2] ['impɔ:t] *n* import *c*, invoer *c*;
~ duty invoerrecht *nt*

importance [im'pɔ:təns] *n* belang *nt*

important [im'pɔ:tənt] *adj* gewichtig,
belangrijk

importer [im'pɔ:tə] *n* importeur *c*

imposing [im'pouziŋ] *adj* indrukwekkend

impossible [im'pɔsəbəl] *adj* onmogelijk

impotence ['impətəns] *n* impotentie *c*

impotent ['impətənt] *adj* impotent

impound [im'paund] *v* beslag leggen
op

impress [im'pres] *v* imponeren, indruk
maken op

impression [im'preʃən] *n* indruk *c*

impressive [im'presiv] *adj* indrukwekkend

imprison [im'prizən] *v* gevangen zetten

imprisonment [im'prizənmənt] *n* gevangenschap *c*

improbable [im'prɔbəbəl] *adj* onwaarschijnlijk

improper [im'prɔpə] *adj* ongepast

improve [im'pru:v] *v* verbeteren

improvement [im'pru:vmənt] *n* verbetering *c*

improvise ['imprəvaiz] *v* improviseren

impudent ['impjudənt] *adj* onbeschaamd

impulse ['impʌls] *n* impuls *c*; prikkel
c

impulsive [im'pʌlsiv] *adj* impulsief

in [in] *prep* in; over, op; *adv* binnen

inaccessible [i,næk'sesəbəl] *adj* ontoegankelijk

inaccurate [i'nækjurət] *adj* onnauwkeurig

inadequate [i'nædikwət] *adj* onvoldoende

incapable [iŋ'keipəbəl] *adj* onbekwaam

incense ['insens] *n* wierook *c*

incident ['insidənt] *n* incident *nt*

incidental [,insi'dentəl] *adj* toevallig

incite [in'sait] *v* aansporen

inclination [,inkli'neiʃən] *n* neiging *c*

incline [in'klain] *n* helling *c*

inclined [in'klaind] *adj* genegen, geneigd; *be ~ to *v neigen

include [in'klu:d] *v* bevatten, *insluiten; included inbegrepen

inclusive [in'klu:siv] *adj* inclusief

income ['inkəm] *n* inkomen *nt*

income-tax ['inkəmtæks] *n* inkomstenbelasting *c*

incompetent [in'kɔmpətənt] *adj* onbekwaam

incomplete [,inkəm'pli:t] *adj* onvolledig, incompleet

inconceivable [,inkən'si:vəbəl] *adj* ondenkbaar

inconspicuous [,inkən'spikjuəs] *adj* onopvallend

inconvenience [,inkən'vi:njəns] *n* ongemak *nt*, ongerief *nt*

inconvenient [,inkən'vi:njənt] *adj* ongelegen; lastig

incorrect [,inkə'rekt] *adj* onnauwkeurig, onjuist

increase¹ [in'kri:s] *v* vermeerderen; *oplopen, *toenemen

increase² ['inkri:s] *n* toename *c*; verhoging *c*

incredible [in'kredəbəl] *adj* ongelofelijk

incurable [in'kjuərəbəl] *adj* ongeneeslijk

indecent [in'di:sənt] *adj* onfatsoenlijk

indeed [in'di:d] *adv* inderdaad

indefinite [in'definit] *adj* onbepaald

indemnity [in'demnəti] *n* schadeloosstelling *c*, schadevergoeding *c*

independence [,indi'pendəns] *n* onafhankelijkheid *c*

independent [,indi'pendənt] *adj* onafhankelijk; zelfstandig

index ['indeks] *n* register *nt*, index *c*; ~ finger wijsvinger *c*

India ['indiə] India

Indian ['indiən] *adj* Indisch; Indiaans; *n* Indiër *c*; Indiaan *c*

indicate ['indikeit] *v* *aangeven, aanduiden

indication [,indi'keiʃən] *n* teken *nt*, aanwijzing *c*

indicator ['indikeitə] *n* richtingaanwijzer *c*

indifferent [in'difərənt] *adj* onverschillig

indigestion [,indi'dʒestʃən] *n* indigestie *c*

indignation [,indig'neiʃən] *n* verontwaardiging *c*

indirect [,indi'rekt] *adj* indirect

individual [,indi'vidʒuəl] *adj* afzonderlijk, individueel; *n* enkeling *c*, individu *nt*

Indonesia [,ində'ni:ziə] Indonesië

Indonesian [,ində'ni:ziən] *adj* Indonesisch; *n* Indonesiër *c*

indoor ['indɔ:] *adj* binnen

indoors [,in'dɔ:z] *adv* binnen

indulge [in'dʌldʒ] *v* *toegeven

industrial [in'dʌstriəl] *adj* industrieel; ~ area industriegebied *nt*

industrious [in'dʌstriəs] *adj* vlijtig

industry ['indəstri] *n* industrie *c*

inedible [i'nedibəl] *adj* oneetbaar

inefficient [,ini'fiʃənt] *adj* ondoeltreffend

inevitable [i'nevitəbəl] *adj* onvermijdelijk

inexpensive [,inik'spensiv] *adj* goedkoop

inexperienced [,inik'spiəriənst] *adj* onervaren

infant ['infənt] *n* zuigeling *c*

infantry ['infəntri] *n* infanterie *c*

infect [in'fekt] *v* besmetten, *aansteken

infection [in'fekʃən] n infectie c

infectious [in'fekʃəs] adj besmettelijk

infer [in'fə:] v afleiden

inferior [in'fiəriə] adj inferieur, minderwaardig; lager

infinite ['infinət] adj oneindig

infinitive [in'finitiv] n onbepaalde wijs

infirmary [in'fə:məri] n ziekenzaal c

inflammable [in'flæməbəl] adj ontvlambaar

inflammation [,inflə'meiʃən] n ontsteking c

inflatable [in'fleitəbəl] adj opblaasbaar

inflate [in'fleit] v *opblazen

inflation [in'fleiʃən] n inflatie c

influence ['influəns] n invloed c; v beïnvloeden

influential [,influ'enʃəl] adj invloedrijk

influenza [,influ'enzə] n griep c

inform [in'fɔ:m] v informeren; inlichten, mededelen

informal [in'fɔ:məl] adj informeel

information [,infə'meiʃən] n informatie c; inlichting c, mededeling c; ~ bureau inlichtingenkantoor nt

infra-red [,infrə'red] adj infrarood

infrequent [in'fri:kwənt] adj zeldzaam

ingredient [in'gri:diənt] n ingrediënt nt, bestanddeel nt

inhabit [in'hæbit] v bewonen

inhabitable [in'hæbitəbəl] adj bewoonbaar

inhabitant [in'hæbitənt] n inwoner c; bewoner c

inhale [in'heil] v inademen

inherit [in'herit] v erven

inheritance [in'heritəns] n erfenis c

initial [i'niʃəl] adj begin-, eerst; n voorletter c; v paraferen

initiative [i'niʃətiv] n initiatief nt

inject [in'dʒekt] v *inspuiten

injection [in'dʒekʃən] n injectie c

injure ['indʒə] v verwonden, kwetsen; krenken

injured ['indʒəd] adj gewond

injury ['indʒəri] n verwonding c; letsel nt, blessure c

injustice [in'dʒʌstis] n onrecht nt

ink [iŋk] n inkt c

inlet ['inlet] n inham c

inn [in] n herberg c

inner ['inə] adj inwendig; ~ tube binnenband c

inn-keeper ['in,ki:pə] n herbergier c

innocence ['inəsəns] n onschuld c

innocent ['inəsənt] adj onschuldig

inoculate [i'nɔkjuleit] v inenten

inoculation [i,nɔkju'leiʃən] n inenting c

inquire [iŋ'kwaiə] v *navragen, informatie *inwinnen

inquiry [iŋ'kwaiəri] n vraag c, navraag c; onderzoek nt; ~ office informatiebureau nt

inquisitive [iŋ'kwizətiv] adj nieuwsgierig

insane [in'sein] adj krankzinnig

inscription [in'skripʃən] n inscriptie c

insect ['insekt] n insekt nt; ~ repellent insektenwerend middel

insecticide [in'sektisaid] n insekticide c

insensitive [in'sensətiv] adj ongevoelig

insert [in'sə:t] v invoegen

inside [,in'said] n binnenkant c; adj binnenst; adv binnen; van binnen; prep in, binnen; ~ out binnenste buiten; insides ingewanden pl

insight ['insait] n inzicht nt

insignificant [,insig'nifikənt] adj onbelangrijk; onbeduidend, nietsbetekenend; nietig

insist [in'sist] v *aandringen; *aanhouden, *volhouden

insolence ['insələns] n onbeschaamdheid c

insolent ['insələnt] adj brutaal, onbeschaamd

insomnia [in'sɔmniə] n slapeloosheid c

inspect [in'spekt] v inspecteren

inspection [in'spekʃən] n inspectie c; controle c

inspector [in'spektə] n inspecteur c

inspire [in'spaiə] v bezielen

install [in'stɔ:l] v installeren

installation [,instə'leiʃən] n installatie c

instalment [in'stɔ:lmənt] n afbetaling c

instance ['instəns] n voorbeeld nt; geval nt; for ~ bijvoorbeeld

instant ['instənt] n ogenblik nt

instantly ['instəntli] adv ogenblikkelijk, onmiddellijk, meteen

instead of [in'sted ɔv] in plaats van

instinct ['instiŋkt] n instinct nt

institute ['institju:t] n instituut nt; instelling c; v instellen

institution [,insti'tju:ʃən] n inrichting c, instelling c

instruct [in'strʌkt] v onderrichten

instruction [in'strʌkʃən] n onderwijs nt

instructive [in'strʌktiv] adj leerzaam

instructor [in'strʌktə] n leraar c

instrument ['insə'fiʃənt] n instrument nt; musical ~ muziekinstrument nt

insufficient ['insə'fiʃənt] adj onvoldoende

insulate ['insjuleit] v isoleren

insulation [,insju'leiʃən] n isolatie c

insulator ['insjuleitə] n isolator c

insult[1] [in'sʌlt] v beledigen

insult[2] ['insʌlt] n belediging c

insurance [in'ʃuərəns] n assurantie c, verzekering c; ~ policy verzekeringspolis c

insure [in'ʃuə] v verzekeren

intact [in'tækt] adj intact

intellect ['intəlekt] n intellect nt

intellectual [,intə'lektʃuəl] adj intellectueel

intelligence [in'telidʒəns] n intelligentie c

intelligent [in'telidʒənt] adj intelligent

intend [in'tend] v van plan *zijn, bedoelen

intense [in'tens] adj intens; hevig

intention [in'tenʃən] n bedoeling c

intentional [in'tenʃənəl] adj opzettelijk

intercourse ['intəkɔ:s] n omgang c

interest ['intrəst] n interesse c, belangstelling c; belang nt; rente c; v interesseren; interested geïnteresseerd, belangstellend

interesting ['intrəstiŋ] adj interessant

interfere [,intə'fiə] v tussenbeide *komen; ~ with zich bemoeien met

interference [,intə'fiərəns] n inmenging c

interim ['intərim] n tussentijd c

interior [in'tiəriə] n binnenkant c

interlude ['intəlu:d] n intermezzo nt

intermediary [,intə'mi:djəri] n tussenpersoon c

intermission [,intə'miʃən] n pauze c

internal [in'tə:nəl] adj intern, inwendig

international [,intə'næʃənəl] adj internationaal

interpret [in'tə:prit] v tolken; vertolken

interpreter [in'tə:pritə] n tolk c

interrogate [in'terəgeit] v *ondervragen

interrogation [in,terə'geiʃən] n verhoor nt

interrogative [,intə'rɔgətiv] adj vragend

interrupt [,intə'rʌpt] v *onderbreken

interruption [,intə'rʌpʃən] n onderbreking c

intersection [,intə'sekʃən] n kruispunt nt

interval ['intəvəl] n pauze c; tussenpoos c

intervene [,intə'vi:n] v *ingrijpen

interview ['intəvju:] *n* interview *nt*, vraaggesprek *nt*

intestine [in'testin] *n* darm *c*; **intestines** ingewanden *pl*

intimate ['intimət] *adj* intiem

into ['intu] *prep* in

intolerable [in'tɔlərəbəl] *adj* onuitstaanbaar

intoxicated [in'tɔksikeitid] *adj* dronken

intrigue [in'tri:g] *n* komplot *nt*

introduce [,intrə'dju:s] *v* introduceren, voorstellen; inleiden; invoeren

introduction [,intrə'dʌkʃən] *n* inleiding *c*

invade [in'veid] *v* *binnenvallen

invalid¹ ['invəli:d] *n* invalide *c*; *adj* invalide

invalid² [in'vælid] *adj* ongeldig

invasion [in'veizən] *n* inval *c*, invasie *c*

invent [in'vent] *v* *uitvinden; *verzinnen

invention [in'venʃən] *n* uitvinding *c*

inventive [in'ventiv] *adj* vindingrijk

inventor [in'ventə] *n* uitvinder *c*

inventory ['invəntri] *n* inventaris *c*

invert [in'və:t] *v* omdraaien

invest [in'vest] *v* investeren; beleggen

investigate [in'vestigeit] *v* *onderzoeken

investigation [in,vesti'geiʃən] *n* onderzoek *nt*

investment [in'vestmənt] *n* investering *c*; belegging *c*, geldbelegging *c*

investor [in'vestə] *n* investeerder *c*

invisible [in'vizəbəl] *adj* onzichtbaar

invitation [,invi'teiʃən] *n* uitnodiging *c*

invite [in'vait] *v* inviteren, uitnodigen

invoice ['invɔis] *n* factuur *c*

involve [in'vɔlv] *v* impliceren; **involved** betrokken

inwards ['inwədz] *adv* naar binnen

iodine ['aiədi:n] *n* jodium *nt*

Iran [i'rɑ:n] Iran

Iranian [i'reiniən] *adj* Iraans; *n* Iraniër *c*

Iraq [i'rɑ:k] Irak

Iraqi [i'rɑ:ki] *adj* Iraaks; *n* Irakees *c*

irascible [i'ræsibəl] *adj* driftig

Ireland ['aiələnd] Ierland

Irish ['aiəriʃ] *adj* Iers

Irishman ['aiəriʃmən] *n* (pl -men) Ier *c*

iron ['aiən] *n* ijzer *nt*; strijkijzer *nt*; ijzeren; *v* *strijken

ironical [ai'rɔnikəl] *adj* ironisch

ironworks ['aiənwə:ks] *n* hoogovens *pl*

irony ['aiərəni] *n* ironie *c*

irregular [i'regjulə] *adj* onregelmatig

irreparable [i'repərəbəl] *adj* onherstelbaar

irrevocable [i'revəkəbəl] *adj* onherroepelijk

irritable ['iritəbəl] *adj* prikkelbaar

irritate ['iriteit] *v* prikkelen, irriteren

is [iz] *v* (pr be)

island ['ailənd] *n* eiland *nt*

isolate ['aisəleit] *v* isoleren

isolation [,aisə'leiʃən] *n* isolement *nt*; isolatie *c*

Israel ['izreil] Israël

Israeli [iz'reili] *adj* Israëlisch; *n* Israëliër *c*

issue ['iʃu:] *v* *uitgeven; *n* uitgifte *c*, oplage *c*, uitgave *c*; kwestie *c*, punt *nt*; uitkomst *c*, resultaat *nt*, gevolg *nt*, slot *nt*, einde *nt*; uitgang *c*

isthmus ['isməs] *n* landengte *c*

it [it] *pron* het

Italian [i'tæljən] *adj* Italiaans; *n* Italiaan *c*

italics [i'tæliks] *pl* cursiefschrift *nt*

Italy ['itəli] Italië

itch [itʃ] *n* jeuk *c*; kriebel *c*; *v* jeuken

item ['aitəm] *n* artikel *nt*; punt *nt*

itinerant [ai'tinərənt] *adj* rondreizend

itinerary [ai'tinərəri] *n* reisplan *nt*, reisroute *c*

ivory ['aivəri] *n* ivoor *nt*

ivy ['aivi] *n* klimop *c*

J

jack [dʒæk] *n* krik *c*

jacket ['dʒækit] *n* jasje *nt*, colbert *c*, vest *nt*; omslag *c/nt*

jade [dʒeid] *n* jade *nt/c*

jail [dʒeil] *n* gevangenis *c*

jailer ['dʒeilə] *n* cipier *c*

jam [dʒæm] *n* jam *c*; verkeersopstopping *c*

janitor ['dʒænitə] *n* concierge *c*

January ['dʒænjuəri] januari

Japan [dʒə'pæn] Japan

Japanese [,dʒæpə'ni:z] *adj* Japans; *n* Japanner *c*

jar [dʒa:] *n* pot *c*

jaundice ['dʒɔ:ndis] *n* geelzucht *c*

jaw [dʒɔ:] *n* kaak *c*

jealous ['dʒeləs] *adj* jaloers

jealousy ['dʒeləsi] *n* jaloezie *c*

jeans [dʒi:nz] *pl* spijkerbroek *c*

jelly ['dʒeli] *n* gelei *c*

jelly-fish ['dʒelifiʃ] *n* kwal *c*

jersey ['dʒə:zi] *n* jersey *c*; trui *c*

jet [dʒet] *n* straal *c*; straalvliegtuig *nt*

jetty ['dʒeti] *n* pier *c*

Jew [dʒu:] *n* jood *c*

jewel ['dʒu:əl] *n* juweel *nt*

jeweller ['dʒu:ələ] *n* juwelier *c*

jewellery ['dʒu:əlri] *n* juwelen; bijouterie *c*

Jewish ['dʒu:iʃ] *adj* joods

job [dʒɔb] *n* karwei *nt*; betrekking *c*, baan *c*

jockey ['dʒɔki] *n* jockey *c*

join [dʒɔin] *v* *verbinden; zich voegen bij, zich *aansluiten bij; samenvoegen, verenigen

joint [dʒɔint] *n* gewricht *nt*; las *c*; *adj* verenigd, gezamenlijk

jointly ['dʒɔintli] *adv* gezamenlijk

joke [dʒouk] *n* mop *c*, grap *c*

jolly ['dʒɔli] *adj* leuk

Jordan ['dʒɔ:dən] Jordanië

Jordanian [dʒɔ:'deiniən] *adj* Jordaans; *n* Jordaniër *c*

journal ['dʒə:nəl] *n* tijdschrift *nt*

journalism ['dʒə:nəlizəm] *n* journalistiek *c*

journalist ['dʒə:nəlist] *n* journalist *c*

journey ['dʒə:ni] *n* reis *c*

joy [dʒɔi] *n* genot *nt*, vreugde *c*

joyful ['dʒɔifəl] *adj* blij, vrolijk

jubilee ['dʒu:bili:] *n* jubileum *nt*

judge [dʒʌdʒ] *n* rechter *c*; *v* oordelen; beoordelen

judgment ['dʒʌdʒmənt] *n* oordeel *nt*; beoordeling *c*

jug [dʒʌg] *n* kan *c*

Jugoslav [,ju:gə'sla:v] *adj* Joegoslavisch; *n* Joegoslaaf *c*

Jugoslavia [,ju:gə'sla:viə] Joegoslavië

juice [dʒu:s] *n* sap *nt*

juicy ['dʒu:si] *adj* sappig

July [dʒu'lai] juli

jump [dʒʌmp] *v* *springen; *n* sprong *c*

jumper ['dʒʌmpə] *n* jumper *c*

junction ['dʒʌŋkʃən] *n* kruising *c*; knooppunt *nt*

June [dʒu:n] juni

jungle ['dʒʌŋgəl] *n* oerwoud *nt*, jungle *c*

junior ['dʒu:njə] *adj* jonger

junk [dʒʌŋk] *n* rommel *c*

jury ['dʒuəri] *n* jury *c*

just [dʒʌst] *adj* terecht, rechtvaardig; juist; *adv* pas; precies

justice ['dʒʌstis] *n* recht *nt*; gerechtigheid *c*, rechtvaardigheid *c*

juvenile ['dʒu:vənail] *adj* jeugdig

K

kangaroo [,kæŋgə'ru:] n kangoeroe c
keel [ki:l] n kiel c
keen [ki:n] adj enthousiast; scherp
*keep [ki:p] v *houden; bewaren;
 *blijven; ~ away from niet *betre-
 den; ~ off *afblijven; ~ on *doorgaan met; ~ quiet *zwijgen; ~ up
 *volhouden; ~ up with *bijhouden
keg [keg] n vaatje nt
kennel ['kenəl] n hondehok nt; kennel
 c
Kenya ['kenjə] Kenya
kerosene ['kerəsi:n] n petroleum c
kettle ['ketəl] n ketel c
key [ki:] n sleutel c
keyhole ['ki:houl] n sleutelgat nt
khaki ['ka:ki] n kaki nt
kick [kik] v trappen, schoppen; n trap
 c, schop c
kick-off [,ki'kɔf] n aftrap c
kid [kid] n kind nt; geiteleer nt; v
 *beetnemen
kidney ['kidni] n nier c
kill [kil] v *ombrengen, doden
kilogram ['kiləgræm] n kilo nt
kilometre ['kilə,mi:tə] n kilometer c
kind [kaind] adj aardig, vriendelijk;
 goed; n soort c/nt
kindergarten ['kində,ga:tən] n kleuterschool c
king [kiŋ] n koning c
kingdom ['kiŋdəm] n koninkrijk nt;
 rijk nt
kiosk ['ki:ɔsk] n kiosk c
kiss [kis] n zoen c, kus c; v kussen
kit [kit] n uitrusting c
kitchen ['kitʃin] n keuken c; ~ garden moestuin c
kleenex ['kli:neks] n papieren zakdoek
knapsack ['næpsæk] n knapzak c
knave [neiv] n boer c

knee [ni:] n knie c
kneecap ['ni:kæp] n knieschijf c
*kneel [ni:l] v knielen
knew [nju:] v (p know)
knickers ['nikəz] pl onderbroek c
knife [naif] n (pl knives) mes nt
knight [nait] n ridder c
*knit [nit] v breien
knob [nɔb] n knop c
knock [nɔk] v kloppen; n klop c; ~
 against *stoten tegen; ~ down
 *neerslaan
knot [nɔt] n knoop c; v knopen
*know [nou] v *weten, kennen
knowledge ['nɔlidʒ] n kennis c
knuckle ['nʌkəl] n knokkel c

L

label ['leibəl] n etiket nt; v etiketteren
laboratory [lə'bɔrətəri] n laboratorium
 nt
labour ['leibə] n werk nt, arbeid c;
 weeën pl; v zwoegen; labor permit
 Am werkvergunning c
labourer ['leibərə] n arbeider c
labour-saving ['leibə,seiviŋ] adj arbeidbesparend
labyrinth ['læbərinθ] n doolhof c
lace [leis] n kant c; veter c
lack [læk] n gemis nt, gebrek nt; v
 missen
lacquer ['lækə] n lak c
lad [læd] n jongen c, joch nt
ladder ['lædə] n ladder c
lady ['leidi] n dame c; ladies' room
 damestoilet nt
lagoon [lə'gu:n] n lagune c
lake [leik] n meer nt
lamb [læm] n lam nt; lamsvlees nt
lame [leim] adj lam, mank, kreupel
lamentable ['læməntəbəl] adj erbarme-

lijk

lamp [læmp] n lamp c

lamp-post ['læmppoust] n lantaarnpaal c

lampshade ['læmpʃeid] n lampekap c

land [lænd] n land nt; v landen; aan land *gaan

landlady ['lænd,leidi] n hospita c

landlord ['lændlɔ:d] n huisbaas c; hospes c

landmark ['lændmɑ:k] n baken nt; mijlpaal c

landscape ['lændskeip] n landschap nt

lane [lein] n steeg c, pad nt; rijstrook c

language ['læŋgwidʒ] n taal c; ~ **laboratory** talenpracticum nt

lantern ['læntən] n lantaarn c

lapel [lə'pel] n revers c

larder ['lɑ:də] n provisiekast c

large [lɑ:dʒ] adj groot; ruim

lark [lɑ:k] n leeuwerik c

laryngitis [,lærin'dʒaitis] n keelontsteking c

last [lɑ:st] adj laatst; vorig; v duren; **at ~** eindelijk; tenslotte, uiteindelijk

lasting ['lɑ:stiŋ] adj blijvend, duurzaam

latchkey ['lætʃki:] n huissleutel c

late [leit] adj laat; te laat

lately ['leitli] adv de laatste tijd, onlangs, laatst

lather ['lɑ:ðə] n schuim nt

Latin America ['lætin ə'merikə] Latijns-Amerika

Latin-American [,lætinə'merikən] adj Latijns-Amerikaans

latitude ['lætitju:d] n breedtegraad c

laugh [lɑ:f] v *lachen; n lach c

laughter ['lɑ:ftə] n gelach nt

launch [lɔ:ntʃ] v inzetten; lanceren; n motorschip nt

launching ['lɔ:ntʃiŋ] n tewaterlating c

launderette [,lɔ:ndə'ret] n wasserette c

laundry ['lɔ:ndri] n wasserij c; was c

lavatory ['lævətəri] n toilet nt

lavish ['læviʃ] adj kwistig

law [lɔ:] n wet c; recht nt; ~ **court** gerecht nt

lawful ['lɔ:fəl] adj wettig

lawn [lɔ:n] n grasveld nt, gazon nt

lawsuit ['lɔ:su:t] n proces nt, geding nt

lawyer ['lɔ:jə] n advocaat c; jurist c

laxative ['læksətiv] n laxeermiddel nt

lay [lei] v plaatsen, zetten, leggen; ~ **bricks** metselen

layer [leiə] n laag c

layman ['leimən] n leek c

lazy ['leizi] adj lui

lead[1] [li:d] n voorsprong c; leiding c; riem c

lead[2] [led] n lood nt

lead [li:d] v leiden

leader ['li:də] n aanvoerder c, leider c

leadership ['li:dəʃip] n leiderschap nt

leading ['li:diŋ] adj vooraanstaand, voornaamst

leaf [li:f] n (pl leaves) blad nt

league [li:g] n bond c

leak [li:k] v lekken; n lek nt

leaky ['li:ki] adj lek

lean [li:n] adj mager

lean [li:n] v leunen

leap [li:p] n sprong c

leap [li:p] v *springen

leap-year ['li:pjiə] n schrikkeljaar nt

learn [lə:n] v leren

learner ['lə:nə] n beginneling c, beginner c

lease [li:s] n huurcontract nt; pacht c; v verpachten, verhuren; huren

leash [li:ʃ] n lijn c

least [li:st] adj geringst, minst; kleinst; **at ~** minstens; tenminste

leather ['leðə] n leer nt; lederen, leren

leave [li:v] n verlof nt

*leave [li:v] v *vertrekken, *verlaten; *laten; ~ behind *achterlaten; ~ out *weglaten

Lebanese [,lebə'ni:z] adj Libanees; n Libanees c

Lebanon ['lebənən] Libanon

lecture ['lektʃə] n college nt, lezing c

left¹ [left] adj links

left² [left] v (p, pp leave)

left-hand [,left'hænd] adj links

left-handed [,left'hændid] adj linkshandig

leg [leg] n poot c, been nt

legacy ['legəsi] n erfenis c

legal ['li:gəl] adj wettig, wettelijk; juridisch

legalization [,li:gəlai'zeiʃən] n legalisatie c

legation [li'geiʃən] n legatie c

legible ['ledʒibəl] adj leesbaar

legitimate [li'dʒitimət] adj wettig

leisure ['leʒə] n vrije tijd; gemak nt

lemon ['lemən] n citroen c

lemonade [,lemə'neid] n limonade c

*lend [lend] v lenen, uitlenen

length [leŋθ] n lengte c

lengthen ['leŋθən] v verlengen

lengthways ['leŋθweiz] adv in de lengte

lens [lenz] n lens c; telephoto ~ telelens c; zoom ~ zoomlens c

leprosy ['leprəsi] n lepra c

less [les] adv minder

lessen ['lesən] v verminderen

lesson ['lesən] n les c

*let [let] v *laten; verhuren; ~ down teleurstellen

letter ['letə] n brief c; letter c; ~ of credit kredietbrief c; ~ of recommendation aanbevelingsbrief c

letter-box ['letəbɔks] n brievenbus c

lettuce ['letis] n sla c

level ['levəl] adj egaal; plat, vlak, effen, gelijk; n peil nt, niveau nt; wa-

terpas c; v egaliseren, nivelleren; ~ crossing overweg c

lever ['li:və] n hefboom c, hendel c

Levis ['li:vaiz] pl jeans pl

liability [,laiə'biləti] n aansprakelijkheid c

liable ['laiəbəl] adj aansprakelijk; ~ to onderhevig aan

liberal ['libərəl] adj liberaal; mild, royaal, vrijgevig

liberation [,libə'reiʃən] n bevrijding c

Liberia [lai'biəriə] Liberia

Liberian [lai'biəriən] adj Liberiaans; n Liberiaan c

liberty ['libəti] n vrijheid c

library ['laibrəri] n bibliotheek c

licence ['laisəns] n licentie c; vergunning c; driving ~ rijbewijs nt; ~ number Am kenteken nt; ~ plate Am nummerbord nt

license ['laisəns] v een vergunning verlenen

lick [lik] v likken

lid [lid] n deksel nt

lie [lai] v *liegen; n leugen c

*lie [lai] v *liggen; ~ down *gaan liggen

life [laif] n (pl lives) leven nt; ~ insurance levensverzekering c

lifebelt ['laifbelt] n reddingsgordel c

lifetime ['laiftaim] n leven nt

lift [lift] v optillen; n lift c

light [lait] n licht nt; adj licht; ~ bulb peer c

*light [lait] v *aansteken

lighter ['laitə] n aansteker c

lighthouse ['laithaus] n vuurtoren c

lighting ['laitiŋ] n verlichting c

lightning ['laitniŋ] n bliksem c

like [laik] v *houden van; *mogen, lusten; adj gelijk; conj zoals; prep als

likely ['laikli] adj waarschijnlijk

like-minded [,laik'maindid] adj gelijk-

gezind
likewise ['laikwaiz] *adv* evenzo, eveneens
lily ['lili] *n* lelie *c*
limb [lim] *n* ledemaat *c*
lime [laim] *n* kalk *c*; linde *c*; limoen *c*
limetree ['laimtri:] *n* linde *c*
limit ['limit] *n* limiet *c*; *v* beperken
limp [limp] *v* hinken; *adj* slap
line [lain] *n* regel *c*; streep *c*; snoer *nt*; lijn *c*; rij *c*; **stand in** ~ *Am* in de rij *staan
linen ['linin] *n* linnen *nt*; linnengoed *nt*
liner ['lainə] *n* lijnboot *c*
lingerie ['lɔ̃ʒəri:] *n* lingerie *c*
lining ['lainiŋ] *n* voering *c*
link [liŋk] *v* *verbinden; *n* verbinding *c*; schakel *c*
lion ['laiən] *n* leeuw *c*
lip [lip] *n* lip *c*
lipsalve ['lipsa:v] *n* lippenboter *c*
lipstick ['lipstik] *n* lippenstift *c*
liqueur [li'kjuə] *n* likeur *c*
liquid ['likwid] *adj* vloeibaar; *n* vloeistof *c*
liquor ['likə] *n* sterke drank
liquorice ['likəris] *n* drop *c*
list [list] *n* lijst *c*; *v* noteren
listen ['lisən] *v* aanhoren, luisteren
listener ['lisnə] *n* luisteraar *c*
literary ['litrəri] *adj* letterkundig, literair
literature ['litrətʃə] *n* literatuur *c*
litre ['li:tə] *n* liter *c*
litter ['litə] *n* afval *nt*; rommel *c*; nest *nt*
little ['litəl] *adj* klein; weinig
live[1] [liv] *v* leven; wonen
live[2] [laiv] *adj* levend
livelihood ['laivlihud] *n* kost *c*
lively ['laivli] *adj* levendig
liver ['livə] *n* lever *c*
living-room ['liviŋru:m] *n* huiskamer *c*,

woonkamer *c*
load [loud] *n* lading *c*; last *c*; *v* *laden
loaf [louf] *n* (pl loaves) brood *nt*
loan [loun] *n* lening *c*
lobby ['lɔbi] *n* hal *c*; foyer *c*
lobster ['lɔbstə] *n* kreeft *c*
local ['loukəl] *adj* lokaal, plaatselijk; ~ **call** lokaal gesprek; ~ **train** stoptrein *c*
locality [lou'kæləti] *n* plaats *c*
locate [lou'keit] *v* plaatsen
location [lou'keiʃən] *n* ligging *c*
lock [lɔk] *v* op slot *doen; *n* slot *nt*; sluis *c*; ~ **up** *opsluiten
locomotive [,loukə'moutiv] *n* locomotief *c*
lodge [lɔdʒ] *v* herbergen; *n* jachthuis *nt*
lodger ['lɔdʒə] *n* kamerbewoner *c*
lodgings ['lɔdʒiŋz] *pl* logies *nt*
log [lɔg] *n* houtblok *nt*
logic ['lɔdʒik] *n* logica *c*
logical ['lɔdʒikəl] *adj* logisch
lonely ['lounli] *adj* eenzaam
long [lɔŋ] *adj* lang; langdurig; ~ **for** verlangen naar; **no longer** niet meer
longing ['lɔŋiŋ] *n* verlangen *nt*
longitude ['lɔndʒitju:d] *n* lengtegraad *c*
look [luk] *v* *kijken; *lijken, er uit *zien; *n* kijkje *nt*, blik *c*; uiterlijk *nt*, voorkomen *nt*; ~ **after** verzorgen, zorgen voor, passen op; ~ **at** *aankijken, *kijken naar; ~ **for** *zoeken; ~ **out** *uitkijken, oppassen; ~ **up** *opzoeken
looking-glass ['lukiŋgla:s] *n* spiegel *c*
loop [lu:p] *n* lus *c*
loose [lu:s] *adj* los
loosen ['lu:sən] *v* losmaken
lord [lɔ:d] *n* lord *c*
lorry ['lɔri] *n* vrachtwagen *c*
***lose** [lu:z] *v* kwijtraken, *verliezen
loss [lɔs] *n* verlies *nt*

lost [lɔst] *adj* verdwaald; weg; ~ **and found** gevonden voorwerpen; ~ **property office** bureau voor gevonden voorwerpen

lot [lɔt] *n* lot *nt*; hoop *c*, boel *c*

lotion ['louʃən] *n* lotion *c*; **aftershave** ~ after shave

lottery ['lɔtəri] *n* loterij *c*

loud [laud] *adj* hard, luid

loud-speaker [,laud'spi:kə] *n* luidspreker *c*

lounge [laundʒ] *n* salon *c*

louse [laus] *n* (pl lice) luis *c*

love [lʌv] *v* *houden van, *liefhebben; *n* liefde *c*; **in** ~ verliefd

lovely ['lʌvli] *adj* heerlijk, prachtig, mooi

lover ['lʌvə] *n* minnaar *c*

love-story ['lʌv,stɔ:ri] *n* liefdesgeschiedenis *c*

low [lou] *adj* laag; diep; neerslachtig; ~ **tide** eb *c*

lower ['louə] *v* *neerlaten; verlagen; *strijken; *adj* onderst, lager

lowlands ['louləndz] *pl* laagland *nt*

loyal ['lɔiəl] *adj* loyaal

lubricate ['lu:brikeit] *v* oliën, smeren

lubrication [,lu:bri'keiʃən] *n* smering *c*; ~ **oil** smeerolie *c*; ~ **system** smeersysteem *nt*

luck [lʌk] *n* geluk *nt*; toeval *nt*; **bad** ~ pech *c*

lucky charm amulet *c*

ludicrous ['lu:dikrəs] *adj* belachelijk, bespottelijk

luggage ['lʌgidʒ] *n* bagage *c*; **hand** ~ handbagage *c*; **left** ~ **office** bagagedepot *nt*; ~ **rack** bagagerek *nt*, bagagenet *nt*; ~ **van** bagagewagen *c*

lukewarm ['lu:kwɔ:m] *adj* lauw

lumbago [lʌm'beigou] *n* spit *nt*

luminous ['lu:minəs] *adj* lichtgevend

lump [lʌmp] *n* brok *nt*, klont *c*, stuk *nt*; bult *c*; ~ **of sugar** suikerklontje *nt*; ~ **sum** ronde som

lumpy ['lʌmpi] *adj* klonterig

lunacy ['lu:nəsi] *n* krankzinnigheid *c*

lunatic ['lu:nətik] *adj* krankzinnig; *n* krankzinnige *c*

lunch [lʌntʃ] *n* lunch *c*, middageten *nt*

luncheon ['lʌntʃən] *n* middageten *nt*

lung [lʌŋ] *n* long *c*

lust [lʌst] *n* wellust *c*

luxurious [lʌg'ʒuəriəs] *adj* luxueus

luxury ['lʌkʃəri] *n* luxe *c*

M

machine [mə'ʃi:n] *n* apparaat *nt*, machine *c*

machinery [mə'ʃi:nəri] *n* machinerie *c*; mechanisme *nt*

mackerel ['mækrəl] *n* (pl ~) makreel *c*

mackintosh ['mækintɔʃ] *n* regenjas *c*

mad [mæd] *adj* krankzinnig, waanzinnig, gek; kwaad

madam ['mædəm] *n* mevrouw

madness ['mædnəs] *n* waanzin *c*

magazine [,mægə'zi:n] *n* blad *nt*

magic ['mædʒik] *n* toverkunst *c*, magie *c*; *adj* tover-

magician [mə'dʒiʃən] *n* goochelaar *c*

magistrate ['mædʒistreit] *n* magistraat *c*

magnetic [mæg'netik] *adj* magnetisch

magneto [mæg'ni:tou] *n* (pl ~s) magneet *c*

magnificent [mæg'nifisənt] *adj* prachtig; groots, luisterrijk

magpie ['mægpai] *n* ekster *c*

maid [meid] *n* meid *c*

maiden name ['meidən neim] meisjesnaam *c*

mail [meil] *n* post *c*; *v* posten; ~ **order** *Am* postwissel *c*

mailbox ['meilbɔks] *nAm* brievenbus *c*

main [mein] *adj* hoofd-, voornaamst; grootst; ~ **deck** bovendek *nt*; ~ **line** hoofdlijn *c*; ~ **road** hoofdweg *c*; ~ **street** hoofdstraat *c*

mainland ['meinlənd] *n* vasteland *nt*

mainly ['meinli] *adv* hoofdzakelijk

mains [meinz] *pl* hoofdleiding *c*

maintain [mein'tein] *v* handhaven

maintenance ['meintənəns] *n* onderhoud *nt*

maize [meiz] *n* maïs *c*

major ['meidʒə] *adj* groter; grootst; *n* majoor *c*

majority [mə'dʒɔrəti] *n* meerderheid *c*

***make** [meik] *v* maken; verdienen; halen; ~ **do with** zich *behelpen met; ~ **good** vergoeden; ~ **up** opstellen

make-up ['meikʌp] *n* make-up *c*

malaria [mə'lɛəriə] *n* malaria *c*

Malay [mə'lei] *n* Maleis *nt*

Malaysia [mə'leiziə] Maleisië

Malaysian [mə'leiziən] *adj* Maleisisch

male [meil] *adj* mannelijk

malicious [mə'liʃəs] *adj* boosaardig

malignant [mə'lignənt] *adj* kwaadaardig

mallet ['mælit] *n* houten hamer

malnutrition [,mælnju'triʃən] *n* ondervoeding *c*

mammal ['mæməl] *n* zoogdier *nt*

mammoth ['mæməθ] *n* mammoet *c*

man [mæn] *n* (pl men) man *c*; mens *c*; **men's room** herentoilet *nt*

manage ['mænidʒ] *v* beheren; slagen

manageable ['mænidʒəbəl] *adj* hanteerbaar

management ['mænidʒmənt] *n* directie *c*; beheer *nt*

manager ['mænidʒə] *n* chef *c*, directeur *c*

mandarin ['mændərin] *n* mandarijn *c*

mandate ['mændeit] *n* mandaat *nt*

manger ['meindʒə] *n* kribbe *c*

manicure ['mænikjuə] *n* manicure *c*; *v* manicuren

mankind [mæn'kaind] *n* mensheid *c*

mannequin ['mænəkin] *n* mannequin *c*

manner ['mænə] *n* wijze *c*, manier *c*; **manners** *pl* manieren

man-of-war [,mænəv'wɔ:] *n* oorlogsschip *nt*

manor-house ['mænəhaus] *n* herenhuis *nt*

mansion ['mænʃən] *n* herenhuis *nt*

manual ['mænjuəl] *adj* hand-

manufacture [,mænju'fæktʃə] *v* vervaardigen, fabriceren

manufacturer [,mænju'fæktʃərə] *n* fabrikant *c*

manure [mə'njuə] *n* mest *c*

manuscript ['mænjuskript] *n* manuscript *nt*

many ['meni] *adj* veel

map [mæp] *n* kaart *c*; landkaart *c*; plattegrond *c*

maple ['meipəl] *n* esdoorn *c*

marble ['ma:bəl] *n* marmer *nt*; knikker *c*

March [ma:tʃ] maart

march [ma:tʃ] *v* marcheren; *n* mars *c*

mare [mɛə] *n* merrie *c*

margarine [,ma:dʒə'ri:n] *n* margarine *c*

margin ['ma:dʒin] *n* kantlijn *c*, marge *c*

maritime ['mæritaim] *adj* maritiem

mark [ma:k] *v* aankruisen; merken; kenmerken; *n* merkteken *nt*; cijfer *nt*; schietschijf *c*

market ['ma:kit] *n* markt *c*

market-place ['ma:kitpleis] *n* marktplein *nt*

marmalade ['ma:məleid] *n* marmelade *c*

marriage ['mæridʒ] *n* huwelijk *nt*

marrow ['mærou] n merg nt

marry ['mæri] v huwen, trouwen;
married couple echtpaar nt

marsh [ma:ʃ] n moeras nt

marshy ['ma:ʃi] adj moerassig

martyr ['ma:tə] n martelaar c

marvel ['ma:vəl] n wonder nt; v zich
verbazen

marvellous ['ma:vələs] adj prachtig

mascara [mæ'ska:rə] n mascara c

masculine ['mæskjulin] adj mannelijk

mash [mæʃ] v fijnstampen

mask [ma:sk] n masker nt

Mass [mæs] n mis c

mass [mæs] n massa c; ~ production
massaproduktie c

massage ['mæsa:ʒ] n massage c; v
masseren

masseur [mæ'sə:] n masseur c

massive ['mæsiv] adj massief

mast [ma:st] n mast c

master ['ma:stə] n meester c; baas c;
leraar c, onderwijzer c; v beheersen

masterpiece ['ma:stəpi:s] n meesterwerk nt

mat [mæt] n mat c; adj mat, dof

match [mætʃ] n lucifer c; wedstrijd c;
v passen bij

match-box ['mætʃbɔks] n lucifersdoosje nt

material [mə'tiəriəl] n materiaal nt;
stof c; adj stoffelijk, materieel

mathematical [,mæθə'mætikəl] adj
wiskundig

mathematics [,mæθə'mætiks] n wiskunde c

matrimonial [,mætri'mouniəl] adj echtelijk

matrimony ['mætriməni] n echt c

matter ['mætə] n stof c, materie c;
aangelegenheid c, kwestie c, zaak c;
v van belang *zijn; as a ~ of fact
feitelijk, eigenlijk

matter-of-fact [,mætərəv'fækt] adj
nuchter

mattress ['mætrəs] n matras c

mature [mə'tjuə] adj rijp

maturity [mə'tjuərəti] n rijpheid c

mausoleum [,mɔ:sə'li:əm] n mausoleum nt

mauve [mouv] adj lichtpaars

May [mei] mei

*may [mei] v *kunnen; *mogen

maybe ['meibi:] adv misschien

mayor [mɛə] n burgemeester c

maze [meiz] n doolhof nt

me [mi:] pron me

meadow ['medou] n wei c

meal [mi:l] n maaltijd c, maal nt

mean [mi:n] adj gemeen; n gemiddelde nt

*mean [mi:n] v betekenen; bedoelen;
menen

meaning ['mi:niŋ] n betekenis c

meaningless ['mi:niŋləs] adj nietszeggend

means [mi:nz] n middel nt; by no ~
zeker niet, geenszins

in the meantime [in ðə 'mi:ntaim] inmiddels, ondertussen

meanwhile ['mi:nwail] adv intussen,
ondertussen

measles ['mi:zəlz] n mazelen pl

measure ['meʒə] v *meten; n maat c;
maatregel c

meat [mi:t] n vlees nt

mechanic [mi'kænik] n monteur c

mechanical [mi'kænikəl] adj mechanisch

mechanism ['mekənizəm] n mechanisme nt

medal ['medəl] n medaille c

mediaeval [,medi'i:vəl] adj middeleeuws

mediate ['mi:dieit] v bemiddelen

mediator ['mi:dieitə] n bemiddelaar c

medical ['medikəl] adj geneeskundig,
medisch

medicine ['medsin] *n* geneesmiddel *nt*; geneeskunde *c*

meditate ['mediteit] *v* mediteren

Mediterranean [,meditə'reiniən] Middellandse Zee

medium ['mi:diəm] *adj* middelmatig, gemiddeld, midden-

*****meet** [mi:t] *v* ontmoeten; *****tegenkomen

meeting ['mi:tiŋ] *n* vergadering *c*, bijeenkomst *c*; ontmoeting *c*

meeting-place ['mi:tiŋpleis] *n* trefpunt *nt*

melancholy ['melənkəli] *n* weemoed *c*

mellow ['melou] *adj* zacht

melodrama ['melə,dra:mə] *n* melodrama *nt*

melody ['melədi] *n* melodie *c*

melon ['melən] *n* meloen *c*

melt [melt] *v* *****smelten

member ['membə] *n* lid *nt*; **Member of Parliament** kamerlid *nt*

membership ['membəʃip] *n* lidmaatschap *nt*

memo ['memou] *n* (pl ~s) memorandum *nt*

memorable ['memərəbəl] *adj* gedenkwaardig

memorial [mə'mɔ:riəl] *n* gedenkteken *nt*

memorize ['meməraiz] *v* uit het hoofd leren

memory ['meməri] *n* geheugen *nt*; herinnering *c*; nagedachtenis *c*

mend [mend] *v* herstellen, repareren

menstruation [,menstru'eiʃən] *n* menstruatie *c*

mental ['mentəl] *adj* geestelijk

mention ['menʃən] *v* noemen, vermelden; *n* melding *c*, vermelding *c*

menu ['menju:] *n* spijskaart *c*, menukaart *c*

merchandise ['mə:tʃəndaiz] *n* handelswaar *c*, koopwaar *c*

merchant ['mə:tʃənt] *n* handelaar *c*, koopman *c*

merciful ['mə:sifəl] *adj* barmhartig

mercury ['mə:kjuri] *n* kwik *nt*

mercy ['mə:si] *n* genade *c*, clementie *c*

mere [miə] *adj* louter

merely ['miəli] *adv* slechts

merger ['mə:dʒə] *n* fusie *c*

merit ['merit] *v* verdienen; *n* verdienste *c*

mermaid ['mə:meid] *n* zeemeermin *c*

merry ['meri] *adj* vrolijk

merry-go-round ['merigou,raund] *n* draaimolen *c*

mesh [meʃ] *n* maas *c*

mess [mes] *n* rommel *c*, warboel *c*; ~ **up** *****bederven

message ['mesidʒ] *n* boodschap *c*, bericht *nt*

messenger ['mesindʒə] *n* bode *c*

metal ['metəl] *n* metaal *nt*; metalen

meter ['mi:tə] *n* meter *c*

method ['meθəd] *n* aanpak *c*, methode *c*; orde *c*

methodical [mə'θɔdikəl] *adj* methodisch

methylated spirits ['meθəleitid 'spirits] brandspiritus *c*

metre ['mi:tə] *n* meter *c*

metric ['metrik] *adj* metrisch

Mexican ['meksikən] *adj* Mexicaans; *n* Mexicaan *c*

Mexico ['meksikou] Mexico

mezzanine ['mezəni:n] *n* entresol *c*

microphone ['maikrəfoun] *n* microfoon *c*

midday ['middei] *n* middag *c*

middle ['midəl] *n* midden *nt*; *adj* middelst; **Middle Ages** middeleeuwen *pl*; **middle-class** *adj* burgerlijk

midnight ['midnait] *n* middernacht *c*

midst [midst] *n* midden *nt*

midsummer ['mid,sʌmə] *n* midzomer *c*

midwife ['midwaif] *n* (pl -wives) vroedvrouw c

might [mait] n macht c

*might [mait] v *kunnen

mighty ['maiti] adj machtig

migraine ['migrein] n migraine c

mild [maild] adj zacht

mildew ['mildju] n schimmel c

mile [mail] n mijl c

mileage ['mailidʒ] n afstand in mijlen

milepost ['mailpoust] n wegwijzer c

milestone ['mailstoun] n mijlpaal c

milieu ['mi:ljə:] n milieu nt

military ['militəri] adj militair; ~ force krijgsmacht c

milk [milk] n melk c

milkman ['milkmən] n (pl -men) melkboer c

milk-shake ['milkʃeik] n milk shake c

mill [mil] n molen c; fabriek c

miller ['milə] n molenaar c

milliner ['milinə] n modiste c

million ['miljən] n miljoen nt

millionaire [,miljə'neə] n miljonair c

mince [mins] v fijnhakken

mind [maind] n geest c; v bezwaar *hebben tegen; letten op, *geven om

mine [main] n mijn c

miner ['mainə] n mijnwerker c

mineral ['minərəl] n delfstof c, mineraal nt; ~ water mineraalwater nt

miniature ['minjətʃə] n miniatuur c

minimum ['miniməm] n minimum nt

mining ['mainiŋ] n mijnbouw c

minister ['ministə] n minister c; predikant c; **Prime Minister** premier c

ministry ['ministri] n ministerie nt

mink [miŋk] n nerts nt

minor ['mainə] adj klein, gering, kleiner; ondergeschikt; n minderjarige c

minority [mai'nɔrəti] n minderheid c

mint [mint] n munt c

minus ['mainəs] prep min

minute[1] ['minit] n minuut c; **minutes** notulen pl

minute[2] [mai'nju:t] adj minuscuul

miracle ['mirəkəl] n wonder nt

miraculous [mi'rækjuləs] adj wonderbaarlijk

mirror ['mirə] n spiegel c

misbehave [,misbi'heiv] v zich *misdragen

miscarriage [mis'kæridʒ] n miskraam c

miscellaneous [,misə'leiniəs] adj gemengd

mischief ['mistʃif] n kattekwaad nt; onheil nt, schade c, kwaad nt

mischievous ['mistʃivəs] adj ondeugend

miserable ['mizərəbəl] adj beroerd, ellendig

misery ['mizəri] n narigheid c, ellende c; nood c

misfortune [mis'fɔ:tʃen] n tegenslag c, ongeluk nt

*mislay [mis'lei] v kwijtraken

misplaced [mis'pleist] adj misplaatst

mispronounce [,misprə'nauns] v verkeerd *uitspreken

miss[1] [mis] mejuffrouw, juffrouw c

miss[2] [mis] v missen

missing ['misiŋ] adj ontbrekend; ~ person vermiste c

mist [mist] n nevel c, mist c

mistake [mi'steik] n abuis nt, vergissing c, fout c

*mistake [mi'steik] v verwarren

mistaken [mi'steikən] adj fout; ***be ~** zich vergissen

mister ['mistə] n meneer, mijnheer c

mistress ['mistrəs] n vrouw des huizes; meesteres c; maîtresse c

mistrust [mis'trʌst] v wantrouwen

misty ['misti] adj mistig

*misunderstand [,misʌndə'stænd] v *misverstaan

misunderstanding [ˌmisʌndə'stændiŋ] *n* misverstand *nt*

misuse [mis'ju:s] *n* misbruik *nt*

mittens ['mitənz] *pl* wanten *pl*

mix [miks] *v* mengen; ~ **with** *omgaan met

mixed [mikst] *adj* gemêleerd, gemengd

mixer ['miksə] *n* mixer *c*

mixture ['mikstʃə] *n* mengsel *nt*

moan [moun] *v* kreunen

moat [mout] *n* gracht *c*

mobile ['moubail] *adj* beweeglijk, mobiel

mock [mɔk] *v* bespotten

mockery ['mɔkəri] *n* spot *c*

model ['mɔdəl] *n* model *nt*; mannequin *c*; *v* modelleren, boetseren

moderate ['mɔdərət] *adj* gematigd, matig; middelmatig

modern ['mɔdən] *adj* modern

modest ['mɔdist] *adj* discreet, bescheiden

modesty ['mɔdisti] *n* bescheidenheid *c*

modify ['mɔdifai] *v* wijzigen

mohair ['mouhεə] *n* mohair *nt*

moist [mɔist] *adj* nat, vochtig

moisten ['mɔisən] *v* bevochtigen

moisture ['mɔistʃə] *n* vochtigheid *c*; **moisturizing cream** vochtinbrengende crème

molar ['moulə] *n* kies *c*

moment ['moumənt] *n* moment *nt*, ogenblik *nt*

momentary ['mouməntəri] *adj* kortstondig

monarch ['mɔnək] *n* vorst *c*

monarchy ['mɔnəki] *n* monarchie *c*

monastery ['mɔnəstri] *n* klooster *nt*

Monday ['mʌndi] maandag *c*

monetary ['mʌnitəri] *adj* monetair; ~ **unit** munteenheid *c*

money ['mʌni] *n* geld *nt*; ~ **exchange** wisselkantoor *nt*; ~ **order** overschrijving *c*

monk [mʌŋk] *n* monnik *c*

monkey ['mʌŋki] *n* aap *c*

monologue ['mɔnɔlɔg] *n* monoloog *c*

monopoly [mə'nɔpəli] *n* monopolie *nt*

monotonous [mə'nɔtənəs] *adj* eentonig

month [mʌnθ] *n* maand *c*

monthly ['mʌnθli] *adj* maandelijks; ~ **magazine** maandblad *nt*

monument ['mɔnjumənt] *n* gedenkteken *nt*, monument *nt*

mood [mu:d] *n* humeur *nt*, stemming *c*

moon [mu:n] *n* maan *c*

moonlight ['mu:nlait] *n* maanlicht *nt*

moor [muə] *n* heide *c*, veen *nt*

moose [mu:s] *n* (pl ~, ~s) eland *c*

moped ['mouped] *n* bromfiets *c*

moral ['mɔrəl] *n* moraal *c*; *adj* zedelijk, moreel; **morals** zeden *pl*

morality [mə'ræləti] *n* moraliteit *c*

more [mɔ:] *adj* meer; **once** ~ nogmaals

moreover [mɔ:'rouvə] *adv* voorts, bovendien

morning ['mɔ:niŋ] *n* ochtend *c*, morgen *c*; ~ **paper** ochtendblad *nt*; **this** ~ vanmorgen

Moroccan [mə'rɔkən] *adj* Marokkaans; *n* Marokkaan *c*

Morocco [mə'rɔkou] Marokko

morphia ['mɔ:fiə] *n* morfine *c*

morphine ['mɔ:fi:n] *n* morfine *c*

morsel ['mɔ:səl] *n* brok *nt*

mortal ['mɔ:təl] *adj* dodelijk, sterfelijk

mortgage ['mɔ:gidʒ] *n* hypotheek *c*

mosaic [mə'zeiik] *n* mozaïek *nt*

mosque [mɔsk] *n* moskee *c*

mosquito [mə'ski:tou] *n* (pl ~es) mug *c*; muskiet *c*

mosquito-net [mə'ski:tounet] *n* muskietennet *nt*

moss [mɔs] *n* mos *nt*

most [moust] *adj* meest; **at** ~ hoogstens, hooguit; ~ **of all** vooral

mostly ['moustli] *adv* meestal

motel [mou'tel] *n* motel *nt*

moth [mɔθ] *n* mot *c*

mother ['mʌðə] *n* moeder *c*; ~ **tongue** moedertaal *c*

mother-in-law ['mʌðərinlɔ:] *n* (pl mothers-) schoonmoeder *c*

mother-of-pearl [,mʌðərəv'pə:l] *n* paarlemoer *nt*

motion ['mouʃən] *n* beweging *c*; motie *c*

motive ['moutiv] *n* motief *nt*

motor ['moutə] *n* motor *c*; *v* *autorijden; ~ **body** *Am* carrosserie *c*; **starter** ~ startmotor *c*

motorbike ['moutəbaik] *nAm* brommer *c*

motor-boat ['moutəbout] *n* motorboot *c*

motor-car ['moutəkɑ:] *n* auto *c*

motor-cycle ['moutə,saikəl] *n* motorfiets *c*

motoring ['moutəriŋ] *n* automobilisme *nt*

motorist ['moutərist] *n* automobilist *c*

motorway ['moutəwei] *n* snelweg *c*

motto ['mɔtou] *n* (pl ~es, ~s) devies *nt*

mouldy ['mouldi] *adj* beschimmeld

mound [maund] *n* heuvel *c*

mount [maunt] *v* *bestijgen; *n* berg *c*

mountain ['mauntin] *n* berg *c*; ~ **pass** bergpas *c*; ~ **range** bergketen *c*

mountaineering [,maunti'niəriŋ] *n* bergsport *c*

mountainous ['mauntinəs] *adj* bergachtig

mourning ['mɔ:niŋ] *n* rouw *c*

mouse [maus] *n* (pl mice) muis *c*

moustache [mə'stɑ:ʃ] *n* snor *c*

mouth [mauθ] *n* mond *c*; muil *c*, bek *c*; monding *c*

mouthwash ['mauθwɔʃ] *n* mondspoeling *c*

movable ['mu:vəbəl] *adj* roerend

move [mu:v] *v* *bewegen; verplaatsen; verhuizen; ontroeren; *n* zet *c*, stap *c*; verhuizing *c*

movement ['mu:vmənt] *n* beweging *c*

movie ['mu:vi] *n* film *c*; **movies** *Am* bioscoop *c*; ~ **theater** *Am* bioscoop *c*

much [mʌtʃ] *adj* veel; **as** ~ evenveel; evenzeer

muck [mʌk] *n* drek *c*

mud [mʌd] *n* modder *c*

muddle ['mʌdəl] *n* wirwar *c*, warboel *c*; *v* verknoeien

muddy ['mʌdi] *adj* modderig

mud-guard ['mʌdgɑ:d] *n* spatbord *nt*

muffler ['mʌflə] *nAm* knalpot *c*

mug [mʌg] *n* beker *c*, kroes *c*

mulberry ['mʌlbəri] *n* moerbei *c*

mule [mju:l] *n* muildier *nt*, muilezel *c*

mullet ['mʌlit] *n* mul *c*

multiplication [,mʌltipli'keiʃən] *n* vermenigvuldiging *c*

multiply ['mʌltiplai] *v* vermenigvuldigen

mumps [mʌmps] *n* bof *c*

municipal [mju:'nisipəl] *adj* gemeentelijk

municipality [mju:,nisi'pæləti] *n* gemeentebestuur *nt*

murder ['mə:də] *n* moord *c*; *v* vermoorden

murderer ['mə:dərə] *n* moordenaar *c*

muscle ['mʌsəl] *n* spier *c*

muscular ['mʌskjulə] *adj* gespierd

museum [mju:'zi:əm] *n* museum *nt*

mushroom ['mʌʃru:m] *n* champignon *c*; paddestoel *c*

music ['mju:zik] *n* muziek *c*; ~ **academy** conservatorium *nt*

musical ['mju:zikəl] *adj* muzikaal; *n* musical *c*

music-hall ['mju:zikhɔ:l] *n* variététheater *nt*

musician [mju:'ziʃən] *n* musicus *c*

muslin ['mʌzlin] *n* mousseline *c*

mussel ['mʌsəl] *n* mossel *c*

***must** [mʌst] *v* *moeten

mustard ['mʌstəd] *n* mosterd *c*

mute [mju:t] *adj* stom

mutiny ['mju:tini] *n* muiterij *c*

mutton ['mʌtən] *n* schapevlees *nt*

mutual ['mju:tʃuəl] *adj* onderling, wederzijds

my [mai] *adj* mijn

myself [mai'self] *pron* me; zelf

mysterious [mi'stiəriəs] *adj* mysterieus, geheimzinnig

mystery ['mistəri] *n* raadsel *nt*, mysterie *nt*

myth [miθ] *n* mythe *c*

N

nail [neil] *n* nagel *c*; spijker *c*

nailbrush ['neilbrʌʃ] *n* nagelborstel *c*

nail-file ['neilfail] *n* nagelvijl *c*

nail-polish ['neil,poliʃ] *n* nagellak *c*

nail-scissors ['neil,sizəz] *pl* nagelschaar *c*

naïve [nɑ:'i:v] *adj* naïef

naked ['neikid] *adj* bloot, naakt; kaal

name [neim] *n* naam *c*; *v* noemen; **in the ~ of** namens

namely ['neimli] *adv* namelijk

nap [næp] *n* dutje *nt*

napkin ['næpkin] *n* servet *nt*

nappy ['næpi] *n* luier *c*

narcosis [nɑ:'kousis] *n* (pl -ses) narcose *c*

narcotic [nɑ:'kotik] *n* narcoticum *nt*

narrow ['nærou] *adj* eng, smal, nauw

narrow-minded [,nærou'maindid] *adj* bekrompen

nasty ['nɑ:sti] *adj* naar, akelig

nation ['neiʃən] *n* natie *c*; volk *nt*

national ['næʃənəl] *adj* nationaal; volks-; staats-; ~ **anthem** volkslied *nt*; ~ **dress** nationale klederdracht; ~ **park** natuurreservaat *nt*

nationality [,næʃə'næləti] *n* nationaliteit *c*

nationalize ['næʃənəlaiz] *v* nationaliseren

native ['neitiv] *n* inboorling *c*; *adj* inheems; ~ **country** vaderland *nt*, geboorteland *nt*; ~ **language** moedertaal *c*

natural ['nætʃərəl] *adj* natuurlijk; aangeboren

naturally ['nætʃərəli] *adv* natuurlijk, uiteraard

nature ['neitʃə] *n* natuur *c*; aard *c*

naughty ['nɔ:ti] *adj* ondeugend, stout

nausea ['nɔ:siə] *n* misselijkheid *c*

naval ['neivəl] *adj* marine-

navel ['neivəl] *n* navel *c*

navigable ['nævigəbəl] *adj* bevaarbaar

navigate ['nævigeit] *v* *varen; sturen

navigation [,nævi'geiʃən] *n* navigatie *c*; scheepvaart *c*

navy ['neivi] *n* marine *c*

near [niə] *prep* bij; *adj* nabij, dichtbij

nearby ['niəbai] *adj* nabijzijnd

nearly ['niəli] *adv* haast, bijna

neat [ni:t] *adj* keurig, net; puur

necessary ['nesəsəri] *adj* nodig, noodzakelijk

necessity [nə'sesəti] *n* noodzaak *c*

neck [nek] *n* hals *c*; **nape of the ~** nek *c*

necklace ['nekləs] *n* halsketting *c*

necktie ['nektai] *n* das *c*

need [ni:d] *v* hoeven, behoeven, nodig *hebben; *n* nood *c*, behoefte *c*; noodzaak *c*; ~ **to** *moeten

needle ['ni:dəl] *n* naald *c*

needlework ['ni:dəlwə:k] *n* handwerk *nt*

negative ['negətiv] *adj* ontkennend,

negatief; *n* negatief *nt*

neglect [ni'glekt] *v* verwaarlozen; *n* verwaarlozing *c*

neglectful [ni'glektfəl] *adj* nalatig

negligee ['negliʒei] *n* negligé *nt*

negotiate [ni'gouʃieit] *v* onderhandelen

negotiation [ni,gouʃi'eiʃən] *n* onderhandeling *c*

Negro ['ni:grou] *n* (pl ~es) neger *c*

neighbour ['neibə] *n* buur *c*, buurman *c*

neighbourhood ['neibəhud] *n* buurt *c*

neighbouring ['neibəriŋ] *adj* aangrenzend, naburig

neither ['naiðə] *pron* geen van beide; **neither ... nor** noch ... noch

neon ['ni:ɔn] *n* neon *nt*

nephew ['nefju:] *n* neef *c*

nerve [nə:v] *n* zenuw *c*; durf *c*

nervous ['nə:vəs] *adj* nerveus, zenuwachtig

nest [nest] *n* nest *nt*

net [net] *n* net *nt*; *adj* netto

the Netherlands ['neðələndz] Nederland

network ['netwə:k] *n* netwerk *nt*

neuralgia [njuə'rældʒə] *n* zenuwpijn *c*

neurosis [njuə'rousis] *n* neurose *c*

neuter ['nju:tə] *adj* onzijdig

neutral ['nju:trəl] *adj* neutraal

never ['nevə] *adv* nimmer, nooit

nevertheless [,nevəðə'les] *adv* niettemin

new [nju:] *adj* nieuw; **New Year** nieuwjaar

news [nju:z] *n* nieuwsberichten *pl*, nieuws *nt*; journaal *nt*

newsagent ['nju:,zeidʒənt] *n* krantenverkoper *c*

newspaper ['nju:z,peipə] *n* krant *c*

newsreel ['nju:zri:l] *n* filmjournaal *nt*

newsstand ['nju:zstænd] *n* krantenkiosk *c*

New Zealand [nju: 'zi:lənd] Nieuw-Zeeland

next [nekst] *adj* volgend; ~ **to** naast

nice [nais] *adj* aardig, mooi, prettig; lekker; sympathiek

nickel ['nikəl] *n* nikkel *nt*

nickname ['nikneim] *n* bijnaam *c*

nicotine ['nikəti:n] *n* nicotine *c*

niece [ni:s] *n* nicht *c*

Nigeria [nai'dʒiəriə] Nigeria

Nigerian [nai'dʒiəriən] *adj* Nigeriaans; *n* Nigeriaan *c*

night [nait] *n* nacht *c*; avond *c*; **by** ~ 's nachts; ~ **flight** nachtvlucht *c*; ~ **rate** nachttarief *nt*; ~ **train** nachttrein *c*

nightclub ['naitklʌb] *n* nachtclub *c*

night-cream ['naitkri:m] *n* nachtcrème *c*

nightdress ['naitdres] *n* nachtjapon *c*

nightingale ['naitiŋgeil] *n* nachtegaal *c*

nightly ['naitli] *adj* nachtelijk

nil [nil] niets

nine [nain] *num* negen

nineteen [,nain'ti:n] *num* negentien

nineteenth [,nain'ti:nθ] *num* negentiende

ninety ['nainti] *num* negentig

ninth [nainθ] *num* negende

nitrogen ['naitrədʒən] *n* stikstof *c*

no [nou] neen, nee; *adj* geen; ~ **one** niemand

nobility [nou'biləti] *n* adel *c*

noble ['noubəl] *adj* adellijk; edel

nobody ['noubɔdi] *pron* niemand

nod [nɔd] *n* knik *c*; *v* knikken

noise [nɔiz] *n* geluid *nt*; herrie *c*, rumoer *nt*, lawaai *nt*

noisy ['nɔizi] *adj* lawaaierig; gehorig

nominal ['nɔminəl] *adj* nominaal

nominate ['nɔmineit] *v* benoemen

nomination [,nɔmi'neiʃən] *n* nominatie *c*; benoeming *c*

none [nʌn] *pron* geen

nonsense ['nɔnsəns] n onzin c

noon [nu:n] n middag c

normal ['nɔ:məl] adj gewoon, normaal

north [nɔ:θ] n noorden nt; noord c; adj noordelijk; **North Pole** noordpool c

north-east [,nɔ:θ'i:st] n noordoosten nt

northerly ['nɔ:ðəli] adj noordelijk

northern ['nɔ:ðən] adj noordelijk

north-west [,nɔ:θ'west] n noordwesten nt

Norway ['nɔ:wei] Noorwegen

Norwegian [nɔ:'wi:dʒən] adj Noors; n Noor c

nose [nouz] n neus c

nosebleed ['nouzbli:d] n neusbloeding c

nostril ['nɔstril] n neusgat nt

not [nɔt] adv niet

notary ['noutəri] n notaris c

note [nout] n aantekening c, notitie c; noot c; toon c; v noteren; opmerken, constateren

notebook ['noutbuk] n notitieboek nt

noted ['noutid] adj befaamd

notepaper ['nout,peipə] n schrijfpapier nt, briefpapier nt

nothing ['nʌθiŋ] n niks, niets

notice ['noutis] v bemerken, merken, opmerken; *zien; n aankondiging c, bericht nt; notitie c, aandacht c

noticeable ['noutisəbəl] adj merkbaar; opmerkelijk

notify ['noutifai] v mededelen; waarschuwen

notion ['noufən] n begrip nt, notie c

notorious [nou'tɔ:riəs] adj berucht

nougat ['nu:gɑ:] n noga c

nought [nɔ:t] n nul c

noun [naun] n zelfstandig naamwoord c

nourishing ['nʌriʃiŋ] adj voedzaam

novel ['nɔvəl] n roman c

novelist ['nɔvəlist] n romanschrijver c

November [nou'vembə] november

now [nau] adv nu; thans; ~ **and then** nu en dan

nowadays ['nauədeiz] adv tegenwoordig

nowhere ['nouwɛə] adv nergens

nozzle ['nɔzəl] n tuit c

nuance [nju:'ɑ̃:s] n nuance c

nuclear ['nju:kliə] adj kern-, nucleair; ~ **energy** kernenergie c

nucleus ['nju:kliəs] n kern c

nude [nju:d] adj naakt; n naakt nt

nuisance ['nju:səns] n last c

numb [nʌm] adj gevoelloos; verstijfd

number ['nʌmbə] n nummer nt; cijfer nt, getal nt; aantal nt

numeral ['nju:mərəl] n telwoord nt

numerous ['nju:mərəs] adj talrijk

nun [nʌn] n non c

nunnery ['nʌnəri] n nonnenklooster nt

nurse [nə:s] n zuster c, verpleegster c; kinderjuffrouw c; v verplegen; zogen

nursery ['nə:səri] n kinderkamer c; crèche c; boomkwekerij c

nut [nʌt] n noot c; moer c

nutcrackers ['nʌt,krækəz] pl notekraker c

nutmeg ['nʌtmeg] n nootmuskaat c

nutritious [nju:'triʃəs] adj voedzaam

nutshell ['nʌtʃel] n notedop c

nylon ['nailən] n nylon nt

O

oak [ouk] n eik c

oar [ɔ:] n roeiriem c

oasis [ou'eisis] n (pl oases) oase c

oath [ouθ] n eed c

oats [outs] pl haver c

obedience [ə'bi:diəns] n gehoorzaamheid c

obedient [ə'bi:diənt] *adj* gehoorzaam

obey [ə'bei] *v* gehoorzamen

object[1] ['ɔbdʒikt] *n* object *nt*; voorwerp *nt*; doel *nt*

object[2] [əb'dʒekt] *v* *tegenwerpen; ~ to bezwaar *hebben tegen

objection [əb'dʒekʃən] *n* bezwaar *nt*, tegenwerping *c*

objective [əb'dʒektiv] *adj* objectief; *n* doel *nt*

obligatory [ə'bligətəri] *adj* verplicht

oblige [ə'blaidʒ] *v* verplichten; *be obliged to* verplicht *zijn om; *moeten

obliging [ə'blaidʒiŋ] *adj* voorkomend

oblong ['ɔblɔŋ] *adj* langwerpig; *n* rechthoek *c*

obscene [əb'si:n] *adj* obsceen

obscure [əb'skjuə] *adj* obscuur, duister

observation [,ɔbzə'veiʃən] *n* observatie *c*, waarneming *c*

observatory [əb'zə:vətri] *n* observatorium *nt*

observe [əb'zə:v] *v* observeren, *waarnemen

obsession [əb'seʃən] *n* obsessie *c*

obstacle ['ɔbstəkəl] *n* hindernis *c*

obstinate ['ɔbstinət] *adj* koppig; hardnekkig

obtain [əb'tein] *v* behalen, *verkrijgen

obtainable [əb'teinəbəl] *adj* verkrijgbaar

obvious ['ɔbviəs] *adj* duidelijk

occasion [ə'keiʒən] *n* gelegenheid *c*; aanleiding *c*

occasionally [ə'keiʒənəli] *adv* af en toe, nu en dan

occupant ['ɔkjupənt] *n* bewoner *c*

occupation [,ɔkju'peiʃən] *n* werk *nt*; bezetting *c*

occupy ['ɔkjupai] *v* *innemen, bezetten; *occupied* adj* bezet

occur [ə'kə:] *v* gebeuren, *voorkomen, zich *voordoen

occurrence [ə'kʌrəns] *n* gebeurtenis *c*

ocean ['ouʃən] *n* oceaan *c*

October [ɔk'toubə] oktober

octopus ['ɔktəpəs] *n* octopus *c*

oculist ['ɔkjulist] *n* oogarts *c*

odd [ɔd] *adj* raar, vreemd; oneven

odour ['oudə] *n* geur *c*

of [ɔv, əv] *prep* van

off [ɔf] *adv* af; weg; *prep* van

offence [ə'fens] *n* overtreding *c*; belediging *c*, aanstoot *c*

offend [ə'fend] *v* krenken, beledigen; *overtreden

offensive [ə'fensiv] *adj* offensief; beledigend, aanstootgevend; *n* offensief *nt*

offer ['ɔfə] *v* *aanbieden; *bieden; *n* aanbieding *c*, aanbod *nt*

office ['ɔfis] *n* bureau *nt*, kantoor *nt*; ambt *nt*; ~ hours kantooruren *pl*

officer ['ɔfisə] *n* officier *c*

official [ə'fiʃəl] *adj* officieel

off-licence [,ɔf,laisəns] *n* slijterij *c*

often ['ɔfən] *adv* vaak, dikwijls

oil [ɔil] *n* olie *c*; fuel ~ stookolie *c*; ~ filter oliefilter *nt*; ~ pressure oliedruk *c*

oil-painting [,ɔil'peintiŋ] *n* olieverfschilderij *nt*

oil-refinery ['ɔilri,fainəri] *n* olieraffinaderij *c*

oil-well ['ɔilwel] *n* oliebron *c*

oily ['ɔili] *adj* olieachtig

ointment ['ɔintmənt] *n* zalf *c*

okay! [,ou'kei] in orde!

old [ould] *adj* oud; ~ age ouderdom *c*

old-fashioned [,ould'fæʃənd] *adj* ouderwets

olive ['ɔliv] *n* olijf *c*; ~ oil olijfolie *c*

omelette ['ɔmlət] *n* omelet *nt*

ominous ['ɔminəs] *adj* onheilspellend

omit [ə'mit] *v* *weglaten

omnipotent [ɔm'nipətənt] *adj* almachtig

on [ɔn] *prep* op; aan

once [wʌns] *adv* eenmaal, eens; **at ~** meteen, dadelijk; **~ more** nog eens

oncoming ['ɔn,kʌmiŋ] *adj* tegemoetkomend, naderend

one [wʌn] *num* een; *pron* men

oneself [wʌn'self] *pron* zelf

onion ['ʌnjən] *n* ui *c*

only ['ounli] *adj* enig; *adv* slechts, alleen, maar; *conj* maar

onwards ['ɔnwədz] *adv* voorwaarts

onyx ['ɔniks] *n* onyx *nt*

opal ['oupəl] *n* opaal *c*

open ['oupən] *v* openen; *adj* open; openhartig

opening ['oupəniŋ] *n* opening *c*

opera ['ɔpərə] *n* opera *c*; **~ house** opera *c*

operate ['ɔpəreit] *v* opereren, werken

operation [,ɔpə'reiʃən] *n* werking *c*; operatie *c*

operator ['ɔpəreitə] *n* telefoniste *c*

operetta [,ɔpə'retə] *n* operette *c*

opinion [ə'pinjən] *n* opinie *c*, mening *c*

opponent [ə'pounənt] *n* tegenstander *c*

opportunity [,ɔpə'tju:nəti] *n* gelegenheid *c*, kans *c*

oppose [ə'pouz] *v* zich verzetten

opposite ['ɔpəzit] *prep* tegenover; *adj* tegengesteld

opposition [,ɔpə'ziʃən] *n* oppositie *c*

oppress [ə'pres] *v* beklemmen, verdrukken

optician [ɔp'tiʃən] *n* opticien *c*

optimism ['ɔptimizəm] *n* optimisme *nt*

optimist ['ɔptimist] *n* optimist *c*

optimistic [,ɔpti'mistik] *adj* optimistisch

optional ['ɔpʃənəl] *adj* facultatief

or [ɔ:] *conj* of

oral ['ɔ:rəl] *adj* mondeling

orange ['ɔrindʒ] *n* sinaasappel *c*; *adj* oranje

orchard ['ɔ:tʃəd] *n* boomgaard *c*

orchestra ['ɔ:kistrə] *n* orkest *nt*; **~ seat** *Am* stalles *pl*

order ['ɔ:də] *v* *bevelen; bestellen; *n* volgorde *c*, orde *c*; opdracht *c*, bevel *nt*; bestelling *c*; **in ~** in orde; **in ~ to** om te; **made to ~** op maat gemaakt; **out of ~** buiten werking; **postal ~** postwissel *c*

order-form ['ɔ:dəfɔ:m] *n* bestelformulier *nt*

ordinary ['ɔ:dənri] *adj* alledaags, gewoon

ore [ɔ:] *n* erts *nt*

organ ['ɔ:gən] *n* orgaan *nt*; orgel *nt*

organic [ɔ:'gænik] *adj* organisch

organization [,ɔ:gənai'zeiʃən] *n* organisatie *c*

organize ['ɔ:gənaiz] *v* organiseren

Orient ['ɔ:riənt] *n* Oosten *nt*

oriental [,ɔ:ri'entəl] *adj* oosters

orientate ['ɔ:riənteit] *v* zich oriënteren

origin ['ɔridʒin] *n* origine *c*, oorsprong *c*; afstamming *c*, herkomst *c*

original [ə'ridʒinəl] *adj* oorspronkelijk, origineel

originally [ə'ridʒinəli] *adv* aanvankelijk

orlon ['ɔ:lɔn] *n* orlon *nt*

ornament ['ɔ:nəmənt] *n* versiersel *nt*

ornamental [,ɔ:nə'mentəl] *adj* ornamenteel

orphan ['ɔ:fən] *n* wees *c*

orthodox ['ɔ:θədɔks] *adj* orthodox

ostrich ['ɔstritʃ] *n* struisvogel *c*

other ['ʌðə] *adj* ander

otherwise ['ʌðəwaiz] *conj* anders

***ought to** [ɔ:t] *moeten

our [auə] *adj* ons

ourselves [auə'selvz] *pron* ons; zelf

out [aut] *adv* buiten, uit; **~ of** buiten, uit

outbreak ['autbreik] *n* uitbarsting *c*

outcome ['autkʌm] *n* resultaat *nt*

***outdo** [,aut'du:] *v* *overtreffen

outdoors [,aut'dɔːz] *adv* buiten

outer ['autə] *adj* buitenst

outfit ['autfit] *n* uitrusting *c*

outline ['autlain] *n* omtrek *c*; *v* schetsen

outlook ['autluk] *n* verwachting *c*; zienswijze *c*

output ['autput] *n* produktie *c*

outrage ['autreidʒ] *n* gewelddaad *c*

outside [,aut'said] *adv* buiten; *prep* buiten; *n* uiterlijk *nt*, buitenkant *c*

outsize ['autsaiz] *n* extra grote maat

outskirts ['autskəːts] *pl* buitenwijk *c*

outstanding [,aut'stændiŋ] *adj* eminent, vooraanstaand

outward ['autwəd] *adj* uiterlijk

outwards ['autwədz] *adv* naar buiten

oval ['ouvəl] *adj* ovaal

oven ['ʌvən] *n* oven *c*

over ['ouvə] *prep* boven, over; meer dan; *adv* over; omver; *adj* voorbij; ~ there ginds

overall ['ouvərɔːl] *adj* totaal

overalls ['ouvərɔːlz] *pl* overall *c*

overcast ['ouvəkaːst] *adj* betrokken

overcoat ['ouvəkout] *n* overjas *c*

* overcome [,ouvə'kʌm] *v* *overwinnen

overdue [,ouvə'djuː] *adj* te laat; achterstallig

overgrown [,ouvə'groun] *adj* begroeid

overhaul [,ouvə'hɔːl] *v* reviseren

overlook [,ouvə'luk] *v* over het hoofd *zien

overnight [,ouvə'nait] *adv* 's nachts

overseas [,ouvə'siːz] *adj* overzees

oversight ['ouvəsait] *n* vergissing *c*

* oversleep [,ouvə'sliːp] *v* zich *verslapen

overstrung [,ouvə'strʌŋ] *adj* overspannen

* overtake [,ouvə'teik] *v* inhalen; no overtaking inhalen verboden

over-tired [,ouvə'taiəd] *adj* oververmoeid

overture ['ouvətʃə] *n* ouverture *c*

overweight ['ouvəweit] *n* bagageoverschot *nt*

overwhelm [,ouvə'welm] *v* onthutsen, overweldigen

overwork [,ouvə'wəːk] *v* zich overwerken

owe [ou] *v* verschuldigd *zijn, schuldig *zijn; te danken *hebben aan; owing to vanwege, ten gevolge van

owl [aul] *n* uil *c*

own [oun] *v* *bezitten; *adj* eigen

owner ['ounə] *n* bezitter *c*, eigenaar *c*

ox [ɔks] *n* (pl oxen) os *c*

oxygen ['ɔksidʒən] *n* zuurstof *c*

oyster ['ɔistə] *n* oester *c*

P

pace [peis] *n* gang *c*; schrede *c*, stap *c*; tempo *nt*

Pacific Ocean [pə'sifik 'ouʃən] Stille Oceaan

pacifism ['pæsifizəm] *n* pacifisme *nt*

pacifist ['pæsifist] *n* pacifist *c*; pacifistisch

pack [pæk] *v* inpakken; ~ up inpakken

package ['pækidʒ] *n* pak *nt*

packet ['pækit] *n* pakje *nt*

packing ['pækiŋ] *n* verpakking *c*

pad [pæd] *n* kussentje *nt*; blocnote *c*

paddle ['pædəl] *n* peddel *c*

padlock ['pædlɔk] *n* hangslot *nt*

pagan ['peigən] *adj* heidens; *n* heiden *c*

page [peidʒ] *n* pagina *c*, bladzijde *c*

page-boy ['peidʒbɔi] *n* piccolo *c*

pail [peil] *n* emmer *c*

pain [pein] *n* pijn *c*; pains moeite *c*

painful ['peinfəl] *adj* pijnlijk

painless ['peinləs] *adj* pijnloos

paint [peint] n verf c; v schilderen; verven

paint-box ['peintbɒks] n verfdoos c

paint-brush ['peintbrʌʃ] n penseel nt

painter ['peintə] n schilder c

painting ['peintiŋ] n schilderij nt

pair [peə] n paar nt

Pakistan [ˌpɑːkiˈstɑːn] Pakistan

Pakistani [ˌpɑːkiˈstɑːni] adj Pakistaans; n Pakistaan c

palace ['pæləs] n paleis nt

pale [peil] adj bleek; licht

palm [pɑːm] n palm c; handpalm c

palpable ['pælpəbəl] adj tastbaar

palpitation [ˌpælpiˈteiʃən] n hartklopping c

pan [pæn] n pan c

pane [pein] n ruit c

panel ['pænəl] n paneel nt

panelling ['pænəliŋ] n lambrizering c

panic ['pænik] n paniek c

pant [pænt] v hijgen

panties ['pæntiz] pl onderbroek c, slip c

pants [pænts] pl onderbroek c; plAm broek c

pant-suit ['pæntsuːt] n broekpak nt

panty-hose ['pæntihouz] n panty c

paper ['peipə] n papier nt; krant c; papieren; **carbon** ~ carbonpapier nt; ~ **bag** papieren zak; ~ **napkin** papieren servet; **typing** ~ schrijfmachinepapier nt; **wrapping** ~ pakpapier nt

paperback ['peipəbæk] n pocketboek nt

paper-knife ['peipənaif] n briefopener c

parade [pəˈreid] n parade c, optocht c

paraffin ['pærəfin] n petroleum c

paragraph ['pærəɡrɑːf] n alinea c, paragraaf c

parakeet ['pærəkiːt] n parkiet c

paralise ['pærəlaiz] v verlammen

parallel ['pærəlel] adj evenwijdig, parallel; n parallel c

parcel ['pɑːsəl] n pakket nt, pakje nt

pardon ['pɑːdən] n vergiffenis c; gratie c

parents ['peərənts] pl ouders pl

parents-in-law ['peərəntsinlɔː] pl schoonouders pl

parish ['pæriʃ] n parochie c

park [pɑːk] n park nt; v parkeren; **no parking** verboden te parkeren; **parking fee** parkeertarief nt; **parking light** stadslicht nt; **parking lot** Am parkeerplaats c; **parking meter** parkeermeter c; **parking zone** parkeerzone c

parliament ['pɑːləmənt] n parlement nt

parliamentary [ˌpɑːləˈmentəri] adj parlementair

parrot ['pærət] n papegaai c

parsley ['pɑːsli] n peterselie c

parson ['pɑːsən] n dominee c

parsonage ['pɑːsənidʒ] n pastorie c

part [pɑːt] n gedeelte nt, deel nt; stuk nt; v *scheiden; **spare** ~ onderdeel nt

partial ['pɑːʃəl] adj gedeeltelijk; partijdig

participant [pɑːˈtisipənt] n deelnemer c

participate [pɑːˈtisipeit] v *deelnemen

particular [pəˈtikjulə] adj bijzonder, speciaal; kieskeurig; **in** ~ in het bijzonder

parting ['pɑːtiŋ] n afscheid nt; scheiding c

partition [pɑːˈtiʃən] n tussenschot nt

partly ['pɑːtli] adv deels, gedeeltelijk

partner ['pɑːtnə] n partner c; compagnon c

partridge ['pɑːtridʒ] n patrijs c

party ['pɑːti] n partij c; fuif c, feestje nt; groep c

pass [pa:s] v *voorbijgaan, passeren; *aangeven; slagen; vAm inhalen; **no passing** Am inhalen verboden; ~ **by** passeren; ~ **through** *gaan door

passage ['pæsidʒ] n doorgang c; overtocht c; passage c; doorreis c

passenger ['pæsəndʒə] n passagier c; ~ **car** Am wagon c; ~ **train** personentrein c

passer-by [,pa:sə'bai] n voorbijganger c

passion ['pæʃən] n hartstocht c, passie c; drift c

passionate ['pæʃənət] adj hartstochtelijk

passive ['pæsiv] adj passief

passport ['pa:spɔ:t] n paspoort nt; ~ **control** paspoortcontrole c; ~ **photograph** pasfoto c

password ['pa:swə:d] n wachtwoord nt

past [pa:st] n verleden nt; adj vorig, afgelopen, voorbij; prep langs, voorbij

paste [peist] n pasta c; v plakken

pastry ['peistri] n gebak nt; ~ **shop** banketbakkerij c

pasture ['pa:stʃə] n weiland nt

patch [pætʃ] v verstellen

patent ['peitənt] n patent nt, octrooi nt

path [pa:θ] n pad nt

patience ['peiʃəns] n geduld nt

patient ['peiʃənt] adj geduldig; n patiënt c

patriot ['peitriət] n patriot c

patrol [pə'troul] n patrouille c; v patrouilleren; surveilleren

pattern ['pætən] n motief nt, patroon nt

pause [pɔ:z] n pauze c; v pauzeren

pave [peiv] v plaveien, bestraten

pavement ['peivmənt] n trottoir nt;

plaveisel nt

pavilion [pə'viljən] n paviljoen nt

paw [pɔ:] n poot c

pawn [pɔ:n] v verpanden; n pion c

pawnbroker ['pɔ:n,broukə] n pandjesbaas c

pay [pei] n salaris nt, loon nt

*pay [pei] v betalen; lonen; ~ **attention to** letten op; **paying** rendabel; ~ **off** aflossen; ~ **on account** afbetalen

pay-desk ['peidesk] n kassa c

payee [pei'i:] n begunstigde c

payment ['peimənt] n betaling c

pea [pi:] n erwt c

peace [pi:s] n vrede c

peaceful ['pi:sfəl] adj vreedzaam

peach [pi:tʃ] n perzik c

peacock ['pi:kɔk] n pauw c

peak [pi:k] n top c; spits c; ~ **hour** spitsuur nt; ~ **season** hoogseizoen nt

peanut ['pi:nʌt] n pinda c

pear [pɛə] n peer c

pearl [pə:l] n parel c

peasant ['pezənt] n boer c

pebble ['pebəl] n kiezel c

peculiar [pi'kju:ljə] adj eigenaardig; speciaal, bijzonder

peculiarity [pi,kju:li'ærəti] n eigenaardigheid c

pedal ['pedəl] n pedaal nt/c

pedestrian [pi'destriən] n voetganger c; **no pedestrians** verboden voor voetgangers; ~ **crossing** zebrapad nt

pedicure ['pedikjuə] n pedicure c

peel [pi:l] v schillen c; n schil c

peep [pi:p] v gluren

peg [peg] n klerenhaak c

pelican ['pelikən] n pelikaan c

pelvis ['pelvis] n bekken nt

pen [pen] n pen c

penalty ['penəlti] n boete c; straf c; ~

kick strafschop c

pencil ['pensəl] n potlood nt

pencil-sharpener ['pensəl,ʃɑːpnə] n punteslijper c

penetrate ['penitreit] v *doordringen

penguin ['peŋgwin] n pinguin c

penicillin [,peni'silin] n penicilline c

peninsula [pə'ninsjulə] n schiereiland nt

penknife ['pennaif] n (pl -knives) zakmes nt

pension¹ ['pãːsiɔ̃ː] n pension nt

pension² ['penʃən] n pensioen nt

people ['piːpəl] pl mensen; n volk nt

pepper ['pepə] n peper c

peppermint ['pepəmint] n pepermunt c

perceive [pə'siːv] v bemerken

percent [pə'sent] n procent nt

percentage [pə'sentidʒ] n percentage nt

perceptible [pə'septibəl] adj merkbaar

perception [pə'sepʃən] n gewaarwording c

perch [pəːtʃ] (pl ~) baars c

percolator ['pəːkəleitə] n percolator c

perfect ['pəːfikt] adj volkomen, volmaakt

perfection [pə'fekʃən] n perfectie c, volmaaktheid c

perform [pə'fɔːm] v uitvoeren, verrichten

performance [pə'fɔːməns] n voorstelling c

perfume ['pəːfjuːm] n parfum nt

perhaps [pə'hæps] adv misschien; wellicht

peril ['peril] n gevaar nt

perilous ['periləs] adj gevaarlijk

period ['piəriəd] n tijdperk nt, periode c; punt c

periodical [,piəri'ɔdikəl] n tijdschrift nt; adj periodiek

perish ['periʃ] v *omkomen

perishable ['periʃəbəl] adj aan bederf onderhevig

perjury ['pəːdʒəri] n meineed c

permanent ['pəːmənənt] adj blijvend, permanent, duurzaam; bestendig, vast; ~ **press** plooihoudend; ~ **wave** permanent c

permission [pə'miʃən] n toestemming c, permissie c; verlof nt, vergunning c

permit¹ [pə'mit] v *toestaan, veroorloven

permit² ['pəːmit] n vergunning c

peroxide [pə'rɔksaid] n waterstofperoxyde nt

perpendicular [,pəːpən'dikjulə] adj loodrecht

Persia ['pəːʃə] Perzië

Persian ['pəːʃən] adj Perzisch; n Pers c

person ['pəːsən] n persoon c; per ~ per persoon

personal ['pəːsənəl] adj persoonlijk

personality [,pəːsə'næləti] n persoonlijkheid c

personnel [,pəːsə'nel] n personeel nt

perspective [pə'spektiv] n perspectief nt

perspiration [,pəːspə'reiʃən] n transpiratie c, zweet nt

perspire [pə'spaiə] v transpireren, zweten

persuade [pə'sweid] v overreden, overhalen; overtuigen

persuasion [pə'sweiʒən] n overtuiging c

pessimism ['pesimizəm] n pessimisme nt

pessimist ['pesimist] n pessimist c

pessimistic [,pesi'mistik] adj pessimistisch

pet [pet] n huisdier nt; lieveling c

petal ['petəl] n bloemblad nt

petition [pi'tiʃən] n petitie c

petrol ['petrəl] *n* benzine *c*; ~ **pump** benzinepomp *c*; ~ **station** benzinestation *nt*; ~ **tank** benzinetank *c*
petroleum [pi'trouliəm] *n* petroleum *c*
petty ['peti] *adj* klein, nietig, onbeduidend; ~ **cash** kleingeld *nt*
pewit ['pi:wit] *n* kievit *c*
pewter ['pju:tə] *n* tin *nt*
phantom ['fæntəm] *n* spook *nt*
pharmacology [,fɑ:mə'kɔlədʒi] *n* farmacologie *c*
pharmacy ['fɑ:məsi] *n* apotheek *c*; drogisterij *c*
phase [feiz] *n* fase *c*
pheasant ['fezənt] *n* fazant *c*
Philippine ['filipain] *adj* Filippijns
Philippines ['filipi:nz] *pl* Filippijnen *pl*
philosopher [fi'lɔsəfə] *n* wijsgeer *c*, filosoof *c*
philosophy [fi'lɔsəfi] *n* wijsbegeerte *c*, filosofie *c*
phone [foun] *n* telefoon *c*; *v* opbellen, telefoneren
phonetic [fə'netik] *adj* fonetisch
photo ['foutou] *n* (pl ~s) foto *c*
photograph ['foutəgrɑ:f] *n* foto *c*; *v* fotograferen
photographer [fə'tɔgrəfə] *n* fotograaf *c*
photography [fə'tɔgrəfi] *n* fotografie *c*
photostat ['foutəstæt] *n* fotocopie *c*
phrase [freiz] *n* uitdrukking *c*
phrase-book ['freizbuk] *n* taalgids *c*
physical ['fizikəl] *adj* fysiek
physician [fi'ziʃən] *n* dokter *c*
physicist ['fizisist] *n* natuurkundige *c*
physics ['fiziks] *n* fysica *c*, natuurkunde *c*
physiology [,fizi'ɔlədʒi] *n* fysiologie *c*
pianist ['pi:ənist] *n* pianist *c*
piano [pi'ænou] *n* piano *c*; **grand** ~ vleugel *c*
pick [pik] *v* plukken; *kiezen; *n* keus *c*; ~ **up** oprapen; ophalen; **pick-up**

van bestelauto *c*
pick-axe ['pikæks] *n* houweel *nt*
pickles ['pikəlz] *pl* zoetzuur *nt*, pickles *pl*
picnic ['piknik] *n* picknick *c*; *v* picknicken
picture ['piktʃə] *n* schilderij *nt*; plaat *c*, prent *c*; beeld *nt*, afbeelding *c*; ~ **postcard** ansichtkaart *c*, prentbriefkaart *c*; **pictures** bioscoop *c*
picturesque [,piktʃə'resk] *adj* pittoresk, schilderachtig
piece [pi:s] *n* stuk *nt*
pier [piə] *n* pier *c*
pierce [piəs] *v* doorboren
pig [pig] *n* varken *nt*; zwijn *c*
pigeon ['pidʒən] *n* duif *c*
pig-headed [,pig'hedid] *adj* eigenwijs
piglet ['piglət] *n* big *c*
pigskin ['pigskin] *n* varkensleer *nt*
pike [paik] (pl ~) snoek *c*
pile [pail] *n* stapel *c*; *v* opstapelen; **piles** *pl* aambeien *pl*
pilgrim ['pilgrim] *n* pelgrim *c*
pilgrimage ['pilgrimidʒ] *n* bedevaart *c*
pill [pil] *n* pil *c*
pillar ['pilə] *n* zuil *c*, pilaar *c*
pillar-box ['piləbɔks] *n* brievenbus *c*
pillow ['pilou] *n* kussen *nt*, hoofdkussen *nt*
pillow-case ['piloukeis] *n* kussensloop *c/nt*
pilot ['pailət] *n* piloot *c*; loods *c*
pimple ['pimpəl] *n* puistje *nt*
pin [pin] *n* speld *c*; *v* vastspelden; **bobby** ~ *Am* haarspeld *c*
pincers ['pinsəz] *pl* nijptang *c*
pinch [pintʃ] *v* *knijpen
pineapple ['pai,næpəl] *n* ananas *c*
ping-pong ['piŋpɔŋ] *n* tafeltennis *nt*
pink [piŋk] *adj* roze
pioneer [,paiə'niə] *n* pionier *c*
pious ['paiəs] *adj* vroom
pip [pip] *n* pit *c*

pipe [paip] *n* pijp *c*; leiding *c*; ~ **cleaner** pijpestoker *c*; ~ **tobacco** pijptabak *c*

pirate ['paiərət] *n* piraat *c*

pistol ['pistəl] *n* pistool *nt*

piston ['pistən] *n* zuiger *c*; ~ **ring** zuigerring *c*

piston-rod ['pistənrɔd] *n* zuigerstang *c*

pit [pit] *n* kuil *c*; groeve *c*

pitcher ['pitʃə] *n* kruik *c*

pity ['piti] *n* medelijden *nt*; *v* medelijden *hebben met, beklagen; **what a pity!** jammer!

placard ['plæka:d] *n* aanplakbiljet *nt*

place [pleis] *n* plaats *c*; *v* zetten, plaatsen; ~ **of birth** geboorteplaats *c*; *take ~ *plaatshebben

plague [pleig] *n* plaag *c*

plaice [pleis] (pl ~) schol *c*

plain [plein] *adj* duidelijk; gewoon, eenvoudig; *n* vlakte *c*

plan [plæn] *n* plan *nt*; plattegrond *c*; *v* plannen

plane [plein] *adj* vlak; *n* vliegtuig *nt*; ~ **crash** vliegramp *c*

planet ['plænit] *n* planeet *c*

planetarium [,plæni'teəriəm] *n* planetarium *nt*

plank [plæŋk] *n* plank *c*

plant [pla:nt] *n* plant *c*; bedrijf *nt*; *v* planten

plantation [plæn'teiʃən] *n* plantage *c*

plaster ['pla:stə] *n* pleister *nt*, gips *nt*; plcistcr *c*

plastic ['plæstik] *adj* plastic; *n* plastic *nt*

plate [pleit] *n* bord *nt*; plaat *c*

plateau ['plætou] *n* (pl ~x, ~s) hoogvlakte *c*

platform ['plætfɔ:m] *n* perron *nt*; ~ **ticket** perronkaartje *nt*

platinum ['plætinəm] *n* platina *nt*

play [plei] *v* spelen; bespelen; *n* spel *nt*; toneelstuk *nt*; **one-act ~** eenakter *c*; ~ **truant** spijbelen

player [pleiə] *n* speler *c*

playground ['pleigraund] *n* speelplaats *c*

playing-card ['pleiiŋka:d] *n* speelkaart *c*

playwright ['pleirait] *n* toneelschrijver *c*

plea [pli:] *n* pleidooi *nt*

plead [pli:d] *v* pleiten

pleasant ['plezənt] *adj* prettig, aardig, aangenaam

please [pli:z] alstublieft; *v* *bevallen; **pleased** ingenomen; **pleasing** aangenaam

pleasure ['pleʒə] *n* genoegen *nt*, pret *c*, plezier *nt*

plentiful ['plentifəl] *adj* overvloedig

plenty ['plenti] *n* overvloed *c*; heleboel *c*

pliers [plaiəz] *pl* tang *c*

plimsolls ['plimsəlz] *pl* gymschoenen *pl*

plot [plɔt] *n* samenzwering *c*, komplot *nt*; handeling *c*; perceel *nt*

plough [plau] *n* ploeg *c*; *v* ploegen

plucky ['plʌki] *adj* flink

plug [plʌg] *n* stekker *c*; ~ **in** inschakelen

plum [plʌm] *n* pruim *c*

plumber ['plʌmə] *n* loodgieter *c*

plump [plʌmp] *adj* mollig

plural ['pluərəl] *n* meervoud *nt*

plus [plʌs] *prep* plus

pneumatic [nju:'mætik] *adj* pneumatisch

pneumonia [nju:'mouniə] *n* longontsteking *c*

poach [poutʃ] *v* stropen

pocket ['pɔkit] *n* zak *c*

pocket-book ['pɔkitbuk] *n* portefeuille *c*

pocket-comb ['pɔkitkoum] *n* zakkam *c*

pocket-knife ['pɔkitnaif] *n* (pl -knives)

zakmes *nt*

pocket-watch ['pɔkitwɔtʃ] *n* zakhorloge *nt*

poem ['pouim] *n* gedicht *nt*

poet ['pouit] *n* dichter *c*

poetry ['pouitri] *n* dichtkunst *c*

point [pɔint] *n* punt *nt*; punt *c*; *v* *wijzen; ~ **of view** standpunt *nt*; ~ **out** *aanwijzen

pointed ['pɔintid] *adj* spits

poison ['pɔizən] *n* vergif *nt*; *v* vergiftigen

poisonous ['pɔizənəs] *adj* giftig

Poland ['poulənd] Polen

Pole [poul] *n* Pool *c*

pole [poul] *n* paal *c*

police [pə'li:s] *pl* politie *c*

policeman [pə'li:smən] *n* (pl -men) agent *c*, politieagent *c*

police-station [pə'li:s,steiʃən] *n* politiebureau *nt*

policy ['pɔlisi] *n* beleid *nt*, politiek *c*; polis *c*

polio ['pouliou] *n* polio *c*, kinderverlamming *c*

Polish ['pouliʃ] *adj* Pools

polish ['pɔliʃ] *v* poetsen

polite [pə'lait] *adj* beleefd

political [pə'litikəl] *adj* politiek

politician [,pɔli'tiʃən] *n* politicus *c*

politics ['pɔlitiks] *n* politiek *c*

pollution [pə'lu:ʃən] *n* vervuiling *c*, verontreiniging *c*

pond [pɔnd] *n* vijver *c*

pony ['pouni] *n* pony *c*

poor [puə] *adj* arm; armoedig; slecht

pope [poup] *n* paus *c*

poplin ['pɔplin] *n* popeline *nt/c*

pop music [pɔp 'mju:zik] popmuziek *c*

poppy ['pɔpi] *n* klaproos *c*; papaver *c*

popular ['pɔpjulə] *adj* populair; volks-

population [,pɔpju'leiʃən] *n* bevolking *c*

populous ['pɔpjuləs] *adj* dichtbevolkt

porcelain ['pɔ:səlin] *n* porselein *nt*

porcupine ['pɔ:kjupain] *n* stekelvarken *nt*

pork [pɔ:k] *n* varkensvlees *nt*

port [pɔ:t] *n* haven *c*; bakboord *nt*

portable ['pɔ:təbəl] *adj* draagbaar

porter ['pɔ:tə] *n* kruier *c*; portier *c*

porthole ['pɔ:thoul] *n* patrijspoort *c*

portion ['pɔ:ʃən] *n* portie *c*

portrait ['pɔ:trit] *n* portret *nt*

Portugal ['pɔ:tjugəl] Portugal

Portuguese [,pɔ:tju'gi:z] *adj* Portugees; *n* Portugees *c*

position [pə'ziʃən] *n* positie *c*; houding *c*; betrekking *c*

positive ['pɔzətiv] *adj* positief; *n* positief *nt*

possess [pə'zes] *v* *bezitten; **possessed** *adj* bezeten

possession [pə'zeʃən] *n* bezit *nt*; **possessions** eigendom *nt*

possibility [,pɔsə'biləti] *n* mogelijkheid *c*

possible ['pɔsəbəl] *adj* mogelijk; eventueel

post [poust] *n* paal *c*; betrekking *c*; post *c*; *v* posten; **post-office** postkantoor *nt*

postage ['poustidʒ] *n* frankering *c*; ~ **paid** franko; ~ **stamp** postzegel *c*

postcard ['poustka:d] *n* briefkaart *c*; ansichtkaart *c*

poster ['poustə] *n* affiche *nt*, poster *c*

poste restante [poust re'stã:t] poste restante

postman ['poustmən] *n* (pl -men) postbode *c*

post-paid [,poust'peid] *adj* franko

postpone [pə'spoun] *v* uitstellen

pot [pɔt] *n* pot *c*

potato [pə'teitou] *n* (pl ~es) aardappel *c*

pottery ['pɔtəri] *n* aardewerk *nt*

pouch [pautʃ] *n* buidel *c*

poulterer ['poultərə] n poelier c
poultry ['poultri] n gevogelte nt
pound [paund] n pond nt
pour [pɔ:] v *inschenken, *schenken, *gieten
poverty ['pɔvəti] n armoede c
powder ['paudə] n poeder nt/c; ~ compact poederdoos c; talc ~ talkpoeder nt/c
powder-puff ['paudəpʌf] n poederdons c
powder-room ['paudəru:m] n damestoilet nt
power [pauə] n kracht c; energie c; macht c; mogendheid c
powerful ['pauəfəl] adj machtig; sterk
powerless ['pauələs] adj machteloos
power-station ['pauə,steiʃən] n elektriciteitscentrale c
practical ['præktikəl] adj praktisch
practically ['præktikli] adv vrijwel
practice ['præktis] n praktijk c
practise ['præktis] v beoefenen; oefenen
praise [preiz] v *prijzen; n lof c
pram [præm] n kinderwagen c
prawn [prɔ:n] n garnaal c, steurgarnaal c
pray [prei] v *bidden
prayer [preə] n gebed nt
preach [pri:tʃ] v preken
precarious [pri'keəriəs] adj hachelijk
precaution [pri'kɔ:ʃən] n voorzorg c; voorzorgsmaatregel c
precede [pri'si:d] v *voorafgaan
preceding [pri'si:diŋ] adj voorgaand
precious ['preʃəs] adj kostbaar; dierbaar
precipice ['presipis] n afgrond c
precipitation [pri,sipi'teiʃən] n neerslag c
precise [pri'sais] adj precies, exact, nauwkeurig; secuur
predecessor ['pri:disesə] n voorganger

c
predict [pri'dikt] v voorspellen
prefer [pri'fə:] v de voorkeur *geven aan, liever *hebben
preferable ['prefərəbəl] adj te verkiezen, verkieselijker, de voorkeur verdienend
preference ['prefərəns] n voorkeur c
prefix ['pri:fiks] n voorvoegsel c
pregnant ['pregnənt] adj in verwachting, zwanger
prejudice ['predʒədis] n vooroordeel nt
preliminary [pri'liminəri] adj inleidend; voorlopig
premature ['premətʃuə] adj voorbarig
premier ['premiə] n premier c
premises ['premisiz] pl pand nt
premium ['pri:miəm] n premie c
prepaid [,pri:'peid] adj vooruitbetaald
preparation [,prepə'reiʃən] n voorbereiding c
prepare [pri'peə] v voorbereiden; klaarmaken
prepared [pri'peəd] adj bereid
preposition [,prepə'ziʃən] n voorzetsel nt
prescribe [pri'skraib] v *voorschrijven
prescription [pri'skripʃən] n recept nt
presence ['prezəns] n aanwezigheid c; tegenwoordigheid c
present[1] ['prezənt] n geschenk nt, cadeau nt; heden nt; adj tegenwoordig; aanwezig
present[2] [pri'zent] v voorstellen; *aanbieden
presently ['prezəntli] adv meteen, dadelijk
preservation [,prezə'veiʃən] n bewaring c
preserve [pri'zə:v] v bewaren; inmaken
president ['prezidənt] n president c; voorzitter c
press [pres] n pers c; v indrukken,

drukken; persen; ~ **conference**
persconferentie *c*

pressing ['presiŋ] *adj* urgent, dringend

pressure ['preʃə] *n* druk *c*; spanning
c; **atmospheric** ~ luchtdruk *c*

pressure-cooker ['preʃə,kukə] *n* snelkookpan *c*

prestige [pre'sti:ʒ] *n* prestige *nt*

presumable [pri'zju:məbəl] *adj* vermoedelijk

presumptuous [pri'zʌmpʃəs] *adj* overmoedig; arrogant

pretence [pri'tens] *n* voorwendsel *nt*

pretend [pri'tend] *v* *doen alsof, voorwenden

pretext ['pri:tekst] *n* voorwendsel *nt*

pretty ['priti] *adj* mooi, knap; *adv*
vrij, tamelijk, nogal

prevent [pri'vent] *v* beletten, verhinderen; *voorkomen

preventive [pri'ventiv] *adj* preventief

previous ['pri:viəs] *adj* verleden, vroeger, voorgaand

pre-war [,pri:'wɔ:] *adj* vooroorlogs

price [prais] *v* prijzen; ~ **list** prijslijst
c

priceless ['praisləs] *adj* onschatbaar

price-list ['prais,list] *n* prijs *c*

prick [prik] *v* prikken

pride [praid] *n* trots *c*

priest [pri:st] *n* priester *c*

primary ['praiməri] *adj* primair; eerst,
hoofd-; elementair

prince [prins] *n* prins *c*

princess [prin'ses] *n* prinses *c*

principal ['prinsəpəl] *adj* voornaamst;
n rector *c*, directeur *c*

principle ['prinsəpəl] *n* beginsel *nt*,
principe *nt*

print [print] *v* drukken; *n* afdruk *c*;
prent *c*; **printed matter** drukwerk
nt

prior [praiə] *adj* vroeger

priority [prai'ɔrəti] *n* prioriteit *c*, voor-

rang *c*

prison ['prizən] *n* gevangenis *c*

prisoner ['prizənə] *n* gedetineerde *c*,
gevangene *c*; ~ **of war** krijgsgevangene *c*

privacy ['praivəsi] *n* privacy *c*, privéleven *nt*

private ['praivit] *adj* particulier, privé;
persoonlijk

privilege ['privilidʒ] *n* voorrecht *nt*

prize [praiz] *n* prijs *c*; beloning *c*

probable ['probəbəl] *adj* vermoedelijk,
waarschijnlijk

probably ['probəbli] *adv* waarschijnlijk

problem ['probləm] *n* probleem *nt*;
vraagstuk *nt*

procedure [prə'si:dʒə] *n* procedure *c*

proceed [prə'si:d] *v* *voortgaan; te
werk *gaan

process ['prouses] *n* proces *nt*, procédé *nt*

procession [prə'seʃən] *n* processie *c*,
stoet *c*

proclaim [prə'kleim] *v* afkondigen

produce[1] [prə'dju:s] *v* produceren

produce[2] ['prodju:s] *n* opbrengst *c*,
produkt *nt*

producer [prə'dju:sə] *n* producent *c*

product ['prodʌkt] *n* produkt *nt*

production [prə'dʌkʃən] *n* produktie *c*

profession [prə'feʃən] *n* vak *nt*, beroep
nt

professional [prə'feʃənəl] *adj* beroeps-

professor [prə'fesə] *n* hoogleraar *c*,
professor *c*

profit ['profit] *n* voordeel *nt*, winst *c*;
baat *c*; *v* profiteren

profitable ['profitəbəl] *adj* winstgevend

profound [prə'faund] *adj* diepzinnig

programme ['prougræm] *n* programma
nt

progress[1] ['prougres] *n* vooruitgang *c*

progress[2] [prə'gres] *v* vorderen

progressive [prə'gresiv] *adj* vooruit-

strevend, progressief; toenemend
prohibit [prə'hibit] v *verbieden
prohibition [,proui'biʃən] n verbod nt
prohibitive [prə'hibitiv] adj onoverkomelijk
project ['prɔdʒekt] n plan nt, project nt
promenade [,prɔmə'na:d] n promenade c
promise ['prɔmis] n belofte c; v beloven
promote [prə'mout] v bevorderen
promotion [prə'mouʃən] n promotie c
prompt [prɔmpt] adj onmiddellijk, prompt
pronoun ['prounaun] n voornaamwoord nt
pronounce [prə'nauns] v *uitspreken
pronunciation [,prənʌnsi'eiʃən] n uitspraak c
proof [pru:f] n bewijs nt
propaganda [,prɔpə'gændə] n propaganda c
propel [prə'pel] v *aandrijven
propeller [prə'pelə] n schroef c, propeller c
proper ['prɔpə] adj juist; behoorlijk, passend, geschikt, gepast
property ['prɔpəti] n bezit nt, eigendom nt; eigenschap c
prophet ['prɔfit] n profeet c
proportion [prə'pɔ:ʃən] n proportie c
proportional [prə'pɔ:ʃənəl] adj evenredig
proposal [prə'pouzəl] n voorstel nt
propose [prə'pouz] v voorstellen
proposition [,prɔpə'ziʃən] n voorstel nt
proprietor [prə'praiətə] n eigenaar c
prospect ['prɔspekt] n vooruitzicht nt
prospectus [prə'spektəs] n prospectus c
prosperity [prɔ'sperəti] n voorspoed c, welvaart c
prosperous ['prɔspərəs] adj welvarend

prostitute ['prɔstitju:t] n prostituée c
protect [prə'tekt] v beschermen
protection [prə'tekʃən] n bescherming c
protein ['prouti:n] n eiwit nt
protest[1] ['proutest] n protest nt
protest[2] [prə'test] v protesteren
Protestant ['prɔtistənt] adj protestants
proud [praud] adj trots; hoogmoedig
prove [pru:v] v aantonen, *bewijzen; *blijken
proverb ['prɔvə:b] n spreekwoord nt
provide [prə'vaid] v leveren, verschaffen; **provided that** mits
province ['prɔvins] n provincie c; gewest nt
provincial [prə'vinʃəl] adj provinciaal
provisional [prə'viʒənəl] adj voorlopig
provisions [prə'viʒənz] pl voorraad c
prune [pru:n] n pruim c
psychiatrist [sai'kaiətrist] n psychiater c
psychic ['saikik] adj psychisch
psychoanalyst [,saikou'ænəlist] n analyticus c
psychological [,saikə'lɔdʒikəl] adj psychologisch
psychologist [sai'kɔlədʒist] n psycholoog c
psychology [sai'kɔlədʒi] n psychologie c
pub [pʌb] n café nt; kroeg c
public ['pʌblik] adj publiek, openbaar; algemeen; n publiek nt; ~ **garden** plantsoen nt; ~ **house** café nt
publication [,pʌbli'keiʃən] n publikatie c
publicity [pʌ'blisəti] n reclame c
publish ['pʌbliʃ] v publiceren, *uitgeven
publisher ['pʌbliʃə] n uitgever c
puddle ['pʌdəl] n plas c
pull [pul] v *trekken; ~ **out** *vertrekken; ~ **up** stoppen

pulley ['puli] *n* (pl ~s) katrol *c*
Pullman ['pulmən] *n* slaaprijtuig *nt*
pullover ['pu,louvə] *n* pullover *c*
pulpit ['pulpit] *n* kansel *c*, preekstoel *c*
pulse [pʌls] *n* polsslag *c*, pols *c*
pump [pʌmp] *n* pomp *c*; *v* pompen
punch [pʌntʃ] *v* stompen; *n* vuistslag *c*
punctual ['pʌŋktʃuəl] *adj* stipt, punctueel
puncture ['pʌŋktʃə] *n* lekke band, bandepech *c*
punctured ['pʌŋktʃəd] *adj* lek
punish ['pʌniʃ] *v* straffen
punishment ['pʌniʃmənt] *n* straf *c*
pupil ['pju:pəl] *n* leerling *c*
puppet-show ['pʌpitʃou] *n* poppenkast *c*
purchase ['pə:tʃəs] *v* *kopen; *n* aankoop *c*, koop *c*; ~ **price** koopprijs *c*; ~ **tax** omzetbelasting *c*
purchaser ['pə:tʃəsə] *n* koper *c*
pure [pjuə] *adj* rein, zuiver
purple ['pə:pəl] *adj* paars
purpose ['pə:pəs] *n* bedoeling *c*, doel *nt*; **on** ~ opzettelijk
purse [pə:s] *n* beurs *c*, portemonnee *c*
pursue [pə'sju:] *v* vervolgen; nastreven
pus [pʌs] *n* etter *c*
push [puʃ] *n* zet *c*, duw *c*; *v* duwen; *schuiven; *dringen
push-button ['puʃ,bʌtən] *n* drukknop *c*
***put** [put] *v* plaatsen, leggen, zetten, stoppen; stellen; ~ **away** *opbergen; ~ **off** opschorten; ~ **on** *aantrekken; ~ **out** *uitdoen
puzzle ['pʌzəl] *n* puzzel *c*; raadsel *nt*; *v* in verwarring *brengen; **jigsaw** ~ legpuzzel *c*
puzzling ['pʌzliŋ] *adj* onbegrijpelijk
pyjamas [pə'dʒɑ:məz] *pl* pyjama *c*

Q

quack [kwæk] *n* kwakzalver *c*, charlatan *c*
quail [kweil] *n* (pl ~, ~s) kwartel *c*
quaint [kweint] *adj* raar; ouderwets
qualification [,kwɔlifi'keiʃən] *n* bevoegdheid *c*; voorbehoud *nt*, restrictie *c*
qualified ['kwɔlifaid] *adj* gediplomeerd; bevoegd
qualify ['kwɔlifai] *v* geschikt *zijn
quality ['kwɔləti] *n* kwaliteit *c*; eigenschap *c*
quantity ['kwɔntəti] *n* hoeveelheid *c*; aantal *nt*
quarantine ['kwɔrənti:n] *n* quarantaine *c*
quarrel ['kwɔrəl] *v* twisten, ruzie maken; *n* twist *c*, ruzie *c*
quarry ['kwɔri] *n* steengroeve *c*
quarter ['kwɔ:tə] *n* kwart *nt*; kwartaal *nt*; wijk *c*; ~ **of an hour** kwartier *nt*
quarterly ['kwɔ:təli] *adj* driemaandelijks
quay [ki:] *n* kade *c*
queen [kwi:n] *n* koningin *c*
queer [kwiə] *adj* zonderling, raar; vreemd
query ['kwiəri] *n* vraag *c*; *v* *navragen; betwijfelen
question ['kwestʃən] *n* vraag *c*; kwestie *c*, vraagstuk *nt*; *v* *ondervragen; in twijfel *trekken; ~ **mark** vraagteken *nt*
queue [kju:] *n* rij *c*; *v* in de rij *staan
quick [kwik] *adj* vlug
quick-tempered [,kwik'tempəd] *adj* driftig
quiet ['kwaiət] *adj* stil, kalm, bedaard, rustig; *n* stilte *c*, rust *c*

quilt [kwilt] *n* sprei *c*

quinine [kwi'ni:n] *n* kinine *c*

quit [kwit] *v* *ophouden met, *uitscheiden

quite [kwait] *adv* helemaal; tamelijk, vrij, nogal; zeer, heel

quiz [kwiz] *n* (pl ~zes) quiz *c*

quota ['kwoutə] *n* quota *c*

quotation [kwou'teiʃən] *n* citaat *nt*; ~ **marks** aanhalingstekens *pl*

quote [kwout] *v* citeren, aanhalen

R

rabbit ['ræbit] *n* konijn *nt*

rabies ['reibiz] *n* hondsdolheid *c*

race [reis] *n* wedloop *c*, race *c*; ras *nt*

race-course ['reiskɔ:s] *n* renbaan *c*

race-horse ['reishɔ:s] *n* renpaard *nt*

race-track ['reistræk] *n* renbaan *c*

racial ['reiʃəl] *adj* rassen-

racket ['rækit] *n* kabaal *nt*

racquet ['rækit] *n* racket *nt*

radiator ['reidieitə] *n* radiator *c*

radical ['rædikəl] *adj* radicaal

radio ['reidiou] *n* radio *c*

radish ['rædiʃ] *n* radijs *c*

radius ['reidiəs] *n* (pl radii) straal *c*

raft [rɑ:ft] *n* vlot *nt*

rag [ræg] *n* vod *nt*

rage [reidʒ] *n* razernij *c*, woede *c*; *v* razen, woeden

raid [reid] *n* inval *c*

rail [reil] *n* leuning *c*, reling *c*

railing ['reiliŋ] *n* hek *nt*

railroad ['reilroud] *nAm* spoorbaan *c*, spoorweg *c*

railway ['reilwei] *n* spoorweg *c*, spoorbaan *c*

rain [rein] *n* regen *c*; *v* regenen

rainbow ['reinbou] *n* regenboog *c*

raincoat ['reinkout] *n* regenjas *c*

rainproof ['reinpru:f] *adj* waterdicht

rainy ['reini] *adj* regenachtig

raise [reiz] *v* optillen; verhogen; *grootbrengen, verbouwen, fokken; *heffen; *nAm* loonsverhoging *c*, opslag *c*

raisin ['reizən] *n* rozijn *c*

rake [reik] *n* hark *c*

rally ['ræli] *n* bijeenkomst *c*

ramp [ræmp] *n* glooiing *c*

ramshackle ['ræm,ʃækəl] *adj* gammel

rancid ['rænsid] *adj* ranzig

rang [ræŋ] *v* (p ring)

range [reindʒ] *n* bereik *nt*

range-finder ['reindʒ,faində] *n* afstandsmeter *c*

rank [ræŋk] *n* rang *c*; rij *c*

ransom ['rænsəm] *n* losgeld *nt*

rape [reip] *v* verkrachten

rapid ['ræpid] *adj* vlug, snel

rapids ['ræpidz] *pl* stroomversnelling *c*

rare [rɛə] *adj* zeldzaam

rarely ['rɛəli] *adv* zelden

rascal ['rɑ:skəl] *n* schelm *c*, deugniet *c*

rash [ræʃ] *n* uitslag *c*, huiduitslag *c*; *adj* overhaast, onbezonnen

raspberry ['rɑ:zbəri] *n* framboos *c*

rat [ræt] *n* rat *c*

rate [reit] *n* prijs *c*, tarief *nt*; snelheid *c*; **at any** ~ hoe dan ook, in elk geval; ~ **of exchange** wisselkoers *c*

rather ['rɑ:ðə] *adv* vrij, tamelijk, nogal; liever, eerder

ration ['ræʃən] *n* rantsoen *c*

rattan [ræ'tæn] *n* rotan *c*

raven ['reivən] *n* raaf *c*

raw [rɔ:] *adj* rauw; ~ **material** grondstof *c*

ray [rei] *n* straal *c*

rayon ['reiən] *n* kunstzijde *c*

razor ['reizə] *n* scheerapparaat *nt*

razor-blade ['reizəbleid] *n* scheermesje *nt*

reach [ri:tʃ] *v* bereiken; *n* bereik *nt*

reaction [ri'ækʃən] n reactie c
*read [ri:d] v *lezen
reading-lamp ['ri:diŋlæmp] n leeslamp c
reading-room ['ri:diŋru:m] n leeszaal c
ready ['redi] adj gereed, klaar
ready-made [,redi'meid] adj confectie-real [riəl] adj echt
reality [ri'æləti] n werkelijkheid c
realizable ['riəlaizəbəl] adj haalbaar
realize ['riəlaiz] v beseffen; tot stand *brengen, verwezenlijken
really ['riəli] adv echt, werkelijk; eigenlijk
rear [riə] n achterkant c; v *groot-brengen
rear-light [riə'lait] n achterlicht nt
reason ['ri:zən] n oorzaak c, reden c; verstand nt, rede c; v redeneren
reasonable ['ri:zənəbəl] adj redelijk; billijk
reassure [,ri:ə'ʃuə] v geruststellen
rebate ['ri:beit] n korting c, reductie c
rebellion [ri'beljən] n opstand c, op-roer nt
recall [ri'kɔ:l] v zich herinneren; *te-rugroepen; *herroepen
receipt [ri'si:t] n kwitantie c, reçu nt; ontvangst c
receive [ri'si:v] v *krijgen, *ontvangen
receiver [ri'si:və] n telefoonhoorn c
recent ['ri:sənt] adj recent
recently ['ri:səntli] adv kort geleden, onlangs
reception [ri'sepʃən] n ontvangst c; onthaal nt; ~ office receptie c
receptionist [ri'sepʃənist] n receptioni-ste c
recession [ri'seʃən] n teruggang c
recipe ['resipi] n recept nt
recital [ri'saitəl] n recital nt
reckon ['rekən] v rekenen; beschou-wen; *denken
recognition [,rekəg'niʃən] n erkenning

c
recognize ['rekəgnaiz] v herkennen; erkennen
recollect [,rekə'lekt] v zich herinneren
recommence [,ri:kə'mens] v hervatten
recommend [,rekə'mend] v *aanprij-zen, *aanbevelen; *aanraden
recommendation [,rekəmen'deiʃən] n aanbeveling c
reconciliation [,rekənsili'eiʃən] n ver-zoening c
record[1] ['rekɔ:d] n grammofoonplaat c; record nt; register nt; long-playing ~ langspeelplaat c
record[2] [ri'kɔ:d] v aantekenen
recorder [ri'kɔ:də] n bandrecorder c
recording [ri'kɔ:diŋ] n opname c
record-player ['rekɔ:d,pleiə] n platen-speler c, pick-up c
recover [ri'kʌvə] v *terugvinden; zich herstellen, *genezen
recovery [ri'kʌvəri] n genezing c, her-stel nt
recreation [,rekri'eiʃən] n recreatie c, ontspanning c; ~ centre recreatie-centrum nt; ~ ground speelterrein nt
recruit [ri'kru:t] n rekruut c
rectangle ['rektæŋgəl] n rechthoek c
rectangular [rek'tæŋgulə] adj recht-hoekig
rector ['rektə] n predikant c, dominee c
rectory ['rektəri] n pastorie c
rectum ['rektəm] n endeldarm c
red [red] adj rood
redeem [ri'di:m] v verlossen
reduce [ri'dju:s] v reduceren, vermin-deren, verlagen
reduction [ri'dʌkʃən] n korting c, re-ductie c
redundant [ri'dʌndənt] adj overbodig
reed [ri:d] n riet nt
reef [ri:f] n rif nt

reference ['refrəns] n referentie c, verwijzing c; betrekking c; **with ~ to** met betrekking tot

refer to [ri'fə:] *verwijzen naar

refill ['ri:fil] n vulling c

refinery [ri'fainəri] n raffinaderij c

reflect [ri'flekt] v weerkaatsen

reflection [ri'flekʃən] n weerkaatsing c; spiegelbeeld c

reflector [ri'flektə] n reflector c

reformation [,refə'meiʃən] n reformatie c

refresh [ri'freʃ] v verfrissen

refreshment [ri'freʃmənt] n verfrissing c

refrigerator [ri'fridʒəreitə] n koelkast c, ijskast c

refund[1] [ri'fʌnd] v terugbetalen

refund[2] ['ri:fʌnd] n terugbetaling c

refusal [ri'fju:zəl] n weigering c

refuse[1] [ri'fju:z] v weigeren

refuse[2] ['refju:s] n afval nt

regard [ri'gɑ:d] v beschouwen; *bekijken; n respect nt; **as regards** betreffende, aangaande, wat betreft

regarding [ri'gɑ:diŋ] prep met betrekking tot, betreffende; ten aanzien van

regatta [ri'gætə] n regatta c

régime [rei'ʒi:m] n regime nt

region ['ri:dʒən] n streek c; gebied nt

regional ['ri:dʒənəl] adj plaatselijk

register ['redʒistə] v zich *inschrijven; aantekenen; **registered letter** aangetekende brief

registration [,redʒi'streiʃən] n registratie c; ~ **form** inschrijvingsformulier nt; ~ **number** kenteken nt; ~ **plate** nummerbord nt

regret [ri'gret] v betreuren; n spijt c

regular ['regjulə] adj geregeld, regelmatig; gewoon, normaal

regulate ['regjuleit] v regelen

regulation [,regju'leiʃən] n reglement

nt, voorschrift nt; regeling c

rehabilitation [,ri:hə,bili'teiʃən] n revalidatie c

rehearsal [ri'hə:səl] n repetitie c

rehearse [ri'hə:s] v repeteren

reign [rein] n regering c; v regeren

reimburse [,ri:im'bə:s] v terugbetalen, vergoeden

reindeer ['reindiə] n (pl ~) rendier nt

reject [ri'dʒekt] v *afwijzen, *verwerpen; afkeuren

relate [ri'leit] v vertellen

related [ri'leitid] adj verwant

relation [ri'leiʃən] n relatie c, verband nt; verwante c

relative ['relətiv] n familielid nt; adj betrekkelijk, relatief

relax [ri'læks] v zich ontspannen

relaxation [,rilæk'seiʃən] n ontspanning c

reliable [ri'laiəbəl] adj betrouwbaar

relic ['relik] n relikwie c

relief [ri'li:f] n verademing c, verlichting c; steun c; reliëf nt

relieve [ri'li:v] v verlichten; aflossen

religion [ri'lidʒən] n godsdienst c

religious [ri'lidʒəs] adj godsdienstig

rely on [ri'lai] vertrouwen op

remain [ri'mein] v *blijven; *overblijven

remainder [ri'meində] n restant nt, rest c

remaining [ri'meiniŋ] adj overig, overblijvend

remark [ri'mɑ:k] n opmerking c; v opmerken

remarkable [ri'mɑ:kəbəl] adj opmerkelijk

remedy ['remədi] n geneesmiddel nt; middel nt

remember [ri'membə] v zich herinneren; *onthouden

remembrance [ri'membrəns] n aandenken nt, herinnering c

remind [ri'maind] v herinneren

remit [ri'mit] v overmaken

remittance [ri'mitəns] n storting c

remnant ['remnənt] n overblijfsel nt, restant nt, rest c

remote [ri'mout] adj afgelegen, ver

removal [ri'mu:vəl] n verwijdering c

remove [ri'mu:v] v verwijderen

remunerate [ri'mju:nəreit] v vergoeden

remuneration [ri,mju:nə'reiʃən] n vergoeding c

renew [ri'nju:] v vernieuwen; verlengen

rent [rent] v huren; n huur c

repair [ri'peə] v herstellen, repareren; n herstel nt

reparation [repə'reiʃən] n reparatie c

*repay [ri'pei] v terugbetalen

repayment [ri'peimənt] n terugbetaling c

repeat [ri'pi:t] v herhalen

repellent [ri'pelənt] adj weerzinwekkend, afstotelijk

repentance [ri'pentəns] n berouw nt

repertory ['repətəri] n repertoire nt

repetition [,repə'tiʃən] n herhaling c

replace [ri'pleis] v *vervangen

reply [ri'plai] v antwoorden; n antwoord nt; in ~ als antwoord

report [ri'pɔ:t] v rapporteren; melden; zich aanmelden; n verslag nt, rapport nt

reporter [ri'pɔ:tə] n verslaggever c

represent [,repri'zent] v vertegenwoordigen; voorstellen

representation [,reprizen'teiʃən] n vertegenwoordiging c

representative [,repri'zentətiv] adj representatief

reprimand ['reprima:nd] v berispen

reproach [ri'proutʃ] n verwijt nt; v *verwijten

reproduce [,ri:prə'dju:s] v reproduceren

reproduction [,ri:prə'dʌkʃən] n reproduktie c

reptile ['reptail] n reptiel nt

republic [ri'pʌblik] n republiek c

republican [ri'pʌblikən] adj republikeins

repulsive [ri'pʌlsiv] adj weerzinwekkend

reputation [,repju'teiʃən] n reputatie c; naam c

request [ri'kwest] n verzoek nt; v *verzoeken

require [ri'kwaiə] v vereisen

requirement [ri'kwaiəmənt] n vereiste c

requisite ['rekwizit] adj vereist

rescue ['reskju:] v redden; n redding c

research [ri'sə:tʃ] n onderzoek nt

resemblance [ri'zembləns] n gelijkenis c

resemble [ri'zembəl] v *lijken op

resent [ri'zent] v kwalijk *nemen

reservation [,rezə'veiʃən] n reservering c

reserve [ri'zə:v] v reserveren; *bespreken; n reserve c

reserved [ri'zə:vd] adj gereserveerd

reservoir ['rezəvwa:] n reservoir nt

reside [ri'zaid] v wonen

residence ['rezidəns] n woonplaats c; ~ permit verblijfsvergunning c

resident ['rezidənt] n inwoner c; adj woonachtig; intern

resign [ri'zain] v ontslag *nemen

resignation [,rezig'neiʃən] n ontslagneming c

resin ['rezin] n hars nt/c

resist [ri'zist] v zich verzetten

resistance [ri'zistəns] n verzet nt

resolute ['rezəlu:t] adj resoluut, vastberaden

respect [ri'spekt] n respect nt; ontzag nt, achting c, eerbied c; v respecteren

respectable [ri'spektəbəl] *adj* eerzaam, respectabel

respectful [ri'spektfəl] *adj* eerbiedig

respective [ri'spektiv] *adj* respectievelijk

respiration [,respə'reiʃən] *n* ademhaling *c*

respite ['respait] *n* uitstel *nt*

responsibility [ri,spɔnsə'biləti] *n* verantwoordelijkheid *c*; aansprakelijkheid *c*

responsible [ri'spɔnsəbəl] *adj* verantwoordelijk; aansprakelijk

rest [rest] *n* rust *c*; rest *c*; *v* uitrusten, rusten

restaurant ['restərɔ̃:] *n* restaurant *nt*

restful ['restfəl] *adj* rustig

rest-home ['resthoum] *n* rusthuis *nt*

restless ['restləs] *adj* onrustig; ongedurig

restrain [ri'strein] *v* *inhouden, *weerhouden

restriction [ri'strikʃən] *n* beperking *c*

result [ri'zʌlt] *n* resultaat *nt*; gevolg *nt*; uitslag *c*; *v* resulteren

resume [ri'zju:m] *v* hervatten

résumé ['rezjumei] *n* samenvatting *c*

retail ['ri:teil] *v* in het klein *verkopen*; ~ **trade** kleinhandel *c*, detailhandel *c*

retailer ['ri:teilə] *n* detaillist *c*, kleinhandelaar *c*; wederverkoper *c*

retina ['retinə] *n* netvlies *nt*

retired [ri'taiəd] *adj* gepensioneerd

return [ri'tə:n] *v* *terugkomen, terugkeren; *n* terugkeer *c*; ~ **flight** retourvlucht *c*; ~ **journey** terugreis *c*

reunite [,ri:ju:'nait] *v* herenigen

reveal [ri'vi:l] *v* openbaren, onthullen

revelation [,revə'leiʃən] *n* onthulling *c*

revenge [ri'vendʒ] *n* wraak *c*

revenue ['revənju:] *n* inkomen *nt*

reverse [ri'və:s] *n* tegendeel *nt*; keerzijde *c*; omkeer *c*, tegenslag *c*; *adj*

omgekeerd; *v* *achteruitrijden

review [ri'vju:] *n* bespreking *c*; tijdschrift *nt*

revise [ri'vaiz] *v* *herzien

revision [ri'viʒən] *n* herziening *c*

revival [ri'vaivəl] *n* herstel *nt*

revolt [ri'voult] *v* in opstand *komen; *n* opstand *c*, oproer *nt*

revolting [ri'voultiŋ] *adj* walgelijk, stuitend, weerzinwekkend

revolution [,revə'lu:ʃən] *n* revolutie *c*; omwenteling *c*

revolutionary [,revə'lu:ʃənəri] *adj* revolutionair

revolver [ri'vɔlvə] *n* revolver *c*

revue [ri'vju:] *n* revue *c*

reward [ri'wɔ:d] *n* beloning *c*; *v* belonen

rheumatism ['ru:mətizəm] *n* reumatiek *c*

rhinoceros [rai'nɔsərəs] *n* (pl ~, ~es) neushoorn *c*

rhubarb ['ru:bɑ:b] *n* rabarber *c*

rhyme [raim] *n* rijm *nt*

rhythm ['riðəm] *n* ritme *nt*

rib [rib] *n* rib *c*

ribbon ['ribən] *n* lint *c*

rice [rais] *n* rijst *c*

rich [ritʃ] *adj* rijk

riches ['ritʃiz] *pl* rijkdom *c*

riddle ['ridəl] *n* raadsel *nt*

ride [raid] *n* rit *c*

***ride** [raid] *v* *rijden; *paardrijden

rider ['raidə] *n* ruiter *c*

ridge [ridʒ] *n* bergrug *c*

ridicule ['ridikju:l] *v* bespotten

ridiculous [ri'dikjuləs] *adj* bespottelijk, belachelijk

riding ['raidiŋ] *n* paardesport *c*

riding-school ['raidiŋsku:l] *n* manege *c*

rifle ['raifəl] *v* geweer *c*

right [rait] *n* recht *nt*; *adj* goed, juist; recht; rechts; billijk, rechtvaardig; **all right!** in orde!; * **be** ~ gelijk *hebben; ~ **of way** voorrang *c*

righteous ['raitʃəs] *adj* rechtvaardig

right-hand ['raithænd] *adj* rechter, rechts

rightly ['raitli] *adv* terecht

rim [rim] *n* velg *c*; rand *c*

ring [riŋ] *n* ring *c*; kring *c*; piste *c*

* **ring** [riŋ] *v* bellen; ~ **up** opbellen

rinse [rins] *v* spoelen; *n* spoeling *c*

riot ['raiət] *n* rel *c*

rip [rip] *v* scheuren

ripe [raip] *adj* rijp

rise [raiz] *n* opslag *c*, verhoging *c*; stijging *c*; opkomst *c*

* **rise** [raiz] *v* *opstaan; *opgaan; *stijgen

rising ['raiziŋ] *n* opstand *c*

risk [risk] *n* risico *nt*; gevaar *nt*; *v* wagen

risky ['riski] *adj* gewaagd, riskant

rival ['raivəl] *n* rivaal *c*; concurrent *c*; *v* rivaliseren

rivalry ['raivəlri] *n* rivaliteit *c*; concurrentie *c*

river ['rivə] *n* rivier *c*; ~ **bank** oever *c*

riverside ['rivəsaid] *n* rivieroever *c*

roach [routʃ] *n* (pl ~) blankvoren *c*

road [roud] *n* straat *c*, weg *c*; ~ **fork** *n* tweesprong *c*; ~ **map** wegenkaart *c*; ~ **system** wegennet *nt*; ~ **up** werk in uitvoering

roadhouse ['roudhaus] *n* wegrestaurant *nt*

roadside ['roudsaid] *n* wegkant *c*; ~ **restaurant** wegrestaurant *nt*

roadway ['roudwei] *nAm* rijbaan *c*

roam [roum] *v* *zwerven

roar [rɔ:] *v* loeien, brullen; *n* gebrul *nt*, geraas *c*

roast [roust] *v* *braden, roosteren

rob [rɔb] *v* beroven

robber ['rɔbə] *n* dief *c*

robbery ['rɔbəri] *n* roof *c*, diefstal *c*, beroving *c*

robe [roub] *n* jurk *c*; gewaad *nt*

robin ['rɔbin] *n* roodborstje *nt*

robust [rou'bʌst] *adj* fors

rock [rɔk] *n* rots *c*; *v* schommelen

rocket ['rɔkit] *n* raket *c*

rock-'n-roll [,rɔkən'roul] *n* rock en roll *c*

rocky ['rɔki] *adj* rotsachtig

rod [rɔd] *n* stang *c*, roede *c*

roe [rou] *n* kuit *c*, viskuit *c*

roll [roul] *v* rollen; *n* rol *c*; broodje *nt*

Roman Catholic ['roumən 'kæθəlik] rooms-katholiek

romance [rə'mæns] *n* romance *c*

romantic [rə'mæntik] *adj* romantisch

roof [ru:f] *n* dak *nt*; **thatched** ~ strodak *nt*

room [ru:m] *n* vertrek *nt*, kamer *c*; ruimte *c*, plaats *c*; ~ **and board** kost en inwoning; ~ **service** bediening op de kamer; ~ **temperature** kamertemperatuur *c*

roomy ['ru:mi] *adj* ruim

root [ru:t] *n* wortel *c*

rope [roup] *n* touw *c*

rosary ['rouzəri] *n* rozenkrans *c*

rose [rouz] *n* roos *c*; *adj* roze

rotten ['rɔtən] *adj* rot

rouge [ru:ʒ] *n* rouge *c*/*nt*

rough [rʌf] *adj* ruw

roulette [ru:'let] *n* roulette *c*

round [raund] *adj* rond; *prep* rondom, om; *n* ronde *c*; ~ **trip** *Am* retour

roundabout ['raundəbaut] *n* rotonde *c*

rounded ['raundid] *adj* afgerond

route [ru:t] *n* route *c*

routine [ru:'ti:n] *n* routine *c*

row[1] [rou] *n* rij *c*; *v* roeien

row[2] [rau] *n* ruzie *c*

rowdy ['raudi] *adj* baldadig

rowing-boat ['rouiŋbout] *n* roeiboot *c*

royal ['rɔiəl] *adj* koninklijk

rub [rʌb] *v* *wrijven

rubber ['rʌbə] *n* rubber *nt*; vlakgom

c/nt; ~ **band** elastiek *nt*
rubbish ['rʌbiʃ] *n* afval *nt*; geklets *nt*, onzin *c*; **talk** ~ kletsen
rubbish-bin ['rʌbiʃbin] *n* vuilnisbak *c*
ruby ['ru:bi] *n* robijn *c*
rucksack ['rʌksæk] *n* rugzak *c*
rudder ['rʌdə] *n* roer *nt*
rude [ru:d] *adj* grof
rug [rʌg] *n* kleedje *nt*
ruin ['ru:in] *v* ruïneren; *n* ondergang *c*; **ruins** ruïne *c*
ruination [,ru:i'neiʃən] *n* ondergang *c*
rule [ru:l] *n* regel *c*; bewind *nt*, bestuur *nt*, heerschappij *c*; *v* heersen, regeren; **as a** ~ gewoonlijk, in de regel
ruler ['ru:lə] *n* vorst *c*, heerser *c*; liniaal *c*
Rumania [ru:'meiniə] Roemenië
Rumanian [ru:'meiniən] *adj* Roemeens; *n* Roemeen *c*
rumour ['ru:mə] *n* gerucht *nt*
*****run** [rʌn] *v* rennen; ~ **into** *****tegenkomen
runaway ['rʌnəwei] *n* ontsnapte gevangene
rung [rʌn] *v* (pp ring)
runway ['rʌnwei] *n* startbaan *c*
rural ['ruərəl] *adj* plattelands-
ruse [ru:z] *n* list *c*
rush [rʌʃ] *v* zich haasten; *n* bies *c*
rush-hour ['rʌʃauə] *n* spitsuur *nt*
Russia ['rʌʃə] Rusland
Russian ['rʌʃən] *adj* Russisch; *n* Rus *c*
rust [rʌst] *n* roest *nt*
rustic ['rʌstik] *adj* rustiek
rusty ['rʌsti] *adj* roestig

S

saccharin ['sækərin] *n* sacharine *c*
sack [sæk] *n* zak *c*
sacred ['seikrid] *adj* heilig
sacrifice ['sækrifais] *n* offer *nt*; *v* offeren
sacrilege ['sækrilidʒ] *n* heiligschennis *c*
sad [sæd] *adj* bedroefd; verdrietig, droevig, treurig
saddle ['sædəl] *n* zadel *nt*
sadness ['sædnəs] *n* bedroefdheid *c*
safe [seif] *adj* veilig; *n* brandkast *c*, kluis *c*
safety ['seifti] *n* veiligheid *c*
safety-belt ['seiftibelt] *n* veiligheidsgordel *c*
safety-pin ['seiftipin] *n* veiligheidsspeld *c*
safety-razor ['seifti,reizə] *n* scheerapparaat *nt*
sail [seil] *v* *****bevaren, *****varen; *n* zeil *nt*
sailing-boat ['seiliŋbout] *n* zeilboot *c*
sailor ['seilə] *n* matroos *c*
saint [seint] *n* heilige *c*
salad ['sæləd] *n* sla *c*
salad-oil ['sælədɔil] *n* slaolie *c*
salary ['sæləri] *n* loon *nt*, salaris *nt*
sale [seil] *n* verkoop *c*; **clearance** ~ opruiming *c*; **for** ~ te koop; **sales** uitverkoop *c*; **sales tax** omzetbelasting *c*
saleable ['seiləbəl] *adj* verkoopbaar
salesgirl ['seilzgə:l] *n* verkoopster *c*
salesman ['seilzmən] *n* (pl -men) verkoper *c*
salmon ['sæmən] *n* (pl ~) zalm *c*
salon ['sælɔ̃:] *n* salon *c*
saloon [sə'lu:n] *n* bar *c*
salt [sɔ:lt] *n* zout *nt*
salt-cellar ['sɔ:lt,selə] *n* zoutvaatje *nt*
salty ['sɔ:lti] *adj* zout

salute [sə'lu:t] v groeten

salve [sɑ:v] n zalf c

same [seim] adj zelfde

sample ['sɑ:mpəl] n monster nt

sanatorium [,sænə'tɔ:riəm] n (pl ~s, -ria) sanatorium nt

sand [sænd] n zand nt

sandal ['sændəl] n sandaal c

sandpaper ['sænd,peipə] n schuurpapier nt

sandwich ['sænwidʒ] n boterham c

sandy ['sændi] adj zanderig

sanitary ['sænitəri] adj sanitair; ~ towel maandverband nt

sapphire ['sæfaiə] n saffier nt

sardine [sɑ:'di:n] n sardine c

satchel ['sætʃəl] n schooltas c

satellite ['sætəlait] n satelliet c

satin ['sætin] n satijn nt

satisfaction [,sætis'fækʃən] n bevrediging c, voldoening c

satisfy ['sætisfai] v bevredigen; satisfied voldaan, tevreden

Saturday ['sætədi] zaterdag c

sauce [sɔ:s] n saus c

saucepan ['sɔ:spən] n steelpan c

saucer ['sɔ:sə] n schoteltje nt

Saudi Arabia [,saudi'reibiə] Saoedi-Arabië

Saudi Arabian [,saudi'reibiən] adj Saoedi-Arabisch

sauna ['sɔ:nə] n sauna c

sausage ['sɔsidʒ] n worst c

savage ['sævidʒ] adj wild

save [seiv] v redden; sparen

savings ['seiviŋz] pl spaargeld nt; ~ bank spaarbank c

saviour ['seivjə] n redder c

savoury ['seivəri] adj smakelijk; pikant

saw[1] [sɔ:] v (p see)

saw[2] [sɔ:] n zaag c

sawdust ['sɔ:dʌst] n zaagsel nt

saw-mill ['sɔ:mil] n houtzagerij c

*say [sei] v *zeggen

scaffolding ['skæfəldiŋ] n steigers pl

scale [skeil] n schaal c; toonladder c; schub c; scales pl weegschaal c

scandal ['skændəl] n schandaal nt

Scandinavia [,skændi'neiviə] Scandinavië

Scandinavian [,skændi'neiviən] adj Scandinavisch; n Scandinaviër c

scapegoat ['skeipgout] n zondebok c

scar [skɑ:] n litteken nt

scarce [skɛəs] adj schaars

scarcely ['skɛəsli] adv nauwelijks

scarcity ['skɛəsəti] n schaarste c

scare [skɛə] v *doen schrikken; n schrik c

scarf [skɑ:f] n (pl ~s, scarves) das c, sjaal c

scarlet ['skɑ:lət] adj vuurrood

scary ['skɛəri] adj griezelig

scatter ['skætə] v verspreiden

scene [si:n] n scène c

scenery ['si:nəri] n landschap nt

scenic ['si:nik] adj schilderachtig

scent [sent] n geur c

schedule ['ʃedju:l] n dienstregeling c, rooster nt

scheme [ski:m] n schema nt; plan nt

scholar ['skɔlə] n geleerde c; leerling c

scholarship ['skɔləʃip] n studiebeurs c

school [sku:l] n school c

schoolboy ['sku:lbɔi] n schooljongen c

schoolgirl ['sku:lgə:l] n schoolmeisje nt

schoolmaster ['sku:l,mɑ:stə] n onderwijzer c, meester c

schoolteacher ['sku:l,ti:tʃə] n onderwijzer c

science ['saiəns] n wetenschap c

scientific [,saiən'tifik] adj wetenschappelijk

scientist ['saiəntist] n geleerde c

scissors ['sizəz] pl schaar c

scold [skould] v berispen; *schelden

scooter ['sku:tə] n scooter c; autoped c

score [skɔ:] n stand c; v scoren

scorn [skɔ:n] n hoon c, verachting c; v verachten

Scot [skɔt] n Schot c

Scotch [skɔtʃ] adj Schots; scotch tape plakband nt

Scotland ['skɔtlənd] Schotland

Scottish ['skɔtiʃ] adj Schots

scout [skaut] n padvinder c

scrap [skræp] n snipper c

scrap-book ['skræpbuk] n plakboek nt

scrape [skreip] v schrappen

scrap-iron ['skræpaiən] n schroot nt

scratch [skrætʃ] v krassen, krabben; n kras c, schram c

scream [skri:m] v gillen, schreeuwen; n gil c, schreeuw c

screen [skri:n] n scherm nt; beeldscherm nt

screw [skru:] n schroef c; v schroeven

screw-driver ['skru:,draivə] n schroevedraaier c

scrub [skrʌb] v schrobben; n struik c

sculptor ['skʌlptə] n beeldhouwer c

sculpture ['skʌlptʃə] n beeldhouwwerk nt

sea [si:] n zee c

sea-bird ['si:bə:d] n zeevogel c

sea-coast ['si:koust] n zeekust c

seagull ['si:gʌl] n meeuw c, zeemeeuw c

seal [si:l] n zegel nt; rob c, zeehond c

seam [si:m] n naad c

seaman ['si:mən] n (pl -men) zeeman c

seamless ['si:mləs] adj naadloos

seaport ['si:pɔ:t] n zeehaven c

search [sə:tʃ] v *zoeken; fouilleren, *doorzoeken

searchlight ['sə:tʃlait] n schijnwerper c

seascape ['si:skeip] n zeegezicht nt

sea-shell ['si:ʃel] n zeeschelp c

seashore ['si:ʃɔ:] n kust c

seasick ['si:sik] adj zeeziek

seasickness ['si:,siknəs] n zeeziekte c

seaside ['si:said] n kust c; ~ resort badplaats c

season ['si:zən] n jaargetijde nt, seizoen nt; high ~ hoogseizoen nt; low ~ naseizoen nt; off ~ buiten het seizoen

season-ticket ['si:zən,tikit] n abonnementskaart c

seat [si:t] n stoel c; plaats c, zitplaats c; zetel c

seat-belt ['si:tbelt] n veiligheidsgordel c

sea-urchin ['si:,ə:tʃin] n zeeëgel c

sea-water ['si:,wɔ:tə] n zeewater nt

second ['sekənd] num tweede; n seconde c; tel c

secondary ['sekəndəri] adj secundair, ondergeschikt; ~ school middelbare school

second-hand [,sekənd'hænd] adj tweedehands

secret ['si:krət] n geheim nt; adj geheim

secretary ['sekrətri] n secretaresse c; secretaris c

section ['sekʃən] n sectie c; afdeling c, vak nt

secure [si'kjuə] adj veilig; v bemachtigen

security [si'kjuərəti] n veiligheid c; pand nt

sedate [si'deit] adj kalm

sedative ['sedətiv] n kalmerend middel

seduce [si'dju:s] v verleiden

* see [si:] v *zien; *begrijpen, *inzien; ~ to zorgen voor

seed [si:d] n zaad nt

* seek [si:k] v *zoeken

seem [si:m] v *lijken, *schijnen

seen [si:n] v (pp see)

seesaw ['si:sɔ:] *n* wip *c*

seize [si:z] *v* *grijpen

seldom ['seldəm] *adv* zelden

select [si'lekt] *v* selecteren, *uitkiezen; *adj* select, uitgelezen

selection [si'lekʃən] *n* keuze *c*, selectie *c*

self-centred [,self'sentəd] *adj* egocentrisch

self-employed [,selfim'plɔid] *adj* zelfstandig

self-evident [,sel'fevidənt] *adj* vanzelfsprekend

self-government [,self'gʌvəmənt] *n* zelfbestuur *nt*

selfish ['selfiʃ] *adj* egoïstisch

selfishness ['selfiʃnəs] *n* egoïsme *nt*

self-service [,self'sə:vis] *n* zelfbediening *c*; ~ **restaurant** zelfbedieningsrestaurant *nt*

* **sell** [sel] *v* *verkopen

semblance ['sembləns] *n* schijn *c*

semi- ['semi] half

semicircle ['semi,sə:kəl] *n* halve cirkel

semi-colon [,semi'koulən] *n* puntkomma *c*

senate ['senət] *n* senaat *c*

senator ['senətə] *n* senator *c*

* **send** [send] *v* sturen, *zenden; ~ **back** terugsturen, *terugzenden; ~ **for** *laten halen; ~ **off** versturen

senile ['si:nail] *adj* seniel

sensation [sen'seiʃən] *n* sensatie *c*; gewaarwording *c*, gevoel *nt*

sensational [sen'seiʃənəl] *adj* sensationeel, opzienbarend

sense [sens] *n* zintuig *nt*; gezond verstand, rede *c*; zin *c*, betekenis *c*; *v* voelen; ~ **of honour** eergevoel *nt*

senseless ['sensləs] *adj* zinloos

sensible ['sensəbəl] *adj* verstandig

sensitive ['sensitiv] *adj* gevoelig

sentence ['sentəns] *n* zin *c*; vonnis *nt*; *v* veroordelen

sentimental [,senti'mentəl] *adj* sentimenteel

separate¹ ['sepəreit] *v* *scheiden

separate² ['sepərət] *adj* afzonderlijk, gescheiden

separately ['sepərətli] *adv* apart

September [sep'tembə] september

septic ['septik] *adj* septisch; * **become** ~ *ontsteken

sequel ['si:kwəl] *n* vervolg *nt*

sequence ['si:kwəns] *n* volgorde *c*; reeks *c*

serene [sə'ri:n] *adj* kalm; helder

serial ['siəriəl] *n* feuilleton *nt*

series ['siəri:z] *n* (pl ~) reeks *c*, serie *c*

serious ['siəriəs] *adj* serieus, ernstig

seriousness ['siəriəsnəs] *n* ernst *c*

sermon ['sə:mən] *n* preek *c*

serum ['siərəm] *n* serum *nt*

servant ['sə:vənt] *n* bediende *c*

serve [sə:v] *v* bedienen

service ['sə:vis] *n* dienst *c*; bediening *c*; ~ **charge** bedieningsgeld *nt*; ~ **station** benzinestation *nt*

serviette [,sə:vi'et] *n* servet *nt*

session ['seʃən] *n* zitting *c*

set [set] *n* stel *nt*, groep *c*

* **set** [set] *v* zetten; ~ **menu** vast menu; ~ **out** *vertrekken

setting ['setiŋ] *n* omgeving *c*; ~ **lotion** haarversteviger *c*

settle ['setəl] *v* afhandelen, regelen; ~ **down** zich vestigen

settlement ['setəlmənt] *n* regeling *c*, schikking *c*, overeenkomst *c*

seven ['sevən] *num* zeven

seventeen [,sevən'ti:n] *num* zeventien

seventeenth [,sevən'ti:nθ] *num* zeventiende

seventh ['sevənθ] *num* zevende

seventy ['sevənti] *num* zeventig

several ['sevərəl] *adj* ettelijk, verscheidene

severe [si'viə] *adj* hevig, streng, ernstig

sew [sou] *v* naaien; ~ **up** hechten
sewer ['su:ə] *n* riool *nt*
sewing-machine ['souiŋmə,ʃi:n] *n* naaimachine *c*
sex [seks] *n* geslacht *nt*; sex *c*
sexton ['sekstən] *n* koster *c*
sexual ['sekʃuəl] *adj* seksueel
sexuality [,sekʃu'æləti] *n* seksualiteit *c*
shade [ʃeid] *n* schaduw *c*; tint *c*
shadow ['ʃædou] *n* schaduw *c*
shady ['ʃeidi] *adj* schaduwrijk
***shake** [ʃeik] *v* schudden
shaky ['ʃeiki] *adj* gammel
***shall** [ʃæl] *v* *zullen; *moeten
shallow ['ʃælou] *adj* ondiep
shame [ʃeim] *n* schaamte *c*; schande *c*; shame! foei!
shampoo [ʃæm'pu:] *n* shampoo *c*
shamrock ['ʃæmrɔk] *n* klaver *c*
shape [ʃeip] *n* vorm *c*; *v* vormen
share [ʃɛə] *v* delen; *n* deel *nt*; aandeel *nt*
shark [ʃɑ:k] *n* haai *c*
sharp [ʃɑ:p] *adj* scherp
sharpen ['ʃɑ:pən] *v* *slijpen
shave [ʃeiv] *v* zich *scheren
shaver ['ʃeivə] *n* scheerapparaat *nt*
shaving-brush ['ʃeiviŋbrʌʃ] *n* scheerkwast *c*
shaving-cream ['ʃeiviŋkri:m] *n* scheercrème *c*
shaving-soap ['ʃeiviŋsoup] *n* scheerzeep *c*
shawl [ʃɔ:l] *n* omslagdoek *c*, sjaal *c*
she [ʃi:] *pron* ze
shed [ʃed] *n* schuur *c*
***shed** [ʃed] *v* storten; verspreiden
sheep [ʃi:p] *n* (pl ~) schaap *nt*
sheer [ʃiə] *adj* absoluut, puur; dun, doorzichtig
sheet [ʃi:t] *n* laken *nt*; blad *nt*; plaat *c*
shelf [ʃelf] *n* (pl shelves) plank *c*
shell [ʃel] *n* schelp *c*; dop *c*

shellfish ['ʃelfiʃ] *n* schaaldier *nt*
shelter ['ʃeltə] *n* beschutting *c*, schuilplaats *c*; *v* beschutten
shepherd ['ʃepəd] *n* herder *c*
shift [ʃift] *n* ploeg *c*
***shine** [ʃain] *v* *schijnen; glanzen, *blinken
ship [ʃip] *n* schip *nt*; *v* verschepen; **shipping line** scheepvaartlijn *c*
shipowner ['ʃi,pounə] *n* reder *c*
shipyard ['ʃipjɑ:d] *n* scheepswerf *c*
shirt [ʃə:t] *n* hemd *nt*, overhemd *nt*
shiver ['ʃivə] *v* bibberen, rillen; *n* rilling *c*
shivery ['ʃivəri] *adj* rillerig
shock [ʃɔk] *n* schok *c*; *v* schokken; ~ **absorber** schokbreker *c*
shocking ['ʃɔkiŋ] *adj* schokkend
shoe [ʃu:] *n* schoen *c*; **gym shoes** gymschoenen *pl*; ~ **polish** schoensmeer *c*
shoe-lace ['ʃu:leis] *n* schoenveter *c*
shoemaker ['ʃu:,meikə] *n* schoenmaker *c*
shoe-shop ['ʃu:ʃɔp] *n* schoenwinkel *c*
shook [ʃuk] *v* (p shake)
***shoot** [ʃu:t] *v* *schieten
shop [ʃɔp] *n* winkel *c*; *v* winkelen; ~ **assistant** verkoper *c*; **shopping bag** boodschappentas *c*; **shopping centre** winkelcentrum *nt*
shopkeeper ['ʃɔp,ki:pə] *n* winkelier *c*
shop-window [,ʃɔp'windou] *n* etalage *c*
shore [ʃɔ:] *n* oever *c*, kust *c*
short [ʃɔ:t] *adj* kort; klein; ~ **circuit** kortsluiting *c*
shortage ['ʃɔ:tidʒ] *n* tekort *nt*, gebrek *nt*
shortcoming ['ʃɔ:t,kʌmiŋ] *n* tekortkoming *c*
shorten ['ʃɔ:tən] *v* verkorten
shorthand ['ʃɔ:thænd] *n* stenografie *c*
shortly ['ʃɔ:tli] *adv* weldra, binnenkort, spoedig

shorts [ʃɔ:ts] pl korte broek; plAm onderbroek c

short-sighted [ˌʃɔ:t'saitid] adj bijziend

shot [ʃɔt] n schot nt; injectie c; opname c

* **should** [ʃud] v *moeten

shoulder [ˈʃouldə] n schouder c

shout [ʃaut] v schreeuwen, *roepen; n schreeuw c

shovel [ˈʃʌvəl] n schop c

show [ʃou] n voorstelling c; tentoonstelling c

* **show** [ʃou] v tonen; *laten zien, tentoonstellen; aantonen

show-case [ˈʃoukeis] n vitrine c

shower [ˈʃauə] n douche c; bui c, regenbui c

showroom [ˈʃouru:m] n toonzaal c

shriek [ʃri:k] v gillen; n gil c

shrimp [ʃrimp] n garnaal c

shrine [ʃrain] n heiligdom nt, schrijn c

* **shrink** [ʃriŋk] v *krimpen

shrinkproof [ˈʃriŋkpru:f] adj krimpvrij

shrub [ʃrʌb] n struik c

shudder [ˈʃʌdə] n rilling c

shuffle [ˈʃʌfəl] v schudden

* **shut** [ʃʌt] v *sluiten; **shut** dicht, gesloten; ~ **in** *insluiten

shutter [ˈʃʌtə] n luik nt, blind nt

shy [ʃai] adj schuw, verlegen

shyness [ˈʃainəs] n verlegenheid c

Siam [sai'æm] Siam

Siamese [ˌsaiə'mi:z] adj Siamees; n Siamees c

sick [sik] adj ziek; misselijk

sickness [ˈsiknəs] n ziekte c; misselijkheid c

side [said] n kant c, zijde c; partij c; **one-sided** adj eenzijdig

sideburns [ˈsaidbə:nz] pl bakkebaarden pl

sidelight [ˈsaidlait] n zijlicht nt

side-street [ˈsaidstri:t] n zijstraat c

sidewalk [ˈsaidwɔ:k] nAm stoep c,

trottoir nt

sideways [ˈsaidweiz] adv opzij

siege [si:dʒ] n belegering c

sieve [siv] n zeef c; v zeven

sift [sift] v zeven

sight [sait] n zicht nt; gezicht nt, aanblik c; bezienswaardigheid c

sign [sain] n teken nt; gebaar nt, wenk c; v ondertekenen, tekenen

signal [ˈsignəl] n signaal nt; sein nt, teken nt; v seinen

signature [ˈsignətʃə] n handtekening c

significant [sigˈnifikənt] adj veelbetekenend

signpost [ˈsainpoust] n wegwijzer c

silence [ˈsailəns] n stilte c; v tot zwijgen *brengen

silencer [ˈsailənsə] n knalpot c

silent [ˈsailənt] adj zwijgend, stil; * **be** ~ *zwijgen

silk [silk] n zijde c

silken [ˈsilkən] adj zijden

silly [ˈsili] adj mal, dwaas

silver [ˈsilvə] n zilver nt; zilveren

silversmith [ˈsilvəsmiθ] n zilversmid c

silverware [ˈsilvəweə] n zilverwerk nt

similar [ˈsimilə] adj dergelijk, overeenkomstig

similarity [ˌsimiˈlærəti] n gelijkenis c

simple [ˈsimpəl] adj simpel, eenvoudig; gewoon

simply [ˈsimpli] adv eenvoudig, gewoonweg

simulate [ˈsimjuleit] v huichelen

simultaneous [ˌsiməlˈteiniəs] adj gelijktijdig; **simultaneously** adv tegelijkertijd

sin [sin] n zonde c

since [sins] prep sedert; adv sindsdien; conj sinds; aangezien

sincere [sinˈsiə] adj oprecht

sinew [ˈsinju:] n pees c

* **sing** [siŋ] v *zingen

singer [ˈsiŋə] n zanger c; zangeres c

single ['siŋgəl] *adj* enkel; ongetrouwd

singular ['siŋgjulə] *n* enkelvoud *nt*; *adj* eigenaardig

sinister ['sinistə] *adj* onheilspellend

sink [siŋk] *n* gootsteen *c*

*sink [siŋk] *v* *zinken

sip [sip] *n* slokje *nt*

siphon ['saifən] *n* sifon *c*

sir [sə:] meneer

siren ['saiərən] *n* sirene *c*

sister ['sistə] *n* zuster *c*, zus *c*

sister-in-law ['sistərinlɔ:] *n* (pl sisters-) schoonzuster *c*

*sit [sit] *v* *zitten; ~ **down** *gaan zitten

site [sait] *n* plaats *c*; ligging *c*

sitting-room ['sitiŋru:m] *n* zitkamer *c*

situated ['sitʃueitid] *adj* gelegen

situation [,sitʃu'eiʃən] *n* situatie *c*; ligging *c*

six [siks] *num* zes

sixteen [,siks'ti:n] *num* zestien

sixteenth [,siks'ti:nθ] *num* zestiende

sixth [siksθ] *num* zesde

sixty ['siksti] *num* zestig

size [saiz] *n* grootte *c*, maat *c*; afmeting *c*, omvang *c*; formaat *nt*

skate [skeit] *v* schaatsen; *n* schaats *c*

skating-rink ['skeitiŋriŋk] *n* kunstijsbaan *c*, ijsbaan *c*

skeleton ['skelitən] *n* skelet *nt*, geraamte *nt*

sketch [sketʃ] *n* tekening *c*, schets *c*; *v* tekenen, schetsen

sketch-book ['sketʃbuk] *n* schetsboek *nt*

ski¹ [ski:] *v* skiën

ski² [ski:] *n* (pl ~, ~s) ski *c*; ~ **boots** skischoenen *pl*; ~ **pants** skibroek *c*; ~ **poles** *Am* skistokken *pl*; ~ **sticks** skistokken *pl*

skid [skid] *v* slippen

skier ['ski:ə] *n* skiër *c*

skilful ['skilfəl] *adj* bekwaam, behen-

dig, vaardig

ski-lift ['ski:lift] *n* skilift *c*

skill [skil] *n* vaardigheid *c*

skilled [skild] *adj* vaardig, vakkundig

skin [skin] *n* vel *nt*, huid *c*; schil *c*; ~ **cream** huidcrème *c*

skip [skip] *v* huppelen; *overslaan

skirt [skə:t] *n* rok *c*

skull [skʌl] *n* schedel *c*

sky [skai] *n* hemel *c*; lucht *c*

skyscraper ['skai,skreipə] *n* wolkenkrabber *c*

slack [slæk] *adj* traag

slacks [slæks] *pl* broek *c*

slam [slæm] *v* *dichtslaan

slander ['slɑ:ndə] *n* laster *c*

slant [slɑ:nt] *v* hellen

slanting ['slɑ:ntiŋ] *adj* schuin, hellend, scheef

slap [slæp] *v* *slaan; *n* klap *c*

slate [sleit] *n* lei *nt*

slave [sleiv] *n* slaaf *c*

sledge [sledʒ] *n* slee *c*, slede *c*

sleep [sli:p] *n* slaap *c*

*sleep [sli:p] *v* *slapen

sleeping-bag ['sli:piŋbæg] *n* slaapzak *c*

sleeping-car ['sli:piŋka:] *n* slaapwagen *c*

sleeping-pill ['sli:piŋpil] *n* slaappil *c*

sleepless ['sli:pləs] *adj* slapeloos

sleepy ['sli:pi] *adj* slaperig

sleeve [sli:v] *n* mouw *c*; hoes *c*

sleigh [slei] *n* slee *c*, ar *c*

slender ['slendə] *adj* slank

slice [slais] *n* snee *c*

slide [slaid] *n* glijbaan *c*; dia *c*

*slide [slaid] *v* *glijden

slight [slait] *adj* licht; gering

slim [slim] *adj* slank; *v* vermageren

slip [slip] *v* slippen, *uitglijden; ontglippen; *n* misstap *c*; onderrok *c*

slipper ['slipə] *n* slof *c*, pantoffel *c*

slippery ['slipəri] *adj* glibberig, glad

slogan ['slougən] *n* leus *c*, slagzin *c*

slope [sloup] *n* helling *c*; *v* glooien

sloping ['sloupiŋ] *adj* afhellend

sloppy ['slɔpi] *adj* slordig

slot [slɔt] *n* gleuf *c*

slot-machine ['slɔt,məʃi:n] *n* automaat *c*

slovenly ['slʌvənli] *adj* slordig

slow [slou] *adj* traag, langzaam; ~ **down** vertragen; afremmen

sluice [slu:s] *n* sluis *c*

slum [slʌm] *n* achterbuurt *c*

slump [slʌmp] *n* prijsdaling *c*

slush [slʌʃ] *n* sneeuwslik *nt*

sly [slai] *adj* listig

smack [smæk] *v* *slaan; *n* klap *c*

small [smɔ:l] *adj* klein; gering

smallpox ['smɔ:lpɔks] *n* pokken *pl*

smart [smɑ:t] *adj* chic; knap, pienter

smell [smel] *n* geur *c*

***smell** [smel] *v* *ruiken; *stinken

smelly ['smeli] *adj* stinkend

smile [smail] *v* glimlachen; *n* glimlach *c*

smith [smiθ] *n* smid *c*

smoke [smouk] *v* roken; *n* rook *c*; **no smoking** verboden te roken

smoker ['smoukə] *n* roker *c*; rookcoupé *c*

smoking-compartment ['smoukiŋkəm,pa:tmənt] *n* coupé voor rokers

smoking-room ['smoukiŋru:m] *n* rookkamer *c*

smooth [smu:ð] *adj* effen, vlak, glad; zacht

smuggle ['smʌgəl] *v* smokkelen

snack [snæk] *n* snack *c*

snack-bar ['snækba:] *n* snackbar *c*

snail [sneil] *n* slak *c*

snake [sneik] *n* slang *c*

snapshot ['snæpʃɔt] *n* kiekje *nt*, momentopname *c*

sneakers ['sni:kəz] *plAm* gymschoenen *pl*

sneeze [sni:z] *v* niezen

sniper ['snaipə] *n* sluipschutter *c*

snooty ['snu:ti] *adj* verwaand

snore [snɔ:] *v* snurken

snorkel ['snɔ:kəl] *n* snorkel *c*

snout [snaut] *n* snuit *c*

snow [snou] *n* sneeuw *c*; *v* sneeuwen

snowstorm ['snoustɔ:m] *n* sneeuwstorm *c*

snowy ['snoui] *adj* besneeuwd

so [sou] *conj* dus; *adv* zo; dermate; **and ~ on** enzovoort; ~ **far** tot zover; ~ **that** zodat, opdat

soak [souk] *v* weken, doorweken

soap [soup] *n* zeep *c*; ~ **powder** zeeppoeder *nt*

sober ['soubə] *adj* nuchter; bezonnen

so-called [,sou'kɔ:ld] *adj* zogenaamd

soccer ['sɔkə] *n* voetbal *nt*; ~ **team** elftal *nt*

social ['souʃəl] *adj* maatschappelijk, sociaal

socialism ['souʃəlizəm] *n* socialisme *nt*

socialist ['souʃəlist] *adj* socialistisch; *n* socialist *c*

society [sə'saiəti] *n* maatschappij *c*; genootschap *nt*, vereniging *c*; gezelschap *nt*

sock [sɔk] *n* sok *c*

socket ['sɔkit] *n* fitting *c*

soda-water ['soudə,wɔ:tə] *n* spuitwater *nt*, sodawater *nt*

sofa ['soufə] *n* sofa *c*

soft [sɔft] *adj* zacht; ~ **drink** frisdrank *c*

soften ['sɔfən] *v* verzachten

soil [sɔil] *n* grond *c*; bodem *c*, aarde *c*

soiled [sɔild] *adj* bevuild

sold [sould] *v* (p, pp sell); ~ **out** uitverkocht

solder ['sɔldə] *v* solderen

soldering-iron ['sɔldəriŋaiən] *n* soldeerbout *c*

soldier ['souldʒə] *n* militair *c*, soldaat *c*

sole¹ [soul] *adj* enig

sole² [soul] *n* zool *c* ; tong *c*

solely ['soulli] *adv* uitsluitend

solemn ['soləm] *adj* plechtig

solicitor [sə'lisitə] *n* raadsman *c*, advocaat *c*

solid ['solid] *adj* stevig, solide; massief; *n* vaste stof

soluble ['soljubəl] *adj* oplosbaar

solution [sə'lu:ʃən] *n* oplossing *c*

solve [solv] *v* oplossen

sombre ['sombə] *adj* somber

some [sʌm] *adj* enige, enkele; *pron* sommige; iets; ~ **day** eens; ~ **more** nog wat; ~ **time** eens

somebody ['sʌmbədi] *pron* iemand

somehow ['sʌmhau] *adv* op de een of andere manier

someone ['sʌmwʌn] *pron* iemand

something ['sʌmθiŋ] *pron* iets

sometimes ['sʌmtaimz] *adv* soms

somewhat ['sʌmwɔt] *adv* enigszins

somewhere ['sʌmweə] *adv* ergens

son [sʌn] *n* zoon *c*

song [sɔŋ] *n* lied *nt*

son-in-law ['sʌninlɔ:] *n* (pl sons-) schoonzoon *c*

soon [su:n] *adv* vlug, gauw, weldra, spoedig; **as** ~ **as** zodra

sooner ['su:nə] *adv* liever

sore [sɔ:] *adj* pijnlijk, zeer; *n* zere plek; zweer *c* ; ~ **throat** keelpijn *c*

sorrow ['sorou] *n* droefheid, leed *nt*, verdriet *nt*

sorry ['sori] *adj* bedroefd; **sorry!** neem me niet kwalijk!, sorry!, pardon!

sort [sɔ:t] *v* sorteren, rangschikken; *n* slag *nt*, soort *c/nt* ; **all sorts of** allerlei

soul [soul] *n* ziel *c* ; geest *c*

sound [saund] *n* klank *c*, geluid *nt* ; *v* *klinken; *adj* degelijk

soundproof ['saundpru:f] *adj* geluiddicht

soup [su:p] *n* soep *c*

soup-plate ['su:ppleit] *n* soepbord *nt*

soup-spoon ['su:pspu:n] *n* soeplepel *c*

sour [sauə] *adj* zuur

source [sɔ:s] *n* bron *c*

south [sauθ] *n* zuid *c*, zuiden *nt* ; **South Pole** zuidpool *c*

South Africa [sauθ 'æfrikə] Zuid-Afrika

south-east [,sauθ'i:st] *n* zuidoosten *nt*

southerly ['sʌðəli] *adj* zuidelijk

southern ['sʌðən] *adj* zuidelijk

south-west [,sauθ'west] *n* zuidwesten *nt*

souvenir ['su:vəniə] *n* souvenir *nt*

sovereign ['sovrin] *n* vorst *c*

Soviet ['souviət] *adj* Sovjet-

Soviet Union ['souviət 'ju:njən] Sovjet-Unie

*sow** [sou] *v* zaaien

spa [spa:] *n* geneeskrachtige bron

space [speis] *n* ruimte *c* ; afstand *c*, tussenruimte *c* ; *v* spatiëren

spacious ['speiʃəs] *adj* ruim

spade [speid] *n* schop *c*, spade *c*

Spain [spein] Spanje

Spaniard ['spænjəd] *n* Spanjaard *c*

Spanish ['spæniʃ] *adj* Spaans

spanking ['spæŋkiŋ] *n* pak slaag

spanner ['spænə] *n* schroefsleutel *c*

spare [speə] *adj* reserve-, extra; *v* missen; ~ **part** onderdeel *nt* ; ~ **room** logeerkamer *c* ; ~ **time** vrije tijd; ~ **tyre** reserveband *c* ; ~ **wheel** reservewiel *nt*

spark [spa:k] *n* vonk *c*

sparking-plug ['spa:kiŋplʌg] *n* bougie *c*

sparkling ['spa:kliŋ] *adj* fonkelend; mousserend

sparrow ['spærou] *n* mus *c*

*speak** [spi:k] *v* *spreken

spear [spiə] *n* speer *c*

special ['speʃəl] *adj* bijzonder, spe-

ciaal; ~ **delivery** expresse-
specialist ['speʃəlist] n specialist c
speciality [,speʃi'æləti] n specialiteit c
specialize ['speʃəlaiz] v zich specialiseren
specially ['speʃəli] adv in het bijzonder
species ['spi:ʃi:z] n (pl ~) soort c/nt
specific [spə'sifik] adj specifiek
specimen ['spesimən] n exemplaar nt,
specimen nt
speck [spek] n spat c
spectacle ['spektəkəl] n schouwspel
nt; **spectacles** bril c
spectator [spek'teitə] n kijker c, toeschouwer c
speculate ['spekjuleit] v speculeren
speech [spi:tʃ] n spraak c; rede c, toespraak c; taal c
speechless ['spi:tʃləs] adj sprakeloos
speed [spi:d] n snelheid c; vaart c,
spoed c; **cruising** ~ kruissnelheid
c; ~ **limit** maximum snelheid, snelheidsbeperking c
* **speed** [spi:d] v hard *rijden; te hard
*rijden
speeding ['spi:diŋ] n snelheidsovertreding c
speedometer [spi:'dɔmitə] n snelheidsmeter c
spell [spel] n betovering c
* **spell** [spel] v spellen
spelling ['speliŋ] n spelling c
* **spend** [spend] v *uitgeven, besteden;
*doorbrengen
sphere [sfiə] n bol c; sfeer c
spice [spais] n specerij c; **spices** kruiden
spiced [spaist] adj gekruid
spicy ['spaisi] adj pikant
spider ['spaidə] n spin c; **spider's
web** spinneweb nt
* **spill** [spil] v morsen
* **spin** [spin] v *spinnen; draaien
spinach ['spinidʒ] n spinazie c

spine [spain] n ruggegraat c
spinster ['spinstə] n oude vrijster
spire [spaiə] n spits c
spirit ['spirit] n geest c; bui c; **spirits**
sterke drank; stemming c; ~ **stove**
spiritusbrander c
spiritual ['spiritʃuəl] adj geestelijk
spit [spit] n spuug nt, speeksel nt;
spit nt
* **spit** [spit] v spuwen
in spite of [in spait ɔv] ongeacht, ondanks
spiteful ['spaitfəl] adj hatelijk
splash [splæʃ] v spatten
splendid ['splendid] adj schitterend,
prachtig
splendour ['splendə] n pracht c
splint [splint] n spalk c
splinter ['splintə] n splinter c
* **split** [split] v *splijten
* **spoil** [spɔil] v *bederven; verwennen
spoke[1] [spouk] v (p speak)
spoke[2] [spouk] n spaak c
sponge [spʌndʒ] n spons c
spook [spu:k] n spook nt
spool [spu:l] n spoel c
spoon [spu:n] n lepel c
sport [spɔ:t] n sport c
sports-car ['spɔ:tska:] n sportwagen c
sports-jacket ['spɔ:ts,dʒækit] n sportjasje nt
sportsman ['spɔ:tsmən] n (pl -men)
sportman c
sportswear ['spɔ:tsweə] n sportkleding
c
spot [spɔt] n spat c, vlek c; plek c,
plaats c
spotless ['spɔtləs] adj vlekkeloos
spotlight ['spɔtlait] n schijnwerper c
spotted ['spɔtid] adj gespikkeld
spout [spaut] n straal c
sprain [sprein] v verstuiken, verzwikken; n verstuiking c
* **spread** [spred] v spreiden

spring [spriŋ] *n* voorjaar *nt*, lente *c*; veer *c*; bron *c*

springtime ['spriŋtaim] *n* voorjaar *nt*

sprouts [sprauts] *pl* spruitjes *pl*

spy [spai] *n* spion *c*

squadron ['skwɔdrən] *n* eskader *nt*

square [skweə] *adj* vierkant; *n* kwadraat *nt*, vierkant *nt*; plein *nt*

squash [skwɔʃ] *n* vruchtensap *nt*

squirrel ['skwirəl] *n* eekhoorn *c*

squirt [skwə:t] *n* straal *c*

stable ['steibəl] *adj* stabiel; *n* stal *c*

stack [stæk] *n* stapel *c*

stadium ['steidiəm] *n* stadion *nt*

staff [sta:f] *n* staf *c*

stage [steidʒ] *n* toneel *nt*; fase *c*, stadium *nt*; etappe *c*

stain [stein] *v* vlekken; *n* spat *c*, vlek *c*; **stained glass** gebrandschilderd glas; ~ **remover** vlekkenwater *nt*

stainless ['steinləs] *adj* vlekkeloos; ~ **steel** roestvrij staal

staircase ['steəkeis] *n* trap *c*

stairs [steəz] *pl* trap *c*

stale [steil] *adj* oudbakken

stall [stɔ:l] *n* kraam *c*; stalles *pl*

stamina ['stæminə] *n* uithoudingsvermogen *nt*

stamp [stæmp] *n* postzegel *c*; stempel *c*; *v* frankeren; stampen; ~ **machine** postzegelautomaat *c*

stand [stænd] *n* kraam *c*; tribune *c*

* stand [stænd] *v* *staan

standard ['stændəd] *n* norm *c*, maatstaf *c*; standaard-; ~ **of living** levensstandaard *c*

stanza ['stænzə] *n* couplet *nt*

staple ['steipəl] *n* nietje *nt*

star [sta:] *n* ster *c*

starboard ['sta:bəd] *n* stuurboord *nt*

starch [sta:tʃ] *n* stijfsel *c*; *v* *stijven

stare [steə] *v* staren

starling ['sta:liŋ] *n* spreeuw *c*

start [sta:t] *v* *beginnen; *n* begin *nt*;

starter motor startmotor *c*

starting-point ['sta:tiŋpɔint] *n* uitgangspunt *nt*

state [steit] *n* staat *c*; toestand *c*; *v* verklaren

the States Verenigde Staten

statement ['steitmənt] *n* verklaring *c*

statesman ['steitsmən] *n* (pl -men) staatsman *c*

station ['steiʃən] *n* station *nt*; plaats *c*

stationary ['steiʃənəri] *adj* stilstaand

stationer's ['steiʃənəz] *n* kantoorboekhandel *c*

stationery ['steiʃənəri] *n* schrijfbehoeften *pl*

station-master ['steiʃən,ma:stə] *n* stationschef *c*

statistics [stə'tistiks] *pl* statistiek *c*

statue ['stætʃu:] *n* standbeeld *nt*

stay [stei] *v* *blijven; logeren, *verblijven; *n* verblijf *nt*

steadfast ['stedfa:st] *adj* standvastig

steady ['stedi] *adj* vast

steak [steik] *n* biefstuk *c*

* steal [sti:l] *v* *stelen

steam [sti:m] *n* stoom *c*

steamer ['sti:mə] *n* stoomboot *c*

steel [sti:l] *n* staal *nt*

steep [sti:p] *adj* steil

steeple ['sti:pəl] *n* kerktoren *c*

steering-column ['stiəriŋ,kɔləm] *n* stuurkolom *c*

steering-wheel ['stiəriŋwi:l] *n* stuurwiel *nt*

steersman ['stiəzmən] *n* (pl -men) stuurman *c*

stem [stem] *n* steel *c*

stenographer [ste'nɔgrəfə] *n* stenograaf *c*

step [step] *n* pas *c*, stap *c*; trede *c*; *v* stappen

stepchild ['steptʃaild] *n* (pl -children) stiefkind *nt*

stepfather ['step,fa:ðə] *n* stiefvader *c*

stepmother ['step,mʌðə] n stiefmoeder c

sterile ['sterail] adj steriel

sterilize ['sterilaiz] v steriliseren

steward ['stju:əd] n steward c

stewardess ['stju:ədes] n stewardess c

stick [stik] n stok c

*stick [stik] v kleven, plakken

sticky ['stiki] adj kleverig

stiff [stif] adj stijf

still [stil] adv nog; toch; adj stil

stillness ['stilnəs] n stilte c

stimulant ['stimjulənt] n stimulerend middel

stimulate ['stimjuleit] v stimuleren

sting [stiŋ] n prik c, steek c

*sting [stiŋ] v *steken

stingy ['stindʒi] adj gierig

*stink [stiŋk] v *stinken

stipulate ['stipjuleit] v bepalen

stipulation [,stipju'leiʃən] n bepaling c

stir [stə:] v *bewegen; roeren

stirrup ['stirəp] n stijgbeugel c

stitch [stitʃ] n steek c; hechting c

stock [stɔk] n voorraad c; v in voorraad *hebben; ~ exchange effectenbeurs c, beurs c; ~ market effectenbeurs c; stocks and shares effecten

stocking ['stɔkiŋ] n kous c

stole[1] [stoul] v (p steal)

stole[2] [stoul] n stola c

stomach ['stʌmək] n maag c

stomach-ache ['stʌməkeik] n buikpijn c, maagpijn c

stone [stoun] n steen c; edelsteen c; pit c; stenen; pumice ~ puimsteen nt

stood [stud] v (p, pp stand)

stop [stɔp] v stoppen; *ophouden met, staken; n halte c; stop! halt!

stopper ['stɔpə] n stop c

storage ['stɔ:ridʒ] n opslag c

store [stɔ:] n voorraad c; winkel c; v *opslaan

store-house ['stɔ:haus] n magazijn nt

storey ['stɔ:ri] n etage c, verdieping c

stork [stɔ:k] n ooievaar c

storm [stɔ:m] n storm c

stormy ['stɔ:mi] adj stormachtig

story ['stɔ:ri] n verhaal nt

stout [staut] adj dik, gezet, corpulent

stove [stouv] n kachel c; fornuis nt

straight [streit] adj recht; eerlijk; adv recht; ~ ahead rechtdoor; ~ away direct, meteen; ~ on rechtdoor

strain [strein] n inspanning c; spanning c; v forceren; zeven

strainer ['streinə] n vergiet nt

strange [streindʒ] adj vreemd; raar

stranger ['streindʒə] n vreemdeling c; vreemde c

strangle ['stræŋgəl] v wurgen

strap [stræp] n riem c

straw [strɔ:] n stro nt

strawberry ['strɔ:bəri] n aardbei c

stream [stri:m] n beek c; stroom c; v stromen

street [stri:t] n straat c

streetcar ['stri:tka:] nAm tram c

street-organ ['stri:,tɔ:gən] n draaiorgel nt

strength [streŋθ] n sterkte c, kracht c

stress [stres] n spanning c; nadruk c, v benadrukken

stretch [stretʃ] v rekken; n stuk nt

strict [strikt] adj strikt; streng

strife [straif] n strijd c

strike [straik] n staking c

*strike [straik] v *slaan; *toeslaan; *treffen; staken; *strijken

striking ['straikiŋ] adj frappant, opmerkelijk, opvallend

string [striŋ] n touw nt; snaar c

strip [strip] n strook c

stripe [straip] n streep c

striped [straipt] adj gestreept

stroke [strouk] n beroerte c

stroll [stroul] v wandelen; n wandeling c

strong [strɔŋ] adj sterk; krachtig

stronghold ['strɔŋhould] n burcht c

structure ['strʌktʃə] n structuur c

struggle ['strʌgəl] n strijd c, worsteling c; v worstelen, *strijden

stub [stʌb] n controlestrook c

stubborn ['stʌbən] adj hardnekkig

student ['stju:dənt] n student c; studente c

study ['stʌdi] v studeren; n studie c; studeerkamer c

stuff [stʌf] n stof c; spul nt

stuffed [stʌft] adj gevuld

stuffing ['stʌfiŋ] n vulling c

stuffy ['stʌfi] adj benauwd

stumble ['stʌmbəl] v struikelen

stung [stʌŋ] v (p, pp sting)

stupid ['stju:pid] adj dom

style [stail] n stijl c

subject[1] ['sʌbdʒikt] n onderwerp nt; onderdaan c; ~ **to** onderhevig aan

subject[2] [səb'dʒekt] v *onderwerpen

submit [səb'mit] v zich *onderwerpen

subordinate [sə'bɔ:dinət] adj ondergeschikt; bijkomstig

subscriber [səb'skraibə] n abonnee c

subscription [səb'skripʃən] n abonnement nt

subsequent ['sʌbsikwənt] adj volgend

subsidy ['sʌbsidi] n subsidie c

substance ['sʌbstəns] n substantie c

substantial [səb'stænʃəl] adj stoffelijk; werkelijk; aanzienlijk

substitute ['sʌbstitju:t] v *vervangen; n vervanging c; plaatsvervanger c

subtitle ['sʌb,taitəl] n ondertitel c

subtle ['sʌtəl] adj subtiel

subtract [səb'trækt] v *aftrekken

suburb ['sʌbə:b] n buitenwijk c, voorstad c

suburban [sə'bə:bən] adj van de voorstad

subway ['sʌbwei] nAm ondergrondse c

succeed [sək'si:d] v slagen; opvolgen

success [sək'ses] n succes nt

successful [sək'sesfəl] adj succesvol

succumb [sə'kʌm] v *bezwijken

such [sʌtʃ] adj dergelijk, zulk; adv zo; ~ **as** zoals

suck [sʌk] v *zuigen

sudden ['sʌdən] adj plotseling

suddenly ['sʌdənli] adv opeens

suede [sweid] n suède nt/c

suffer ['sʌfə] v *lijden; *ondergaan

suffering ['sʌfəriŋ] n lijden nt

suffice [sə'fais] v voldoende *zijn

sufficient [sə'fiʃənt] adj voldoende, genoeg

suffrage ['sʌfridʒ] n stemrecht nt, kiesrecht nt

sugar ['ʃugə] n suiker c

suggest [sə'dʒest] v voorstellen

suggestion [sə'dʒestʃən] n voorstel nt

suicide ['su:isaid] n zelfmoord c

suit [su:t] v schikken; aanpassen; goed *staan; n kostuum nt

suitable ['su:təbəl] adj gepast, geschikt

suitcase ['su:tkeis] n koffer c

suite [swi:t] n suite c

sum [sʌm] n som c

summary ['sʌməri] n resumé nt, samenvatting c

summer ['sʌmə] n zomer c; ~ **time** zomertijd c

summit ['sʌmit] n top c

summons ['sʌmənz] n (pl ~es) dagvaarding c

sun [sʌn] n zon c

sunbathe ['sʌnbeið] v zonnebaden

sunburn ['sʌnbə:n] n zonnebrand c

Sunday ['sʌndi] zondag c

sun-glasses ['sʌn,gla:siz] pl zonnebril c

sunlight ['sʌnlait] n zonlicht nt

sunny ['sʌni] adj zonnig

sunrise ['sʌnraiz] n zonsopgang c
sunset ['sʌnset] n zonsondergang c
sunshade ['sʌnʃeid] n parasol c
sunshine ['sʌnʃain] n zonneschijn c
sunstroke ['sʌnstrouk] n zonnesteek c
suntan oil ['sʌntænɔil] zonnebrandolie c

superb [su'pə:b] adj groots, prachtig
superficial [,su:pə'fiʃəl] adj oppervlakkig
superfluous [su'pə:fluəs] adj overbodig
superior [su'piəriə] adj beter, groter, hoger, superieur
superlative [su'pə:lətiv] adj overtreffend; n superlatief c
supermarket ['su:pə,ma:kit] n supermarkt c
superstition [,su:pə'stiʃən] n bijgeloof nt
supervise ['su:pəvaiz] v toezicht *houden op
supervision [,su:pə'viʒən] n controle c, toezicht nt
supervisor ['su:pəvaizə] n opzichter c
supper ['sʌpə] n avondeten nt
supple ['sʌpəl] adj soepel, lenig, buigzaam
supplement ['sʌplimənt] n supplement nt
supply [sə'plai] n aanvoer c, levering c; voorraad c; aanbod nt; v leveren, bezorgen
support [sə'pɔ:t] v ondersteunen, steunen; n steun c; ~ hose steunkousen pl
supporter [sə'pɔ:tə] n supporter c
suppose [sə'pouz] v *aannemen, veronderstellen; supposing that aangenomen dat
suppository [sə'pɔzitəri] n zetpil c
suppress [sə'pres] v onderdrukken
surcharge ['sə:tʃa:dʒ] n toeslag c
sure [ʃuə] adj zeker
surely ['ʃuəli] adv zeker

surface ['sə:fis] n oppervlakte c
surf-board ['sə:fbɔ:d] n surfplank c
surgeon ['sə:dʒən] n chirurg c; veterinary ~ veearts c
surgery ['sə:dʒəri] n operatie c; spreekkamer c
surname ['sə:neim] n achternaam c
surplus ['sə:pləs] n overschot nt
surprise [sə'praiz] n verrassing c; verbazing c; v verrassen; verbazen
surrender [sə'rendə] v zich *overgeven; n overgave c
surround [sə'raund] v omringen, *omgeven
surrounding [sə'raundiŋ] adj omliggend
surroundings [sə'raundiŋz] pl omgeving c
survey ['sə:vei] n overzicht nt
survival [sə'vaivəl] n overleving c
survive [sə'vaiv] v overleven
suspect[1] [sə'spekt] v *verdenken; vermoeden
suspect[2] ['sʌspekt] n verdachte c
suspend [sə'spend] v schorsen
suspenders [sə'spendəz] plAm bretels pl; suspender belt jarretelgordel c
suspension [sə'spenʃən] n vering c, ophanging c; ~ bridge hangbrug c
suspicion [sə'spiʃən] n verdenking c; wantrouwen nt, argwaan c
suspicious [sə'spiʃəs] adj verdacht; argwanend, achterdochtig
sustain [sə'stein] v *verdragen
Swahili [swɑ'hi:li] n Swahili nt
swallow ['swɔlou] v inslikken, slikken; n zwaluw c
swam [swæm] v (p swim)
swamp [swɔmp] n moeras nt
swan [swɔn] n zwaan c
swap [swɔp] v ruilen
*swear [sweə] v *zweren; vloeken
sweat [swet] n zweet nt; v zweten
sweater ['swetə] n sweater c

Swede [swi:d] *n* Zweed *c*

Sweden ['swi:dən] Zweden

Swedish ['swi:diʃ] *adj* Zweeds

*****sweep** [swi:p] *v* vegen

sweet [swi:t] *adj* zoet; lief; *n* snoepje *nt*; toetje *nt*; **sweets** snoep *nt*, snoepgoed *nt*

sweeten ['swi:tən] *v* zoet maken

sweetheart ['swi:tha:t] *n* liefje *nt*, lieveling *c*

sweetshop ['swi:tʃɔp] *n* snoepwinkel *c*

swell [swel] *adj* prachtig

*****swell** [swel] *v* *zwellen

swelling ['sweliŋ] *n* zwelling *c*

swift [swift] *adj* snel

*****swim** [swim] *v* *zwemmen

swimmer ['swimə] *n* zwemmer *c*

swimming ['swimiŋ] *n* zwemsport *c*; **~ pool** zwembad *nt*

swimming-trunks ['swimiŋtrʌŋks] *n* zwembroek *c*

swim-suit ['swimsu:t] *n* zwempak *nt*

swindle ['swindəl] *v* oplichten; *n* zwendelarij *c*

swindler ['swindlə] *n* oplichter *c*

swing [swiŋ] *n* schommel *c*

*****swing** [swiŋ] *v* zwaaien; schommelen

Swiss [swis] *adj* Zwitsers; *n* Zwitser *c*

switch [switʃ] *n* schakelaar *c*; *v* omwisselen; **~ off** uitschakelen; **~ on** inschakelen

switchboard ['switʃbɔ:d] *n* schakelbord *nt*

Switzerland ['switsələnd] Zwitserland

sword [sɔ:d] *n* zwaard *nt*

swum [swʌm] *v* (pp swim)

syllable ['siləbəl] *n* lettergreep *c*

symbol ['simbəl] *n* symbool *nt*

sympathetic [,simpə'θetik] *adj* hartelijk, begrijpend

sympathy ['simpəθi] *n* sympathie *c*; medegevoel *nt*

symphony ['simfəni] *n* symfonie *c*

symptom ['simtəm] *n* symptoom *nt*

synagogue ['sinəgɔg] *n* synagoge *c*

synonym ['sinənim] *n* synoniem *nt*

synthetic [sin'θetik] *adj* synthetisch

syphon ['saifən] *n* sifon *c*

Syria ['siriə] Syrië

Syrian ['siriən] *adj* Syrisch; *n* Syriër *c*

syringe [si'rindʒ] *n* spuit *c*

syrup ['sirəp] *n* stroop *c*, siroop *c*

system ['sistəm] *n* systeem *nt*; stelsel *nt*; **decimal ~** tientallig stelsel

systematic [,sistə'mætik] *adj* systematisch

T

table ['teibəl] *n* tafel *c*; tabel *c*; **~ of contents** inhoudsopgave *c*; **~ tennis** tafeltennis *nt*

table-cloth ['teibəlklɔθ] *n* tafellaken *nt*

tablespoon ['teibəlspu:n] *n* eetlepel *c*

tablet ['tæblit] *n* tablet *c*

taboo [tə'bu:] *n* taboe *nt*

tactics ['tæktiks] *pl* tactiek *c*

tag [tæg] *n* etiket *nt*

tail [teil] *n* staart *c*

tail-light ['teillait] *n* achterlicht *nt*

tailor ['teilə] *n* kleermaker *c*

tailor-made ['teiləmeid] *adj* op maat gemaakt

*****take** [teik] *v* *nemen; pakken; *brengen; *begrijpen, snappen; **~ away** *meenemen; *afnemen, *wegnemen; **~ off** starten; **~ out** *wegnemen; **~ over** *overnemen; **~ place** *plaatshebben; **~ up** *innemen

take-off ['teikɔf] *n* start *c*

tale [teil] *n* verhaal *nt*, vertelling *c*

talent ['tælənt] *n* aanleg *c*, talent *nt*

talented ['tæləntid] *adj* begaafd

talk [tɔ:k] *v* *spreken, praten; *n* gesprek *nt*

talkative ['tɔːkətiv] *adj* spraakzaam

tall [tɔːl] *adj* hoog; lang, groot

tame [teim] *adj* mak, tam; *v* temmen

tampon ['tæmpən] *n* tampon *c*

tangerine [,tændʒə'riːn] *n* mandarijn *c*

tangible ['tændʒibəl] *adj* tastbaar

tank [tæŋk] *n* tank *c*

tanker ['tæŋkə] *n* tankschip *nt*

tanned [tænd] *adj* gebruind

tap [tæp] *n* kraan *c*; klop *c*; *v* kloppen

tape [teip] *n* band *c*; lint *nt*; **adhesive** ~ plakband *nt*; hechtpleister *c*

tape-measure ['teip,meʒə] *n* centimeter *c*

tape-recorder ['teipri,kɔːdə] *n* bandrecorder *c*

tapestry ['tæpistri] *n* wandkleed *nt*, gobelin *c*

tar [taː] *n* teer *c/nt*

target ['taːgit] *n* doel *nt*, mikpunt *nt*

tariff ['tærif] *n* tarief *nt*

tarpaulin [taː'pɔːlin] *n* dekzeil *nt*

task [taːsk] *n* taak *c*

taste [teist] *n* smaak *c*; *v* smaken; proeven

tasteless ['teistləs] *adj* smakeloos

tasty ['teisti] *adj* lekker, smakelijk

taught [tɔːt] *v* (p, pp teach)

tavern ['tævən] *n* herberg *c*

tax [tæks] *n* belasting *c*; *v* belasten

taxation [tæk'seiʃən] *n* belasting *c*

tax-free ['tæksfriː] *adj* belastingvrij

taxi ['tæksi] *n* taxi *c*; ~ **rank** taxistandplaats *c*; ~ **stand** *Am* taxistandplaats *c*

taxi-driver ['tæksi,draivə] *n* taxichauffeur *c*

taxi-meter ['tæksi,miːtə] *n* taximeter *c*

tea [tiː] *n* thee *c*

*tea teach [tiːtʃ] *v* leren, *onderwijzen

teacher ['tiːtʃə] *n* docent *c*, leraar *c*; lerares *c*; onderwijzer *c*, meester *c*, schoolmeester *c*

teachings ['tiːtʃiŋz] *pl* leer *c*

tea-cloth ['tiːklɔθ] *n* theedoek *c*

teacup ['tiːkʌp] *n* theekopje *nt*

team [tiːm] *n* equipe *c*, ploeg *c*

teapot ['tiːpɔt] *n* theepot *c*

tear¹ [tiə] *n* traan *c*

tear² [teə] *n* scheur *c*; *tear *v* scheuren

tear-jerker ['tiə,dʒəːkə] *n* smartlap *c*

tease [tiːz] *v* plagen

tea-set ['tiːset] *n* theeservies *nt*

tea-shop ['tiːʃɔp] *n* tearoom *c*

teaspoon ['tiːspuːn] *n* theelepel *c*

teaspoonful ['tiːspuːn,ful] *n* theelepel *c*

technical ['teknikəl] *adj* technisch

technician [tek'niʃən] *n* technicus *c*

technique [tek'niːk] *n* techniek *c*

technology [tek'nɔlədʒi] *n* technologie *c*

teenager ['tiː,neidʒə] *n* tiener *c*

teetotaller [tiː'toutələ] *n* geheelonthouder *c*

telegram ['teligræm] *n* telegram *c*

telegraph ['teligraːf] *v* telegraferen

telepathy [ti'lepəθi] *n* telepathie *c*

telephone ['telifoun] *n* telefoon *c*; ~ **book** *Am* telefoongids *c*, telefoonboek *nt*; ~ **booth** telefooncel *c*; ~ **call** telefoongesprek *nt*; ~ **directory** telefoonboek *nt*, telefoongids *c*; ~ **exchange** telefooncentrale *c*; ~ **operator** telefoniste *c*

telephonist [ti'lefənist] *n* telefoniste *c*

television ['teliviʒən] *n* televisie *c*; ~ **set** televisietoestel *nt*

telex ['teleks] *n* telex *c*

*tell [tel] *v* *zeggen; vertellen

temper ['tempə] *n* boosheid *c*

temperature ['temprətʃə] *n* temperatuur *c*

tempest ['tempist] *n* storm *c*

temple ['templəl] *n* tempel *c*; slaap *c*

temporary ['tempərəri] *adj* voorlopig, tijdelijk

tempt [tempt] v *aantrekken

temptation [temp'teiʃən] n verleiding c

ten [ten] num tien

tenant ['tenənt] n huurder c

tend [tend] v de neiging *hebben; verzorgen; ~ to neigen tot

tendency ['tendənsi] n neiging c, tendens c

tender ['tendə] adj teder, teer; mals

tendon ['tendən] n pees c

tennis ['tenis] n tennis nt; ~ shoes tennisschoenen pl

tennis-court ['teniskɔːt] n tennisbaan c

tense [tens] adj gespannen

tension ['tenʃən] n spanning c

tent [tent] n tent c

tenth [tenθ] num tiende

tepid ['tepid] adj lauw

term [təːm] n term c; periode c, termijn c; voorwaarde c

terminal ['təːminəl] n eindpunt nt

terrace ['terəs] n terras nt

terrain [te'rein] n terrein nt

terrible ['teribəl] adj verschrikkelijk, ontzettend, vreselijk

terrific [tə'rifik] adj geweldig

terrify ['terifai] v schrik *aanjagen; terrifying angstwekkend

territory ['teritəri] n gebied nt

terror ['terə] n angst c

terrorism ['terərizəm] n terrorisme nt, terreur c

terrorist ['terərist] n terrorist c

terylene ['teriliːn] n terylene nt

test [test] n proef c, test c; v proberen, testen

testify ['testifai] v getuigen

text [tekst] n tekst c

textbook ['teksbuk] n leerboek nt

textile ['tekstail] n textiel c/nt

texture ['tekstʃə] n structuur c

Thai [tai] adj Thailands; n Thailander c

Thailand ['tailænd] Thailand

than [ðæn] conj dan

thank [θæŋk] v bedanken, danken; ~ you dank u

thankful ['θæŋkfəl] adj dankbaar

that [ðæt] adj die, dat; conj dat

thaw [θɔː] v dooien, ontdooien; n dooi c

the [ðə,ði] art de art; the ... the hoe ... hoe

theatre ['θiətə] n schouwburg c, theater nt

theft [θeft] n diefstal c

their [ðeə] adj hun

them [ðem] pron hen

theme [θiːm] n thema nt, onderwerp nt

themselves [ðəm'selvz] pron zich; zelf

then [ðen] adv toen; vervolgens, dan

theology [θi'ɔlədʒi] n theologie c

theoretical [θiə'retikəl] adj theoretisch

theory ['θiəri] n theorie c

therapy ['θerəpi] n therapie c

there [ðeə] adv daar; daarheen

therefore ['ðeəfɔː] conj daarom

thermometer [θə'mɔmitə] n thermometer c

thermostat ['θəːməstæt] n thermostaat c

these [ðiːz] adj deze

thesis ['θiːsis] n (pl theses) stelling c

they [ðei] pron ze

thick [θik] adj dik; dicht

thicken ['θikən] v verdikken

thickness ['θiknəs] n dikte c

thief [θiːf] n (pl thieves) dief c

thigh [θai] n dij c

thimble ['θimbəl] n vingerhoed c

thin [θin] adj dun; mager

thing [θiŋ] n ding nt

*think [θiŋk] v *denken; *nadenken; ~ of *denken aan; *bedenken; ~ over *overdenken

thinker ['θiŋkə] n denker c

third [θə:d] *num* derde

thirst [θə:st] *n* dorst *c*

thirsty ['θə:sti] *adj* dorstig

thirteen [,θə:'ti:n] *num* dertien

thirteenth [,θə:'ti:nθ] *num* dertiende

thirtieth ['θə:tiəθ] *num* dertigste

thirty ['θə:ti] *num* dertig

this [ðis] *adj* dit, deze

thistle ['θisəl] *n* distel *c*

thorn [θɔ:n] *n* doorn *c*

thorough ['θʌrə] *adj* grondig, degelijk

thoroughbred ['θʌrəbred] *adj* volbloed

thoroughfare ['θʌrəfɛə] *n* hoofdweg *c*, hoofdstraat *c*

those [ðouz] *adj* die

though [ðou] *conj* hoewel, ofschoon, alhoewel; *adv* overigens

thought¹ [θɔ:t] *v* (p, pp think)

thought² [θɔ:t] *n* gedachte *c*

thoughtful ['θɔ:tfəl] *adj* nadenkend; zorgzaam

thousand ['θauzənd] *num* duizend

thread [θred] *n* draad *c*; garen *nt*; *v* *rijgen

threadbare ['θredbɛə] *adj* versleten

threat [θret] *n* dreigement *nt*, bedreiging *c*

threaten ['θretən] *v* dreigen, bedreigen; threatening dreigend

three [θri:] *num* drie

three-quarter [,θri:'kwɔ:tə] *adj* driekwart

threshold ['θreʃould] *n* drempel *c*

threw [θru:] *v* (p throw)

thrifty ['θrifti] *adj* zuinig

throat [θrout] *n* keel *c*; hals *c*

throne [θroun] *n* troon *c*

through [θru:] *prep* door

throughout [θru:'aut] *adv* overal

throw [θrou] *n* gooi *c*

*throw [θrou] *v* *werpen, gooien

thrush [θrʌʃ] *n* lijster *c*

thumb [θʌm] *n* duim *c*

thumbtack ['θʌmtæk] *nAm* punaise *c*

thump [θʌmp] *v* stampen

thunder ['θʌndə] *n* donder *c*; *v* donderen

thunderstorm ['θʌndəstɔ:m] *n* onweer *nt*

thundery ['θʌndəri] *adj* onweerachtig

Thursday ['θə:zdi] donderdag *c*

thus [ðʌs] *adv* zo

thyme [taim] *n* tijm *c*

tick [tik] *n* streepje *nt*; ~ off aanstrepen

ticket ['tikit] *n* kaartje *nt*; bon *c*; ~ collector conducteur *c*; ~ machine kaartenautomaat *c*

tickle ['tikəl] *v* kietelen

tide [taid] *n* getij *nt*; high ~ hoog water; low ~ laag water

tidings ['taidiŋz] *pl* nieuws *nt*

tidy ['taidi] *adj* net; ~ up opruimen

tie [tai] *v* knopen, *binden; *n* das *c*

tiger ['taigə] *n* tijger *c*

tight [tait] *adj* strak; nauw, krap; *adv* vast

tighten ['taitən] *v* aanhalen, *aantrekken; strakker maken; strakker *worden

tights [taits] *pl* maillot *c*

tile [tail] *n* tegel *c*; dakpan *c*

till [til] *prep* tot aan, tot; *conj* tot, tot dat

timber ['timbə] *n* timmerhout *nt*

time [taim] *n* tijd *c*; maal *c*, keer *c*; all the ~ aldoor; in ~ op tijd; ~ of arrival aankomsttijd *c*; ~ of departure vertrektijd *c*

time-saving ['taim,seiviŋ] *adj* tijdbesparend

timetable ['taim,teibəl] *n* dienstregeling *c*

timid ['timid] *adj* bedeesd

timidity [ti'midəti] *n* verlegenheid *c*

tin [tin] *n* tin *nt*; bus *c*, blik *nt*; tinned food conserven *pl*

tinfoil ['tinfɔil] *n* zilverpapier *nt*

tin-opener ['ti,noupənə] *n* blikopener *c*

tiny ['taini] *adj* minuscuul

tip [tip] *n* punt *c*; fooi *c*

tire[1] [taiə] *n* band *c*

tire[2] [taiə] *v* vermoeien

tired [taiəd] *adj* vermoeid, moe; ~ **of** beu

tiring ['taiəriŋ] *adj* vermoeiend

tissue ['tiʃuː] *n* weefsel *nt*; papieren zakdoek

title ['taitəl] *n* titel *c*

to [tuː] *prep* tot; aan, voor, bij, naar; om te

toad [toud] *n* pad *c*

toadstool ['toudstuːl] *n* paddestoel *c*

toast [toust] *n* toast *c*

tobacco [tə'bækou] *n* (pl ~s) tabak *c*; ~ **pouch** tabakszak *c*

tobacconist [tə'bækənist] *n* sigaren-winkelier *c*; **tobacconist's** tabaks-winkel *c*

today [tə'dei] *adv* vandaag

toddler ['tɔdlə] *n* peuter *c*

toe [tou] *n* teen *c*

toffee ['tɔfi] *n* toffee *c*

together [tə'geðə] *adv* bijeen, samen

toilet ['tɔilət] *n* toilet *nt*; ~ **case** toi-lettas *c*

toilet-paper ['tɔilət,peipə] *n* closetpa-pier *nt*, toiletpapier *nt*

toiletry ['tɔilətri] *n* toiletbenodigdhe-den *pl*

token ['toukən] *n* teken *nt*; bewijs *nt*; munt *c*

told [tould] *v* (p, pp tell)

tolerable ['tɔlərəbəl] *adj* draaglijk

toll [toul] *n* tol *c*

tomato [tə'mɑːtou] *n* (pl ~es) tomaat *c*

tomb [tuːm] *n* graf *nt*

tombstone ['tuːmstoun] *n* grafsteen *c*

tomorrow [tə'mɔrou] *adv* morgen

ton [tʌn] *n* ton *c*

tone [toun] *n* toon *c*; klank *c*

tongs [tɔŋz] *pl* tang *c*

tongue [tʌŋ] *n* tong *c*

tonic ['tɔnik] *n* tonicum *nt*

tonight [tə'nait] *adv* vannacht, van-avond

tonsilitis [,tɔnsə'laitis] *n* amandelont-steking *c*

tonsils ['tɔnsəlz] *pl* amandelen

too [tuː] *adv* te; ook

took [tuk] *v* (p take)

tool [tuːl] *n* werktuig *nt*, gereedschap *nt*; ~ **kit** gereedschapskist *c*

toot [tuːt] *vAm* claxonneren

tooth [tuːθ] *n* (pl teeth) tand *c*

toothache ['tuːθeik] *n* tandpijn *c*

toothbrush ['tuːθbrʌʃ] *n* tandenborstel *c*

toothpaste ['tuːθpeist] *n* tandpasta *c/nt*

toothpick ['tuːθpik] *n* tandestoker *c*

toothpowder ['tuːθ,paudə] *n* tandpoe-der *nt/c*

top [tɔp] *n* top *c*; bovenkant *c*; deksel *nt*; bovenst; **on** ~ **of** bovenop; ~ **side** bovenkant *c*

topcoat ['tɔpkout] *n* overjas *c*

topic ['tɔpik] *n* onderwerp *nt*

topical ['tɔpikəl] *adj* actueel

torch [tɔːtʃ] *n* fakkel *c*; zaklantaarn *c*

torment[1] [tɔː'ment] *v* kwellen

torment[2] ['tɔːment] *n* kwelling *c*

torture ['tɔːtʃə] *n* marteling *c*; *v* mar-telen

toss [tɔs] *v* gooien

tot [tɔt] *n* kleuter *c*

total ['toutəl] *adj* totaal; geheel, vol-slagen; *n* totaal *nt*

totalitarian [,toutæli'tɛəriən] *adj* totali-tair

totalizator ['toutəlaizeitə] *n* totalisator *c*

touch [tʌtʃ] *v* aanraken; *betreffen; *n* contact *nt*, aanraking *c*; tastzin *c*

touching ['tʌtʃiŋ] *adj* aandoenlijk

tough [tʌf] *adj* taai
tour [tuə] *n* rondreis *c*
tourism ['tuərizəm] *n* toerisme *nt*
tourist ['tuərist] *n* toerist *c*; ~ **class** toeristenklasse *c*; ~ **office** verkeersbureau *nt*
tournament ['tuənəmənt] *n* toernooi *nt*
tow [tou] *v* slepen
towards [tə'wɔ:dz] *prep* naar; jegens
towel [tauəl] *n* handdoek *c*
towelling ['tauəliŋ] *n* badstof *c*
tower [tauə] *n* toren *c*
town [taun] *n* stad *c*; ~ **centre** stadscentrum *nt*; ~ **hall** stadhuis *nt*
townspeople ['taunz,pi:pəl] *pl* stadsmensen *pl*
toxic ['tɔksik] *adj* vergiftig
toy [tɔi] *n* speelgoed *nt*
toyshop ['tɔiʃɔp] *n* speelgoedwinkel *c*
trace [treis] *n* spoor *nt*; *v* opsporen
track [træk] *n* spoor *nt*; renbaan *c*
tractor ['træktə] *n* tractor *c*
trade [treid] *n* koophandel *c*, handel *c*; ambacht *nt*, vak *nt*; *v* handel *drijven
trademark ['treidma:k] *n* handelsmerk *nt*
trader ['treidə] *n* handelaar *c*
tradesman ['treidzmən] *n* (pl -men) handelaar *c*
trade-union [,treid'ju:njən] *n* vakbond *c*
tradition [trə'diʃən] *n* traditie *c*
traditional [trə'diʃənəl] *adj* traditioneel
traffic ['træfik] *n* verkeer *nt*; ~ **jam** verkeersopstopping *c*; ~ **light** stoplicht *nt*
trafficator ['træfikeitə] *n* richtingaanwijzer *c*
tragedy ['trædʒədi] *n* tragedie *c*
tragic ['trædʒik] *adj* tragisch
trail [treil] *n* spoor *nt*, pad *nt*
trailer ['treilə] *n* aanhangwagen *c*;

nAm kampeerwagen *c*
train [trein] *n* trein *c*; *v* dresseren, trainen; **stopping** ~ stoptrein *c*; **through** ~ doorgaande trein
training ['treiniŋ] *n* training *c*
trait [treit] *n* trek *c*
traitor ['treitə] *n* verrader *c*
tram [træm] *n* tram *c*
tramp [træmp] *n* landloper *c*, vagebond *c*; *v* *rondtrekken
tranquil ['træŋkwil] *adj* rustig
tranquillizer ['træŋkwilaizə] *n* kalmerend middel
transaction [træn'zækʃən] *n* transactie *c*
transatlantic [,trænzət'læntik] *adj* transatlantisch
transfer [træns'fə:] *v* *overbrengen
transform [træns'fɔ:m] *v* veranderen
transformer [træns'fɔ:mə] *n* transformator *c*
transition [træn'siʃən] *n* overgang *c*
translate [træns'leit] *v* vertalen
translation [træns'leiʃən] *n* vertaling *c*
translator [træns'leitə] *n* vertaler *c*
transmission [trænz'miʃən] *n* uitzending *c*
transmit [trænz'mit] *v* *uitzenden
transmitter [trænz'mitə] *n* zender *c*
transparent [træn'spɛərənt] *adj* doorzichtig
transport¹ ['trænspɔ:t] *n* vervoer *nt*
transport² [træn'spɔ:t] *v* transporteren
transportation [,trænspɔ:'teiʃən] *n* transport *nt*
trap [træp] *n* val *c*
trash [træʃ] *n* rommel *c*; ~ **can** *Am* vuilnisbak *c*
travel ['trævəl] *v* reizen; ~ **agency** reisbureau *nt*; ~ **agent** reisagent *c*; ~ **insurance** reisverzekering *c*; **travelling expenses** reiskosten *pl*
traveller ['trævələ] *n* reiziger *c*; **traveller's cheque** reischeque *c*

tray [trei] *n* dienblad *nt*

treason ['tri:zən] *n* verraad *nt*

treasure ['treʒə] *n* schat *c*

treasurer ['treʒərə] *n* penningmeester *c*

treasury ['treʒəri] *n* schatkist *c*

treat [tri:t] *v* behandelen

treatment ['tri:tmənt] *n* behandeling *c*

treaty ['tri:ti] *n* verdrag *nt*

tree [tri:] *n* boom *c*

tremble ['trembəl] *v* rillen, beven; trillen

tremendous [tri'mendəs] *adj* enorm

trespasser ['trespəsə] *n* indringer *c*

trial [traiəl] *n* rechtszaak *c*; proef *c*

triangle ['traiæŋgəl] *n* driehoek *c*

triangular [trai'æŋgjulə] *adj* driehoekig

tribe [traib] *n* stam *c*

tributary ['tribjutəri] *n* zijrivier *c*

tribute ['tribju:t] *n* hulde *c*

trick [trik] *n* streek *c*; foefje *nt*, kunstje *nt*

trigger ['trigə] *n* trekker *c*

trim [trim] *v* bijknippen

trip [trip] *n* uitstapje *nt*, reis *c*

triumph ['traiəmf] *n* triomf *c*; *v* zegevieren

triumphant [trai'ʌmfənt] *adj* triomfantelijk

trolley-bus ['trɔlibʌs] *n* trolleybus *c*

troops [tru:ps] *pl* troepen *pl*

tropical ['trɔpikəl] *adj* tropisch

tropics ['trɔpiks] *pl* tropen *pl*

trouble ['trʌbəl] *n* zorg *c*, moeite *c*, last *c*; *v* storen

troublesome ['trʌbəlsəm] *adj* lastig

trousers ['trauzəz] *pl* broek *c*

trout [traut] *n* (pl ~) forel *c*

truck [trʌk] *nAm* vrachtwagen *c*

true [tru:] *adj* waar; werkelijk, echt; getrouw, trouw

trumpet ['trʌmpit] *n* trompet *c*

trunk [trʌŋk] *n* koffer *c*; stam *c*; *nAm* kofferruimte *c*; **trunks** *pl*
gymnastiekbroek *c*

trunk-call ['trʌŋkkɔ:l] *n* interlokaal gesprek

trust [trʌst] *v* vertrouwen; *n* vertrouwen *nt*

trustworthy ['trʌst,wə:ði] *adj* betrouwbaar

truth [tru:θ] *n* waarheid *c*

truthful ['tru:θfəl] *adj* waarheidsgetrouw

try [trai] *v* proberen; trachten, pogen; *n* poging *c*; ~ **on** passen

tube [tju:b] *n* pijp *c*, buis *c*; tube *c*

tuberculosis [tju:,bə:kju'lousis] *n* tuberculose *c*

Tuesday ['tju:zdi] dinsdag *c*

tug [tʌg] *v* slepen; *n* sleepboot *c*; ruk *c*

tuition [tju:'iʃən] *n* onderwijs *nt*

tulip ['tju:lip] *n* tulp *c*

tumbler ['tʌmblə] *n* beker *c*

tumour ['tju:mə] *n* gezwel *nt*, tumor *c*

tuna ['tju:nə] *n* (pl ~, ~s) tonijn *c*

tune [tju:n] *n* wijs *c*, melodie *c*; ~ **in**
afstemmen

tuneful ['tju:nfəl] *adj* melodieus

tunic ['tju:nik] *n* tuniek *c*

Tunisia [tju:'niziə] Tunesië

Tunisian [tju:'niziən] *adj* Tunesisch; *n*
Tunesiër *c*

tunnel ['tʌnəl] *n* tunnel *c*

turbine ['tə:bain] *n* turbine *c*

turbojet [,tə:bou'dʒet] *n* straalvliegtuig *nt*

Turk [tə:k] *n* Turk *c*

Turkey ['tə:ki] Turkije

turkey ['tə:ki] *n* kalkoen *c*

Turkish ['tə:kiʃ] *adj* Turks; ~ **bath**
Turks bad

turn [tə:n] *v* draaien, keren; omkeren,
omdraaien; *n* wending *c*, draai *c*;
bocht *c*; beurt *c*; ~ **back** terugkeren; ~ **down** *verwerpen; ~ **into**
veranderen in; ~ **off** dichtdraaien;

~ **on** aanzetten; opendraaien; ~
over omkeren; ~ **round** omkeren;
zich omdraaien

turning ['tə:niŋ] *n* bocht *c*

turning-point ['tə:niŋpɔint] *n* keerpunt
nt

turnover ['tə:,nouvə] *n* omzet *c*; ~ **tax**
omzetbelasting *c*

turnpike ['tə:npaik] *nAm* tolweg *c*

turpentine ['tə:pəntain] *n* terpentijn *c*

turtle ['tə:təl] *n* schildpad *c*

tutor ['tju:tə] *n* huisonderwijzer *c*;
voogd *c*

tuxedo [tʌk'si:dou] *nAm* (pl ~s, ~es)
smoking *c*

tweed [twi:d] *n* tweed *nt*

tweezers ['twi:zəz] *pl* pincet *c*

twelfth [twelfθ] *num* twaalfde

twelve [twelv] *num* twaalf

twentieth ['twentiəθ] *num* twintigste

twenty ['twenti] *num* twintig

twice [twais] *adv* tweemaal

twig [twig] *n* twijg *c*

twilight ['twailait] *n* schemering *c*

twine [twain] *n* touw *nt*

twins [twinz] *pl* tweeling *c*; **twin beds**
lits-jumeaux *c*

twist [twist] *v* *winden; draaien; *n*
draai *c*

two [tu:] *num* twee

two-piece [,tu:'pi:s] *adj* tweedelig

type [taip] *v* tikken, typen; *n* type *nt*

typewriter ['taipraitə] *n* schrijfmachine *c*

typewritten ['taipritən] getypt

typhoid ['taifɔid] *n* tyfus *c*

typical ['tipikəl] *adj* kenmerkend, typisch

typist ['taipist] *n* typiste *c*

tyrant ['taiərənt] *n* tiran *c*

tyre [taiə] *n* band *c*; ~ **pressure** bandenspanning *c*

U

ugly ['ʌgli] *adj* lelijk

ulcer ['ʌlsə] *n* zweer *c*

ultimate ['ʌltimət] *adj* laatst

ultraviolet [,ʌltrə'vaiələt] *adj* ultraviolet

umbrella [ʌm'brelə] *n* paraplu *c*

umpire ['ʌmpaiə] *n* scheidsrechter *c*

unable [ʌ'neibəl] *adj* onbekwaam

unacceptable [,ʌnək'septəbəl] *adj* onaanvaardbaar

unaccountable [,ʌnə'kauntəbəl] *adj* onverklaarbaar

unaccustomed [,ʌnə'kʌstəmd] *adj* niet
gewend

unanimous [ju:'næniməs] *adj* unaniem

unanswered [,ʌ'nɑ:nsəd] *adj* onbeantwoord

unauthorized [,ʌ'nɔ:θəraizd] *adj* onbevoegd

unavoidable [,ʌnə'vɔidəbəl] *adj* onvermijdelijk

unaware [,ʌnə'weə] *adj* onbewust

unbearable [ʌn'beərəbəl] *adj* ondraaglijk

unbreakable [,ʌn'breikəbəl] *adj* onbreekbaar

unbroken [,ʌn'broukən] *adj* heel

unbutton [,ʌn'bʌtən] *v* losknopen

uncertain [ʌn'sə:tən] *adj* onzeker

uncle ['ʌŋkəl] *n* oom *c*

unclean [,ʌn'kli:n] *adj* onrein

uncomfortable [ʌn'kʌmfətəbəl] *adj* ongemakkelijk

uncommon [ʌn'kɔmən] *adj* ongewoon,
zeldzaam

unconditional [,ʌnkən'diʃənəl] *adj* onvoorwaardelijk

unconscious [ʌn'kɔnʃəs] *adj* bewusteloos

uncork [,ʌn'kɔ:k] *v* ontkurken

uncover [ʌn'kʌvə] *v* blootleggen

uncultivated [ˌʌn'kʌltiveitid] *adj* onbebouwd

under ['ʌndə] *prep* beneden, onder

undercurrent ['ʌndə,kʌrənt] *n* onderstroom *c*

underestimate [ˌʌndə'restimeit] *v* onderschatten

underground ['ʌndəgraund] *adj* ondergronds; *n* metro *c*

underline [ˌʌndə'lain] *v* onderstrepen

underneath [ˌʌndə'ni:θ] *adv* beneden

underpants ['ʌndəpænts] *plAm* onderbroek *c*

undershirt ['ʌndəʃə:t] *n* hemd *nt*

undersigned ['ʌndəsaind] *n* ondergetekende *c*

* understand [ˌʌndə'stænd] *v* *begrijpen

understanding [ˌʌndə'stændiŋ] *n* begrip *nt*

* undertake [ˌʌndə'teik] *v* *ondernemen

undertaking [ˌʌndə'teikiŋ] *n* onderneming *c*

underwater ['ʌndə,wɔ:tə] *adj* onderwater-

underwear ['ʌndəweə] *n* ondergoed *nt*

undesirable [ˌʌndi'zaiərəbəl] *adj* ongewenst

* undo [ˌʌn'du:] *v* losmaken

undoubtedly [ʌn'dautidli] *adv* ongetwijfeld

undress [ˌʌn'dres] *v* zich uitkleden

undulating ['ʌndjuleitiŋ] *adj* golvend

unearned [ˌʌ'nə:nd] *adj* onverdiend

uneasy [ʌ'ni:zi] *adj* onbehaaglijk

uneducated [ˌʌ'nedjukeitid] *adj* ongeschoold

unemployed [ˌʌnim'plɔid] *adj* werkeloos

unemployment [ˌʌnim'plɔimənt] *n* werkeloosheid *c*

unequal [ˌʌ'ni:kwəl] *adj* ongelijk

uneven [ˌʌ'ni:vən] *adj* ongelijk, onef-

fen

unexpected [ˌʌnik'spektid] *adj* onvoorzien, onverwacht

unfair [ˌʌn'feə] *adj* oneerlijk, onbillijk

unfaithful [ˌʌn'feiθfəl] *adj* ontrouw

unfamiliar [ˌʌnfə'miljə] *adj* onbekend

unfasten [ˌʌn'fɑ:sən] *v* losmaken

unfavourable [ˌʌn'feivərəbəl] *adj* ongunstig

unfit [ˌʌn'fit] *adj* ongeschikt

unfold [ʌn'fould] *v* ontvouwen

unfortunate [ʌn'fɔ:tʃənət] *adj* ongelukkig

unfortunately [ʌn'fɔ:tʃənətli] *adv* helaas, ongelukkigerwijs

unfriendly [ˌʌn'frendli] *adj* onvriendelijk

unfurnished [ˌʌn'fə:niʃt] *adj* ongemeubileerd

ungrateful [ʌn'greitfəl] *adj* ondankbaar

unhappy [ʌn'hæpi] *adj* ongelukkig

unhealthy [ʌn'helθi] *adj* ongezond

unhurt [ˌʌn'hə:t] *adj* heelhuids

uniform ['ju:nifɔ:m] *n* uniform *nt/c*; *adj* uniform

unimportant [ˌʌnim'pɔ:tənt] *adj* onbelangrijk

uninhabitable [ˌʌnin'hæbitəbəl] *adj* onbewoonbaar

uninhabited [ˌʌnin'hæbitid] *adj* onbewoond

unintentional [ˌʌnin'tenʃənəl] *adj* onopzettelijk

union ['ju:njən] *n* vereniging *c*; verbond *nt*, unie *c*

unique [ju:'ni:k] *adj* uniek

unit ['ju:nit] *n* eenheid *c*

unite [ju:'nait] *v* verenigen

United States [ju:'naitid steits] Verenigde Staten

unity ['ju:nəti] *n* eenheid *c*

universal [ju:ni'və:səl] *adj* algemeen, universeel

universe ['ju:nivə:s] *n* heelal *nt*

university [,ju:ni'və:səti] *n* universiteit *c*

unjust [,ʌn'dʒʌst] *adj* onrechtvaardig

unkind [ʌn'kaind] *adj* onaardig, onvriendelijk

unknown [,ʌn'noun] *adj* onbekend

unlawful [,ʌn'lɔ:fəl] *adj* onwettig

unlearn [,ʌn'lə:n] *v* afleren

unless [ən'les] *conj* tenzij

unlike [,ʌn'laik] *adj* verschillend

unlikely [ʌn'laikli] *adj* onwaarschijnlijk

unlimited [ʌn'limitid] *adj* grenzeloos, onbeperkt

unload [,ʌn'loud] *v* lossen, *uitladen

unlock [,ʌn'lɔk] *v* openen

unlucky [ʌn'lʌki] *adj* ongelukkig

unnecessary [ʌn'nesəsəri] *adj* onnodig

unoccupied [,ʌ'nɔkjupaid] *adj* onbezet

unofficial [,ʌnə'fiʃəl] *adj* officieus

unpack [ʌn'pæk] *v* uitpakken

unpleasant [ʌn'plezənt] *adj* onaangenaam, onplezierig; naar, vervelend

unpopular [,ʌn'pɔpjulə] *adj* impopulair, onbemind

unprotected [,ʌnprə'tektid] *adj* onbeschermd

unqualified [,ʌn'kwɔlifaid] *adj* onbevoegd

unreal [,ʌn'riəl] *adj* onwerkelijk

unreasonable [ʌn'ri:zənəbəl] *adj* onredelijk

unreliable [,ʌnri'laiəbəl] *adj* onbetrouwbaar

unrest [,ʌn'rest] *n* onrust *c*; rusteloosheid *c*

unsafe [,ʌn'seif] *adj* onveilig

unsatisfactory [,ʌnsætis'fæktəri] *adj* onbevredigend

unscrew [,ʌn'skru:] *v* losschroeven

unselfish [,ʌn'selfiʃ] *adj* onzelfzuchtig

unskilled [,ʌn'skild] *adj* ongeschoold

unsound [,ʌn'saund] *adj* ongezond

unstable [,ʌn'steibəl] *adj* labiel

unsteady [,ʌn'stedi] *adj* wankel, onvast; onevenwichtig

unsuccessful [,ʌnsək'sesfəl] *adj* mislukt

unsuitable [,ʌn'su:təbəl] *adj* ongepast

unsurpassed [,ʌnsə'pa:st] *adj* onovertroffen

untidy [ʌn'taidi] *adj* slordig

untie [,ʌn'tai] *v* losknopen

until [ən'til] *prep* tot

untrue [,ʌn'tru:] *adj* onwaar

untrustworthy [,ʌn'trʌst,wə:ði] *adj* onbetrouwbaar

unusual [ʌn'ju:ʒuəl] *adj* ongebruikelijk, ongewoon

unwell [,ʌn'wel] *adj* onwel

unwilling [,ʌn'wiliŋ] *adj* onwillig

unwise [,ʌn'waiz] *adj* onverstandig

unwrap [,ʌn'ræp] *v* uitpakken

up [ʌp] *adv* naar boven, omhoog, op

upholster [ʌp'houlstə] *v* bekleden

upkeep ['ʌpki:p] *n* onderhoud *nt*

uplands ['ʌpləndz] *pl* hoogvlakte *c*

upon [ə'pɔn] *prep* op

upper ['ʌpə] *adj* hoger, bovenst

upright ['ʌprait] *adj* rechtopstaand; *adv* overeind

upset [ʌp'set] *v* verstoren; *adj* overstuur

upside-down [,ʌpsaid'daun] *adv* onderstebovn

upstairs [,ʌp'steəz] *adv* boven; naar boven

upstream [,ʌp'stri:m] *adv* stroomopwaarts

upwards ['ʌpwədz] *adv* naar boven

urban ['ə:bən] *adj* stedelijk

urge [ə:dʒ] *v* aansporen; *n* drang *c*

urgency ['ə:dʒənsi] *n* urgentie *c*

urgent ['ə:dʒənt] *adj* dringend

urine ['juərin] *n* urine *c*

Uruguay ['juərəgwai] Uruguay

Uruguayan [,juərə'gwaiən] *adj* Uruguayaans; *n* Uruguayaan *c*

us [ʌs] *pron* ons

usable ['ju:zəbəl] *adj* bruikbaar

usage ['ju:zidʒ] *n* gebruik *nt*

use¹ [ju:z] *v* gebruiken; *be used to gewoon *zijn; ~ up verbruiken

use² [ju:s] *n* gebruik *nt*; nut *nt*; *be of ~ baten

useful ['ju:sfəl] *adj* bruikbaar, nuttig

useless ['ju:sləs] *adj* nutteloos

user ['ju:zə] *n* gebruiker *c*

usher ['ʌʃə] *n* suppoost *c*

usherette [,ʌʃə'ret] *n* ouvreuse *c*

usual ['ju:ʒuəl] *adj* gebruikelijk

usually ['ju:ʒuəli] *adv* gewoonlijk

utensil [ju:'tensəl] *n* gereedschap *nt*, werktuig *nt*; gebruiksvoorwerp *nt*

utility [ju:'tiləti] *n* nut *nt*

utilize ['ju:tilaiz] *v* benutten

utmost ['ʌtmoust] *adj* uiterst

utter ['ʌtə] *adj* volslagen, totaal; *v* uiten

V

vacancy ['veikənsi] *n* vacature *c*

vacant ['veikənt] *adj* vacant

vacate [və'keit] *v* ontruimen

vacation [və'keiʃən] *n* vakantie *c*

vaccinate ['væksineit] *v* inenten

vaccination [,væksi'neiʃən] *n* inenting *c*

vacuum ['vækjuəm] *n* vacuüm *nt*; *vAm* stofzuigen; ~ **cleaner** stofzuiger *c*; ~ **flask** thermosfles *c*

vagrancy ['veigrənsi] *n* landloperij *c*

vague [veig] *adj* vaag

vain [vein] *adj* ijdel; vergeefs; **in** ~ vergeefs, tevergeefs

valet ['vælit] *n* bediende *c*

valid ['vælid] *adj* geldig

valley ['væli] *n* dal *nt*, vallei *c*

valuable ['væljubəl] *adj* waardevol, kostbaar; **valuables** *pl* kostbaarheden *pl*

value ['vælju:] *n* waarde *c*; *v* schatten

valve [vælv] *n* ventiel *nt*

van [væn] *n* bestelauto *c*

vanilla [və'nilə] *n* vanille *c*

vanish ['væniʃ] *v* *verdwijnen

vapour ['veipə] *n* damp *c*

variable ['vɛəriəbəl] *adj* veranderlijk

variation [,vɛəri'eiʃən] *n* afwisseling *c*; verandering *c*

varied ['vɛərid] *adj* gevarieerd

variety [və'raiəti] *n* verscheidenheid *c*; ~ **show** variétévoorstelling *c*; ~ **theatre** variététheater *nt*

various ['vɛəriəs] *adj* allerlei, verscheidene

varnish ['vɑ:niʃ] *n* lak *c*, vernis *nt/c*; *v* lakken

vary ['vɛəri] *v* variëren, afwisselen; veranderen; verschillen

vase [vɑ:z] *n* vaas *c*

vaseline ['væsəli:n] *n* vaseline *c*

vast [vɑ:st] *adj* onmetelijk, uitgestrekt

vault [vɔ:lt] *n* gewelf *nt*; kluis *c*

veal [vi:l] *n* kalfsvlees *nt*

vegetable ['vedʒətəbəl] *n* groente *c*; ~ **merchant** groenteboer *c*

vegetarian [,vedʒi'tɛəriən] *n* vegetariër *c*

vegetation [,vedʒi'teiʃən] *n* plantengroei *c*

vehicle ['vi:əkəl] *n* voertuig *nt*

veil [veil] *n* sluier *c*

vein [vein] *n* ader *c*; **varicose** ~ spatader *c*

velvet ['velvit] *n* fluweel *nt*

velveteen [,velvi'ti:n] *n* katoenfluweel *nt*

venerable ['venərəbəl] *adj* eerbiedwaardig

venereal disease [vi'niəriəl di'zi:z] geslachtsziekte *c*

Venezuela [ˌveniˈzweilə] Venezuela

Venezuelan [ˌveniˈzweilən] *adj* Venezolaans; *n* Venezolaan *c*

ventilate [ˈventileit] *v* ventileren; luchten

ventilation [ˌventiˈleiʃən] *n* ventilatie *c*; luchtverversing *c*

ventilator [ˈventileitə] *n* ventilator *c*

venture [ˈventʃə] *v* wagen

veranda [vəˈrændə] *n* veranda *c*

verb [vəːb] *n* werkwoord *nt*

verbal [ˈvəːbəl] *adj* mondeling

verdict [ˈvəːdikt] *n* vonnis *nt*, uitspraak *c*

verge [vəːdʒ] *n* rand *c*

verify [ˈverifai] *v* verifiëren

verse [vəːs] *n* vers *nt*

version [ˈvəːʃən] *n* versie *c*; vertaling *c*

versus [ˈvəːsəs] *prep* contra

vertical [ˈvəːtikəl] *adj* verticaal

vertigo [ˈvəːtigou] *n* duizeling *c*

very [ˈveri] *adv* erg, zeer; *adj* precies, waar, werkelijk; uiterst

vessel [ˈvesəl] *n* vaartuig *nt*, schip *nt*; vat *nt*

vest [vest] *n* hemd *nt*; *nAm* vest *nt*

veterinary surgeon [ˈvetrinəri ˈsəːdʒən] dierenarts *c*

via [vaiə] *prep* via

viaduct [ˈvaiədʌkt] *n* viaduct *c/nt*

vibrate [vaiˈbreit] *v* trillen

vibration [vaiˈbreiʃən] *n* vibratie *c*

vicar [ˈvikə] *n* predikant *c*

vicarage [ˈvikəridʒ] *n* pastorie *c*

vice-president [ˌvaisˈprezidənt] *n* vicepresident *c*

vicinity [viˈsinəti] *n* nabijheid *c*, buurt *c*

vicious [ˈviʃəs] *adj* boosaardig

victim [ˈviktim] *n* slachtoffer *nt*; dupe *c*

victory [ˈviktəri] *n* overwinning *c*

view [vjuː] *n* uitzicht *nt*; opvatting *c*,

mening *c*; *v* *bekijken

view-finder [ˈvjuːˌfaində] *n* zoeker *c*

vigilant [ˈvidʒilənt] *adj* waakzaam

villa [ˈvilə] *n* villa *c*

village [ˈvilidʒ] *n* dorp *nt*

villain [ˈvilən] *n* boef *c*

vine [vain] *n* wijnstok *c*

vinegar [ˈvinigə] *n* azijn *c*

vineyard [ˈvinjəd] *n* wijngaard *c*

vintage [ˈvintidʒ] *n* wijnoogst *c*

violation [vaiəˈleiʃən] *n* schending *c*

violence [ˈvaiələns] *n* geweld *nt*

violent [ˈvaiələnt] *adj* gewelddadig; hevig, heftig

violet [ˈvaiələt] *n* viooltje *nt*; *adj* violet

violin [vaiəˈlin] *n* viool *c*

virgin [ˈvəːdʒin] *n* maagd *c*

virtue [ˈvəːtʃuː] *n* deugd *c*

visa [ˈviːzə] *n* visum *nt*

visibility [ˌvizəˈbiləti] *n* zicht *nt*

visible [ˈvizəbəl] *adj* zichtbaar

vision [ˈviʒən] *n* visie *c*

visit [ˈvizit] *v* *bezoeken; *n* visite *c*, bezoek *nt*; **visiting hours** bezoekuren *pl*

visiting-card [ˈvizitiŋkaːd] *n* visitekaartje *nt*

visitor [ˈvizitə] *n* bezoeker *c*

vital [ˈvaitəl] *adj* essentieel

vitamin [ˈvitəmin] *n* vitamine *c*

vivid [ˈvivid] *adj* levendig

vocabulary [vəˈkæbjuləri] *n* vocabulaire *nt*, woordenschat *c*; woordenlijst *c*

vocal [ˈvoukəl] *adj* vocaal

vocalist [ˈvoukəlist] *n* zanger *c*

voice [vɔis] *n* stem *c*

void [vɔid] *adj* nietig

volcano [vɔlˈkeinou] *n* (pl ~es, ~s) vulkaan *c*

volt [voult] *n* volt *c*

voltage [ˈvoultidʒ] *n* voltage *c/nt*

volume [ˈvɔljum] *n* volume *nt*; deel *nt*

voluntary ['vɔləntəri] adj vrijwillig
volunteer [,vɔlən'tiə] n vrijwilliger c
vomit ['vɔmit] v braken, *overgeven
vote [vout] v stemmen; n stem c;
stemming c
voucher ['vautʃə] n bon c, bewijs nt
vow [vau] n gelofte c, eed c; v *zweren
vowel [vauəl] n klinker c
voyage ['vɔiidʒ] n reis c
vulgar ['vʌlgə] adj vulgair; volks-, ordinair
vulnerable ['vʌlnərəbəl] adj kwetsbaar
vulture ['vʌltʃə] n gier c

W

wade [weid] v waden
wafer ['weifə] n wafel c
waffle ['wɔfəl] n wafel c
wages ['weidʒiz] pl loon nt
waggon ['wægən] n wagon c
waist [weist] n taille c, middel nt
waistcoat ['weiskout] n vest nt
wait [weit] v wachten; ~ on bedienen
waiter ['weitə] n ober c, kelner c
waiting n het wachten
waiting-list ['weitiŋlist] n wachtlijst c
waiting-room ['weitiŋru:m] n wachtkamer c
waitress ['weitris] n serveerster c
*wake [weik] v wekken; ~ up ontwa-
ken, wakker *worden
walk [wɔ:k] v *lopen; wandelen; n
wandeling c; loop c; walking te
voet
walker ['wɔ:kə] n wandelaar c
walking-stick ['wɔ:kiŋstik] n wandelstok c
wall [wɔ:l] n muur c; wand c
wallet ['wɔlit] n portefeuille c
wallpaper ['wɔ:l,peipə] n behang nt

walnut ['wɔ:lnʌt] n walnoot c
waltz [wɔ:ls] n wals c
wander ['wɔndə] v *rondzwerven,
*zwerven
want [wɔnt] v *willen; wensen; n behoefte c; gebrek nt, gemis nt
war [wɔ:] n oorlog c
warden ['wɔ:dən] n bewaker c, opzichter c
wardrobe ['wɔ:droub] n klerenkast c,
garderobe c
warehouse ['wɛəhaus] n magazijn nt,
pakhuis nt
wares [wɛəz] pl waren pl
warm [wɔ:m] adj heet, warm; v verwarmen
warmth [wɔ:mθ] n warmte c
warn [wɔ:n] v waarschuwen
warning ['wɔ:niŋ] n waarschuwing c
wary ['wɛəri] adj behoedzaam
was [wɔz] v (p be)
wash [wɔʃ] v *wassen; ~ and wear
zelfstrijkend; ~ up afwassen
washable ['wɔʃəbəl] adj wasbaar
wash-basin ['wɔʃ,beisən] n wasbekken
nt
washing ['wɔʃiŋ] n was c; wasgoed nt
washing-machine ['wɔʃiŋmə,ʃi:n] n
wasmachine c
washing-powder ['wɔʃiŋ,paudə] n waspoeder nt
washroom ['wɔʃru:m] nAm toilet nt
wash-stand ['wɔʃstænd] n wastafel c
wasp [wɔsp] n wesp c
waste [weist] v verspillen; n verspilling c; adj braak
wasteful ['weistfəl] adj verkwistend
wastepaper-basket [weist'peipə,ba:-
skit] n prullenmand c
watch [wɔtʃ] v *kijken naar, *gadeslaan; letten op; n horloge nt; ~
for *uitkijken naar; ~ out *uitkijken
watch-maker ['wɔtʃ,meikə] n horloge-

maker c

watch-strap ['wɔtʃstræp] n horlogebandje nt

water ['wɔ:tə] n water nt; **iced** ~ ijswater nt; **running** ~ stromend water; ~ **pump** waterpomp c; ~ **ski**
waterski c

water-colour ['wɔ:tə,kʌlə] n waterverf
c; aquarel c

watercress ['wɔ:təkres] n waterkers c

waterfall ['wɔ:təfɔ:l] n waterval c

watermelon ['wɔ:tə,melən] n watermeloen c

waterproof ['wɔ:təpru:f] adj waterdicht

water-softener [,wɔ:tə,sɔfnə] n wasverzachter c

waterway ['wɔ:təwei] n vaarwater c

watt [wɔt] n watt c

wave [weiv] n golf c; v zwaaien

wave-length ['weivleŋθ] n golflengte c

wavy ['weivi] adj golvend

wax [wæks] n was c

waxworks ['wækswə:ks] pl wassenbeeldenmuseum nt

way [wei] n manier c, wijze c; weg c;
kant c, richting c; afstand c; **any** ~
hoe dan ook; **by the** ~ tussen twee
haakjes; **one-way traffic** eenrichtingsverkeer nt; **out of the** ~ afgelegen; **the other** ~ **round** andersom; ~ **back** terugweg c; ~ **in** ingang c; ~ **out** uitgang c

wayside ['weisaid] n wegkant c

we [wi:] pron wij

weak [wi:k] adj zwak; slap

weakness ['wi:knəs] n zwakheid c

wealth [welθ] n rijkdom c

wealthy ['welθi] adj rijk

weapon ['wepən] n wapen nt

*wear [weə] v *aanhebben, *dragen;
~ **out** *verslijten

weary ['wiəri] adj moe, vermoeid

weather ['weðə] n weer nt; ~ **fore-**

cast weerbericht nt

*weave [wi:v] v *weven

weaver ['wi:və] n wever c

wedding ['wediŋ] n huwelijk nt, bruiloft c

wedding-ring ['wediŋriŋ] n trouwring
c

wedge [wedʒ] n wig c

Wednesday ['wenzdi] woensdag c

weed [wi:d] n onkruid nt

week [wi:k] n week c

weekday ['wi:kdei] n weekdag c

weekly ['wi:kli] adj wekelijks

*weep [wi:p] v huilen

weigh [wei] v *wegen

weighing-machine ['weiŋmə,ʃi:n] n
weegschaal c

weight [weit] n gewicht nt

welcome ['welkəm] adj welkom; n
welkom nt; v verwelkomen

weld [weld] v lassen

welfare ['welfeə] n welzijn nt

well[1] [wel] adv goed; adj gezond; **as**
~ ook, eveneens; **as** ~ **as** evenals;
well! welnu!

well[2] [wel] n bron c, put c

well-founded [,wel'faundid] adj gegrond

well-known ['welnoun] adj bekend

well-to-do [,weltə'du:] adj bemiddeld

went [went] v (p go)

were [wə:] v (p be)

west [west] n west c, westen nt

westerly ['westəli] adj westelijk

western ['westən] adj westers

wet [wet] adj nat; vochtig

whale [weil] n walvis c

wharf [wɔ:f] n (pl ~s, wharves) kade c

what [wɔt] pron wat; ~ **for** waarom

whatever [wɔ'tevə] pron wat dan ook

wheat [wi:t] n tarwe c

wheel [wi:l] n wiel nt

wheelbarrow ['wi:l,bærou] n kruiwagen c

wheelchair ['wi:ltʃɛə] n rolstoel c

when [wen] adv wanneer; conj als, toen, wanneer

whenever [we'nevə] conj wanneer ook

where [wɛə] adv waar; conj waar

wherever [wɛə'revə] conj waar ook

whether ['weðə] conj of; **whether ... or** of ... of

which [witʃ] pron welk; dat

whichever [wi'tʃevə] adj welk ook

while [wail] conj terwijl; n poosje nt

whilst [wailst] conj terwijl

whim [wim] n gril c, bevlieging c

whip [wip] n zweep c; v kloppen

whiskers ['wiskəz] pl bakkebaarden pl

whisper ['wispə] v fluisteren; n gefluister nt

whistle ['wisəl] v *fluiten; n fluitje nt

white [wait] adj wit; blank

whitebait ['waitbeit] n witvis c

whiting ['waitiŋ] n (pl ~) wijting c

Whitsun ['witsən] Pinksteren

who [hu:] pron wie; die

whoever [hu:'evə] pron wie ook

whole [houl] adj geheel, heel; n geheel nt

wholesale ['houlseil] n groothandel c; ~ **dealer** grossier c

wholesome ['houlsəm] adj gezond

wholly ['houlli] adv helemaal

whom [hu:m] pron wie

whore [hɔ:] n hoer c

whose [hu:z] pron wiens; van wie

why [wai] adv waarom

wicked ['wikid] adj slecht

wide [waid] adj wijd, breed

widen ['waidən] v verwijden

widow ['widou] n weduwe c

widower ['widouə] n weduwnaar c

width [widθ] n breedte c

wife [waif] n (pl wives) echtgenote c, vrouw c

wig [wig] n pruik c

wild [waild] adj wild; woest

will [wil] n wil c; testament nt

*will [wil] v *willen; *zullen

willing ['wiliŋ] adj bereid

willingly ['wiliŋli] adv graag

will-power ['wilpauə] n wilskracht c

*win [win] v *winnen

wind [wind] n wind c

*wind [waind] v kronkelen; *opwinden, *winden

winding ['waindiŋ] adj kronkelig

windmill ['windmil] n molen c, windmolen c

window ['windou] n raam nt

window-sill ['windousil] n vensterbank c

windscreen ['windskri:n] n voorruit c; ~ **wiper** ruitenwisser c

windshield ['windʃi:ld] nAm voorruit c; ~ **wiper** Am ruitenwisser c

windy ['windi] adj winderig

wine [wain] n wijn c

wine-cellar ['wain,selə] n wijnkelder c

wine-list ['wainlist] n wijnkaart c

wine-merchant ['wain,mə:tʃənt] n wijnkoper c

wine-waiter ['wain,weitə] n wijnkelner c

wing [wiŋ] n vleugel c

winkle ['wiŋkəl] n alikruik c

winner ['winə] n winnaar c

winning ['winiŋ] adj winnend; **winnings** pl winst c

winter ['wintə] n winter c; ~ **sports** wintersport c

wipe [waip] v vegen, afvegen

wire [waiə] n draad c; ijzerdraad nt

wireless ['waiələs] n radio c

wisdom ['wizdəm] n wijsheid c

wise [waiz] adj wijs

wish [wiʃ] v verlangen, wensen; n verlangen nt, wens c

witch [witʃ] n heks c

with [wið] prep met; bij; van

*withdraw [wið'drɔ:] v *terugtrekken

within [wi'ðin] *prep* binnen; *adv* van binnen

without [wi'ðaut] *prep* zonder

witness ['witnəs] *n* getuige *c*

wits [wits] *pl* verstand *nt*

witty ['witi] *adj* geestig

wolf [wulf] *n* (pl wolves) wolf *c*

woman ['wumən] *n* (pl women) vrouw *c*

womb [wu:m] *n* baarmoeder *c*

won [wʌn] *v* (p, pp win)

wonder ['wʌndə] *n* wonder *nt*; verwondering *c*; *v* zich *afvragen

wonderful ['wʌndəfəl] *adj* prachtig, verrukkelijk; heerlijk

wood [wud] *n* hout *nt*; bos *nt*

wood-carving ['wud,kɑ:viŋ] *n* houtsnijwerk *nt*

wooded ['wudid] *adj* bebost

wooden ['wudən] *adj* houten; ~ shoe klomp *c*

woodland ['wudlənd] *n* bebost gebied *nt*

wool [wul] *n* wol *c*; darning ~ stopgaren *nt*

woollen ['wulən] *adj* wollen

word [wə:d] *n* woord *nt*

wore [wɔ:] *v* (p wear)

work [wə:k] *n* werk *nt*; arbeid *c*; *v* werken; functioneren; working day werkdag *c*; ~ of art kunstwerk *nt*; ~ permit werkvergunning *c*

worker ['wə:kə] *n* arbeider *c*

working ['wə:kiŋ] *n* werking *c*

workman ['wə:kmən] *n* (pl -men) arbeider *c*

works [wə:ks] *pl* fabriek *c*

workshop ['wə:kʃɔp] *n* werkplaats *c*

world [wə:ld] *n* wereld *c*; ~ war wereldoorlog *c*

world-famous [,wə:ld'feiməs] *adj* wereldberoemd

world-wide ['wə:ldwaid] *adj* wereldomvattend

worm [wə:m] *n* worm *c*

worn [wɔ:n] *adj* (pp wear) versleten

worn-out [,wɔ:n'aut] *adj* versleten

worried ['wʌrid] *adj* ongerust

worry ['wʌri] *v* zich ongerust maken; *n* zorg *c*, bezorgdheid *c*

worse [wə:s] *adj* slechter; *adv* erger

worship ['wə:ʃip] *v* *aanbidden; *n* eredienst *c*

worst [wə:st] *adj* slechtst; *adv* ergst

worsted ['wustid] *n* kamgaren *nt*

worth [wə:θ] *n* waarde *c*; *be ~ waard *zijn; *be worth-while de moeite waard *zijn

worthless ['wə:θləs] *adj* waardeloos

worthy of ['wə:ði əv] waard

would [wud] *v* (p will) gewoon *zijn

wound¹ [wu:nd] *n* wond *c*; *v* kwetsen, verwonden

wound² [waund] *v* (p, pp wind)

wrap [ræp] *v* inpakken

wreck [rek] *n* wrak *nt*; *v* vernielen

wrench [rentʃ] *n* sleutel *c*; ruk *c*; *v* verdraaien

wrinkle ['riŋkəl] *n* rimpel *c*

wrist [rist] *n* pols *c*

wrist-watch ['ristwɔtʃ] *n* polshorloge *nt*

*write [rait] *v* *schrijven; in writing schriftelijk; ~ down *opschrijven

writer ['raitə] *n* schrijver *c*

writing-pad ['raitiŋpæd] *n* blocnote *c*, schrijfblok *nt*

writing-paper ['raitiŋ,peipə] *n* schrijfpapier *nt*

written ['ritən] *adj* (pp write) schriftelijk

wrong [rɔŋ] *adj* verkeerd, fout; *n* onrecht *nt*; *v* onrecht *aandoen; *be ~ ongelijk *hebben

wrote [rout] *v* (p write)

X

Xmas ['krisməs] Kerstmis
X-ray ['eksrei] *n* röntgenfoto *c*; *v* doorlichten

Y

yacht [jɔt] *n* jacht *nt*
yacht-club ['jɔtklʌb] *n* zeilclub *c*
yachting ['jɔtiŋ] *n* zeilsport *c*
yard [jɑːd] *n* erf *nt*
yarn [jɑːn] *n* garen *nt*
yawn [jɔːn] *v* gapen, geeuwen
year [jiə] *n* jaar *nt*
yearly ['jiəli] *adj* jaarlijks
yeast [jiːst] *n* gist *c*
yell [jel] *v* gillen; *n* gil *c*
yellow ['jelou] *adj* geel
yes [jes] ja
yesterday ['jestədi] *adv* gisteren
yet [jet] *adv* nog; *conj* toch, echter, maar
yield [jiːld] *v* *opbrengen; *toegeven
yoke [jouk] *n* juk *nt*

yolk [jouk] *n* dooier *c*
you [juː] *pron* je; jou; u; jullie
young [jʌŋ] *adj* jong
your [jɔː] *adj* uw; jouw; jullie
yourself [jɔː'self] *pron* je; zelf
yourselves [jɔː'selvz] *pron* je; zelf
youth [juːθ] *n* jeugd *c*; ~ **hostel** jeugdherberg *c*
Yugoslav [ˌjuːgə'slɑːv] *n* Joegoslaaf *c*
Yugoslavia [ˌjuːgə'slɑːviə] Joegoslavië

Z

zeal [ziːl] *n* ijver *c*
zealous ['zeləs] *adj* ijverig
zebra ['ziːbrə] *n* zebra *c*
zenith ['zeniθ] *n* zenit *nt*; toppunt *nt*
zero ['ziərou] *n* (pl ~s) nul *c*
zest [zest] *n* animo *c*
zinc [ziŋk] *n* zink *nt*
zip [zip] *n* ritssluiting *c*; ~ **code** *Am* postcode *c*
zipper ['zipə] *n* ritssluiting *c*
zodiac ['zoudiæk] *n* dierenriem *c*
zone [zoun] *n* zone *c*; gebied *nt*
zoo [zuː] *n* (pl ~s) dierentuin *c*
zoology [zouˈɔlədʒi] *n* zoölogie *c*

Culinaire woordenlijst

Spijzen

almond amandel
anchovy ansjovis
angel food cake witte, ronde cake, gemaakt van suiker, eiwit en bloem
angels on horseback geroosterde, met spek omwikkelde oesters
appetizer borrelhapje
apple appel
~ **charlotte** lagen van appels en sneetjes boord met vanille en slagroom
~ **dumpling** appelbol
~ **sauce** appelmoes
apricot abrikoos
Arbroath smoky gerookte schelvis
artichoke artisjok
asparagus asperge
~ **tip** aspergepunt
aspic koude schotel in gelei
assorted gevarieerd, gemengd
bacon spek
~ **and eggs** spiegeleieren met spek
bagel klein kransvormig broodje
baked in de oven gebakken, gebraden
~ **Alaska** omelette sibérienne
~ **beans** witte bonen in tomatensaus

~ **potato** hele, ongeschilde aardappel, in de oven gebakken
Bakewell tart amandeltaart met jam
baloney worstsoort
banana banaan
~ **split** in de lengte gehalveerde banaan met ijs, noten en overgoten met vruchtensiroop of vloeibare chocolade
barbecue 1) gehakt rundvlees in tomatensaus in een broodje geserveerd 2) maaltijd van geroosterd vlees in de open lucht
~ **sauce** zeer scherpe tomatensaus
barbecued geroosterd op houtskool
basil basilicum
bass baars
bean boon
beef rundvlees
~ **olive** blinde vink
beefburger gehakte, geroosterde biefstuk geserveerd in een broodje
beet, beetroot rode biet
bilberry blauwe bosbes
bill rekening
~ **of fare** menu

biscuit 1) koekje (GB) 2) broodje (US)

black pudding bloedworst

blackberry braam

blackcurrant zwarte bes

bloater verse bokking

blood sausage bloedworst

blueberry blauwe bosbes

boiled gekookt

Bologna (sausage) worstsoort

bone bot

boned ontbeend

Boston baked beans witte bonen met stukjes spek en stroop

Boston cream pie taart met vlavulling en chocoladeglazuur

brains hersenen

braised gestoofd

bramble pudding bramenpudding, vaak met schijfjes appel erin

braunschweiger gerookte leverworst

bread brood

breaded gepaneerd

breakfast ontbijt

bream brasem

breast borst (stuk)

brisket borststuk

broad bean tuinboon

broth bouillon

brown Betty afwisselende lagen appel, perzik of kers en paneermeel, met suiker en kruiderijen, in de oven gebakken

brunch ontbijt en lunch gecombineerd

brussels sprout spruitje

bubble and squeak soort pannekoek van gebakken aardappelen en kool, soms met vlees

bun 1) krentebroodje (GB) 2) klein, luchtig broodje (US)

butter boter

buttered beboterd

cabbage kool

Caesar salad sla met geroosterde, naar knoflook smakende brooddobbelsteentjes, anjovis en geraspte kaas

cake gebak, koek, cake, taart

cakes koekjes, taartjes

calf kalfsvlees

Canadian bacon gerookt spek in dikke plakken gesneden

canapé belegd sneetje brood

cantaloupe wratmeloen, kanteloep

caper kappertje

capercaillie, capercailzie auerhoen

carp karper

carrot wortel

cashew vrucht van de cajouboom

casserole gestoofd

catfish meerval (vis)

catsup ketchup

cauliflower bloemkool

celery selderie

cereal graansoorten voor bij het ontbijt, zoals maïsvlokken, havermout, met melk en suiker
hot ~ havermoutpap

chateaubriand dubbele biefstuk van de haas

check rekening

Cheddar (cheese) stevige kaas met een milde, zurige smaak

cheese kaas
~ **board** kaasassortiment
~ **cake** kaaskoekje

cheeseburger gehakte, geroosterde biefstuk met schijfje kaas, opgediend in een broodje

chef's salad salade van ham, kip, eieren, tomaten, sla en kaas

cherry kers

chestnut tamme kastanje

chicken kip

chicory 1) Brussels lof (GB) 2) andijvie (US)

chili con carne gehakt rundvlees gestoofd met bruine bonen, Spaanse pepers en komijn

chili pepper rode Spaanse pepers

chips 1) patates frites (GB) 2) aardappel chips (US)

chitt(er)lings varkenspens

chive bieslook

chocolate chocolade
  ~ **pudding** 1) chocoladepudding bereid met verkruimelde koekjes, suiker, eieren en bloem (GB) 2) chocolademousse (US)

choice keus

chop kotelet
  ~ **suey** gerecht, bereid uit fijngesneden varkensvlees en kip, groenten en rijst (tjap tjoy)

chopped fijngehakt

chowder dikke soep van vis, schaal- en schelpdieren of kip, met groenten

Christmas pudding speciaal Kerstgebak, soms geflambeerd

chutney sterke Indische kruiderij

cinnamon kaneel

clam steenmossel

club sandwich dubbele sandwich met kip, spek, sla, tomaat en mayonaise

cobbler vruchtenmoes met deeg, soms met ijs

cock-a-leekie soup preisoep met kip

coconut kokosnoot

cod kabeljauw

Colchester oyster beste soort Engelse oester

cold cuts/meat koud vlees

coleslaw koolsla

compote vruchten op sap

condiment kruiderij

consommé heldere soep

cooked gekookt

cookie koekje

corn 1) koren (GB) 2) maïs (US)
  ~ **on the cob** maïskolf

cornflakes maïsvlokken

cottage cheese witte, verse kaas

cottage pie gehakt vlees met uien, bedekt met aardappelpuree in de oven gebakken

course gerecht

cover charge couvert

crab krab

cracker droog beschuit van bladerdeeg

cranberry veenbes
  ~ **sauce** veenbessengelei

crawfish, crayfish 1) rivierkreeft 2) langoest (GB) 3) steurgarnaal (US)

cream 1) room 2) vlaai (dessert) 3) gebonden soep
  ~ **cheese** roomkaas
  ~ **puff** roomsoes

creamed potatoes aardappelen in witte roomsaus

creole op Creoolse wijze bereid; over het algemeen zeer pikant, met tomaten, paprika's en uien, geserveerd met rijst

cress waterkers

crisps chips

croquette kroket

crumpet rond, licht broodje, geroosterd en beboterd

cucumber komkommer

Cumberland ham zeer fijne, gerookte Engelse ham

Cumberland sauce rode bessengelei, op smaak gemaakt met wijn, sinaasappelsap en kruiderijen

cupcake klein rond gebakje

cured gezouten, gerookt, gepekeld (vis en vlees)

currant krent
curried met kerrie
curry kerrie
custard custardvla
cutlet vleeslapje, kotelet
dab schar
Danish pastry soort luchtig koffie-
brood
date dadel
Derby cheese gele kaas met pi-
kante smaak
devilled sterk gekruid
devil's food cake machtige choco-
ladetaart
devils on horseback gekookte
pruimen, gevuld met amandelen en ansjovis, omwikkeld met
spek, geroosterd en geserveerd
op toost
Devonshire cream dikke, klonte-
rige room
diced in dobbelsteentjes gesneden
diet food volgens voedselleer bereid
dill dille
dinner diner, avondeten
dish schotel, gerecht
donut, doughnut soort oliebol
double cream volle room
Dover sole tong uit Dover, in Engeland zeer gewaardeerd
dressing 1) slasaus 2) vulsel voor
kalkoen (US)
Dublin Bay prawn steurgarnaal
duck eend
duckling jonge eend
dumpling knoedel
Dutch apple pie appeltaart bedekt
met een mengsel van boter en
bruine suiker
éclair langwerpig, met chocolade
of caramel geglaceerd room-
taartje
eel paling

egg ei
  boiled ~ gekookt
  fried ~ spiegelei
  hard-boiled ~ hardgekookt
  poached ~ gepocheerd
  scrambled ~ roerei
  soft-boiled ~ zachtgekookt
eggplant aubergine, eierplant
endive 1) andijvie (GB) 2) Brussels lof (US)
entrecôte tussenrib
entrée 1) voorgerecht (GB) 2)
hoofdgerecht (US)
escalope schnitzel
fennel venkel
fig vijg
filet mignon kalfs- of varkens-
haasje
fillet filet van vlees of vis
finnan haddock gerookte schelvis
fish vis
  ~ **and chips** gebakken vis met
frites
  ~ **cake** viskoekje
flan vla, ronde taart met vruchten
flapjack (appel)flap
flounder bot
forcemeat farce, gehakt
fowl gevogelte
frankfurter knakworst
French bean slaboon
French bread stokbrood
French dressing 1) slasaus in olie,
azijn en tuinkruiden (GB) 2)
romige slasaus met ketchup
(US)
french fries patates frites
French toast wentelteefje
fresh vers
fricassée ragoût, vleeshachee
fried gebakken in een koekepan of
in de olie
fritter beignet, poffertje
frogs' legs kikkerbilletjes

frosting suikerglazuur
fruit vrucht
fry bakken
game wild
gammon gerookte ham
garfish geep (snoekachtige zeevis)
garlic knoflook
garnish garnituur
gherkin augurkje
giblets afval van gevogelte
ginger gember
goose gans
　～**berry** kruisbes
grape druif
　～**fruit** pompelmoes
grated geraspt
gravy vleesjus
grayling vlagzalm
green bean slaboon
green pepper groene paprika
green salad sla
greens groenten
grilled geroosterd
grilse jonge zalm
grouse korhoen
gumbo 1) groente van Afrikaanse afkomst 2) Creools gerecht van vlees, kip of vis, met *okra*zaden, uien, tomaten en kruiden
haddock gerookte schelvis
haggis hart, longen en lever van een schaap fijn gehakt en in de maag gekookt met reuzel, havermeel en uien
hake stokvis
halibut heilbot
ham and eggs spiegeleieren met ham
hamburger gehakt, geroosterd rundvlees opgediend in een broodje
hare haas
haricot bean prinsessenboon, witte boon

hash 1) gehakt of fijngesneden vlees 2) hachee met aardappelen en groenten
hazelnut hazelnoot
heart hart
herb tuinkruid
herring haring
home-made eigengemaakt, van het huis
hominy grits brij van maïsgrutten
honey honing
　～**dew melon** zoete meloen met geelgroen vruchtvlees
hors-d'œuvre voorgerecht (Engeland)
horse-radish mierikswortel
hot 1) heet, warm 2) sterk gekruid
　～**cross bun** fijn broodje gevuld met rozijnen en kruisvormig bedekt met glazuur, wordt in de vastentijd gegeten (brioche)
　～**dog** hot dog, warme worst in een broodje
huckleberry blauwe bosbes
hush puppy beignet van maïsmeel en uien
ice-cream ijs
iced gekoeld
icing suikerglazuur
Idaho baked potato soort bintje, ongeschild in de oven gepoft
Irish stew hutspot van schapevlees, aardappelen en uien
Italian dressing slasaus van olie, azijn en tuinkruiden
jellied in gelei
Jell-O gelatinedessert
jelly jam; gelei
Jerusalem artichoke aardpeer
John Dory zonnevis (zeevis)
jugged hare hazepeper
juice sap
juniper berry jeneverbes
junket gestremde melk (wrongel),

144

gesuikerd
kale boerenkool
kedgeree stukjes vis met rijst, eieren, boter, wordt vaak als warm gerecht aan het ontbijt geserveerd
kidney nier
kipper bokking
lamb lamsvlees
Lancashire hot pot schotel in de oven van ragoût van lamsvlees en nieren met uien, kruiderijen en aardappelen
larded gelardeerd
lean mager
leek prei
leg bout
lemon citroen
~ **sole** scharretong
lentil linze
lettuce kropsla, veldsla
lima bean tuinboon
lime limoen, kleine groene citroen
liver lever
loaf brood
lobster kreeft
loin lendestuk
Long Island duck eend van Long Island, in de VS zeer goed bekend staande soort
low-calorie laag caloriegehalte
lox gerookte zalm
macaroon bitterkoekje
mackerel makreel
maize maïs
mandarin mandarijntje
maple syrup ahornstroop
marinated gemarineerd
marjoram marjolein
marmalade marmelade van sinaasappelen of andere citrusvruchten
marrow beenmerg
~ **bone** mergpijp

marshmallow Amerikaans snoepgoed; *marshmallows* worden vaak aan warme chocola en allerlei soorten desserts toegevoegd
marzipan marsepein
mashed potatoes aardappelpuree
meal maaltijd
meat vlees
~ **ball** gehaktbal
~ **loaf** gehaktbrood
~ **pâté** vleespastei
medium (done) net gaar
melon meloen
melted gesmolten
Melton Mowbray pie pastei bestaande uit gehakt vlees en kruiden
meringue schuimgebak, schuimpje
milk melk
mince fijnhakken
~ **pie** pasteitje met krenten, rozijnen, fijngehakte geconfijte vruchten en appelen (met of zonder vlees)
minced fijngehakt
~ **meat** fijngehakt vlees
mint munt (kruid)
minute steak kort gebakken biefstuk
mixed gemengd
~ **grill** aan een stokje geregen, geroosterde stukjes vlees
molasses melasse, stroop
morel morille, zeer gewaardeerde paddestoelsoort
mousse 1) dessert van geklopte eieren en slagroom 2) luchtig pasteitje
mulberry moerbei
mullet harder (vis gelijkend op een karper)
mulligatawny soup zeer sterk ge-

kruide soep van Indische afkomst met wortels, uien, *chutney* en kip met kerrie
mushroom paddestoel
muskmelon meloen
mussel mossel
mustard mosterd
mutton schapevlees
noodle noedel
nut noot
oatmeal (porridge) havermoutpap
oil olie
okra zaad van de *gumbo*, wordt
gebruikt om soepen en ragoût-
sausen aan te dikken
olive olijf
onion ui
orange sinaasappel
ox tongue ossetong
oxtail ossestaart
oyster oester
pancake pannekoek
Parmesan (cheese) Parmezaanse
kaas
parsley peterselie
parsnip pastinaak, witte peen
partridge patrijs
pastry banket, gebakje, taartje
pasty pastei
pea doperwt
peach perzik
peanut olienoot, pinda
    ~ **butter** pindakaas
pear peer
pearl barley parelgerst
pepper peper
    ~**mint** pepermunt
perch baars
persimmon dadelpruim
pheasant fazant
pickerel jonge snoek
pickle 1) groente of geconfijte
vrucht in pekelzuur 2) in het
bijzonder augurkje (US)

pickled in pekel bewaard
pie pastei, vaak met een deksel
van bladerdeeg, gevuld met
vlees, groenten of vruchten
pig varken
pigeon duif
pike snoek
pineapple ananas
plaice schol
plain natuur, zonder iets erin
plate bord, schaal
plum pruim
    ~ **pudding** speciaal Kerstge-
bak, soms geflambeerd
poached gepocheerd
popcorn gepofte maïskorrels
popover klein, luchtig broodje
pork varkensvlees
porridge havermoutpap
porterhouse steak biefstuk van de
haas
pot roast met groenten gesmoord
rundvlees
potato aardappel
    ~ **chips** 1) patates frites (GB)
2) aardappel chips (US)
    ~ **in its jacket** aardappel in de
schil gekookt en opgediend
potted shrimps garnalen in gesmolten boter, koud opgediend
in een vorm
poultry gevogelte, pluimvee
prawn grote garnaal
prune gedroogde pruim
ptarmigan sneeuwhoen
pudding soepel of stevig beslag
van meel en eieren, gegarneerd
met vlees, vis, groenten of
vruchten, in de oven gebakken
of gaargestoomd; nagerecht
pumpernickel zwart roggebrood
pumpkin pompoen
quail kwartel
quince kweepeer

rabbit konijn
radish radijs
rainbow trout regenboogforel
raisin rozijn
rare ongaar
raspberry framboos
raw rauw
red mullet soort harder (zeevis)
red (sweet) pepper rode paprika
redcurrant rode bes
relish kruiderij gemaakt van fijngesneden groente in azijn
rhubarb rabarber
rib (of beef) ribstuk (van het rund)
ribe-eye steak entrecôte
rice rijst
rissole vlees- of viskroket
river trout rivierforel
roast braadstuk
roasted gebraden
Rock Cornish hen piepkuiken
roe viskuit
roll broodje
rollmop herring rolmops, gemari-
neerde haringfilet
round steak runderschijf
Rubens sandwich cornedbeef op
een toostje, met zuurkool, kaas
en slasaus, warm opgediend
rump steak biefstuk
rusk beschuit
rye bread roggebrood
saddle lendestuk
saffron saffraan
sage salie
salad sla
 ~ **bar** verschillende soorten
slaatjes, tomaten, prinsessen-
bonen
 ~ **cream** slasaus, licht gezoet
 ~ **dressing** slasaus
salmon zalm
 ~ **trout** zalmforel
salt zout

salted gezouten
sardine sardien
sauce saus
sauerkraut zuurkool
sausage worst
sauté(ed) snel in boter, olie of vet
gebakken
scallop 1) kamschelp 2) kalfslapje
scampi steurgarnaal
scone zacht broodje, warm geserveerd, met boter en jam
Scotch broth runder- of schape-
bouillon met groenten
Scotch woodcock toost met roerei
en ansjovis
sea bass zeebaars
sea kale zeekool
seafood zeebanket
(in) season (in het) seizoen
seasoning kruiderij
service bediening
 ~ **charge** bedieningstarief
 ~ **included** inclusief bediening
 ~ **not included** exclusief bediening
set menu menu van de dag
shad elft (zeevis)
shallot sjalot
shellfish schelp- en schaaldieren
sherbet sorbet
shoulder schouderstuk
shredded wheat gesponnen tarwe,
wordt bij het ontbijt gegeten
shrimp garnaal
silverside (of beef) onderste deel
van runderschenkel
sirloin steak lendestuk (van het
rund)
skewer vleespen
slice sneet(je), plak
sliced in plakken gesneden
sloppy Joe gehakt vlees in scherpe
tomatensaus, geserveerd in een
broodje

smelt spiering
smoked gerookt
snack hapje, snack
sole tong (vis)
soup soep
sour zuur
soused herring gepekelde haring
spare rib krabbetje
spice kruiderij
spinach spinazie
spiny lobster langoest
(on a) spit (aan het) spit
sponge cake Moscovisch gebak
sprat sprot
squash mergpompoen
starter voorgerecht
steak and kidney pie pastei in bladerdeeg van niertjes en rundvlees
steamed gekookt
stew stoofschotel
Stilton (cheese) een van de beste Engelse kazen, wit of blauw geaderd
strawberry aardbei
string bean slaboon
stuffed gevuld
stuffing vulling
suck(l)ing pig speenvarken
sugar suiker
sugarless zonder suiker
sundae roomijs met vruchten, noten, slagroom en siroop
supper avondmaaltijd
swede knolraap
sweet 1) zoet 2) dessert
~ **corn** zoete maïs
~ **potato** bataat, knol van een oorspronkelijk tropisch gewas, rijk aan zetmeel en suiker
sweetbread zwezerik
Swiss cheese Emmentaler kaas
Swiss roll opgerold gebak met jam ertussen (koninginnebrood)

Swiss steak met groenten en kruiderijen gestoofde runderlappen
T-bone steak lendestuk van het rund met een T-vormig bot erin
table d'hôte open tafel in een hotel
tangerine mandarijntje
tarragon dragon
tart (vruchten)taart
tenderloin filet van vlees
Thousand Island dressing slasaus, bestaande uit mayonaise met piment, noten, olijven, selderie, uien, peterselie en eieren
thyme tijm
toad-in-the-hole rundvlees (of worstjes) in beslag gedoopt en in de oven gebakken
toast geroosterd brood
toasted getoost
~ **cheese** toost met gesmolten kaas
tomato tomaat
tongue tong (vlees)
tournedos ossehaas in dikke plakken
treacle melasse, stroop
trifle cake met amandelen en gelei, in sherry (of brandewijn) gedrenkt, opgediend met vla of slagroom
tripe pens
trout forel
truffle truffel (paddestoel)
tuna, tunny tonijn
turbot tarbot
turkey kalkoen
turnip raap, knol
turnover flap
turtle schildpad
underdone ongaar
vanilla vanille
veal kalfsvlees
~ **bird** blinde vink
~ **escalope** kalfsoester

vegetable groente
~ **marrow** mergpompoen, courgette
venison wildbraad
vichyssoise preisoep, koud geserveerd
vinegar azijn
Virginia baked ham ham in de
oven geroosterd, in inkepingen
in het vel worden stukjes ananas, kersen en kruidnagels
gestoken waarna de ham
met het vruchtesap geglaceerd
wordt
wafer wafeltje
waffle warme wafel met boter,
stroop of honing
walnut walnoot
water ice sorbet
watercress waterkers

watermelon watermeloen
well-done gaar
Welsh rabbit/rarebit gesmolten
kaas op geroosterd brood
whelk kinkhoorn (wulk)
whipped cream slagroom
whitebait witvis
wine list wijnkaart
woodcock (hout)snip
Worcestershire sauce zoetzure
saus bestaande uit soja en vele
andere ingrediënten
York ham zeer goed bekend staande ham, opgediend in dunne
plakken
Yorkshire pudding knappend gebakken deeg, geserveerd met
rosbief
zucchini mergpompoen, courgette
zwieback beschuit

Dranken

ale donker, zoetachtig bier, onder
hoge temperatuur gegist
bitter ~ bitter bier, nogal zwaar
brown ~ gebotteld, zoetachtig
donker bier
light ~ gebotteld licht bier
mild ~ donker bier van het
vat met een zeer uitgesproken
smaak
pale ~ gebotteld licht bier
applejack Amerikaanse appel-
brandewijn
Athol Brose haver vermengd met
kokend water, honing en whisky

Bacardi cocktail cocktail van rum
en gin met grenadinesiroop en
limoensap
barley water frisdrank gemaakt
van parelgerst met citroen-
smaak
barley wine donker bier met hoog
alcoholgehalte
beer bier
bottled ~ gebotteld bier
draft, draught ~ getapt bier,
bier van het vat
bitters kruidenaperitieven, de
spijsvertering bevorderende
alcoholische dranken

black velvet champagne met toevoeging van *stout* (vaak ter begeleiding van oesters)

bloody Mary cocktail van wodka, tomatesap en kruiderijen

bourbon Amerikaanse whisky, hoofdzakelijk van maïs gestookt

brandy 1) verzamelnaam voor brandewijnsoorten gemaakt van druiven en andere vruchten 2) cognac

~ **Alexander** cocktail van brandewijn, crème de cacao en room

British wines wijnen in Engeland gegist; gemaakt van geïmporteerde druiven (of van geïmporteerd druivesap)

cherry brandy kersenlikeur

chocolate chocolademelk

cider cider

~ **cup** mengsel van cider, kruiderijen, suiker en ijs

claret rode Bordeauxwijn

cobbler *long drink* gemaakt van vruchten, waaraan men wijn of alcohol toevoegt

coffee koffie

~ **with cream** met room

black ~ zonder melk

caffeine-free ~ cafeïnevrij

white ~ half koffie, half melk; koffie verkeerd

cordial hartversterking

cream room

cup verfrissende drank gemaakt van gekoelde wijn, sodawater en een likeur of andere sterkedrank met een schijfje citroen of sinaasappel

daiquiri cocktail van rum, suiker, limoensap

double dubbele portie

Drambuie likeur gemaakt van whisky en honing

dry martini 1) droge vermouth (GB) 2) cocktail van droge vermouth en gin (US)

egg-nog alcoholische drank op basis van rum of andere sterkedrank, vermengd met geklopt eigeel en suiker

gin and it gin met Italiaanse vermouth

gin-fizz gin met citroensap, sodawater en suiker

ginger ale frisdrank met gembersmaak

ginger beer gemberbier

grasshopper cocktail van crème de menthe, crème de cacao en room

Guinness (stout) donker zoetsmakend bier met een hoog mout- en hopgehalte

half pint ongeveer 3 dl

highball alcoholische drank, zoals whisky, vermengd met water, sodawater of *ginger ale*

iced gekoeld, ijskoud

Irish coffee koffie met suiker en slagroom, waaraan men een scheut Ierse whisky toevoegt

Irish Mist Ierse likeur van whisky en honing

Irish whiskey Ierse whisky minder scherp dan Schotse whisky, bevat naast gerst ook rogge, haver en tarwe

juice sap

lager licht bier, koud geserveerd

lemon squash kwast

lemonade limonade

lime juice limoensap

liqueur likeur

liquor sterkedrank

long drink sterkedrank met tonic, sodawater of gewoon water en

ijsblokjes
madeira madera
Manhattan cocktail van Amerikaanse whisky en vermouth met
angostura
milk melk
mineral water mineraalwater
mulled wine bisschopswijn; warme, gekruide wijn
neat onvermengd. puur, zonder
water of ijs
old-fashioned cocktail van whisky,
angostura, sinaasappel schijfje,
suiker en maraskijnkersen
on the rocks met ijsblokjes
Ovaltine ovomaltine
Pimm's cup(s) sterkedrank met
vruchtesap, eventueel aange-
lengd met sodawater
~ **No. 1** met gin
~ **No. 2** met whisky
~ **No. 3** met rum
~ **No. 4** met brandewijn
pink champagne roze champagne
pink lady cocktail van eiwit, calva-
dos, citroensap, grenadine en
gin
pint ongeveer 6 dl
porter donker, bitter bier
quart 1,14 l (US 0,95 l)
root beer gezoete frisdrank met
aromat uit plantenwortels en
kruiden
rye (whiskey) whisky uit rogge
gestookt; zwaarder en scherper
van smaak dan *bourbon*
scotch (whisky) Schotse whisky,
een uit gerst en maïs (grain
whisky) gestookte sterkedrank,

vaak vermengd met malt whisky, uitsluitend uit gemoute gerst
gestookt
screwdriver wodka met sinaasappelsap
shandy *bitter ale* vermengd met
limonade of met *ginger beer*
short drink sterkedrank, onverdund gedronken
shot scheut sterkedrank
sloe **gin-fizz** sleepruimlikeur
(vrucht van de sleedoorn) met
citroensap en sodawater
soda water sodawater, spuitwater
soft drink frisdrank
spirits spiritualiën, gedistilleerde
dranken
stinger cognac en crème de
menthe
stout donker bier met veel hop
gebrouwen
straight sterkedrank onverdund
gedronken, puur
tea thee
toddy grog
Tom Collins *long drink* van gin,
citroensap, spuitwater en suiker
tonic (water) tonic, spuitwater met
kininesmaak
vodka wodka
whisky sour whisky, citroensap,
suiker en sodawater
wine wijn
dessert ~ zoete
dry ~ droge
red ~ rode
sparkling ~ mousserende
sweet ~ zoete (dessertwijn)
white ~ witte

Engelse onregelmatige werkwoorden

De onderstaande lijst geeft de Engelse onregelmatige werkwoorden aan. De samengestelde werkwoorden of werkwoorden met een voorvoegsel worden als de grondwerkwoorden vervoegd, bijvoorbeeld: *withdraw* wordt vervoegd als *draw* en *rebuild* als *build*.

Onbepaalde wijs	Onvoltooid verleden tijd	Verleden deelwoord	
arise	arose	arisen	*opstaan*
awake	awoke	awoken	*ontwaken*
be	was	been	*zijn*
bear	bore	borne	*dragen*
beat	beat	beaten	*slaan*
become	became	become	*worden*
begin	began	begun	*aanvangen*
bend	bent	bent	*buigen*
bet	bet	bet	*wedden*
bid	bade/bid	bidden/bid	*verzoeken*
bind	bound	bound	*binden*
bite	bit	bitten	*bijten*
bleed	bled	bled	*bloeden*
blow	blew	blown	*blazen*
break	broke	broken	*breken*
breed	bred	bred	*fokken*
bring	brought	brought	*brengen*
build	built	built	*bouwen*
burn	burnt/burned	burnt/burned	*branden*
burst	burst	burst	*barsten*
buy	bought	bought	*kopen*
can*	could	—	*kunnen*
cast	cast	cast	*werpen*
catch	caught	caught	*vangen*
choose	chose	chosen	*kiezen*
cling	clung	clung	*vastklemmen*
clothe	clothed/clad	clothed/clad	*kleden*
come	came	come	*komen*
cost	cost	cost	*kosten*
creep	crept	crept	*kruipen*
cut	cut	cut	*snijden*
deal	dealt	dealt	*uitdelen*
dig	dug	dug	*graven*
do (he does)	did	done	*doen*
draw	drew	drawn	*trekken*
dream	dreamt/dreamed	dreamt/dreamed	*dromen*
drink	drank	drunk	*drinken*
drive	drove	driven	*rijden*
dwell	dwelt	dwelt	*vertoeven*

* tegenwoordige tijd

eat	ate	eaten	*eten*
fall	fell	fallen	*vallen*
feed	fed	fed	*voeden*
feel	felt	felt	*voelen*
fight	fought	fought	*vechten*
find	found	found	*vinden*
flee	fled	fled	*vluchten*
fling	flung	flung	*werpen*
fly	flew	flown	*vliegen*
forsake	forsook	forsaken	*verzaken*
freeze	froze	frozen	*vriezen*
get	got	got	*krijgen*
give	gave	given	*geven*
go	went	gone	*gaan*
grind	ground	ground	*malen*
grow	grew	grown	*groeien*
hang	hung	hung	*(op)hangen*
have	had	had	*hebben*
hear	heard	heard	*horen*
hew	hewed	hewed/hewn	*hakken*
hide	hid	hidden	*verstoppen*
hit	hit	hit	*slaan*
hold	held	held	*houden*
hurt	hurt	hurt	*pijn doen*
keep	kept	kept	*houden*
kneel	knelt	knelt	*knielen*
knit	knitted/knit	knitted/knit	*breien*
know	knew	known	*weten*
lay	laid	laid	*leggen*
lead	led	led	*leiden*
lean	leant/leaned	leant/leaned	*leunen*
leap	leapt/leaped	leapt/leaped	*springen*
learn	learnt/learned	learnt/learned	*leren*
leave	left	left	*verlaten*
lend	lent	lent	*lenen(aan)*
let	let	let	*laten*
lie	lay	lain	*liggen*
light	lit/lighted	lit/lighted	*aansteken*
lose	lost	lost	*verliezen*
make	made	made	*maken*
may*	might	—	*mogen, kunnen*
mean	meant	meant	*bedoelen*
meet	met	met	*ontmoeten*
mow*	mowed	mowed/mown	*maaien*
must*	—	—	*moeten*
ought (to)*	—	—	*moeten*
pay	paid	paid	*betalen*
put	put	put	*zetten*
read	read	read	*lezen*

* tegenwoordige tijd

rid	rid	rid	*zich ontdoen (van)*
ride	rode	ridden	*rijden*
ring	rang	rung	*bellen*
rise	rose	risen	*opstaan*
run	ran	run	*rennen*
saw	sawed	sawn	*zagen*
say	said	said	*zeggen*
see	saw	seen	*zien*
seek	sought	sought	*zoeken*
sell	sold	sold	*verkopen*
send	sent	sent	*verzenden*
set	set	set	*zetten*
sew	sewed	sewed/sewn	*naaien*
shake	shook	shaken	*schudden*
shall*	should	—	*zullen*
shed	shed	shed	*vergieten*
shine	shone	shone	*schijnen*
shoot	shot	shot	*schieten*
show	showed	shown	*tonen*
shrink	shrank	shrunk	*krimpen*
shut	shut	shut	*sluiten*
sing	sang	sung	*zingen*
sink	sank	sunk	*zinken*
sit	sat	sat	*zitten*
sleep	slept	slept	*slapen*
slide	slid	slid	*glijden*
sling	slung	slung	*slingeren*
slink	slunk	slunk	*sluipen*
slit	slit	slit	*opensnijden*
smell	smelled/smelt	smelled/smelt	*ruiken*
sow	sowed	sown/sowed	*zaaien*
speak	spoke	spoken	*spreken*
speed	sped/speeded	sped/speeded	*zich haasten*
spell	spelt/spelled	spelt/spelled	*spellen*
spend	spent	spent	*uitgeven*
spill	spilt/spilled	spilt/spilled	*morsen*
spin	spun	spun	*spinnen*
spit	spat	spat	*spuwen*
split	split	split	*splijten*
spoil	spoilt/spoiled	spoilt/spoiled	*bederven*
spread	spread	spread	*spreiden*
spring	sprang	sprung	*ontspringen*
stand	stood	stood	*staan*
steal	stole	stolen	*stelen*
stick	stuck	stuck	*kleven*
sting	stung	stung	*steken*
stink	stank/stunk	stunk	*stinken*
strew	strewed	strewed/strewn	*strooien*
stride	strode	stridden	*schrijden*

---

* tegenwoordige tijd

strike	struck	struck/stricken	*slaan*
string	strung	strung	*rijgen*
strive	strove	striven	*streven*
swear	swore	sworn	*zweren*
sweep	swept	swept	*vegen*
swell	swelled	swollen	*zwellen*
swim	swam	swum	*zwemmen*
swing	swung	swung	*slingeren*
take	took	taken	*nemen*
teach	taught	taught	*onderwijzen*
tear	tore	torn	*scheuren*
tell	told	told	*vertellen*
think	thought	thought	*denken*
throw	threw	thrown	*werpen*
thrust	thrust	thrust	*duwen*
tread	trod	trodden	*treden*
wake	woke/waked	woken/waked	*wekken*
wear	wore	worn	*dragen*
weave	wove	woven	*weven*
weep	wept	wept	*huilen*
will*	would	—	*zullen*
win	won	won	*winnen*
wind	wound	wound	*opwinden*
wring	wrung	wrung	*wringen*
write	wrote	written	*schrijven*

---

* tegenwoordige tijd

Engelse afkortingen

AA	*Automobile Association*	Britse Automobielclub
AAA	*American Automobile Association*	Amerikaanse Automobielclub
ABC	*American Broadcasting Company*	Amerikaanse radio- en televisiemaatschappij
A.D.	*anno Domini*	na Christus
Am.	*America; American*	Amerika; Amerikaans
a.m.	*ante meridiem (before noon)*	de tijd tussen 0 en 12 uur
Amtrak	*American railroad corporation*	Amerikaanse spoorwegmaatschappij
AT & T	*American Telephone and Telegraph Company*	Amerikaanse telefoon- en telegraafmaatschappij
Ave.	*avenue*	avenue
BBC	*British Broadcasting Corporation*	Britse radio- en televisie- maatschappij
B.C.	*before Christ*	voor Christus
bldg.	*building*	gebouw
Blvd.	*boulevard*	boulevard
B.R.	*British Rail*	Britse Spoorwegen
Brit.	*Britain; British*	Groot-Brittannië, Brits
Bros.	*brothers*	gebroeders
¢	*cent*	1/100 van een dollar
Can.	*Canada; Canadian*	Canada; Canadees
CBS	*Columbia Broadcasting System*	Amerikaanse radio- en televisiemaatschappij
CID	*Criminal Investigation Department*	afdeling criminele recherche van Scotland Yard
CNR	*Canadian National Railway*	Canadese Nationale Spoorwegen
c/o	*(in) care of*	per adres
Co.	*company*	maatschappij
Corp.	*corporation*	vennootschap
CPR	*Canadian Pacific Railways*	Canadese spoorweg- maatschappij
D.C.	*District of Columbia*	district in de V.S. waarin de hoofdstad Washington ligt
DDS	*Doctor of Dental Science*	doctor in de tandheelkunde
dept.	*department*	departement, afdeling
EEC	*European Economic Community*	EEG, Europese Economische Gemeenschap
e.g.	*for instance*	bijvoorbeeld

Eng.	*England; English*	Engeland; Engels
excl.	*excluding; exclusive*	exclusief
ft.	*foot/feet*	voet
GB	*Great Britain*	Groot-Brittannië
H.E.	*His/Her Excellency;*	Zijne/Hare Excellentie;
	His Eminence	Zijne Eminentie
H.H.	*His Holiness*	Zijne Heiligheid
H.M.	*His/Her Majesty*	Zijne/Hare Majesteit
H.M.S.	*Her Majesty's ship*	Harer Majesteits schip
		(Brits oorlogsschip)
hp	*horsepower*	paardekracht
Hwy	*highway*	autoweg
i.e.	*that is to say*	d.w.z., dat wil zeggen
in.	*inch*	duim (2,54 cm)
Inc.	*incorporated*	naamloze vennootschap
incl.	*including, inclusive*	inclusief
£	*pound sterling*	pond sterling
L.A.	*Los Angeles*	Los Angeles
Ltd.	*limited*	naamloze vennootschap
M.D.	*Doctor of Medicine*	arts
M.P.	*Member of Parliament*	lid van het Lagerhuis
		(Engeland)
mph	*miles per hour*	Engelse mijl per uur
Mr.	*Mister*	meneer
Mrs.	*Missis*	mevrouw
Ms.	*Missis/Miss*	mevrouw/mejuffrouw
nat.	*national*	nationaal
NBC	*National Broadcasting*	Amerikaanse radio- en
	Company	televisiemaatschappij
No.	*number*	nummer
N.Y.C.	*New York City*	New York City
O.B.E.	*Officer (of the Order)*	Officier in de Orde
	of the British Empire	van het Britse Imperium
p.	*page; penny/pence*	bladzijde; 1/100 van een pond
p.a.	*per annum*	per jaar
Ph.D.	*Doctor of Philosophy*	doctor in de wijsbegeerte
p.m.	*post meridiem*	de tijd tussen 12 en 24 uur
	(after noon)	
PO	*post office*	postkantoor
POO	*post office order*	postorder
pop.	*population*	bevolking
P.T.O.	*please turn over*	zie ommezijde, a.u.b.
RAC	*Royal Automobile Club*	Koninklijke Britse
		Automobielclub

C°	F°
100	212
40	105
36,9	98,6
35	90
30	
25	80
20	70
15	60
10	50
5	40
0	32
	30
−5	20
10	
−15	10
−20	0

Conversion tables/Omrekentabelle

Meters en voeten
Het middelste cijfer geeft zowel meters ...
voeten aan, bijvoorbeeld 1 meter = 3,2...
voet en 1 voet = 0,30 m.

Metres and feet
The figure in the middle stands for b...
metres and feet, e.g. 1 metre = 3.281
and 1 foot = 0.30 m.

Meters/Metres		Voeten/Fee...
0.30	**1**	3.281
0.61	**2**	6.563
0.91	**3**	9.843
1.22	**4**	13.124
1.52	**5**	16.403
1.83	**6**	19.686
2.13	**7**	22.967
2.44	**8**	26.248
2.74	**9**	29.529
3.05	**10**	32.810
3.66	**12**	39.372
4.27	**14**	45.934
6.10	**20**	65.620
7.62	**25**	82.023
15.24	**50**	164.046
22.86	**75**	246.069
30.48	**100**	328.092

Temperatuur
Voor het omrekenen van Celsius in Fahr...
heit, moet u het aantal graden Celsius m...
1,8 vermenigvuldigen en er dan 32 bij o...
tellen.
Voor het omrekenen van Fahrenheit ...
Celsius, moet u 32 van het aantal grad...
Fahrenheit aftrekken en dan delen door 1,...

Temperature
To convert Centigrade to Fahrenheit, mu...
tiply by 1.8 and add 32.
To convert Fahrenheit to Centigrade, su...
tract 32 from Fahrenheit and divide by 1.

RCMP	Royal Canadian Mounted Police	Koninklijke Canadese Bereden Politie
Rd.	road	weg
ref.	reference	verwijzing
Rev.	reverend	dominee
RFD	rural free delivery	landelijke postbus
RR	railroad	spoorweg
RSVP	please reply	verzoeke gaarne antwoord
$	dollar	dollar
Soc.	society	maatschappij, genootschap
St.	saint; street	sint; straat
STD	Subscriber Trunk Dialling	automatisch telefoonverkeer
UN	United Nations	V.N., Verenigde Naties
UPS	United Parcel Service	Amerikaanse pakketdienst
US	United States	Verenigde Staten
USS	United States Ship	Amerikaans oorlogsschip
VAT	value added tax	B.T.W.
VIP	very important person	zeer belangrijke persoon
Xmas	Christmas	Kerstmis
yd.	yard	yard (91,44 cm)
YMCA	Young Men's Christian Association	Christelijke Jongeren Vereniging
YWCA	Young Women's Christian Association	Christelijke Meisjes Vereniging
ZIP	ZIP code	postnummer

Telwoorden

Hoofdtelwoorden		Rangtelwoorden	
0	zero	1st	first
1	one	2nd	second
2	two	3rd	third
3	three	4th	fourth
4	four	5th	fifth
5	five	6th	sixth
6	six	7th	seventh
7	seven	8th	eighth
8	eight	9th	ninth
9	nine	10th	tenth
10	ten	11th	eleventh
11	eleven	12th	twelfth
12	twelve	13th	thirteenth
13	thirteen	14th	fourteenth
14	fourteen	15th	fifteenth
15	fifteen	16th	sixteenth
16	sixteen	17th	seventeenth
17	seventeen	18th	eighteenth
18	eighteen	19th	nineteenth
19	nineteen	20th	twentieth
20	twenty	21st	twenty-first
21	twenty-one	22nd	twenty-second
22	twenty-two	23rd	twenty-third
23	twenty-three	24th	twenty-fourth
24	twenty-four	25th	twenty-fifth
25	twenty-five	26th	twenty-sixth
30	thirty	27th	twenty-seventh
40	forty	28th	twenty-eighth
50	fifty	29th	twenty-ninth
60	sixty	30th	thirtieth
70	seventy	40th	fortieth
80	eighty	50th	fiftieth
90	ninety	60th	sixtieth
100	a/one hundred	70th	seventieth
230	two hundred and thirty	80th	eightieth
		90th	ninetieth
1,000	a/one thousand	100th	hundredth
10,000	ten thousand	230th	two hundred and thirtieth
100,000	a/one hundred thousand		
1,000,000	a/one million	1,000th	thousandth

Tijd

De Engelsen en Amerikanen gebruiken het twaalf-uren systeem. De uitdrukking *a.m. (ante meridiem)* duidt op de uren tussen middernacht en 12 uur 's middags; *p.m. (post meridiem)* op de uren tussen 12 uur 's middags en middernacht. Engeland gaat momenteel geleidelijk over op het continentale systeem.

I'll come at seven a.m. — Ik kom om 7 uur 's morgens.
I'll come at two p.m. — Ik kom om 2 uur 's middags.
I'll come at eight p.m. — Ik kom om 8 uur 's avonds.

Dagen van de week

Sunday	zondag	*Thursday*	donderdag
Monday	maandag	*Friday*	vrijdag
Tuesday	dinsdag	*Saturday*	zaterdag
Wednesday	woensdag		

Enkele nuttige zinnen	**Some Basic Phrases**
Alstublieft.	Please.
Hartelijk dank.	Thank you very much.
Niets te danken.	Don't mention it.
Goedemorgen.	Good morning.
Goedemiddag.	Good afternoon.
Goedenavond.	Good evening.
Goedenacht.	Good night.
Tot ziens.	Good-bye.
Tot straks.	See you later.
Waar is/Waar zijn...?	Where is/Where are...?
Hoe noemt u dit?	What do you call this?
Wat betekent dat?	What does that mean?
Spreekt u Engels?	Do you speak English?
Spreekt u Duits?	Do you speak German?
Spreekt u Frans?	Do you speak French?
Spreekt u Spaans?	Do you speak Spanish?
Spreekt u Italiaans?	Do you speak Italian?
Kunt u wat langzamer spreken, alstublieft?	Could you speak more slowly, please?
Ik begrijp het niet.	I don't understand.
Mag ik...hebben?	Can I have...?
Kunt u mij...tonen?	Can you show me...?
Kunt u mij zeggen...?	Can you tell me...?
Kunt u me helpen?	Can you help me, please?
Ik wil graag...	I'd like...
Wij willen graag...	We'd like...
Geeft u me..., alstublieft.	Please give me...
Brengt u me..., alstublieft.	Please bring me...
Ik heb honger.	I'm hungry.
Ik heb dorst.	I'm thirsty.
Ik ben verdwaald.	I'm lost.
Vlug!	Hurry up!
Er is/Er zijn...	There is/There are...
Er is geen/Er zijn geen...	There isn't/There aren't...

Aankomst

Uw paspoort, alstublieft.

Hebt u iets aan te geven?

Nee, helemaal niets.

Kunt u me met mijn bagage helpen, alstublieft?

Waar is de bus naar het centrum?

Hierlangs, alstublieft.

Waar kan ik een taxi krijgen?

Wat kost het naar…?

Breng me naar dit adres, alstublieft.

Ik heb haast.

Arrival

Your passport, please.

Have you anything to declare?

No, nothing at all.

Can you help me with my luggage, please?

Where's the bus to the centre of town, please?

This way, please.

Where can I get a taxi?

What's the fare to…?

Take me to this address, please.

I'm in a hurry.

Hotel

Mijn naam is…

Hebt u gereserveerd?

Ik wil graag een kamer met bad.

Hoeveel kost het per nacht?

Mag ik de kamer zien?

Wat is mijn kamernummer?

Er is geen warm water.

Mag ik de directeur spreken, alstublieft?

Heeft er iemand voor mij opgebeld?

Is er post voor mij?

Mag ik de rekening, alstublieft?

Hotel

My name is…

Have you a reservation?

I'd like a room with a bath.

What's the price per night?

May I see the room?

What's my room number, please?

There's no hot water.

May I see the manager, please?

Did anyone telephone me?

Is there any mail for me?

May I have my bill (check), please?

Uit eten

Hebt u een menu à prix fixe?

Mag ik de spijskaart zien?

Kunt u ons een asbak brengen, alstublieft?

Eating out

Do you have a fixed-price menu?

May I see the menu?

May we have an ashtray, please?

Waar is het toilet? — Where's the toilet, please?

Ik wil graag een voorgerecht. — I'd like an hors d'œuvre (starter).

Hebt u soep? — Have you any soup?

Ik wil graag vis. — I'd like some fish.

Wat voor vis hebt u? — What kind of fish do you have?

Ik wil graag een biefstuk. — I'd like a steak.

Wat voor groenten hebt u? — What vegetables have you got?

Niets meer, dank u. — Nothing more, thanks.

Wat wilt u drinken? — What would you like to drink?

Een pils, alstublieft. — I'll have a beer, please.

Ik wil graag een fles wijn. — I'd like a bottle of wine.

Mag ik de rekening, alstublieft? — May I have the bill (check), please?

Is de bediening inbegrepen? — Is service included?

Dank u, het was een uitstekende maaltijd. — Thank you, that was a very good meal.

Reizen — Travelling

Waar is het station? — Where's the railway station, please?

Waar is het loket? — Where's the ticket office, please?

Ik wil graag een kaartje naar... — I'd like a ticket to...

Eerste of tweede klas? — First or second class?

Eerste klas, alstublieft. — First class, please.

Enkele reis of retour? — Single or return (one way or roundtrip)?

Moet ik overstappen? — Do I have to change trains?

Van welk perron vertrekt de trein naar...? — What platform does the train for... leave from?

Waar is het dichtstbijzijnde metrostation? — Where's the nearest underground (subway) station?

Waar is het busstation? — Where's the bus station, please?

Hoe laat vertrekt de eerste bus naar...? — When's the first bus to...?

Wilt u me bij de volgende halte laten uitstappen? — Please let me off at the next stop.

Ontspanning

Wat wordt er in de bioscoop
gegeven?

Hoe laat begint de film?

Zijn er nog plaatsen vrij voor
vanavond?

Waar kunnen we gaan dansen?

Relaxing

What's on at the cinema (movies)?

What time does the film begin?

Are there any tickets for tonight?

Where can we go dancing?

Ontmoetingen

Dag mevrouw/juffrouw/
mijnheer.

Hoe maakt u het?

Uitstekend, dank u. En u?

Mag ik u... voorstellen?

Mijn naam is...

Prettig kennis met u te maken.

Hoelang bent u al hier?

Het was mij een genoegen.

Hindert het u als ik rook?

Hebt u een vuurtje, alstublieft?

Mag ik u iets te drinken
aanbieden?

Mag ik u vanavond ten eten
uitnodigen?

Waar spreken we af?

Meeting people

How do you do.

How are you?

Very well, thank you. And you?

May I introduce...?

My name is...

I'm very pleased to meet you.

How long have you been here?

It was nice meeting you.

Do you mind if I smoke?

Do you have a light, please?

May I get you a drink?

May I invite you for dinner
tonight?

Where shall we meet?

Winkels en diensten

Waar is de dichtstbijzijnde bank?

Waar kan ik reischeques
inwisselen?

Kunt u me wat kleingeld geven,
alstublieft?

Waar is de dichtstbijzijnde
apotheek?

Hoe kom ik daar?

Is het te lopen?

Shops, stores and services

Where's the nearest bank, please?

Where can I cash some travellers'
cheques?

Can you give me some small
change, please?

Where's the nearest chemist's
(pharmacy)?

How do I get there?

Is it within walking distance?

Kunt u mij helpen, alstublieft?   Can you help me, please?

Hoeveel kost dit? En dat?   How much is this? And that?

Het is niet precies wat ik zoek.   It's not quite what I want.

Het bevalt me.   I like it.

Kunt u mij iets tegen zonnebrand aanbevelen?   Can you recommend something for sunburn?

Knippen, alstublieft.   I'd like a haircut, please.

Ik wil een manicure, alstublieft.   I'd like a manicure, please.

De weg vragen

Street directions

Kunt u mij op de kaart aanwijzen waar ik ben?   Can you show me on the map where I am?

U bent op de verkeerde weg.   You are on the wrong road.

Rij/Ga rechtuit.   Go/Walk straight ahead.

Het is aan de linkerkant/aan de rechterkant.   It's on the left/on the right.

Spoedgevallen

Emergencies

Roep vlug een dokter.   Call a doctor quickly.

Roep een ambulance.   Call an ambulance.

Roep de politie, alstublieft.   Please call the police.

dutch-english

nederlands-engels

Introduction

The dictionary has been designed so that it best meets your practical needs. Unnecessary linguistic information has been avoided. The entries are listed in alphabetical order regardless of whether the entry word is printed in a single word, is hyphened or is in two or more separate words. The only exception to this rule, reflexive verbs, are listed as main entries alphabetically according to the verb, e.g. *zich afvragen* is found under **a.**

When an entry is followed by sub-entries such as expressions and locutions, these, too, have been listed in alphabetical order.

Each main-entry word is followed by a phonetic transcription (see Guide to pronunciation). Following the transcription is the part of speech of the entry word whenever applicable. When an entry word may be used as more then one part of speech, the translations are grouped together after the respective part of speech.

Considering the complexity of the rules for constructing the plural of Dutch nouns, we have supplied the plural form whenever in current use.

Each time an entry word is repeated in plurals or in sub-entries, a tilde (~) is used to represent the full entry word.

In plurals of long words, only the part that changes is written out fully, whereas the unchanged part is represented by a hyphen.

Entry: beker (pl ~s)	Plural: bekers
kind (pl ~eren)	kinderen
leslokaal (pl -kalen)	leslokalen

An asterisk (*) in front of a verb indicates that the verb is irregular. For details, refer to the lists of irregular verbs.

Abbreviations

adj	adjective	*p*	past tense
adv	adverb	*pl*	plural
Am	American	*plAm*	plural (American)
art	article	*pp*	past participle
c	common gender	*pr*	present tense
conj	conjunction	*pref*	prefix
n	noun	*prep*	preposition
nAm	noun (American)	*pron*	pronoun
nt	neuter	*v*	verb
num	numeral	*vAm*	verb (American)

Guide to Pronunciation

Each main entry in this part of the dictionary is followed by a phonetic transcription which shows you how to pronounce the words. This transcription should be read as if it were English. It is based on Standard British pronunciation, though we have tried to take account of General American pronunciation also. Below, only those letters and symbols are explained which we consider likely to be ambiguous or not immediately understood.

The syllables are separated by hyphens, and stressed syllables are printed in *italics*.

Of course, the sounds of any two languages are never exactly the same, but if you follow carefully our indications, you should be able to pronounce the foreign words in such a way that you'll be understood. To make your task easier, our transcriptions occasionally simplify slightly the sound system of the language while still reflecting the essential sound differences.

Consonants

g   a g-sound where the tongue doesn't quite close the air passage between itself and the roof of the mouth, so that the escaping air produces audible friction; often fairly hard, so that it resembles **kh**

kh   like **g**, but based on a **k**-sound; therefore hard and voiceless, like **ch** in Scottish lo**ch**

ñ   as in Spanish se**ñ**or, or like **ni** in o**ni**on

s   always hard, as in **s**o

zh   a soft, voiced **sh**, like **s** in plea**s**ure

1) In everyday speech, the **n** in the ending of verbs and plurals of nouns is usually dropped.

2) We use the transcription **v** for two different sounds (written **v** and **w** in Dutch) because the difference between them is often inaudible to foreigners.

Vowels and Diphthongs

aa   like **a** in c**a**r

ah   a short version of **aa**; between **a** in c**a**t and **u** in c**u**t

ai   like **air**, without any **r**-sound

eh	like **e** in g**e**t
er	as in oth**er**, without any **r**-sound
ew	a "rounded **ee**-sound"; say the vowel sound **ee** (as in s**ee**), and while saying it, round your lips as for **oo** (as in s**oo**n), without moving your tongue; when your lips ar in the **oo** position, but your tongue is in the **ee** position, you should be pronouncing the correct sound
ı	like **i** in b**i**t
igh	as in s**igh**
o	always as in h**o**t (British pronunciation)
ou	as in l**ou**d
ur	as in f**ur**, but with rounded lips and no **r**-sound

1) A bar over a vowel symbol (e.g. $\overline{oo}$) shows that this sound is long.

2) Raised letters (e.g. **aa**^{ee}, **t**^{y}, ^{y}**eh**) should be pronounced only fleetingly.

3) Dutch vowels (i.e. not diphthongs) are pure. Therefore, you should try to read a transcription like $\overline{oa}$ without moving tongue or lips while pronouncing the sound.

4) Some Dutch words borrowed from French contain nasal vowels, which we transcribe with a vowel symbol plus ~~ng~~ (e.g. **ahng**). This ~~ng~~ should *not* be pronounced, and serves solely to indicate nasal quality of the preceding vowel. A nasal vowel is pronounced simultaneously through the mouth and the nose.

A

aal (aal) *c* (pl alen) eel

aambeien (*aam*-bay-ern) *pl* haemorrhoids *pl*, piles *pl*

aan (aan) *prep* to; on

aanbetaling (*aam*-ber-taa-ling) *c* (pl ~en) down payment

***aanbevelen** (*aam*-ber-vāy-lern) *v* recommend

aanbeveling (*aam*-ber-vāy-ling) *c* (pl ~en) recommendation

aanbevelingsbrief (*aam*-ber-vāy-lings-breef) *c* (pl -brieven) letter of recommendation

***aanbidden** (*aam*-bi-dern) *v* worship

***aanbieden** (*aam*-bee-dern) *v* offer; present

aanbieding (*aam*-bee-ding) *c* (pl ~en) offer

aanblik (*aam*-blik) *c* sight; appearance

aanbod (*aam*-bot) *nt* offer; supply

aanbranden (*aam*-brahn-dern) *v* *burn

aandacht (*aan*-dahkht) *c* attention; notice, consideration; ~ **besteden aan** attend to

aandeel (*aan*-dāyl) *nt* (pl -delen) share

aandenken (*aan*-dehng-kern) *nt* (pl ~s) remembrance

aandoening (*aan*-dōō-ning) *c* (pl ~en) affection

aandoenlijk (aan-*dōōn*-lerk) *adj* touching

***aandrijven** (*aan*-dray-vern) *v* propel

***aandringen** (*aan*-dri-ngern) *v* insist

aanduiden (*aan*-dur^ew^-dern) *v* indicate

***aangaan** (*aang*-gaan) *v* concern

aangaande (aang-*gaan*-der) *prep* as regards

aangeboren (*aang*-ger-bōā-rern) *adj* natural

aangelegenheid (*aang*-ger-*lāy*-gern-hayt) *c* (pl -heden) matter, concern; affair, business

aangenaam (*aang*-ger-naam) *adj* agreeable, pleasing, pleasant

aangesloten (*aang*-ger-slōā-tern) *adj* affiliated

***aangeven** (*aang*-gāy-vern) *v* indicate; declare; *give, hand, pass

aangezien (aang-ger-*zeen*) *conj* as, since; because

aangifte (*aang* gif-ter) *c* (pl ~n) declaration

aangrenzend (aang-*grehn*-zernt) *adj* neighbouring

aanhalen (*aan*-haa-lern) *v* tighten; quote

aanhalingstekens (*aan*-haa-lings-tāy-kerns) *pl* quotation marks

aanhangwagen (*aan*-hahng-vaa-gern) *c* (pl ~s) trailer

aanhankelijk (aan-*hahng*-ker-lerk) *adj*

affectionate

*aanhebben (*aan*-heh-bern) *v* *wear

aanhechten (*aan*-hehkh-tern) *v* attach

aanhoren (*aan*-hōā-rern) *v* listen

*aanhouden (*aan*-hou-dern) *v* insist;
aanhoudend constant

aanhouding (*aan*-hou-dıng) *c* (pl ~en)
arrest

*aankijken (*aang*-kay-kern) *v* look at

aanklacht (*aang*-klahkht) *c* (pl ~en)
charge

aanklagen (*aang*-klaa-gern) *v* accuse,
charge

aankleden (*aang*-klāȳ-dern) *v* dress;
*get dressed

*aankomen (*aang*-kōā-mern) *v* arrive

aankomst (*aang*-komst) *c* arrival

aankomsttijd (*aang*-koms-tayt) *c* (pl
~en) time of arrival

aankondigen (*aang*-kon-der-gern) *v*
announce

aankondiging (*aang*-kon-der-gıng) *c*
(pl ~en) notice, announcement

aankoop (*aang*-kōāp) *c* (pl -kopen)
purchase

aankruisen (*aang*-krur^{ew}-sern) *v* mark

aanleg (*aan*-lehkh) *c* talent

aanleggen (*aan*-leh-gern) *v* dock

aanleiding (*aan*-lay-dıng) *c* (pl ~en)
cause, occasion

aanlengen (*aan*-leh-ngern) *v* dilute

zich aanmelden (*aan*-mehl-dern) report

aanmerkelijk (aa-*mehr*-ker-lerk) *adj*
considerable

aanmerken (aa-*mehr*-kern) *v* comment

aanmoedigen (aa-*mōō*-der-gern) *v* encourage

*aannemen (aa-*nāȳ*-mern) *v* accept;
assume, suppose; adopt; **aangenomen dat** supposing that

aannemer (aa-*nāȳ*-merr) *c* (pl ~s)
contractor

aanpak (*aam*-pahk) *c* method, approach

aanpassen (*aam*-pah-sern) *v* adapt;
suit; adjust

aanplakbiljet (*aam*-plahk-bıl-^yeht) *nt*
(pl ~ten) placard

*aanprijzen (*aam*-pray-zern) *v* recommend

*aanraden (*aan*-raa-dern) *v* advise,
recommend

aanraken (*aan*-raa-kern) *v* touch

aanraking (*aan*-raa-kıng) *c* (pl ~en)
touch; contact

aanranden (*aan*-rahn-dern) *v* assault

aanrichten (*aan*-rıkh-tern) *v* cause

aanrijding (*aan*-ray-dıng) *c* (pl ~en)
collision

aanschaffen (*aan*-skhah-fern) *v* *buy

*aansluiten (*aan*-slur^{ew}-tern) *v* connect

aansluiting (*aan*-slur^{ew}-tıng) *c* (pl
~en) connection

aansporen (*aan*-spōā-rern) *v* incite;
urge

aanspraak (*aan*-spraak) *c* (pl -spraken) claim

aansprakelijk (aan-*spraa*-ker-lerk) *adj*
liable; responsible

aansprakelijkheid (aan-*spraa*-ker-lerk-
hayt) *c* liability; responsibility

*aanspreken (*aan*-sprāȳ-kern) *v* address

aanstekelijk (aan-*stāȳ*-ker-lerk) *adj*
contagious

*aansteken (*aan*-stāȳ-kern) *v* *light;
infect

aansteker (*aan*-stāȳ-kerr) *c* (pl ~s)
lighter, cigarette-lighter

aanstellen (*aan*-steh-lern) *v* appoint

aanstoot (*aan*-stōāt) *c* offence

aanstootgevend (aan-stōāt-*khāȳ*-vernt)
adj offensive

aanstrepen (*aan*-strāȳ-pern) *v* tick off

aantal (*aan*-tahl) *nt* (pl ~len) number; quantity

aantekenen (*aan*-tāy-ker-nern) v record; register

aantekening (*aan*-tāy-ker-nɪng) c (pl ~en) note

aantonen (*aan*-tōa-nern) v prove; demonstrate, *show

aantrekkelijk (aan-*treh*-ker-lerk) adj attractive

*****aantrekken** (*aan*-treh-kern) v attract; tempt; *put on; tighten

aantrekking (*aan*-treh-kɪng) c attraction

aanvaarden (aan-*vaar*-dern) v accept

aanval (*aan*-vahl) c (pl ~len) attack; fit

*****aanvallen** (*aan*-vah-lern) v attack; assault

aanvang (*aan*-vahng) c beginning

*****aanvangen** (*aan*-vah-ngern) v *begin

aanvankelijk (aan-*vahng*-ker-lerk) adv originally, at first

aanvaring (*aan*-vaa-rɪng) c (pl ~en) collision

aanvoer (*aan*-vōōr) c supply

aanvoerder (*aan*-vōōr-derr) c (pl ~s) leader

aanvraag (*aan*-vraakh) c (pl -vragen) application

aanwezig (aan-*vāy*-zerkh) adj present

aanwezigheid (aan-*vāy*-zerkh-hayt) c presence

*****aanwijzen** (*aan*-vay-zern) v point out; designate

aanwijzing (*aan*-vay-zɪng) c (pl ~en) indication

aanzetten (*aan*-zeh-tern) v turn on

aanzien (*aan*-zeen) nt aspect; esteem; **ten ~ van** regarding

aanzienlijk (aan-*zeen*-lerk) adj considerable, substantial

aap (aap) c (pl apen) monkey

aard (aart) c nature

aardappel (*aar*-dah-perl) c (pl ~s, ~en) potato

aardbei (*aart*-bay) c (pl ~en) strawberry

aardbeving (*aart*-bāy-vɪng) c (pl ~en) earthquake

aardbol (*aart*-bol) c globe

aarde (*aar*-der) c earth; soil

aardewerk (*aar*-der-vehrk) nt crockery, pottery, faience, earthenware, ceramics pl

aardig (*aar*-derkh) adj pleasant; nice, kind

aardrijkskunde (*aar*-drayks-kern-der) c geography

aartsbisschop (*aarts*-bɪ-skhop) c (pl ~pen) archbishop

aarzelen (*aar*-zer-lern) v hesitate

aas (aass) nt bait

abces (ahp-*sehss*) nt (pl ~sen) abscess

abdij (ahb-*day*) c (pl ~en) abbey

abnormaal (ahp-nor-*maal*) adj abnormal

abonnee (ah-bo-*nāy*) c (pl ~s) subscriber

abonnement (ah-bo-ner-*mehnt*) nt (pl ~en) subscription

abonnementskaart (ah-bo-ner-*mehnts*-kaart) c (pl ~en) season-ticket

abortus (ah-*bor*-terss) c (pl ~sen) abortion

abrikoos (ah-bree-*kōass*) c (pl -kozen) apricot

absoluut (ahp-sōa-*lēwt*) adj sheer; adv absolutely

abstract (ahp-*strahkt*) adj abstract

absurd (ahp-*serrt*) adj absurd

abuis (aa-*bur^(ew)ss*) nt (pl abuizen) mistake

academie (aa-kaa-*dāy*-mee) c (pl ~s) academy

accent (ahk-*sehnt*) nt (pl ~en) accent

accepteren (ahk-sehp-*tāy*-rern) v accept

accessoires (ahk-seh-*svaa*-rerss) pl accessories pl

accijns (ahk-*sayns*) *c* (pl -cijnzen)
Customs duty

accommodatie (ah-ko-mōa-*daa*-tsee) *c*
accommodation

accu (*ah*-kew) *c* (pl ~'s) battery

acht (ahkht) *num* eight

achteloos (*ahkh*-ter-lōass) *adj* careless

achten (*ahkh*-tern) *v* esteem; count

achter (*ahkh*-terr) *prep* behind; after

achteraan (ahkh-ter-*raan*) *adv* behind

achterbuurt (*ahkh*-terr-bewrt) *c* (pl
~en) slum

achterdochtig (ahkh-terr-*dokh*-terkh)
adj suspicious

achtergrond (*ahkh*-terr-gront) *c* (pl
~en) background

achterkant (*ahkh*-terr-kahnt) *c* (pl
~en) rear

*****achterlaten** (*ahkh*-terr-laa-tern) *v*
*leave behind

achterlicht (*ahkh*-terr-lıkht) *nt* (pl
~en) tail-light, rear-light

achternaam (*ahkh*-terr-naam) *c* (pl
-namen) family name, surname

achterstallig (ahkh-terr-*stah*-lerkh) *adj*
overdue

achteruit (ahkh-ter-*rur^(ew)*t) *adv* backwards

*****achteruitrijden** (ahkh-ter-*rur^(ew)*t-ray-
dern) *v* reverse

achterwerk (*ahkh*-terr-vehrk) *nt* (pl
~en) bottom

achting (*ahkh*-tıng) *c* respect, esteem

achtste (*ahkht*-ster) *num* eighth

achttien (*ahkh*-teen) *num* eighteen

achttiende (*ahkh*-teen-der) *num* eighteenth

acne (*ahk*-nāy) *c* acne

acquisitie (ah-kvee-*zee*-tsee) *c* (pl ~s)
acquisition

acteur (ahk-*tŭrr*) *c* (pl ~s) actor

actie (*ahk*-see) *c* (pl ~s) action

actief (ahk-*teef*) *adj* active

activiteit (ahk-tee-vee-*tayt*) *c* (pl ~en)
activity

actrice (ahk-*tree*-ser) *c* (pl ~s) actress

actueel (ahk-tēw-*vāyl*) *adj* topical

acuut (ah-*kēwt*) *adj* acute

adel (*aa*-derl) *c* nobility

adellijk (*aa*-der-lerk) *adj* noble

adem (*aa*-derm) *c* breath

ademen (*aa*-der-mern) *v* breathe

ademhaling (*aa*-derm-haa-lıng) *c*
breathing, respiration

adequaat (ah-*dāy*-kvaat) *adj* adequate

ader (*aa*-derr) *c* (pl ~s, ~en) vein

administratie (aht-mee-nee-*straa*-tsee)
c (pl ~s) administration

administratief (aht-mee-nee-straa-*teef*)
adj administrative

admiraal (aht-mee-*raal*) *c* (pl ~s) admiral

adopteren (ah-dop-*tāy*-rern) *v* adopt

adres (aa-*drehss*) *nt* (pl ~sen) address

adresseren (aa-dreh-*sāy*-rern) *v* address

advertentie (aht-ferr-*tehn*-see) *c* (pl
~s) advertisement

advies (aht-*feess*) *nt* (pl adviezen) advice

adviseren (aht-fee-*zāy*-rern) *v* advise

advocaat (aht-fōa-*kaat*) *c* (pl -caten)
lawyer; barrister; solicitor; attorney

af (ahf) *adv* off; finished; ~ **en toe**
occasionally

afbeelding (*ahf*-bāyl-dıng) *c* (pl ~en)
picture

afbetalen (*ahf*-ber-taa-lern) *v* *pay on
account

afbetaling (*ahf*-ber-taa-lıng) *c* (pl ~en)
instalment

*****afblijven** (*ahf*-blay-vern) *v* *keep off

afbraak (*ahf*-braak) *c* demolition

*****afbreken** (*ahf*-brāy-kern) *v* chip

afdaling (*ahf*-daa-lıng) *c* (pl ~en) descent

afdanken (*ahf*-dahng-kern) *v* discard

afdeling (ahf-dāy-lıng) c (pl ~en) division, department; section

*afdingen (ahf-dı-ngern) v bargain

afdrogen (ahf-drōa-gern) v dry

afdruk (ahf-drerk) c (pl ~ken) print

*afdwingen (ahf-dvı-ngern) v extort

affaire (ah-fai-rer) c (pl ~s) deal; affair

affiche (ah-fee-sher) nt (pl ~s) poster

afgeladen (ahf-kher-laa-dern) adj chock-full

afgelegen (ahf-kher-lāy-gern) adj remote, far-off, out of the way

afgelopen (ahf-kher-lōa-pern) adj past

afgerond (ahf-kher-ront) adj rounded

afgevaardigde (ahf-kher-vaar-derg-der) c (pl ~n) deputy

afgezien van (ahf-kher-zeen vahn) apart from

afgod (ahf-khot) c (pl ~en) idol

afgrijzen (ahf-khray-zern) nt horror

afgrond (ahf-khront) c (pl ~en) precipice, abyss

afgunst (ahf-khernst) c envy

afgunstig (ahf-khern-sterkh) adj envious

afhalen (ahf-haa-lern) v collect, fetch

afhandelen (ahf-hahn-der-lern) v settle

*afhangen van (ahf-hah-ngern) depend on

afhankelijk (ahf-hahng-ker-lerk) adj dependant

afhellend (ahf-heh-lernt) adj sloping

afkeer (ahf-kāyr) c dislike; antipathy

afkerig (ahf-kāy-rerkh) adj averse

afkeuren (ahf-kūr-rern) v disapprove; reject

afknippen (ahf-knı-pern) v *cut off

afkondigen (ahf-kon-der-gern) v proclaim

afkorting (ahf-kor-tıng) c (pl ~en) abbreviation

afleiden (ahf-lay-dern) v deduce, infer

afleiding (ahf-lay-dıng) c diversion

afleren (ahf-lāy-rern) v unlearn

afleveren (ahf-lāy-ver-rern) v deliver

afloop (ahf-lōap) c expiry

*aflopen (ahf-lōa-pern) v end; expire

aflossen (ahf-lo-sern) v relieve; *pay off

afluisteren (ahf-lur^{ew}-ster-rern) v eavesdrop

afmaken (ahf-maa-kern) v finish

afmeting (ahf-māy-tıng) c (pl ~en) size

*afnemen (ahf-nāy-mern) v decrease; *take away

afpersing (ahf-pehr-sıng) c (pl ~en) extortion

*afraden (ahf-raa-dern) v dissuade from

afremmen (ahf-reh-mern) v slow down

Afrika (aa-free-kaa) Africa

Afrikaan (aa-free-kaan) c (pl -kanen) African

Afrikaans (aa-free-kaans) adj African

afschaffen (ahf-skhah-fern) v abolish

afscheid (ahf-skhayt) nt parting

afschrift (ahf-skhrıft) nt (pl ~en) copy

afschuw (ahf-skhew^{oo}) c horror

afschuwelijk (ahf-skhew-ver-lerk) adj horrible, awful; hideous

*afsluiten (ahf-slur^{ew}-tern) v *cut off

*afsnijden (ahf-snay-dern) v *cut off; chip

afspraak (ahf-spraak) c (pl -spraken) date, appointment; engagement

afstammeling (ahf-stah-mer-lıng) c (pl ~en) descendant

afstamming (ahf-stah-mıng) c origin

afstand (ahf-stahnt) c (pl ~en) distance; space, way

afstandsmeter (ahf-stahnts-māy-terr) c (pl ~s) range-finder

afstellen (ahf-steh-lern) v adjust

afstemmen (ahf-steh-mern) v tune in

afstotelijk (ahf-stōa-ter-lerk) adj repellent

aftekenen (*ahf*-tāy-ker-nern) *v* endorse

aftrap (*ahf*-trahp) *c* kick-off

***aftrekken** (*ahf*-treh-kern) *v* deduct ; subtract

afvaardiging (*ah*-faar-der-ging) *c* (pl ~en) delegation

afval (*ah*-fahl) *nt* garbage, litter, rubbish, refuse

afvegen (*ah*-fāy-gern) *v* wipe

afvoer (*ah*-fōōr) *c* drain

zich *afvragen (*ah*-fraa-gern) wonder

afwachten (*ahf*-vahkh-tern) *v* await

afwassen (*ahf*-vah-sern) *v* wash up

afwateren (*ahf*-vaa-ter-rern) *v* drain

afwenden (*ahf*-vehn-dern) *v* avert

afwezig (ahf-*vāy*-zerkh) *adj* absent

afwezigheid (ahf-*vāy*-zerkh-hayt) *c* absence

***afwijken** (*ahf*-vay-kern) *v* deviate

afwijking (*ahf*-vay-king) *c* (pl ~en) aberration

***afwijzen** (*ahf*-vay-zern) *v* reject

afwisselen (*ahf*-vi-ser-lern) *v* vary ; **afwisselend** alternate

afwisseling (*ahf*-vi-ser-ling) *c* variation

***afzeggen** (*ahf*-seh-gern) *v* cancel

afzetting (*ahf*-seh-ting) *c* (pl ~en) deposit

afzonderlijk (ahf-*son*-derr-lerk) *adj* individual ; separate ; *adv* apart

agenda (aa-*gehn*-daa) *c* (pl ~'s) diary ; agenda

agent (aa-*gehnt*) *c* (pl ~en) policeman ; distributor, agent

agentschap (aa-*gehnt*-skhahp) *nt* (pl ~pen) agency

agrarisch (aa-*graa*-reess) *adj* agrarian

agressief (ah-greh-*seef*) *adj* aggressive

akelig (*aa*-ker-lerkh) *adj* nasty

akker (*ah*-kerr) *c* (pl ~s) field

akkoord (ah-*kōart*) *nt* (pl ~en) agreement

akte (*ahk*-ter) *c* (pl ~n, ~s) act, certificate

aktentas (*ahk*-tern-tahss) *c* (pl ~sen) briefcase, attaché case

al (ahl) *adj* all ; *adv* already

alarm (aa-*lahrm*) *nt* alarm

alarmeren (aa-lahr-*māy*-rern) *v* alarm

album (*ahl*-berm) *nt* (pl ~s) album

alcohol (*ahl*-kōa-hol) *c* alcohol

alcoholisch (ahl-kōa-*hōa*-leess) *adj* alcoholic

aldoor (*ahl*-dōar) *adv* all the time

alfabet (*ahl*-faa-beht) *nt* alphabet

algebra (*ahl*-ger-braa) *c* algebra

algemeen (ahl-ger-*māyn*) *adj* general ; universal, public ; **in het ~** in general

Algerije (ahl-ger-*ray*-er) Algeria

Algerijn (ahl-ger-*rayn*) *c* (pl ~en) Algerian

Algerijns (ahl-ger-*rayns*) *adj* Algerian

alhoewel (ahl-hōō-*vehl*) *conj* though

alikruik (*aa*-lee-krur^{ew}k) *c* (pl ~en) winkle

alimentatie (ah-lee-mehn-*taa*-tsee) *c* alimony

alinea (aa-*lee*-nāy-aa) *c* (pl ~'s) paragraph

alledaags (ah-ler-*daakhs*) *adj* ordinary ; everyday

alleen (ah-*lāyn*) *adv* only ; alone

allemaal (ah-ler-*maal*) *num* ALL

allergie (ah-lehr-*gee*) *c* (pl ~ën) allergy

allerlei (*ah*-lerr-lay) *adj* various ; all sorts of

alles (*ah*-lerss) *pron* everything

almachtig (ahl-*mahkh*-terkh) *adj* omnipotent

almanak (*ahl*-maa-nahk) *c* (pl ~ken) almanac

als (ahls) *conj* if ; when ; as, like

alsof (ahl-*zof*) *conj* as if ; ***doen ~** pretend

alstublieft (ahl-stew-*bleeft*) here you

are; please

alt (ahlt) *c* (pl ~en) alto

altaar (*ahl*-taar) *nt* (pl altaren) altar

alternatief (ahl-terr-naa-*teef*) *nt* (pl -tieven) alternative

altijd (*ahl*-tayt) *adv* always, ever

amandel (aa-*mahn*-derl) *c* (pl ~en, ~s) almond; **amandelen** tonsils *pl*

amandelontsteking (aa-*mahn*-derl-ont-stāy-kɪng) *c* (pl ~en) tonsilitis

ambacht (*ahm*-bahkht) *nt* (pl ~en) trade

ambassade (ahm-bah-*saa*-der) *c* (pl ~s) embassy

ambassadeur (ahm-bah-saa-*dūr*) *c* (pl ~s) ambassador

ambitieus (ahm-bee-*ts*ⁱ*ūrss*) *adj* ambitious

ambt (ahmt) *nt* (pl ~en) office

ambtenaar (*ahm*-ter-naar) *c* (pl -naren) civil servant

ambulance (ahm-bēw-*lahn*-ser) *c* (pl ~s) ambulance

Amerika (aa-*māy*-ree-kaa) America

Amerikaan (aa-māy-ree-*kaan*) *c* (pl -kanen) American

Amerikaans (aa-māy-ree-*kaans*) *adj* American

amethist (ah-mer-*tist*) *c* (pl ~en) amethyst

amicaal (aa-mee-*kaal*) *adj* friendly

ammonia (ah-*mōa*-nee-ʸaa) *c* ammonia

amnestie (ahm-nehss-*tee*) *c* amnesty

amulet (aa-mēw-*leht*) *c* (pl ~ten) lucky charm, charm

amusant (aa-mēw-*zahnt*) *adj* amusing; entertaining

amusement (aa-mēw-zer-*mehnt*) *nt* amusement; entertainment

amuseren (aa-mēw-*zāy*-rern) *v* amuse

analfabeet (ahn-ahl-faa-*bāy*t) *c* (pl -beten) illiterate

analist (ah-naa-*list*) *c* (pl ~en) analyst

analyse (ah-naa-*lee*-zer) *c* (pl ~n, ~s) analysis

analyseren (ah-naa-lee-*zāy*-rern) *v* analyse

analyticus (ah-naa-*lee*-tee-kerss) *c* (pl -ci) analyst, psychoanalyst

ananas (*ah*-nah-nahss) *c* (pl ~sen) pineapple

anarchie (ah-nahr-*khee*) *c* anarchy

anatomie (ah-naa-tōa-*mee*) *c* anatomy

ander (*ahn*-derr) *adj* other; different; **een ~** another; **onder andere** among other things

anders (*ahn*-derrs) *adv* else; otherwise

andersom (ahn-derr-*som*) *adv* the other way round

angst (ahngst) *c* (pl ~en) fright, fear; terror

angstig (*ahng*-sterkh) *adj* afraid

angstwekkend (ahngst-*veh*-kernt) *adj* terrifying

animo (*aa*-nee-mōa) *c* zest

anker (*ahng*-kerr) *nt* (pl ~s) anchor

annexeren (ah-nehk-*sāy*-rern) *v* annex

annonce (ah-*nawng*-ser) *c* (pl ~s) advertisement

annuleren (ah-nēw-*lāy*-rern) *v* cancel

annulering (ah-nēw-*lāy*-rɪng) *c* (pl ~en) cancellation

anoniem (ah-nōa-*neem*) *adj* anonymous

ansichtkaart (*ahn*-zɪkht-kaart) *c* (pl ~en) postcard, picture postcard

ansjovis (ahn-*shōa*-vɪss) *c* (pl ~sen) anchovy

antenne (ahn-*teh*-ner) *c* (pl ~s) aerial

antibioticum (ahn-tee-bee-ʸ*ōa*-tee-kerm) *nt* (pl -ca) antibiotic

antiek (ahn-*teek*) *adj* antique

antipathie (ahn-tee-paa-*tee*) *c* dislike

antiquair (ahn-tee-*kair*) *c* (pl ~s) antique dealer

antiquiteit (ahn-tee-kvee-*tayt*) *c* (pl ~en) antique

antivries (ahn-tee-*vreess*) *c* antifreeze

antwoord (*ahnt*-vōart) *nt* (pl ~en) reply, answer; als ~ in reply

antwoorden (*ahnt*-vōar-dern) *v* reply, answer

apart (aa-*pahrt*) *adv* apart, separately

aperitief (aa-pāy-ree-*teef*) *nt/c* (pl -tieven) aperitif

apotheek (aa-pōa-*tāyk*) *c* (pl -theken) pharmacy, chemist's; drugstore *nAm*

apotheker (aa-pōa-*tāy*-kerr) *c* (pl ~s) chemist

apparaat (ah-paa-*raat*) *nt* (pl -raten) appliance; machine; apparatus

appartement (ah-pahr-ter-*mehnt*) *nt* (pl ~en) apartment *nAm*

appel (*ah*-perl) *c* (pl ~s) apple

applaudisseren (ah-plou-dee-*sāy*-rern) *v* clap

applaus (ah-*plouss*) *nt* applause

april (ah-*pril*) April

aquarel (aa-kvaa-*rehl*) *c* (pl ~len) water-colour

ar (ahr) *c* (pl ~ren) sleigh

Arabier (aa-raa-*beer*) *c* (pl ~en) Arab

Arabisch (aa-*raa*-beess) *adj* Arab

arbeid (*ahr*-bayt) *c* labour, work

arbeidbesparend (*ahr*-bayt-ber-spaa-rernt) *adj* labour-saving

arbeider (*ahr*-bay-derr) *c* (pl ~s) labourer, workman, worker

arbeidsbureau (*ahr*-bayts-bēw-rōa) *nt* (pl ~s) employment exchange

archeologie (ahr-khāy-ōa-lōa-*gee*) *c* archaeology

archeoloog (ahr-khāy-ōa-*lōākh*) *c* (pl -logen) archaeologist

archief (ahr-*kheef*) *nt* (pl -chieven) archives *pl*

architect (ahr-shee-*tehkt*) *c* (pl ~en) architect

architectuur (ahr-shee-tehk-*tēwr*) *c* architecture

arena (aa-*rāy*-naa) *c* (pl ~'s) bullring

arend (*aa*-rernt) *c* (pl ~en) eagle

Argentijn (ahr-gern-*tayn*) *c* (pl ~en) Argentinian

Argentijns (ahr-gern-*tayns*) *adj* Argentinian

Argentinië (ahr-gern-*tee*-nee-Yer) Argentina

argument (ahr-gēw-*mehnt*) *nt* (pl ~en) argument

argumenteren (ahr-gēw-mehn-*tāy*-rern) *v* argue

argwaan (*ahrkh*-vaan) *c* suspicion

argwanend (ahrkh-*vaa*-nernt) *adj* suspicious

arm¹ (ahrm) *adj* poor

arm² (ahrm) *c* (pl ~en) arm

armband (*ahrm*-bahnt) *c* (pl ~en) bracelet; bangle

armoede (*ahr*-mōō-der) *c* poverty

armoedig (ahr-*mōō*-derkh) *adj* poor

aroma (aa-*rōa*-maa) *nt* aroma

arrestatie (ah-rehss-*taa*-tsee) *c* (pl ~s) arrest

arresteren (ah-rehss-*tāy*-rern) *v* arrest

arrogant (ah-rōa-*gahnt*) *adj* presumptuous

artikel (ahr-*tee*-kerl) *nt* (pl ~en, ~s) article; item

artisjok (ahr-tou-*shok*) *c* (pl ~ken) artichoke

artistiek (ahr-tiss-*teek*) *adj* artistic

arts (ahrts) *c* (pl ~en) doctor

as¹ (ahss) *c* (pl ~sen) axle

as² (ahss) *c* ash

asbak (*ahss*-bahk) *c* (pl ~ken) ashtray

asbest (*ahss*-behst) *nt* asbestos

asfalt (*ahss*-fahlt) *nt* asphalt

asiel (aa-*zeel*) *nt* asylum

aspect (ahss-*pehkt*) *nt* (pl ~en) aspect

asperge (ahss-*pehr*-zher) *c* (pl ~s) asparagus

aspirine (ahss-pee-*ree*-ner) *c* aspirin

assistent (ah-see-*stehnt*) *c* (pl ~en)

assistant

associëren (ah-sōa-*shay*-rern) *v* associate

assortiment (ah-sor-tee-*mehnt*) *nt* (pl ~en) assortment

assurantie (ah-sēw-*rahn*-see) *c* (pl -ties, -tiën) insurance

astma (*ahss*-maa) *nt* asthma

atheïst (aa-tāy-*ist*) *c* (pl ~en) atheist

Atlantische Oceaan (aht-*lahn*-tee-ser ōa-say-*aan*) Atlantic

atleet (aht-*layt*) *c* (pl -leten) athlete

atletiek (aht-lāy-*teek*) *c* athletics *pl*

atmosfeer (aht-moss-*fayr*) *c* atmosphere

atomisch (aa-*tōa*-meess) *adj* atomic

atoom (aa-*tōam*) *nt* (pl atomen) atom; **atoom-** atomic

attent (ah-*tehnt*) *adj* considerate

attest (ah-*tehst*) *nt* (pl ~en) certificate

attractie (ah-*trahk*-see) *c* (pl ~s) attraction

aubergine (ōa-behr-*zhee*-ner) *c* (pl ~s) eggplant

augustus (ou-*gerss*-terss) August

aula (*ou*-laa) *c* (pl ~'s) auditorium

Australië (ou-*straa*-lee-Yer) Australia

Australiër (ou-*straa*-lee-Yerr) *c* (pl ~s) Australian

Australisch (ou-*straa*-leess) *adj* Australian

auteur (ōa-*tūrr*) *c* (pl ~s) author

authentiek (ōa-tehn-*teek*) *adj* authentic

auto (*ōa*-tōa) *c* (pl ~'s) car; motorcar, automobile

automaat (ōa-tōa-*maat*) *c* (pl -maten) slot-machine

automatisch (ōa-tōa-*maa*-teess) *adj* automatic

automatisering (ōa-tōa-maa-tee-*zāy*-ring) *c* automation

automobielclub (ōa-tōa-mōa-*beel*-

klerp) *c* (pl ~s) automobile club

automobilisme (ōa-tōa-mōa-bee-*liss*-mer) *nt* motoring

automobilist (ōa-tōa-mōa-bee-*list*) *c* (pl ~en) motorist

autonoom (ōa-tōa-*nōam*) *adj* autonomous

autoped (*ōa*-tōa-peht) *c* (pl ~s) scooter

autopsie (ōa-top-*see*) *c* autopsy

* **autorijden** (*ōa*-tōa-ray-dern) *v* motor

autorit (*ōa*-tōa-rit) *c* (pl ~ten) drive

autoritair (ōa-tōa-ree-*tair*) *adj* authoritarian

autoriteiten (ōa-tōa-ree-*tay*-tern) *pl* authorities *pl*

autoverhuur (*ōa*-tōa-verr-hewr) *c* car hire; car rental *Am*

autoweg (*ōa*-tōa-vehkh) *c* (pl ~en) highway *nAm*

avond *c* (pl ~en) night, evening

avondeten (*aa*-vernt-ay-tern) *nt* dinner; supper

avondkleding (*aa*-vernt-klay-ding) *c* evening dress

avondschemering (*aa*-vernt-skhay-mer-ring) *c* dusk

avontuur (aa-von-*tewr*) *nt* (pl -turen) adventure

Aziaat (aa-zee-*Yaat*) *c* (pl Aziaten) Asian

Aziatisch (aa-zee-*Yaa*-teess) *adj* Asian

Azië (*aa*-zee-Yer) Asia

azijn (aa-*zayn*) *c* vinegar

B

baai (baa^ee) *c* (pl ~en) bay

baan (baan) *c* (pl banen) job

baard (baart) *c* (pl ~en) beard

baarmoeder (*baar*-mōō-derr) *c* womb

baars (baars) *c* (pl baarzen) bass,

perch

baas (baass) c (pl bazen) boss; master

baat (baat) c benefit; profit

babbelen (bah-ber-lern) v chat

babbelkous (bah-berl-kouss) c (pl ~en) chatterbox

babbeltje (bah-berl-tᵞer) nt (pl ~s) chat

baby (bāy̆-bee) c (pl ~'s) baby

bacil (bah-sil) c (pl ~len) germ

bacterie (bahk-tāy̆-ree) c (pl -riën) bacterium

bad (baht) nt (pl ~en) bath; **een ~ *nemen** bathe

baden (baa-dern) v bathe

badhanddoek (baht-hahn-dōōk) c (pl ~en) bath towel

badjas (baht-ᵞahss) c (pl ~sen) bathrobe

badkamer (baht-kaa-merr) c (pl ~s) bathroom

badmuts (baht-merts) c (pl ~en) bathing-cap

badpak (baht-pahk) nt (pl ~ken) bathing-suit

badplaats (baht-plaats) c (pl ~en) seaside resort

badstof (baht-stof) c towelling

badzout (baht-sout) nt bath salts

bagage (bah-gaa-zher) c baggage; luggage

bagagedepot (bah-gaa-zher-dāy̆-pōā) nt (pl ~s) left luggage office; baggage deposit office Am

bagagenet (bah-gaa-zher-neht) nt (pl ~ten) luggage rack

bagageoverschot (bah-gaa-zher-ōā-verr-skhot) nt overweight

bagagerek (bah-gaa-zher-rehk) nt (pl ~ken) luggage rack

bagageruimte (bah-gaa-zher-rur-ewm-ter) c (pl ~n, ~s) boot

bagagewagen (bah-gaa-zher-vaa-gern) c (pl ~s) luggage van

bakboord (bahk-bōārt) nt port

baken (baa-kern) nt (pl ~s) landmark

bakermat (baa-kerr-maht) c cradle

bakkebaarden (bah-ker-baar-dern) pl whiskers pl, sideburns pl

*bakken (bah-kern) v bake; fry

bakker (bah-kerr) c (pl ~s) baker

bakkerij (bah-ker-ray) c (pl ~en) bakery

baksteen (bahk-stāy̆n) c (pl -stenen) brick

bal¹ (bahl) c (pl ~len) ball

bal² (bahl) nt (pl ~s) ball

balans (bah-lahns) c (pl ~en) balance

baldadig (bahl-daa-derkh) adj rowdy

balie (baa-lee) c (pl ~s) counter

balk (bahlk) c (pl ~en) beam

balkon (bahl-kon) nt (pl ~s) balcony; circle

ballet (bah-leht) nt (pl ~ten) ballet

balling (bah-ling) c (pl ~en) exile

ballingschap (bah-ling-skhahp) c exile

ballon (bah-lon) c (pl ~s) balloon

ballpoint (bol-poᵞnt) c (pl ~s) ballpoint-pen; Biro

bamboe (bahm-bōō) nt bamboo

banaan (baa-naan) c (pl bananen) banana

band (bahnt) c (pl ~en) tape; band; tyre, tire; **lekke ~** flat tyre, puncture

bandenspanning (bahn-der-spah-ning) c tyre pressure

bandepech (bahn-der-pehkh) c blowout, puncture

bandiet (bahn-deet) c (pl ~en) bandit

bandrecorder (bahnt-rer-kor-derr) c (pl ~s) tape-recorder, recorder

bang (bahng) adj frightened, afraid

bank (bahngk) c (pl ~en) bank; bench

bankbiljet (bahngk-bil-ᵞeht) nt (pl ~ten) banknote

banket (bahng-keht) nt (pl ~ten) banquet

banketbakker (bahng-*keht*-bah-kerr) *c* (pl ~s) confectioner

banketbakkerij (bahng-keht-bah-ker-*ray*) *c* (pl ~en) pastry shop

banketzaal (bahng-*keht*-saal) *c* (pl -zalen) banqueting-hall

bankrekening (*bahngk*-rāȳ-ker-nǐng) *c* (pl ~en) bank account

bankroet (bahngk-*rōōt*) *adj* bankrupt

bar (bahr) *c* (pl ~s) bar; saloon

baret (baa-*reht*) *c* (pl ~ten) beret

bariton (*baa*-ree-ton) *c* (pl ~s) baritone

barjuffrouw (*bahr*-ʸer-frou) *c* (pl ~en) barmaid

barman (*bahr*-mahn) *c* (pl ~nen) bartender, barman

barmhartig (bahr-*mahr*-terkh) *adj* merciful

barnsteen (*bahrn*-stāȳn) *nt* amber

barok (baa-*rok*) *adj* baroque

barometer (bah-rōā-*māȳ*-terr) *c* (pl ~s) barometer

barrière (bah-ree-ʸai-rer) *c* (pl ~s) barrier

barst (bahrst) *c* (pl ~en) crack

*__barsten__ (*bahrs*-tern) *v* crack, *burst, *split; *get cracked

bas (bahss) *c* (pl ~sen) bass

baseren (baa-*zāȳ*-rern) *v* base

basiliek (baa-zee-*leek*) *c* (pl ~en) basilica

basis (*baa*-zerss) *c* (pl bases) basis; base

basiscrème (*baa*-zerss-kraim) *c* (pl ~s) foundation cream

bast (bahst) *c* (pl ~en) bark

bastaard (*bahss*-taart) *c* (pl ~en, ~s) bastard

baten (*baa*-tern) *v* *be of use

batterij (bah-ter-*ray*) *c* (pl ~en) battery

beambte (ber-*ahm*-ter) *c* (pl ~n) clerk

beantwoorden (ber-*ahnt*-vōār-dern) *v* answer

bebost (ber-*bost*) *adj* wooded

bebouwen (ber-*bou*-ern) *v* cultivate

bed (beht) *nt* (pl ~den) bed

bedaard (ber-*daart*) *adj* quiet

bedachtzaam (ber-*dahkht*-saam) *adj* cautious

bedanken (ber-*dahng*-kern) *v* thank

bedaren (ber-*daa*-rern) *v* calm down

beddegoed (*beh*-der-gōōt) *nt* bedding

bedeesd (ber-*dāȳst*) *adj* timid

bedekken (ber-*deh*-kern) *v* cover

bedelaar (*bāȳ*-der-laar) *c* (pl ~s) beggar

bedelen (*bāȳ*-der-lern) *v* beg

*__bedelven__ (ber-*dehl*-vern) *v* bury

*__bedenken__ (ber-*dehng*-kern) *v* *think of

*__bederven__ (ber-*dehr*-vern) *v* *spoil; mess up

bedevaart (*bāȳ*-der-vaart) *c* (pl ~en) pilgrimage

bediende (ber-*deen*-der) *c* (pl ~n, ~s) domestic, servant; valet; boy

bedienen (ber-*dee*-nern) *v* serve; wait on; attend on

bediening (ber-*dee*-nǐng) *c* service

bedieningsgeld (ber-*dee*-nǐngs-khehlt) *nt* service charge

bedoelen (ber-*dōō*-lern) *v* *mean; intend

bedoeling (ber-*dōō*-lǐng) *c* (pl ~en) purpose, intention

bedrag (ber-*drahkh*) *nt* (pl ~en) amount

*__bedragen__ (ber-*draa*-gern) *v* amount to

bedreigen (ber-*dray*-gern) *v* threaten

bedreiging (ber-*dray*-gǐng) *c* (pl ~en) threat

*__bedriegen__ (ber-*dree*-gern) *v* deceive; cheat

bedrijf (ber-*drayf*) *nt* (pl bedrijven)

business, concern; plant; act

bedrijvig (ber-*dray*-verkh) *adj* active

bedroefd (ber-*drōōft*) *adj* sad, sorry

bedroefdheid (ber-*drōōft*-hayt) *c* sadness; grief

bedrog (ber-*drokh*) *nt* deceit; fraud

beëindigen (ber-*ayn*-der-gern) *v* end, finish

beek (bāyk) *c* (pl beken) brook, stream

beeld (bāylt) *nt* (pl ~en) picture, image

beeldhouwer (*bāylt*-hou-err) *c* (pl ~s) sculptor

beeldhouwwerk (*bāylt*-hou-vehrk) *nt* (pl ~en) sculpture

beeldscherm (*bāylt*-skhehrm) *nt* (pl ~en) screen

been[1] (bāyn) *nt* (pl benen) leg

been[2] (bāyn) *nt* (pl beenderen, benen) bone

beer (bāyr) *c* (pl beren) bear

beest (bāyst) *nt* (pl ~en) beast

beestachtig (*bāyst*-ahkh-terkh) *adj* brutal

beet (bāyt) *c* (pl beten) bite

beetje (*bāy*-tᵛer) *nt* bit

***beetnemen** (*bāyt*-nāy-mern) *v* kid

beetwortel (*bāyt*-vor-terl) *c* (pl ~s, ~en) beetroot

befaamd (ber-*faamt*) *adj* noted

begaafd (ber-*gaaft*) *adj* gifted, talented

***begaan** (ber-*gaan*) *v* commit

begeerlijk (ber-*gāyr*-lerk) *adj* desirable

begeerte (ber-*gāyr*-ter) *c* (pl ~n) desire

begeleiden (ber-ger-*lay*-dern) *v* accompany; conduct

begeren (ber-*gāy*-rern) *v* desire

begin (ber-*gin*) *nt* start, beginning; **begin-** initial

beginneling (ber-*gi*-ner-ling) *c* (pl ~en) learner, beginner

***beginnen** (ber-*gi*-nern) *v* start, commence, *begin

beginner (ber-*gi*-nerr) *c* (pl ~s) learner

beginsel (ber-*gin*-serl) *nt* (pl ~en, ~s) principle

begraafplaats (ber-*graaf*-plaats) *c* (pl ~en) cemetery

begrafenis (ber-*graa*-fer-niss) *c* (pl ~sen) burial; funeral

***begraven** (ber-*graa*-vern) *v* bury

***begrijpen** (ber-*gray*-pern) *v* *understand; *see, *take; **begrijpend** sympathetic

begrip (ber-*grip*) *nt* (pl ~pen) notion; idea, conception; understanding

begroeid (ber-*grōō*ᵉᵉt) *adj* overgrown

begroting (ber-*grōā*-ting) *c* (pl ~en) budget

begunstigde (ber-*gern*-sterkh-der) *c* (pl ~n) payee

begunstigen (ber-*gern*-ster-gern) *v* favour

beha (bāy-*haa*) *c* (pl ~s) brassiere, bra

behalen (ber-*haa*-lern) *v* obtain

behalve (ber--*hahl*-ver) *prep* but, except; beyond, besides

behandelen (ber-*hahn*-der-lern) *v* treat, handle

behandeling (ber-*hahn*-der-ling) *c* (pl ~en) treatment

behang (ber-*hahng*) *nt* wallpaper

beheer (ber-*hāyr*) *nt* management; administration

beheersen (ber-*hāyr*-sern) *v* master

beheksen (ber-*hehk*-sern) *v* bewitch

zich *behelpen met (ber-*hehl*-pern) *make do with

behendig (ber-*hehn*-derkh) *adj* skilful

beheren (ber-*hāy*-rern) *v* manage

behoedzaam (ber-*hōōt*-saam) *adj* wary

behoefte (ber-*hōōf*-ter) *c* (pl ~n) need, want

behoeven (ber-*hoo*-vern) *v* need; **ten behoeve van** on behalf of

behoorlijk (ber-*hoar*-lerk) *adj* proper

behoren (ber-*hoa*-rern) *v* belong to; *ought

behoudend (ber-*hou*-dernt) *adj* conservative

beide (*bay*-der) *adj* both; either; **een van ~** either; **geen van ~** neither

beige (*bai*-zher) *adj* beige

beïnvloeden (ber-*in*-vloo-dern) *v* influence; affect

beitel (*bay*-terl) *c* (pl ~s) chisel

bejaard (ber-*Yaart*) *adj* aged; elderly

bek (behk) *c* (pl ~ken) mouth; beak

bekend (ber-*kehnt*) *adj* well-known

bekende (ber-*kehn*-der) *c* (pl ~n) acquaintance

bekendmaken (ber-*kehnt*-maa-kern) *v* announce

bekendmaking (ber-*kehnt*-maa-king) *c* (pl ~en) announcement

bekennen (ber-*keh*-nern) *v* admit, confess

bekentenis (ber-*kehn*-ter-niss) *c* (pl ~sen) confession

beker (*bay*-kerr) *c* (pl ~s) mug; tumbler; cup

bekeren (ber-*kay*-rern) *v* convert

*bekijken (ber-*kay*-kern) *v* regard, view

bekken (*beh*-kern) *nt* (pl ~s) basin; pelvis

beklagen (ber-*klaa*-gern) *v* pity

bekleden (ber-*klay*-dern) *v* upholster

beklemmen (ber-*kleh*-mern) *v* oppress

*beklimmen (ber-*kli*-mern) *v* ascend

beklimming (ber-*kli*-ming) *c* (pl ~en) ascent

beknopt (ber-*knopt*) *adj* concise; brief

zich bekommeren om (ber-*ko*-mer-rern) care about

bekoring (ber-*koa*-ring) *c* (pl ~en) attraction, charm

bekritiseren (ber-kree-tee-*zay*-rern) *v* criticize

bekrompen (ber-*krom*-pern) *adj* narrow-minded

bekronen (ber-*kroa*-nern) *v* crown

bekwaam (ber-*kvaam*) *adj* able, capable; skilful

bekwaamheid (ber-*kvaam*-hayt) *c* (pl -heden) ability, faculty, capacity

bel (behl) *c* (pl ~len) bell; bubble

belachelijk (ber-*lah*-kher-lerk) *adj* ridiculous, ludicrous

belang (ber-*lahng*) *nt* (pl ~en) interest; importance; **van ~** *zijn* matter

belangrijk (ber-*lahng*-rayk) *adj* important; capital

belangstellend (ber-lahng-*steh*-lernt) *adj* interested

belangstelling (ber-*lahng*-steh-ling) *c* interest

belastbaar (ber-*lahst*-baar) *adj* dutiable

belasten (ber-*lahss*-tern) *v* charge; tax; **belast met** in charge of

belasting (ber-*lahss*-ting) *c* (pl ~en) charge; tax; taxation

belastingvrij (ber-lahss-ting-*vray*) *adj* duty-free; tax-free

beledigen (ber-*lay*-der-gern) *v* insult; offend; **beledigend** offensive

belediging (ber-*lay*-der-ging) *c* (pl ~en) insult; offence

beleefd (ber-*layft*) *adj* polite; civil

belegering (ber-*lay*-ger-ring) *c* (pl ~en) siege

beleggen (ber-*leh*-gern) *v* invest

belegging (ber-*leh*-ging) *c* (pl ~en) investment

beleid (ber-*layt*) *nt* policy

belemmeren (ber-*leh*-mer-rern) *v* impede

beletsel (ber-*leht*-serl) *nt* (pl ~s, ~en) impediment

beletten (ber-*leh*-tern) *v* prevent

beleven (ber-*lāy*-vern) *v* experience

Belg (behlkh) *c* (pl ~en) Belgian

België (*behl*-gee-^Yer) Belgium

Belgisch (*behl*-geess) *adj* Belgian

belichting (ber-*likh*-ting) *c* exposure

belichtingsmeter (ber-*likh*-tings-māy-terr) *c* (pl ~s) exposure meter

***belijden** (ber-*lay*-dern) *v* confess

bellen (*beh*-lern) *v* *ring

belofte (ber-*lof*-ter) *c* (pl ~n) promise

belonen (ber-*lōa*-nern) *v* reward

beloning (ber-*lōa*-ning) *c* (pl ~en) reward; prize

beloven (ber-*lōa*-vern) *v* promise

bemachtigen (ber-*mahkh*-ter-gern) *v* secure

bemanning (ber-*mah*-ning) *c* (pl ~en) crew

bemerken (ber-*mehr*-kern) *v* notice; perceive

bemiddelaar (ber-*mi*-der-laar) *c* (pl ~s) mediator

bemiddeld (ber-*mi*-derlt) *adj* well-to-do

bemiddelen (ber-*mi*-der-lern) *v* mediate

bemind (ber-*mint*) *adj* beloved

zich bemoeien met (ber-*mōō*^{ee}-ern) interfere with

benadrukken (ber-*naa*-drer-kern) *v* emphasize, stress

benaming (ber-*naa*-ming) *c* (pl ~en) denomination

benauwd (ber-*nout*) *adj* stuffy

bende (*behn*-der) *c* (pl ~n, ~s) gang

beneden (ber-*nāy*-dern) *prep* under, below; *adv* underneath, beneath; below; downstairs; **naar** ~ downwards, down; downstairs

benieuwd (ber-*nee*^{oo}t) *adj* curious

benijden (ber-*nay*-dern) *v* envy

benoemen (ber-*nōō*-mern) *v* nominate, appoint

benoeming (ber-*nōō*-ming) *c* (pl ~en) nomination, appointment

benutten (ber-*ner*-tern) *v* utilize

benzine (behn-*zee*-ner) *c* petrol; fuel; gasoline *nAm*, gas *nAm*

benzinepomp (behn-*zee*-ner-pomp) *c* (pl ~en) petrol pump; fuel pump *Am*; gas pump *Am*

benzinestation (behn-*zee*-ner-staa-shon) *nt* (pl ~s) service station, petrol station, filling station; gas station *Am*

benzinetank (behn-*zee*-ner-tehngk) *c* (pl ~s) petrol tank

beoefenen (ber-*ōō*-fer-nern) *v* practise

beogen (ber-*ōa*-gern) *v* aim at

beoordelen (ber-*ōar*-dāy-lern) *v* judge

beoordeling (ber-*ōar*-dāy-ling) *c* (pl ~en) judgment

bepaald (ber-*paalt*) *adj* definite; certain

bepalen (ber-*paa*-lern) *v* define, determine; stipulate

bepaling (ber-*paa*-ling) *c* (pl ~en) stipulation; definition

beperken (ber-*pehr*-kern) *v* limit

beperking (ber-*pehr*-king) *c* (pl ~en) restriction

beproeven (ber-*prōō*-vern) *v* attempt

beraad (ber-*raat*) *nt* deliberation

beraadslagen (ber-*raat*-slaa-gern) *v* deliberate

beramen (ber-*raa*-mern) *v* devise

bereid (ber-*rayt*) *adj* prepared, willing

bereiden (ber-*ray*-dern) *v* cook

bereidwillig (ber-*rayt*-vi-lerkh) *adj* co-operative

bereik (ber-*rayk*) *nt* reach; range

bereikbaar (ber-*rayk*-baar) *adj* attainable

bereiken (ber-*ray*-kern) *v* reach; achieve, accomplish, attain

berekenen (ber-*rāy*-ker-nern) *v* calculate; charge

berekening (ber-*rāy*-ker-nɪng) *c* (pl ~en) calculation

berg (behrkh) *c* (pl ~en) mountain; mount

bergachtig (*behrkh*-ahkh-terkh) *adj* mountainous

bergketen (*behrkh*-kāy-tern) *c* (pl ~s) mountain range

bergkloof (*behrkh*-klōāf) *c* (pl -kloven) glen

bergpas (*behrkh*-pahss) *c* (pl ~sen) mountain pass

bergplaats (*behrkh*-plaats) *c* (pl ~en) depository

bergrug (*behrkh*-rerg) *c* (pl ~gen) ridge

bergsport (*behrkh*-sport) *c* mountaineering

bericht (ber-*rɪkht*) *nt* (pl ~en) message; notice

berispen (ber-*rɪss*-pern) *v* reprimand, scold

berk (behrk) *c* (pl ~en) birch

beroemd (ber-*rōōmt*) *adj* famous

beroep (ber-*rōōp*) *nt* (pl ~en) profession; appeal; **beroeps-** professional

beroerd (ber-*rōōrt*) *adj* miserable

beroerte (ber-*rōōr*-ter) *c* (pl ~n, ~s) stroke

berouw (ber-*rou*) *nt* repentance

beroven (ber-*rōā*-vern) *v* rob

beroving (ber-*rōā*-vɪng) *c* (pl ~en) robbery

berucht (ber-*rerkht*) *adj* notorious

bes (behss) *c* (pl ~sen) berry; currant; **zwarte ~** black-currant

beschaafd (ber-*skhaaft*) *adj* civilized; cultured

beschaamd (ber-*skhaamt*) *adj* ashamed

beschadigen (ber-*skhaa*-der-gern) *v* damage

beschaving (ber-*skhaa*-vɪng) *c* (pl ~en) civilization; culture

bescheiden (ber-*skhay*-dern) *adj* modest

bescheidenheid (ber-*skhay*-dern-hayt) *c* modesty

beschermen (ber-*skhehr*-mern) *v* protect

bescherming (ber-*skhehr*-mɪng) *c* protection

beschikbaar (ber-*skhɪk*-baar) *adj* available

beschikken over (ber-*skhɪ*-kern) dispose of

beschikking (ber-*skhɪ*-kɪng) *c* disposal

beschimmeld (ber-*skhɪ*-merlt) *adj* mouldy

beschouwen (ber-*skhou*-ern) *v* consider; regard; reckon

*** beschrijven** (ber-*skhray*-vern) *v* describe

beschrijving (ber-*skhray*-vɪng) *c* (pl ~en) description

beschuldigen (ber-*skherl*-der-gern) *v* accuse; blame

beschutten (ber-*skher*-tern) *v* shelter

beschutting (ber-*skher*-tɪng) *c* cover, shelter

beseffen (ber-*seh*-fern) *v* realize

beslag (ber-*slahkh*) *nt* batter; **beslag leggen op** impound, confiscate

beslissen (ber-*slɪ*-sern) *v* decide

beslissing (ber-*slɪ*-sɪng) *c* (pl ~en) decision

beslist (ber-*slɪst*) *adv* without fail

besluit (ber-*slur*ᵉʷt) *nt* (pl ~en) decision

*** besluiten** (ber-*slur*ᵉʷ-tern) *v* decide

besmettelijk (ber-*smeh*-ter-lerk) *adj* contagious, infectious

besmetten (ber-*smeh*-tern) *v* infect

besneeuwd (ber-*snāy*ᵒᵒt) *adj* snowy

bespelen (ber-*spāy*-lern) *v* play

bespottelijk (ber-*spo*-ter-lerk) *adj* ridiculous, ludicrous

bespotten (ber-*spo*-tern) v ridicule;
mock

*__bespreken__ (ber-*spray*-kern) v engage,
reserve; discuss

bespreking (ber-*spray*-kıng) c (pl ~en)
booking; review; discussion

best (behst) adj best

bestaan (ber-*staan*) nt existence

*__bestaan__ (ber-*staan*) v exist; ~ uit
consist of

bestanddeel (ber-stahn-dayl) nt (pl
-delen) ingredient; element

besteden (ber-*stay*-dern) v *spend

bestek (ber-*stehk*) nt (pl ~ken) cutlery

bestelauto (ber-*stehl*-oa-toa) c (pl ~'s)
van; delivery van, pick-up van

bestelformulier (ber-*stehl*-for-mew-
leer) nt (pl ~en) order-form

bestellen (ber-*steh*-lern) v order

bestelling (ber-*steh*-lıng) c (pl ~en)
order

bestemmen (ber-*steh*-mern) v destine

bestemming (ber-*steh*-mıng) c (pl
~en) destination

bestendig (ber-*stehn*-derkh) adj permanent

*__bestijgen__ (ber-*stay*-gern) v mount

bestraten (ber-*straa*-tern) v pave

*__bestrijden__ (ber-*stray*-dern) v combat

besturen (ber-*stew*-rern) v *drive

bestuur (ber-*stewr*) nt (pl besturen)
direction; board; rule

bestuurlijk (ber-*stewr*-lerk) adj administrative

bestuursrecht (ber-*stewrs*-rehkht) nt
administrative law

betalen (ber-*taa*-lern) v *pay

betaling (ber-*taa*-lıng) c (pl ~en) payment

betasten (ber-*tahss*-tern) v *feel

betekenen (ber-*tay*-ker-nern) v *mean

betekenis (ber-*tay*-ker-nıss) c (pl
~sen) meaning; sense

beter (*bay*-terr) adj better; superior

beteugelen (ber-*tur*-ger-lern) v curb

betogen (ber-*toa*-gern) v demonstrate

betoging (ber-*toa*-gıng) c (pl ~en)
demonstration

beton (ber-*ton*) nt concrete

betoveren (ber-*toa*-ver-rern) v bewitch; **betoverend** enchanting,
glamorous

betovering (ber-*toa*-ver-rıng) c (pl
~en) spell

betrappen (ber-*trah*-pern) v *catch

*__betreden__ (ber-*tray*-dern) v enter

*__betreffen__ (ber-*treh*-fern) v concern;
affect, touch; **wat betreft** as regards

betreffende (ber-*treh*-fern-der) prep as
regards, regarding, about, concerning

betrekkelijk (ber-*treh*-ker-lerk) adj
relative

*__betrekken__ (ber-*treh*-kern) v impli-
cate, *get involved; obtain

betrekking (ber-*treh*-kıng) c (pl ~en)
post, position, job; reference; **met
~ tot** regarding, with reference to

betreuren (ber-*trur*-rern) v regret

betrokken (ber-*tro*-kern) adj cloudy,
overcast; concerned, involved

botrouwbaar (ber-*trou*-baar) adj trustworthy, reliable

betuigen (ber-*tur*ew-gern) v express

betwijfelen (ber-*tvay*-fer-lern) v doubt,
query

betwisten (ber-*tvıss*-tern) v dispute

beu (bur) adj tired of, fed up with

beuk (burk) c (pl ~en) beech

beul (burl) c (pl ~en) executioner

beurs (burrs) c (pl beurzen) purse;
stock exchange; fair; grant

beurt (burrt) c (pl ~en) turn

bevaarbaar (ber-*vaar*-baar) adj navigable

*__bevallen__ (ber-*vah*-lern) v please

bevallig (ber-*vah*-lerkh) *adj* graceful

bevalling (ber-*vah*-ling) *c* (pl ~en) delivery, childbirth

*bevaren (ber-*vaa*-rern) *v* sail

bevatten (ber-*vah*-tern) *v* contain; include

bevel (ber-*vehl*) *nt* (pl ~en) command, order

*bevelen (ber-*vā̄y*-lern) *v* command, order

bevelhebber (ber-*vehl*-heh-berr) *c* (pl ~s) commander

beven (*bā̄y*-vern) *v* tremble

bever (*bā̄y*-verr) *c* (pl ~s) beaver

bevestigen (ber-*vehss*-ter-gern) *v* acknowledge, confirm; fasten; bevestigend affirmative

bevestiging (ber-*vehss*-ter-ging) *c* (pl ~en) confirmation

zich *bevinden (ber-*vin*-dern) *be

bevlieging (ber-*vlee*-ging) *c* (pl ~en) whim

bevochtigen (ber-*vokh*-ter-gern) *v* damp, moisten

bevoegd (ber-*vōōkht*) *adj* qualified

bevoegdheid (ber-*vōōkht*-hayt) *c* (pl -heden) qualification

bevolking (ber-*vol*-king) *c* population

bevoorrechten (ber-*vōā*-raykh-tern) *v* favour

bevorderen (ber-*vor*-der-rern) *v* promote

bevredigen (ber-*vrā̄y*-der-gern) *v* satisfy

bevrediging (ber-*vrā̄y*-der-ging) *c* (pl ~en) satisfaction

*bevriezen (ber-*vree*-zern) *v* *freeze

bevrijding (ber-*vray*-ding) *c* liberation

bevuild (ber-*vur*ᵉʷ/t) *adj* soiled

bewaken (ber-*vaa*-kern) *v* guard

bewaker (ber-*vaa*-kerr) *c* (pl ~s) guard; warden

bewapenen (ber-*vaa*-per-nern) *v* arm

bewaren (ber-*vaa*-rern) *v* *hold; preserve; *keep

bewaring (ber-*vaa*-ring) *c* preservation

beweeglijk (ber-*vā̄ykh*-lerk) *adj* mobile

beweegreden (ber-*vā̄ykh*-rā̄y-dern) *c* (pl ~en) cause

*bewegen (ber-*vā̄y*-gern) *v* move; stir

beweging (ber-*vā̄y*-ging) *c* (pl ~en) movement; motion

beweren (ber-*vā̄y*-rern) *v* claim

bewijs (ber-*vayss*) *nt* (pl bewijzen) proof, evidence; token; voucher

*bewijzen (ber-*vay*-zern) *v* prove

bewind (ber-*vint*) *nt* rule, government

bewolking (ber-*vol*-king) *c* clouds

bewolkt (ber-*volkt*) *adj* cloudy

bewonderen (ber-*von*-der-rern) *v* admire

bewondering (ber-*von*-der-ring) *c* admiration

bewonen (ber-*vōā*-nern) *v* inhabit

bewoner (ber-*vōā*-nerr) *c* (pl ~s) inhabitant; occupant

bewoonbaar (ber-*vōān*-baar) *adj* habitable, inhabitable

bewust (ber-*verst*) *adj* conscious, aware

bewusteloos (ber-*verss*-ter-lōāss) *adj* unconscious

bewustzijn (ber-*verst*-sayn) *nt* consciousness

bezem (*bā̄y*-zerm) *c* (pl ~s) broom

bezeren (ber-*zā̄y*-rern) *v* *hurt

bezet (ber-*zeht*) *adj* engaged, occupied

bezetten (ber-*zeh*-tern) *v* occupy

bezetting (ber-*zeh*-ting) *c* (pl ~en) occupation

bezielen (ber-*zee*-lern) *v* inspire

bezienswaardigheid (ber-zeen-*svaar*-derkh-hayt) *c* (pl -heden) sight

bezig (*bā̄y*-zerkh) *adj* engaged, busy

zich *bezighouden met (*bā̄y*-zerkh-hou-dern) attend to

bezinksel (ber-*zingk*-serl) *nt* (pl ~s) deposit

bezit (ber-*zit*) *nt* property; possession

* **bezitten** (ber-*zi*-tern) *v* possess, own

bezitter (ber-*zi*-terr) *c* (pl ~s) owner

bezittingen (ber-*zi*-ting-ern) *pl* belongings *pl*

bezoek (ber-*zōōk*) *nt* (pl ~en) call, visit

* **bezoeken** (ber-*zōō*-kern) *v* visit; call on

bezoeker (ber-*zōō*-kerr) *c* (pl ~s) visitor

bezoekuren (ber-*zōōk*-ēw-rern) *pl* visiting hours

bezonnen (ber-*zo*-nern) *adj* sober

bezorgd (ber-*zorkht*) *adj* anxious, concerned

bezorgdheid (ber-*zorkht*-hayt) *c* worry, anxiety

bezorgen (ber-*zor*-gern) *v* deliver; supply

bezorging (ber-*zor*-ging) *c* delivery

bezwaar (ber-*zvaar*) *nt* (pl bezwaren) objection; ~ * **hebben tegen** object to; mind

* **bezwijken** (ber-*zvay*-kern) *v* collapse; succumb

bibberen (*bi*-ber-rern) *v* shiver

bibliotheek (bee-blee-ᵞōa-*tāyk*) *c* (pl -theken) library

* **bidden** (*bi*-dern) *v* pray

biecht (beekht) *c* (pl ~en) confession

biechten (*beekh*-tern) *v* confess

* **bieden** (*bee*-dern) *v* offer

biefstuk (*beef*-sterk) *c* (pl ~ken) steak

bier (beer) *nt* (pl ~en) beer; ale

bies (beess) *c* (pl biezen) rush

bieslook (*beess*-lōak) *nt* chives *pl*

biet (beet) *c* (pl ~en) beet

big (bikh) *c* (pl ~gen) piglet

bij¹ (bay) *prep* near, at, with, by; to

bij² (bay) *c* (pl ~en) bee

bijbel (*bay*-berl) *c* (pl ~s) bible

bijbetekenis (*bay*-ber-tāy-ker-niss) *c* (pl ~sen) connotation

bijdrage (*bay*-draa-ger) *c* (pl ~n) contribution

bijeen (bay-*āyn*) *adv* together

* **bijeenbrengen** (bay-*āyn*-breh-ngern) *v* assemble

* **bijeenkomen** (bay-*āyng*-kōa-mern) *v* gather

bijeenkomst (bay-*āyng*-komst) *c* (pl ~en) meeting; rally; assembly, congress

bijenkorf (*bay*-er-korf) *c* (pl -korven) beehive

bijgebouw (*bay*-ger-bou) *nt* (pl ~en) annex

bijgeloof (*bay*-ger-lōaf) *nt* superstition

bijgevolg (*bay*-ger-*volkh*) *adv* consequently

* **bijhouden** (*bay*-hou-dern) *v* * keep up with

bijknippen (*bay*-kni-pern) *v* trim

bijkomend (*bay*-kōa-mernt) *adj* additional

bijkomstig (bay-*kom*-sterkh) *adj* additional; subordinate

bijl (bayl) *c* (pl ~en) axe

bijlage (*bay*-laa-ger) *c* (pl ~n) annex; enclosure

bijna (*bay*-naa) *adv* nearly, almost

bijnaam (*bay*-naam) *c* (pl -namen) nickname

bijouterie (bee-zhōō-ter-*ree*) *c* jewellery

* **bijsluiten** (*bay*-slur^ew-tern) *v* enclose

* **bijstaan** (*bay*-staan) *v* assist, aid

bijstand (*bay*-stahnt) *c* assistance

* **bijten** (*bay*-tern) *v* * bite

bijvoegen (*bay*-vōō-gern) *v* attach

bijvoeglijk naamwoord (bay-*vōōkh*-lerk *naam*-vōart) adjective

bijvoorbeeld (ber-*vōar*-bāylt) *adv* for instance, for example

bijwonen (*bay*-vōa-nern) *v* assist at, attend

bijwoord (*bay*-vōart) *nt* (pl ~en) adverb

bijziend (bay-*zeent*) *adj* short-sighted

bijzonder (bee-*zon*-derr) *adj* special, particular; peculiar; **in het ~** in particular, specially

bijzonderheid (bee-*zon*-derr-hayt) *c* (pl -heden) detail

bil (bɪl) *c* (pl ~len) buttock

biljart (bɪl-*Yahrt*) *nt* billiards *pl*

billijk (bɪ-lerk) *adj* right, fair, reasonable

*binden (bɪn-dern) *v* *bind; tie

binnen (bɪ-nern) *prep* within, inside; *adv* inside, indoors; in; indoor; **naar ~** inwards; **van ~** within, inside

binnenband (bɪ-ner-bahnt) *c* (pl ~en) inner tube

*binnengaan (bɪ-ner-gaan) *v* enter, *go in

binnenkant (bɪ-ner-kahnt) *c* interior, inside

*binnenkomen (bɪ-nern-kōa-mern) *v* enter

binnenkomst (bɪ-nern-komst) *c* entrance

binnenkort (bɪ-ner-*kort*) *adv* shortly

binnenlands (bɪ-ner-lahnts) *adj* domestic

binnenst (bɪ-nerst) *adj* inside; **binnenste buiten** *adv* inside out

*binnenvallen (bɪ-ner-vah-lern) *v* invade

biologie (bee-Yōa-lōa-*gee*) *c* biology

bioscoop (bee-Yoss-*kōap*) *c* (pl -scopen) cinema; pictures; movie theater *Am*, movies *Am*

biscuit (bɪss-*kvee*) *nt* (pl ~s) cookie *nAm*

bisschop (*bɪss*-khop) *c* (pl ~pen) bishop

bitter (bɪ-terr) *adj* bitter

blaar (blaar) *c* (pl blaren) blister

blaas (blaass) *c* (pl blazen) bladder;

blister

blaasontsteking (*blaass*-ont-stāy-kɪng) *c* (pl ~en) cystitis

blad¹ (blaht) *nt* (pl ~eren, blaren) leaf

blad² (blaht) *nt* (pl ~en) sheet; magazine

bladgoud (*blaht*-khout) *nt* gold leaf

bladzijde (*blaht*-say-der) *c* (pl ~n) page

blaffen (*blah*-fern) *v* bark; bay

blanco (*blahng*-kōa) *adj* blank

blank (blahngk) *adj* white

blankvoren (*blahngk*-fōa-rern) *c* (pl ~s) roach

blauw (blou) *adj* blue

*blazen (*blaa*-zern) *v* *blow

blazer (*blāy*-zerr) *c* (pl ~s) blazer

bleek (blāyk) *adj* pale

bleken (*blāy*-kern) *v* bleach

blessure (bleh-*sēw*-rer) *c* (pl ~s) injury

blij (blay) *adj* glad; happy, joyful

blijkbaar (*blayk*-baar) *adv* apparently

*blijken (*blay*-kern) *v* prove; appear

blijspel (*blay*-spehl) *nt* (pl ~en) comedy

*blijven (*blay*-vern) *v* stay, remain; *keep; **blijvend** lasting; permanent

blik (blɪk) *nt* (pl ~ken) tin, can; *c* look; glimpse, glance; **een ~ *werpen** glance

blikopener (*blɪk*-ōa-per-nerr) *c* (pl ~s) tin-opener, can opener

bliksem (*blɪk*-serm) *c* lightning

blind¹ (blɪnt) *nt* (pl ~en) shutter

blind² (blɪnt) *adj* blind

blindedarm (blɪn-der-*dahrm*) *c* (pl ~en) appendix

blindedarmontsteking (blɪn-der-*dahrm*-ont-stāy-kɪng) *c* (pl ~en) appendicitis

*blinken (*blɪng*-kern) *v* *shine; **blinkend** bright

blocnote (*blok*-nōat) *c* (pl ~s) writing-pad

bloed (bloot) *nt* blood

bloedarmoede (*bloot*-ahr-moo-der) *c* anaemia

bloeddruk (*bloo*-drerk) *c* blood pressure

bloeden (*bloo*-dern) *v* *bleed

bloeding (*bloo*-ding) *c* (pl ~en) haemorrhage

bloedsomloop (*bloot*-som-loap) *c* circulation

bloedvat (*bloot*-faht) *nt* (pl ~en) blood-vessel

bloedvergiftiging (*bloot*-ferr-gif-ter-ging) *c* blood-poisoning

bloem¹ (bloom) *c* flour

bloem² (bloom) *c* (pl ~en) flower

bloemblad (*bloom*-blaht) *nt* (pl ~en) petal

bloembol (*bloom*-bol) *c* (pl -len) bulb

bloemenwinkel (*bloo*-mer-ving-kerl) *c* (pl ~s) flower-shop

bloemist (bloo-*mist*) *c* (pl ~en) florist

bloemkool (*bloom*-koal) *c* (pl -kolen) cauliflower

bloemlezing (*bloom*-lay-zing) *c* (pl ~en) anthology

bloemperk (*bloom*-pehrk) *nt* (pl ~en) flowerbed

blok (blok) *nt* (pl ~ken) block; **blokje** *nt* cube

blokkeren (blo-*kay*-rern) *v* block

blond (blont) *adj* fair

blondine (blon-*dee*-ner) *c* (pl ~s) blonde

bloot (bloat) *adj* bare; naked

blootleggen (*bloat*-leh-gern) *v* uncover

blootstelling (*bloat*-steh-ling) *c* (pl ~en) exposure

blouse (*bloo*-zer) *c* (pl ~s) blouse

blozen (*bloa*-zern) *v* blush

blussen (*bler*-sern) *v* extinguish

bocht (bokht) *c* (pl ~en) turning, bend; curve, turn

bode (*boa*-der) *c* (pl ~n, ~s) messenger

bodem (*boa*-derm) *c* (pl ~s) bottom; ground; soil

boef (boof) *c* (pl boeven) villain

boei (boo^ee) *c* (pl ~en) buoy

boeien (*boo^ee*-ern) *v* fascinate

boek (book) *nt* (pl ~en) book

boeken (*boo*-kern) *v* book

boekenstalletje (*boo*-ker-stah-ler-t^yer) *nt* (pl ~s) bookstand

boeket (boo-*keht*) *nt* (pl ~ten) bouquet

boekhandel (*book*-hahn-derl) *c* (pl ~s) bookstore

boekhandelaar (*book*-hahn-der-laar) *c* (pl -laren) bookseller

boekwinkel (*book*-ving-kerl) *c* (pl ~s) bookstore

boel (bool) *c* lot

boer (boor) *c* (pl ~en) farmer; peasant; knave

boerderij (boor-der-*ray*) *c* (pl ~en) farm; farmhouse

boerin (boo-*rin*) *c* (pl ~nen) farmer's wife

boete (*boo*-ter) *c* (pl ~n, ~s) penalty, fine

boetseren (boot-*say*-rern) *v* model

bof (bof) *c* mumps

bok (bok) *c* (pl ~ken) goat

boksen (*bok*-sern) *v* box

bokswedstrijd (*boks*-veht-strayt) *c* (pl ~en) boxing match

bol (bol) *c* (pl ~len) bulb; sphere

Boliviaan (boa-lee-vee-*ƴaan*) *c* (pl -vianen) Bolivian

Boliviaans (boa-lee-vee-*ƴaans*) *adj* Bolivian

Bolivië (boa-*lee*-vee-ƴer) Bolivia

bom (bom) *c* (pl ~men) bomb

bombarderen (bom-bahr-*day*-rern) *v* bomb

bon (bon) *c* (pl ~nen) coupon; ticket; voucher

bonbon (bom-*bon*) *c* (pl ~s) chocolate

bond (bont) *c* (pl ~en) league, federation

bondgenoot (*bont*-kher-nōat) *c* (pl -noten) associate

bondgenootschap (*bont*-kher-nōat-skhahp) *nt* (pl ~pen) alliance

bons (bons) *c* (pl bonzen) bump

bont (bont) *adj* gay, colourful; *nt* furs

bontjas (*bont*-t^yahss) *c* (pl ~sen) fur coat

bontwerker (*bon*-tvehr-kerr) *c* (pl ~s) furrier

bonzen (*bon*-zern) *v* bump

boodschap (*bōat*-skhahp) *c* (pl ~pen) errand; message

boodschappentas (*bōat*-skhah-per-tahss) *c* (pl ~sen) shopping bag

boog (bōakh) *c* (pl bogen) arch; bow

boogvormig (*bōakh*-for-merkh) *adj* arched

boom (bōam) *c* (pl bomen) tree

boomgaard (*bōam*-gaart) *c* (pl ~en) orchard

boomkwekerij (bōam-kvāy-ker-*ray*) *c* (pl ~en) nursery

boon (bōan) *c* (pl bonen) bean

boor (bōar) *c* (pl boren) drill

boord (bōart) *nt/c* (pl ~en) collar; **aan boord** aboard; **van boord *gaan** disembark

boordeknoopje (*bōar*-der-knōa-p^yer) *nt* (pl ~s) collar stud

boos (bōass) *adj* cross

boosaardig (bōa-*zaar*-derkh) *adj* malicious, vicious

boosheid (*bōass*-hayt) *c* anger, temper

boot (bōat) *c* (pl boten) boat

bootje (*bōa*-t^yer) *nt* (pl ~s) dinghy

boottocht (*bōa*-tokht) *c* (pl ~en) cruise

bord (bort) *nt* (pl ~en) dish, plate; board

bordeel (bor-*dāyl*) *nt* (pl -delen) brothel

borduren (bor-*dēw*-rern) *v* embroider

borduurwerk (bor-*dēwr*-vehrk) *nt* (pl ~en) embroidery

boren (*bōa*-rern) *v* drill, bore

borg (borkh) *c* (pl ~en) guarantor

borgsom (*borkh*-som) *c* (pl ~men) bail

borrel (*boa*-rerl) *c* (pl ~s) drink

borrelhapje (bo-rerl-hahp-^yer) *nt* (pl ~s) appetizer

borst (borst) *c* (pl ~en) chest; breast, bosom

borstel (*bor*-sterl) *c* (pl ~s) brush

borstelen (*bor*-ster-lern) *v* brush

borstkas (*borst*-kahss) *c* (pl ~sen) chest

bos (boss) *nt* (pl ~sen) forest, wood; *c* bunch

bosje (*bo*-sher) *nt* (pl ~s) grove

boswachter (*boss*-vahkh-terr) *c* (pl ~s) forester

bot¹ (bot) *adj* dull, blunt

bot² (bot) *nt* (pl ~ten) bone

boter (*bōa*-terr) *c* butter

boterham (*bōa*-terr-hahm) *c* (pl ~men) sandwich

botsen (*bot*-sern) *v* bump; collide, crash

botsing (*bot*-sɪng) *c* (pl ~en) collision, crash

bougie (bōo-*zhee*) *c* (pl ~s) sparking-plug

bout (bout) *c* (pl ~en) bolt

boutique (bōo-*teek*) *c* (pl ~s) boutique

bouw (bou) *c* construction

bouwen (*bou*-ern) *v* *build; construct

bouwkunde (*bou*-kern-der) *c* architecture

bouwvallig (bou-*vah*-lerkh) *adj* dilapidated

boven (*bōa*-vern) *prep* above, over;

adv above; upstairs; **naar** ~ upwards, up; upstairs

bovendek (bōa-vern-dehk) *nt* main deck

bovendien (bōa-vern-*deen*) *adv* furthermore, moreover, besides

bovenkant (bōa-verng-kahnt) *c* (pl ~en) top side, top

bovenop (bōa-vern-*op*) *prep* on top of

bovenst (bōa-verst) *adj* upper, top

braaf (braaf) *adj* good

braak (braak) *adj* waste

braam (braam) *c* (pl bramen) blackberry

*braden (braa-dern) *v* fry; roast

braken (braa-kern) *v* vomit

brand (brahnt) *c* (pl ~en) fire

brandalarm (brahnt-aa-lahrm) *nt* fire-alarm

brandblusapparaat (brahnt-blerss-ah-paa-raat) *nt* (pl -raten) fire-extinguisher

branden (brahn-dern) *v* *burn

brandkast (brahnt-kahst) *c* (pl ~en) safe

brandmerk (brahnt-mehrk) *nt* (pl ~en) brand

brandpunt (brahnt-pernt) *nt* (pl ~en) focus

brandspiritus (brahnt-spee-ree-terss) *c* methylated spirits

brandstof (brahnt-stof) *c* (pl ~fen) fuel

brandtrap (brahn-trahp) *c* (pl ~pen) fire-escape

brandvrij (brahnt-fray) *adj* fireproof

brandweer (brahn-tvāyr) *c* fire-brigade

brandwond (brahn-tvont) *c* (pl ~en) burn

brasem (braa-serm) *c* (pl ~s) bream

Braziliaan (braa-zee-lee-*Yaan*) *c* (pl -lianen) Brazilian

Braziliaans (braa-zee-lee-*Yaans*) *adj* Brazilian

Brazilië (braa-*zee*-lee-Yer) Brazil

breed (brāyt) *adj* broad, wide

breedte (brāy-ter) *c* (pl ~n, ~s) breadth, width

breedtegraad (brāy-ter-graat) *c* (pl -graden) latitude

breekbaar (brāyk-baar) *adj* fragile

breekijzer (brāy-kay-zerr) *nt* (pl ~s) crowbar

breien (bray-ern) *v* *knit

*breken (brāy-kern) *v* *break; *burst, crack; fracture

brengen (breh-ngern) *v* *bring; *take

bres (brehss) *c* (pl ~sen) gap, breach

bretels (brer-tehls) *pl* braces *pl*; suspenders *plAm*

breuk (brurk) *c* (pl ~en) break; fracture; hernia

brief (breef) *c* (pl brieven) letter; **aangetekende** ~ registered letter

briefkaart (breef-kaart) *c* (pl ~en) card, postcard

briefopener (breef-ōa-per-nerr) *c* (pl ~s) paper-knife

briefpapier (breef-paa-peer) *nt* notepaper

briefwisseling (breef-vi-ser-ling) *c* correspondence

bries (breess) *c* breeze

brievenbus (bree-ver-berss) *c* (pl ~sen) letter-box, pillar-box; mailbox *nAm*

bril (bril) *c* (pl ~len) spectacles, glasses

briljant (bril-*Yahnt*) *adj* brilliant

Brit (brit) *c* (pl ~ten) Briton

Brits (brits) *adj* British

broche (bro-sher) *c* (pl ~s) brooch

brochure (bro-*shew*-rer) *c* (pl ~s) brochure

broeder (brōō-derr) *c* (pl ~s) brother

broederschap (brōō-derr-skhahp) *c*

fraternity
broeikas (*broo^ee*-kahss) *c* (pl ~sen)
greenhouse
broek (brook) *c* (pl ~en) trousers *pl*,
slacks *pl*; pants *plAm*; **korte ~**
shorts *pl*
broekpak (*brook*-pahk) *nt* (pl ~ken)
pant-suit
broer (broor) *c* (pl ~s) brother
brok (brok) *nt* (pl ~ken) morsel;
lump
bromfiets (*brom*-feets) *c* (pl ~en) moped
brommer (*bro*-merr) *c* (pl ~s) motorbike *nAm*
bron (bron) *c* (pl ~nen) well; fountain, source, spring; **geneeskrachtige ~** spa
bronchitis (brong-*khee*-terss) *c* bronchitis
brons (brons) *nt* bronze
bronzen (*bron*-zern) *adj* bronze
brood (broat) *nt* (pl broden) bread;
loaf
broodje (*broa*-t^Yer) *nt* (pl ~s) roll, bun
broos (broass) *adj* fragile
brouwen (*brou*-ern) *v* brew
brouwerij (brou-er-*ray*) *c* (pl ~en)
brewery
brug (brerkh) *c* (pl ~gen) bridge
bruid (brur^ew t) *c* (pl ~en) bride
bruidegom (*brur^ew*-der-gom) *c* (pl ~s)
bridegroom
bruikbaar (*brur^ew k*-baar) *adj* usable;
useful
bruiloft (*brur^ew*-loft) *c* (pl ~en) wedding
bruin (brur^ew n) *adj* brown
brullen (*brer*-lern) *v* roar
brunette (brew-*neh*-ter) *c* (pl ~s) brunette
brutaal (brew-*taal*) *adj* bold, impertinent, insolent
bruto (*broo*-toa) *adj* gross

budget (ber-*jeht*) *nt* (pl ~ten, ~s)
budget
buffet (bew-*feht*) *nt* (pl ~ten) buffet
bui (bur^ew) *c* (pl ~en) shower; spirit
buidel (*bur^ew*-derl) *c* (pl ~s) pouch
buigbaar (*bur^ew kh*-baar) *adj* flexible
***buigen** (*bur^ew*-gern) *v* *bend; bow
buigzaam (*bur^ew kh*-saam) *adj* supple
buik (bur^ew k) *c* (pl ~en) belly
buikpijn (*bur^ew k*-payn) *c* stomach-
ache
buis (bur^ew ss) *c* (pl buizen) tube
buiten (*bur^ew*-tern) *prep* outside, out
of; *adv* out; outside, outdoors;
naar ~ outwards
buitengewoon (*bur^ew*-ter-ger-voan)
adj extraordinary, exceptional
buitenhuis (*bur^ew*-ter-hur^ew ss) *nt* (pl
-huizen) cottage
buitenkant (*bur^ew*-ter-kahnt) *c* (pl
~en) outside, exterior
in het buitenland (in ert bur^ew-tern-
lahnt) abroad
buitenlander (*bur^ew*-ter-lahn-derr) *c*
(pl ~s) alien, foreigner
buitenlands (*bur^ew*-ter-lahnts) *adj*
alien, foreign
buitensporig (bur^ew-ter-*spoa*-rerkh)
adj excessive
buitenwijk (*bur^ew*-ter-vayk) *c* (pl ~en)
suburb; outskirts *pl*
zich bukken (ber-kern) *v* *bend down
Bulgaar (berl-*gaar*) *c* (pl -garen) Bulgarian
Bulgaars (berl-*gaars*) *adj* Bulgarian
Bulgarije (berl-gaa-*ray*-er) Bulgaria
bult (berlt) *c* (pl ~en) lump
bumper (*berm*-perr) *c* (pl ~s) bumper,
fender
bundel (*bern*-derl) *c* (pl ~s) bundle
bundelen (*bern*-der-lern) *v* bundle
burcht (berrkht) *c* (pl ~en) stronghold
bureau (bew-*roa*) *nt* (pl ~s) agency,
office; bureau, desk; ~ **voor ge-**

vonden voorwerpen lost property office

bureaucratie (bew-rōa-kraa-*tsee*) *c* bureaucracy

burgemeester (berr-ger-*māyss*-terr) *c* (pl ~s) mayor

burger (*berr*-gerr) *c* (pl ~s) citizen; civilian; **burger-** civilian, civic

burgerlijk (*berr*-gerr-lerk) *adj* bourgeois, middle-class; ~ **recht** civil law

bus (berss) *c* (pl ~sen) coach, bus; tin, canister

buste (*bew*-ster) *c* (pl ~s, ~n) bust

bustehouder (*bew*-ster-hou-derr) *c* (pl ~s) brassiere, bra

buur (bewr) *c* (pl buren) neighbour

buurman (*bewr*-mahn) *c* neighbour

buurt (bewrt) *c* (pl ~en) neighbourhood, vicinity

C

cabaret (kaa-baa-*reht*) *nt* (pl ~s) cabaret

cabine (kaa-*bee*-ner) *c* (pl ~s) cabin

cadeau (kaa-*dōa*) *nt* (pl ~s) gift, present

café (kah-*fāy*) *nt* (pl ~s) café; public house, pub

cafetaria (kah-fer-*taa*-ree-Yaa) *c* (pl ~'s) cafeteria

caissière (kah-*shai*-rer) *c* (pl ~s) cashier

cake (kāyk) *c* (pl ~s) cake

calcium (*kahl*-see-Yerm) *nt* calcium

calorie (kah-lōa-*ree*) *c* (pl ~ën) calorie

calvinisme (kahl-vee-*niss*-mer) *nt* Calvinism

camee (kaa-*māy*) *c* (pl ~ën) cameo

campagne (kahm-*pah*-ñer) *c* (pl ~s) campaign

camping (*kehm*-pïng) *c* (pl ~s) camping site, camping

Canada (*kaa*-naa-daa) Canada

Canadees (kaa-naa-*dāyss*) *adj* Canadian

capabel (kaa-*paa*-berl) *adj* able

capaciteit (kaa-paa-see-*tayt*) *c* (pl ~en) capacity

cape (kāyp) *c* (pl ~s) cape

capitulatie (kah-pee-tew-*laa*-tsee) *c* (pl ~s) capitulation

capsule (kahp-*sew*-ler) *c* (pl ~s) capsule

caravan (*keh*-rer-vern) *c* (pl ~s) caravan

carbonpapier (kahr-*bon*-paa-peer) *nt* carbon paper

carburateur (kahr-bew-raa-*tūrr*) *c* (pl ~s) carburettor

carillon (kaa-rïl-*Yon*) *nt* (pl ~s) chimes *pl*

carnaval (*kahr*-naa-vahl) *nt* carnival

carrière (kah-ree-*Yai*-rer) *c* (pl ~s) career

carrosserie (kah-ro-ser-*ree*) *c* (pl ~ën) coachwork; motor body *Am*

carter (*kahr*-terr) *nt* crankcase

casino (kaa-*zee*-nōa) *nt* (pl ~'s) casino

catacombe (kah-tah-*kom*-ber) *c* (pl ~n) catacomb

catalogus (kah-*taa*-lōa-gerss) *c* (pl -gussen, -gi) catalogue

catarre (kaa-*tahr*) *c* catarrh

catastrofe (kaa-taa-*straw*-fer) *c* (pl ~s) catastrophe, disaster

categorie (kaa-ter-gōa-*ree*) *c* (pl ~ën) category

cavia (*kaa*-vee-Yaa) *c* (pl ~'s) guinea-pig

cel (sehl) *c* (pl ~len) cell

celibaat (sāy-lee-*baat*) *nt* celibacy

cellofaan (seh-loa-*faan*) *nt* cellophane

celsius (*sehl*-see-Yerss) centigrade

cement (ser-*mehnt*) *nt* cement

censuur (sehn-*zewr*) *c* censorship

centimeter (*sehn*-tee-may-terr) *c* (pl ~s) centimetre; tape-measure

centraal (sehn-*traal*) *adj* central; ~ **station** central station; **centrale verwarming** central heating

centraliseren (sehn-traa-lee-*zay*-rern) *v* centralize

centrifuge (sehn-tree-*few*-zher) *c* (pl ~s) dryer

centrum (*sehn*-trerm) *nt* (pl centra) centre

ceramiek (say-raa-*meek*) *c* ceramics *pl*

ceremonie (say-rer-*moā*-nee) *c* (pl -niën, -nies) ceremony

certificaat (sehr-tee-fee-*kaat*) *nt* (pl -caten) certificate

chalet (shaa-*leht*) *nt* (pl ~s) chalet

champagne (shahm-*pah*-ñer) *c* (pl ~s) champagne

champignon (shahm-pee-*ñon*) *c* (pl ~s) mushroom

chantage (shahn-*taa*-zher) *c* blackmail

chanteren (shahn-*tay*-rern) *v* blackmail

chaos (*khaa*-oss) *c* chaos

chaotisch (khaa-*oā*-teess) *adj* chaotic

charlatan (*shahr*-laa-tahn) *c* (pl ~s) quack

charmant (shahr-*mahnt*) *adj* charming

charme (*shahr*-mer) *c* (pl ~s) charm; glamour

chartervlucht (*chahr*-terr-vlerkht) *c* (pl ~en) charter flight

chassis (shah-*see*) *nt* (pl ~) chassis

chauffeur (shoā-*fürr*) *c* (pl ~s) driver, chauffeur

chef (shehf) *c* (pl ~s) boss, manager, chief

chef-kok (shehf-*kok*) *c* (pl ~s) chef

chemie (khay-*mee*) *c* chemistry

chemisch (*khay*-meess) *adj* chemical

cheque (shehk) *c* (pl ~s) cheque; check *nAm*

chequeboekje (*shehk*-boō-k^yer) *nt* (pl ~s) cheque-book; check-book *nAm*

chic (sheek) *adj* smart

Chileen (shee-*layn*) *c* (pl -lenen) Chilean

Chileens (shee-*layns*) *adj* Chilean

Chili (*shee*-lee) Chile

China (*shee*-naa) China

Chinees (shee-*nayss*) *adj* Chinese

chirurg (shee-*rerrkh*) *c* (pl ~en) surgeon

chloor (khloār) *nt* chlorine

chocola (shoā-koā-*laa*) *c* chocolate

chocolademelk (shoā-koā-*laa*-der-mehlk) *c* chocolate

christelijk (*kriss*-ter-lerk) *adj* Christian

christen (*kriss*-tern) *c* (pl ~en) Christian

Christus (*kriss*-terss) Christ

chronisch (*khroā*-neess) *adj* chronic

chronologisch (khroā-noā-*loā*-geess) *adj* chronological

chroom (khroām) *nt* chromium

cijfer (*say*-ferr) *nt* (pl ~s) number, figure; digit; mark

cilinder (see-*lin*-derr) *c* (pl ~s) cylinder

cilinderkop (see-*lin*-derr-kop) *c* (pl ~pen) cylinder head

cipier (see-*peer*) *c* (pl ~s) jailer

circa (*sir*-kaa) *adv* approximately

circulatie (sir-kew-*laa*-tsee) *c* circulation

circus (*sir*-kerss) *nt* (pl ~sen) circus

cirkel (*sir*-kerl) *c* (pl ~s) circle

citaat (see-*taat*) *nt* (pl citaten) quotation

citeren (see-*tay*-rern) *v* quote

citroen (see-*troōn*) *c* (pl ~en) lemon

civiel (see-*veel*) *adj* civil

clausule (klou-*sew*-ler) *c* (pl ~s) clause

clavecimbel (klaa-ver-*sim*-berl) *c* (pl ~s) harpsichord

claxon (*klahk*-son) *c* (pl ~s) horn, hooter

claxonneren (klahk-so-*nāy*-rern) *v* hoot ; toot *vAm*, honk *vAm*

clementie (klāy-*mehn*-tsee) *c* mercy

cliënt (klee-*Yehnt*) *c* (pl ~en) customer, client

closetpapier (klōa-*zeht*-pah-peer) *nt* toilet-paper

cocaïne (kōa-kaa-*ee*-ner) *c* cocaine

code (*kōa*-der) *c* (pl ~s) code

coffeïne (ko-fāy-*ee*-ner) *c* caffeine

coffeïnevrij (ko-fāy-*ee*-ner-vray) *adj* decaffeinated

cognac (ko-*ñahk*) *c* cognac

coiffure (kvah-*fēw*-rer) *c* (pl ~s) hairdo

colbert (kol-*bair*) *c* (pl ~s) jacket

collectant (ko-lehk-*tahnt*) *c* (pl ~en) collector

collecteren (ko-lehk-*tāy*-rern) *v* collect

collectie (ko-*lehk*-see) *c* (pl ~s) collection

collectief (ko-lehk-*teef*) *adj* collective

collega (ko-*lāy*-gaa) *c* (pl ~'s) colleague

college (ko-*lāy*-zher) *nt* (pl ~s) lecture

Colombia (kōa-*lom*-bee-Yaa) Colombia

Colombiaan (kōa-lom-bee-Yaan) *c* (pl -bianen) Colombian

Colombiaans (kōa-lom-bee-Yaans) *adj* Colombian

coma (*kōa*-maa) *nt* coma

combinatie (kom-bee-*naa*-tsee) *c* (pl ~s) combination

combineren (kom-bee-*nāy*-rern) *v* combine

comfortabel (kom-for-*taa*-berl) *adj* comfortable

comité (ko-mee-*tāy*) *nt* (pl ~s) committee

commentaar (ko-mehn-*taar*) *nt* (pl -taren) comment

commercieel (ko-mehr-*shāyl*) *adj* commercial

commissie (ko-*mi*-see) *c* (pl ~s) committee ; commission

commode (ko-*mōa*-der) *c* (pl ~s) bureau *nAm*

commune (ko-*mēw*-ner) *c* (pl ~s) commune

communicatie (ko-mew-nee-*kaa*-tsee) *c* communication

communiqué (ko-mēw-nee-*kāy*) *nt* (pl ~s) communiqué

communisme (ko-mēw-*niss*-mer) *nt* communism

communist (ko-mēw-*nist*) *c* (pl ~en) communist

compact (kom-*pahkt*) *adj* compact

compagnon (kom-pah-*ñon*) *c* (pl ~s) partner

compensatie (kom-pehn-*zaa*-tsee) *c* (pl ~s) compensation

compenseren (kom-pehn-*zāy*-rern) *v* compensate

compleet (kom-*plāyt*) *adj* complete

complex (kom-*plehks*) *nt* (pl ~en) complex

compliment (kom-plee-*mehnt*) *nt* (pl ~en) compliment

componist (kom-pōa-*nist*) *c* (pl ~en) composer

compositie (kom-pōa-*zee*-tsee) *c* (pl ~s) composition

compromis (kom-prōa-*mee*) *nt* (pl ~sen) compromise

concentratie (kon-sehn-*traa*-tsee) *c* (pl ~s) concentration

concentreren (kon-sehn-*trāy*-rern) *v* concentrate

conceptie (kon-*sehp*-see) *c* conception

concert (kon-*sehrt*) *nt* (pl ~en) concert

concertzaal (kon-*sehrt*-saal) *c* (pl -zalen) concert hall

concessie (kon-*seh*-see) *c* (pl ~s) concession

concierge (kon-*shehr*-zheh) *c* (pl ~s)
janitor; caretaker, concierge

conclusie (kong-*klew*-zee) *c* (pl ~s)
conclusion

concreet (kong-*krayt*) *adj* concrete

concurrent (kong-kew-*rehnt*) *c* (pl
~en) competitor; rival

concurrentie (kong-kew-*rehn*-tsee) *c*
competition; rivalry

conditie (kon-*dee*-tsee) *c* (pl ~s) condition

conducteur (kon-derk-*türr*) *c* (pl ~s)
conductor; ticket collector

conferencier (kon-fer-rahng-*shay*) *c* (pl
~s) entertainer

conferentie (kon-fer-*rehn*-see) *c* (pl
~s) conference

conflict (kon-*flikt*) *nt* (pl ~en) conflict

congregatie (kong-gray-*gaa*-tsee) *c* (pl
~s) congregation

congres (kong-*grehss*) *nt* (pl ~sen)
congress

consequentie (kon-ser-*kvehn*-see) *c*
(pl ~s) consequence

conservatief (kon-zerr-vaa-*teef*) *adj*
conservative

conservatorium (kon-zerr-vaa-*tōa*-ree-
Yerm) *nt* (pl -ria) music academy

conserven (kon-*sehr*-vern) *pl* tinned
food

consideratie (kon-see-der-*raa*-tsee) *c*
consideration

constant (kon-*stahnt*) *adj* even

constateren (koan-staa-*tay*-rern) *v*
note, ascertain; diagnose

constipatie (kon-stee-*paa*-tsee) *c* constipation

constructie (kon-*strerk*-see) *c* (pl ~s)
construction

construeren (kon-strew^{oo}-*ay*-rern) *v*
construct

consul (*kon*-zerl) *c* (pl ~s) consul

consulaat (kon-zew-*laat*) *nt* (pl -laten)
consulate

consult (kon-*zerlt*) *nt* (pl ~en) consultation

consultatiebureau (kon-zerl-*taa*-tsee-
bew-rōa) *nt* (pl ~s) health centre

consument (kon-zew-*mehnt*) *c* (pl
~en) consumer

contact (kon-*tahkt*) *nt* (pl ~en) contact; touch

contactlenzen (kon-*tahkt*-lehn-zern) *pl*
contact lenses

contanten (kon-*tahn*-tern) *pl* cash

continent (kon-tee-*nehnt*) *nt* (pl ~en)
continent

continentaal (kon-tee-nehn-*taal*) *adj*
continental

contra (*kon*-traa) *prep* versus

contract (kon-*trahkt*) *nt* (pl ~en)
agreement, contract

contrast (kon-*trahst*) *nt* (pl ~en) contrast

controle (kon-*traw*-ler) *c* (pl ~s) control; supervision, inspection

controleren (kon-trōa-*lay*-rern) *v* control, check

controlestrook (kon-*traw*-ler-strōak) *c*
(-stroken) counterfoil, stub

controversieel (kon-trōa-vehr-*zhayl*)
adj controversial

conversatie (kon-verr-*zaa*-tsee) *c* (pl
~s) conversation

coöperatie (kōa-ōa-per-*raa*-tsee) *c* (pl
~s) co-operative

coöperatief (kōa-ōa-per-raa-*teef*) *adj*
co-operative

coördinatie (kōa-or-dee-*naa*-tsee) *c* co-
ordination

coördineren (kōa-or-dee-*nay*-rern) *v*
co-ordinate

corpulent (kor-pew-*lehnt*) *adj* corpulent, stout

correct (ko-*rehkt*) *adj* correct

correctie (ko-*rehk*-see) *c* (pl ~s) correction

correspondent (ko-rehss-pon-*dehnt*) *c*

(pl ~en) correspondent

correspondentie (ko-rehss-pon-*dehn*-see) *c* correspondence

corresponderen (ko-rehss-pon-*day*-rern) *v* correspond

corrigeren (ko-ree-*zhay*-rern) *v* correct

corrupt (ko-*rerpt*) *adj* corrupt

couchette (koo-*sheh*-ter) *c* (pl ~s) berth

coupé (koo-*pay*) *c* (pl ~s) compartment; ~ **voor rokers** smoking-compartment

couplet (koo-*pleht*) *nt* (pl ~ten) stanza

coupon (koo-*pon*) *c* (pl ~s) coupon

crèche (krehsh) *c* (pl ~s) nursery

crediteren (kray-dee-*tay*-rern) *v* credit

creëren (kray-*ay*-rern) *v* create

crematie (kray-*maa*-tsee) *c* (pl ~s) cremation

crème (kraim) *c* (pl ~s) cream; **vochtinbrengende** ~ moisturizing cream

cremeren (kray-*may*-rern) *v* cremate

criminaliteit (kree-mee-naa-lee-*tayt*) *c* criminality

crimineel (kree-mee-*nayl*) *adj* criminal

crisis (*kree*-serss) *c* (pl -ses) crisis

criticus (*kree*-tee-kerss) *c* (pl -ci) critic

croquant (kroa-*kahnt*) *adj* crisp

Cuba (*kew*-baa) Cuba

Cubaan (kew-*baan*) *c* (pl -banen) Cuban

Cubaans (kew-*baans*) *adj* Cuban

cultuur (kerl-*tewr*) *c* (pl -turen) culture

cursiefschrift (kerr-*zeef*-skhrift) *nt* italics *pl*

cursus (*kerr*-zerss) *c* (pl ~sen) course

cyclus (*see*-klerss) *c* (pl ~sen) cycle

D

daad (daat) *c* (pl daden) deed, act

daar (daar) *adv* there

daarheen (*daar*-hayn) *adv* there

daarom (*daa*-rom) *conj* therefore

dadel (*daa*-derl) *c* (pl ~s) date

dadelijk (*daa*-der-lerk) *adv* at once, immediately; presently

dag (dahkh) *c* (pl ~en) day; **dag!** hello!; good-bye!; **per** ~ per day

dagblad (*dahkh*-blaht) *nt* (pl ~en) daily

dagboek (*dahkh*-book) *nt* (pl ~en) diary

dagelijks (*daa*-ger-lerks) *adj* daily

dageraad (*daa*-ger-raat) *c* daybreak, dawn

daglicht (*dahkh*-likht) *nt* daylight

dagvaarding (*dahkh*-vaar-ding) *c* (pl ~en) summons

dak (dahk) *nt* (pl ~en) roof

dakpan (*dahk*-pahn) *c* (pl ~nen) tile

dal (dahl) *nt* (pl ~en) valley

dalen (*daa*-lern) *v* descend

dam (dahm) *c* (pl ~men) dam; dike

dambord (*dahm*-bort) *nt* (pl ~en) draught-board

dame (*daa*-mer) *c* (pl ~s) lady

damestoilet (*daa*-merss-tvah-leht) *nt* (pl ~ten) powder-room, ladies' room

damp (dahmp) *c* (pl ~en) vapour

damspel (*dahm*-spehl) *nt* draughts; checkers *plAm*

dan (dahn) *adv* then; *conj* than; **nu en** ~ occasionally

dankbaar (*dahngk*-baar) *adj* grateful, thankful

dankbaarheid (*dahngk*-baar-hayt) *c* gratitude

danken (*dahng*-kern) *v* thank; **dank u**

thank you; **te ~ *hebben aan** owe

dans (dahns) *c* (pl ~en) dance

dansen (dahn-sern) *v* dance

danszaal (dahn-saal) *c* (pl -zalen) ballroom

dapper (dah-perr) *adj* brave, courageous

dapperheid (dah-perr-hayt) *c* courage

darm (dahrm) *c* (pl ~en) gut, intestine; **darmen** bowels *pl*

das (dahss) *c* (pl ~sen) necktie, tie; scarf

dat (daht) *pron* which; *conj* that

datum (daa-term) *c* (pl data) date

dauw (dou) *c* dew

de (der) *art* the *art*

debat (der-baht) *nt* (pl ~ten) discussion, debate

debatteren (dāy-bah-tāy-rern) *v* argue

debet (dāy-beht) *nt* debit

december (dāy-sehm-berr) December

deeg (dāykh) *nt* dough

deel (dāyl) *nt* (pl delen) part; share; volume

***deelnemen** (dāyl-nāy-mern) *v* participate

deelnemer (dāyl-nāy-merr) *c* (pl ~s) participant

deels (dāyls) *adv* partly

Deen (dāyn) *c* (pl Denen) Dane

Deens (dāyns) *adj* Danish

defect[1] (der-fehkt) *adj* defective, faulty

defect[2] (der-fehkt) *nt* (pl ~en) fault

defensie (dāy-fehn-zee) *c* defence

definiëren (dāy-fi-ni-āy-rern) *v* define

definitie (dāy-fee-nee-tsee) *c* (pl ~s) definition

degelijk (dāy-ger-lerk) *adj* thorough; sound

dek (dehk) *nt* deck

deken (dāy-kern) *c* (pl ~s) blanket

dekhut (dehk-hert) *c* (pl ~ten) deck cabin

deksel (dehk-serl) *nt* (pl ~s) lid; cover, top

dekzeil (dehk-sayl) *nt* (pl ~en) tarpaulin

delegatie (dāy-ler-gaa-tsee) *c* (pl ~s) delegation

delen (dāy-lern) *v* divide; share

delfstof (dehlf-stof) *c* (pl ~fen) mineral

delicatessen (dāy-lee-kaa-teh-sern) *pl* delicatessen

delicatessenwinkel (dāy-lee-kaa-teh-ser-ving-kerl) *c* (pl ~s) delicatessen

delikaat (dāy-lee-kaat) *adj* delicate

deling (dāy-ling) *c* (pl ~en) division

delinquent (dāy-ling-kvehnt) *c* (pl ~en) criminal

***delven** (dehl-vern) *v* *dig

democratie (dāy-mōa-kraa-tsee) *c* (pl ~ën) democracy

democratisch (dāy-mōa-kraa-teess) *adj* democratic

demonstratie (dāy-mon-straa-tsee) *c* (pl ~s) demonstration

demonstreren (dāy-mon-strāy-rern) *v* demonstrate

den (dehn) *c* (pl ~nen) fir-tree

Denemarken (dāy-ner-mahr-kern) Denmark

denkbeeld (dehngk-bāyld) *nt* (pl ~en) idea

denkbeeldig (dehngk-bāyl-derkh) *adj* imaginary

***denken** (dehng-kern) *v* *think; guess, reckon; ~ **aan** *think of

denker (dehng-kerr) *c* (pl ~s) thinker

denneboom (deh-ner-bōam) *c* (pl -bomen) fir-tree

deodorant (dāy-yōa-dōa-rahnt) *c* deodorant

departement (dāy-pahr-ter-mehnt) *nt* (pl ~en) department

deponeren (dāy-pōa-nāy-rern) *v* bank

depressie (dāy-preh-see) *c* (pl ~s) depression

deprimeren (dāy-pree-*māy*-rern) *v* depress

derde (*dehr*-der) *num* third

dergelijk (*dehr*-ger-lerk) *adj* such; similar

dermate (*dehr*-maa-ter) *adv* so

dertien (*dehr*-teen) *num* thirteen

dertiende (*dehr*-teen-der) *num* thirteenth

dertig (*dehr*-terkh) *num* thirty

dertigste (*dehr*-terkh-ster) *num* thirtieth

deserteren (dāy-zehr-*tāy*-rern) *v* desert

deskundig (dehss-*kern*-derkh) *adj* expert

deskundige (dehss-*kern*-der-ger) *c* (pl ~n) expert

dessert (deh-*sair*) *nt* (pl ~s) dessert

detail (dāy-*tigh*) *nt* (pl ~s) detail

detailhandel (dāy-*tigh*-hahn-derl) *c* retail trade

detaillist (dāy-tah-*Y*ıst) *c* (pl ~en) retailer

detectiveroman (dāy-*tehk*-tıf-rōā-mahn) *c* (pl ~s) detective story

deugd (dūrkht) *c* (pl ~en) virtue

deugniet (*dūr*kh-neet) *c* (pl ~en) rascal

deuk (dūrk) *c* (pl ~en) dent

deur (dūrr) *c* (pl ~en) door

deurbel (*dūr*r-behl) *c* (pl ~len) doorbell

deurwaarder (*dūr*r-vaar-derr) *c* (pl ~s) bailiff

devaluatie (dāy-vaa-lew-*vaa*-tsee) *c* (pl ~s) devaluation

devalueren (dāy-vaa-lew-*vāy*-rern) *v* devalue

devies (der-*veess*) *nt* (pl deviezen) motto

deze (*dāy*-zer) *pron* this; these

dia (*dee*-Yaa) *c* (pl ~'s) slide

diabetes (dee-Yaa-*bāy*-terss) *c* diabetes

diabeticus (dee-Yaa-*bāy*-tee-kerss) *c* (pl -ci) diabetic

diagnose (dee-Yahkh-*nōā*-zer) *c* (pl ~n, ~s) diagnosis; **een ~ stellen** diagnose

diagonaal[1] (dee-Yaa-gōā-*naal*) *adj* diagonal

diagonaal[2] (dee-Yaa-gōā-*naal*) *c* (pl -nalen) diagonal

dialect (dee-Yaa-*lehkt*) *nt* (pl ~en) dialect

diamant (dee-Yaa-*mahnt*) *c* (pl ~en) diamond

diarree (dee-Yah-*rāy*) *c* diarrhoea

dicht (dıkht) *adj* dense; thick; closed, shut

dichtbevolkt (dıkht-ber-*volkt*) *adj* populous

dichtbij (dıkht-*bay*) *adj* near

dichtdraaien (*dıkh*-draa^(ee)-ern) *v* turn off

dichter (*dıkh*-terr) *c* (pl ~s) poet

dichtkunst (*dıkht*-kernst) *c* poetry

***dichtslaan** (*dıkht*-slaan) *v* slam

dictaat (dık-*taat*) *nt* (pl -taten) dictation

dictafoon (dık-taa-*fōān*) *c* (pl ~s) dictaphone

dictator (dık-*taa*-tor) *c* (pl ~s) dictator

dictee (dık-*tay*) *nt* (pl ~s) dictation

dicteren (dık-*tāy*-rern) *v* dictate

die (dee) *pron* that; those; who

dieet (dee-*Yāyt*) *nt* diet

dief (deef) *c* (pl dieven) robber, thief

diefstal (*deef*-stahl) *c* (pl ~len) robbery, theft

dienblad (*deen*-blaht) *nt* (pl ~en) tray

dienen (*dee*-nern) *v* serve

dienst (deenst) *c* (pl ~en) service; **in ~ *nemen** engage

dienstplichtige (deenst-*plıkh*-ter-ger) *c* (pl ~n) conscript

dienstregeling (deenst-*rāy*-ger-lıng) *c* (pl ~en) schedule, timetable

diep (deep) *adj* deep; low

diepte (*deep*-ter) *c* (pl ~n, ~s) depth

diepvrieskast (*deep*-freess-kahst) *c* (pl ~en) deep-freeze

diepzinnig (deep-*sı*-nerkh) *adj* profound

dier (deer) *nt* (pl ~en) animal

dierbaar (*deer*-baar) *adj* dear; precious

dierenarts (*dee*-rern-ahrts) *c* (pl ~en) veterinary surgeon

dierenriem (*dee*-rer-reem) *c* zodiac

dierentuin (*dee*-rer-tur^ewn) *c* (pl ~en) zoological gardens; zoo

diesel (*dee*-serl) *c* diesel

difterie (dif-ter-*ree*) *c* diphtheria

dij (day) *c* (pl ~en) thigh

dijk (dayk) *c* (pl ~en) dike; dam

dik (dık) *adj* corpulent; thick; fat, stout, big

dikte (*dık*-ter) *c* (pl ~n, ~s) thickness; fatness

dikwijls (*dık*-verls) *adv* frequently, often

ding (dıng) *nt* (pl ~en) thing

dinsdag (*dıns*-dahkh) *c* Tuesday

diploma (dee-*plōa*-maa) *nt* (pl ~'s) certificate, diploma; **een ~ behalen** graduate

diplomaat (dee-plōa-*maat*) *c* (pl -maten) diplomat

direct (dee-*rehkt*) *adj* direct; *adv* straight away

directeur (dee-rerk-*tūrr*) *c* (pl ~en, ~s) executive, manager, director; headmaster, principal

directie (dee-*rehk*-see) *c* (pl ~s) management

dirigent (dee-ree-*gehnt*) *c* (pl ~en) conductor

dirigeren (dee-ree-*gāy*-rern) *v* conduct

discipline (di-see-*plee*-ner) *c* discipline

disconto (dıss-*kon*-tōa) *nt* (pl ~'s) bank-rate

discreet (dıss-*krāyt*) *adj* modest

discussie (dıss-*ker*-see) *c* (pl ~s) discussion, argument

discussiëren (dıss-ker-*shāy*-rern) *v* discuss; argue

distel (*dıss*-terl) *c* (pl ~s) thistle

district (dıss-*trıkt*) *nt* (pl ~en) district

dit (dıt) *pron* this

divan (*dee*-vahn) *c* (pl ~s) couch

docent (dōa-*sehnt*) *c* (pl ~en) teacher

doch (dokh) *conj* but

dochter (*dokh*-terr) *c* (pl ~s) daughter

doctor (*dok*-tor) *c* (pl ~en, ~s) doctor

document (dōa-kew-*mehnt*) *nt* (pl ~en) document

dodelijk (*dōa*-der-lerk) *adj* mortal, fatal

doden (*dōa*-dern) *v* kill

doek (dōōk) *c* (pl ~en) cloth; *nt* curtain

doel (dōōl) *nt* (pl ~en) objective, aim, purpose; object, goal, design, target

doelman (*dōōl*-mahn) *c* (pl ~nen) goalkeeper

doelmatig (dōōl-*maa*-terkh) *adj* efficient

doelpunt (*dōōl*-pernt) *nt* (pl ~en) goal

doeltreffend (dōōl-*treh*-fernt) *adj* effective

***doen** (dōōn) *v* *do; cause to

dof (dof) *adj* mat, dim

dok (dok) *nt* (pl ~ken) dock

dokter (*dok*-terr) *c* (pl ~s) doctor, physician

dom[1] (dom) *adj* dumb, stupid

dom[2] (dom) *c* cathedral

dominee (*dōa*-mee-nāy) *c* (pl ~s) clergyman, parson, rector

dompelaar (*dom*-per-laar) *c* (pl ~s) immersion heater

donateur (dōa-naa-*tūrr*) *c* (pl ~s) donor

donder (*don*-derr) *c* thunder

donderdag (*don*-derr-dahkh) *c* Thursday

donderen (*don*-der-rern) v thunder

donker (*dong*-kerr) adj dark, dim

dons (dons) nt down; **donzen dek-bed** eiderdown

dood (dōāt) adj dead; c death

doodstraf (*dōāt*-strahf) c death penalty

doof (dōāf) adj deaf

dooi (dōāee) c thaw

dooien (*dōāee*-ern) v thaw

dooier (*dōāee*-err) c (pl ~s) yolk

doolhof (*dōāl*-hof) nt (pl -hoven) maze; labyrinth

doop (dōāp) c baptism, christening

doopsel (*dōāp*-serl) nt baptism

door (dōār) prep through; by

doorboren (dōār-*bōā*-rern) v pierce

* **doorbrengen** (*dōār*-breh-ngern) v *spend

doordat (dōār-*daht*) conj because

* **doordringen** (*dōār*-drı-ngern) v penetrate

* **doorgaan** (*dōār*-gaan) v continue, *go on; carry on; *go ahead; ~ met *keep on

doorgang (*dōār*-gahng) c (pl ~en) passage

doorlichten (*dōār*-lıkh-tern) v X-ray

doorlopend (doar-*lōā*-pernt) adj continuous

doormaken (*dōār*-maa-kern) v *go through

doorn (dōārn) c (pl ~en, ~s) thorn

doorreis (*dōā*-rayss) c passage

doorslag (*dōār*-slahkh) c (pl ~en) carbon copy

doorweken (dōār-*vāy*-kern) v soak

doorzichtig (dōār-*zıkh*-terkh) adj transparent, sheer

* **doorzoeken** (dōār-*zōō*-kern) v search

doos (dōāss) c (pl dozen) box

dop (dop) c (pl ~pen) shell

dopen (*dōā*-pern) v baptize, christen

dor (dor) adj arid

dorp (dorp) nt (pl ~en) village

dorst (dorst) c thirst

dorstig (*dors*-terkh) adj thirsty

dosis (*dōā*-zerss) c (pl doses) dose

dossier (do-*shāy*) nt (pl ~s) file

douane (dōō-*vaa*-ner) c Customs pl

douanebeambte (dōō-*vaa*-ner-ber-ahm-ter) c (pl ~n) Customs officer

douche (dōōsh) c (pl ~s) shower

doven (*dōā*-vern) v extinguish

dozijn (dōā-*zayn*) nt (pl ~en) dozen

draad (draat) c (pl draden) thread; wire

draagbaar (*draakh*-baar) adj portable

draaglijk (*draakh*-lerk) adj tolerable

draai (draaee) c (pl ~en) turn; twist

draaideur (draaee-*dūrr*) c (pl ~en) revolving door

draaien (*draaee*-ern) v turn; twist; *spin

draaimolen (*draaee*-mōā-lern) c (pl ~s) merry-go-round

draaiorgel (*draaee*-or-gerl) nt (pl ~s) street-organ

draak (draak) c (pl draken) dragon

* **dragen** (*draa*-gern) v carry, *bear; *wear

drager (*draa*-gerr) c (pl ~s) bearer

drama (*draa*-maa) nt (pl ~'s) drama

dramatisch (draa-*maa*-teess) adj dramatic

drang (drahng) c urge

drank (drahngk) c (pl ~en) drink, beverage; **sterke ~** spirits, liquor

dreigement (dray-ger-*mernt*) nt (pl ~en) threat

dreigen (*dray*-gern) v threaten

drek (drehk) c muck

drempel (*drehm*-perl) c (pl ~s) threshold

dresseren (dreh-*sāy*-rern) v train

drie (dree) num three

driehoek (*dree*-hōōk) c (pl ~en) triangle

driehoekig (dree-*hoo*-kerkh) *adj* tri-angular

driekwart (*dree*-kvahrt) *adj* three-quarter

driemaandelijks (*dree*-maan-der-lerks) *adj* quarterly

drift (drɪft) *c* passion

driftig (*drɪf*-terkh) *adj* quick-tempered; hot-tempered, irascible

drijfkracht (*drayf*-krahkht) *c* driving force

****drijven** (*dray*-vern) *v* float

****dringen** (*drɪ*-ngern) *v* push; **dringend** pressing, urgent

drinkbaar (*drɪngk*-baar) *adj* for drinking

****drinken** (*drɪng*-kern) *v* **drink

drinkwater (*drɪngk*-vaa-terr) *nt* drinking-water

droefheid (*droof*-hayt) *c* sorrow

droevig (*droo*-verkh) *adj* sad

drogen (*droa*-gern) *v* dry

drogisterij (droa-gɪss-ter-*ray*) *c* (pl ~en) pharmacy, chemist's; drugstore *nAm*

dromen (*droa*-mern) *v* **dream

dronken (*drong*-kern) *adj* drunk; intoxicated

droog (droakh) *adj* dry

droogleggen (*droakh*-leh-gern) *v* drain

droogte (*droakh*-ter) *c* drought

droom (droam) *c* (pl dromen) dream

droombeeld (*droam*-baylt) *nt* (pl ~en) illusion

drop (drop) *c* liquorice

druiven (*druɪ*ᵉʷ-vern) *pl* grapes *pl*

druk (drerk) *adj* busy; crowded; *c* pressure

drukken (*drer*-kern) *v* press; print

drukknop (*drer*-knop) *c* (pl ~pen) push-button

drukte (*drerk*-ter) *c* bustle; fuss, excitement

drukwerk (*drerk*-vehrk) *nt* printed matter

druppel (*drer*-perl) *c* (pl ~s) drop

dubbel (*der*-berl) *adj* double

dubbelzinnig (der-berl-*zɪ*-nerkh) *adj* ambiguous

duidelijk (*durᵉʷ*-der-lerk) *adj* distinct, plain, clear; apparent, evident; obvious

duif (durᵉʷf) *c* (pl duiven) pigeon

duikbril (*durᵉʷk*-brɪl) *c* (pl ~len) goggles *pl*

****duiken** (*durᵉʷ*-kern) *v* dive

duim (durᵉʷm) *c* (pl ~en) thumb

duin (durᵉʷn) *nt* (pl ~en) dune

duister (*durᵉʷ*-sterr) *adj* obscure, dark; *nt* gloom

duisternis (*durᵉʷ*-sterr-nɪss) *c* dark

Duits (durᵉʷts) *adj* German

Duitser (*durᵉʷt*-serr) *c* (pl ~s) German

Duitsland (*durᵉʷts*-lahnt) Germany

duivel (*durᵉʷ*-verl) *c* (pl ~s) devil

duizelig (*durᵉʷ*-zer-lerkh) *adj* giddy, dizzy

duizeligheid (*durᵉʷ*-zer-lerkh-hayt) *c* giddiness, dizziness

duizeling (*durᵉʷ*-zer-lɪng) *c* (pl ~en) vertigo

duizend (*durᵉʷ*-zernt) *num* thousand

dulden (*derl*-dern) *v* **bear

dun (dern) *adj* thin; sheer

dupe (de*w*-per) *c* (pl ~s) victim

duren (de*w*-rern) *v* last

durf (derrf) *c* nerve

durven (*derr*-vern) *v* dare

dus (derss) *conj* so

dutje (*der*-tʸer) *nt* (pl ~s) nap

duur (dewr) *adj* dear, expensive; *c* duration

duurzaam (*dewr*-zaam) *adj* lasting, permanent

duw (dewᵒᵒ) *c* (pl ~en) push

duwen (*dewᵒᵒ*-ern) *v* push

dwaas¹ (dvaass) *adj* foolish, crazy, silly

dwaas² (dvaass) *c* (pl dwazen) fool

dwalen (dvaa-lern) *v* err

dwerg (dvehrkh) *c* (pl ~en) dwarf

*dwingen (dvı-ngern) *v* force; compel

dynamo (dee-*naa*-mōa) *c* (pl ~'s) dynamo

dysenterie (dee-sehn-ter-*ree*) *c* dysentery

E

eb (ehp) *c* low tide

ebbehout (*eh*-ber-hout) *nt* ebony

echo (*eh*-khōa) *c* (pl ~'s) echo

echt (ehkht) *adj* genuine, true, authentic, real; *adv* really; *c* matrimony

echtelijk (*ehkh*-ter-lerk) *adj* matrimonial

echter (*ehkh*-terr) *conj* however, yet

echtgenoot (*ehkht*-kher-nōat) *c* (pl -noten) husband

echtgenote (*ehkht*-kher-nōa-ter) *c* (pl ~n) wife

echtpaar (*ehkht*-paar) *nt* (pl -paren) married couple

echtscheiding (*ehkht*-skhay-dıng) *c* (pl ~en) divorce

economie (āy-kōa-nōa-*mee*) *c* economy

economisch (āy-kōa-*nōa*-meess) *adj* economic

econoom (āy-kōa-*nōam*) *c* (pl -nomen) economist

Ecuador (āy-kvaa-*dor*) Ecuador

Ecuadoriaan (āy-kvaa-dōa-ree-ʸaan) *c* (pl -rianen) Ecuadorian

eczeem (ehk-*sāym*) *nt* eczema

edel (*āy*-derl) *adj* noble

edelmoedigheid (āy-derl-*mōō*-derkh-hayt) *c* generosity

edelsteen (*āy*-derl-stāyn) *c* (pl -stenen) gem, stone

editie (āy-*dee*-tsee) *c* (pl ~s) edition

eed (āyt) *c* (pl eden) oath, vow

eekhoorn (*āyk*-hōarn) *c* (pl ~s) squirrel

eelt (āylt) *nt* callus

een¹ (ern) *art a* art

een² (āyn) *num* one

eenakter (*āyn*-ahk-terr) *c* (pl ~s) one-act play

eend (āynt) *c* (pl ~en) duck

eender (*āyn*-derr) *adj* alike

eenheid (*āyn*-hayt) *c* (pl -heden) unit; unity

eenmaal (*āyn*-maal) *adv* once

eenrichtingsverkeer (āyn-*rıkh*-tıngs-ferr-kāyr) *nt* one-way traffic

eens (āyns) *adv* once; some time, some day; **het ~ *zijn** agree

eentonig (āyn-*tōa*-nerkh) *adj* monotonous

eenvoudig (āyn-*vou*-derkh) *adj* plain, simple; *adv* simply

eenzaam (*āyn*-zaam) *adj* lonely

eenzijdig (āyn-*zay*-derkh) *adj* one-sided

eer (āyr) *c* honour; glory

eerbied (*āyr*-beet) *c* respect

eerbiedig (āyr-*bee*-derkh) *adj* respectful

eerbiedwaardig (āyr-beet-*vaar*-derkh) *adj* venerable

eerder (*āyr*-derr) *adv* before; rather

eergevoel (*āyr*-ger-vōol) *nt* sense of honour

eergisteren (*āyr*-gıss-ter-rern) *adv* the day before yesterday

eerlijk (*āyr*-lerk) *adj* honest; fair, straight

eerlijkheid (*āyr*-lerk-hayt) *c* honesty

eerst (āyrst) *adj* first; primary, initial; *adv* at first

eersteklas (*āyr*-ster-klahss) *adj* first-class

eersterangs (āyr-ster-rahngs) *adj* first-rate

eerstvolgend (āyrst-*fol*-gernt) *adj* following

eervol (āyr-vol) *adj* honourable

eerzaam (āyr-zaam) *adj* respectable; honourable

eerzuchtig (āyr-*zerkh*-terkh) *adj* ambitious

eetbaar (āyt-baar) *adj* edible

eetkamer (āyt-kaa-merr) *c* (pl ~s) dining-room

eetlepel (āyt-lāy-perl) *c* (pl ~s) tablespoon

eetlust (āyt-lerst) *c* appetite

eetservies (āyt-sehr-veess) *nt* (pl -viezen) dinner-service

eetzaal (āyt-saal) *c* (pl -zalen) dining-room

eeuw (āy°°) *c* (pl ~en) century

eeuwig (āy°°-erkh) *adj* eternal

eeuwigheid (āy°°-erkh-hayt) *c* eternity

effect (eh-*fehkt*) *nt* (pl ~en) effect; **effecten** stocks and shares

effectenbeurs (eh-*fehk*-term-būrrs) *c* (pl -beurzen) stock market, stock exchange

effectief (eh-fehk-*teef*) *adj* effective

effen (eh-fern) *adj* level; smooth, even

efficiënt (eh-fee-*shehnt*) *adj* efficient

egaal (āy-*gaal*) *adj* level

egaliseren (āy-gaa-lee-*zāy*-rern) *v* level

egel (āy-gerl) *c* (pl ~s) hedgehog

egocentrisch (āy-gōa-*sehn*-treess) *adj* self-centred

egoïsme (āy-gōa-*viss*-mer) *nt* selfishness

egoïstisch (āy-gōa-*viss*-teess) *adj* selfish

Egypte (āy-*gip*-ter) Egypt

Egyptenaar (āy-*gip*-ter-naar) *c* (pl -naren) Egyptian

Egyptisch (āy-*gip*-teess) *adj* Egyptian

ei (ay) *nt* (pl ~eren) egg

eierdooier (ay-err-dōa°°-err) *c* (pl ~s) egg-yolk

eierdopje (ay-err-dop-ʸer) *nt* (pl ~s) egg-cup

eigen (ay-gern) *adj* own

eigenaar (ay-ger-naar) *c* (pl ~s, -naren) owner, proprietor

eigenaardig (ay-ger-*naar*-derkh) *adj* singular, peculiar

eigenaardigheid (ay-ger-*naar*-derkh-hayt) *c* (pl -heden) peculiarity

eigendom (ay-gern-dom) *nt* (pl ~men) property; possessions

eigengemaakt (ay-gern-ger-maakt) *adj* home-made

eigenlijk (ay-gern-lerk) *adj* actual; *adv* as a matter of fact, really

eigenschap (ay-gern-skhahp) *c* (pl ~pen) property, quality

eigentijds (ay-gern-*tayts*) *adj* contemporary

eigenwijs (ay-gern-*vayss*) *adj* pigheaded

eik (ayk) *c* (pl ~en) oak

eikel (ay-kerl) *c* (pl ~s) acorn

eiland (ay-lahnt) *nt* (pl ~en) island

einde (ayn-der) *nt* end, finish; ending, issue

eindelijk (ayn-der-lerk) *adv* at last

eindigen (ayn-der-gern) *v* finish

eindpunt (aynt-pernt) *nt* (pl ~en) terminal

eindstreep (aynt-strāyp) *c* (pl -strepen) finish

eis (ayss) *c* (pl ~en) demand, claim

eisen (ay-sern) *v* demand

eiwit (ay-vit) *nt* (pl ~ten) protein

ekster (ehk-sterr) *c* (pl ~s) magpie

eksteroog (ehk-sterr-ōakh) *nt* (pl -ogen) corn

eland (āy-lahnt) *c* (pl ~en) moose

elastiek (āy-lahss-*teek*) *nt* (pl ~en) rubber band, elastic

elastisch (āy-*lahss*-teess) *adj* elastic

elders (ehl-derrs) *adv* elsewhere

elegant (āy-ler-*gahnt*) *adj* elegant

elegantie (āy-ler-*gahnt*-see) *c* elegance

elektricien (āy-lehk-tree-*shang*) *c* (pl ~s) electrician

elektriciteit (āy-lehk-tree-see-*tayt*) *c* electricity

elektriciteitscentrale (āy-lehk-tree-see-*tayt*-sehn-traa-ler) *c* power-station

elektrisch (āy-*lehk*-treess) *adj* electric

elektronisch (āy-lehk-*trōa*-neess) *adj* electronic

element (āy-ler-*mehnt*) *nt* (pl ~en) element

elementair (āy-ler-mehn-*tair*) *adj* primary

elf[1] (ehlf) *num* eleven

elf[2] (ehlf) *c* (pl ~en) elf

elfde (*ehlf*-der) *num* eleventh

elftal (*ehlf*-tahl) *nt* (pl ~len) soccer team

elimineren (āy-lee-mee-*nāy*-rern) *v* eliminate

elk (ehlk) *adj* each, every

elkaar (ehl-*kaar*) *pron* each other

elleboog (*eh*-ler-bōakh) *c* (pl -bogen) elbow

ellende (eh-*lehn*-der) *c* misery

ellendig (eh-*lehn*-derkh) *adj* miserable

email (āy-*migh*) *nt* enamel

emailleren (āy-migh-*āy*-rern) *v* glaze

emancipatie (āy-mahn-see-*paa*-tsee) *c* emancipation

embargo (ehm-*bahr*-gōa) *nt* embargo

embleem (ehm-*blāym*) *nt* (pl -blemen) emblem

emigrant (āy-mee-*grahnt*) *c* (pl ~en) emigrant

emigratie (āy-mee-*graa*-tsee) *c* emigration

emigreren (āy-mee-*grāy*-rern) *v* emigrate

eminent (āy-mee-*nehnt*) *adj* outstanding

emmer (*eh*-merr) *c* (pl ~s) bucket, pail

emotie (āy-*mōa*-tsee) *c* (pl ~s) emotion

employé (ahm-plvah-*Yāy*) *c* (pl ~s) employee

en (ehn) *conj* and

encyclopedie (ehn-see-klōa-pāy-*dee*) *c* (pl ~ën) encyclopaedia

endeldarm (*ehn*-derl-dahrm) *c* (pl ~en) rectum

endosseren (ahn-do-*sāy*-rern) *v* endorse

energie (āy-nehr-*zhee*) *c* energy; power

energiek (āy-nehr-*zheek*) *adj* energetic

eng (ehng) *adj* narrow; creepy

engel (*eh*-ngerl) *c* (pl ~en) angel

Engeland (*eh*-nger-lahnt) England; Britain

Engels (*eh*-ngerls) *adj* English; British

Engelsman (*eh*-ngerls-mahn) *c* (pl Engelsen) Englishman; Briton

enig (*āy*-nerkh) *adj* sole, only; *pron* any; **enige** *pron* some

enigszins (*āy*-nerkh-sins) *adv* somewhat

enkel[1] (*ehng*-kerl) *adj* single; **enkele** *pron* some

enkel[2] (*ehng*-kerl) *c* (pl ~s) ankle

enkeling (*ehng*-ker-ling) *c* (pl ~en) individual

enkelvoud (*ehng*-kerl-vout) *nt* singular

enorm (āy-*norm*) *adj* tremendous, enormous, huge

enquête (ahng-*kai*-ter) *c* (pl ~s) enquiry

enthousiasme (ahn-tōō-*zhahss*-mer) *nt* enthusiasm

enthousiast (ahn-tōō-*zhahst*) *adj* enthusiastic; keen

entree (ahn-*trāy*) *c* entry; entrance-fee

entresol (ahng-trer-*sol*) *c* (pl ~s)
mezzanine

envelop (ahng-ver-*lop*) *c* (pl ~pen)
envelope

enzovoort (*ehn*-zoa-voart) *and so on,*
etcetera

epidemie (ay-pee-der-*mee*) *c* (pl ~ën)
epidemic

epilepsie (ay-pee-lehp-*see*) *c* epilepsy

epiloog (ay-pee-*loakh*) *c* (pl -logen)
epilogue

episch (*ay*-peess) *adj* epic

episode (ay-pee-*zoa*-der) *c* (pl ~n, ~s)
episode

epos (*ay*-poss) *nt* (pl epen, ~sen) epic

equipe (ay-*keep*) *c* (pl ~s) team

equivalent (ay-kvee-vaa-*lehnt*) *adj*
equivalent

er (ehr) *adv* there; *pron* of them

erbarmelijk (ehr-*bahr*-mer-lerk) *adj*
lamentable

eredienst (*ay*-rer-deenst) *c* (pl ~en)
worship

eren (*ay*-rern) *v* honour

erf (ehrf) *nt* (pl erven) yard

erfelijk (*ehr*-fer-lerk) *adj* hereditary

erfenis (ehr-fer-niss) *c* (pl ~sen) inheritance; legacy

erg (ehrkh) *adj* bad; *adv* very; **erger**
worse; **ergst** worst

ergens (*ehr*-gerns) *adv* somewhere

ergeren (*ehr*-ger-rern) *v* annoy

ergernis (*ehr*-gerr-niss) *c* annoyance

erkennen (ehr-*keh*-nern) *v* recognize;
acknowledge

erkenning (ehr-*keh*-ning) *c* (pl ~en)
recognition

erkentelijk (ehr-*kehn*-ter-lerk) *adj*
grateful

ernst (ehrnst) *c* seriousness; gravity

ernstig (*ehrn*-sterkh) *adj* serious;
grave, bad, severe

erts (ehrts) *nt* (pl ~en) ore

***ervaren** (ehr-*vaa*-rern) *v* experience

ervaring (ehr-*vaa*-ring) *c* (pl ~en) experience

erven (*ehr*-vern) *v* inherit

erwt (ehrt) *c* (pl ~en) pea

escorte (ehss-*kor*-ter) *nt* (pl ~s) escort

escorteren (ehss-kor-*tay*-rern) *v* escort

esdoorn (*ehss*-doarn) *c* (pl ~s) maple

eskader (ehss-*kaa*-derr) *nt* (pl ~s)
squadron

essay (eh-*say*) *nt* (pl ~s) essay

essentie (eh-*sehn*-see) *c* essence

essentieel (eh-sehn-*shayl*) *adj* vital,
essential

etage (ay-*taa*-zher) *c* (pl ~s) floor,
storey; apartment *nAm*

etalage (ay-taa-*laa*-zher) *c* (pl ~s)
shop-window

etappe (ay-*tah*-per) *c* (pl ~n, ~s)
stage

eten (*ay*-tern) *nt* food

***eten** (*ay*-tern) *v* *eat

ether (*ay*-terr) *c* ether

Ethiopië (ay-tee-*Yoa*-pee-Yer) Ethiopia

Ethiopiër (ay-tee-*Yoa*-pee-Yerr) *c* (pl
~s) Ethiopian

Ethiopisch (ay-tee-*Yoa*-peess) *adj*
Ethiopian

etiket (ay-tee-*keht*) *nt* (pl ~ten) label,
tag

etiketteren (ay-tee-keh-*tay*-rern) *v*
label

etmaal (*eht*-maal) *nt* (pl -malen)
twenty-four hours

ets (ehts) *c* (pl ~en) etching

ettelijk (*eh*-ter-lerk) *adj* several

etter (*eh*-terr) *c* pus

etui (ay-*tvee*) *nt* (pl ~s) case

Europa (ur-*roa*-paa) Europe

Europeaan (ur-roa-pay-*aan*) *c* (pl
-anen) European

Europees (ur-roa-*payss*) *adj* European

evacueren (ay-vaa-kew-*vay*-rern) *v*
evacuate

evangelie (ay-vahng-*gay*-lee) *nt* (pl -liën, ~s) gospel

even (*āy*-vern) *adj* even; *adv* equally, as

evenaar (*āy*-ver-naar) *c* equator

evenals (*āy*-ver-nahls) *conj* as well as

evenaren (*āy*-ver-*naa*-rern) *v* equal

eveneens (*āy*-ver-*nāyns*) *adv* as well, likewise, also

evenredig (*āy*-ver-*rāy*-derkh) *adj* proportional

eventueel (*āy*-vern-tēw-*vāyl*) *adj* possible, eventual

evenveel (*āy*-ver-*vāyl*) *adv* as much

evenwel (*āy*-ver-*vehl*) *adv* however

evenwicht (*āy*-ver-vıkht) *nt* balance

evenwijdig (*āy*-ver-*vay*-derkh) *adj* parallel

evenzeer (*āy*-ver-*zāyr*) *adv* as much

evenzo (*āy*-ver-*zōā*) *adv* likewise

evolutie (*āy*-vōā-*lēw*-tsee) *c* (pl ~s) evolution

exact (ehk-*sahkt*) *adj* precise

examen (ehk-*saa*-mern) *nt* (pl ~s) examination

excentriek (ehk-sehn-*treek*) *adj* eccentric

exces (ehk-*sehss*) *nt* (pl ~sen) excess

exclusief (ehks-klēw-*zeef*) *adj* exclusive

excursie (ehks-*kerr*-zee) *c* (pl ~s) day trip, excursion

excuseren (ehks-kēw-*zāy*-rern) *v* excuse

excuus (ehks-*kēwss*) *nt* (pl excuses) apology, excuse

exemplaar (ehk-serm-*plaar*) *nt* (pl -plaren) specimen; copy

exotisch (ehk-*sōā*-teess) *adj* exotic

expeditie (ehks-per-*dee*-tsee) *c* (pl ~s) expedition

experiment (ehks-pāy-ree-*mehnt*) *nt* (pl ~en) experiment

experimenteren (ehks-pāy-ree-mehn-*tāy*-rern) *v* experiment

expert (ehks-*pair*) *c* (pl ~s) expert

expliciet (ehks-plee-*seet*) *adj* explicit

exploiteren (ehks-plvah-*tāy*-rern) *v* exploit

explosie (ehks-*plōā*-zee) *c* (pl ~s) blast, explosion

explosief (ehks-plōā-*zeef*) *adj* explosive

export (*ehk*-sport) *c* exports *pl*, export

exporteren (ehk-spor-*tāy*-rern) *v* export

expositie (ehk-spōā-*zee*-tsee) *c* (pl ~s) exhibition; display

expresse- (ehk-*spreh*-ser) express; special delivery

extase (ehk-*staa*-zer) *c* ecstasy

extra (*ehk*-straa) *adj* additional, extra; spare

extravagant (ehk-straa-vaa-*gahnt*) *adj* extravagant

extreem (ehk-*strāym*) *adj* extreme

ezel (*āy*-zerl) *c* (pl ~s) ass; donkey

F

faam (faam) *c* fame

fabel (*faa*-berl) *c* (pl ~s, ~en) fable

fabriceren (faa-bree-*sāy*-rern) *v* manufacture

fabriek (faa-*breek*) *c* (pl ~en) factory; mill, works *pl*

fabrikant (faa-bree-*kahnt*) *c* (pl ~en) manufacturer

faciliteit (faa-see-lee-*tayt*) *c* (pl ~en) facility

factor (*fahk*-tor) *c* (pl ~en) factor

factureren (fahk-tēw-*rāy*-rern) *v* bill

factuur (fahk-*tēwr*) *c* (pl -turen) invoice

facultatief (faa-kerl-taa-*teef*) *adj* optional

faculteit (faa-kerl-*tayt*) *c* (pl ~en) faculty

faience (faa-*Yahng*-ser) *c* faience

failliet (fah-*Yeet*) *adj* bankrupt

fakkel (*fah*-kerl) *c* (pl ~s) torch

falen (*faa*-lern) *v* fail

familiaar (fah-mee-lee-*Yaar*) *adj* familiar

familie (faa-*mee*-lee) *c* (pl ~s) family

familielid (faa-*mee*-le-lɪt) *nt* (pl -leden) relative

fanatiek (faa-naa-*teek*) *adj* fanatical

fanfarekorps (fahm-*faa*-rer-korps) *nt* (pl ~en) brass band

fantasie (fahn-taa-*zee*) *c* (pl ~ën) fantasy, fancy

fantastisch (fahn-*tahss*-teess) *adj* fantastic

farce (fahrs) *c* (pl ~n) farce

farmacologie (fahr-maa-kōa-lōa-*gee*) *c* pharmacology

fascinerend (fah-see-*nāy*-rernt) *adj* glamorous

fascisme (fah-*sɪss*-mer) *nt* fascism

fascist (fah-*sɪst*) *c* (pl ~en) fascist

fascistisch (fah-*sɪss*-teess) *adj* fascist

fase (*faa*-zer) *c* (pl ~s, ~n) stage, phase

fataal (faa-*taal*) *adj* fatal

fatsoen (faht-*sōōn*) *nt* decency

fatsoenlijk (faht-*sōōn*-lerk) *adj* decent

fauteuil (fōa-*turew*) *c* (pl ~s) armchair

favoriet (faa-vōa-*reet*) *c* (pl ~en) favourite

fazant (faa-*zahnt*) *c* (pl ~en) pheasant

februari (fāy-brew-*vaa*-ree) February

federaal (fāy-der-*raal*) *adj* federal

federatie (fāy-der-*raa*-tsee) *c* (pl ~s) federation

fee (fāy) *c* (pl ~ën) fairy

feest (fāyst) *nt* (pl ~en) feast

feestdag (*fāyss*-dahkh) *c* (pl ~en) holiday

feestelijk (*fāy*-ster-lerk) *adj* festive

feestje (*fāy*-sher) *nt* (pl ~s) party

feilloos (fay-*lōass*) *adj* faultless

feit (fayt) *nt* (pl ~en) fact; **in feite** in fact

feitelijk (*fay*-ter-lerk) *adj* factual; *adv* as a matter of fact, actually, in effect

fel (fehl) *adj* fierce

felicitatie (fāy-lee-see-*taa*-tsee) *c* (pl ~s) congratulation

feliciteren (fāy-lee-see-*tāy*-rern) *v* congratulate; compliment

feodaal (fāy-*Yōa-daal*) *adj* feudal

festival (*fehss*-tee-vahl) *nt* (pl ~s) festival

feuilleton (fur*ew*-er-*ton*) *nt* (pl ~s) serial

fiasco (fee-*Yahss*-kōa) *nt* (pl ~'s) failure

fiche (*fee*-sher) *c* (pl ~s) chip

fictie (*fɪk*-see) *c* (pl ~s) fiction

fiets (feets) *c* (pl ~en) cycle, bicycle

fietser (*fee*-tserr) *c* (pl ~s) cyclist

figuur (fee-*gēwr*) *c* (pl -guren) figure; diagram

fijn (fayn) *adj* enjoyable; fine; delicate

fijnhakken (*fayn*-hah-kern) *v* mince

*fijnmalen (*fayn*-maa-lern) *v* *grind

fijnproever (*faym*-prōō-verr) *c* (pl ~s) gourmet

fijnstampen (*fayn*-stahm-pern) *v* mash

filiaal (fee-lee-*Yaal*) *nt* (-ialen) branch

Filippijn (fee-lɪ-*payn*) *c* (pl ~en) Filipino

Filippijnen (fee-lɪ-*pay*-nern) *pl* Philippines *pl*

Filippijns (fee-lɪ-*payns*) *adj* Philippine

film (fɪlm) *c* (pl ~s) film; movie

filmcamera (*fɪlm*-kaa-mer-raa) *c* (pl ~'s) camera

filmen (*fɪl*-mern) *v* film

filmjournaal (*fɪlm*-zhōōr-naal) *nt* newsreel

filosofie (fee-lōa-zōa-*fee*) *c* (pl ~ën) philosophy

filosoof (fee-lōā-*zōāf*) *c* (pl -sofen) philosopher

filter (*fil*-terr) *nt* (pl ~s) filter

Fin (fin) *c* (pl ~nen) Finn

financieel (fee-nahn-*shāyl*) *adj* financial

financiën (fee-*nahn*-see-Yern) *pl* finances *pl*

financieren (fee-nahn-*see*-rern) *v* finance

Finland (*fin*-lahnt) Finland

Fins (fins) *adj* Finnish

firma (*fir*-maa) *c* (pl ~'s) company, firm

fitting (*fi*-ting) *c* (pl ~en) socket

fjord (fYort) *c* (pl ~en) fjord

flacon (flaa-*kon*) *c* (pl ~s) flask

flamingo (flaa-*ming*-gōā) *c* (pl ~'s) flamingo

flanel (flaa-*nehl*) *nt* flannel

flat (fleht) *c* (pl ~s) flat; apartment *nAm*

flatgebouw (*fleht*-kher-bou) *nt* (pl ~en) block of flats; apartment house *Am*

flauw (flou) *adj* faint

*****flauwvallen** (*flou*-vah-lern) *v* faint

fles (flehss) *c* (pl ~sen) bottle

flesopener (*fleh*-zōā-per-nerr) *c* (pl ~s) bottle opener

flessehals (*fleh*-ser-hahls) *c* bottleneck

flets (flehts) *adj* dull

flink (flingk) *adj* considerable; brave, plucky

flits (flits) *c* (pl ~en) flash

flitslampje (*flits*-lahm-pYer) *nt* (pl ~s) flash-bulb

fluisteren (*flurew*ss-ter-rern) *v* whisper

fluit (flurewt) *c* (pl ~en) flute

*****fluiten** (*flurew*-tern) *v* whistle

fluitje (*flurew*-tYer) *nt* (pl ~s) whistle

fluweel (flew-*vāyl*) *nt* velvet

foefje (*fōō*-fYer) *nt* (pl ~s) trick

foei! (fōōee) shame!

fok (fok) *c* (pl ~ken) foresail

fokken (*fo*-kern) *v* *breed; raise

folklore (fol-*klōā*-rer) *c* folklore

fonds (fons) *nt* (pl ~en) fund

fonetisch (fōā-*nāy*-teess) *adj* phonetic

fonkelend (*fong*-ker-lernt) *adj* sparkling

fontein (fon-*tayn*) *c* (pl ~en) fountain

fooi (fōāee) *c* (pl ~en) tip; gratuity

foppen (*fo*-pern) *v* fool

forceren (for-*sāy*-rern) *v* strain; force

forel (fōā-*rehl*) *c* (pl ~len) trout

forens (fōā-*rehns*) *c* (pl ~en, forenzen) commuter

formaat (for-*maat*) *nt* (pl -maten) size

formaliteit (for-maa-lee-*tayt*) *c* (pl ~en) formality

formeel (for-*māyl*) *adj* formal

formule (for-*mew*-ler) *c* (pl ~s) formula

formulier (for-mew-*leer*) *nt* (pl ~en) form

fornuis (for-*nurew*ss) *nt* (pl -nuizen) cooker, stove

fors (fors) *adj* robust

fort (fort) *nt* (pl ~en) fort

fortuin (for-*turew*n) *nt* (pl ~en) fortune

foto (*fōā*-tōā) *c* (pl ~'s) photograph, photo

fotocopie (fōā-tōā-kōā-*pee*) *c* (pl ~ën) photostat

fotograaf (fōā-tōā-*graaf*) *c* (pl -grafen) photographer

fotograferen (fōā-tōā-graa-*fāy*-rern) *v* photograph

fotografie (fōā-tōā-graa-*fee*) *c* photography

fototoestel (*fōā*-tōā-tōō-stehl) *nt* (pl ~len) camera

fotowinkel (*fōā*-tōā-ving-kerl) *c* (pl ~s) camera shop

fouilleren (fōō-Y*āy*-rern) *v* search

fout¹ (fout) *adj* mistaken, wrong

fout² (fout) *c* (pl ~en) error, mistake, fault

foutloos (fout-lōass) *adj* faultless

foyer (fvah-ʸaȳ) *c* (pl ~s) foyer; lobby

fractie (frahk-see) *c* (pl ~s) fraction

fragment (frahkh-*mehnt*) *nt* (pl ~en) fragment; extract

framboos (frahm-*bōass*) *c* (pl -bozen) raspberry

franje (frah-ñer) *c* (pl ~s) fringe

frankeren (frahng-*kaȳ*-rern) *v* stamp

frankering (frahng-*kaȳ*-rıng) *c* (pl ~en) postage

franko (frahng-kōa) *adj* postage paid, post-paid

Frankrijk (*frahng*-krayk) France

Frans (frahns) *adj* French

Fransman (*frahns*-mahn) *c* (pl Fransen) Frenchman

frappant (frah-*pahnt*) *adj* striking

fraude (frou-der) *c* (pl ~s) fraud

frequent (frer-*kvehnt*) *adj* frequent

frequentie (frer-*kvehn*-tsee) *c* (pl ~s) frequency

fris (friss) *adj* fresh

frisdrank (*friss*-drahngk) *c* soft drink

frites (freet) *pl* chips

fruit (frurᵉʷt) *nt* fruit

fuif (furᵉʷf) *c* (pl fuiven) party

functie (*ferngk*-see) *c* (pl ~s) function

functioneren (ferngk-shōa-*naȳ*-rern) *v* work

fundamenteel (fern-daa-mehn-*taȳl*) *adj* fundamental, basic

fusie (fēw-zee) *c* (pl ~s) merger

fysica (fee-zee-kaa) *c* physics

fysiek (fee-*zeek*) *adj* physical

fysiologie (fee-zee-ʸōa-lōa-*gee*) *c* physiology

G

*****gaan** (gaan) *v* *go; *~ **door** pass through

gaarne (*gaar*-ner) *adv* gladly

gaas (gaass) *nt* gauze

*****gadeslaan** (*gaa*-der-slaan) *v* watch

gal (gahl) *c* gall, bile

galblaas (*gahl*-blaass) *c* (pl -blazen) gall bladder

galerij (gah-ler-*ray*) *c* (pl ~en) arcade; gallery

galg (gahlkh) *c* (pl ~en) gallows *pl*

galop (gaa-*lop*) *c* gallop

galsteen (*gahl*-staȳn) *c* (pl -stenen) gallstone

gammel (*gah*-merl) *adj* ramshackle, shaky

gang (gahng) *c* (pl ~en) corridor; gait, pace; course

gangbaar (*gahng*-baar) *adj* current

gangpad (*gahng*-paht) *nt* (pl ~en) aisle

gans (gahns) *c* (pl ganzen) goose

gapen (*gaa*-pern) *v* yawn

garage (gaa-*raa*-zher) *c* (pl ~s) garage

garanderen (gaa-rahn-*daȳ*-rern) *v* guarantee

garantie (gaa-*rahn*-tsee) *c* (pl ~s) guarantee

garderobe (gahr-der-*raw*-ber) *c* (pl ~s) wardrobe, cloakroom; checkroom *nAm*

garen (*gaa*-rern) *nt* (pl ~s) thread, yarn; **garen- en bandwinkel** haberdashery

garnaal (gahr-*naal*) *c* (pl -nalen) prawn, shrimp

gas (gahss) *nt* (pl ~sen) gas

gasfabriek (*gahss*-faa-breek) *c* (pl ~en) gasworks

gasfornuis (*gahss*-for-nurᵉʷss) *nt* (pl

-nuizen) gas cooker

gaskachel (*gahss*-kah-kherl) c (pl ~s) gas stove

gaspedaal (*gahss*-per-daal) nt (pl -dalen) accelerator

gasstel (*gah*-stehl) nt (pl ~len) gas cooker

gast (gahst) c (pl ~en) guest

gastheer (*gahst*-hāyr) c (pl -heren) host

gastvrij (gahst-*fray*) adj hospitable

gastvrijheid (gahst-*fray*-hayt) c hospitality

gastvrouw (*gahst*-frou) c (pl ~en) hostess

gat (gaht) nt (pl ~en) hole

gauw (gou) adv soon

gave (*gaa*-ver) c (pl ~n) gift, faculty

gazon (gaa-*zon*) nt (pl ~s) lawn

geadresseerde (ger-ah-dreh-*sāyr*-der) c (pl ~n) addressee

geaffecteerd (ger-ah-fehk-*tāyrt*) adj affected

Geallieerden (ger-ah-lee-^Yāyr-dern) pl Allies pl

gearmd (ger-*ahrmt*) adv arm-in-arm

gebaar (ger-*baar*) nt (pl gebaren) sign

gebak (ger-*bahk*) nt cake, pastry

gebaren (ger-*baa*-rern) v gesticulate

gebed (ger-*beht*) nt (pl ~en) prayer

gebergte nt mountain range

gebeuren (ger-*būr*-rern) v occur; happen

gebeurtenis (ger-*būrr*-ter-nɪss) c (pl ~sen) event; happening, occurrence

gebied (ger-*beet*) nt (pl ~en) region; zone, area, field, territory

geblokt (ger-*blokt*) adj chequered

gebogen (ger-*bōa*-gern) adj curved

geboorte (ger-*bōar*-ter) c (pl ~n) birth

geboorteland (ger-*bōar*-ter-lahnt) nt native country

geboorteplaats (ger-*bōar*-ter-plaats) c place of birth

geboren (ger-*bōa*-rern) adj born

gebouw (ger-*bou*) nt (pl ~en) construction, building

gebrek (ger-*brehk*) nt (pl ~en) deficiency, fault; want, lack, shortage

gebrekkig (ger-*breh*-kerkh) adj defective, faulty

gebruik (ger-*brur^{ew}k*) nt (pl ~en) use, usage; custom

gebruikelijk (ger-*brur^{ew}*-ker-lerk) adj customary; common, usual

gebruiken (ger-*brur^{ew}*-kern) v use; employ; apply

gebruiker (ger-*brur^{ew}*-kerr) c (pl ~s) user

gebruiksaanwijzing (ger-*brur^{ew}k*-saan-vay-zɪng) c (pl ~en) directions for use

gebruiksvoorwerp (ger-*brur^{ew}ks*-fōar-vehrp) nt (pl ~en) utensil

gebruind (ger-*brur^{ew}nt*) adj tanned

gebrul (ger-*brerl*) nt roar

gecompliceerd (ger-kom-plee-*sāyrt*) adj complicated

gedachte (ger-*dahkh*-ter) c (pl ~n) thought; idea

gedachtenstreepje (ger-*dahkh*-ter-strāyp-^Yer) nt (pl ~s) dash

gedeelte (ger-*dāyl*-ter) nt (pl ~n, ~s) part

gedeeltelijk (ger-*dāyl*-ter-lerk) adj partial; adv partly

gedelegeerde (ger-*dāy*-ler-gāyr-der) c (pl ~n) delegate

gedenkteken (ger-*dehngk*-tāy-kern) nt (pl ~s) memorial; monument

gedenkwaardig (ger-*dehngk*-vaar-derkh) adj memorable

gedetailleerd (ger-*dāy*-tah-^Yāyrt) adj detailed

gedetineerde (ger-*dāy*-tee-nāyr-der) c (pl ~n) prisoner

gedicht (ger-*dɪkht*) nt (pl ~en) poem

geding (ger-*dɪng*) nt (pl ~en) lawsuit

gediplomeerd (ger-dee-plōa-*māȳrt*) *adj* qualified

gedrag (ger-*drahkh*) *nt* conduct, behaviour

zich *gedragen (ger-*draa*-gern) act, behave

geduld (ger-*derlt*) *nt* patience

geduldig (ger-*derl*-derkh) *adj* patient

gedurende (ger-*dēw̄*-rern-der) *prep* during; for

gedurfd (ger-*derrft*) *adj* daring

geel (gāȳl) *adj* yellow

geelkoper (*gāȳl*-kōa-perr) *nt* brass

geelzucht (*gāȳl*-zerkht) *c* jaundice

geëmailleerd (ger-āȳ-mah-*ȳāȳrt*) *adj* enamelled

geen (gāȳn) *adj* no

geenszins (*gāȳn*-sıns) *adv* by no means

geest (gāȳst) *c* (pl ~en) spirit, mind; soul; ghost

geestelijk (*gāȳ*-ster-lerk) *adj* spiritual, mental

geestelijke (*gāȳ*-ster-ler-ker) *c* (pl ~n) clergyman

geestig (*gāȳ*-sterkh) *adj* witty, humorous

geeuwen (*gāȳ*ᵒᵒ-ern) *v* yawn

gefluister (ger-*flur*ᵉʷ-sterr) *nt* whisper

gegadigde (ger-*gaa*-derkh-der) *c* (pl ~n) candidate

gegeneerd (ger-zher-*nāȳrt*) *adj* embarrassed

gegeven (ger-*gāȳ*-vern) *nt* (pl ~s) data *pl*

gegrond (ger-*gront*) *adj* well-founded

gehandicapt (ger-*hehn*-dee-kehpt) *adj* disabled

geheel (ger-*hāȳl*) *adj* entire, whole, total; *adv* completely; *nt* whole

geheelonthouder (ger-*hāȳl*-ont-hou-derr) *c* (pl ~s) teetotaller

geheim¹ (ger-*haym*) *adj* secret

geheim² (ger-*haym*) *nt* (pl ~en) secret

geheimzinnig (ger-haym-zı-nerkh) *adj* mysterious

geheugen (ger-*hūȳ*-gern) *nt* memory

gehoor (ger-*hōar*) *nt* hearing

gehoorzaam (ger-*hōar*-zaam) *adj* obedient

gehoorzaamheid (ger-*hōar*-zaam-hayt) *c* obedience

gehoorzamen (ger-*hōar*-zaa-mern) *v* obey

gehorig (ger-*hōa*-rerkh) *adj* noisy

gehucht (ger-*herkht*) *nt* (pl ~en) hamlet

geïnteresseerd (ger-ın-trer-*sāȳrt*) *adj* interested

geïsoleerd (ger-ee-zōa-*lāȳrt*) *adj* isolated

geit (gayt) *c* (pl ~en) goat

geiteleer (*gay*-ter-lāȳr) *nt* kid

gek¹ (gehk) *adj* crazy, mad

gek² (gehk) *c* (pl ~ken) fool

geklets (ger-*klehts*) *nt* chat; rubbish

gekleurd (ger-*klūrrt*) *adj* coloured

gekraak (ger-*kraak*) *nt* crack

gekruid (ger-*krur*ᵉʷt) *adj* spiced

gelaatstrek (ger-*laats*-trehk) *c* (pl ~ken) feature

gelach (ger-*lahkh*) *nt* laughter

geld (gehlt) *nt* money; **buitenlands** ~ foreign currency; **contant** ~ cash

geldbelegging (*gehlt*-ber-leh-gıng) *c* (pl ~en) investment

*gelden (*gehl*-dern) *v* apply

geldig (*gehl*-derkh) *adj* valid

geldstuk (*gehlt*-sterk) *nt* (pl ~ken) coin

geleden (ger-*lāȳ*-dern) ago; **kort** ~ recently

geleerde (ger-*lāȳr*-der) *c* (pl ~n) scholar, scientist

gelegen (ger-*lay*-gern) *adj* situated

gelegenheid (ger-*lāȳ*-gern-hayt) *c* (pl -heden) occasion, chance, opportunity

gelei (zher-*lay*) *c* (pl ~en) jelly

geleidehond (ger-*lay*-der-hont) *c* (pl ~en) guide-dog

geleidelijk (ger-*lay*-der-lerk) *adj* gradual

gelijk (ger-*layk*) *adj* equal, like, alike; level, even; ~ **hebben ** be right; ~ maken equalize

gelijkenis (ger-*lay*-ker-nıss) *c* (pl ~sen) resemblance, similarity

gelijkgezind (ger-layk-kher-zınt) *adj* like-minded

gelijkheid (ger-*layk*-hayt) *c* equality

gelijkstroom (ger-*layk*-stroam) *c* direct current

gelijktijdig (ger-layk-*tay*-derkh) *adj* simultaneous

gelijkwaardig (ger-layk-*vaar*-derkh) *adj* equivalent

gelofte (ger-*lof*-ter) *c* (pl ~n) vow

geloof (ger-*loaf*) *nt* belief; faith

geloofwaardig (ger-loaf-*vaar*-derkh) *adj* credible

geloven (ger-*loa*-vern) *v* believe

geluid (ger-lur\[ew\]t) *nt* (pl ~en) sound; noise

geluiddicht (ger-lur\[ew\]-*dıkht*) *adj* soundproof

geluk (ger-*lerk*) *nt* happiness; luck, fortune

gelukkig (ger-*ler*-kerkh) *adj* happy; fortunate

gelukwens (ger-*lerk*-vehns) *c* (pl ~en) congratulation

gelukwensen (ger-*lerk*-vehn-sern) *v* congratulate, compliment

gemak (ger-*mahk*) *nt* leisure; ease; comfort

gemakkelijk (ger-*mah*-ker-lerk) *adj* easy; convenient

gematigd (ger-*maa*-terkht) *adj* moderate

gember (*gehm*-berr) *c* ginger

gemeen (ger-*mayn*) *adj* foul, mean

gemeenschap (ger-*mayn*-skhahp) *c* (pl ~pen) community

gemeenschappelijk (ger-mayn-*skhah*-per-lerk) *adj* common

gemeente (ger-*mayn*-ter) *c* (pl ~n, ~s) congregation

gemeentebestuur (ger-*mayn*-ter-ber-stewr) *nt* municipality

gemeentelijk (ger-*mayn*-ter-lerk) *adj* municipal

gemêleerd (ger-meh-*layrt*) *adj* mixed

gemengd (ger-*mehngt*) *adj* mixed; miscellaneous

gemiddeld (ger-*mı*-derlt) *adj* average, medium; *adv* on the average

gemiddelde (ger-*mı*-derl-der) *nt* (pl ~n) average, mean

gemis (ger-*mıss*) *nt* want, lack

genade (ger-*naa*-der) *c* mercy; grace

geneeskunde (ger-*nayss*-kern-der) *c* medicine

geneeskundig (ger-nayss-*kern*-derkh) *adj* medical

geneesmiddel (ger-*nayss*-mı-derl) *nt* (pl ~en) medicine; remedy, drug

genegen (ger-*nay*-gern) *adj* inclined

genegenheid (ger-*nay*-gern-hayt) *c* affection

geneigd (ger-*naykht*) *adj* inclined

generaal (gay-ner-*raal*) *c* (pl ~s) general

generatie (gay-ner-*raa*-tsee) *c* (pl ~s) generation

generator (gay-ner-*raa*-tor) *c* (pl ~en, ~s) generator

*genezen (ger-*nay*-zern) *v* heal; cure; recover

genezing (ger-*nay*-zıng) *c* (pl ~en) cure; recovery

genie (zher-*nee*) *nt* (pl ~ën) genius

*genieten van (ger-*nee*-tern) enjoy

genoeg (ger-*nookh*) *adv* enough; sufficient

genoegen (ger-*noo*-gern) *nt* (pl ~s)

pleasure

genootschap (ger-*nōāt*-skhahp) *nt* (pl ~pen) society; association

genot (ger-*not*) *nt* joy; delight; enjoyment

geologie (gāy-*Yōā*-lōā-*gee*) *c* geology

gepast (ger-*pahst*) *adj* suitable, proper

gepensioneerd (ger-pehn-shōā-*nāyrt*) *adj* retired

geraamte (ger-*raam*-ter) *nt* (pl ~n, ~s) skeleton

geraas (ger-*raass*) *nt* roar

gerecht (ger-*rehkht*) *nt* (pl ~en) dish; law court

gerechtigheid (ger-*rehkh*-terkh-hayt) *c* justice

gereed (ger-*rāyt*) *adj* ready

gereedschap (ger-*rāyt*-skhahp) *nt* (pl ~pen) tool; utensil, implement

gereedschapskist (ger-*rāyt*-skhahps-kist) *c* (pl ~en) tool kit

geregeld (ger-*rāy*-gerlt) *adj* regular

gereserveerd (ger-rāy-zehr-*vāyrt*) *adj* reserved

gerief (ger-*reef*) *nt* comfort

gerieflijk (ger-*ree*-fer-lerk) *adj* comfortable, easy; convenient

gering (ger-*ring*) *adj* minor; slight, small; **geringst** least

geroddel (ger-*ro*-derl) *nt* gossip

gerst (gehrst) *c* barley

gerucht (ger-*rerkht*) *nt* (pl ~en) rumour

geruit (ger-*rur^{ew}t*) *adj* chequered

gerust (ger-*rerst*) *adj* confident

geruststellen (ger-*rerst*-steh-lern) *v* reassure

gescheiden (ger-*skhay*-dern) *adj* separate

geschenk (ger-*skhehngk*) *nt* (pl ~en) gift, present

geschiedenis (ger-*skhee*-der-niss) *c* history

geschiedkundig (ger-*skheet*-kern-

derkh) *adj* historical

geschiedkundige (ger-*skheet*-*kern*-der-ger) *c* (pl ~n) historian

geschikt (ger-*skhikt*) *adj* convenient, suitable, proper, appropriate, fit; ~ *zijn qualify

geschil (ger-*skhil*) *nt* (pl ~len) dispute

geslacht (ger-*slahkht*) *nt* (pl ~en) sex; gender

geslachtsziekte (ger-*slahkht*-seek-ter) *c* (pl ~n, ~s) venereal disease

gesloten (ger-*slōā*-tern) *adj* closed, shut

gesp (gehsp) *c* (pl ~en) buckle

gespannen (ger-*spah*-nern) *adj* tense

gespierd (ger-*speert*) *adj* muscular

gespikkeld (ger-*spi*-kerlt) *adj* spotted

gesprek (ger-*sprehk*) *nt* (pl ~ken) discussion, conversation, talk; **interlokaal** ~ trunk-call; **lokaal** ~ local call

gestalte (ger-*stahl*-ter) *c* (pl ~n, ~s) figure

gesticht (ger-*stikht*) *nt* (pl ~en) asylum

gestorven (ger-*stor*-vern) *adj* dead

gestreept (ger-*strāypt*) *adj* striped

getal (ger-*tahl*) *nt* (pl ~len) number

getij (ger-*tay*) *nt* (pl ~en) tide

getrouw (ger-*trou*) *adj* true

getuige (ger-*tur^{ew}*-ger) *c* (pl ~n) witness

getuigen (ger-*tur^{ew}*-gern) *v* testify

getuigschrift (ger-*tur^{ew}kh*-skhrift) *nt* (pl ~en) certificate

getypt (ger-*teept*) *adj* typewritten

geur (gürr) *c* (pl ~en) smell, odour; scent

gevaar (ger-*vaar*) *nt* (pl -varen) danger; risk, peril

gevaarlijk (ger-*vaar*-lerk) *adj* dangerous; perilous

geval (ger-*vahl*) *nt* (pl ~len) case; instance; event; **in elk** ~ at any rate, anyway; **in ~ van** in case of

gevangene (ger-*vah*-nger-ner) *c* (pl ~n) prisoner

gevangenis (ger-*vah*-nger-niss) *c* (pl ~sen) prison; gaol, jail

gevangenschap (ger-*vah*-ngern-skhahp) *c* imprisonment

gevarieerd (ger-vaa-ree-*Yayrt*) *adj* varied

gevecht (ger-*vehkht*) *nt* (pl ~en) combat, battle, fight

gevel (*gay*-verl) *c* (pl ~s) façade

geveltop (*gay*-verl-top) *c* (pl ~pen) gable

*****geven** (*gay*-vern) *v* *give; ~ **om** mind

gevoel (ger-*vool*) *nt* feeling; sensation

gevoelig (ger-*voo*-lerkh) *adj* sensitive

gevoelloos (ger-*voo*-loass) *adj* numb

gevogelte (ger-*voa*-gerl-ter) *nt* fowl; poultry

gevolg (ger-*volkh*) *nt* (pl ~en) result, consequence; issue, effect; **ten gevolge van** owing to

gevolgtrekking (ger-*volkh*-treh-king) *c* (pl ~en) conclusion

gevorderd (ger-*vor*-derrt) *adj* advanced

gevuld (ger-*verlt*) *adj* stuffed

gewaad (ger-*vaat*) *nt* (pl gewaden) robe

gewaagd (ger-*vaakht*) *adj* risky

gewaarwording (ger-*vaar*-vor-ding) *c* (pl ~en) perception; sensation

gewapend (ger-*vaa*-pernt) *adj* armed

geweer (ger-*vayr*) *nt* (pl geweren) rifle, gun

gewei (ger-*vay*) *nt* (pl ~en) antlers *pl*

geweld (ger-*vehlt*) *nt* violence; force

gewelddaad (ger-*vehl*-daat) *c* (pl -daden) outrage

gewelddadig (ger-vehl-*daa*-derkh) *adj* violent

geweldig (ger-*vehl*-derkh) *adj* terrific;

huge

gewelf (ger-*vehlf*) *nt* (pl gewelven) arch, vault

gewend (ger-*vehnt*) *adj* accustomed

gewest (ger-*vehst*) *nt* (pl ~en) province

geweten (ger-*vay*-tern) *nt* conscience

gewicht (ger-*vikht*) *nt* (pl ~en) weight

gewichtig (ger-*vikh*-terkh) *adj* important; big

gewillig (ger-*vi*-lerkh) *adj* co-operative

gewond (ger-*vont*) *adj* injured

gewoon (ger-*voan*) *adj* normal, ordinary; common, regular, plain, simple; customary, habitual; accustomed; ~ *****zijn** *be used to; would

gewoonlijk (ger-*voan*-lerk) *adj* customary; *adv* as a rule, usually

gewoonte (ger-*voan*-ter) *c* (pl ~n, ~s) habit; custom

gewoonweg (ger-*voan*-vehkh) *adv* simply

gewricht (ger-*vrikht*) *nt* (pl ~en) joint

gezag (ger-*zahkh*) *nt* authority

gezagvoerder (ger-*zahkh*-foor-derr) *c* (pl ~s) captain

gezamenlijk (ger-*zaa*-mer-lerk) *adj* joint

gezang (ger-*zahng*) *nt* (pl ~en) hymn

gezant (ger-*zahnt*) *c* (pl ~en) envoy

gezellig (ger-*zeh*-lerkh) *adj* cosy

gezelschap (ger-*zehl*-skhahp) *nt* (pl ~pen) company; society

gezet (ger-*zeht*) *adj* corpulent; stout

gezicht (ger-*zikht*) *nt* (pl ~en) face; sight

gezichtscrème (ger-*zikhts*-kraim) *c* (pl ~s) face-cream

gezichtsmassage (ger-*zikhts*-mah-saa-zher) *c* (pl ~s) face massage

gezichtspoeder (ger-*zikhts*-poo-derr) *nt/c* (pl ~s) face-powder

gezien (ger-*zeen*) *prep* considering

gezin (ger-*zin*) *nt* (pl ~nen) family

gezond (ger-*zont*) *adj* healthy; well; wholesome

gezondheid (ger-*zont*-hayt) *c* health

gezondheidsattest (ger-*zont*-hayts-ah-tehst) *nt* (pl ~en) health certificate

gezwel (ger-*zvehl*) *nt* (pl ~len) tumour, growth

gids (gɪts) *c* (pl ~en) guide; guide-book

giechelen (*gee*-kher-lern) *v* giggle

gier (geer) *c* (pl ~en) vulture

gierig (*gee*-rerkh) *adj* avaricious; stingy

*__gieten__ (*gee*-tern) *v* pour

gietijzer (*gee*-tay-zerr) *nt* cast iron

gift (gɪft) *c* (pl ~en) donation

giftig (*gɪf*-terkh) *adj* poisonous

gijzelaar (*gay*-zer-laar) *c* (pl ~s) hostage

gil (gɪl) *c* (pl ~len) scream, yell, shriek

gillen (*gɪ*-lern) *v* scream, yell, shriek

ginds (gɪns) *adv* over there

gips (gɪps) *nt* plaster

gissen (*gɪ*-sern) *v* guess

gissing (*gɪ*-sɪng) *c* (pl ~en) guess

gist (gɪst) *c* yeast

gisten (*gɪss*-tern) *v* ferment

gisteren (*gɪss*-ter-rern) *adv* yesterday

gitaar (gee-*taar*) *c* (pl -taren) guitar

glad (glaht) *adj* slippery; smooth

glans (glahns) *c* gloss

glanzen (*glahn*-zern) *v* *__shine; **glanzend** glossy

glas (glahss) *nt* (pl glazen) glass; **gebrandschilderd** ~ stained glass

glazen (*glaa*-zern) *adj* glass

gletsjer (*gleht*-sherr) *c* (pl ~s) glacier

gleuf (glürf) *c* (pl gleuven) slot

glibberig (*glɪ*-ber-rerkh) *adj* slippery

glijbaan (*glay*-baan) *c* (pl -banen) slide

*__glijden__ (*glay*-dern) *v* glide, *__slide

glimlach (*glɪm*-lahkh) *c* smile

glimlachen (*glɪm*-lah-khern) *v* smile

glimp (glɪmp) *c* glimpse

globaal (gloa-*baal*) *adj* broad

gloed (glōōt) *c* glow

gloeien (*glōō*ᵉᵉ-ern) *v* glow

gloeilamp (*glōō*ᵉᵉ-lahmp) *c* (pl ~en) light bulb

glooien (*glōa*ᵉᵉ-ern) *v* slope

glooiing (*glōa*ᵉᵉ-ɪng) *c* (pl ~en) ramp

glorie (*glōa*-ree) *c* glory

gluren (*glēw*-rern) *v* peep

gobelin (gōa-ber-*laŋ*) *c* (pl ~s) tapestry

god (got) *c* (pl ~en) god

goddelijk (go-der-lerk) *adj* divine

godin (gōa-*dɪn*) *c* (pl ~nen) goddess

godsdienst (gots-deenst) *c* (pl ~en) religion

godsdienstig (gots-*deen*-sterkh) *adj* religious

goed (gōōt) *adj* good; right, correct; kind; *adv* well; **goed!** all right!

goederen (*gōō*-der-rern) *pl* goods *pl*

goederentrein (*gōō*-der-rern-trayn) *c* (pl ~en) goods train; freight-train *nAm*

goedgelovig (gōōt-kher-*lōa*-verkh) *adj* credulous

goedgestemd (gōōt-kher-*stehmt*) *adj* good-tempered

goedhartig (gōōt-*hahr*-terkh) *adj* good-natured

goedkeuren (*gōōt*-kūr-rern) *v* approve

goedkeuring (*gōōt*-kur-rɪng) *c* (pl ~en) approval

goedkoop (gōōt-*kōap*) *adj* cheap; inexpensive

gok (gok) *c* chance

golf¹ (golf) *c* (pl golven) wave; gulf

golf² (golf) *nt* golf

golfbaan (*golf*-baan) *c* (pl -banen) golf-links, golf-course

golfclub (*golf*-klerp) *c* (pl ~s) golf-club

golflengte (*golf*-lehng-ter) *c* (pl ~n, ~s) wave-length

golvend (*gol*-vernt) *adj* wavy, undulating

gom (gom) *c/nt* (pl ~men) eraser

gondel (*gon*-derl) *c* (pl ~s) gondola

goochelaar (*gōa*-kher-laar) *c* (pl ~s) magician

gooi (gōa^ee) *c* (pl ~en) throw

gooien (*gōa*^ee-ern) *v* *throw; *cast; toss

goot (gōat) *c* (pl goten) gutter

gootsteen (*gōat*-stāyn) *c* (pl -stenen) sink

gordijn (gor-*dayn*) *nt* (pl ~en) curtain

gorgelen (*gor*-ger-lern) *v* gargle

goud (gout) *nt* gold

gouden (*gou*-dern) *adj* golden

goudmijn (*gout*-mayn) *c* (pl ~en) goldmine

goudsmid (*gout*-smit) *c* (pl -smeden) goldsmith

gouvernante (gōo-verr-*nahn*-ter) *c* (pl ~s) governess

gouverneur (gōo-verr-*nūrr*) *c* (pl ~s) governor

graad (graat) *c* (pl graden) degree; grade

graaf (graaf) *c* (pl graven) count; earl

graafschap (*graaf*-skhahp) *nt* (pl ~pen) county

graag (graakh) *adv* gladly, willingly

graan (graan) *nt* (pl granen) corn, grain

graat (graat) *c* (pl graten) bone, fish-bone

gracht (grahkht) *c* (pl ~en) canal; moat

graf (grahf) *nt* (pl graven) grave; tomb

grafiek (graa-*feek*) *c* (pl ~en) graph, diagram; chart

grafisch (*graa*-feess) *adj* graphic

grafsteen (*grahf*-stāyn) *c* (pl -stenen) tombstone, gravestone

gram (grahm) *nt* (pl ~men) gram

grammatica (grah-*maa*-tee-kaa) *c* grammar

grammaticaal (grah-maa-tee-*kaal*) *adj* grammatical

grammofoon (grah-mōa-*fōan*) *c* (pl ~s) gramophone

grammofoonplaat (grah-mōa-*fōan*-plaat) *c* (pl -platen) disc, record

graniet (graa-*neet*) *nt* granite

grap (grahp) *c* (pl ~pen) joke

grappig (*grah*-perkh) *adj* funny, humorous

gras (grahss) *nt* grass

grasspriet (*grahss*-spreet) *c* (pl ~en) blade of grass

grasveld (*grahss*-fehlt) *nt* (pl ~en) lawn

gratie (*graa*-tsee) *c* grace; pardon

gratis (*graa*-terss) *adv* free of charge, free, gratis

grauw (grou) *adj* grey

***graven** (*graa*-vern) *v* *dig

graveren (graa-*vāy*-rern) *v* engrave

graveur (graa-*vūrr*) *c* (pl ~s) engraver

gravin (graa-*vin*) *c* (pl ~nen) countess

gravure (graa-*vēw*-rer) *c* (pl ~s, ~n) engraving

grazen (*graa*-zern) *v* graze

greep (grāyp) *c* (pl grepen) grip; grasp, clutch

grendel (*grehn*-derl) *c* (pl ~s) bolt

grens (grehns) *c* (pl grenzen) frontier, border; boundary, bound

grenzeloos (*grehn*-zer-lōass) *adj* unlimited

greppel (*greh*-perl) *c* (pl ~s) ditch

Griek (greek) *c* (pl ~en) Greek

Griekenland (*gree*-kern-lahnt) Greece

Grieks (greeks) *adj* Greek

griep (greep) *c* flu, influenza

griet (greet) *c* (pl ~en) brill

griezelig (*gree*-zer-lerkh) *adj* scary,

creepy

grijns (grayns) *c* grin

grijnzen (*grayn*-zern) *v* grin

*****grijpen** (*gray*-pern) *v* *catch, grip, grasp, seize

grijs (grayss) *adj* grey

gril (grɪl) *c* (pl ~len) whim, fancy, fad

grind (grɪnt) *nt* gravel

grinniken (*grɪ*-ner-kern) *v* chuckle

groef (grōof) *c* (pl groeven) groove

groei (grōoee) *c* growth

groeien (grōoee-ern) *v* *grow

groen (grōon) *adj* green

groente *c* (pl ~n, ~s) greens *pl*, vegetable

groenteboer (*grōon*-ter-bōor) *c* (pl ~en) greengrocer; vegetable merchant

groep (grōop) *c* (pl ~en) group; bunch, set, party

groet (grōot) *c* (pl ~en) greeting

groeten (*grōo*-tern) *v* greet; salute

groeve (*grōo*-ver) *c* (pl ~n) pit

grof (grof) *adj* gross, coarse; rude

grommen (*gro*-mern) *v* growl

grond (gront) *c* ground; earth, soil; **begane** ~ ground floor

grondig (*gron*-derkh) *adj* thorough

grondslag (*gront*-slahkh) *c* (pl ~en) basis, base

grondstof (*gront*-stof) *c* (pl ~fen) raw material

grondwet (*gront*-veht) *c* (pl ~ten) constitution

groot (grōat) *adj* big; great, large, tall; major; **grootst** major, main; **groter** major; superior

*****grootbrengen** (*grōat*-breh-ngern) *v* *bring up, raise; rear

Groot-Brittannië (grōat-brɪ-*tah*-nee-Yer) Great Britain

groothandel (*grōat*-hahn-derl) *c* wholesale

grootmoeder (*grōat*-mōo-derr) *c* (pl

~s) grandmother

grootouders (*grōat*-ou-derrs) *pl* grandparents *pl*

groots (grōats) *adj* grand, superb, magnificent

grootte (*grōa*-ter) *c* (pl ~n, ~s) size

grootvader (*grōat*-faa-derr) *c* (pl ~s) grandfather

gros (gross) *nt* (pl ~sen) gross

grossier (gro-*seer*) *c* (pl ~s) wholesale dealer

grot (grot) *c* (pl ~ten) cave; grotto

gruis (grurewss) *nt* grit

gruwelijk (*grēw*-ver-lerk) *adj* horrible

gul (gerl) *adj* generous

gulp (gerlp) *c* (pl ~en) fly

gulzig (*gerl*-zerkh) *adj* greedy

gunnen (*ger*-nern) *v* grant

gunst (gernst) *c* (pl ~en) favour

gunstig (*gern*-sterkh) *adj* favourable

guur (gēwr) *adj* bleak

gymnast (gɪm-*nahst*) *c* (pl ~en) gymnast

gymnastiek (gɪm-nahss-*teek*) *c* gymnastics *pl*

gymnastiekbroek (gɪm-nahss-*teek*-brōok) *c* (pl ~en) trunks *pl*

gymnastiekzaal (gɪm-nahss-*teek*-saal) *c* (pl -zalen) gymnasium

gymschoenen (*gɪm*-skhōo-nern) *pl* gym shoes, plimsolls *pl*; sneakers *plAm*

gynaecoloog (gee-nāy-kōa-*lōakh*) *c* (pl -logen) gynaecologist

H

haai (haaee) *c* (pl ~en) shark

haak (haak) *c* (pl haken) hook; **tussen twee haakjes** by the way

haalbaar (*haal*-baar) *adj* attainable, realizable

haan (haan) c (pl hanen) cock

haar¹ (haar) nt (pl haren) hair

haar² (haar) pron her

haarborstel (haar-bor-sterl) c (pl ~s) hairbrush

haarcrème (haar-kraim) c (pl ~s) hair cream

haard (haart) c (pl ~en) hearth, fireplace

haardroger (haar-drōa-gerr) c (pl ~s) hair-dryer

haarlak (haar-lahk) c (pl ~ken) hairspray

haarnetje (haar-neh-tᵛer) nt (pl ~s) hair-net

haarolie (haar-ōa-lee) c hair-oil

haarspeld (haar-spehlt) c (pl ~en) hairpin, hair-grip; bobby pin Am

haarstukje (haar-ster-kᵛer) nt (pl ~s) hair piece

haarversteviger (haar-verr-stāy-ver-gerr) c setting lotion

haas (haass) c (pl hazen) hare

haast¹ (haast) adv nearly, almost

haast² (haast) c haste, hurry

zich haasten (haass-tern) hasten, rush, hurry

haastig (haass-terkh) adj hasty; adv in a hurry

haat (haat) c hatred, hate

hachelijk (hah-kher-lerk) adj precarious, critical

hagel (haa-gerl) c hail

hak (hahk) c (pl ~ken) heel

haken (haa-kern) v crochet

hakken (hah-kern) v chop

hal (hahl) c (pl ~len) lobby, hall

halen (haa-lern) v *get, fetch; *make; *catch; *laten ~ *send for

half (hahlf) adj half; semi-; adv half

hallo! (hah-lōā) hello!

hals (hahls) c (pl halzen) throat; neck

halsband (hahls-bahnt) c (pl ~en) collar

halsketting (hahls-keh-tɪng) c (pl ~en) necklace

halt! (hahlt) stop!

halte (hahl-ter) c (pl ~n, ~s) stop

halveren (hahl-vāy-rern) v halve

halverwege (hahl-verr-vāy-ger) adv halfway

ham (hahm) c (pl ~men) ham

hamer (haa-merr) c (pl ~s) hammer; **houten** ~ mallet

hand (hahnt) c (pl ~en) hand; **hand-** manual; **met de** ~ **gemaakt** handmade

handbagage (hahnt-bah-gaa-zher) c hand luggage; hand baggage Am

handboeien (hahnt-bōōᵉᵉ-ern) pl handcuffs pl

handboek (hahnt-bōōk) nt (pl ~en) handbook

handcrème (hahnt-kraim) c (pl ~s) hand cream

handdoek (hahn-dōōk) c (pl ~en) towel

handdruk (hahn-drerk) c handshake

handel (hahn-derl) c commerce, trade; business; ~ *drijven trade; **handels-** commercial

handelaar (hahn-der-laar) c (pl ~s, -laren) tradesman, merchant; dealer, trader

handelen (hahn-der-lern) v act

handeling (hahn-der-lɪng) c (pl ~en) action; deed, plot

handelsmerk (hahn-derls-mehrk) nt (pl ~en) trademark

handelsrecht (hahn-derls-rehkht) nt commercial law

handelswaar (hahn-derls-vaar) c merchandise

handenarbeid (hahn-der-nahr-bayt) c handicraft

handhaven (hahnt-haa-vern) v maintain

handig (hahn-derkh) adj handy

handkoffertje (hahnt-ko-ferr-t^yer) nt (pl ~s) grip nAm

handpalm (hahnt-pahlm) c (pl ~en) palm

handrem (hahnt-rehm) c (pl ~men) hand-brake

handschoen (hahnt-skhoon) c (pl ~en) glove

handschrift (hahnt-skhrift) nt (pl ~en) handwriting

handtas (hahn-tahss) c (pl ~sen) handbag, bag

handtekening (hahn-tāy-ker-nɪng) v (pl ~en) signature

handvat (hahnt-faht) nt (pl ~ten) handle

handvol (hahnt-fol) c handful

handwerk (hahnt-vehrk) nt handwork, handicraft; needlework

hangbrug (hahng-brerkh) c (pl ~gen) suspension bridge

*** hangen** (hah-ngern) v *hang

hangmat (hahng-maht) c (pl ~ten) hammock

hangslot (hahng-slot) nt (pl ~en) padlock

hanteerbaar (hahn-tāyr-baar) adj manageable

hanteren (hahn-tāy-rern) v handle

hap (hahp) c (pl ~pen) bite

hard (hahrt) adj hard; loud

harddraverij (hahr-draa-ver-ray) c (pl ~en) horserace

hardnekkig (hahrt-neh-kerkh) adj obstinate, dogged, stubborn

hardop (hahrt-op) adv aloud

harig (haa-rerkh) adj hairy

haring (haa-rɪng) c (pl ~en) herring

hark (hahrk) c (pl ~en) rake

harmonie (hahr-mōa-nee) c harmony

harnas (hahr-nahss) nt (pl ~sen) armour

harp (hahrp) c (pl ~en) harp

hars (hahrs) nt/c resin

hart (hahrt) nt (pl ~en) heart

hartaanval (hahr-taan-vahl) c (pl ~len) heart attack

hartelijk (hahr-ter-lerk) adj hearty, cordial; sympathetic

harteloos (hahr-ter-lōass) adj heartless

hartklopping (hahrt-klo-pɪng) c (pl ~en) palpitation

hartstocht (hahrts-tokht) c passion

hartstochtelijk (hahrts-tokh-ter-lerk) adj passionate

hatelijk (haa-ter-lerk) adj spiteful

haten (haa-tern) v hate

haven (haa-vern) c (pl ~s) port, harbour

havenarbeider (haa-vern-ahr-bay-derr) c (pl ~s) docker

haver (haa-verr) c oats pl

havik (haa-vɪk) c (pl ~en) hawk

hazelnoot (haa-zerl-nōat) c (pl -noten) hazelnut

hazewind (haa-zer-vɪnt) c (pl ~en) greyhound

*** hebben** (heh-bern) v *have

Hebreeuws (hāy-brāy^{oo}ss) nt Hebrew

hebzucht (hehp-serkht) c greed

hebzuchtig (hehp-serkh-terkh) adj greedy

hechten (hehkh-tern) v attach; sew up

hechtenis (hehkh-ter-nɪss) c custody

hechting (hehkh-tɪng) c (pl ~en) stitch

hechtpleister (hehkht-play-sterr) c (pl ~s) adhesive tape

heden (hāy-dern) nt present

hedendaags (hāy-dern-daakhs) adj contemporary

heel (hāyl) adj entire, whole; unbroken; adv quite

heelal (hāy-lahl) nt universe

heelhuids (hāyl-hur^{ew}ts) adj unhurt

*** heengaan** (hāyng-gaan) v depart

heer (hāyr) c (pl heren) gentleman

heerlijk (hāyr-lerk) adj lovely, wonderful; delightful, delicious

heerschappij (hāyr-skhah-*pay*) c (pl ~en) rule; dominion

heersen (hāyr-sern) v rule

heerser (hāyr-serr) c (pl ~s) ruler

hees (hāyss) adj hoarse

heet (hāyt) adj hot; warm

hefboom (hehf-bōam) c (pl -bomen) lever

*****heffen** (heh-fern) v raise

heftig (hehf-terkh) adj violent

heg (hehkh) c (pl ~gen) hedge

heide (hay-der) c (pl ~n) heath; moor; heather

heiden (hay-dern) c (pl ~en) heathen, pagan

heidens (hay-derns) adj heathen, pagan

heiig (hay-erkh) adj hazy

heilbot (hayl-bot) c (pl ~ten) halibut

heilig (hay-lerkh) adj holy, sacred

heiligdom (hay-lerkh-dom) nt (pl ~men) shrine

heilige (hay-ler-ger) c (pl ~n) saint

heiligschennis (hay-lerkh-skheh-nerss) c sacrilege

heimwee (haym-vāy) nt homesickness

hek (hehk) nt (pl ~ken) fence; gate; railing

hekel (hāy-kerl) c dislike, aan

*****hebben aan** hate, dislike

heks (hehks) c (pl ~en) witch

hel (hehl) c hell

helaas (hāy-laass) adv unfortunately

held (hehlt) c (pl ~en) hero

helder (hehl-derr) adj clear; serene; bright

heleboel (hāy-ler-bōōl) c plenty

helemaal (hāy-ler-maal) adv entirely, altogether, completely, wholly; quite; at all

helft (hehlft) c (pl ~en) half

hellen (heh-lern) v slant; **hellend** slanting

helling (heh-ling) c (pl ~en) slope; hillside; gradient, incline

helm (hehlm) c (pl ~en) helmet

*****helpen** (hehl-pern) v help; assist, aid

helper (hehl-perr) c (pl ~s) helper

hem (hehm) pron him

hemd (hehmt) nt (pl ~en) shirt; vest; undershirt

hemel (hāy-merl) c (pl ~s, ~en) sky; heaven

hen[1] (hehn) pron them

hen[2] (hehn) c (pl ~nen) hen

hendel (hehn-derl) c (pl ~s) lever

hengel (heh-ngerl) c (pl ~s) fishing rod

hengelen (heh-nger-lern) v angle, fish

hennep (heh-nerp) c hemp

herberg (hehr-behrkh) c (pl ~en) hostel, tavern, inn

herbergen (hehr-behr-gern) v lodge

herbergier (hehr-behr-geer) c (pl ~s) inn-keeper

herdenking (hehr-dehng-king) c (pl ~en) commemoration

herder (hehr-derr) c (pl ~s) shepherd

herenhuis (hāy-rern-hur^(ew)ss) nt (pl -huizen) mansion, manor-house

herenigen (heh-rāy-ner-gern) v reunite

herentoilet (hāy-rern-tvah-leht) nt (pl ~ten) men's room

herfst (hehrfst) c autumn; fall nAm

herhalen (hehr-haa-lern) v repeat

herhaling (hehr-haa-ling) c (pl ~en) repetition

herinneren (heh-ri-ner-rern) v remind; **zich** ~ remember, recollect, recall

herinnering (heh-ri-ner-ring) c (pl ~en) memory; remembrance

herkennen (hehr-keh-nern) v recognize

herkomst (hehr-komst) c origin

hernia (hehr-nee-Yaa) c slipped disc

herrie (heh-ree) c noise; fuss

*****herroepen** (heh-rōō-pern) v recall

hersenen (*hehr*-ser-nern) *pl* brain

hersenschudding (*hehr*-sern-skher-dıng) *c* (pl ~en) concussion

herstel (hehr-*stehl*) *nt* repair; recovery; revival

herstellen (hehr-*steh*-lern) *v* repair, mend; **zich** ~ recover

hert (hehrt) *nt* (pl ~en) deer

hertog (*hehr*-tokh) *c* (pl ~en) duke

hertogin (hehr-tōa-*gın*) *c* (pl ~nen) duchess

hervatten (hehr-*vah*-tern) *v* resume, recommence

*****herzien** (hehr-*zeen*) *v* revise

herziening (hehr-*zee*-nıng) *c* (pl ~en) revision

het (heht, ert) *art* the; *pron* it

*****heten** (*hāy*-tern) *v* *be called

heteroseksueel (hāy-ter-rōa-sehk-sēw-*vāyl*) *adj* heterosexual

hetzij ... hetzij (heht-*say*) either ... or

heup (hūrp) *c* (pl ~en) hip

heuvel (*hūr*-verl) *c* (pl ~s) hill; mound

heuvelachtig (*hūr*-ver-lahkh-terkh) *adj* hilly

heuveltop (*hūr*-verl-top) *c* (pl ~pen) hilltop

hevig (*hāy*-verkh) *adj* severe, violent; intense

hiel (heel) *c* (pl ~en) heel

hier (heer) *adv* here

hiërarchie (hee-Yer-rahr-*khee*) *c* (pl ~ën) hierarchy

hij (hay) *pron* he

hijgen (*hay*-gern) *v* pant

*****hijsen** (*hay*-sern) *v* hoist

hijskraan (*hayss*-kraan) *c* (pl -kranen) crane

hik (hık) *c* hiccup

hinderen (*hın*-der-rern) *v* hinder; bother, embarrass

hinderlaag (*hın*-derr-laakh) *c* (pl -lagen) ambush

hinderlijk (*hın*-derr-lerk) *adj* annoying

hindernis (*hın*-derr-nıss) *c* (pl ~sen) obstacle

hinken (*hıng*-kern) *v* limp

historisch (hee-*stōa*-reess) *adj* historic

hitte (*hı*-ter) *c* heat

hobbelig (*ho*-ber-lerkh) *adj* bumpy

hobby (*ho*-bee) *c* (pl ~'s) hobby

hoe (hōo) *adv* how; ~ ... **hoe** the ... the; ~ **dan ook** anyhow, any way; at any rate

hoed (hōot) *c* (pl ~en) hat

hoede (*hōo*-der) *c* custody

zich hoeden (*hōo*-dern) beware

hoef (hōof) *c* (pl hoeven) hoof

hoefijzer (*hōof*-ay-zerr) *nt* (pl ~s) horseshoe

hoek (hōok) *c* (pl ~en) corner; angle

hoer (hōor) *c* (pl ~en) whore

hoes (hōoss) *c* (pl hoezen) sleeve

hoest (hōost) *c* cough

hoesten (*hōoss*-tern) *v* cough

hoeveel (hōo-*vāyl*) *pron* how much; how many

hoeveelheid (hōo-*vāyl*-hayt) *c* (pl -heden) quantity; amount

hoeven (*hōo*-vern) *v* need

hoewel (hōo-*vehl*) *conj* although, though

hof (hof) *nt* (pl hoven) court

hoffelijk (*ho*-fer-lerk) *adj* courteous

hokje (*ho*-kYer) *nt* (pl ~s) booth

hol¹ (hol) *nt* (pl ~en) den; cavern

hol² (hol) *adj* hollow

Holland (*ho*-lahnt) Holland

Hollander (*ho*-lahn-derr) *c* (pl ~s) Dutchman

Hollands (*ho*-lahnts) *adj* Dutch

holte (*hol*-ter) *c* (pl ~s, ~n) cavity

homoseksueel (hōa-mōa-sehk-sēw-*vāyl*) *adj* homosexual

hond (hont) *c* (pl ~en) dog

hondehok (*hon*-der-hok) *nt* (pl ~ken) kennel

honderd (*hon*-derrt) *num* hundred

hondsdolheid (honts-*dol*-hayt) *c* rabies

Hongaar (hong-*gaar*) *c* (pl -garen) Hungarian

Hongaars (hong-*gaars*) *adj* Hungarian

Hongarije (hong-gaa-*ray*-er) Hungary

honger (*ho*-ngerr) *c* hunger

hongerig (*ho*-nger-rerkh) *adj* hungry

honing (*hōa*-ning) *c* honey

honkbal (*hongk*-bahl) *nt* baseball

honorarium (hōa-nōa-*raa*-ree-Yerm) *nt* (pl -ria) fee

hoofd (hōaft) *nt* (pl ~en) head; het ~ * bieden aan face; hoofd- primary, main, chief; cardinal, capital; over het ~ * zien overlook; uit het ~ by heart; uit het ~ leren memorize

hoofdkussen (*hōaft*-ker-sern) *nt* (pl ~s) pillow

hoofdkwartier (*hōaft*-kvahr-teer) *nt* (pl ~en) headquarters *pl*

hoofdleiding (*hōaft*-lay-ding) *c* (pl ~en) mains *pl*

hoofdletter (*hōaft*-leh-terr) *c* (pl ~s) capital letter

hoofdlijn (*hōaft*-layn) *c* (pl ~en) main line

hoofdonderwijzer (*hōaft*-on-derr-vay-zerr) *c* (pl ~s) head teacher

hoofdpijn (*hōaft*-payn) *c* headache

hoofdstad (*hōaft*-staht) *c* (pl -steden) capital

hoofdstraat (*hōaft*-straat) *c* (pl -straten) main street, thoroughfare

hoofdweg (*hōaft*-vehkh) *c* (pl ~en) main road, thoroughfare; highway

hoofdzakelijk (hōaft-*saa*-ker-lerk) *adv* mainly

hoog (hōakh) *adj* high; tall; hoger upper; superior; hoogst foremost, extreme

hooghartig (hōakh-*hahr*-terkh) *adj* haughty

hoogleraar (hōakh-*lāy*-raar) *c* (pl -lera-

ren, ~s) professor

hoogmoedig (hōakh-*mōo*-derkh) *adj* proud

hoogovens (*hōakh*-ōa-verns) *pl* iron-works

hoogseizoen (*hōakh*-say-zōōn) *nt* high season, peak season

hoogstens (*hōakh*-sterns) *adv* at most

hoogte (*hōakh*-ter) *c* (pl ~n, ~s) height; altitude

hoogtepunt (*hōakh*-ter-pernt) *nt* (pl ~en) height

hooguit (*hōakh*-ur^(ewt)) *adv* at most

hoogvlakte (*hōakh*-flahk-ter) *c* (pl ~n, ~s) uplands *pl*; plateau

hooi (hōa^(ee)) *nt* hay

hooikoorts (hōa^(ee)-kōarts) *c* hay fever

hoon (hōan) *c* scorn

hoop[1] (hōap) *c* (pl hopen) heap, lot

hoop[2] (hōap) *c* hope

hoopvol (*hōap*-fol) *adj* hopeful

hoorbaar (*hōar*-baar) *adj* audible

hoorn (*hōa*-rern) *c* (pl ~en, ~s) horn

hop (hop) *c* hop

hopeloos (hōa-per-*lōass*) *adj* hopeless

hopen (*hōa*-pern) *v* hope

horen (*hōa*-rern) *v* * hear

horizon (*hōa*-ree-zon) *c* horizon

horizontaal (hōa-ree-zon-*taal*) *adj* horizontal

horloge (hor-*lōa*-zher) *nt* (pl ~s) watch

horlogebandje (hor-*lōa*-zher-bahn-t^(Y)er) *nt* (pl ~s) watch-strap

horlogemaker (hor-*lōa*-zher-maa-kerr) *c* (pl ~s) watch-maker

hors d'œuvre (awr-*dur̄*-vrer) *c* (pl ~s) hors-d'œuvre

hospes (*hoss*-perss) *c* (pl ~sen) land-lord

hospita (*hoss*-pee-taa) *c* (pl ~'s) land-lady

hospitaal (*hoss*-pee-taal) *nt* (pl -talen) hospital

hotel (hōā-*tehl*) *nt* (pl ~s) hotel

*houden (*hou*-dern) *v* *hold; *keep; ~ van love; like, care for, *be fond of; niet ~ van dislike

houding (*hou*-dɪng) *c* (pl ~en) position; attitude

hout (hout) *nt* wood

houtblok (*hout*-blok) *nt* (pl ~ken) log

houten (*hou*-tern) *adj* wooden

houtskool (*houts*-kōāl) *c* charcoal

*houtsnijden (*hout*-snay-dern) *v* carve

houtsnijwerk (*hout*-snay-vehrk) *nt* wood-carving

houtzagerij (hout-saa-ger-*ray*) *c* (pl ~en) saw-mill

houvast (hou-*vahst*) *nt* grip

houweel (hou-*vāy*l) *nt* (pl -welen) pick-axe

huichelaar (*hur*ew-kher-laar) *c* (pl ~s) hypocrite

huichelachtig (*hur*ew-kherl-ahkh-terkh) *adj* hypocritical

huichelarij (hur*ew*-kher-laa-*ray*) *c* hypocrisy

huichelen (*hur*ew-kher-lern) *v* simulate

huid (hur*ew*t) *c* (pl ~en) skin; hide

huidcrème (*hur*ew*t-kraim) *c* (pl ~s) skin cream

huidig (*hur*ew-derkh) *adj* current

huiduitslag (*hur*ew*t-ur*ew*t-slahkh) *c* rash

huilen (*hur*ew-lern) *v* cry, *weep

huis (hur*ew*ss) *nt* (pl huizen) house; home; naar ~ home

huisarts (*hur*ew*ss-ahrts) *c* (pl ~en) general practitioner

huisbaas (*hur*ew*ss-baass) *c* (pl -bazen) landlord

huisdier (*hur*ew*ss-deer) *nt* (pl ~en) pet

huiselijk (*hur*ew-ser-lerk) *adj* domestic

huishouden (*hur*ew*ss-hou-dern) *nt* (pl ~s) household; housework, housekeeping

huishoudster (*hur*ew*ss-hout-sterr) *c* (pl ~s) housekeeper

huiskamer (*hur*ew*ss-kaa-merr) *c* (pl ~s) living-room

huisonderwijzer (*hur*ew*ss-on-derr-vay-zerr) *c* (pl ~s) tutor

huissleutel (*hur*ew-slur-terl) *c* (pl ~s) latchkey

huisvrouw (*hur*ew*ss-frou) *c* (pl ~en) housewife

huizenblok (*hur*ew-zern-blok) *nt* (pl ~ken) house block *Am*

hulde (*herl*-der) *c* tribute, homage

huldigen (*herl*-der-gern) *v* honour

hulp (herlp) *c* help; assistance, aid; eerste ~ first-aid; eerste hulppost first-aid post

hulpvaardig (herlp-*faar*-derkh) *adj* helpful

humeur (hew-*mūrr*) *nt* (pl ~en) mood

humor (*hew*-mor) *c* humour

humoristisch (hew-mōā-*rɪss*-teess) *adj* humorous

hun (hern) *pron* their

huppelen (*her*-per-lern) *v* hop, skip

huren (*hew*-rern) *v* hire, rent; lease

hut (hert) *c* (pl ~ten) hut; cabin

huur (hewr) *c* (pl huren) rent; te ~ for hire

huurcontract (*hewr*-kon-trahkt) *nt* (pl ~en) lease

huurder (*hewr*-derr) *c* (pl ~s) tenant

huurkoop (*hewr*-kōāp) *c* hire-purchase

huwelijk (*hew*-ver-lerk) *nt* (pl ~en) wedding, marriage

huwelijksreis (*hew*-ver-lerks-rayss) *c* (pl -reizen) honeymoon

huwen (*hew*ᵒᵒ-ern) *v* marry

hygiëne (hee-gee-*ᵞāy*-ner) *c* hygiene

hygiënisch (hee-gee-*ᵞāy*-neess) *adj* hygienic

hypocriet (hee-pōā-*kreet*) *adj* hypocritical

hypotheek (hee-pōā-*tāyk*) *c* (pl -theken) mortgage

hysterisch (hee-*stāy*-reess) *adj* hysterical

I

ideaal[1] (ee-dāy-*Yaal*) *adj* ideal
ideaal[2] (ee-dāy-*Yaal*) *nt* (pl idealen) ideal
idee (ee-*dāy*) *nt/c* (pl ~ën, ~s) idea
identiek (ee-dehn-*teek*) *adj* identical
identificatie (ee-dehn-tee-fi-*kaa*-tsee) *c* identification
identificeren (ee-dehn-tee-fee-*sāy*-rern) *v* identify
identiteit (ee-dehn-ti-*tayt*) *c* identity
identiteitskaart (ee-dehn-tee-*tayts*-kaart) *c* (pl ~en) identity card
idiomatisch (ee-dee-Yōa-*maa*-teess) *adj* idiomatic
idioom (ee-dee-*Yōam*) *nt* (pl idiomen) idiom
idioot[1] (ee-dee-*Yōat*) *adj* idiotic
idioot[2] (ee-dee-*Yōat*) *c* (pl idioten) idiot
idool (ee-*dōal*) *nt* (pl idolen) idol
ieder (*ee*-derr) *pron* each, every; everyone
iedereen (ee-dur-*rāyn*) *pron* everyone, everybody; anyone
iemand (*ee*-mahnt) *pron* someone, somebody
iep (eep) *c* (pl ~en) elm
Ier (eer) *c* (pl ~en) Irishman
Ierland (*eer*-lahnt) Ireland
Iers (eers) *adj* Irish
iets (eets) *pron* something; some
ijdel (*ay*-derl) *adj* vain; idle
ijs (ayss) *nt* ice; ice-cream
ijsbaan (*ayss*-baan) *c* (pl -banen) skating-rink
ijsje (*ay*-sher) *nt* (pl ~s) ice-cream
ijskast (*ayss*-kahst) *c* (pl ~en) fridge,

refrigerator
ijskoud (ayss-kout) *adj* freezing
IJsland (ayss-lahnt) Iceland
IJslander (ayss-lahn-derr) *c* (pl ~s) Icelander
IJslands (ayss-lahnts) *adj* Icelandic
ijswater (ayss-vaa-terr) *nt* iced water
ijver (ay-verr) *c* zeal; diligence
ijverig (ay-ver-rerkh) *adj* zealous; diligent
ijzer (ay-zerr) *nt* iron
ijzerdraad (ay-zerr-draat) *nt* wire
ijzeren (ay-zer-rern) *adj* iron
ijzerwaren (ay-zerr-vaa-rern) *pl* hardware
ik (ik) *pron* I
ikoon (ee-*kōan*) *c* (pl ikonen) icon
illegaal (ee-ler-*gaal*) *adj* illegal
illusie (i-*lēw*-zee) *c* (pl ~s) illusion
illustratie (i-lēw-*straa*-tsee) *c* (pl ~s) illustration
illustreren (i-lēw-*strāy*-rern) *v* illustrate
imitatie (ee-mee-*taa*-tsee) *c* (pl ~s) imitation
imiteren (ee-mee-*tāy*-rern) *v* imitate
immigrant (i-mee-*grahnt*) *c* (pl ~en) immigrant
immigratie (i-mee-*graa*-tsee) *c* immigration
immigreren (i-mee-*grāy*-rern) *v* immigrate
immuniteit (i-mēw-nee-*tayt*) *c* immunity
impliceren (im-plee-*sāy*-rern) *v* imply, involve
imponeren (im-pōa-*nāy*-rern) *v* impress
impopulair (im-pōa-pēw-*lair*) *adj* unpopular
import (*im*-port) *c* import
importeren (im-por-*tāy*-rern) *v* import
importeur (im-por-*tūrr*) *c* (pl ~s) importer

impotent (im-pōā-*tehnt*) *adj* impotent

impotentie (im-pōā-*tehn*-see) *c* impotence

improviseren (im-prōā-vee-*sāy*-rern) *v* improvise

impuls (im-*perls*) *c* (pl ~en) impulse

impulsief (im-perl-*zeef*) *adj* impulsive

in (in) *prep* in; into, inside; at

inademen (*in*-aa-der-mern) *v* inhale

inbegrepen (*in*-ber-grāy-pern) *adj* included; alles ~ all in

inboorling (im-*bōar*-ling) *c* (pl ~en) native

*inbreken (im-*brāy*-kern) *v* burgle

inbreker (im-*brāy*-kerr) *c* (pl ~s) burglar

incasseren (ing-kah-*sāy*-rern) *v* cash

incident (in-see-*dehnt*) *nt* (pl ~en) incident

inclusief (ing-klew-*zeef*) *adv* inclusive

incompleet (ing-kom-*plāyt*) *adj* incomplete

indelen (*in*-dāy-lern) *v* classify

zich *indenken (*in*-dehng-kern) *v* imagine

inderdaad (in-derr-*daat*) *adv* indeed

index (*in*-dehks) *c* (pl ~en) index

India (*in*-dee-ʸah) India

Indiaan (in-dee-ʸaan) *c* (pl Indianen) Indian

Indiaans (in-dee-ʸaans) *adj* Indian

indien (in-*deen*) *conj* in case, if

Indiër (*in*-dee-ʸerr) *c* (pl ~s) Indian

indigestie (in-dee-*gehss*-tee) *c* indigestion

indirect (*in*-dee-rehkt) *adj* indirect

Indisch (*in*-deess) *adj* Indian

individu (in-dee-vee-*dew*) *nt* (pl ~en, ~'s) individual

individueel (in-dee-vee-dew-*vāyl*) *adj* individual

Indonesië (in-dōā-*nāy*-zee-ʸer) Indonesia

Indonesiër (in-dōā-*nāy*-zee-ʸerr) *c* (pl ~s) Indonesian

Indonesisch (in-dōā-*nāy*-zeess) *adj* Indonesian

indringer (*in*-dri-ngerr) *c* (pl ~s) trespasser

indruk (*in*-drerk) *c* (pl ~ken) impression; ~ maken op impress

indrukken (*in*-drer-kern) *v* press

indrukwekkend (in-drerk-*veh*-kernt) *adj* impressive, imposing

industrie (in-derss-*tree*) *c* (pl ~ën) industry

industrieel (in-derss-tree-ʸāyl) *adj* industrial

industriegebied (in-derss-*tree*-ger-beet) *nt* (pl ~en) industrial area

ineens (i-*nāyns*) *adv* suddenly; at once

inenten (*in*-ehn-tern) *v* vaccinate, inoculate

inenting (*in*-ehn-ting) *c* (pl ~en) vaccination, inoculation

infanterie (*in*-fahn-ter-ree) *c* infantry

infectie (in-*fehk*-see) *c* (pl ~s) infection

inferieur (in-fāy-ree-ʸurr) *adj* inferior

inflatie (in-*flaa*-tsee) *c* inflation

informatie (in-for-*maa*-tsee) *c* (pl ~s) information; enquiry; ~ *inwinnen *v* inquire

informatiebureau (in-for-*maa*-tsee-bew-rōā) *nt* (pl ~s) inquiry office

informeel (in-for-*māyl*) *adj* informal

informeren (in-for-*māy*-rern) *v* enquire; inform

infrarood (*in*-fraa-rōāt) *adj* infra-red

*ingaan (*ing*-gaan) *v* enter; *take effect

ingang (*ing*-gahng) *c* (pl ~en) entrance, way in; entry; met ~ van as from

ingenieur (in-zhern-ʸurr) *c* (pl ~s) engineer

ingenomen (*ing*-ger-nōā-mern) *adj*

pleased

ingevolge (ing-ger-*vol*-ger) *prep* in accordance with

ingewanden (*ing*-ger-vahn-dern) *pl* bowels *pl*, intestines, insides

ingewikkeld (ing-ger-*vi*-kerlt) *adj* complicated; complex

ingrediënt (ing-gray-dee-Yehnt) *nt* (pl ~en) ingredient

*ingrijpen** (*ing*-gray-pern) *v* intervene

inhalen (*in*-haa-lern) *v* *overtake; pass vAm; ~ **verboden** no overtaking; no passing *Am*

inham (*in*-hahm) *c* (pl ~men) creek, inlet

inheems (in-*hayms*) *adj* native

inhoud (*in*-hout) *c* contents *pl*

*inhouden** (*in*-hou-dern) *v* contain; imply; restrain

inhoudsopgave (*in*-houts-op-khaa-ver) *c* (pl ~n) table of contents

initiatief (ee-nee-shaa-*teef*) *nt* (pl -tieven) initiative

injectie (in-Yehk-see) *c* (pl ~s) shot, injection

inkomen (*ing*-kōa-mern) *nt* (pl ~s) revenue, income

inkomsten (*ing*-kom-stern) *pl* earnings *pl*

inkomstenbelasting (*ing*-kom-ster-ber-lahss-ting) *c* income-tax

inkt (ingkt) *c* ink

inleiden (*in*-lay-dern) *v* introduce; **inleidend** preliminary

inleiding (*in*-lay-ding) *c* (pl ~en) introduction

inlichten (*in*-likh-tern) *v* inform

inlichting (*in*-likh-ting) *c* (pl ~en) information

inlichtingenkantoor (*in*-likh-ti-nger-kahn-tōar) *nt* (pl -toren) information bureau

inmaken (*in*-maa-kern) *v* preserve

inmenging (*in*-mehng-ing) *c* (pl ~en) interference

inmiddels (in-*mi*-derls) *adv* in the meantime

*innemen** (*i*-nāy-mern) *v* *take up; occupy; capture

inneming (*i*-nāy-ming) *c* capture

innen (*i*-nern) *v* cash

inpakken (*im*-pah-kern) *v* wrap; pack up, pack

inrichten (*in*-rikh-tern) *v* furnish

inrichting (*in*-rikh-ting) *c* (pl ~en) institution

inschakelen (*in*-skhaa-ker-lern) *v* switch on; plug in

*inschenken** (*in*-skhehng-kern) *v* pour

inschepen (*in*-skhāy-pern) *v* embark

inscheping (*in*-skhāy-ping) *c* embarkation

*inschrijven** (*in*-skhray-vern) *v* enter, book; zich ~ register, check in

inschrijvingsformulier (*in*-skhray-vings-for-mēw-leer) *nt* (pl ~en) registration form

inscriptie (in-*skrip*-see) *c* (pl ~s) inscription

insekt (in-*sehkt*) *nt* (pl ~en) insect; bug *nAm*

insekticide (in-sehk-tee-*see*-der) *c* (pl ~n) insecticide

inslikken (*in*-sli-kern) *v* swallow

*insluiten** (*in*-slur^ew-tern) *v* *shut in, encircle; include; enclose

inspanning (*in*-spah-ning) *c* (pl ~en) strain, effort

inspecteren (in-spehk-*tāy*-rern) *v* inspect

inspecteur (in-spehk-*tūr*) *c* (pl ~s) inspector

inspectie (in-*spehk*-see) *c* (pl ~s) inspection

*inspuiten** (*in*-spur^ew-tern) *v* inject

installatie (in-stah-*laa*-tsee) *c* (pl ~s) installation

installeren (in-stah-*lāy*-rern) *v* install

instappen (ın-stah-pern) *v* *get on; embark

instellen (ın-steh-lern) *v* institute

instelling (ın-steh-lıng) *c* (pl ~en) institution, institute

instemmen (ın-steh-mern) *v* consent; ~ **met** approve of

instemming (ın-steh-mıng) *c* approval, consent

instinct (ın-stıngkt) *nt* (pl ~en) instinct

instituut (ın-stee-tēwt) *nt* (pl -tuten) institute

instorten (ın-stor-tern) *v* collapse

instructie (ın-strerk-see) *c* (pl ~s) direction

instrument (ın-strēw-mehnt) *nt* (pl ~en) instrument

intact (ın-tahkt) *adj* intact

integendeel (ın-tāy-gern-dāyl) on the contrary

intellect (ın-ter-lehkt) *nt* intellect

intellectueel (ın-ter-lehk-tēw-vāyl) *adj* intellectual

intelligent (ın-ter-lee-gehnt) *adj* clever, intelligent

intelligentie (ın-ter-lee-gehn-see) *c* intelligence

intens (ın-tehns) *adj* intense

interessant (ın-ter-rer-sahnt) *adj* interesting

interesse (ın-ter-reh-ser) *c* interest

interesseren (ın-ter-reh-sāy-rern) *v* interest

intermezzo (ın-terr-mehd-zōā) *nt* (pl ~'s) interlude

intern (ın-tehrn) *adj* internal; resident

internaat (ın-terr-naat) *nt* (pl -naten) boarding-school

internationaal (ın-terr-naht-shōā-naal) *adj* international

intiem (ın-teem) *adj* intimate

introduceren (ın-trōā-dēw-sāy-rern) *v* introduce

intussen (ın-ter-sern) *adv* meanwhile

inval (ın-vahl) *c* (pl ~len) brain-wave, idea; raid, invasion

invalide[1] (ın-vaa-lee-der) *adj* disabled, invalid

invalide[2] (ın-vaa-lee-der) *c* (pl ~n) invalid

invasie (ın-vaa-zee) *c* (pl ~s) invasion

inventaris (ın-vehn-taa-rerss) *c* (pl ~sen) inventory

investeerder (ın-vehss-tāyr-derr) *c* (pl ~s) investor

investeren (ın-vehss-tāy-rern) *v* invest

investering (ın-vehss-tāy-rıng) *c* (pl ~en) investment

inviteren (ın-vee-tāy-rern) *v* invite

invloed (ın-vlōōt) *c* (pl ~en) influence

invloedrijk (ın-vlōōt-rayk) *adj* influential

invoegen (ın-vōō-gern) *v* insert

invoer (ın-vōōr) *c* import

invoeren (ın-vōō-rern) *v* introduce; import

invoerrecht (ın-vōō-rehkht) *nt* (pl ~en) duty, import duty

invullen (ın-ver-lern) *v* fill in; fill out *Am*

inwendig (ın-vehn-derkh) *adj* inner; internal

inwilligen (ın-vı-ler-gern) *v* grant

inwoner (ın-vōā-nerr) *c* (pl ~s) inhabitant; resident

inzet (ın-zeht) *c* (pl ~ten) bet

inzetten (ın-zeh-tern) *v* launch

inzicht (ın-zıkht) *nt* (pl ~en) insight

*inzien** (ın-zeen) *v* *see

Iraaks (ee-raaks) *adj* Iraqi

Iraans (ee-raans) *adj* Iranian

Irak (ee-raak) Iraq

Irakees (ee-raa-kāyss) *c* (pl -kezen) Iraqi

Iran (ee-raan) Iran

Iraniër (ee-raa-nee-Yerr) *c* (pl ~s) Iranian

ironie (ee-rō̄a-*nee*) *c* irony

ironisch (ee-*rō̄a*-neess) *adj* ironical

irriteren (ı-ree-*tāy*-rern) *v* annoy, irritate

isolatie (ee-zōa-*laa*-tsee) *c* insulation; isolation

isolator (ee-zōa-*laa*-tor) *c* (pl ~en, ~s) insulator

isolement (ee-zōa-ler-*mehnt*) *nt* isolation

isoleren (ee-zōa-*lāy*-rern) *v* insulate; isolate

Israël (*ıss*-raa-ehl) Israel

Israëliër (ıss-raa-*āy*-lee-Yerr) *c* (pl ~s) Israeli

Israëlisch (ıss-raa-*āy*-leess) *adj* Israeli

Italiaan (ee-taa-lee-Yaan) *c* (pl -lianen) Italian

Italiaans (ee-taa-lee-Yaans) *adj* Italian

Italië (ee-*taa*-lee-Yer) Italy

ivoor (ee-*vōar*) *nt* ivory

J

ja (Yaa) yes

jaar (Yaar) *nt* (pl jaren) year

jaarboek (Yaar-bōōk) *nt* (pl ~en) annual

jaargetijde (Yaar-ger-tay-der) *nt* (pl ~n) season

jaarlijks (Yaar-lerks) *adj* annual, yearly; *adv* per annum

jacht[1] (Yahkht) *c* hunt; chase

jacht[2] (Yahkht) *nt* (pl ~en) yacht

jachthuis (Yahkht-hurewss) *nt* (pl -huizen) lodge

jade (Yaa-der) *nt/c* jade

jagen (Yaa-gern) *v* hunt

jager (Yaa-gerr) *c* (pl ~s) hunter

jaloers (Yaa-lōōrs) *adj* envious, jealous

jaloezie (Yaa-lōō-zee) *c* (pl ~ën) jealousy; blind

jam (zhehm) *c* jam

jammer! (Yah-merr) what a pity!

januari (Yah-nēw-vaa-ree) January

Japan (Yaa-pahn) Japan

Japanner (Yaa-pah-nerr) *c* (pl ~s) Japanese

Japans (Yaa-pahns) *adj* Japanese

japon (Yaa-pon) *c* (pl ~nen) dress; gown

jarretelgordel (zhah-rer-tehl-gor-derl) *c* (pl ~s) suspender belt; garter belt *Am*

jas (Yahss) *c* (pl ~sen) coat

jasje (Yah-sher) *nt* (pl ~s) jacket

je (Yer) *pron* you; yourself; yourselves

jegens (Yāy-gerns) *prep* towards

jeugd (Yūrkht) *c* youth

jeugdherberg (Yūrkht-hehr-behrkh) *c* (pl ~en) youth hostel

jeugdig (Yūrkh-derkh) *adj* juvenile

jeuk (Yūrk) *c* itch

jeuken (Yūr-kern) *v* itch

jicht (Yıkht) *c* gout

joch (Yokh) *nt* boy, lad

jodium (Yōa-dee-Yerm) *nt* iodine

Joegoslaaf (Yōō-gōa-slaaf) *c* (pl -slaven) Jugoslav, Yugoslav

Joegoslavië (Yōō-gōa-slaa-vee-er) Jugoslavia, Yugoslavia

Joegoslavisch (Yōō-gōa-slaa-veess) *adj* Jugoslav

jong (Yong) *adj* young; **jonger** junior

jongen (Yo-ngern) *c* (pl ~s) boy; lad

jood (Yōat) *c* (pl joden) Jew

joods (Yōats) *adj* Jewish

Jordaans (Yor-daans) *adj* Jordanian

Jordanië (Yor-daa-nee-Yer) Jordan

Jordaniër (Yor-daa-nee-Yerr) *c* (pl ~s) Jordanian

jou (You) *pron* you

journaal (zhōōr-naal) *nt* news

journalist (zhōōr-naa-lıst) *c* (pl ~en) journalist

journalistiek (zhōōr-naa-lıss-*teek*) *c* journalism

jouw (^You) *pron* your

jubileum (^Yēw-bee-*lā̄y*-^Yerm) *nt* (pl ~s, -lea) jubilee

juffrouw (^Yer-frou) *c* (pl ~en) miss

juichen (^Yur^{ew}-khern) *v* cheer

juist (^Yur^{ew}st) *adj* right, correct, just; proper, appropriate

juistheid (^Yur^{ew}st-hayt) *c* correctness

juk (^Yerk) *nt* (pl ~ken) yoke

jukbeen (^Yerk-bā̄yn) *nt* (pl ~deren, -benen) cheek-bone

juli (^Yēw-lee) July

jullie (^Yer-lee) *pron* you; your

juni (^Yēw-nee) June

juridisch (^Yēw-*ree*-deess) *adj* legal

jurist (^Yēw-rıst) *c* (pl ~en) lawyer

jurk (^Yerrk) *c* (pl ~en) frock, robe, dress

jury (zhēw-ree) *c* (pl ~'s) jury

jus (zhēw) *c* gravy

juweel (^Yēw-*vā̄yl*) *nt* (pl -welen) jewel; gem; **juwelen** jewellery

juwelier (^Yēw-ver-*leer*) *c* (pl ~s) jeweller

K

kaak (kaak) *c* (pl kaken) jaw

kaal (kaal) *adj* bald; naked, bare

kaap (kaap) *c* (pl kapen) cape

kaars (kaars) *c* (pl ~en) candle

kaart (kaart) *c* (pl ~en) map; card; **groene** ~ green card

kaartautomaat (*kaar*-tern-ōā-tōā-maat) *c* (pl -maten) ticket machine

kaartje (*kaar*-t^Yer) *nt* (pl ~s) ticket

kaas (kaass) *c* (pl kazen) cheese

kabaal (kaa-*baal*) *nt* racket

kabel (*kaa*-berl) *c* (pl ~s) cable

kabeljauw (kah-berl-*You*) *c* (pl ~en) cod

kabinet (kaa-bee-*neht*) *nt* (pl ~ten) cabinet

kachel (*kah*-kherl) *c* (pl ~s) heater; stove

kade (*kaa*-der) *c* (pl ~n) quay; embankment; dock, wharf

kader (*kaa*-derr) *nt* (pl ~s) cadre

kajuit (kaa-*Yur^{ew}t*) *c* (pl ~en) cabin

kaki (*kaa*-kee) *nt* khaki

kalender (kaa-*lehn*-derr) *c* (pl ~s) calendar

kalf (kahlf) *nt* (pl kalveren) calf

kalfsleer (*kahlfs*-lā̄yr) *nt* calf skin

kalfsvlees (*kahlfs*-flā̄yss) *nt* veal

kalk (kahlk) *c* lime

kalkoen (kahl-*kōōn*) *c* (pl ~en) turkey

kalm (kahlm) *adj* calm; sedate, quiet, serene

kalmeren (kahl-*mā̄y*-rern) *v* calm down

kam (kahm) *c* (pl ~men) comb

kameel (kaa-*mā̄yl*) *c* (pl kamelen) camel

kamer (*kaa*-merr) *c* (pl ~s) room; chamber

kameraad (kah-mer-*raat*) *c* (pl -raden) comrade

kamerbewoner (*kaa*-merr-ber-vōā-nerr) *c* (pl ~s) lodger

kamerjas (*kaa*-merr-^Yahss) *c* (pl ~sen) dressing-gown

kamerlid (*kaa*-merr-lıt) *nt* (pl -leden) Member of Parliament

kamermeisje (*kaa*-merr-may-sher) *nt* (pl ~s) chambermaid

kamertemperatuur (*kaa*-merr-tehm-per-raa-tēwr) *c* room temperature

kamgaren (*kahm*-gaa-rern) *nt* worsted

kammen (*kah*-mern) *v* comb

kamp (kahmp) *nt* (pl ~en) camp

kampeerder (kahm-*pā̄yr*-derr) *c* (pl ~s) camper

kampeerterrein (kahm-*pā̄yr*-teh-rayn)

nt (pl ~en) camping site

kampeerwagen (kahm-*pāyr*-vaa-gern) *c* (pl ~s) trailer *nAm*

kamperen (kahm-*pāy*-rern) *v* camp

kampioen (kahm-pee-*ᵉōōn*) *c* (pl ~en) champion

kan (kahn) *c* (pl ~nen) jug

kanaal (kaa-*naal*) *nt* (pl kanalen) canal; channel; **het Kanaal** English Channel

kanarie (kaa-*naa*-ree) *c* (pl ~s) canary

kandelaber (kahn-der-*laa*-berr) *c* (pl ~s) candelabrum

kandidaat (kahn-dee-*daat*) *c* (pl -daten) candidate

kaneel (kaa-*nāyl*) *c* cinnamon

kangoeroe (*kahng*-ger-rōō) *c* (pl ~s) kangaroo

kanker (*kahng*-kerr) *c* cancer

kano (*kaa*-nōa) *c* (pl ~'s) canoe

kanon (kaa-*non*) *nt* (pl ~nen) gun

kans (kahns) *c* (pl ~en) chance; opportunity

kansel (*kahn*-serl) *c* (pl ~s) pulpit

kant[1] (kahnt) *c* (pl ~en) side; way; edge; **aan de andere ~ van** across

kant[2] (kahnt) *nt* lace

kantine (kahn-*tee*-ner) *c* (pl ~s) canteen

kantlijn (*kahnt*-layn) *c* (pl ~en) margin

kantoor (kahn-*tōar*) *nt* (pl -toren) office

kantoorbediende (kahn-*tōar*-ber-deen-der) *c* (pl ~n, ~s) clerk

kantoorboekhandel (kahn-*tōar*-bōōk-hahn-derl) *c* (pl ~s) stationer's

kantooruren (kahn-*tōar*-ēw-rern) *pl* business hours, office hours

kap (kahp) *c* (pl ~pen) hood

kapel (kaa-*pehl*) *c* (pl ~len) chapel

kapelaan (kah-per-*laan*) *c* (pl ~s) chaplain

kapen (*kaa*-pern) *v* hijack

kaper (*kaa*-perr) *c* (pl ~s) hijacker

kapitaal (kah-pee-*taal*) *nt* capital

kapitalisme (kah-pee-taa-*liss*-mer) *nt* capitalism

kapitein (kah-pee-*tayn*) *c* (pl ~s) captain

kapot (kaa-*pot*) *adj* broken

kapper (*kah*-perr) *c* (pl ~s) barber; hairdresser

kapsel (*kahp*-serl) *nt* (pl ~s) hair-do

kapstok (*kahp*-stok) *c* (pl ~ken) hat rack

kar (kahr) *c* (pl ~ren) cart

karaat (kaa-*raat*) *nt* carat

karaf (kaa-*rahf*) *c* (pl ~fen) carafe

karakter (kaa-*rahk*-terr) *nt* (pl ~s) character

karakteristiek (kaa-rahk-ter-riss-*teek*) *adj* characteristic

karaktertrek (kaa-*rahk*-terr-trehk) *c* (pl ~ken) characteristic

karamel (kaa-raa-*mehl*) *c* (pl ~s, ~len) caramel

karbonade (kahr-bōa-*naa*-der) *c* (pl ~s) cutlet, chop

kardinaal[1] (kahr-dee-*naal*) *c* (pl -nalen) cardinal

kardinaal[2] (kahr-dee-*naal*) *adj* cardinal

karper (*kahr*-perr) *c* (pl ~s) carp

karton (kahr-*ton*) *nt* cardboard

kartonnen (kahr-*to*-nern) *adj* cardboard; **~ doos** carton

karwei (kahr-*vay*) *nt* (pl ~en) job

kas (kahss) *c* (pl ~sen) greenhouse

kasjmier (*kahsh*-meer) *nt* cashmere

kassa (*kah*-saa) *c* (pl ~'s) pay-desk; box-office

kassier (kah-*seer*) *c* (pl ~s) cashier

kast (kahst) *c* (pl ~en) cupboard, closet

kastanje (kahss-*tah*-ñer) *c* (pl ~s) chestnut

kastanjebruin (kahss-*tah*-ñer-brur*ᵉʷ*n) *adj* auburn

kasteel (kahss-*tayl*) *nt* (pl -telen) castle

kat (kaht) *c* (pl ~ten) cat

kathedraal (kaa-tay-*draal*) *c* (pl -dralen) cathedral

katholiek (kaa-tōa-*leek*) *adj* catholic

katoen (kaa-*tōōn*) *nt/c* cotton

katoenen (kaa-*tōō*-nern) *adj* cotton

katoenfluweel (kaa-*tōōn*-flew-*vayl*) *nt* velveteen

katrol (kaa-*trol*) *c* (pl ~len) pulley

kattekwaad (*kah*-ter-kvaat) *nt* mischief

kauwen (*kou*-ern) *v* chew

kauwgom (*kou*-gom) *c/nt* chewing-gum

kaviaar (*kaa*-vee-Ɣaar) *c* caviar

kazerne (kaa-*zehr*-ner) *c* (pl ~s, ~n) barracks *pl*

keel (kayl) *c* (pl kelen) throat

keelontsteking (*kayl*-ont-stay-kıng) *c* (pl ~en) laryngitis

keelpijn (*kayl*-payn) *c* sore throat

keer (kayr) *c* (pl keren) time

keerpunt (*kayr*-pernt) *nt* (pl ~en) turning-point

keerzijde (*kayr*-zay-der) *c* (pl ~n) reverse

kegelbaan (*kay*-gerl-baan) *c* (pl -banen) bowling alley

kegelspel (*kay*-gerl-spehl) *nt* bowling

keizer (*kay*-zerr) *c* (pl ~s) emperor

keizerin (kay-zer-*rın*) *c* (pl ~nen) empress

keizerlijk (*kay*-zer-lerk) *adj* imperial

keizerrijk (*kay*-zer-rayk) *nt* (pl ~en) empire

kelder (*kehl*-derr) *c* (pl ~s) cellar

kelner (*kehl*-nerr) *c* (pl ~s) waiter

kenmerk (*kehn*-mehrk) *nt* (pl ~en) characteristic, feature

kenmerken (*kehn*-mehr-kern) *v* characterize, mark; **kenmerkend** characteristic, typical

kennel (*keh*-nerl) *c* (pl ~s) kennel

kennen (*keh*-nern) *v* *know

kenner (*keh*-nerr) *c* (pl ~s) connoisseur

kennis[1] (*keh*-nerss) *c* knowledge

kennis[2] (*keh*-nerss) *c* (pl ~sen) acquaintance

kenteken (*kehn*-tay-kern) *nt* (pl ~s) registration number; licence number *Am*

Kenya (*kay*-nee-Ɣaa) Kenya

kerel (*kay*-rerl) *c* (pl ~s) fellow

keren (*kay*-rern) *v* turn

kerk (kehrk) *c* (pl ~en) church; chapel

kerkhof (*kehrk*-hof) *nt* (pl -hoven) cemetery, graveyard, churchyard

kerktoren (*kehrk*-tōa-rern) *c* (pl ~s) steeple

kermis (*kehr*-merss) *c* (pl ~sen) fair

kern (kehrn) *c* (pl ~en) nucleus; heart, core; essence; **kern-** nuclear

kernenergie (*kehrn*-ay-nehr-zhee) *c* nuclear energy

kerrie (*keh*-ree) *c* curry

kers (kehrs) *c* (pl ~en) cherry

Kerstmis (*kehrs*-merss) Xmas, Christmas

kerven (*kehr*-vern) *v* carve

ketel (*kay*-terl) *c* (pl ~s) kettle

keten (*kay*-tern) *c* (pl ~s, ~en) chain

ketting (*keh*-tıng) *c* (pl ~en) chain

keuken (*kūr*-kern) *c* (pl ~s) kitchen

keurig (*kūr*-rerkh) *adj* neat

keus (kūrss) *c* (keuzen) pick, choice

keuze (*kūr*-zer) *c* (pl ~n) selection, choice

kever (*kay*-verr) *c* (pl ~s) beetle; bug

kiekje (*keek*-Ɣer) *nt* (pl ~s) snapshot

kiel (keel) *c* (pl ~en) keel

kiem (keem) *c* (pl ~en) germ

kier (keer) *c* (pl ~en) chink

kies (keess) *c* (pl kiezen) molar

kiesdistrict (*keess*-dıss-trıkt) *nt* (pl

~en) constituency

kieskeurig (keess-*kūr*-rerkh) *adj* particular

kiesrecht (*keess*-rehkht) *nt* franchise, suffrage

kietelen (*kee*-ter-lern) *v* tickle

kieuw (kee°°) *c* (pl ~en) gill

kievit (*kee*-veet) *c* (pl ~en) pewit

kiezel (*kee*-zerl) *c* (pl ~s) pebble; gravel

*****kiezen** (*kee*-zern) *v* *choose; pick; elect

*****kijken** (*kay*-kern) *v* look; ~ **naar** look at; watch

kijker (*kay*-kerr) *c* (pl ~s) spectator

kijkje (*kayk*-Yer) *nt* (pl ~s) look

kikker (*kɪ*-kerr) *c* (pl ~s) frog

kil (kɪl) *adj* chilly

kilo (*kee*-lōā) *nt* (pl ~'s) kilogram

kilometer (*kee*-lōā-māy-terr) *c* (pl ~s) kilometre

kilometertal (*kee*-lōā-māy-terr-tahl) *nt* distance in kilometres

kim (kɪm) *c* horizon

kin (kɪn) *c* (pl ~nen) chin

kind (kɪnt) *nt* (pl ~eren) child; kid

kinderjuffrouw (*kɪn*-derr-Yer-frou) *c* (pl ~en) nurse

kinderkamer (*kɪn*-derr-kaa-merr) *c* (pl ~s) nursery

kinderverlamming (*kɪn*-derr-verr-lah-mɪng) *c* polio

kinderwagen (*kɪn*-derr-vaa-gern) *c* (pl ~s) pram; baby carriage *Am*

kinine (kee-*nee*-ner) *c* quinine

kiosk (kee-Yosk) *c* (pl ~en) kiosk

kip (kɪp) *c* (pl ~pen) hen; chicken

kippevel (*kɪ*-per-vehl) *nt* goose-flesh

kist (kɪst) *c* (pl ~en) chest

klaar (klaar) *adj* ready

klaarblijkelijk (klaar-*blay*-ker-lerk) *adv* apparently

klaarmaken (*klaar*-maa-kern) *v* prepare; cook

klacht (klahkht) *c* (pl ~en) complaint

klachtenboek (*klahkh*-tern-bōōk) *nt* (pl ~en) complaints book

klagen (*klaa*-gern) *v* complain

klank (klahngk) *c* (pl ~en) sound; tone

klant (klahnt) *c* (pl ~en) customer; client

klap (klahp) *c* (pl ~pen) blow; smack, slap

klappen (*klah*-pern) *v* clap

klaproos (*klahp*-rōāss) *c* (pl -rozen) poppy

klas (klahss) *c* (pl ~sen) class; form

klasgenoot (*klahss*-kher-nōāt) *c* (pl -noten) class-mate

klasse (*klah*-ser) *c* (pl ~n) class

klassiek (klah-*seek*) *adj* classical

klauw (klou) *c* (pl ~en) claw

klaver (*klaa*-verr) *c* (pl ~s) clover; shamrock

zich kleden (*klāy*-dern) dress

kleding (*klāy*-dɪng) *c* clothes *pl*

kleedhokje (*klāyt*-hok-Yer) *nt* (pl ~s) cabin

kleedje (*klāy*-tYer) *nt* (pl ~s) rug

kleedkamer (*klāyt*-kaa-merr) *c* (pl ~s) dressing-room

kleerborstel (*klāyr*-bor-sterl) *c* (pl ~s) clothes-brush

kleerhanger (*klāyr*-hah-ngerr) *c* (pl ~s) hanger, coat-hanger

kleerkast (*klāyr*-kahst) *c* (pl ~en) closet *nAm*

kleermaker (*klāyr*-maa-kerr) *c* (pl ~s) tailor

klei (klay) *c* clay

klein (klayn) *adj* little, small; minor, petty, short; **kleiner** minor; **kleinst** least

kleindochter (*klayn*-dokh-terr) *c* (pl ~s) granddaughter

kleingeld (*klayn*-gehlt) *nt* change, petty cash

kleinhandel (*klayn*-hahn-derl) *c* retail trade

kleinhandelaar (*klayn*-hahn-der-laar) *c* (pl -laren, ~s) retailer

kleinood (*klay*-nōat) *nt* (pl -noden) gem

kleinzoon (*klayn*-zōan) *c* (pl -zonen) grandson

klem (klehm) *c* (pl ~men) clamp

klemschroef (*klehm*-skhrōof) *c* (pl -schroeven) clamp

kleren (*kláy*-rern) *pl* clothes *pl*

klerenhaak (*kláy*-rern-haak) *c* (pl -haken) peg

klerenkast (*kláy*-rer-kahst) *c* (pl ~en) wardrobe

klerk (klehrk) *c* (pl ~en) clerk

kletsen (*kleht*-sern) *v* chat; talk rubbish

kleur (klurr) *c* (pl ~en) colour

kleurecht (*klúrr*-ehkht) *adj* fast-dyed

kleurenblind (*klúr*-rerm-blint) *adj* colour-blind

kleurenfilm (*klúr*-rer-film) *c* (pl ~s) colour film

kleurrijk (*klúr*-rayk) *adj* colourful

kleurstof (*klúrr*-stof) *c* (pl ~fen) colourant

kleuter (*klúr*-terr) *c* (pl ~s) tot

kleuterschool (*klúr*-terr-skhōal) *c* (pl -scholen) kindergarten

kleven (*kláy*-vern) *v* *stick

kleverig (*kláy*-ver-rerkh) *adj* sticky

klier (kleer) *c* (pl ~en) gland

klimaat (klee-*maat*) *nt* (pl -maten) climate

***klimmen** (*klı*-mern) *v* climb

klimop (klı-*mop*) *c* ivy

kliniek (klee-*neek*) *c* (pl ~en) clinic

***klinken** (*kling*-kern) *v* sound

klinker (*kling*-kerr) *c* (pl ~s) vowel

klip (klip) *c* (pl ~pen) cliff

klok (klok) *c* (pl ~ken) clock; bell

klokhuis (*klok*-hur^{ew}ss) *nt* (pl -huizen) core

klomp (klomp) *c* (pl ~en) wooden shoe

klont (klont) *c* (pl ~en) lump

klonterig (*klon*-ter-rerkh) *adj* lumpy

kloof (klōaf) *c* (pl kloven) cleft; chasm

klooster (*klōa*-sterr) *nt* (pl ~s) monastery; convent, cloister

klop (klop) *c* (pl ~pen) knock, tap

kloppen (*klo*-pern) *v* knock, tap; whip

klucht (klerkht) *c* (pl ~en) farce

kluis (klur^{ew}ss) *c* (pl kluizen) safe, vault

knaap (knaap) *c* (pl knapen) boy

knalpot (*knahl*-pot) *c* (pl ~ten) silencer; muffler *nAm*

knap (knahp) *adj* smart, clever; pretty, handsome, good-looking

knappend (*knah*-pernt) *adj* crisp

knapzak (*knahp*-sahk) *c* (pl ~ken) knapsack

kneuzen (*knúr*-zern) *v* bruise

kneuzing (*knúr*-zıng) *c* (pl ~en) bruise

knie (knee) *c* (pl ~ën) knee

knielen (*knee*-lern) *v* *kneel

knieschijf (*knee*-skhayf) *c* (pl -schijven) kneecap

***knijpen** (*knay*-pern) *v* pinch

knik (knık) *c* nod

knikken (*knı*-kern) *v* nod

knikker (*knı*-kerr) *c* (pl ~s) marble

knippen (*knı*-pern) *v* *cut

knoflook (*knof*-lōak) *nt*/*c* garlic

knokkel (*kno*-kerl) *c* (pl ~s) knuckle

knoop (knōap) *c* (pl knopen) button; knot

knooppunt (*knōa*-pernt) *nt* (pl ~en) junction

knoopsgat (*knōaps*-khaht) *nt* (pl ~en) buttonhole

knop (knop) *c* (pl ~pen) bud; knob

knopen (*knōa*-pern) *v* button; tie, knot

knots (knots) *c* (pl ~en) club
knuffelen (*kner*-fer-lern) *v* cuddle
knuppel (*kner*-perl) *c* (pl ~s) club ; cudgel
knus (knerss) *adj* cosy
koe (kōō) *c* (pl koeien) cow
koeiehuid (*kōō*ᵉᵉ-er-hurᵉʷt) *c* (pl ~en) cow-hide
koek (kōōk) *c* (pl ~en) cake
koekepan (*kōō*-ker-pahn) *c* (pl ~nen) frying-pan
koekje (kōōk-ʸer) *nt* (pl ~s) biscuit ; cracker *nAm*
koekoek (*kōō*-kōōk) *c* (pl ~en) cuckoo
koel (kōōl) *adj* cool
koelkast (*kōōl*-kahst) *c* (pl ~en) fridge, refrigerator
koelsysteem (*kōōl*-see-stāym) *nt* (pl -temen) cooling system
koeltas (*kōōl*-tahss) *c* (pl ~sen) ice-bag
koepel (*kōō*-perl) *c* (pl ~s) dome
koers (kōōrs) *c* (pl ~en) exchange rate ; course
koets (kōōts) *c* (pl ~en) carriage, coach
koffer (*ko*-ferr) *c* (pl ~s) case, suitcase, bag ; trunk
kofferruimte (*ko*-fer-rurᵉʷm-ter) *c* trunk *nAm*
koffie (*ko*-fee) *c* coffee
kogel (*kōā*-gerl) *c* (pl ~s) bullet
kok (kok) *c* (pl ~s) cook
koken (*kōā*-kern) *v* cook ; boil
kokosnoot (*kōā*-koss-nōāt) *c* (pl -noten) coconut
kolen (*kōā*-lern) *pl* coal
kolom (kōā-*lom*) *c* (pl ~men) column
kolonel (kōā-lōā-*nehl*) *c* (pl ~s) colonel
kolonie (kōā-*lōā*-nee) *c* (pl ~s, -niën) colony
kolonne (kōā-*lo*-ner) *c* (pl ~s) column
kom (kom) *c* (pl ~men) basin

komedie (kōa-*māy*-dee) *c* (pl ~s) comedy
***komen** (*kōā*-mern) *v* *come
komfort (koam-*fōār*) *nt* comfort
komiek (kōā-*meek*) *c* (pl ~en) comedian
komisch (*kōā*-meess) *adj* comic
komkommer (kom-*ko*-merr) *c* (pl ~s) cucumber
komma (*ko*-maa) *c* (pl ~'s) comma
kompas (kom-*pahss*) *nt* (pl ~sen) compass
komplot (kom-*plot*) *nt* (pl ~ten) plot, intrigue
komst (komst) *c* coming ; arrival
konijn (kōā-*nayn*) *nt* (pl ~en) rabbit
koning (*kōā*-nıng) *c* (pl ~en) king
koningin (kōā-nı-*ngın*) *c* (pl ~nen) queen
koninklijk (*kōā*-nıng-klerk) *adj* royal
koninkrijk (*kōā*-nıng-krayk) *nt* (pl ~en) kingdom
kooi (kōāᵉᵉ) *c* (pl ~en) cage ; bunk, berth
kookboek (*kōāk*-bōōk) *nt* (pl ~en) cookery-book ; cookbook *nAm*
kool (kōāl) *c* (pl kolen) cabbage
koop (kōāp) *c* purchase ; **te** ~ for sale
koophandel (*kōāp*-hahn-derl) *c* trade
koopje (*kōāp*-ʸer) *nt* (pl ~s) bargain
koopman (*kōāp*-mahn) *c* (pl kooplieden) dealer, merchant
koopprijs (*kōā*-prayss) *c* (pl -prijzen) purchase price
koopwaar (*kōāp*-vaar) *c* merchandise
koor (kōār) *nt* (pl koren) choir
koord (kōārt) *nt* (pl ~en) cord
koorts (kōārts) *c* fever
koortsig (*kōārt*-serkh) *adj* feverish
kop (kop) *c* (pl ~pen) head ; headline
***kopen** (*kōā*-pern) *v* *buy ; purchase
koper[1] (*kōā*-perr) *nt* brass ; copper
koper[2] (*kōā*-perr) *c* (pl ~s) buyer, purchaser

koperwerk (kōā-perr-vehrk) nt brass-ware

kopie (kōā-*pee*) c (pl ~ën) copy

kopiëren (kōā-pee-*Yāy*-rern) v copy

kopje (*kop-*Yer) nt (pl ~s) cup

koplamp (*kop*-lahmp) c (pl ~en) headlight, headlamp

koppeling (*ko*-per-lıng) c clutch

koppelteken (*ko*-perl-tāy-kern) nt (pl ~s) hyphen

koppig (*ko*-perkh) adj obstinate, headstrong

koraal (kōā-*raal*) c (pl ~ralen) coral

koren (*kōā*-rern) nt corn, grain

korenveld (*kōā*-rer-vehlt) nt (pl ~en) cornfield

korhoen (kor-hōōn) nt (pl ~ders) grouse

korrel (*ko*-rerl) c (pl ~s) corn, grain

korset (kor-*seht*) nt (pl ~ten) corset

korst (korst) c (pl ~en) crust

kort (kort) adj brief, short

korting (*kor*-tıng) c (pl ~en) discount, reduction, rebate

kortsluiting (*kort*-slur^ew-tıng) c short circuit

kortstondig (kort-*ston*-derkh) adj momentary

kosmetica (koss-*māy*-tee-kaa) pl cosmetics pl

kost (kost) c food, fare; livelihood; ~ **en inwoning** room and board, board and lodging, bed and board

kostbaar (*kost*-baar) adj precious, valuable, expensive

kostbaarheden (*kost*-baar-hāy-dern) pl valuables pl

kosteloos (*koss*-ter-lōāss) adj free of charge

kosten (*koss*-tern) v *cost; pl cost, expenditure

koster (*koss*-terr) c (pl ~s) sexton

kostganger (*kost*-khah-ngerr) c (pl ~s) boarder

kostuum (koss-tewm) nt (pl ~s) suit

kotelet (kōā-ter-*leht*) c (pl ~ten) chop

kou (kou) c cold; ~ **vatten** catch a cold

koud (kout) adj cold

kous (kouss) c (pl ~en) stocking

kraag (kraakh) c (pl kragen) collar

kraai (kraa^ee) c (pl ~en) crow

kraakbeen (*kraak*-bāyn) nt cartilage

kraal (kraal) c (pl kralen) bead

kraam (kraam) c (pl kramen) stand, stall; booth

kraan (kraan) c (pl kranen) tap; faucet nAm

krab (krahp) c (pl ~ben) crab

krabben (*krah*-bern) v scratch

kracht (krahkht) c (pl ~en) force, strength; energy, power

krachtig (*krahkh*-terkh) adj strong

kraken (*kraa*-kern) v creak, crack

kralensnoer (*kraa*-ler-snōōr) nt (pl ~en) beads pl

kramp (krahmp) c (pl ~en) cramp; convulsion

krankzinnig (krahngk-*sı*-nerkh) adj insane; lunatic, crazy, mad

krankzinnige (krahngk-*sı*-ner-ger) c (pl ~n) lunatic

krankzinnigheid (krahngk-*sı*-nerkh-hayt) c lunacy

krant (krahnt) c (pl ~en) newspaper, paper

krantenkiosk (*krahn*-ter-kee-Yosk) c (pl ~en) newsstand

krantenverkoper (*krahn*-ter-verr-kōā-perr) c (pl ~s) newsagent

krap (krahp) adj tight

kras (krahss) c (pl ~sen) scratch

krassen (*krah*-sern) v scratch

krat (kraht) nt (pl ~ten) crate

krater (*kraa*-terr) c (pl ~s) crater

krediet (krer-*deet*) nt (pl ~en) credit

kredietbrief (krer-*deet*-breef) c (pl -brieven) letter of credit

kreeft (krayft) c (pl ~en) lobster

kreek (krayk) c (pl kreken) creek

kreet (krayt) c (pl kreten) cry

krekel (kray-kerl) c (pl ~s) cricket

krenken (krehng-kern) v offend, injure

krent (krehnt) c (pl ~en) currant

kreuken (krūr-kern) v crease

kreunen (krūr-nern) v moan, groan

kreupel (krūr-perl) adj lame, crippled

kribbe (kri-ber) c (pl ~n) manger

kriebel (kree-berl) c (pl ~s) itch

* **krijgen** (kray-gern) v *get; receive

krijgsgevangene (kraykhs-kher-vah-nger-ner) c (pl ~n) prisoner of war

krijgsmacht (kraykhs-mahkht) c (pl ~en) military force

krijt (krayt) nt chalk

krik (krik) c (pl ~ken) jack

* **krimpen** (krim-pern) v *shrink

krimpvrij (krimp-vray) adj shrinkproof

kring (kring) c (pl ~en) ring, circle

kringloop (kring-lōap) c (pl -lopen) cycle

kristal (kriss-tahl) nt (pl ~len) crystal

kristallen (kriss-tah-lern) adj crystal

kritiek (kree-teek) adj critical; c criticism

kritisch (kree-teess) adj critical

kroeg (krōokh) c (pl ~en) public house; pub

kroes (krōoss) c (pl kroezen) mug

krokodil (krōa-kōa-dil) c (pl ~len) crocodile

krom (krom) adj crooked; curved, bent

kromming (kro-ming) c (pl ~en) curve, bend

kronen (krōa-nern) v crown

kronkelen (krong-ker-lern) v *wind

kronkelig (krong-ker-lerkh) adj winding

kroon (krōan) c (pl kronen) crown

kruid (krurewt) nt (pl ~en) herb; kruiden spices; v flavour

kruidenier (krurew-der-neer) c (pl ~s) grocer

kruidenierswaren (krurew-der-neers-vaa-rern) pl groceries pl

kruidenierswinkel (krurew-der-neers-ving-kerl) c (pl ~s) grocer's

kruier (krurew-err) c (pl ~s) porter

kruik (krurewk) c (pl ~en) pitcher

kruimel (krurew-merl) c (pl ~s) crumb

* **kruipen** (krurew-pern) v *creep, crawl

kruis (krurewss) nt (pl ~en) cross

kruisbeeld (krurewss-bāylt) nt (pl ~en) crucifix

kruisbes (krurewss-behss) c (pl ~sen) gooseberry

kruisigen (krurew-ser-gern) v crucify

kruisiging (krurew-ser-ging) c (pl ~en) crucifixion

kruising (krurew-sing) c (pl ~en) crossing, junction

kruispunt (krurewss-pernt) nt (pl ~en) crossroads, intersection

kruissnelheid (krurew-snehl-hayt) c cruising speed

kruistocht (krurewss-tokht) c (pl ~en) crusade

kruit (krurewt) nt gunpowder

kruiwagen (krurew-vaa-gern) c (pl ~s) wheelbarrow

kruk (krerk) c (pl ~ken) crutch

krukas (krerk-ahss) c crankshaft

krul (krerl) c (pl ~len) curl

krullen (krer-lern) v curl; krullend curly

krulspeld (krerl-spehlt) c (pl ~en) curler

krultang (krerl-tahng) c (pl ~en) curling-tongs pl

kubus (kew-berss) c (pl ~sen) cube

kudde (ker-der) c (pl ~n, ~s) herd, flock

kuiken (kurew-kern) nt (pl ~s) chicken

kuil (kurewl) c (pl ~en) hole; pit

kuis (kurewss) adj chaste

kuit[1] (kur*ew*t) *c* roe

kuit[2] (kur*ew*t) *c* (pl ~en) calf

kundig (*kern*-derkh) *adj* capable

*kunnen (*ker*-nern) *v* *can, *be able to; *might, *may

kunst (kernst) *c* (pl ~en) art; **schone kunsten** fine arts

kunstacademie (*kernst*-ah-kaa-dāy-mee) *c* (pl ~s) art school

kunstenaar (*kern*-ster-naar) *c* (pl ~s) artist

kunstenares (kern-ster-naa-*rehss*) *c* (pl ~sen) artist

kunstgalerij (*kernst*-khah-ler-ray) *c* (pl ~en) art gallery

kunstgebit (*kernst*-kher-bit) *nt* (pl ~ten) denture, false teeth

kunstgeschiedenis (*kernst*-kher-skhee-der-niss) *c* art history

kunstijsbaan (*kernst*-ayss-baan) *c* (pl -banen) skating-rink

kunstje (*kern*-sher) *nt* (pl ~s) trick

kunstmatig (kernst-*maa*-terkh) *adj* artificial

kunstnijverheid (kernst-*nay*-verr-hayt) *c* arts and crafts

kunsttentoonstelling (kerns-tern-tōän-steh-ling) *c* (pl ~en) art exhibition

kunstverzameling (kernst-ferr-zaa-mer-ling) *c* (pl ~en) art collection

kunstwerk (*kernst*-vehrk) *nt* (pl ~en) work of art

kunstzijde (*kernst*-say-der) *c* rayon

kunstzinnig (kernst-*si*-nerkh) *adj* artistic

kurk (kerrk) *c* (pl ~en) cork

kurketrekker (*kerr*-ker-treh-kerr) *c* (pl ~s) corkscrew

kus (kerss) *c* (pl ~sen) kiss

kussen[1] (*ker*-sern) *v* kiss

kussen[2] (*ker*-sern) *nt* (pl ~s) cushion; pillow; **kussentje** *nt* pad

kussensloop (*ker*-ser-slōap) *c/nt* (pl -slopen) pillow-case

kust (kerst) *c* (pl ~en) coast, shore; seaside, seashore

kuur (kēwr) *c* (pl kuren) cure

kwaad[1] (kvaat) *adj* angry, cross; mad; ill

kwaad[2] (kvaat) *nt* (pl kwaden) evil; mischief, harm

kwaadaardig (kvaa-*daar*-derkh) *adj* malignant

kwaal (kvaal) *c* (pl kwalen) ailment

kwadraat (kvaa-*draat*) *nt* (pl -draten) square

kwakzalver (*kvahk*-sahl-verr) *c* (pl ~s) quack

kwal (kvahl) *c* (pl ~len) jelly-fish

kwalijk *nemen (*kvaa*-lerk *nāy*-mern) resent; **neem me niet kwalijk!** sorry!

kwaliteit (kvaa-lee-*tayt*) *c* (pl ~en) quality

kwart (kvahrt) *nt* (pl ~en) quarter

kwartaal (kvahr-*taal*) *nt* (pl -talen) quarter

kwartel (*kvahr*-terl) *c* (pl ~s) quail

kwartier (kvahr-*teer*) *nt* quarter of an hour

kwast (kvahst) *c* (pl ~en) brush

kweken (*kvāy*-kern) *v* cultivate, *grow

kwellen (*kveh*-lern) *v* torment

kwelling (*kveh*-ling) *c* (pl ~en) torment

kwestie (*kvehss*-tee) *c* (pl ~s) matter, question, issue

kwetsbaar (*kvehts*-baar) *adj* vulnerable

kwetsen (*kveht*-sern) *v* injure; *hurt, wound

kwijtraken (*kvayt*-raa-kern) *v* *lose; *mislay

kwik (kvik) *nt* mercury

kwistig (*kviss*-terkh) *adj* lavish

kwitantie (kvee-*tahn*-see) *c* (pl ~s) receipt

L

la (laa) *c* (pl ~den) drawer

laag[1] (laakh) *adj* low; **lager** *adj* inferior

laag[2] (laakh) *c* (pl lagen) layer

laagland (*laakh*-lahnt) *nt* lowlands *pl*

laan (laan) *c* (pl lanen) avenue

laars (laars) *c* (pl laarzen) boot

laat (laat) *adj* late; **laatst** *adj* last; ultimate, final; *adv* lately; **later** *adv* afterwards; **te** ~ late; overdue

labiel (laa-*beel*) *adj* unstable

laboratorium (laa-bōa-raa-*tōa*-ree-ᵞerm) *nt* (pl -ria) laboratory

lach (lahkh) *c* laugh

***lachen** (*lah*-khern) *v* laugh

ladder (*lah*-derr) *c* (pl ~s) ladder

lade (*laa*-der) *c* (pl ~n) drawer

***laden** (*laa*-dern) *v* load; charge

ladenkast (*laa*-der-kahst) *c* (pl ~en) chest of drawers

lading (*laa*-ding) *c* (pl ~en) charge, load; freight, cargo

laf (lahf) *adj* cowardly

lafaard (*lah*-faart) *c* (pl ~s) coward

lagune (laa-*gēw*-ner) *c* (pl ~s) lagoon

lak (lahk) *c* (pl ~ken) lacquer, varnish

laken (*laa*-kern) *nt* (pl ~s) sheet

lakken (*lah*-kern) *v* varnish

lam[1] (lahm) *adj* lame

lam[2] (lahm) *nt* (pl ~meren) lamb

lambrizering (lahm-bree-*zāy*-ring) *c* panelling

lamp (lahmp) *c* (pl ~en) lamp

lampekap (*lahm*-per-kahp) *c* (pl ~pen) lampshade

lamsvlees (*lahms*-flāyss) *nt* lamb

lanceren (lahn-*sāy*-rern) *v* launch

land (lahnt) *nt* (pl ~en) country, land; **aan** ~ ashore; **aan** ~ ***gaan** land

landbouw (*lahnt*-bou) *c* agriculture; **landbouw-** agrarian

landen (*lahn*-dern) *v* land

landengte (*lahnt*-ehng-ter) *c* (pl ~n, ~s) isthmus

landgenoot (*lahnt*-kher-nōat) *c* (pl -noten) countryman

landgoed (*lahnt*-khōot) *nt* (pl ~eren) estate

landhuis (*lahnt*-hurᵉʷss) *nt* (pl -huizen) country house

landkaart (*lahnt*-kaart) *c* (pl ~en) map

landloper (*lahnt*-lōa-perr) *c* (pl ~s) tramp

landloperij (lahnt-lōa-per-*ray*) *c* vagrancy

landschap (*lahnt*-skhahp) *nt* (pl ~pen) scenery, landscape

landsgrens (*lahnts*-khrehns) *c* (pl -grenzen) boundary

landtong (*lahn*-tong) *c* (pl ~en) headland

lang (lahng) *adj* long; tall

langdurig (lahng-*dēw*-rerkh) *adj* long

langs (lahngs) *prep* along; past

langspeelplaat (*lahng*-spāyl-plaat) *c* (pl -platen) long-playing record

langwerpig (lahng-*vehr*-perkh) *adj* oblong

langzaam (*lahng*-zaam) *adj* slow

langzamerhand (lahng-zaa-merr-*hahnt*) *adv* gradually

lantaarn (lahn-*taa*-rern) *c* (pl ~s) lantern

lantaarnpaal (lahn-*taa*-rerm-paal) *c* (pl -palen) lamp-post

las (lahss) *c* (pl ~sen) joint

lassen (*lah*-sern) *v* weld

last (lahst) *c* (pl ~en) charge; load, burden; trouble, nuisance, bother

laster (*lahss*-terr) *c* slander

lastig (*lahss*-terkh) *adj* troublesome, inconvenient; difficult

***laten** (*laa*-tern) *v* *let; allow to;

*leave; *have

Latijns-Amerika (lah-tayn-zaa-*māy*-ree-kaa) Latin America

Latijns-Amerikaans (lah-tayn-zaa-*māy*-ree-*kaans*) *adj* Latin-American

lauw (lou) *adj* lukewarm, tepid

lawaai (laa-*vaa*ᵉᵉ) *nt* noise

lawaaierig (laa-*vaa*ᵉᵉ-er-rerkh) *adj* noisy

lawine (laa-*vee*-ner) *c* (pl ~s, ~n) avalanche

laxeermiddel (lahk-*sāy*r-mı-derl) *nt* (pl ~en) laxative

ledemaat (*lāy*-der-maat) *c* (pl maten) limb

lederen (*lāy*-der-rern) *adj* leather

ledigen (*lāy*-der-gern) *v* empty

leed (lāyt) *nt* affliction, sorrow

leeftijd (*lāy*f-tayt) *c* (pl ~en) age

leeg (lāykh) *adj* empty

leek (lāyk) *c* (pl leken) layman

leer¹ (lāyr) *c* teachings *pl*

leer² (lāyr) *nt* leather

leerboek (*lāy*r-bōōk) *nt* (pl ~en) textbook

leerling (*lāy*r-lıng) *c* (pl ~en) pupil; scholar

leerzaam (*lāy*r-zaam) *adj* instructive

leesbaar (*lāy*ss-baar) *adj* legible

leeslamp (*lāy*ss-lahmp) *c* (pl ~en) reading-lamp

leeszaal (*lāy*-saal) *c* (pl -zalen) reading-room

leeuw (lāyᵒᵒ) *c* (pl ~en) lion

leeuwerik (*lāy*ᵒᵒ-er-rık) *c* (pl ~en) lark

lef (lehf) *nt* guts

legalisatie (lāy-gaa-lee-*zaa*-tsee) *c* legalization

legatie (ler-*gaa*-tsee) *c* (pl ~s) legation

leger (*lāy*-gerr) *nt* (pl ~s) army

leggen (*leh*-gern) *v* *lay, *put

legpuzzel (*lehkh*-per-zerl) *c* (pl ~s) jig-saw puzzle

lei (lay) *nt* slate

leiden (*lay*-dern) *v* head, direct; guide, *lead, conduct

leider (*lay*-derr) *c* (pl ~s) leader

leiderschap (*lay*-derr-skhahp) *nt* leadership

leiding¹ (*lay*-dıng) *c* lead

leiding² (*lay*-dıng) *c* (pl ~en) pipe

lek¹ (lehk) *adj* leaky; punctured

lek² (lehk) *nt* (pl ~ken) leak

lekken (*leh*-kern) *v* leak

lekker (*leh*-kerr) *adj* good; nice, enjoyable, delicious, tasty

lekkernij (leh-kerr-*nay*) *c* (pl ~en) delicacy

lelie (*lāy*-lee) *c* (pl ~s) lily

lelijk (*lāy*-lerk) *adj* ugly

lemmet (*leh*-mert) *nt* (pl ~en) blade

lenen (*lāy*-nern) *v* *lend; borrow

lengte (*lehng*-ter) *c* (pl ~n, ~s) length; **in de ~** lengthways

lengtegraad (*lehng*-ter-graat) *c* (pl -graden) longitude

lenig (*lāy*-nerkh) *adj* supple

lening (*lāy*-nıng) *c* (pl ~en) loan

lens (lehns) *c* (pl lenzen) lens

lente (*lehn*-ter) *c* (pl ~s) spring

lepel (*lāy*-perl) *c* (pl ~s) spoon; spoonful

lepra (*lāy*-praa) *c* leprosy

leraar (*lāy*-raar) *c* (pl leraren, ~s) master, teacher; instructor

lerares (*lāy*-raa-*rehss*) *c* (pl ~sen) teacher

leren¹ (*lāy*-rern) *v* *teach; *learn

leren² (*lāy*-rern) *adj* leather

les (lehss) *c* (pl ~sen) lesson

leslokaal (*lehss*-lōa-kaal) *nt* (pl -kalen) classroom

lessenaar (*leh*-ser-naar) *c* (pl ~s) desk

letsel (*leht*-serl) *nt* (pl ~s) injury

letten op (*leh*-tern) attend to, *pay attention to; watch, mind

letter (*leh*-terr) *c* (pl ~s) letter

lettergreep (*leh*-terr-grāyp) *c* (pl -grepen) syllable

letterkundig (leh-terr-*kern*-derkh) *adj* literary

leugen (*lūr*-gern) *c* (pl ~s) lie

leuk (lūrk) *adj* enjoyable; funny, jolly

leunen (*lūr*-nern) *v* *lean

leuning (*lūr*-nıng) *c* (pl ~en) arm; rail

leunstoel (*lūrn*-stōōl) *c* (pl ~en) easy chair, armchair

leus (lūrss) *c* (pl leuzen) slogan

leven[1] (*lāy*-vern) *v* live; **levend** alive; live

leven[2] (*lāy*-vern) *nt* (pl ~s) life; lifetime; **in** ~ alive

levendig (*lāy*-vern-derkh) *adj* lively; brisk, vivid

levensmiddelen (*lāy*-verns-mı-der-lern) *pl* foodstuffs *pl*

levensstandaard (*lāy*-vern-stahn-daart) *c* standard of living

levensverzekering (*lāy*-verns-ferr-zāy-ker-rıng) *c* (pl ~en) life insurance

lever (*lāy*-verr) *c* (pl ~s) liver

leveren (*lāy*-ver-rern) *v* furnish, provide, supply

levering (*lāy*-ver-rıng) *c* (pl ~en) delivery, supply

*lezen (*lāy*-zern) *v* *read

lezing (*lāy*-zıng) *c* (pl ~en) lecture

Libanees[1] (lee-baa-*nāy*ss) *adj* Lebanese

Libanees[2] (lee-bah-*nāy*ss) *c* (pl -nezen) Lebanese

Libanon (*lee*-baa-non) Lebanon

liberaal (lee-ber-*raal*) *adj* liberal

Liberia (lee-*bāy*-ree-ʸaa) Liberia

Liberiaan (lee-bāy-ree-ʸaan) *c* (pl -rianen) Liberian

Liberiaans (lee-bāy-ree-ʸaans) *adj* Liberian

licentie (lee-*sehn*-see) *c* (pl ~s) licence

lichaam (*lı*-khaam) *nt* (pl lichamen) body

licht[1] (lıkht) *adj* light; pale; gentle, slight

licht[2] (lıkht) *nt* (pl ~en) light

lichtbruin (*lıkht*-brur^ewn) *adj* fawn

lichtgevend (*lıkht*-kher-vernt) *adj* luminous

lichting (*lıkh*-tıng) *c* (pl ~en) collection

lichtpaars (*lıkht*-paars) *adj* mauve

lid (lıt) *nt* (pl leden) member; associate

lidmaatschap (*lıt*-maat-skhahp) *nt* membership

lidwoord (*lıt*-vōārt) *nt* (pl ~en) article

lied (leet) *nt* (pl ~eren) song

lief (leef) *adj* dear; sweet; affectionate, adorable

liefdadigheid (leef-*daa*-derkh-hayt) *c* charity

liefde (*leef*-der) *c* (pl ~s) love

liefdesgeschiedenis (*leef*-derss-kher-skhee-der-nıss) *c* (pl ~sen) love-story

*liefhebben (*leef*-heh-bern) *v* love

liefhebberij (leef-heh-ber-*ray*) *c* (pl ~en) hobby

liefje (*leef*-ʸer) *nt* (pl ~s) sweetheart

*liegen (*lee*-gern) *v* lie

lies (leess) *c* (pl liezen) groin

lieveling (*lee*-ver-lıng) *c* (pl ~en) darling, sweetheart; favourite, pet; **lievelings**- favourite, pet

liever (*lee*-verr) *adv* sooner, rather; ~ *hebben prefer

lift (lıft) *c* (pl ~en) lift; elevator *nAm*

liften (*lıf*-tern) *v* hitchhike

lifter (*lıf*-terr) *c* (pl ~s) hitchhiker

*liggen (*lı*-gern) *v* *lie; *gaan ~ *lie down

ligging (*lı*-gıng) *c* location; situation, site

ligstoel (*lıkh*-stōōl) *c* (pl ~en) deck chair

lijden (*lay*-dern) *nt* suffering

* **lijden** (*lay*-dern) v suffer

lijf (layf) nt (pl lijven) body

lijfwacht (*layf*-vahkht) c (pl ~en) bodyguard

lijk (layk) nt (pl ~en) corpse

* **lijken** (lay-kern) v seem, appear; look; ~ **op** resemble

lijm (laym) c glue, gum

lijn (layn) c (pl ~en) line; leash

lijnboot (*layn*-bōat) c (pl -boten) liner

lijst (layst) c (pl ~en) list; frame

lijster (*lay*-sterr) c (pl ~s) thrush

lijvig (*lay*-verkh) adj bulky

likdoorn (*lik*-dōa-rern) c (pl ~s) corn

likeur (lee-*kūrr*) c (pl ~en) liqueur

likken (*li*-kern) v lick

limiet (lee-*meet*) c (pl ~en) limit

limoen (lee-*mōon*) c (pl ~en) lime

limonade (lee-mōa-*naa*-der) c (pl ~s) lemonade

linde (*lin*-der) c (pl ~n) limetree, lime

lingerie (lang-zher-*ree*) c lingerie

liniaal (lee-nee-Yaal) c (pl -alen) ruler

links (lingks) adj left; left-hand

linkshandig (lingks-*hahn*-derkh) adj left-handed

linnen (*li*-nern) nt linen

linnengoed (*li*-ner-gōot) nt linen

lint (lint) nt (pl ~en) ribbon; tape

lip (lip) c (pl ~pen) lip

lippenboter (*li*-per-bōa-terr) c lipsalve

lippenstift (*li*-per-stift) c lipstick

list (list) c (pl ~en) ruse, artifice

listig (*liss*-terkh) adj sly

liter (*lee*-terr) c (pl ~s) litre

literair (lee-ter-*rair*) adj literary

literatuur (lee-ter-raa-*tewr*) c literature

lits-jumeaux (lee-zhew-*mōa*) nt twin beds

litteken (*li*-tāy-kern) nt (pl ~s) scar

locomotief (lōa-kōa-mōa-*teef*) c (pl -tieven) engine, locomotive

loeien (*lōoee*-ern) v roar

lof (lof) c glory, praise

logé (lōa-*zhāy*) c (pl ~'s) guest

logeerkamer (lōa-*zhāyr*-kaa-merr) c (pl ~s) spare room, guest-room

logeren (lōa-*zhāy*-rern) v stay

logica (*lōa*-gee-kaa) c logic

logies (lōa-*zheess*) nt lodgings pl, accommodation; ~ **en ontbijt** bed and breakfast

logisch (*lōa*-geess) adj logical

lokaal (lōa-*kaal*) adj local

lol (lol) c fun

lonen (*lōa*-nern) v *pay

long (long) c (pl ~en) lung

longontsteking (*long*-ont-stāy-king) c (pl ~en) pneumonia

lont (lont) c (pl ~en) fuse

lood (lōat) nt lead

loodgieter (*lōat*-khee-terr) c (pl ~s) plumber

loodrecht (*lōat*-rehkht) adj perpendicular

loods (lōats) c (pl ~en) pilot

loon (lōan) nt (pl lonen) wages pl; salary, pay

loonsverhoging (*lōans*-ferr-hōa-ging) c (pl ~en) raise nAm

loop (lōap) c course; gait, walk

loopbaan (*lōa*-baan) c (pl -banen) career

loopplank (*lōa*-plahngk) c (pl ~en) gangway

* **lopen** (*lōa*-pern) v walk; *go

los (loss) adj loose

losgeld (*loass*-khehlt) nt (pl ~en) ransom

losknopen (*loss*-knōa-pern) v unbutton; untie

losmaken (*loss*-maa-kern) v unfasten, *undo, detach; loosen

losschroeven (*lo*-skhrōo-vern) v unscrew

lossen (*lo*-sern) v unload, discharge

lot[1] (lot) nt lot, fortune, destiny, fate

lot[2] (lot) nt (pl ~en) lot

loterij (lōā-ter-*ray*) *c* (pl ~en) lottery
lotion (lōā-*shon*) *c* (pl ~s) lotion
loyaal (lōā-*Yaal*) *adj* loyal
lucht (lerkht) *c* air; breath; sky
luchtdicht (*lerkh*-dɪkht) *adj* airtight
luchtdruk (*lerkh*-drerk) *c* atmospheric pressure
luchten (*lerkh*-tern) *v* air, ventilate
luchtfilter (*lerkht*-fɪl-terr) *nt* (pl ~s) air-filter
luchthaven (*lerkht*-haa-vern) *c* (pl ~s) airport
luchtig (*lerkh*-terkh) *adj* airy
luchtpost (*lerkht*-post) *c* airmail
luchtvaartmaatschappij (*lerkht*-faart-maat-skhah-pay) *c* (pl ~en) airline
luchtverversing (*lerkht*-ferr-vehr-sɪng) *c* air-conditioning, ventilation
luchtziekte (*lerkht*-seek-ter) *c* air-sickness
lucifer (*lēw*-see-fehr) *c* (pl ~s) match
lucifersdoosje (*lēw*-see-fehrs-dōā-sher) *nt* (pl ~s) match-box
lui (lur^ew) *adj* lazy; idle
luid (lur^ewt) *adj* loud
luidspreker (*lur^ew*t-sprāy-kerr) *c* (pl ~s) loud-speaker
luier (*lur^ew*-err) *c* (pl ~s) nappy; diaper *nAm*
luik (lur^ewk) *nt* (pl ~en) hatch; shutter
luis (lur^ewss) *c* (pl luizen) louse
luisteraar (*lur^ew*ss-ter-raar) *c* (pl ~s) listener
luisteren (*lur^ew*ss-ter-rern) *v* listen
luisterrijk (*lur^ew*ss-ter-rayk) *adj* magnificent
lukken (*ler*-kern) *v* succeed
lunch (lernsh) *c* (pl ~es) lunch
lus (lerss) *c* (pl ~sen) loop
lusten (*lerss*-tern) *v* like; fancy
luxe (*lēw*k-ser) *c* luxury
luxueus (lēwk-sēw-*ūrss*) *adj* luxurious

M

maag (maakh) *c* (pl magen) stomach; **maag-** gastric
maagd (maakht) *c* (pl ~en) virgin
maagpijn (*maakh*-payn) *c* stomachache
maagzuur (*maakh*-sēwr) *nt* heartburn
maagzweer (*maakh*-svāyr) *c* (pl -zweren) gastric ulcer
maal¹ (maal) *nt* (pl malen) meal
maal² (maal) *c* (pl malen) time
maal³ (maal) *prep* times
maaltijd (*maal*-tayt) *c* (pl ~en) meal; **warme ~** dinner
maan (maan) *c* (pl manen) moon
maand (maant) *c* (pl ~en) month
maandag (*maan*-dahkh) *c* Monday
maandblad (*maant*-blaht) *nt* (pl ~en) monthly magazine
maandelijks (*maan*-der-lerks) *adj* monthly
maandverband (*maant*-ferr-bahnt) *nt* sanitary towel
maanlicht (*maan*-lɪkht) *nt* moonlight
maar (maar) *conj* but; yet; *adv* only
maart (maart) March
maas (maass) *c* (pl mazen) mesh
maat (maat) *c* (pl maten) size, measure; **extra grote ~** outsize; **op ~ gemaakt** tailor-made; made to order
maatregel (*maat*-rāy-gerl) *c* (pl ~en, ~s) measure
maatschappelijk (maat-*skhah*-per-lerk) *adj* social
maatschappij (maat-skhah-*pay*) *c* (pl ~en) company; society
maatstaf (*maat*-stahf) *c* (pl -staven) standard
machine (mah-*shee*-ner) *c* (pl ~s) engine, machine

machinerie (mah-shee-ner-*ree*) *c* machinery

macht (mahkht) *c* (pl ~en) power; force, might; authority

machteloos (*mahkh*-ter-lōass) *adj* powerless

machtig (*mahkh*-terkh) *adj* powerful, mighty

machtiging (*mahkh*-ter-gɪng) *c* (pl ~en) authorization

magazijn (maa-gaa-*zayn*) *nt* (pl ~en) store-house, warehouse

mager (*maa*-gerr) *adj* lean, thin

magie (maa-*gee*) *c* magic

magistraat (maa-gɪss-*traat*) *c* (pl -straten) magistrate

magneet (mahkh-*nāyt*) *c* (pl -neten) magneto

magnetisch (mahkh-*nāy*-teess) *adj* magnetic

maillot (maa-*Yōā*) *c* (pl ~s) tights *pl*

maïs (mighss) *c* maize

maïskolf (*mighss*-kolf) *c* (pl -kolven) corn on the cob

maître d'hôtel (mai-trer-dōā-*tehl*) head-waiter

maîtresse (meh-*tray*-ser) *c* (pl ~s, ~n) mistress

majoor (maa-*Yōār*) *c* (pl ~s) major

mak (mahk) *adj* tame

makelaar (*maa*-ker-laar) *c* (pl ~s) broker, house agent

maken (*maa*-kern) *v* *make; **te ~** *hebben met *deal with

makreel (maa-*krāyl*) *c* (pl -relen) mackerel

mal (mahl) *adj* foolish, silly

malaria (maa-*laa*-ree-Yaa) *c* malaria

Maleis (maa-*layss*) *nt* Malay

Maleisië (maa-*lay*-zee-Yer) Malaysia

Maleisisch (maa-*lay*-zeess) *adj* Malaysian

*malen (*maa*-lern) *v* *grind

mals (mahls) *adj* tender

mammoet (*mah*-mōōt) *c* (pl ~en, ~s) mammoth

man (mahn) *c* (pl ~nen) man; husband

manchet (mahn-*sheht*) *c* (pl ~ten) cuff

manchetknopen (mahn-*sheht*-knōā-pern) *pl* cuff-links *pl*

mand (mahnt) *c* (pl ~en) hamper, basket

mandaat (mahn-*daat*) *nt* (pl -daten) mandate

mandarijn (mahn-daa-*rayn*) *c* (pl ~en) mandarin, tangerine

manege (maa-*nāy*-zher) *c* (pl ~s) riding-school

manicure (maa-nee-*kēw*-rer) *c* (pl ~s) manicure

manicuren (maa-nee-*kēw*-rern) *v* manicure

manier (maa-*neer*) *c* (pl ~en) manner; way, fashion

mank (mahngk) *adj* lame

mannelijk (*mah*-ner-lerk) *adj* male; masculine

mannequin (mah-ner-*kang*) *c* (pl ~s) model, mannequin

mantel (*mahn*-terl) *c* (pl ~s) coat, cloak

manufacturier (mah-nēw-fahk-tēw-*reer*) *c* (pl ~s) draper

manuscript (maa-nerss-*krɪpt*) *nt* (pl ~en) manuscript

marcheren (mahr-*shāy*-rern) *v* march

margarine (mahr-gaa-*ree*-ner) *c* margarine

marge (*mahr*-zher) *c* (pl ~s) margin

marine (maa-*ree*-ner) *c* navy; **marine**-naval

maritiem (mah-ree-*teem*) *adj* maritime

markt (mahrkt) *c* (pl ~en) market; **zwarte ~** black market

marktplein (*mahrkt*-playn) *nt* (pl ~en) market-place

marmelade (mahr-mer-*laa*-der) *c* (pl ~s, ~n) marmalade

marmer (*mahr*-merr) *nt* marble

Marokkaan (mah-ro-*kaan*) *c* (pl -kanen) Moroccan

Marokkaans (mah-ro-*kaans*) *adj* Moroccan

Marokko (maa-*ro*-kōa) Morocco

mars (mahrs) *c* (pl ~en) march

martelaar (*mahr*-ter-laar) *c* (pl ~s, -laren) martyr

martelen (*mahr*-ter-lern) *v* torture

marteling (*mahr*-ter-lıng) *c* (pl ~en) torture

mascara (mahss-*kaa*-raa) *c* mascara

masker (*mahss*-kerr) *nt* (pl ~s) mask

massa (*mah*-saa) *c* (pl ~'s) bulk, mass; crowd

massage (mah-*saa*-zher) *c* (pl ~s) massage

massaproduktie (*mah*-saa-prōa-derk-see) *c* mass production

masseren (mah-*sāy*-rern) *v* massage

masseur (mah-*sūrr*) *c* (pl ~s) masseur

massief (mah-*seef*) *adj* solid, massive

mast (mahst) *c* (pl ~en) mast

mat[1] (maht) *adj* dull, mat, dim

mat[2] (maht) *c* (pl ~ten) mat

materiaal (maa-tree-*ᵞaal*) *nt* (pl -rialen) material

materie (mah-*tāy*-ree) *c* (pl -riën, ~s) matter

materieel (maa-tree-*ᵞāyl*) *adj* material

matig (*maa*-terkh) *adj* moderate

matras (maa-*trahss*) *c* (pl ~sen) mattress

matroos (maa-*trōass*) *c* (pl matrozen) sailor

mausoleum (mou-sōa-*lāy*-ᵞerm) *nt* (pl ~s, -lea) mausoleum

mazelen (*maa*-zer-lern) *pl* measles

me (mer) *pron* me; myself

mechanisch (māy-*khaa*-neess) *adj* mechanical

mechanisme (māy-khaa-*nıss*-mer) *nt* (pl ~n) mechanism; machinery

medaille (māy-*dah*-ᵞer) *c* (pl ~s) medal

mededelen (*māy*-der-dāy-lern) *v* notify, communicate, inform

mededeling (*māy*-der-dāy-lıng) *c* (pl ~en) communication, information

medegevoel (*māy*-der-ger-vōol) *nt* sympathy

medelijden (*māy*-der-lay-dern) *nt* pity; ~ *hebben met pity

medeplichtige (māy-der-*plıkh*-ter-ger) *c* (pl ~n) accessary

medewerking (*māy*-der-vehr-kıng) *c* co-operation

medisch (*māy*-deess) *adj* medical

mediteren (māy-dee-*tāy*-rern) *v* meditate

meebrengen (*māy*-breh-ngern) *v* *bring

meedelen (*māy*-dāy-lern) *v* communicate

meel (māyl) *nt* flour

meemaken (*māy*-maa-kern) *v* *go through

meenemen (*māy*-nāy-mern) *v* *take away

meer[1] (māyr) *adj* more; ~ *dan* over; **niet** ~ no longer

meer[2] (māyr) *nt* (pl meren) lake

meerderheid (*māyr*-derr-hayt) *c* majority; bulk

meerderjarig (māyr-derr-*ᵞaa*-rerkh) *adj* of age

meervoud (*māyr*-vout) *nt* (pl ~en) plural

meest (māyst) *adj* most

meestal (māy-*stahl*) *adv* mostly

meester (*māy*-sterr) *c* (pl ~s) master; schoolmaster, teacher

meesteres (māy-ster-*rehss*) *c* (pl ~sen) mistress

meesterwerk (*māy*-sterr-vehrk) *nt* (pl

~en) masterpiece

meetellen (*māy*-teh-lern) *v* count

meetkunde (*māyt*-kern-der) *c* geometry

meeuw (māy⁰⁰) *c* (pl ~en) gull; seagull

mei (may) May

meid (mayt) *c* (pl ~en) housemaid, maid

meineed (*may*-nāyt) *c* (pl -eden) perjury

meisje (*may*-sher) *nt* (pl ~s) girl

meisjesnaam (*may*-sherss-naam) *c* (pl -namen) maiden name

mejuffrouw (mer-ʸer-frou) *c* miss

melden (*mehl*-dern) *v* report

melding (*mehl*-dıng) *c* (pl ~en) mention

melk (mehlk) *c* milk

melkboer (*mehlk*-bōōr) *c* (pl ~en) milkman

melodie (māy-lōā-*dee*) *c* (pl ~ën) melody; tune

melodieus (māy-lōā-dee-ʸūrss) *adj* tuneful

melodrama (māy-lōā-*draa*-maa) *nt* (pl ~'s) melodrama

meloen (mer-*lōōn*) *c* (pl ~en) melon

memorandum (māy-mōā-*rahn*-derm) *nt* (pl -randa) memo

men (mehn) *pron* one

meneer (mer-*nāyr*) mister; sir

menen (*māy*-nern) *v* consider; *mean

mengen (*meh*-ngern) *v* mix

mengsel (*mehng*-serl) *nt* (pl ~s) mixture

menigte (*māy*-nerkh-ter) *c* (pl ~n, ~s) crowd

mening (*māy*-nıng) *c* (pl ~en) opinion; view; **van ~ verschillen** disagree

mens (mehns) *c* (pl ~en) man; **mensen** people *pl*

menselijk (*mehn*-ser-lerk) *adj* human;

~ **wezen** human being

mensheid (*mehns*-hayt) *c* humanity, mankind

menstruatie (mehn-strew-*vaa*-tsee) *c* menstruation

menukaart (mer-*new*-kaart) *c* (pl ~en) menu

merel (*māy*-rerl) *c* (pl ~s) blackbird

merg (mehrkh) *nt* marrow

merk (mehrk) *nt* (pl ~en) brand

merkbaar (*mehrk*-baar) *adj* noticeable, perceptible

merken (*mehr*-kern) *v* notice; mark

merkteken (*mehrk*-tāy-kern) *nt* (pl ~s) mark

merrie (*meh*-ree) *c* (pl ~s) mare

mes (mehss) *nt* (pl ~sen) knife

messing (*meh*-sıng) *nt* brass

mest (mehst) *c* dung, manure

mesthoop (*mehst*-hōāp) *c* (pl -hopen) dunghill

met (meht) *prep* with; by

metaal (māy-*taal*) *nt* (pl metalen) metal

metalen (māy-*taa*-lern) *adj* metal

meteen (mer-*tāyn*) *adv* at once, straight away, immediately, instantly; presently

*(**meten** (*māy*-tern) *v* measure

meter (*māy*-terr) *c* (pl ~s) metre; meter; gauge

metgezel (*meht*-kher-zehl) *c* (pl ~len) companion

methode (māy-*tōā*-der) *c* (pl ~n, ~s) method

methodisch (māy-*tōā*-deess) *adj* methodical

metrisch (*māy*-treess) *adj* metric

metro (*māy*-trōā) *c* (pl ~'s) underground

metselaar (*meht*-ser-laar) *c* (pl ~s) bricklayer

metselen (*meht*-ser-lern) *v* *lay bricks

meubilair (mūr-bee-*lair*) *nt* furniture

meubileren (mūr-bee-láy-rern) v furnish

mevrouw (mer-vrou) madam

Mexicaan (mehk-see-kaan) c (pl -canen) Mexican

Mexicaans (mehk-see-kaans) adj Mexican

Mexico (mehk-see-kōā) Mexico

microfoon (mee-krōā-fōān) c (pl ~s) microphone

middag (mi-dahkh) c (pl ~en) afternoon; midday; noon

middageten (mi-dahkh-ay-tern) nt luncheon, lunch; dinner

middel¹ (mi-derl) nt (pl ~en) means; remedy; **antiseptisch** ~ antiseptic; **insektenwerend** ~ insect repellent; **kalmerend** ~ tranquillizer, sedative; **pijnstillend** ~ anaesthetic; **stimulerend** ~ stimulant; **verdovend** ~ drug

middel² (mi-derl) nt (pl ~s) waist

middeleeuwen (mi-derl-ay°°-ern) pl Middle Ages

middeleeuws (mi-derl-ay°°ss) adj mediaeval

Middellandse Zee (mi-der-lahnt-ser-zāy) Mediterranean

middelmatig (mi-derl-maa-terkh) adj moderate, medium

middelpunt (mi-derl-pernt) nt (pl - en) centre

middelst (mi-derlst) adj middle

midden (mi-dern) nt midst, middle; **midden-** medium; ~ **in** amid; **te** ~ **van** amid; among

middernacht (mi-derr-nahkht) c midnight

midzomer (mit-sōā-merr) c midsummer

mier (meer) c (pl ~en) ant

mierikswortel (mee-riks-vor-terl) c (pl ~s) horseradish

migraine (mee-grai-ner) c migraine

mijl (mayl) c (pl ~en) mile

mijlpaal (mayl-paal) c (pl -palen) milestone; landmark

mijn¹ (mayn) pron my

mijn² (mayn) c (pl ~en) mine

mijnbouw (mayn-bou) c mining

mijnheer (mer-nāyr) c mister

mijnwerker (mayn-vehr-kerr) c (pl ~s) miner

mikken op (mi-kern) aim at

mikpunt (mik-pernt) nt (pl ~en) target

mild (milt) adj liberal

milieu (meel-Yúr) nt (pl ~s) milieu; environment

militair¹ (mee-lee-tair) adj military

militair² (mee-lee-tair) c (pl ~en) soldier

miljoen (mil-Yōōn) nt million

miljonair (mil-Yōā-nair) c (pl ~s) millionaire

min (min) prep minus

minachting (min-ahkh-ting) c contempt

minder (min-derr) adv less

minderheid (min-derr-hayt) c (pl -heden) minority

minderjarig (min-derr-Yaa-rerkh) adj under age

minderjarige (min-derr-Yaa-rer-ger) c (pl ~n) minor

minderwaardig (min-derr-vaar-derkh) adj inferior

mineraal (mee-ner-raal) nt (pl -ralen) mineral

mineraalwater (mee-ner-raal-vaa-terr) nt mineral water

miniatuur (mee-nee-Yaa-tewr) c (pl -turen) miniature

minimum (mee-nee-merm) nt (pl -ma) minimum

minister (mee-niss-terr) c (pl ~s) minister

ministerie (mee-niss-tāy-ree) nt (pl

~s) ministry

minnaar (*mı*-naar) *c* (pl ~s) lover

minst (mınst) *adj* least

minstens (*mın*-sterns) *adv* at least

minuscuul (mee-nerss-*kēwl*) *adj* tiny, minute

minuut (mee-*nēwt*) *c* (pl minuten) minute

mis (mıss) *c* (pl ~sen) Mass

misbruik (*mıss*-brur^ewk) *nt* misuse, abuse

misdaad (*mıss*-daat) *c* (pl -daden) crime

misdadig (mıss-*daa*-derkh) *adj* criminal

misdadiger (mıss-*daa*-der-gerr) *c* (pl ~s) criminal

zich ***misdragen** (mıss-*draa*-gern) misbehave

misgunnen (mıss-*kher*-nern) *v* grudge

mishagen (mıss-*haa*-gern) *v* displease

miskraam (*mıss*-kraam) *c* (pl -kramen) miscarriage

mislukking (mıss-*ler*-kıng) *c* (pl ~en) failure

mislukt (mıss-*lerkt*) *adj* unsuccessful

mismaakt (mıss-*maakt*) *adj* deformed

misplaatst (mıss-*plaatst*) *adj* misplaced

misschien (mı-*skheen*) *adv* perhaps; maybe

misselijk (*mı*-ser-lerk) *adj* sick; disgusting

misselijkheid (*mı*-ser-lerk-hayt) *c* nausea, sickness

missen (*mı*-sern) *v* lack; miss; spare

misstap (*mı*-stahp) *c* (pl ~pen) slip

mist (mıst) *c* fog, mist

mistig (*mıss*-terkh) *adj* foggy, misty

mistlamp (*mıst*-lahmp) *c* (pl ~en) foglamp

***misverstaan** (*mıss*-ferr-staan) *v* *misunderstand

misverstand (*mıss*-ferr-stahnt) *nt* (pl

~en) misunderstanding

misvormd (mıss-*formt*) *adj* deformed

mits (mıts) *conj* provided that

mobiel (mōā-*beel*) *adj* mobile

modder (*mo*-derr) *c* mud

modderig (*mo*-der-rerkh) *adj* muddy

mode (*mōā*-der) *c* (pl ~s) fashion

model (mōā-*dehl*) *nt* (pl ~len) model

modelleren (mōā-deh-*lāy*-rern) *v* model

modern (mōā-*dehrn*) *adj* modern

modieus (mōā-dee-*Yūrss*) *adj* fashionable

modiste (mōā-*dıss*-ter) *c* (pl ~s) milliner

moe (mōō) *adj* tired; weary

moed (mōōt) *c* courage

moeder (*mōō*-derr) *c* (pl ~s) mother

moedertaal (*mōō*-derr-taal) *c* native language, mother tongue

moedig (*mōō*-derkh) *adj* brave, courageous

moeilijk (*mōō^ee*-lerk) *adj* difficult; hard

moeilijkheid (*mōō^ee*-lerk-hayt) *c* (pl -heden) difficulty

moeite (*mōō^ee*-ter) *c* (pl ~n) trouble; pains, difficulty; **de ~ waard** ***zijn** *be worth-while; **~** ***doen** bother

moer (mōōr) *c* (pl ~en) nut

moeras (mōō-*rahss*) *nt* (pl ~sen) swamp; bog, marsh

moerassig (mōō-*rah*-serkh) *adj* marshy

moerbei (*mōōr*-bay) *c* (pl ~en) mulberry

moestuin (*mōōss*-tur^ewn) *c* (pl ~en) kitchen garden

***moeten** (*mōō*-tern) *v* *must; *have to; need to, *ought to, *be obliged to, *should

mogelijk (*mōā*-ger-lerk) *adj* possible

mogelijkheid (*mōā*-ger-lerk-hayt) *c* (pl -heden) possibility

***mogen** (*mōā*-gern) *v* *be allowed;

*may; like

mogendheid (*mōa*-gernt-hayt) *c* (pl -heden) power

mohair (*mōa-hair*) *nt* mohair

molen (*mōa*-lern) *c* (pl ~s) mill; windmill

molenaar (*mōa*-ler-naar) *c* (pl ~s) miller

mollig (*mo*-lerkh) *adj* plump

moment (*mōa-mehnt*) *nt* (pl ~en) moment

momentopname (*mōa-mehnt*-op-naa-mer) *c* (pl ~n) snapshot

monarchie (*mōa*-nahr-*khee*) *c* (pl ~ën) monarchy

mond (mont) *c* (pl ~en) mouth

mondeling (*mon*-der-lıng) *adj* oral, verbal

monding (*mon*-dıng) *c* (pl ~en) mouth

mondspoeling (mont-spōō-lıng) *c* mouthwash

monetair (mōa-nāy-*tair*) *adj* monetary

monnik (*mo*-nerk) *c* (pl ~en) monk

monoloog (mōa-nōa-*lōakh*) *c* (pl -logen) monologue

monopolie (mōa-nōa-*pōa*-lee) *nt* (pl ~s) monopoly

monster (*mon*-sterr) *nt* (pl ~s) sample

monteren (mon-*tāy*-rern) *v* assemble

monteur (mon-*tūrr*) *c* (pl ~s) mechanic

montuur (mon-*tewr*) *nt* (pl -turen) frame

monument (mōa-new-*mehnt*) *nt* (pl ~en) monument

mooi (mōa^ee) *adj* beautiful; pretty, fine; nice, lovely, fair

moord (mōart) *c* (pl ~en) assassination, murder

moordenaar (*mōar*-der-naar) *c* (pl ~s) murderer

mop (mop) *c* (pl ~pen) joke

mopperen (*mo*-per-rern) *v* grumble

moraal (mōa-*raal*) *c* moral

moraliteit (mōa-raa-lee-*tayt*) *c* morality

moreel (mōa-*rāyl*) *adj* moral

morfine (mor-*fee*-ner) *c* morphine, morphia

morgen¹ (*mor*-gern) *adv* tomorrow

morgen² (*mor*-gern) *c* (pl ~s) morning

morsen (*mor*-sern) *v* *spill

mos (moss) *nt* (pl ~sen) moss

moskee (moss-*kāy*) *c* (pl ~ën) mosque

mossel (*mo*-serl) *c* (pl ~s, ~en) mussel

mosterd (*moss*-terrt) *c* mustard

mot (mot) *c* (pl ~ten) moth

motel (mōa-*tehl*) *nt* (pl ~s) motel

motie (*mōa*-tsee) *c* (pl ~s) motion

motief (mōa-*teef*) *nt* (pl motieven) motive; pattern

motor (*mōa*-terr) *c* (pl ~en, ~s) engine, motor

motorboot (*mōa*-terr-bōat) *c* (pl -boten) motor-boat

motorfiets (*mōa*-terr-feets) *c* (pl ~en) motor-cycle

motorkap (*mōa*-terr-kahp) *c* (pl ~pen) bonnet; hood *nAm*

motorpech (*mōa*-terr-pehkh) *c* breakdown

motorschip (*mōa*-terr-skhıp) *nt* (pl -schepen) launch

motregen (*mot*-rāy-gern) *c* drizzle

mousseline (mōo-ser-*lee*-ner) *c* muslin

mousserend (mōo-*sāy*-rernt) *adj* sparkling

mouw (mou) *c* (pl ~en) sleeve

mozaïek (mōa-zaa-*eek*) *nt* (pl ~en) mosaic

mug (merkh) *c* (pl ~gen) mosquito

muil (mur^ewl) *c* (pl ~en) mouth

muildier (*mur^ewl*-deer) *nt* (pl ~en) mule

muilezel (*mur^ewl*-ā̄y-zerl) *c* (pl ~s) mule

muis (mur^ewss) *c* (pl muizen) mouse

muiterij (mur^ew-ter-*ray*) *c* (pl ~en) mutiny

mul (merl) *c* mullet

munt (mernt) *c* (pl ~en) coin; token; mint

munteenheid (mernt-ā̄yn-hayt) *c* (pl -heden) monetary unit

muntstuk (*mernt*-sterk) *nt* (pl ~ken) coin

mus (merss) *c* (pl ~sen) sparrow

museum (mew-*zā̄y*-Yerm) *nt* (pl ~s, -sea) museum

musical (*m^Yōō*-zi-kerl) *c* (pl ~s) musical comedy, musical

musicus (*mew*-zee-kerss) *c* (pl -ci) musician

muskiet (merss-*keet*) *c* (pl ~en) mosquito

muskietennet (merss-*kee*-ter-neht) *nt* (pl ~ten) mosquito-net

muts (merts) *c* (pl ~en) cap

muur (mēw̄r) *c* (pl muren) wall

muziek (mew-*zeek*) *c* music

muziekinstrument (mew-*zeek*-ın-strēw̄-mehnt) *nt* (pl ~en) musical instrument

muzikaal (mēw-zee-*kaal*) *adj* musical

mysterie (mee-*stā̄y*-ree) *nt* (pl ~s) mystery

mysterieus (mee-stā̄y-ree-*Yūrss*) *adj* mysterious

mythe (*mee*-ter) *c* (pl ~n) myth

N

na (naa) *prep* after

naad (naat) *c* (pl naden) seam

naadloos (*naat*-lōass) *adj* seamless

naaien (*naa^ee*-ern) *v* sew

naaimachine (*naa^ee*-mah-shee-ner) *c* (pl ~s) sewing-machine

naaister (*naa^ee*-sterr) *c* (pl ~s) dressmaker

naakt (naakt) *adj* nude, naked, bare

naaktstrand (*naakt*-strahnt) *nt* (pl ~en) nudist beach

naald (naalt) *c* (pl ~en) needle

naam (naam) *c* (pl namen) name; reputation; denomination; **in ~ van** on behalf of

naar[1] (naar) *prep* to, towards; at, for

naar[2] (naar) *adj* nasty, unpleasant

naast (naast) *prep* next to, beside

nabij (naa-*bay*) *adj* near, close

nabijheid (naa-*bay*-hayt) *c* vicinity

nabijzijnd (naa-*bay*-zaynt) *adj* nearby

nabootsen (*naa*-bōat-sern) *v* imitate

naburig (naa-*bōō*-rerkh) *adj* neighbouring

nacht (nahkht) *c* (pl ~en) night; **'s nachts** by night; overnight

nachtclub (*nahkht*-klerp) *c* (pl ~s) nightclub, cabaret

nachtcrème (*nahkht*-kraim) *c* (pl ~s) night-cream

nachtegaal (*nahkh*-ter-gaal) *c* (pl -galen) nightingale

nachtelijk (*nahkh*-ter-lerk) *adj* nightly

nachtjapon (*nahkht*-Yaa-pon) *c* (pl ~nen) nightdress

nachttarief (*nahkht*-taa-reef) *nt* (pl -rieven) night rate

nachttrein (*nahkht*-trayn) *c* (pl ~en) night train

nachtvlucht (*nahkht*-flerkht) *c* (pl ~en) night flight

nadat (naa-*daht*) *conj* after

nadeel (naa-*dā̄yl*) *nt* (pl -delen) disadvantage

nadelig (naa-*dā̄y*-lerkh) *adj* harmful

***nadenken** (naa-*dehng*-kern) *v* *think; **nadenkend** thoughtful

nader (naa-derr) *adj* further

naderen (naa-der-rern) v approach;
naderend oncoming

naderhand (naa-derr-*hahnt*) adv afterwards

nadien (naa-*deen*) adv afterwards

nadruk (*naa*-drerk) c stress; accent

nagedachtenis (naa-ger-dahkh-ter-nıss) c memory

nagel (*naa*-gerl) c (pl ~s) nail

nagelborstel (*naa*-gerl-bors-terl) c (pl ~s) nailbrush

nagellak (*naa*-ger-lahk) c nail-polish

nagelschaar (*naa*-gerl-skhaar) c (pl -scharen) nail-scissors pl

nagelvijl (*naa*-gerl-vayl) c (pl ~en) nail-file

naïef (naa-*eef*) adj naïve

najaar (*naa*-Yaar) nt autumn

* **najagen** (*naa*-Yaa-gern) v chase

* **nakijken** (*naa*-kay-kern) v check

* **nalaten** (*naa*-laa-tern) v fail

nalatig (naa-*laa*-terkh) adj neglectful

namaak (*naa*-maak) c imitation

namaken (*naa*-maa-kern) v copy

namelijk (*naa*-mer-lerk) adv namely

namens (*naa*-merns) adv on behalf of, in the name of

namiddag (naa-*mı*-dahkh) c (pl ~en) afternoon

narcis (nahr-*sıss*) c (pl ~sen) daffodil

narcose (nahr-*kōā*-zer) c narcosis

narcoticum (nahr-*kōā*-tee-kerm) nt (pl -ca) narcotic

narigheid (*naa*-rerkh-hayt) c (pl -heden) misery

naseizoen (*naa*-say-zōōn) nt low season

nastreven (naa-strāy-vern) v aim at, pursue

nat (naht) adj wet; damp, moist

natie (*naa*-tsee) c (pl ~s) nation

nationaal (naa-tshōā-*naal*) adj national; **nationale klederdracht** national dress

nationaliseren (naa-tshōā-naa-lee-*zāy*-rern) v nationalize

nationaliteit (naa-tshōā-naa-lee-*tayt*) c (pl ~en) nationality

natuur (naa-*tewr*) c nature

natuurkunde (naa-*tewr*-kern-der) c physics

natuurkundige (naa-tewr-*kern*-der-ger) c (pl ~n) physicist

natuurlijk (naa-*tewr*-lerk) adj natural; adv of course, naturally

natuurreservaat (naa-*tew*-rāy-zerr-vaat) nt (pl -vaten) national park

nauw (nou) adj narrow; tight

nauwelijks (*nou*-er-lerks) adv hardly; scarcely, barely

nauwkeurig (nou-*kūr*-rerkh) adj accurate; precise, careful, exact

navel (*naa*-verl) c (pl ~s) navel

navigatie (naa-vee-*gaa*-tsee) c navigation

navraag (*naa*-vraakh) c inquiry; demand

* **navragen** (*naa*-vraa-gern) v query, inquire

* **nazenden** (*naa*-zehn-dern) v forward

nederig (*nāy*-der-rerkh) adj humble

nederlaag (*nāy*-derr-laakh) c (pl -lagen) defeat

Nederland (*nāy* derr lahnt) the Netherlands

Nederlander (*nāy*-derr-lahn-derr) c (pl ~s) Dutchman

Nederlands (*nāy*-derr-lahnts) adj Dutch

nee (nāy) no

neef (nāyf) c (pl neven) cousin; nephew

neen (nāyn) no

neer (nāyr) adv down; downwards

* **neerlaten** (*nāyr*-laa-tern) v lower

* **neerslaan** (*nāyr*-slaan) v knock down

neerslachtig (nāyr-*slahkh*-terkh) adj

down, low, blue, depressed

neerslachtigheid (nāyr-*slahkh*-terkh-hayt) *c* depression

neerslag (nāyr-slahkh) *c* precipitation

neerstorten (nāyr-stor-tern) *v* crash

negatief (nāy-gaa-*teef*) *adj* negative

negen (nāy-gern) *num* nine

negende (nāy-gern-der) *num* ninth

negentien (nāy-gern-teen) *num* nineteen

negentiende (nāy-gern-teen-der) *num* nineteenth

negentig (nāy-gern-terkh) *num* ninety

neger (nāy-gerr) *c* (pl ~s) Negro

negeren (ner-*gāy*-rern) *v* ignore

negligé (nāy-glee-*zhāy*) *nt* (pl ~s) negligee

neigen (nay-gern) *v* *be inclined to; ~ tot *v* tend to

neiging (nay-gɪng) *c* (pl ~en) inclination, tendency; **de ~** *hebben tend

nek (nehk) *c* (pl ~ken) nape of the neck

*nemen (nāy-mern) *v* *take; **op zich ~** *take charge of

neon (nāy-ᵞon) *nt* neon

nergens (nehr-gerns) *adv* nowhere

nerts (nehrts) *nt* (pl ~en) mink

nerveus (nehr-*vūrss*) *adj* nervous

nest (nehst) *nt* (pl ~en) nest; litter

net¹ (neht) *adj* tidy, neat

net² (neht) *nt* (pl ~ten) net

netnummer (*neht*-ner-merr) *nt* (pl ~s) area code

netto (*neh*-tōa) *adj* net

netvlies (*neht*-fleess) *nt* (pl -vliezen) retina

netwerk (*neht*-vehrk) *nt* (pl ~en) network

neuriën (nūr-ree-ᵞern) *v* hum

neurose (nūr-*rōa*-zer) *c* (pl ~n, ~s) neurosis

neus (nūrss) *c* (pl neuzen) nose

neusbloeding (nūrss-blōō-dɪng) *c* (pl ~en) nosebleed

neusgat (*nūrss*-khaht) *nt* (pl ~en) nostril

neushoorn (*nūrss*-hōarn) *c* (pl ~s) rhinoceros

neutraal (nūr-*traal*) *adj* neutral

nevel (nāy-verl) *c* (pl ~s, ~en) haze, mist

nicht (nɪkht) *c* (pl ~en) cousin; niece

nicotine (nee-kōa-*tee*-ner) *c* nicotine

niemand (*nee*-mahnt) *pron* nobody, no one

nier (neer) *c* (pl ~en) kidney

niet (neet) *adv* not

nietig (*nee*-terkh) *adj* petty, insignificant; void

nietje (*nee*-tᵞer) *nt* (pl ~s) staple

niets (neets) *pron* nothing; nil

nietsbetekenend (neets-ber-*tāy*-ker-nernt) *adj* insignificant

nietszeggend (neet-*seh*-gernt) *adj* meaningless

niettemin (nee-ter-*mɪn*) *adv* nevertheless

nieuw (nee°°) *adj* new

nieuwjaar (nee°°-ᵞaar) New Year

nieuws (nee°°ss) *nt* news; tidings *pl*

nieuwsberichten (nee°°ss-ber-rɪkh-tern) *pl* news

nieuwsgierig (nee°°-*skhee*-rerkh) *adj* curious, inquisitive

nieuwsgierigheid (nee°°-*skhee*-rerkh-hayt) *c* curiosity

Nieuw-Zeeland (nee°°-*zāy*-lahnt) New Zealand

niezen (*nee*-zern) *v* sneeze

Nigeria (nee-*gāy*-ree-ᵞaa) Nigeria

Nigeriaan (nee-gāy-ree-ᵞaan) *c* (pl -rianen) Nigerian

Nigeriaans (nee-gāy-ree-ᵞaans) *adj* Nigerian

nijptang (*nayp*-tahng) *c* (pl ~en) pincers *pl*

nikkel (*nɪ*-kerl) *nt* nickel

niks (nıks) *pron* nothing

nimmer (*nı*-merr) *adv* never

niveau (nee-*vōa*) *nt* (pl ~s) level

nivelleren (nee-ver-*lāy*-rern) *v* level

noch ... noch (nokh) neither ... nor

nodig (*nōa*-derkh) *adj* necessary; ~ ***hebben** need

noemen (*nōo*-mern) *v* call; name, mention

nog (nokh) *adv* still, yet; ~ **een** another; ~ **eens** once more; ~ **wat** some more

noga (*nōa*-gaa) *c* nougat

nogal (*no*-gahl) *adv* pretty, fairly, rather, quite

nogmaals (*nokh*-maals) *adv* once more

nokkenas (*no*-ker-nahss) *c* (pl ~sen) camshaft

nominaal (nōa-mee-*naal*) *adj* nominal

nominatie (nōa-mee-*naa*-tsee) *c* (pl ~s) nomination

non (non) *c* (pl ~nen) nun

nonnenklooster (*no*-ner-klōass-terr) *nt* (pl ~s) nunnery

nood (nōat) *c* (pl noden) distress; misery; need

noodgedwongen (nōat-kher-*dvo*-ngern) *adv* by force

noodgeval (*nōat*-kher-yahl) *nt* (pl ~len) emergency

noodlot (*nōat*-lot) *nt* destiny, fate

noodlottig (nōat-*lo*-terkh) *adj* fatal

noodsein (*nōat*-sayn) *nt* (pl ~en) distress signal

noodtoestand (*nōa*-tōo-stahnt) *c* emergency

nooduitgang (*nōat*-ur^(ewt)-khahng) *c* (pl ~en) emergency exit

noodzaak (*nōat*-saak) *c* need, necessity

noodzakelijk (nōat-*saa*-ker-lerk) *adj* necessary

noodzaken (*nōat*-saa-kern) *v* force

nooit (nōa^(eet)) *adv* never

Noor (nōar) *c* (pl Noren) Norwegian

noord (nōart) *c* north

noordelijk (*nōar*-der-lerk) *adj* northern, northerly, north

noorden (*nōar*-dern) *nt* north

noordoosten (nōart-*ōass*-tern) *nt* north-east

noordpool (*nōart*-pōal) *c* North Pole

noordwesten (nōart-*vehss*-tern) *nt* north-west

Noors (nōars) *adj* Norwegian

Noorwegen (*nōar*-vāy-gern) Norway

noot (nōat) *c* (pl noten) nut; note

nootmuskaat (nōat-merss-*kaat*) *c* nutmeg

norm (norm) *c* (pl ~en) standard

normaal (nor-*maal*) *adj* normal, regular

nota (*nōa*-taa) *c* (pl ~'s) bill

notaris (nōa-*taa*-rerss) *c* (pl ~sen) notary

notedop (*nōa*-ter-dop) *c* (pl ~pen) nutshell

notekraker (*nōa*-ter-kraa-kerr) *c* (pl ~s) nutcrackers *pl*

noteren (nōa-*tāy*-rern) *v* note; list

notie (*nōa*-tsee) *c* notion

notitie (nōa-*tee*-tsee) *c* (pl ~s) note

notitieboek (nōa-*tee*-tsee-bōok) *nt* (pl ~en) notebook

notulen (nōa-*tēw*-lern) *pl* minutes

nou (nou) *adv* now

november (nōa-*vehm*-berr) November

nu (nēw) *adv* now; ~ **en dan** now and then; **tot** ~ **toe** so far

nuance (nēw-*ahng*-ser) *c* (pl ~s, ~n) nuance

nuchter (*nerkh*-terr) *adj* sober; down-to-earth, matter-of-fact

nucleair (nēw-klāy-*Yair*) *adj* nuclear

nul (nerl) *c* (pl ~len) nought, zero

nummer (*ner*-merr) *nt* (pl ~s) number; act

nummerbord (*ner*-merr-bort) *nt* (pl
~en) registration plate; licence
plate *Am*

nut (nert) *nt* utility, use

nutteloos (*ner*-ter-lōass) *adj* useless

nuttig (*ner*-terkh) *adj* useful

nylon (*nay*-lon) *nt* nylon

O

oase (ōa-*vaa*-zer) *c* (pl ~n, ~s) oasis

ober (ōa-berr) *c* (pl ~s) waiter

object (op-ᵞ*ehkt*) *nt* (pl ~en) object

objectief (op-ᵞehk-*teef*) *adj* objective

obligatie (ōa-blee-*gaa*-tsee) *c* (pl ~s)
bond

obsceen (op-*sāyn*) *adj* obscene

obscuur (op-*skewr*) *adj* obscure

observatie (op-sehr-*vaa*-tsee) *c* (pl ~s)
observation

observatorium (op-sehr-vaa-*tōā*-ree-
ᵞerm) *nt* (pl -ria) observatory

observeren (op-sehr-*vāy*-rern) *v* observe

obsessie (op-*seh*-see) *c* (pl ~s) obsession

obstipatie (op-stee-*paa*-tsee) *c* constipation

oceaan (ōa-sāy-ᵞ*aan*) *c* (pl oceanen)
ocean

ochtend (*okh*-ternt) *c* (pl ~en) morning

ochtendblad (*okh*-ternt-blaht) *nt* (pl
~en) morning paper

ochtendeditie (*okh*-ternt-āy-dee-tsee) *c*
(pl ~s) morning edition

ochtendschemering (*okh*-ternt-skhāy-
mer-rɪng) *c* dawn

octopus (*ok*-tōā-perss) *c* (pl ~sen) octopus

octrooi (ok-*trōāee*) *nt* (pl ~en) patent

oefenen (*ōō*-fer-nern) *v* practise, exercise

oefening (*ōō*-fer-nɪng) *c* (pl ~en) exercise

oeroud (*ōōr*-out) *adj* ancient

oerwoud (*ōōr*-vout) *nt* (pl ~en) jungle

oester (*ōōss*-terr) *c* (pl ~s) oyster

oever (*ōō*-verr) *c* (pl ~s) river bank;
bank, shore

of (of) *conj* or; whether; ~ ... **of**
either ... or; whether ... or

offensief[1] (o-fehn-*seef*) *adj* offensive

offensief[2] (o-fehn-*seef*) *nt* (pl -sieven)
offensive

offer (*o*-ferr) *nt* (pl ~s) sacrifice

officieel (o-fee-*shāyl*) *adj* official

officier (o-fee-*seer*) *c* (pl ~en, ~s) officer

officieus (o-fee-*shūrss*) *adj* unofficial

ofschoon (of-*skhōān*) *conj* although,
though

ogenblik (*ōā*-germ-blɪk) *nt* (pl ~ken)
moment, instant

ogenblikkelijk (*ōā*-germ-*blɪ*-ker-lerk)
adv instantly

ogenschaduw (*ōā*-ger-skhaa-dēw°°) *c*
eye-shadow

oktober (ok-*tōā*-berr) October

olie (*ōā*-lee) *c* oil

olieachtig (*ōā*-lee-ahkh-terkh) *adj* oily

oliebron (*ōā*-lee-bron) *c* (pl ~nen) oil-
well

oliedruk (*ōā*-lee-drerk) *c* oil pressure

oliefilter (*ōā*-lee-fɪl-terr) *nt* (pl ~s) oil
filter

oliën (*ōā*-lee-ᵞern) *v* lubricate

olieraffinaderij (*ōā*-lee-rah-fee-naa-der-
ray) *c* (pl ~en) oil-refinery

olieverfschilderij (*ōā*-lee-vehrf-skhɪl-
der-ray) *nt* (pl ~en) oil-painting

olifant (*ōā*-lee-fahnt) *c* (pl ~en) elephant

olijf (*ōā*-*layf*) *c* (pl olijven) olive

olijfolie (*ōā*-*layf*-ōā-lee) *c* olive oil

om (om) *prep* round, about, around;

~ **te** to, in order to

oma (ōā-maa) c (pl ~'s) grandmother

*****ombrengen** (om-breh-ngern) v kill

omcirkelen (om-sír-ker-lern) v encircle

omdat (om-*daht*) conj because; as

omdraaien (om-draa^{ee}-ern) v turn; invert; **zich** ~ turn round

omelet (ōā-mer-*leht*) nt (pl ~ten) omelette

*****omgaan met** (om-gaan) associate with, mix with

omgang (om-gahng) c intercourse

omgekeerd (om-ger-kāyrt) adj reverse

*****omgeven** (om-gāy-vern) v surround, circle

omgeving (om-gāy-víng) c environment, surroundings pl; setting

omheen (om-hāyn) adv about

omheining (om-hay-níng) c (pl ~en) fence

omhelzen (om-hehl-zern) v hug, embrace

omhelzing (om-hehl-zíng) c (pl ~en) hug, embrace

omhoog (om-hōākh) adv up; ~

*****gaan** ascend

omkeer (om-kāyr) c reverse

omkeren (om-kāy-rern) v turn over, turn, turn round

*****omkomen** (om-kōā-mern) v perish

*****omkopen** (om-kōā-pern) v bribe, corrupt

omkoping (om-kōā-píng) c (pl ~en) bribery, corruption

omlaag (om-*laakh*) adv down

omleiding (om-lay-díng) c (pl ~en) detour

omliggend (om-lí-gernt) adj surrounding

omloop (om-lōāp) c circulation

omrekenen (om-rāy-ker-nern) v convert

omrekentabel (om-rāy-ker-taa-behl) c (pl ~len) conversion chart

omringen (om-*ríng*-ern) v encircle, surround, circle

*****omschrijven** (oam-*skhray*-vern) v define

omslag (om-slahkh) c/nt (pl ~en) cover, jacket

omslagdoek (om-slahkh-dōōk) c (pl ~en) shawl

omstandigheid (om-*stahn*-derkh-hayt) c (pl -heden) circumstance; condition

omstreden (om-*strāy*-dern) adj controversial

omstreeks (om-*strāyks*) adv about

omtrek (*om*-trehk) c (pl ~ken) contour, outline

omtrent (om-*trehnt*) prep about, concerning

omvang (*om*-vahng) c bulk, size; extent

omvangrijk (om-*vahng*-rayk) adj bulky, big; extensive

omvatten (om-*vah*-tern) v comprise

omver (om-*vehr*) adv down, over

omweg (om-vehkh) c (pl ~en) detour

omwenteling (om-vehn-ter-líng) c (pl ~en) revolution

omwisselen (om-ví-ser-lern) v switch

omzet (om-zeht) c (pl ~ten) turnover

omzetbelasting (om-zeht-ber-lahss-tíng) c turnover tax; sales tax

onaangenaam (on-*aan*-ger-naam) adj unpleasant, disagreeable

onaanvaardbaar (on-aan-*vaart*-baar) adj unacceptable

onaardig (on-*aar*-derkh) adj unkind

onafgebroken (on-*ahf*-kher-brōā-kern) adj continuous

onafhankelijk (on-ahf-*hahng*-ker-lerk) adj independent

onafhankelijkheid (on-ahf-*hahng*-ker-lerk-hayt) c independence

onbeantwoord (om-ber-*ahnt*-vōārt) adj unanswered

onbebouwd (om-ber-*bout*) adj uncultivated

onbeduidend (om-ber-*dur^ew*-dernt) adj petty, insignificant

onbegaanbaar (om-ber-*gaam*-baar) adj impassable

onbegrijpelijk (om-ber-*gray*-per-lerk) adj puzzling

onbehaaglijk (om-ber-*haakh*-lerk) adj uneasy

onbekend (om-ber-*kehnt*) adj unfamiliar, unknown

onbekwaam (om-ber-*kvaam*) adj unable, incompetent, incapable

onbelangrijk (om-ber-*lahng*-rayk) adj unimportant; insignificant

onbeleefd (om-ber-*lāyft*) adj impolite

onbemind (om-ber-*mint*) adj unpopular

onbepaald (om-ber-*paalt*) adj indefinite; onbepaalde wijs infinitive

onbeperkt (om-ber-*pehrkt*) adj unlimited

onbeschaamd (om-ber-*skhaamt*) adj impudent, impertinent, insolent

onbeschaamdheid (om-ber-*skhaamt*-hayt) c impertinence, insolence

onbescheiden (om-ber-*skhay*-dern) adj immodest

onbeschermd (om-ber-*skhehrmt*) adj unprotected

onbeschoft (oam-ber-*skhoft*) adj impertinent

onbetrouwbaar (om-ber-*trou*-baar) adj untrustworthy, unreliable

onbevoegd (om-ber-*vōōkht*) adj unqualified; unauthorized

onbevredigend (om-ber-*vrāy*-der-gernt) adj unsatisfactory

onbewoonbaar (om-ber-*vōām*-baar) adj uninhabitable

onbewoond (om-ber-*vōānt*) adj uninhabited

onbewust (om-ber-*verst*) adj unaware

onbezet (om-ber-*zeht*) adj unoccupied

onbezonnen (om-ber-zo-nern) adj rash

onbezorgd (om-ber-*zorkht*) adj carefree

onbillijk (om-br-lerk) adj unfair

onbreekbaar (om-ber-*brāyk*-baar) adj unbreakable

ondankbaar (on-*dahngk*-baar) adj ungrateful

ondanks (*on*-dahngks) prep despite, in spite of

ondenkbaar (on-*dehngk*-baar) adj inconceivable

onder (*on*-derr) prep under; beneath, below; among, amid

onderaan (on-der-*raan*) adv below

*onderbreken (on-derr-*brāy*-kern) v interrupt

onderbreking (on-derr-*brāy*-king) c (pl ~en) interruption

*onderbrengen (*on*-derr-breh-ngern) v accommodate

onderbroek (*on*-derr-brōōk) c (pl ~en) briefs pl, pants pl, panties pl; shorts plAm; underpants plAm

onderdaan (on-derr-daan) c (pl -danen) subject

onderdak (*on*-derr-dahk) nt accommodation

onderdeel (*on*-derr-dāyl) nt (pl -delen) spare part

onderdrukken (on-derr-*drer*-kern) v suppress

*ondergaan (on-derr-*gaan*) v suffer

ondergang (*on*-derr-gahng) c destruction; ruination, ruin

ondergeschikt (on-derr-ger-*skhikt*) adj subordinate; secondary, minor

ondergetekende (on-derr-ger-*tāy*-kern-der) c (pl ~n) undersigned

ondergoed (*on*-derr-gōōt) nt underwear

ondergronds (on-derr-*gronts*) adj underground

ondergrondse (on-derr-*gron*-tser) *c*
subway *nAm*

onderhandelen (on-derr-*hahn*-der-lern)
v negotiate

onderhandeling (on-derr-*hahn*-der-ling) *c* (pl ~en) negotiation

onderhevig aan (on-derr-*hāy*-verkh
aan) subject to; liable to; **aan bederf onderhevig** perishable

onderhoud (*on*-derr-hout) *nt* upkeep;
maintenance

* **onderhouden** (on-derr-*hou*-dern) *v*
entertain

onderling (*on*-derr-ling) *adj* mutual

* **ondernemen** (on-derr-*nāy*-mern) *v*
*undertake

onderneming (on-derr-*nāy*-ming) *c* (pl
~en) enterprise, undertaking; concern, company

onderrichten (on-der-*rıkh*-tern) *v* instruct

onderrok (*on*-derr-rok) *c* (pl ~ken)
slip

onderschatten (on-derr-*skhah*-tern) *v*
underestimate

onderscheid (*on*-derr-skhayt) *nt* distinction; difference; ~ **maken** distinguish

* **onderscheiden** (on-derr-*skhay*-dern)
v distinguish

onderst (*on*-derrst) *adj* bottom

ondersteboven (on-derr-ster-*bōā*-vern)
adv upside-down

ondersteunen (on-derr-*stŭr*-nern) *v*
*hold up, support

onderstrepen (on-derr-*strāy*-pern) *v*
underline

onderstroom (*on*-derr-strōam) *c* (pl
-stromen) undercurrent

ondertekenen (on-derr-*tāy*-ker-nern) *v*
sign

ondertitel (*on*-derr-tee-terl) *c* (pl ~s)
subtitle

ondertussen (on-derr-*ter*-sern) *adv* in

the meantime, meanwhile

* **ondervinden** (on-derr-*vın*-dern) *v* experience

ondervoeding (on-derr-*vōō*-ding) *c*
malnutrition

* **ondervragen** (on-derr-*vraa*-gern) *v*
interrogate

onderwerp (*on*-derr-vehrp) *nt* (pl ~en)
subject; topic, theme

* **onderwerpen** (on-derr-*vehr*-pern) *v*
subject; **zich** ~ submit

onderwijs (*on*-derr-vayss) *nt* tuition;
education, instruction

* **onderwijzen** (on-derr-*vay*-zern) *v*
*teach

onderwijzer (on-derr-*vay*-zerr) *c* (pl
~s) schoolteacher, schoolmaster,
master, teacher

onderzoek (*on*-derr-zōōk) *nt* (pl ~en)
enquiry, investigation, inquiry;
check-up, examination; research

* **onderzoeken** (on-derr-*zōō*-kern) *v* enquire, investigate, examine; explore

ondeugend (on-*dŭr*-gernt) *adj* naughty, mischievous

ondiep (on-*deep*) *adj* shallow

ondoeltreffend (on-dōōl-*treh*-fehnt)
adj inefficient

ondraaglijk (on-*draakh*-lerk) *adj* unbearable

onduidelijk (on-dur ᵘᵛ-der-lerk) *adj*
ambiguous

onecht (on-*ehkht*) *adj* false

het oneens * **zijn** (ert on-*āyns* zayn)
disagree

oneerlijk (on-*āyr*-lerk) *adj* crooked,
dishonest; unfair

oneetbaar (on-*āyt*-baar) *adj* inedible

oneffen (on-*eh*-fern) *adj* uneven

oneindig (on-*ayn*-derkh) *adj* infinite,
endless; immense

onenigheid (on-*āy*-nerkh-hayt) *c* (pl
-heden) dispute

onervaren (on-ehr-*vaa*-rern) *adj* inexperienced

oneven (on-*āy*-vern) *adj* odd

onevenwichtig (on-*āy*-ver-*vikh*-terkh) *adj* unsteady

onfatsoenlijk (om-faht-*sōōn*-lerk) *adj* indecent

ongeacht (ong-*ger*-ahkht) *prep* in spite of

ongebruikelijk (ong-ger-*brurew*-ker-lerk) *adj* unusual

ongeduldig (ong-ger-*derl*-derkh) *adj* impatient; eager

ongedurig (ong-ger-*dēw*-rerkh) *adj* restless

ongedwongen (ong-ger-*dvo*-ngern) *adj* casual

ongedwongenheid (ong-ger-*dvo*-nger-hayt) *c* ease

ongeldig (ong-*gehl*-derkh) *adj* invalid

ongelegen (ong-ger-*lāy*-gern) *adj* inconvenient

ongelijk (ong-ger-*layk*) *adj* unequal; uneven; ~ **hebben *be wrong

ongelofelijk (ong-ger-*lōa*-fer-lerk) *adj* incredible

ongeluk (*ong*-ger-lerk) *nt* (pl ~ken) accident; misfortune

ongelukkig (ong-ger-*ler*-kerkh) *adj* unhappy; unlucky, unfortunate

ongelukkigerwijs (ong-ger-ler-ker-gerr-*vayss*) *adv* unfortunately

ongemak (*ong*-ger-mahk) *nt* (pl ~ken) inconvenience

ongemakkelijk (ong-ger-*mah*-ker-lerk) *adj* uncomfortable

ongemeubileerd (ong-ger-mūr-bee-*lāyrt*) *adj* unfurnished

ongeneeslijk (ong-ger-*nāyss*-lerk) *adj* incurable

ongepast (ong-ger-*pahst*) *adj* unsuitable; improper

ongerief (*ong*-ger-reef) *nt* inconvenience

ongerijmd (ong-ger-*raymt*) *adj* absurd

ongerust (ong-ger-*rerst*) *adj* worried; zich ~ **maken** worry

ongeschikt (ong-ger-*skhikt*) *adj* unfit

ongeschoold (ong-ger-*skhōalt*) *adj* uneducated; unskilled

ongetrouwd (ong-ger-*trout*) *adj* single

ongetwijfeld (ong-ger-*tvay*-ferlt) *adv* undoubtedly

ongeval (*ong*-ger-vahl) *nt* (pl ~len) accident

ongeveer (ong-ger-*vāyr*) *adv* about, approximately

ongevoelig (ong-ger-*vōō*-lerkh) *adj* insensitive

ongewenst (ong-ger-*vehnst*) *adj* undesirable

ongewoon (ong-ger-*vōān*) *adj* uncommon, unusual

ongezond (ong-ger-*zont*) *adj* unhealthy, unsound

ongunstig (ong-*gerns*-terkh) *adj* unfavourable

onhandig (on-*hahn*-derkh) *adj* clumsy, awkward

onheil (*on*-hayl) *nt* calamity, disaster; mischief

onheilspellend (on-hayl-*speh*-lernt) *adj* sinister; ominous

onherroepelijk (on-heh-*rōō*-per-lerk) *adj* irrevocable

onherstelbaar (on-hehr-*stehl*-baar) *adj* irreparable

onjuist (oñ-*urewst*) *adj* incorrect

onkosten (*ong*-koss-tern) *pl* expenses *pl*

onkruid (*ong*-krur*ew*t) *nt* weed

onlangs (*on*-lahngs) *adv* recently; lately

onleesbaar (on-*lāyss*-baar) *adj* illegible

onmetelijk (o-*māy*-ter-lerk) *adj* vast, immense

onmiddellijk (o-*mı*-der-lerk) *adj* immediate, prompt; *adv* immediately, instantly

onmogelijk (o-*mōa*-ger-lerk) *adj* impossible

onnauwkeurig (o-nou-*kūr*-rerkh) *adj* inaccurate; incorrect

onnodig (o-*nōa*-derkh) *adj* unnecessary

onontbeerlijk (on-ont-*bāyr*-lerk) *adj* essential

onopvallend (on-op-*fah*-lernt) *adj* inconspicuous

onopzettelijk (on-op-*seh*-ter-lerk) *adj* unintentional

onoverkomelijk (on-*ōa*-verr-*kōa*-merlerk) *adj* prohibitive

onovertroffen (on-*ōa*-verr-*tro*-fern) *adj* unsurpassed

onpartijdig (om-pahr-*tay*-derkh) *adj* impartial

onpersoonlijk (om-pehr-*sōan*-lerk) *adj* impersonal

onplezierig (om-pler-*zee*-rerkh) *adj* unpleasant

onrecht (*on*-rehkht) *nt* injustice; wrong; ~ *aandoen wrong

onrechtvaardig (on-rehkht-*faar*-derkh) *adj* unjust

onredelijk (on-*rāy*-der-lerk) *adj* unreasonable

onregelmatig (on-*rāy* gorl *maa*-terkh) *adj* irregular

onrein (on-*rayn*) *adj* unclean

onrust (*on*-rerst) *c* unrest

onrustig (on-*rerss*-terkh) *adj* restless

ons (ons) *pron* our; us; ourselves

onschadelijk (on-*skhaa*-der-lerk) *adj* harmless

onschatbaar (on-*skhaht*-baar) *adj* priceless

onschuld (*on*-skherlt) *c* innocence

onschuldig (on-*skherl*-derkh) *adj* innocent

ontbijt (ont-*bayt*) *nt* breakfast

*ontbinden** (ont-*bin*-dern) *v* dissolve

*ontbreken** (ont-*brāy*-kern) *v* fail; **ontbrekend** missing

ontdekken (on-*deh*-kern) *v* detect, discover

ontdekking (on-*deh*-kıng) *c* (pl ~en) discovery

ontdooien (on-*dōaee*-ern) *v* thaw

ontevreden (on-ter-*vrāy*-dern) *adj* dissatisfied; discontented

*ontgaan** (ont-*khaan*) *v* escape

ontglippen (ont-*khlı*-pern) *v* slip

onthaal (ont-*haal*) *nt* reception

*ontheffen** (ont-*heh*-fern) *v* exempt; ~ *van* discharge of

*onthouden** (ont-*hou*-dern) *v* remember; deny; **zich** ~ **van** abstain from

onthullen (ont-*her*-lern) *v* reveal

onthulling (ont-*her*-lıng) *c* (pl ~en) revelation

onthutsen (ont-*hert*-sern) *v* overwhelm

ontkennen (ont-*keh*-nern) *v* deny; **ontkennend** negative

ontkoppelen (ont-*ko*-per-lern) *v* disconnect

ontkurken (ont-*kerr*-kern) *v* uncork

ontleden (ont-*lāy*-dern) *v* analyse; *break down

ontlenen (ont-*lāy*-nern) *v* borrow

ontmoeten (ont-*mōo*-tern) *v* encounter; *meet

ontmoeting (ont-*mōo*-tıng) *c* (pl ~en) encounter, meeting

*ontnemen** (ont-*nāy*-mern) *v* deprive of

ontoegankelijk (on-tōo-*gahng*-ker-lerk) *adj* inaccessible

ontploffen (ont-*plo*-fern) *v* explode

ontplooien (ont-*plōa ee*-ern) *v* expand

ontroeren (oant-*rōo*-rern) *v* move

ontroering (oant-*rōo*-rıng) *c* emotion

ontrouw (*on*-trou) *adj* unfaithful

ontruimen (ont-*rur ew*-mern) *v* vacate

ontschepen (ont-*skhāy*-pern) *v* disembark

*ontslaan (ont-*slaan*) v dismiss, fire

ontslag *nemen (ont-*slahkh nāy*-mern) resign

ontslagneming (ont-*slahkh*-nāy-ming) c resignation

ontsmetten (ont-*smeh*-tern) v disinfect

ontsmettingsmiddel (ont-*smeh*-tings-mi-derl) nt (pl ~en) disinfectant

ontsnappen (ont-*snah*-pern) v escape

ontsnapping (ont-*snah*-ping) c (pl ~en) escape

ontspannen (ont-*spah*-nern) adj easygoing

zich ontspannen (ont-*spah*-nern) relax

ontspanning (ont-*spah*-ning) c relaxation; recreation

*ontstaan (ont-*staan*) v *arise

*ontsteken (ont-*stāy*-kern) v *become septic

ontsteking (ont-*stāy*-king) c (pl ~en) ignition; ignition coil; inflammation

ontstemmen (ont-*steh*-mern) v displease

*ontvangen (ont-*fah*-ngern) v receive; entertain

ontvangst (ont-*fahngst*) c (pl ~en) receipt; reception

ontvlambaar (ont-*flahm*-baar) adj inflammable

ontvluchten (ont-*flerkh*-tern) v escape

ontvouwen (ont-*fou*-ern) v unfold

ontwaken (ont-*vaa*-kern) v wake up

ontwerp (ont-*vehrp*) nt (pl ~en) design

*ontwerpen (ont-*vehr*-pern) v design

*ontwijken (ont-*vay*-kern) v avoid

ontwikkelen (ont-*vi*-ker-lern) v develop

ontwikkeling (ont-*vi*-ker-ling) c (pl ~en) development

ontwricht (ont-*frikht*) adj dislocated

ontzag (ont-*sahkh*) nt respect

*ontzeggen (ont-*seh*-gern) v deny

ontzettend (ont-*seh*-ternt) adj dreadful, terrible

onuitstaanbaar (on-ur*ewt*-staam-baar) adj intolerable

onvast (*on*-vahst) adj unsteady

onveilig (on-*vay*-lerkh) adj unsafe

onverdiend (*on*-verr-deent) adj unearned

onverklaarbaar (on-verr-*klaar*-baar) adj unaccountable

onvermijdelijk (on-verr-*may*-der-lerk) adj unavoidable, inevitable

onverschillig (on-verr-*skhi*-lerkh) adj indifferent

onverstandig (on-verr-*stahn*-derkh) adj unwise

onverwacht (*on*-verr-vahkht) adj unexpected

onvoldoende (on-vol-*dōōn*-der) adj insufficient; inadequate

onvolledig (on-vo-*lāy*-derkh) adj incomplete

onvolmaakt (on-vol-*maakt*) adj imperfect

onvoorwaardelijk (on-vōar-*vaar*-der-lerk) adj unconditional

onvoorzien (on-vōar-*zeen*) adj unexpected

onvriendelijk (on-*vreen*-der-lerk) adj unkind, unfriendly

onwaar (*on*-vaar) adj untrue, false

onwaarschijnlijk (on-vaar-*skhayn*-lerk) adj unlikely, improbable

onweer (*on*-vāyr) nt thunderstorm

onweerachtig (*on*-vāyr-ahkh-terkh) adj thundery

onwel (on-*vehl*) adj unwell

onwerkelijk (on-*vehr*-ker-lerk) adj unreal

onwetend (on-*vāy*-ternt) adj ignorant

onwettig (on-*veh*-terkh) adj unlawful, illegal

onwillig (on-*vi*-lerkh) *adj* unwilling

onyx (*ōā*-niks) *nt* onyx

onzeker (on-*zāy*-kerr) *adj* doubtful, uncertain

onzelfzuchtig (on-zehlf-*serkh*-terkh) *adj* unselfish

onzichtbaar (on-*zikht*-baar) *adj* invisible

onzijdig (on-*zay*-derkh) *adj* neuter

onzin (*on*-zin) *c* nonsense, rubbish

oog (ōākh) *nt* (pl ogen) eye

oogarts (*ōākh*-ahrts) *c* (pl ~en) oculist

ooggetuige (*ōā*-kher-tur^{ew}-ger) *c* (pl ~n) eye-witness

ooglid (*ōākh*-lit) *nt* (pl -leden) eyelid

oogst (*ōākhst) *c* (pl ~en) harvest; crop

ooievaar (*ōā^{ee}*-er-vaar) *c* (pl ~s) stork

ooit (*ōā^{ee}*t) *adv* ever

ook (*ōāk) *adv* also, too; as well

oom (*ōām) *c* (pl ~s) uncle

oor (*ōār) *nt* (pl oren) ear

oorbel (*ōār*-behl) *c* (pl ~len) earring

oordeel (*ōār*-dāyl) *nt* (pl -delen) judgment

oordelen (*ōār*-dāy-lern) *v* judge

oorlog (*ōār*-lokh) *c* (pl ~en) war

oorlogsschip (*ōār*-lokh-skhip) *nt* (pl -schepen) man-of-war

oorpijn (*ōār*-payn) *c* earache

oorsprong (*ōār*-sprong) *c* (pl ~en) origin

oorspronkelijk (*ōār*-sprong-ker-lerk) *adj* original

oorzaak (*ōār*-zaak) *c* (pl -zaken) cause; reason

oost (*ōāst) *c* east; oost- eastern

oostelijk (*o*-ster-lerk) *adj* eastern, easterly

oosten (*ōā*-stern) *nt* east

Oostenrijk (*ōā*-stern-rayk) Austria

Oostenrijker (*ōā*-stern-ray-kerr) *c* (pl ~s) Austrian

Oostenrijks (*ōā*-stern-rayks) *adj* Aus-

trian

oosters (*ōā*-sterrs) *adj* oriental

op (op) *prep* on, upon; at, in; *adv* up; finished

opa (*ōā*-paa) *c* (pl ~'s) grandfather, granddad

opaal (*ōā*-*paal*) *c* (pl opalen) opal

opbellen (*o*-beh-lern) *v* call, ring up, phone; call up *Am*

*opbergen (*o*-behr-gern) *v* *put away

opblaasbaar (*o*-*blaass*-baar) *adj* inflatable

*opblazen (*o*-blaa-zern) *v* inflate

opbouw (*o*-bou) *c* construction

opbouwen (*o*-bou-ern) *v* erect; construct

opbrengst (*o*-brehngst) *c* (pl ~en) produce

opdat (ob-*daht*) *conj* so that

opdracht (*op*-drahkht) *c* (pl ~en) order; assignment

*opdragen aan (*oap*-draa-gern) assign to

opeens (op-*āyns*) *adv* suddenly

opeisen (*op*-ay-sern) *v* claim

open (*ōā*-pern) *adj* open

openbaar (*ōā*-perm-*baar*) *adj* public

openbaren (*ōā*-perm-*baa*-rern) *v* reveal

opendraaien (*ōā*-per-draa^{ee}ern) *v* turn on

openen (*ōā*-per-nern) *v* unlock; open

openhartig (*ōā*-per-*hahr*-terkh) *adj* open

opening (*ōā*-per-ning) *c* (pl ~en) opening

openingstijden (*ōā*-per-nings-tay-dern) *pl* business hours

opera (*ōā*-per-raa) *c* (pl ~'s) opera; opera house

operatie (*ōā*-per-*raa*-tsee) *c* (pl ~s) operation, surgery

opereren (*ōā*-per-*rāy*-rern) *v* operate

operette (*ōā*-per-*reh*-ter) *c* (pl ~s) operette

*opgaan (*op*-khaan) *v* *rise

opgeruimd (*op*-kher-rur^(ew)mt) *adj* good-humoured

opgetogen (*oap*-kher-tōa-gern) *adj* delighted

*opgeven (*oap*-khāy-vern) *v* declare; *give up

opgewekt (*op*-kher-vehkt) *adj* cheerful

opgraving (*op*-khraa-vɪng) *c* (pl ~en) excavation

ophaalbrug (*op*-haal-brerkh) *c* (pl ~gen) drawbridge

ophalen (*op*-haa-lern) *v* collect, pick up

*ophangen (*op*-hah-ngern) *v* *hang

ophanging (*op*-hah-ngɪng) *c* suspension

ophef (*op*-hehf) *c* fuss

*opheffen (*op*-heh-fern) *v* discontinue

ophelderen (*op*-hehl-der-rern) *v* clarify

*ophouden (*op*-hou-dern) *v* cease; ~ met stop; quit

opinie (ōa-*pee*-nee) *c* (pl ~s) opinion

opkomst (*op*-komst) *c* rise; attendance

oplage (*op*-laa-ger) *c* (pl ~n) issue

opleiden (*op*-lay-dern) *v* educate

opletten (*op*-leh-tern) *v* *pay attention; **oplettend** attentive

oplichten (*op*-lɪkh-tern) *v* cheat, swindle

oplichter (*op*-lɪkh-terr) *c* (pl ~s) swindler

*oplopen (*op*-lōa-pern) *v* increase; contract

oplosbaar (op-*loss*-baar) *adj* soluble

oplossen (*op*-lo-sern) *v* dissolve; solve

oplossing (*op*-lo-sɪng) *c* (pl ~en) solution

opmerkelijk (op-*mehr*-ker-lerk) *adj* remarkable; noticeable, striking

opmerken (*op*-mehr-kern) *v* notice, note; remark

opmerking (*op*-mehr-kɪng) *c* (pl ~en) remark

opname (*op*-naa-mer) *c* (pl ~n) recording; shot

*opnemen (*op*-nāy-mern) *v* *draw

opnieuw (op-*nee*^(oo)) *adv* again

opofferen (*op*-o-fer-rern) *v* sacrifice

oponthoud (*op*-ont-hout) *nt* delay

oppassen (*o*-pah-sern) *v* look out, beware

oppasser (*o*-pah-serr) *c* (pl ~s) attendant

opperhoofd (*o*-perr-hōaft) *nt* (pl ~en) chieftain

oppervlakkig (o-perr-*vlah*-kerkh) *adj* superficial

oppervlakte (*o*-perr-vlahk-ter) *c* (pl ~n, ~s) surface; area

oppositie (o-pōa-*see*-tsee) *c* (pl ~s) opposition

oprapen (*op*-raa-pern) *v* pick up

oprecht (op-*rehkht*) *adj* honest, sincere

oprichten (*op*-rɪkh-tern) *v* found; erect

*oprijzen (*op*-ray-zern) *v* *arise

oproer (*op*-rōor) *nt* revolt, rebellion

opruimen (*op*-rur^(ew)-mern) *v* tidy up

opruiming (*op*-rur^(ew)-mɪng) *c* clearance sale

opscheppen (*op*-skheh-pern) *v* boast

*opschieten (*op*-skhee-tern) *v* hurry

opschorten (*op*-skhor-tern) *v* *put off

*opschrijven (*op*-skhray-vern) *v* *write down

*opslaan (*op*-slaan) *v* store

opslag[1] (*op*-slahkh) *c* storage

opslag[2] (*op*-slahkh) *c* rise; raise *nAm*

opslagplaats (*op*-slahkh-plaats) *c* (pl ~en) depot

*opsluiten (*op*-slur^(ew)-tern) *v* lock up

opsporen (*op*-spōa-rern) *v* trace

*opstaan (*op*-staan) *v* *get up, *rise

opstand (*op*-stahnt) *c* (pl ~en) rising, revolt, rebellion; **in ~ *komen** revolt opstapelen (*op*-staa-per-lern) v pile

opstel (*op*-stehl) nt (pl ~len) essay

opstellen (*op*-steh-lern) v *draw up, *make up

*opstijgen (*op*-stay-gern) v ascend

optellen (*op*-teh-lern) v add; count

optelling (*op*-teh-ling) c (pl ~en) addition

opticien (op-tee-*shang*) c (pl ~s) optician

optillen (*op*-tı-lern) v lift; raise

optimisme (op-tee-*miss*-mer) nt optimism

optimist (op-tee-*mist*) c (pl ~en) optimist

optimistisch (op-tee-*miss*-teess) adj optimistic

optocht (*op*-tokht) c (pl ~en) parade

optreden (*op*-trāy-dern) nt (pl ~s) appearance

*optreden (*op*-trāy-dern) v act; appear

*opvallen (*op*-fah-lern) v attract attention; opvallend striking

opvatten (*op*-fah-tern) v conceive

opvatting (*op*-fah-ting) c (pl ~en) view

opvoeden (*op*-fōō-dern) v *bring up, educate

opvoeding (*op*-fōō-ding) c education

opvolgen (*op*-fol-gern) v succeed

*opvouwen (*op*-fou-ern) v fold

opvrolijken (*op*-frōa-ler-kern) v cheer up

opvullen (*op*-fer-lern) v fill up

*opwinden (*op*-vın-dern) v *wind; excite

opwinding (*op*-vın-ding) c excitement

opzettelijk (op-*seh*-ter-lerk) adj deliberate, intentional; on purpose

opzicht (*op*-sıkht) nt (pl ~en) respect

opzichter (*op*-sıkh-terr) c (pl ~s) supervisor; warden

opzienbarend (op-seen-*baa*-rernt) adj sensational

opzij (op-*say*) adv aside; sideways

*opzoeken (*op*-sōō-kern) v look up

oranje (ōā-*rah*-ñer) adj orange

orde¹ (*or*-der) c order; method; in ~ in order; in orde! okay!, all right!

orde² (*or*-der) c (pl ~n, ~s) congregation

ordenen (*or*-der-nern) v arrange

ordinair (or-dee-*nair*) adj common, vulgar

orgaan (or-*gaan*) nt (pl organen) organ

organisatie (or-gaa-nee-*zaa*-tsee) c (pl ~s) organization

organisch (or-*gaa*-neess) adj organic

organiseren (or-gaa-nee-*zāy*-rern) v organize

orgel (*or*-gerl) nt (pl ~s) organ

zich oriënteren (ōā-ree-Yehn-*tāy*-rern) orientate

origine (ōā-ree-*zhee*-ner) c origin

origineel (ōā-ree-zhee-*nāyl*) adj original

orkaan (or-*kaan*) c (pl orkanen) hurricane

orkest (or-*kehst*) nt (pl ~en) orchestra; band

orlon (*or*-lon) nt orlon

ornamenteel (or-naa-mehn-*tāyl*) adj ornamental

orthodox (or-tōā-*doks*) adj orthodox

os (oss) c (pl ~sen) ox

oud (out) adj old; ancient; aged; ouder elder; oudst eldest, elder

oudbakken (out-*bah*-kern) adj stale

ouderdom (*ou*-derr-dom) c age; old age

ouders (*ou*-derrs) pl parents pl

ouderwets (ou-derr-*vehts*) adj old-fashioned, ancient; out of date; quaint

oudheden (*out*-hāy-dern) pl antiquities pl

Oudheid (*out*-hayt) *c* antiquity

oudheidkunde (*out*-hayt-kern-der) *c* archaeology

ouverture ($\overline{oo}$-verr-*te͞w*-rer) *c* (pl ~s, ~n) overture

ouvreuse ($\overline{oo}$-*vru͞r*-zer) *c* (pl ~s) usherette

ovaal ($\overline{o}$a-*vaal*) *adj* oval

oven ($\overline{o}$a-vern) *c* (pl ~s) oven ; furnace

over ($\overline{o}$a-verr) *prep* about ; over ; across ; in ; *adv* over

overal ($\overline{o}$a-verr-ahl) *adv* everywhere ; anywhere, throughout

overall ($\overline{o}$a-ver-*rahl*) *c* (pl ~s) overalls *pl*

overblijfsel ($\overline{o}$a-verr-blayf-serl) *nt* (pl ~s, ~en) remnant

*overblijven ($\overline{o}$a-verr-blay-vern) *v* remain

overbodig ($\overline{o}$a-verr-*b͞oa*-derkh) *adj* superfluous ; redundant

*overbrengen ($\overline{o}$a-verr-breh-ngern) *v* transfer

overdag ($\overline{o}$a-verr-*dahk*) *adv* by day

*overdenken ($\overline{o}$a-verr-*dehng*-kern) *v* *think over

*overdrijven ($\overline{o}$a-verr-*dray*-vern) *v* exaggerate ; **overdreven** extravagant

*overeenkomen ($\overline{o}$a-verr-*ra͞yng*-k͞oa-mern) *v* agree ; correspond

overeenkomst ($\overline{o}$a-ver-*ra͞yng*-komst) *c* (pl ~en) agreement, settlement

overeenkomstig ($\overline{o}$a-ver-*ra͞yng*-komsterkh) *adj* similar ; *prep* according to

overeenstemming ($\overline{o}$a-ver-*ra͞yn*-steh-mıng) *c* agreement

overeind ($\overline{o}$a-ver-*raynt*) *adv* upright ; erect

overgang ($\overline{o}$a-verr-gahng) *c* (pl ~en) transition

overgave ($\overline{o}$a-verr-gaa-ver) *c* surrender

*overgeven ($\overline{o}$a-verr-*ga͞y*-vern) *v* vom-

it ; zich ***overgeven** surrender

overhaast ($\overline{o}$a-verr-*haast*) *adj* rash

overhalen ($\overline{o}$a-verr-haa-lern) *v* persuade

overheersing ($\overline{o}$a-verr-*ha͞yr*-sıng) *c* domination

overheid ($\overline{o}$a-verr-hayt) *c* (pl -heden) authorities *pl*

overhemd ($\overline{o}$a-verr-hehmt) *nt* (pl ~en) shirt

overig ($\overline{o}$a-ver-rerkh) *adj* remaining

overigens ($\overline{o}$a-ver-rer-gerns) *adv* though

overjas ($\overline{o}$a-verr-^{Y}ahss) *c* (pl ~sen) topcoat, overcoat

aan de overkant (aan der $\overline{o}$a-verr-kahnt) across

overleg ($\overline{o}$a-verr-*lehkh*) *nt* deliberation

overleggen ($\overline{o}$a-verr-*leh*-gern) *v* deliberate

overleven ($\overline{o}$a-verr-*la͞y*-vern) *v* survive

overleving ($\overline{o}$a-verr-*la͞y*vıng) *c* survival

*overlijden ($\overline{o}$a-verr-*lay*-dern) *v* depart, die

overmaken ($\overline{o}$a-verr-maa-kern) *v* remit

overmoedig ($\overline{o}$a-verr-*m͞oo*-derkh) *adj* presumptuous

*overnemen ($\overline{o}$a-verr-*na͞y*-mern) *v* *take over

overreden ($\overline{o}$a-ver-*ra͞y*-dern) *v* persuade

overschot ($\overline{o}$a-verr-skhot) *nt* (pl ~ten) surplus

*overschrijden ($\overline{o}$a-verr-*skhray*-dern) *v* exceed

overschrijving ($\overline{o}$a-verr-skhray-vıng) *c* (pl ~en) money order

*overslaan ($\overline{o}$a-verr-slaan) *v* skip

overspannen ($\overline{o}$a-verr-*spah*-nern) *adj* overstrung

overstappen ($\overline{o}$a-verr-stah-pern) *v* change

oversteekplaats ($\overline{o}$a-verr-sta͞yk-plaats) *c* (pl ~en) crossing

*oversteken (ōā-verr-stāy-kern) v
cross

overstroming (ōā-verr-strōā-mıng) c
(pl ~en) flood

overstuur (ōā-verr-stewr) adj upset

overtocht (ōā-verr-tokht) c (pl ~en)
crossing, passage

*overtreden (ōā-verr-trāy-dern) v offend

overtreding (ōā-verr-trāy-dıng) c (pl
~en) offence

*overtreffen (ōā-verr-treh-fern) v
*outdo, exceed

overtuigen (ōā-verr-tur^ew-gern) v convince; persuade

overtuiging (ōā-verr-tur^ew-gıng) c (pl
~en) conviction; persuasion

overval (ōā-verr-vahl) c (pl ~len)
hold-up

oververmoeid (ōā-verr-verr-mōō^eet)
adj over-tired

overvloed (ōā-verr-vlōōt) c abundance; plenty

overvloedig (ōā-verr-vlōō-derkh) adj
abundant, plentiful

overvol (ōā-verr-vol) adj crowded

overweg (ōā-verr-vehkh) c (pl ~en)
level crossing, crossing

*overwegen (ōā-verr-vāy-gern) v consider

overweging (ōā-verr-vāy-gıng) c (pl
~en) consideration

overweldigen (ōā-verr-vehl-der-gern) v
overwhelm

zich overwerken (ōā-verr-vehr-kern) v
overwork

*overwinnen (ōā-verr-vı-nern) v conquer; *overcome

overwinning (ōā-verr-vı-nıng) c (pl
~en) victory

overzees (ōā-verr-zāyss) adj overseas

overzicht (ōā-verr-zıkht) nt (pl ~en)
survey

P

paal (paal) c (pl palen) post, pole

paar (paar) nt (pl paren) pair; couple

paard (paart) nt (pl ~en) horse

paardebloem (paar-der-blōōm) c (pl
~en) dandelion

paardekracht (paar-der-krahkht) c
horsepower

paardesport (paar-der-sport) c riding

*paardrijden (paart-ray-dern) v *ride

paarlemoer (paar-ler-mōōr) nt mother-
of-pearl

paars (paars) adj purple

pacht (pahkht) c (pl ~en) lease

pacifisme (pah-see-fiss-mer) nt pacifism

pacifist (pah-see-fist) c (pl ~en) pacifist

pacifistisch (pah-see-fiss-teess) adj
pacifist

pad¹ (paht) nt (pl ~en) path; lane,
trail

pad² (paht) c (pl ~den) toad

paddestoel (pah-der-stōōl) c (pl ~en)
toadstool; mushroom

padvinder (paht-fın-derr) c (pl ~s)
scout, boy scout

padvindster (paht-tınt-sterr) c (pl ~s)
girl guide

pagina (paa-gee-naa) c (pl ~'s) page

pak (pahk) nt (pl ~ken) package

pakhuis (pahk-hur^ew ss) nt (pl -huizen)
warehouse

Pakistaan (paa-kee-staan) c (pl -sta-
nen) Pakistani

Pakistaans (paa-kee-staans) adj Pakistani

Pakistan (paa-kıss-tahn) Pakistan

pakje (pahk-Yer) nt (pl ~s) parcel,
packet

pakken (pah-kern) v *take

pakket (pah-*keht*) *nt* (pl ~ten) parcel

pakpapier (*pahk*-paa-peer) *nt* wrapping paper

paleis (paa-*layss*) *nt* (pl paleizen) palace

paling (*paa*-ling) *c* (pl ~en) eel

palm (pahlm) *c* (pl ~en) palm

pan (pahn) *c* (pl ~nen) pan

pand (pahnt) *nt* (pl ~en) security; house, premises *pl*

pandjesbaas (*pahn*-t ʸerss-baass) *c* (pl -bazen) pawnbroker

paneel (paa-*nāyl*) *nt* (pl panelen) panel

paniek (paa-*neek*) *c* panic

panne (*pah*-ner) *c* breakdown

pantoffel (pahn-*to*-ferl) *c* (pl ~s) slipper

panty (*pehn*-tee) *c* (pl panties) panty-hose

papa (*pah*-paa) *c* (pl ~'s) daddy

papaver (paa-*paa*-verr) *c* (pl ~s) poppy

papegaai (pah-per-*gaa*ᵉᵉ) *c* (pl ~en) parrot

papier (paa-*peer*) *nt* (pl ~en) paper

papieren (paa-*pee*-rern) *adj* paper; ~ servet paper napkin; ~ zak paper bag; ~ zakdoek kleenex

parade (paa-*raa*-der) *c* (pl ~s) parade

paraferen (paa-raa-*fāy*-rern) *v* initial

paragraaf (paa-raa-*graaf*) *c* (pl -grafen) paragraph

parallel (paa-raa-*lehl*) *adj* parallel

paraplu (paa-raa-*plēw*) *c* (pl ~'s) umbrella

parasol (paa-raa-*sol*) *c* (pl ~s) sunshade

pardon! (pahr-*don*) sorry!

parel (*paa*-rerl) *c* (pl ~s, ~en) pearl

parfum (pahr-*ferm*) *nt* (pl ~s) perfume

park (pahrk) *nt* (pl ~en) park

parkeermeter (pahr-*kāyr*-māy-terr) *c* (pl ~s) parking meter

parkeerplaats (pahr-*kāyr*-plaats) *c* (pl ~en) car park; parking lot *Am*

parkeertarief (pahr-*kāyr*-taa-reef) *nt* (pl -tarieven) parking fee

parkeerzone (pahr-*kāyr*-zaw-ner) *c* (pl ~s) parking zone

parkeren (pahr-*kāy*-rern) *v* park

parkiet (pahr-*keet*) *c* (pl ~en) parakeet

parlement (pahr-ler-*mehnt*) *nt* (pl ~en) parliament

parlementair (pahr-ler-mehn-*tair*) *adj* parliamentary

parochie (pah-*ro*-khee) *c* (pl ~s) parish

particulier (pahr-tee-kēw-*leer*) *adj* private

partij (pahr-*tay*) *c* (pl ~en) party; side; batch

partijdig (pahr-*tay*-derkh) *adj* partial

partner (*pahrt*-nerr) *c* (pl ~s) partner; associate

pas¹ (pahss) *c* (pl ~sen) step

pas² (pahss) *adv* just

Pasen (*paa*-sern) Easter

pasfoto (*pahss*-fōa-tōa) *c* (pl ~'s) passport photograph

paskamer (*pahss*-kaa-merr) *c* (pl ~s) fitting room

paspoort (*pahss*-pōart) *nt* (pl ~en) passport

paspoortcontrole (*pahss*-pōart-kon-traw-ler) *c* passport control

passage (pah-*saa*-zher) *c* (pl ~s) excerpt; passage

passagier (pah-saa-*zheer*) *c* (pl ~s) passenger

passen (*pah*-sern) *v* try on; fit; ~ bij match; passend appropriate; convenient, adequate, proper; ~ op look after; attend to

passeren (pah-*sāy*-rern) *v* pass; bypass, pass by

passie (*pah*-see) *c* passion

passief (pah-*seef*) *adj* passive

pasta (*pahss*-taa) *c* (pl ~'s) paste

pastorie (pahss-tōā-*ree*) *c* (pl ~ën) parsonage, vicarage, rectory

patent (paa-*tehnt*) *nt* (pl ~en) patent

pater (*paa*-terr) *c* (pl ~s) father

patiënt (paa-*shehnt*) *c* (pl ~en) patient

patrijs (paa-*trayss*) *c* (pl patrijzen) partridge

patrijspoort (paa-*trayss*-pōārt) *c* (pl ~en) porthole

patriot (paa-tree-ᵛot) *c* (pl ~ten) patriot

patroon (paa-trōān) *nt* (pl patronen) pattern; *c* cartridge

patrouille (paa-trōō-ᵛer) *c* (pl ~s) patrol

patrouilleren (paa-trōō-ᵛāy-rern) *v* patrol

paus (pouss) *c* (pl ~en) pope

pauw (pou) *c* (pl ~en) peacock

pauze (*pou*-zer) *c* (pl ~s) pause; break; interval, intermission

pauzeren (pou-zāy-rern) *v* pause

paviljoen (paa-vɪl-ᵛōōn) *nt* (pl ~en, ~s) pavilion

pech (pehkh) *c* bad luck

pedaal (per-*daal*) *nt/c* (pl pedalen) pedal

peddel (*peh*-derl) *c* (pl ~s) paddle

pedicure (pāy-dee-*kēw*-rer) *c* (pl ~s) pedicure, chiropodist

peen (pāyn) *c* (pl penen) carrot

peer (pāyr) *c* (pl peren) pear; light bulb

pees (pāyss) *c* (pl pezen) sinew, tendon

peetvader (*pāyt*-faa-derr) *c* (pl ~s) godfather

peil (payl) *nt* (pl ~en) level

pelgrim (*pehl*-grɪm) *c* (pl ~s) pilgrim

pelikaan (pāy-lee-*kaan*) *c* (pl -kanen) pelican

pels (pehls) *c* (pl pelzen) fur

pen (pehn) *c* (pl ~nen) pen

penicilline (pāy-nee-see-*lee*-ner) *c* penicillin

penningmeester (*peh*-nɪng-māyss-terr) *c* (pl ~s) treasurer

penseel (pehn-*sāyl*) *nt* (pl -selen) paint-brush

pensioen (pehn-*shōōn*) *nt* (pl ~en) pension

pension (pehn-*shon*) *nt* (pl ~s) board; boarding-house, guesthouse, pension; **vol** ~ full board, board and lodging, bed and board

peper (*pāy*-perr) *c* pepper

pepermunt (pāy-perr-*mernt*) *c* peppermint

per (pehr) *prep* by

perceel (pehr-*sāyl*) *nt* (pl -celen) plot

percentage (pehr-sehn-*taa*-zher) *nt* (pl ~s) percentage

percolator (pehr-kōā-*laa*-tor) *c* (pl ~s) percolator

perfectie (pehr-*fehk*-see) *c* perfection

periode (pāy-ree-ᵛōā-der) *c* (pl ~s, ~n) period; term

periodiek (pāy-ree-ᵛōā-*deek*) *adj* periodical

permanent (pehr-maa-*nehnt*) *adj* permanent; *c* permanent wave

permissie (pehr-*mɪ*-see) *c* permission

perron (peh-*ron*) *nt* (pl ~s) platform

perronkaartje (peh-*ron*-kaar-tᵛer) *nt* (pl ~s) platform ticket

Pers (pehrs) *c* (pl Perzen) Persian

pers (pehrs) *c* press

persconferentie (*pehrs*-kon-fer-rehn-tsee) *c* (pl ~s) press conference

persen (*pehr*-sern) *v* press

personeel (pehr-sōā-*nāyl*) *nt* personnel

personentrein (pehr-*sōā*-ner-trayn) *c* (pl ~en) passenger train

persoon (pehr-*sōān*) *c* (pl -sonen) person; **per** ~ per person

persoonlijk (pehr-*sōan*-lerk) *adj* personal; private

persoonlijkheid (pehr-*sōan*-lerk-hayt) *c* (pl -heden) personality

perspectief (pehr-spehk-*teef*) *nt* (pl -tieven) perspective

Perzië (*pehr*-zee-yer) Persia

perzik (*pehr*-zık) *c* (pl ~en) peach

Perzisch (*pehr*-zeess) *adj* Persian

pessimisme (peh-see-*miss*-mer) *nt* pessimism

pessimist (peh-see-*mist*) *c* (pl ~en) pessimist

pessimistisch (peh-see-*miss*-teess) *adj* pessimistic

pet (peht) *c* (pl ~ten) cap

peterselie (pāy-terr-*sāy*-lee) *c* parsley

petitie (per-*tee*-tsee) *c* (pl ~s) petition

petroleum (pāy-*trōa*-lāy-yerm) *c* petroleum; kerosene, paraffin

peuter (*pūr*-terr) *c* (pl ~s) toddler

pianist (pee-yaa-*nist*) *c* (pl ~en) pianist

piano (pee-*yaa*-nōa) *c* (pl ~'s) piano

piccolo (*pee*-kōa-lōa) *c* (pl ~'s) pageboy, bellboy

picknick (*pık*-nık) *c* (pl ~s) picnic

picknicken (*pık*-nı-kern) *v* picnic

pick-up (pık-*erp*) *c* (pl ~s) record-player

pienter (*peen*-terr) *adj* bright, smart, clever

pier (peer) *c* (pl ~en) pier, jetty

pijl (payl) *c* (pl ~en) arrow

pijn (payn) *c* (pl ~en) ache, pain; ~ *doen *hurt; ache

pijnlijk (*payn*-lerk) *adj* sore, painful; embarrassing, awkward

pijnloos (*payn*-lōass) *adj* painless

pijp (payp) *c* (pl ~en) pipe; tube

pijpestoker (*pay*-per-stōa-kerr) *c* (pl ~s) pipe cleaner

pijptabak (*payp*-taa-bahk) *c* pipe tobacco

pikant (pee-*kahnt*) *adj* spicy; savoury

pil (pıl) *c* (pl ~len) pill

pilaar (pee-*laar*) *c* (pl pilaren) column, pillar

piloot (pee-*lōat*) *c* (pl piloten) pilot

pils (pıls) *nt* beer

pincet (pın-*seht*) *c* (pl ~ten) tweezers *pl*

pinda (*pın*-daa) *c* (pl ~'s) peanut

pinguïn (*pın*-gvın) *c* (pl ~s) penguin

pink (pıngk) *c* (pl ~en) little finger

Pinksteren (*pıngk*-ster-rern) Whitsun

pion (pee-*yon*) *c* (pl ~nen) pawn

pionier (pee-yōa-*neer*) *c* (pl ~s) pioneer

piraat (pee-*raat*) *c* (pl piraten) pirate

piste (*peess*-ter) *c* (pl ~s) ring

pistool (peess-*tōal*) *nt* (pl pistolen) pistol

pit (pıt) *c* (pl ~ten) stone, pip

pittoresk (pee-tōa-*rehsk*) *adj* picturesque

plaag (plaakh) *c* (pl plagen) plague

plaat (plaat) *c* (pl platen) plate, sheet; picture

plaats (plaats) *c* (pl ~en) place; spot, locality, site; seat; room; **in ~ van** instead of

plaatselijk (*plaat*-ser-lerk) *adj* local; regional

plaatsen (*plaat*-sern) *v* *lay, *put, place; locate

* plaatshebben (*plaats*-heh-bern) *v* *take place

plaatskaartenbureau (*plaats*-kaar-ter-bēw-rōa) *nt* (pl ~s) box-office

plaatsvervanger (*plaats*-ferr-vah-ngerr) *c* (pl ~s) deputy, substitute

plafond (plaa-*font*) *nt* (pl ~s) ceiling

plagen (*plaa*-gern) *v* tease

plakband (*plahk*-bahnt) *nt* scotch tape, adhesive tape

plakboek (*plahk*-bōok) *nt* (pl ~en)

scrap-book

plakken (*plah*-kern) *v* *stick; paste

plan (plahn) *nt* (pl ~nen) plan; project, scheme; **van ~** *zijn intend

planeet (plaa-*nayt*) *c* (pl -neten) planet

planetarium (plaa-ner-*taa*-ree-^yerm) *nt* (pl ~s, -ria) planetarium

plank (plahngk) *c* (pl ~en) board, plank; shelf

plannen (*pleh*-nern) *v* plan

plant (plahnt) *c* (pl ~en) plant

plantage (plahn-*taa*-zher) *c* (pl ~s) plantation

planten (*plahn*-tern) *v* plant

plantengroei (*plahn*-ter-groo^{ee}) *c* vegetation

plantkunde (*plahnt*-kern-der) *c* botany

plantsoen (plahnt-*soon*) *nt* (pl ~en) public garden

plas (plahss) *c* (pl ~sen) puddle

plastic (*pleh*-stik) *adj* plastic

plat (plaht) *adj* flat; even, level

platenspeler (*plaa*-ter-spay-lerr) *c* (pl ~s) record-player

platina (*plaa*-tee-naa) *nt* platinum

plattegrond (plah-ter-*gront*) *c* (pl ~en) map, plan

platteland (plah-ter-*lahnt*) *nt* country-side, country; **plattelands-** rural

platzak (*plaht*-sahk) broke

plaveien (plaa-*vay*-ern) *v* pave

plaveisel (plaa-*vay*-serl) *nt* pavement

plechtig (*plehkh*-terkh) *adj* solemn

pleegouders (*playkh*-ou-derrs) *pl* foster-parents *pl*

plegen (*play*-gern) *v* commit

pleidooi (play-*doa*^{ee}) *nt* (pl ~en) plea

plein (playn) *nt* (pl ~en) square

pleister[1] (*play*-sterr) *c* (pl ~s) plaster

pleister[2] (*play*-sterr) *nt* plaster

pleiten (*play*-tern) *v* plead

plek (plehk) *c* (pl ~ken) spot; **blauwe ~** bruise; **zere ~** sore

plezier (pler-*zeer*) *nt* pleasure; fun

plicht (plikht) *c* (pl ~en) duty

ploeg[1] (plookh) *c* (pl ~en) plough

ploeg[2] (plookh) *c* (pl ~en) team; shift; gang

ploegen (*ploo*-gern) *v* plough

plooi (ploa^{ee}) *c* (pl ~en) crease

plooihoudend (ploa^{ee}-*hou*-dernt) *adj* permanent press

plotseling (*plot*-ser-ling) *adj* sudden

plukken (*pler*-kern) *v* pick

plus (plerss) *prep* plus

pneumatisch (pnur-*maa*-teess) *adj* pneumatic

pocketboek (*po*-kert-book) *nt* (pl ~en) paperback

poeder (*poo*-derr) *nt/c* (pl ~s) powder

poederdons (*poo*-derr-dons) *c* (pl -donzen) powder-puff

poederdoos (*poo*-derr-doass) *c* (pl -dozen) powder compact

poelier (poo-*leer*) *c* (pl ~s) poulterer

poes (pooss) *c* (pl poezen) pussy-cat

poetsen (*poo*-tsern) *v* brush; polish

pogen (*poa*-gern) *v* try

poging (*poa*-ging) *c* (pl ~en) try, attempt; effort

pokken (*po*-kern) *pl* smallpox

Polen (*poa*-lern) Poland

polio (*poa*-lee-^yoa) *c* polio

polis (*poa*-lerss) *c* (pl ~sen) policy

politicus (poa-*lee*-tee-kerss) *c* (pl -ci) politician

politie (poa-*lee*-tsee) *c* police *pl*

politieagent (poa-*lee*-tsi-aa-gehnt) *c* (pl ~en) policeman

politiebureau (poa-*lee*-tsee-bew-roa) *nt* (pl ~s) police-station

politiek (poa-lee-*teek*) *adj* political; *c* policy; politics

pols (pols) *c* (pl ~en) wrist; pulse

polshorloge (*pols*-hor-loa-zher) *nt* (pl ~s) wrist-watch

polsslag (*pol*-slahkh) *c* pulse

pomp (pomp) *c* (pl ~en) pump
pompelmoes (*pom*-perl-mōōss) *c* (pl -moezen) grapefruit
pompen (*pom*-pern) *v* pump
pond (pont) *nt* pound
Pool (pōal) *c* (pl Polen) Pole
Pools (pōals) *adj* Polish
poort (pōart) *c* (pl ~en) gate
poosje (*pōa*-sher) *nt* while
poot (pōat) *c* (pl poten) leg; paw
pop (pop) *c* (pl ~pen) doll
popeline (*pōa*-per-*lee*-ner) *nt/c* poplin
popmuziek (*pop*-mew̄-zeek) *c* pop music
poppenkast (*po*-per-kahst) *c* puppet-show
populair (pōa-pew̄-*lair*) *adj* popular
porselein (por-seh-*layn*) *nt* porcelain, china
portefeuille (por-ter-*fur*ew̄-yer) *c* (pl ~s) pocket-book, wallet
portemonnee (por-ter-mo-*nāy*) *c* (pl ~s) purse
portie (*por*-see) *c* (pl ~s) portion; helping
portier (por-*teer*) *c* (pl ~s) doorman, door-keeper, porter
portret (por-*treht*) *nt* (pl ~ten) portrait
Portugal (*por*-tew̄-gahl) Portugal
Portugees (por-tew̄-*gāyss*) *adj* Portuguese
positie (pōa-*zee*-tsee) *c* (pl ~s) position
positief (pōa-zee-*teef*) *adj* positive
post[1] (post) *c* mail, post
post[2] (post) *c* (pl ~en) entry
postbode (*post*-bōa-der) *c* (pl ~s, ~n) postman
postcode (*post*-kōa-der) *c* (pl ~s) zip code *Am*
posten (*poss*-tern) *v* mail, post
poste restante (post-rehss-*tahnt*) poste restante

posterijen (poss-ter-*ray*-ern) *pl* postal service
postkantoor (*post*-kahn-tōar) *nt* (pl -toren) post-office
postwissel (*post*-vi-serl) *c* (pl ~s) postal order; mail order *Am*
postzegel (*post*-sāy-gerl) *c* (pl ~s) postage stamp, stamp
postzegelautomaat (*post*-sāy-gerl-ōa-tōa-maat) *c* (pl -maten) stamp machine
pot (pot) *c* (pl ~ten) pot; jar
potlood (*pot*-lōat) *nt* (pl -loden) pencil
praatje (*praa*-t^yer) *nt* (pl ~s) chat
pracht (prahkht) *c* splendour
prachtig (*prahkh*-terkh) *adj* lovely, wonderful, marvellous; splendid, gorgeous, fine
praktijk (prahk-*tayk*) *c* (pl ~en) practice
praktisch (*prahk*-teess) *adj* practical
praten (*praa*-tern) *v* talk
precies (prer-*seess*) *adj* precise, very, exact; *adv* exactly; just
predikant (prāy-dee-*kahnt*) *c* (pl ~en) clergyman, minister, vicar, rector
preek (prāyk) *c* (pl preken) sermon
preekstoel (*prāyk*-stōōl) *c* (pl ~en) pulpit
preken (*prāy*-kern) *v* preach
premie (*prāy*-mee) *c* (pl ~s) premium
premier (prer-m^y*āy*) *c* (pl ~s) premier, Prime Minister
prent (prehnt) *c* (pl ~en) picture; print, engraving
prentbriefkaart (*prehnt*-breef-kaart) *c* (pl ~en) picture postcard
president (prāy-zee-*dehnt*) *c* (pl ~en) president
prestatie (prehss-*taa*-tsee) *c* (pl ~s) achievement; feat
presteren (prehss-*tāy*-rern) *v* achieve
prestige (prehss-*tee*-zher) *nt* prestige
pret (prehnt) *c* fun; gaiety, pleasure

prettig (_preh_-terkh) adj enjoyable, pleasant ; nice

preventief (pray-vehn-_teef_) adj preventive

priester (_pree_-sterr) c (pl ~s) priest

prijs (prayss) c (pl prijzen) price-list ; charge, cost, rate ; prize, award ; **op ~ stellen** appreciate

prijsdaling (_prayss_-daa-lɪng) c (pl ~en) slump

prijslijst (_prayss_-layst) c (pl ~en) price list

prijzen (_pray_-zern) v price

* **prijzen** (_pray_-zern) v praise

prijzig (_pray_-zerkh) adj expensive

prik¹ (prɪk) c (pl ~ken) sting

prik² (prɪk) c fizz

prikkel (_prɪ_-kerl) c (pl ~s) impulse

prikkelbaar (_prɪ_-kerl-baar) adj irritable

prikkelen (_prɪ_-ker-lern) v irritate

prikken (_prɪ_-kern) v prick

prima (_pree_-maa) adj first-rate

primair (_pree_-mair) adj primary

principe (prɪn-_see_-per) nt (pl ~s) principle

prins (prɪns) c (pl ~en) prince

prinses (prɪn-_sehss_) c (pl ~sen) princess

prioriteit (pree-ʸōa-ree-_tayt_) c (pl ~en) priority

privé (pree-_vay_) adj private

privéleven (pree-_vay_-lay-vern) nt privacy

proberen (prōa-_bay_-rern) v try ; attempt ; test

probleem (prōa-_blaym_) nt (pl -blemen) problem

procédé (prōa-ser-_day_) nt (pl ~s) process

procedure (prōa-ser-_dēw_-rer) c (pl ~s) procedure

procent (prōa-_sehnt_) nt (pl ~en) percent

proces (prōa-_sehss_) nt (pl ~sen) process ; lawsuit

processie (prōa-_seh_-see) c (pl ~s) procession

producent (prōa-dēw-_sehnt_) c (pl ~en) producer

produceren (prōa-dēw-_say_-rern) v produce

produkt (prōa-_derkt_) nt (pl ~en) product ; produce

produktie (prōa-_derk_-see) c (pl ~s) production ; output

proef (prōōf) c (pl proeven) experiment ; trial, test

proeven (_prōō_-vern) v taste

profeet (prōa-_fayt_) c (pl -feten) prophet

professor (prōa-_feh_-sor) c (pl ~en, ~s) professor

profiteren (prōa-fee-_tay_-rern) v profit, benefit

programma (prōa-_grah_-maa) nt (pl ~'s) programme

progressief (prōa-greh-_seef_) adj progressive

project (prōa-ʸehkt) nt (pl ~en) project

promenade (pro-mer-_naa_-der) c (pl ~s) esplanade, promenade

promotie (prōa-_mōa_-tsee) c (pl ~s) promotion

prompt (prompt) adj prompt

propaganda (prōa-paa-_gahn_-daa) c propaganda

propeller (prōa-_peh_-lerr) c (pl ~s) propeller

proportie (prōa-_por_-see) c (pl ~s) proportion

prospectus (pro-_spehk_-terss) c (pl ~sen) prospectus

prostituée (pro-stee-tēw-_vay_) c (pl ~s) prostitute

protest (prōa-_tehst_) nt (pl ~en) protest

protestants (prōa-terss-_tahnts_) adj

Protestant

protesteren (prōa-tehss-*tāy*-rern) *v* protest

provinciaal (prōa-vın-*shaal*) *adj* provincial

provincie (prōa-*vın*-see) *c* (pl ~s) province

provisiekast (prōa-*vee*-zee-kahst) *c* (pl ~en) larder

pruik (prur^ew k) *c* (pl ~en) wig

pruim (prur^ew m) *c* (pl ~en) plum; prune

prullenmand (*prer*-ler-mahnt) *c* (pl ~en) wastepaper-basket

psychiater (psee-khee-*Yaa*-terr) *c* (pl ~s) psychiatrist

psychisch (*psee*-kheess) *adj* psychic

psychologie (psee-khōa-lōa-*gee*) *c* psychology

psychologisch (psee-khōa-*lōa*-geess) *adj* psychological

psycholoog (psee-khōa-*lōakh*) *c* (pl -logen) psychologist

publiceren (pēw-blee-*sāy*-rern) *v* publish

publiek (pēw-*bleek*) *adj* public; *nt* audience, public

publikatie (pēw-blee-*kaa*-tsee) *c* (pl ~s) publication

puimsteen (*pur^ew m*-stāyn) *nt* pumice stone

puistje (*pur^ew*-sher) *nt* (pl ~s) pimple

punaise (pēw-*nai*-zer) *c* (pl ~s) drawing-pin; thumbtack *nAm*

punctueel (perngk-tēw-*vāyl*) *adj* punctual

punt (pernt) *nt* (pl ~en) point; item, issue; *c* full stop, period; tip

puntenslijper (*pern*-ter-slay-perr) *c* (pl ~s) pencil-sharpener

puntkomma (pernt-*ko*-maa) *c* semicolon

put (pert) *c* (pl ~ten) well

puur (pēwr) *adj* neat; sheer

puzzel (*per*-zerl) *c* (pl ~s) puzzle

pyjama (pee-*Yaa*-maa) *c* (pl ~'s) pyjamas *pl*

Q

quarantaine (kaa-rahn-*tai*-ner) *c* quarantine

quota (*kvōa*-taa) *c* (pl ~'s) quota

R

raad[1] (raat) *c* advice, counsel

raad[2] (raat) *c* (pl raden) council

raadplegen (*raat*-plāy-gern) *v* consult

raadpleging (*raat*-plāy-gıng) *c* (pl ~en) consultation

raadsel (*raat*-serl) *nt* (pl ~s, ~en) riddle, puzzle; mystery, enigma

raadslid (*raats*-lıt) *nt* (pl -leden) councillor

raadsman (*raats*-mahn) *c* (pl -lieden) counsellor; solicitor

raaf (raaf) *c* (pl raven) raven

raam (raam) *nt* (pl ramen) window

raar (raar) *adj* curious, odd, strange, queer, quaint

rabarber (raa-*bahr*-berr) *c* rhubarb

racket (*reh*-kert) *nt* (pl ~s) racquet

* **raden** (*raa*-dern) *v* guess

radiator (raa-dee-*Yaa*-tor) *c* (pl ~s, ~en) radiator

radicaal (raa-dee-*kaal*) *adj* radical

radijs (raa-*dayss*) *c* (pl radijzen) radish

radio (*raa*-dee-*Yōa*) *c* (pl ~'s) wireless, radio

rafelen (*raa*-fer-lern) *v* fray

raffinaderij (rah-fee-naa-der-*ray*) *c* (pl ~en) refinery

rage (*raa*-zher) *c* (pl ~s) craze

raken (*raa*-kern) *v* *hit

raket (*raa*-*keht*) *c* (pl ~ten) rocket

ramp (rahmp) *c* (pl ~en) calamity, disaster

rampzalig (rahm-*psaa*-lerkh) *adj* disastrous

rand (rahnt) *c* (pl ~en) edge, border; brim, rim, verge

rang (rahng) *c* (pl ~en) rank; class

rangschikken (*rahng*-skhı-kern) *v* arrange; sort, grade

rantsoen (rahnt-*soon*) *nt* (pl ~en) ration

ranzig (*rahn*-zerkh) *adj* rancid

rapport (rah-*port*) *nt* (pl ~en) report

rapporteren (rah-por-*tay*-rern) *v* report

rariteit (raa-ree-*tayt*) *c* (pl ~en) curio

ras (rahss) *nt* (pl ~sen) race; breed; **rassen-** racial

rasp (rahsp) *c* (pl ~en) grater

raspen (*rahss*-pern) *v* grate

rat (raht) *c* (pl ~ten) rat

rauw (rou) *adj* raw

ravijn (raa-*vayn*) *nt* (pl ~en) gorge

razen (*raa*-zern) *v* rage

razend (*raa*-zernt) *adj* furious

razernij (raa-zerr-*nay*) *c* rage

reactie (ray-*Yahk*-see) *c* (pl ~s) reaction

reageren (ray-*Yah*-*gay*-rern) *v* react

recent (rer-*sehnt*) *adj* recent

recept (rer-*sehpt*) *nt* (pl ~en) recipe; prescription

receptie (rer-*sehp*-see) *c* (pl ~s) reception office

receptioniste (rer-sehp-shoa-*niss*-ter) *c* (pl ~s) receptionist

recht¹ (rehkht) *nt* (pl ~en) right; law, justice

recht² (rehkht) *adj* straight

rechtbank (*rehkht*-bahngk) *c* (pl ~en) court

rechtdoor (rehkh-*doar*) *adv* straight on, straight ahead

rechter¹ (*rehkh*-terr) *adj* right-hand

rechter² (*rehkh*-terr) *c* (pl ~s) judge

rechthoek (*rehkht*-hook) *c* (pl ~en) oblong, rectangle

rechthoekig (rehkht-*hoo*-kerkh) *adj* rectangular

rechtopstaand (rehkh-*top*-staant) *adj* erect, upright

rechts (rehkhts) *adj* right-hand, right

rechtschapen (rehkht-*skhaa*-pern) *adj* honourable

rechtstreeks (*rehkh*-strāyks) *adj* direct

rechtszaak (*rehkht*-saak) *c* (pl -zaken) trial

rechtuit (rehkh-*turᵉʷt*) *adv* straight ahead

rechtvaardig (raykht-*faar*-derkh) *adj* just, righteous, right

rechtvaardigheid (rehkht-*faar*-derkh-hayt) *c* justice

reclame (rer-*klaa*-mer) *c* advertising, publicity

reclamespot (rer-*klaa*-mer-spot) *c* (pl ~s) commercial

record (rer-*kawr*) *nt* (pl ~s) record

recreatie (rāy-krāy-*Yaa*-tsee) *c* recreation

recreatiecentrum (rāy-krāy-*Yaa*-tsee-sehn-trerm) *nt* (pl -tra) recreation centre

rector (*rehk*-tor) *c* (pl ~en, ~s) head master, principal

reçu (rer-*sew*) *nt* (pl ~'s) receipt

redakteur (rāy-dahk-*tūrr*) *c* (pl ~en, ~s) editor

redden (*reh*-dern) *v* save, rescue

redder (*reh*-derr) *c* (pl ~s) saviour

redding (*reh*-dıng) *c* (pl ~en) rescue

reddingsgordel (*reh*-dıngs-khor-derl) *c* (pl ~s) lifebelt

rede¹ (*rāy*-der) *c* sense; reason

rede² (*rāy*-der) *c* (pl ~s) speech

redelijk (*rāy*-der-lerk) *adj* reasonable

reden (*rāy*-dern) *c* (pl ~en) reason

redeneren (rāy-der-nāy-rern) v reason

reder (rāy-derr) c (pl ~s) shipowner

redetwisten (rāy-der-tvɪss-tern) v argue

reduceren (rāy-dew-sāy-rern) v reduce

reductie (rer-derk-see) c (pl ~s) discount, reduction, rebate

reeds (rāyts) adv already

reekalf (rāy-kahlf) nt (pl -kalveren) fawn

reeks (rāyks) c (pl ~en) series; sequence

referentie (rer-fer-rehn-tsee) c (pl ~s) reference

reflector (rer-flehk-tor) c (pl ~s, ~en) reflector

reformatie (rāy-for-maa-tsee) c reformation

regel (rāy-gerl) c (pl ~s) line; rule; **in de ~** as a rule

regelen (rāy-ger-lern) v arrange; settle; regulate

regeling (rāy-ger-lɪng) c (pl ~en) arrangement; settlement; regulation

regelmatig (rāy-gerl-maa-terkh) adj regular

regen (rāy-gern) c rain

regenachtig (rāy-gern-ahkh-terkh) adj rainy

regenboog (rāy-ger-bōakh) c (pl -bogen) rainbow

regenbui (rāy-ger-bur^ew) c (pl ~en) shower

regenen (rāy-ger-nern) v rain

regenjas (rāy-ger-ʸahss) c (pl ~sen) mackintosh, raincoat

regeren (rer-gāy-rern) v rule, govern, reign

regering (rer-gāy-rɪng) c (pl ~en) government; reign

regie (rer-gee) c (pl ~s) direction

regime (rer-zheem) nt (pl ~s) régime

regisseren (rāy-gee-sāy-rern) v direct

regisseur (rāy-gee-surr) c (pl ~s) director

register (rer-gɪss-terr) nt (pl ~s) record; index

registratie (rāy-gɪss-traa-tsee) c registration

reglement (rāy-gler-mehnt) nt (pl ~en) regulation

reiger (ray-gerr) c (pl ~s) heron

rein (rayn) adj pure

reinigen (ray-ner-gern) v clean; **chemisch ~** dry-clean

reiniging (ray-ner-gɪng) c cleaning

reinigingsmiddel (ray-ner-gɪngs-mɪderl) nt (pl ~en) cleaning fluid

reis (rayss) c (pl reizen) journey; trip, voyage

reisagent (rayss-aa-gehnt) c (pl ~en) travel agent

reisbureau (rayss-bēw-rōa) nt (pl ~s) travel agency

reischeque (ray-shehk) c (pl ~s) traveller's cheque

reiskosten (rayss-koss-tern) pl fare; travelling expenses

reisplan (rayss-plahn) nt (pl ~nen) itinerary

reisroute (rayss-rōō-ter) c (pl ~s, ~n) itinerary

reisverzekering (rayss-ferr-zāy-ker-rɪng) c travel insurance

reiswieg (rayss-veekh) c (pl ~en) carry-cot

reizen (ray-zern) v travel

reiziger (ray-zer-gerr) c (pl ~s) traveller

rek (rehk) c elasticity

rekbaar (rehk-baar) adj elastic

rekenen (rāy-ker-nern) v reckon

rekening (rāy-ker-nɪng) c (pl ~en) account; bill; check nAm

rekenkunde (rāy-kerng-kern-der) c arithmetic

rekken (reh-kern) v stretch

rekruut (rer-krēwt) c (pl rekruten) recruit

rel (rehl) *c* (pl ~len) riot

relatie (rer-*laa*-tsee) *c* (pl ~s) relation; connection

relatief (rer-laa-*teef*) *adj* relative; comparative

reliëf (rerl-*Yehf*) *nt* (pl ~s) relief

relikwie (rer-ler-*kvee*) *c* (pl ~ën) relic

reling (*rāy*-lıng) *c* (pl ~en) rail

rem (rehm) *c* (pl ~men) brake

remlichten (*rehm*-lıkh-tern) *pl* brake lights

remtrommel (*rehm*-tro-mehl) *c* (pl ~s) brake drum

renbaan (*rehn*-baan) *c* (pl -banen) race-course; track; race-track

rendabel (rehn-*daa*-berl) *adj* paying

rendier (*rehn*-deer) *nt* (pl ~en) rein-deer

rennen (*reh*-nern) *v* *run

renpaard (*rehn*-paart) *nt* (pl ~en) race-horse

rente (*rehn*-ter) *c* (pl ~n, ~s) interest

reparatie (*rāy*-paa-*raa*-tsee) *c* (pl ~s) reparation

repareren (*rāy*-paa-*rāy*-rern) *v* repair, fix; mend

repertoire (rer-pehr-*tvaar*) *nt* (pl ~s) repertory

repeteren (rer-per-*tāy*-rern) *v* rehearse

repetitie (rer-per-*tee*-tsee) *c* (pl ~s) re-hearsal

representatief (rer-prāy-zehn-taa-*teef*) *adj* representative

reproduceren (rāy-prōa-dew-*sāy*-rern) *v* reproduce

reproduktie (rāy-prōa-*derk*-see) *c* (pl ~s) reproduction

reptiel (rehp-*teel*) *nt* (pl ~en) reptile

republiek (rāy-pew-*bleek*) *c* (pl ~en) republic

republikeins (rāy-pew-blee-*kayns*) *adj* republican

reputatie (rāy-pew-*taa*-tsee) *c* reputa-

tion; fame

reserve (rer-*zehr*-ver) *c* (pl ~s) re-serve; reserve- spare

reserveband (rer-*zehr*-ver-bahnt) *c* (pl ~en) spare tyre

reserveren (rer-zehr-*vāy*-rern) *v* re-serve; book

reservering (rer-zehr-*vāy*-rıng) *c* (pl ~en) reservation; booking

reservewiel (rer-*zehr*-ver-veel) *nt* (pl ~en) spare wheel

reservoir (rer-zerr-*vvaar*) *nt* (pl ~s) reservoir; container

resoluut (rāy-zōa-*lōōt*) *adj* resolute

respect (reh-*spehkt*) *nt* respect; es-teem, regard

respectabel (reh-spehk-*taa*-berl) *adj* respectable

respecteren (reh-spehk-*tāy*-rern) *v* re-spect

respectievelijk (reh-spehk-*tee*-ver-lerk) *adj* respective

rest (rehst) *c* (pl ~en) rest; remain-der; remnant

restant (rehss-*tahnt*) *nt* (pl ~en) re-mainder; remnant

restaurant (reh-stōa-*rahnt*) *nt* (pl ~s) restaurant

restauratiewagen (rehss-tōa-*raa*-tsee-vaa-gern) *c* (pl ~s) dining-car

restriktie (rer-*strık*-see) *v* (pl ~s) qualification

resultaat (rāy-zerl-*taat*) *nt* (pl -taten) result; outcome, issue

resulteren (rāy-zerl-*tāy*-rern) *v* result

resumé (rāy-zew-*māy*) *nt* (pl ~s) sum-mary

retour (rer-*tōōr*) round trip *Am*

retourvlucht (rer-*tōōr*-vlerkht) *c* (pl ~en) return flight

reumatiek (rūr-maa-*teek*) *c* rheuma-tism

reus (rūrss) *c* (pl reuzen) giant

reusachtig (rūr-*zahkh*-terkh) *adj* huge;

gigantic, enormous, immense

revalidatie (rāy-vaa-lee-*daa*-tsee) *c* rehabilitation

revers (rer-*vair*) *c* (pl ~) lapel

reviseren (rāy-vee-*zāy*-rern) *v* overhaul

revolutie (rāy-vōa-*lew*-tsee) *c* (pl ~s) revolution

revolutionair (rāy-vōa-lew-tshōa-*nair*) *adj* revolutionary

revolver (rer-*vol*-verr) *c* (pl ~s) gun, revolver

revue (rer-*vew*) *c* (pl ~s) revue

rib (rıp) *c* (pl ~ben) rib

ribfluweel (rıp-flew-vāyl) *nt* corduroy

richten (rıkh-tern) *v* direct; ~ **op** aim at

richting (rıkh-tıng) *c* (pl ~en) direction; way

richtingaanwijzer (rıkh-tıng-aan-vay-zerr) *c* (pl ~s) trafficator, indicator; directional signal *Am*

richtlijn (rıkht-layn) *c* (pl ~en) directive

ridder (rı-derr) *c* (pl ~s) knight

riem (reem) *c* (pl ~en) belt; strap; lead

riet (reet) *nt* reed; cane

rif (rıf) *nt* (pl ~fen) reef

rij (ray) *c* (pl ~en) row, rank; line; file, queue; **in de** ~ *staan* queue; stand in line *Am*

rijbaan (*ray*-baan) *c* (pl -banen) carriageway; roadway n*Am*

rijbewijs (*ray*-ber-vayss) *nt* driving licence

***rijden** (*ray*-dern) *v* *drive; *ride

***rijgen** (*ray*-gern) *v* thread

rijk¹ (rayk) *adj* rich; wealthy

rijk² (rayk) *nt* (pl ~en) kingdom, empire; **rijks-** imperial

rijkdom (*rayk*-dom) *c* (pl ~men) wealth, riches *pl*

rijm (raym) *nt* (pl ~en) rhyme

rijp (rayp) *adj* ripe, mature

rijpheid (*rayp*-hayt) *c* maturity

rijst (rayst) *c* rice

rijstrook (*ray*-strōak) *c* (pl -stroken) lane

rijtuig (*ray*-tur^ew g) *nt* (pl ~en) carriage; coach

rijweg (*ray*-vehk) *c* drive

rijwiel (*ray*-veel) *nt* (pl ~en) cycle; bicycle

rillen (rı-lern) *v* shiver; tremble

rillerig (rı-ler-rerkh) *adj* shivery

rilling (rı-lıng) *c* (pl ~en) chill; shiver, shudder

rimpel (rım-perl) *c* (pl ~s) wrinkle

ring (rıng) *c* (pl ~en) ring

ringweg (rıng-vehk) *c* (pl ~en) bypass

riool (ree-^Y ōal) *nt* (pl riolen) sewer

risico (*ree*-zee-kōa) *nt* (pl ~'s) risk; chance, hazard

riskant (rıss-*kahnt*) *adj* risky

rit (rıt) *c* (pl ~ten) ride

ritme (rıt-mer) *nt* (pl ~n) rhythm

ritssluiting (rıt-slur^ew -tıng) *c* (pl ~en) zipper, zip

rivaal (ree-*vaal*) *c* (pl rivalen) rival

rivaliseren (ree-vaa-lee-*zāy*-rern) *v* rival

rivaliteit (ree-vaa-lee-*tayt*) *c* rivalry

rivier (ree-*veer*) *c* (pl ~en) river

riviermonding (ree-*veer*-mon-dıng) *c* (pl ~en) estuary

rivieroever (ree-*veer*-ōō-verr) *c* (pl ~s) riverside

rob (rop) *c* (pl ~ben) seal

robijn (rōa-*bayn*) *c* (pl ~en) ruby

roddelen (ro-der-lern) *v* gossip

roede (*rōō*-der) *c* (pl ~n) rod

roeiboot (*rōō ^ee*-bōat) *c* (pl -boten) rowing-boat

roeien (*rōō ^ee*-ern) *v* row

roeiriem (*rōō ^ee*-reem) *c* (pl ~en) oar

roem (rōōm) *c* glory; celebrity, fame

Roemeen (rōō-*māyn*) *c* (pl -menen)

Rumanian

Roemeens (rōō-*māy*ns) *adj* Rumanian

Roemenië (rōō-*māy*-nee-ᵞer) Rumania

roep (rōōp) *c* call, cry

* **roepen** (rōō-pern) *v* call; cry, shout

roer (rōōr) *nt* rudder, helm

roeren (rōō-rern) *v* stir

roerend (rōō-rernt) *adj* movable

roest (rōōst) *nt* rust

roestig (rōōss-terkh) *adj* rusty

rok (rok) *c* (pl ~ken) skirt

roken (rōa-kern) *v* smoke

roker (rōa-kerr) *c* (pl ~s) smoker

rol (rol) *c* (pl ~len) roll

rolgordijn (rol-gor-dayn) *nt* (pl ~en) blind

rollen (ro-lern) *v* roll

rolstoel (rol-stōōl) *c* (pl ~en) wheelchair

roltrap (rol-trahp) *c* (pl ~pen) escalator

roman (rōa-*mahn*) *c* (pl ~s) novel

romance (rōa-*mahng*-ser) *c* (pl ~s, ~n) romance

romanschrijver (rōa-*mahn*-skhray-verr) *c* (pl ~s) novelist

romantisch (rōa-*mahn*-teess) *adj* romantic

romig (rōa-merkh) *adj* creamy

rommel (ro-merl) *c* mess; litter; trash, junk

rond (ront) *adj* round; *prep* around

ronde (ron-der) *c* (pl ~n, ~s) round

rondom (ront-*om*) *adv* around; *prep* round

rondreis (ront-rayss) *c* (pl -reizen) tour

rondreizend (ront-ray-zernt) *adj* itinerant

* **rondtrekken** (ron-treh-kern) *v* tramp

* **rondzwerven** (ront-svehr-vern) *v* wander

röntgenfoto (rernt-gern-fōa-tōa) *c* (pl ~'s) X-ray

rood (rōat) *adj* red

roodborstje (rōat-bor-sher) *nt* (pl ~s) robin

roodkoper (rōat-kōa-perr) *nt* copper

roof (rōaf) *c* robbery

roofdier (rōaf-deer) *nt* (pl ~en) beast of prey

rook (rōak) *c* smoke

rookcoupé (rōa-kōo-pāy) *c* (pl ~s) smoker

rookkamer (rōa-kaa-merr) *c* smoking-room

room (rōam) *c* cream

roomkleurig (rōam-*klur*-rerkh) *adj* cream

rooms-katholiek (rōams-kah-tōa-*leek*) *adj* Roman Catholic

roos[1] (rōass) *c* (pl rozen) rose

roos[2] (rōass) *c* dandruff

rooster (rōa-sterr) *nt* (pl ~s) grate; schedule

roosteren (rōa-ster-rern) *v* grill, roast

rot (rot) *adj* rotten

rotan (rōa-tahn) *nt* rattan

rotonde (rōa-ton-der) *c* (pl ~s) roundabout

rots (rots) *c* (pl ~en) rock; cliff

rotsachtig (rot-sahkh-terkh) *adj* rocky

rotsblok (rots-blok) *nt* (pl ~ken) boulder

rouge (rōō-zher) *c/nt* rouge

roulette (rōō-*leh*-ter) *c* roulette

route (rōō-ter) *c* (pl ~s) route

routine (rōō-*tee*-ner) *c* routine

rouw (rou) *c* mourning

royaal (rōa-ᵞaal) *adj* generous; liberal

roze (raw-zer) *adj* rose, pink

rozenkrans (rōa-zer-krahns) *c* (pl ~en) rosary, beads *pl*

rozijn (rōa-zayn) *c* (pl ~en) raisin

rubber (rer-berr) *nt* rubber

rubriek (rew-*breek*) *c* (pl ~en) column

rug (rerkh) *c* (pl ~gen) back

ruggegraat (rer-ger-graat) *c* spine, backbone

rugpijn (*rerkh*-payn) *c* backache
rugzak (*rerkh*-sahk) *c* (pl ~ken) ruck-sack
*ruiken (*rur*ᵉʷ-kern) *v* *smell
ruil (rurᵉʷl) *c* exchange
ruilen (*rur*ᵉʷ-lern) *v* exchange; swap
ruim¹ (rurᵉʷm) *adj* broad, large; roomy, spacious
ruim² (rurᵉʷm) *nt* (pl ~en) hold
ruimte (*rur*ᵉʷm-ter) *c* room, space
ruïne (rēw-*vee*-ner) *c* (pl ~s) ruins
ruïneren (rēw-vee-*nāy*-rern) *v* ruin
ruit (rurᵉʷt) *c* (pl ~en) check; pane
ruitenwisser (*rur*ᵉʷ-ter-vɪ-serr) *c* (pl ~s) windscreen wiper; windshield wiper *Am*
ruiter (*rur*ᵉʷ-terr) *c* (pl ~s) horseman; rider
ruk (rerk) *c* (pl ~ken) tug, wrench
rumoer (rēw-*mōōr*) *nt* noise
rundvlees (*rernt*-flāyss) *nt* beef
Rus (rerss) *c* (pl ~sen) Russian
Rusland (*rerss*-lahnt) Russia
Russisch (*rer*-seess) *adj* Russian
rust (rerst) *c* rest; quiet; half-time
rusteloosheid (rerss-ter-*lōāss*-hayt) *c* unrest
rusten (*rerss*-tern) *v* rest
rusthuis (*rerst*-hurᵉʷss) *nt* (pl -huizen) rest-home
rustiek (rerss-*teek*) *adj* rustic
rustig (*rerss*-terkh) *adj* calm, quiet; restful, tranquil
ruw (rēwᵒᵒ) *adj* rough, harsh
ruzie (*rēw*-zee) *c* (pl ~s) row, quarrel, dispute; ~ **maken** quarrel

S

saai (saaᵉᵉ) *adj* dull, boring
sacharine (sah-khaa-*ree*-ner) *c* saccharin

saffier (sah-*feer*) *nt* sapphire
salaris (saa-*laa*-rɪss) *nt* (pl ~sen) salary; pay
saldo (*sahl*-dōa) *nt* (pl ~'s, saldi) balance
salon (saa-*lon*) *c* (pl ~s) drawing-room, lounge; salon
samen (*saa*-mern) *adv* together
*samenbinden (*saa*-mer-bɪn-dern) *v* bundle
*samenbrengen (*saa*-mer-breh-ngern) *v* combine
samenhang (*saa*-mer-hahng) *c* coherence
samenleving (*saa*-mer-lāy-vɪng) *c* (pl ~en) community
samenloop (*saa*-mer-lōap) *c* concurrence
samenstellen (*saa*-mer-steh-lern) *v* compose, compile
samenstelling (*saa*-mer-steh-lɪng) *c* (pl ~en) composition
*samenvallen (*saa*-mer-vah-lern) *v* coincide
samenvatting (*saa*-mer-vah-tɪng) *c* (pl ~en) résumé, summary
samenvoegen (*saa*-mer-vōō-gern) *v* join
samenwerking (*saa*-mer-vehr-kɪng) *c* co-operation
*samenzweren (*saa*-mer-zvāy-rern) *v* conspire
samenzwering (*saa*-mer-zvāy-rɪng) *c* (pl ~en) plot
sanatorium (saa-naa-*tōā*-ree-ᵞerm) *nt* (pl ~s, -ria) sanatorium
sandaal (sahn-*daal*) *c* (pl -dalen) sandal
sanitair (saa-nee-*tair*) *adj* sanitary
Saoedi-Arabië (saa-ōō-dee-aa-*raa*-bee-ᵞer) Saudi Arabia
Saoedi-Arabisch (saa-ōō-dee-aa-*raa*-beess) *adj* Saudi Arabian
sap (sahp) *nt* (pl ~pen) juice

sappig (*sah*-perkh) *adj* juicy

sardine (sahr-*dee*-ner) *c* (pl ~s) sardine

satelliet (saa-ter-*leet*) *c* (pl ~en) satellite

satijn (saa-*tayn*) *nt* satin

sauna (*sou*-naa) *c* (pl ~'s) sauna

saus (souss) *c* (pl sauzen) sauce

Scandinavië (skahn-dee-*naa*-vee-Yer) Scandinavia

Scandinaviër (skahn-dee-*naa*-vee-Yerr) *c* (pl ~s) Scandinavian

Scandinavisch (skahn-dee-*naa*-veess) *adj* Scandinavian

scène (*sai*-ner) *c* (pl ~s) scene

schaafwond (*skhaaf*-vont) *c* (pl ~en) graze

schaak! (skhaak) check!

schaakbord (*skhaak*-bort) *nt* (pl ~en) checkerboard *nAm*

schaakspel (*skhaak*-spehl) *nt* chess

schaal (skhaal) *c* (pl schalen) dish; bowl; scale

schaaldier (*skhaal*-deer) *nt* (pl ~en) shellfish

schaamte (*skhaam*-ter) *c* shame

schaap (skhaap) *nt* (pl schapen) sheep

schaar (skhaar) *c* (pl scharen) scissors *pl*

schaars (skhaars) *adj* scarce

schaarste (*skhaar*-ster) *c* scarcity

schaats (skhaats) *c* (pl ~en) skate

schaatsen (*skhaat*-sern) *v* skate

schade (*skhaa*-der) *c* damage; harm, mischief

schadelijk (*skhaa*-der-lerk) *adj* harmful; hurtful

schadeloosstelling (*skhaa*-der-lōa-steh-lıng) *c* (pl ~en) indemnity

schaden (*skhaa*-dern) *v* harm

schadevergoeding (*skhaa*-der-verr-gōo-dıng) *c* (pl ~en) compensation, indemnity

schaduw (*skhaa*-dēw⁰⁰) *c* (pl ~en) shade; shadow

schaduwrijk (*skhaa*-dēw⁰⁰-rayk) *adj* shady

schakel (*skhaa*-kerl) *c* (pl ~s) link

schakelaar (*skhaa*-ker-laar) *c* (pl ~s) switch

schakelbord (*skhaa*-kerl-bort) *nt* switchboard

schakelen (*skhaa*-ker-lern) *v* change gear

zich schamen (*skhaa*-mern) *be ashamed

schandaal (skhahn-*daal*) *nt* (pl -dalen) scandal

schande (*skhahn*-deh) *c* disgrace, shame

schapevlees (*skhaa*-per-vlāyss) *nt* mutton

scharnier (skhahr-*neer*) *nt* (pl ~en) hinge

schat (skhaht) *c* (pl ~ten) treasure; darling

schatkist (*skhaht*-kıst) *c* treasury

schatten (*skhah*-tern) *v* evaluate, estimate, value; appreciate

schatting (*skhah*-tıng) *c* (pl ~en) estimate; appreciation

schedel (*skhāy*-derl) *c* (pl ~s) skull

scheef (skhāyf) *adj* slanting

scheel (skhāyl) *adj* cross-eyed

scheepswerf (*skhāyps*-vehrf) *c* (pl -werven) shipyard

scheepvaart (*skhāyp*-faart) *c* navigation

scheepvaartlijn (*skhāyp*-faart-layn) *c* (pl ~en) shipping line

scheerapparaat (*skhāyr*-ah-paa-raat) *nt* (pl -raten) safety-razor, electric razor, shaver

scheercrème (*skhāyr*-kraim) *c* (pl ~s) shaving-cream

scheerkwast (*skhāyr*-kvahst) *c* (pl ~en) shaving-brush

scheermesje (*skhāyr*-meh-sher) *nt* (pl

~s) razor-blade

scheerzeep (*skhāȳr-zāȳp*) *c* shaving-soap

*scheiden (*skhay-*dern) *v* separate; divide, part; divorce

scheiding (*skhay-*dıng) *c* (pl ~en) division; parting

scheidsrechter (*skhayts-*rehkh-terr) *c* (pl ~s) umpire

scheikunde (*skhay-*kern-der) *c* chemistry

scheikundig (skhay-*kern-*derkh) *adj* chemical

*schelden (*skhehl-*dern) *v* scold

schelm (skhehlm) *c* (pl ~en) rascal

schelp (skhehlp) *c* (pl ~en) shell

schelvis (*skhehl-*vıss) *c* haddock

schema (*skhāȳ-*maa) *nt* (pl ~'s, ~ta) diagram; scheme

schemering (*skhāȳ-*mer-ring) *c* twilight

schending (*skhehn-*dıng) *c* (pl ~en) violation

*schenken (*skhehng-*kern) *v* pour; donate

schenking (*skhehng-*kıng) *c* (pl ~en) donation

*scheppen (*skheh-*pern) *v* create

schepsel (*skhehp-*serl) *nt* (pl ~s) creature

zich *scheren (*skhāȳ-*rern) *v* shave

scherm (skhehrm) *nt* (pl ~en) screen

schermen (*skhehr-*mern) *v* fence

scherp (skhehrp) *adj* sharp; keen

schets (skhehts) *c* (pl ~en) sketch

schetsboek (*skhehts-*bōōk) *nt* (pl ~en) sketch-book

schetsen (*skheht-*sern) *v* sketch

scheur (skhūrr) *c* (pl ~en) tear

scheuren (*skhūr-*rern) *v* rip, *tear

schiereiland (*skheer-*ay-lahnt) *nt* peninsula

*schieten (*skhee-*tern) *v* *shoot, fire

schietschijf (*skheet-*skhayf) *c* (pl

-schijven) mark

schijf (skhayf) *c* (pl schijven) disc

schijn (skhayn) *c* semblance

schijnbaar (*skhaym-*baar) *adj* apparent

*schijnen (*skhay-*nern) *v* appear, seem; *shine

schijnheilig (skhayn-*hay-*lerkh) *adj* hypocritical

schijnwerper (*skhayn-*vehr-perr) *c* (pl ~s) spotlight, searchlight

schikken (*skhı-*kern) *v* suit

schikking (*skhı-*kıng) *c* (pl ~en) settlement

schil (skhıl) *c* (pl ~len) skin; peel

schilder (*skhıl-*derr) *c* (pl ~s) painter

schilderachtig (*skhıl-*derr-ahkh-terkh) *adj* scenic, picturesque

schilderen (*skhıl-*der-rern) *v* paint

schilderij (skhıl-der-*ray*) *nt* (pl ~en) painting, picture

schildpad (*skhıl-*paht) *c* (pl ~den) turtle

schilfer (*skhıl-*ferr) *c* (pl ~s) chip

schillen (*skhı-*lern) *c* peel

schimmel (*skhı-*merl) *c* (pl ~s) mildew

schip (skhıp) *nt* (pl schepen) ship; boat, vessel

schitterend (*skhı-*ter-rernt) *adj* brilliant, splendid

schittering (*skhı-*ter-rıng) *c* (pl ~en) glare

schoeisel (*skhōō^{ee}-*serl) *nt* footwear

schoen (skhōōn) *c* (pl ~en) shoe

schoenmaker (*skhōōn-*maa-kerr) *c* (pl ~s) shoemaker

schoensmeer (*skhōōn-*smāȳr) *c* shoe polish

schoenveter (*skhōōn-*fāȳ-terr) *c* (pl ~s) shoe-lace

schoenwinkel (*skhōōn-*vıng-kerl) *c* (pl ~s) shoe-shop

schoft (skhoft) *c* (pl ~en) bastard

schok (skhok) *c* (pl ~ken) shock

schokbreker (*skhok*-brāy-kerr) *c* (pl
~s) shock absorber
schokken (*skho*-kern) *v* shock
schol (skhol) *c* (pl ~len) plaice
schommel (*skho*-merl) *c* (pl ~s) swing
schommelen (*skho*-mer-lern) *v* rock,
*swing
school (skhōal) *c* (pl scholen) school;
college; middelbare ~ secondary
school
schoolbank (*skhōal*-bahngk) *c* (pl
~en) desk
schoolbord (*skhōal*-bort) *nt* (pl ~en)
blackboard
schoolhoofd (*skhōal*-hōaft) *nt* (pl
~en) headmaster, head teacher
schooljongen (*skhōal*-Yo-ngern) *c* (pl
~s) schoolboy
schoolmeester (*skhōal*-māyss-terr) *c*
(pl ~s) teacher
schoolmeisje (*skhōal*-may-sher) *nt* (pl
~s) schoolgirl
schoolslag (*skhōal*-slahkh) *c* breaststroke
schooltas (*skhōal*-tahss) *c* (pl ~sen)
satchel
schoon (skhōan) *adj* clean
schoonheid (*skhōan*-hayt) *c* (pl -he-
den) beauty
schoonheidsbehandeling (*skhōan*-
hayts-ber-hahn-der-ling) *c* (pl ~en)
beauty treatment
schoonheidsmasker (*skhōan*-hayts-
mahss-kerr) *nt* (pl ~s) face-pack
schoonheidsmiddelen (*skhōan*-hayts-
mı-der-lern) *pl* cosmetics *pl*
schoonheidssalon (*skhōan*-hayts-saa-
lon) *c* (pl ~s) beauty salon, beauty
parlour
schoonmaak (*skhōa*-maak) *c* cleaning
schoonmaken (*skhōa*-maa-kern) *v*
clean
schoonmoeder (*skhōa*-mōo-derr) *c* (pl
~s) mother-in-law

schoonouders (*skhōan*-ou-derrs) *pl*
parents-in-law *pl*
schoonvader (*skhōan*-vaa-derr) *c* (pl
~s) father-in-law
schoonzoon (*skhōan*-zōan) *c* (pl -zo-
nen) son-in-law
schoonzuster (*skhōan*-zerss-terr) *c* (pl
~s) sister-in-law
schoorsteen (*skhōar*-stāyn) *c* (pl -ste-
nen) chimney
schop (skhop) *c* (pl ~pen) kick;
spade, shovel
schoppen (*skho*-pern) *v* kick
schor (skhor) *adj* hoarse
schorsen (*skhor*-sern) *v* suspend
schort (skhort) *c* (pl ~en) apron
Schot (skhot) *c* (pl ~ten) Scot
schot (skhot) *nt* (pl ~en) shot
schotel (*skhōa*-terl) *c* (pl ~s) dish;
schoteltje *nt* saucer
Schotland (*skhot*-lahnt) Scotland
Schots (skhots) *adj* Scottish, Scotch
schouder (*skhou*-derr) *c* (pl ~s) shoulder
schouwburg (*skhou*-berrkh) *c* (pl ~en)
theatre
schouwspel (*skhou*-spehl) *nt* (pl ~en)
spectacle
schram (skhrahm) *c* (pl ~men)
scratch
schrappen (*skhrah*-pern) *v* scrape
schrede (*skhrāy*-der) *c* (pl ~n) pace
schreeuw (skhrāy⁰⁰) *c* (pl ~en)
scream, cry, shout
schreeuwen (*skhrāy⁰⁰*-ern) *v* scream,
cry, shout
schriftelijk (*skhrıf*-ter-lerk) *adj* written; *adv* in writing
schrijfbehoeften (*skhrayf*-ber-hōof-
tern) *pl* stationery
schrijfblok (*skhrayf*-blok) *nt* (pl ~ken)
writing-pad
schrijfmachine (*skhrayf*-mah-shee-ner)
c (pl ~s) typewriter

schrijfmachinepapier (*skhrayf*-mah-shee-ner-paa-peer) *nt* typing paper

schrijfpapier (*skhrayf*-paa-peer) *nt* notepaper; writing-paper

schrijftafel (*skhrayf*-taa-ferl) *c* (pl ~s) bureau

schrijn (skhrayn) *c* (pl ~en) shrine

*schrijven (*skhray*-vern) *v* *write

schrijver (*skhray*-vehr) *c* (pl ~s) author, writer

schrik (skhrɪk) *c* fright, scare; ~ ***aanjagen** terrify

schrikkeljaar (*skhrɪ*-kerl-ʸaar) *nt* leap-year

*schrikken (*skhrɪ*-kern) *v* *be frightened; ***doen** ~ frighten, scare

schrobben (*skhro*-bern) *v* scrub

schroef (skhroōf) *c* (pl schroeven) screw; propeller

schroefsleutel (*skhroōf*-slur-terl) *c* (pl ~s) spanner

schroevedraaier (*skhroō*-ver-draa-ʸerr) *c* (pl ~s) screw-driver

schroeven (*skhroō*-vern) *v* screw

schroot (skhroāt) *nt* scrap-iron

schub (skherp) *c* (pl ~ben) scale

schudden (*skher*-dern) *v* *shake; shuffle

schuifdeur (*skhur*ᵉʷf-dūrr) *c* (pl ~en) sliding door

schuilplaats (*skhur*ᵉʷl-plaats) *c* (pl ~en) cover; shelter

schuim (skhur*ᵉʷ*m) *nt* froth, lather, foam

schuimen (*skhur*ᵉʷ-mern) *v* foam

schuimrubber (*skhur*ᵉʷm-rer-berr) *nt* foam-rubber

schuin (skhur*ᵉʷ*n) *adj* slanting

*schuiven (*skhur*ᵉʷ-vern) *v* push

schuld[1] (skherlt) *c* guilt; fault, blame; **de** ~ ***geven aan** blame

schuld[2] (skherlt) *c* (pl ~en) debt

schuldeiser (*skherlt*-ay-serr) *c* (pl ~s) creditor

schuldig (*skherl*-derkh) *adj* guilty; ~ ***bevinden** convict; ~ ***zijn** owe

schuur (skhewr) *c* (pl schuren) barn; shed

schuurpapier (*skhewr*-paa-peer) *nt* sandpaper

schuw (skhewᵒᵒ) *adj* shy

scoren (*skoā*-rern) *v* score

seconde (ser-*kon*-der) *c* (pl ~n) second

secretaresse (sɪ-krer-taa-*reh*-ser) *c* (pl ~n) secretary

secretaris (sɪ-krer-*taa*-rerss) *c* (pl ~sen) secretary; clerk

sectie (*sehk*-see) *c* (pl ~s) section

secundair (saȳ-kern-*dair*) *adj* secondary

secuur (ser-*kewr*) *adj* precise

sedert (*saȳ*-derrt) *prep* since

sein (sayn) *nt* (pl ~en) signal

seinen (*say*-nern) *v* signal

seizoen (say-*zoōn*) *nt* (pl ~en) season; **buiten het** ~ off season

seksualiteit (sehk-sew-vaa-lee-*tayt*) *c* sexuality

sekseel (sehk-sew-*vaȳl*) *adj* sexual

selderij (*sehl*-der-ray) *c* celery

select (ser-*lehkt*) *adj* select

selecteren (saȳ-lehk-*taȳ*-rern) *v* select

selectie (saȳ-*lehk*-see) *c* selection

senaat (ser-*naat*) *c* senate

senator (ser-*naa*-tor) *c* (pl ~en) senator

seniel (ser-*neel*) *adj* senile

sensatie (sehn-*zaa*-tsee) *c* (pl ~s) sensation

sensationeel (sehn-zaa-tshoā-*naȳl*) *adj* sensational

sentimenteel (sehn-tee-mehn-*taȳl*) *adj* sentimental

september (sehp-*tehm*-berr) September

septisch (*sehp*-teess) *adj* septic

serie (*saȳ*-ree) *c* (pl ~s) series

serieus (sāy-ree-^yūrss) adj serious

serum (sāy-rerm) nt (pl ~s, sera) serum

serveerster (sehr-vāyr-sterr) c (pl ~s) waitress

servet (sehr-veht) nt (pl ~ten) napkin, serviette

sfeer (sfāyr) c atmosphere; sphere

shag (shehk) c cigarette tobacco

shampoo (shahm-pōa) c shampoo

Siam (see-^yahm) Siam

Siamees (see-^yaa-māyss) adj Siamese

sifon (see-fon) c (pl ~s) syphon, siphon

sigaar (see-gaar) c (pl sigaren) cigar

sigarenwinkel (see-gaa-rer-vɪng-kerl) c (pl ~s) cigar shop

sigarenwinkelier (see-gaa-rer-vɪng-ker-leer) c (pl ~s) tobacconist

sigaret (see-gaa-reht) c (pl ~ten) cigarette

sigarettenkoker (see-gaa-reh-ter-kōa-kehr) c (pl ~s) cigarette-case

sigarettepijpje (see-gaa-reh-ter-payp-^yer) nt (pl ~s) cigarette-holder

signaal (see-ñaal) nt (pl -nalen) signal

signalement (see-ñaa-ler-mehnt) nt (pl ~en) description

simpel (sɪm-perl) adj simple

sinaasappel (see-naa-sah-perl) c (pl ~en, ~s) orange

sinds (sɪns) conj since

sindsdien (sɪns-deen) adv since

singel (sɪ-ngerl) c (pl ~s) canal

sirene (see-rāy-ner) c (pl ~s) siren

siroop (see-rōap) c syrup

situatie (see-tēw-vaa-tsee) c (pl ~s) situation

sjaal (shaal) c (pl ~s) shawl; scarf

skelet (sker-leht) nt (pl ~ten) skeleton

ski (skee) c (pl ~'s) ski

skibroek (skee-brōōk) c (pl ~en) ski pants

skiën (skee-^yern) v ski

skiër (skee-^yerr) c (pl ~s) skier

skilift (skee-lɪft) c (pl ~en) ski-lift

skischoenen (skee-skhōō-nern) pl ski boots

skistokken (skee-sto-kern) pl ski sticks; ski poles Am

sla (slaa) c lettuce; salad

slaaf (slaaf) c (pl slaven) slave

*slaan (slaan) v *beat; *hit, *strike; smack, slap

slaap¹ (slaap) c sleep; **in ~** asleep

slaap² (slaap) c (pl slapen) temple

slaapkamer (slaap-kaa-merr) c (pl ~s) bedroom

slaappil (slaa-pɪl) c (pl ~len) sleeping-pill

slaapwagen (slaap-vaa-gern) c (pl ~s) sleeping-car

slaapzaal (slaap-saal) c (pl -zalen) dormitory

slaapzak (slaap-sahk) c (pl ~ken) sleeping-bag

slachtoffer (slahkht-o-ferr) nt (pl ~s) victim; casualty

slag¹ (slahkh) c (pl ~en) blow; battle

slag² (slahkh) nt sort

slagader (slahkh-aa-derr) c (pl ~s) artery

slagboom (slahkh-bōam) c (pl -bomen) barrier

slagen (slaa-gern) v manage, succeed; pass

slager (slaa-gerr) c (pl ~s) butcher

slagzin (slahkh-sɪn) c (pl ~nen) slogan

slak (slahk) c (pl ~ken) snail

slang (slahng) c (pl ~en) snake

slank (slahngk) adj slim, slender

slaolie (slaa-ōa-lee) c salad-oil

slap (slahp) adj limp; weak

slapeloos (slaa-per-lōass) adj sleepless

slapeloosheid (slaa-per-lōass-hayt) c insomnia

*slapen (slaa-pern) v *sleep

slaperig (slaa-per-rerkh) adj sleepy

slecht (slehkht) *adj* bad; poor; ill; wicked, evil; **slechter** worse; **slechtst** worst

slechts (slehkhts) *adv* only, merely

slede (slāy-der) *c* (pl ~n) sledge

slee (slāy) *c* (pl ~ën) sleigh, sledge

sleepboot (slāy-bōat) *c* (pl -boten) tug

slepen (slāy-pern) *v* drag, haul; tug, tow

sleutel (slūr-terl) *c* (pl ~s) key; wrench

sleutelbeen (slūr-terl-bāyn) *nt* (pl -beenderen, -benen) collarbone

sleutelgat (slūr-terl-gaht) *nt* (pl ~en) keyhole

***slijpen** (slay-pern) *v* sharpen

slijterij (slay-ter-*ray*) *c* (pl ~en) off-licence

slikken (slı-kern) *v* swallow

slim (slım) *adj* clever

slip (slıp) *c* (pl ~s) briefs *pl*; panties *pl*

slippen (slı-pern) *v* slip; skid

slof (slof) *c* (pl ~fen) slipper; carton

slokje (slok-Yer) *nt* (pl ~s) sip

sloot (slōat) *c* (pl sloten) ditch

slopen (slōa-pern) *v* demolish

slordig (slor-derkh) *adj* untidy; slovenly, sloppy, careless

slot[1] (slot) *nt* (pl ~en) lock; castle; **op** ~ ***doen** lock

slot[2] (slot) *nt* end, issue

sluier (slurew-err) *c* (pl ~s) veil

sluipschutter (slurewp-skher-terr) *c* (pl ~s) sniper

sluis (slurewss) *c* (pl sluizen) lock, sluice

***sluiten** (slurew-tern) *v* close, *shut; fasten

sluiting (slurew-tıng) *c* (pl ~en) fastener

sluw (slewoo) *adj* cunning

smaak (smaak) *c* (pl smaken) taste; flavour

smakelijk (smaa-ker-lerk) *adj* savoury, tasty; appetizing

smakeloos (smaa-ker-lōass) *adj* tasteless

smaken (smaa-kern) *v* taste

smal (smahl) *adj* narrow

smaragd (smaa-*rahkht*) *nt* emerald

smart (smahrt) *c* (pl ~en) grief

smartlap (smahrt-lahp) *c* (pl ~pen) tear-jerker

smeerolie (smāyr-ōa-lee) *c* lubrication oil

smeersysteem (smāyr-see-stāym) *nt* lubrication system

smeken (smāy-kern) *v* beg

***smelten** (smehl-tern) *v* melt

smeren (smāy-rern) *v* lubricate, grease

smerig (smāy-rerkh) *adj* dirty; foul, filthy

smering (smāy-rıng) *c* lubrication

smet (smeht) *c* (pl ~ten) blot

smid (smıt) *c* (pl smeden) smith, blacksmith

smoking (smōa-kıng) *c* (pl ~s) dinner-jacket; tuxedo *nAm*

smokkelen (smo-ker-lern) *v* smuggle

snaar (snaar) *c* (pl snaren) string

snavel (snaa-verl) *c* (pl ~s) beak

snee (snāy) *c* (pl ~ën) cut; slice

sneeuw (snāyoo) *c* snow

sneeuwen (snāyoo-ern) *v* snow

sneeuwslik (snāyoo-slık) *nt* slush

sneeuwstorm (snāyoo-storm) *c* (pl ~en) snowstorm, blizzard

snel (snehl) *adj* fast, swift, rapid

snelheid (snehl-hayt) *c* (pl -heden) speed; **maximum** ~ speed limit

snelheidsbeperking (snehl-hayts-ber-pehr-kıng) *c* speed limit

snelheidsmeter (snehl-hayts-māy-terr) *c* speedometer

snelheidsovertreding (snehl-hayts-ōa-verr-trāy-dıng) *c* speeding

snelkookpan (snehl-kōak-pahn) *c* (pl

~nen) pressure-cooker

snellen (*sneh*-lern) *v* dash

sneltrein (*snehl*-trayn) *c* (pl ~en) express train

snelweg (*snehl*-vehkh) *c* (pl ~en) motorway

*snijden (*snay*-dern) *v* *cut; carve

snijwond (*snay*-vont) *c* (pl ~en) cut

snipper (*sni*-perr) *c* (pl ~s) scrap

snoek (snōōk) *c* (pl ~en) pike

snoep (snōōp) *nt* sweets; candy *nAm*

snoepgoed (*snōōp*-khōōt) *nt* sweets; candy *nAm*

snoepje (*snōōp*-Yer) *nt* (pl ~s) sweet; candy *nAm*

snoepwinkel (*snōōp*-vɪng-kerl) *c* (pl ~s) sweetshop; candy store *Am*

snoer (snōōr) *nt* (pl ~en) line, cord; flex; electric cord

snor (snor) *c* (pl ~ren) moustache

snorkel (*snor*-kerl) *c* (pl ~s) snorkel

snugger (*sner*-gerr) *adj* bright

snuit (snur^{ew}t) *c* (pl ~en) snout

snurken (*snerr*-kern) *v* snore

sociaal (sōa-*shaal*) *adj* social

socialisme (sōa-shaa-*liss*-mer) *nt* socialisme

socialist (sōa-shaa-*list*) *c* (pl ~en) socialist

socialistisch (sōa-shaa-*liss*-teess) *adj* socialist

sociëteit (sōa-see-Yer-*tayt*) *c* (pl ~en) club

sodawater (*sōa*-daa-vaa-terr) *nt* soda-water

soep (sōōp) *c* (pl ~en) soup

soepbord (*sōō*-bort) *nt* (pl ~en) soup-plate

soepel (*sōō*-perl) *adj* supple, flexible

soeplepel (*sōōp*-lāy-perl) *c* (pl ~s) soup-spoon

sofa (*sōa*-faa) *c* (pl ~'s) sofa

sok (sok) *c* (pl ~ken) sock

soldaat (sol-*daat*) *c* (pl -daten) soldier

soldeerbout (sol-*dāyr*-bout) *c* (pl ~en) soldering-iron

solderen (sol-*dāy*-rern) *v* solder

solide (sōa-*lee*-der) *adj* (pl ~en) solid

sollicitatie (so-lee-see-*taa*-tsee) *c* (pl ~s) application

solliciteren (so-lee-see-*tāy*-rern) *v* apply

som (som) *c* (pl ~men) sum; amount; **ronde ~** lump sum

somber (*som*-berr) *adj* gloomy, sombre

sommige (*so*-mer-ger) *pron* some

soms (soms) *adv* sometimes

soort (sōart) *c/nt* (pl ~en) sort, kind; breed, species

sorteren (sor-*tāy*-rern) *v* assort, sort

sortering (sor-*tāy*-rɪng) *c* (pl ~en) assortment

souterrain (sōō-ter-*rang*) *nt* (pl ~s) basement

souvenir (sōō-ver-*neer*) *nt* (pl ~s) souvenir

Sovjet-Unie (*sof*-Yeht-ēw-nee) Soviet Union

spaak (spaak) *c* (pl spaken) spoke

Spaans (spaans) *adj* Spanish

spaarbank (*spaar*-bahngk) *c* (pl ~en) savings bank

spaargeld (*spaar*-gehlt) *nt* savings *pl*

spaarzaam (*spaar*-zaam) *adj* economical

spade (*spaa*-der) *c* (pl ~n) spade

spalk (spahlk) *c* (pl ~en) splint

Spanjaard (*spah*-ñaart) *c* (pl ~en) Spaniard

Spanje (*spah*-ñer) Spain

spannend (*spah*-nernt) *adj* exciting

spanning (*spah*-nɪng) *c* (pl ~en) tension; pressure, strain, stress

sparen (*spaa*-rern) *v* save; economize

spat (spaht) *c* (pl ~ten) stain, spot, speck

spatader (*spaht*-aa-derr) *c* (pl ~s,

~en) varicose vein

spatbord (*spaht*-bort) *nt* (pl ~en) mud-guard

spatiëren (spaa-*tshāy*-rern) *v* space

spatten (*spah*-tern) *v* splash

specerij (spāy-ser-*ray*) *c* (pl ~en) spice

speciaal (spāy-*shaal*) *adj* special; particular, peculiar

zich specialiseren (spāy-shaa-lee-*zāy*-rern) specialize

specialist (spāy-shaa-*list*) *c* (pl ~en) specialist

specialiteit (spāy-shaa-lee-*tayt*) *c* (pl ~en) speciality

specifiek (spāy-see-*feek*) *adj* specific

specimen (*spāy*-see-mehn) *nt* (pl ~s) specimen

speculeren (spāy-kēw-*lāy*-rern) *v* speculate

speeksel (*spāyk*-serl) *nt* spit

speelgoed (*spāyl*-gōōt) *nt* toy

speelgoedwinkel (*spāyl*-gōōt-ving-kerl) *c* (pl ~s) toyshop

speelkaart (*spāyl*-kaart) *c* (pl ~en) playing-card

speelplaats (*spāyl*-plaats) *c* (pl ~en) playground

speelterrein (*spāyl*-teh-rayn) *nt* (pl ~en) recreation ground

speer (spāyr) *c* (pl speren) spear

spek (spehk) *nt* bacon

spel[1] (spehl) *nt* (pl ~en) game

spel[2] (spehl) *nt* (pl ~len) play

speld (spehlt) *c* (pl ~en) pin

spelen (*spāy*-lern) *v* play

speler (*spāy*-lerr) *c* (pl ~s) player

spellen (*speh*-lern) *v* *spell

spelling (*speh*-ling) *c* spelling

spelonk (spāy-*longk*) *c* (pl ~en) cave

spiegel (*spee*-gerl) *c* (pl ~s) looking-glass, mirror

spiegelbeeld (*spee*-gerl-bāylt) *nt* (pl ~en) reflection

spier (speer) *c* (pl ~en) muscle

spijbelen (*spay*-ber-lern) *v* play truant

spijker (*spay*-kerr) *c* (pl ~s) nail

spijkerbroek (*spay*-kerr-brōōk) *c* (pl ~en) jeans *pl*

spijskaart (*spayss*-kaart) *c* (pl ~en) menu

spijsvertering (*spayss*-ferr-tāy-ring) *c* digestion

spijt (spayt) *c* regret

spin (spin) *c* (pl ~nen) spider

spinazie (spee-*naa*-zee) *c* spinach

*spinnen** (*spi*-nern) *v* *spin

spinneweb (*spi*-ner-vehp) *nt* (pl ~ben) spider's web, cobweb

spion (spee-*yon*) *c* (pl ~nen) spy

spiritusbrander (*spee*-ree-terss-brahn-derr) *c* (pl ~s) spirit stove

spit[1] (spit) *nt* (pl ~ten) spit

spit[2] (spit) *nt* lumbago

spits[1] (spits) *adj* pointed

spits[2] (spits) *c* (pl ~en) peak; spire

spitsuur (*spits*-ēwr) *nt* (pl -uren) rush-hour, peak hour

*splijten** (*splay*-tern) *v* *split

splinter (*splin*-terr) *c* (pl ~s) splinter

splinternieuw (*splin*-terr-nee∞) *adj* brand-new

zich splitsen (*split*-sern) fork

spoed (spōōt) *c* haste, speed

spoedcursus (*spōōt*-kerr-zerss) *c* (pl ~sen) intensive course

spoedgeval (*spōōt*-kher-vahl) *nt* (pl ~len) emergency

spoedig (*spōō*-derkh) *adv* soon, shortly

spoel (spōōl) *c* (pl ~en) spool

spoelen (*spōō*-lern) *v* rinse

spoeling (*spōō*-ling) *c* (pl ~en) rinse

spons (spons) *c* (pl sponzen) sponge

spook (spōāk) *nt* (pl spoken) ghost, phantom; spook

spoor (spōār) *nt* (pl sporen) trace; trail, track

spoorbaan (*spōār*-baan) *c* (pl -banen)

railway; railroad *nAm*

spoorweg (*spoōr*-vehkh) *c* (pl ~en) railway; railroad *nAm*

sport (sport) *c* sport

sportjasje (*sport*-Yah-sher) *nt* (pl ~s) sports-jacket, blazer

sportkleding (*sport*-klāy̆-dɪng) *c* sportswear

sportman (*sport*-mahn) *c* (pl ~en) sportsman

sportwagen (*sport*-vaa-gern) *c* (pl ~s) sports-car

spot (spot) *c* mockery

spraak (spraak) *c* speech; **ter sprake** *brengen *bring up

spraakzaam (*spraak*-saam) *adj* talkative

sprakeloos (*spraa*-ker-lōass) *adj* speechless

spreekkamer (*sprāy̆*-kaa-merr) *c* (pl ~s) surgery

spreekuur (*sprāy̆k*-ēwr) *nt* (pl -uren) consultation hours

spreekwoord (*sprāy̆k*-vōart) *nt* (pl ~en) proverb

spreeuw (sprāy̆ᵒᵒ) *c* (pl ~en) starling

sprei (spray) *c* (pl ~en) counterpane, quilt

spreiden (*spray*-dern) *v* *spread

*spreken (*sprāy̆*-kern) *v* *speak, talk

*springen (*sprɪ*-ngern) *v* jump; *leap

springstof (*sprɪng*-stof) *c* (pl ~fen) explosive

sprinkhaan (*sprɪngk*-haan) *c* (pl -hanen) grasshopper

sproeier (*sprōō*ᵉᵉ-err) *c* (pl ~s) atomizer

sprong (sprong) *c* (pl ~en) jump; hop, leap

sprookje (*sprōāk*-Yer) *nt* (pl ~s) fairytale

spruitjes (*sprᵘᵉʷ*-tYerss) *pl* sprouts *pl*

spuit (spurᵉʷt) *c* (pl ~en) syringe

spuitbus (*spurᵉʷt*-berss) *c* (pl ~sen)

atomizer

spuitwater (*spurᵉʷt*-vaa-terr) *nt* soda-water

spuug (spewkh) *nt* spit

spuwen (*spew̄ᵒᵒ*-ern) *v* *spit

staal (staal) *nt* steel; **roestvrij ~** stainless steel

*staan (staan) *v* *stand; **goed ~** *become; suit

staart (staart) *c* (pl ~en) tail

staat (staat) *c* (pl staten) state; **in ~ stellen** enable; **in ~** *zijn om* *be able to; **staats-** national

staatsburgerschap (*staats*-berr-gerr-skhahp) *nt* citizenship

staatshoofd (*staats*-hōaft) *nt* (pl ~en) head of state

staatsman (*staats*-mahn) *c* (pl -lieden) statesman

stabiel (staa-*beel*) *adj* stable

stad (staht) *c* (pl steden) town; city

stadhuis (staht-*hur*ᵉʷss) *nt* (pl -huizen) town hall

stadion (*staa*-dee-Yon) *nt* (pl ~s) stadium

stadium (*staa*-dee-Yerm) *nt* (pl stadia) stage

stadscentrum (*staht*-sehn-trerm) *nt* (pl -tra) town centre

stadslicht (*stahts*-lɪkht) *nt* (pl ~en) parking light

stadsmensen (*stahts*-mehn-sern) *pl* townspeople *pl*

staf (stahf) *c* staff

staken (*staa*-kern) *v* *strike; stop, discontinue

staking (*staa*-kɪng) *c* (pl ~en) strike

stal (stahl) *c* (pl ~len) stable

stallen (*stah*-lern) *v* garage

stalles (*stah*-lerss) *pl* stall; orchestra seat *Am*

stam (stahm) *c* (pl ~men) trunk; tribe

stamelen (*staa*-mer-lern) *v* falter

stampen (*stahm*-pern) v stamp, thump

stampvol (*stahmp*-fol) adj chock-full

stand (stahnt) c score; tot ~ *brengen realize

standbeeld (*stahnt*-bāȳlt) nt (pl ~en) statue

standpunt (*stahnt*-pernt) nt (pl ~en) point of view

standvastig (stahnt-*fahss*-terkh) adj steadfast

stang (stahng) c (pl ~en) rod, bar

stap (stahp) c (pl ~pen) step; pace; move

stapel (*staa*-perl) c (pl ~s) stack, heap, pile

stappen (*stah*-pern) v step

staren (*staa*-rern) v gaze, stare

start (stahrt) c take-off

startbaan (*stahrt*-baan) c runway

starten (*stahr*-tern) v *take off

startmotor (*stahrt*-mōa-terr) c starter motor

statiegeld (*staa*-tsee-gehlt) nt deposit

station (staa-*shon*) nt (pl ~s) station; depot nAm

stationschef (staa-*shon*-shehf) c (pl ~s) station-master

statistiek (staa-tiss-*teek*) c (pl ~en) statistics pl

stedelijk (*stāȳ*-der-lerk) adj urban

steeds (stāȳts) adv continually

steeg (stāȳkh) c (pl stegen) alley, lane

steek (stāȳk) c (pl steken) stitch; sting, bite

steel (stāȳl) c (pl stelen) stem; handle

steelpan (*stāȳl*-pahn) c (pl ~nen) saucepan

steen (stāȳn) c (pl stenen) stone; brick

steengroeve (*stāȳn*-grōō-ver) c (pl ~n) quarry

steenpuist (*stāȳn*-pur^(ew)st) c (pl ~en) boil

steigers (*stay*-gerrs) pl scaffolding

steil (stayl) adj steep

stekelvarken (*stāȳ*-kerl-vahr-kern) nt (pl ~s) porcupine

*steken (*stāȳ*-kern) v *sting

stekker (*steh*-kerr) c (pl ~s) plug

stel (stehl) nt (pl ~len) set

*stelen (*stāȳ*-lern) v *steal

stellen (*steh*-lern) v *put

stelling (*steh*-ling) c (pl ~en) thesis

stelsel (*stehl*-serl) nt (pl ~s) system; tientallig ~ decimal system

stem (stehm) c (pl ~men) voice; vote

stemmen (*steh*-mern) v vote

stemming¹ (*steh*-ming) c mood; atmosphere; spirits

stemming² (*steh*-ming) c (pl ~en) vote

stempel (*stehm*-perl) c (pl ~s) stamp

stemrecht (*stehm*-rehkht) nt suffrage

stenen (*stāȳ*-nern) adj stone

stenograaf (*stāȳ*-nōa-*graaf*) c (pl -grafen) stenographer

stenografie (stāȳ-nōa-graa-*fee*) c shorthand

step-in (stehp-*in*) c (pl ~s) girdle

ster (stehr) c (pl ~ren) star

sterfelijk (*stehr*-fer-lerk) adj mortal

steriel (ster-*reel*) adj sterile

steriliseren (stāȳ-ree-li-*zāȳ*-rern) v sterilize

sterk (stehrk) adj powerful, strong; sterke drank spirits

sterkte (*stehrk*-ter) c strength

sterrenkunde (*steh*-rer-kern-der) c astronomy

*sterven (*stehr*-vern) v die

steun (stūrn) c assistance, support; relief

steunen (*stū̄r*-nern) v support

steunkousen (*stūrn*-kou-sern) pl support hose

steurgarnaal (*stūrr*-gahr-naal) c (pl -nalen) prawn

stevig (*stāȳ*-verkh) adj solid, firm

stichten (stıkh-tern) v found

stichting (stıkh-tıng) c (pl ~en) foundation

stiefkind (steef-kınt) nt (pl ~eren) stepchild

stiefmoeder (steef-mōō-derr) c (pl ~s) stepmother

stiefvader (stee-faa-derr) c (pl ~s) stepfather

stier (steer) c (pl ~en) bull

stierengevecht (stee-rer-ger-vehkht) nt (pl ~en) bullfight

stijf (stayf) adj stiff

stijfsel (stayf-serl) nt starch

stijgbeugel (staykh-bür-gerl) c (pl ~s) stirrup

*stijgen (stay-gern) v *rise; climb

stijging (stay-gıng) c rise; climb, ascent

stijl (stayl) c (pl ~en) style

*stijven (stay-vern) v starch

stikken (stı-kern) v choke

stikstof (stık-stof) c nitrogen

stil (stıl) adj silent; quiet; still

Stille Oceaan (stı-ler ōā-sāy-aan) Pacific Ocean

stilstaand (stıl-staant) adj stationary

stilte (stıl-ter) c (pl ~s) silence; stillness, quiet

stimuleren (stee-mēw-lāy-rern) v stimulate

*stinken (stıng-kern) v *smell; *stink; stinkend smelly

stipt (stıpt) adj punctual

stoel (stōōl) c (pl ~en) chair; seat

stoep (stōōp) c (pl ~en) sidewalk nAm

stoet (stōōt) c (pl ~en) procession

stof[1] (stof) nt dust

stof[2] (stof) c (pl ~fen) fabric, cloth, material; matter; stoffen drapery; vaste ~ solid

stoffelijk (sto-fer-lerk) adj substantial, material

stoffig (sto-ferkh) adj dusty

stofzuigen (stof-sur^ew^-gern) v hoover; vacuum vAm

stofzuiger (stof-sur^ew^-gerr) c (pl ~s) vacuum cleaner

stok (stokl) c (pl ~ken) stick; cane

stokpaardje (stok-paar-t^y^er) nt (pl ~s) hobby-horse

stola (stōā-laa) c (pl ~'s) stole

stollen (sto-lern) v coagulate

stom (stom) adj mute, dumb

stomerij (stōā-mer-ray) c (pl ~en) dry-cleaner's

stomp (stomp) adj blunt

stompen (stom-pern) v punch

stookolie (stōāk-ōā-lee) c fuel oil

stoom (stōām) c steam

stoomboot (stōām-bōāt) c (pl boten) steamer

stoot (stōāt) c (pl stoten) bump

stop (stop) c (pl ~pen) stopper, cork

stopgaren (stop-khaa-rern) nt darning wool

stoplicht (stop-lıkht) nt (pl ~en) traffic light

stoppen (sto-pern) v stop, halt; *put; darn

stoptrein (stop-trayn) c (pl ~en) stopping train, local train

storen (stōā-rern) v disturb; trouble

storing (stōā-rıng) c (pl ~en) disturbance

storm (storm) c (pl ~en) storm; gale, tempest

stormachtig (storm-ahkh-terkh) adj stormy

stormlamp (storm-lahmp) c (pl ~en) hurricane lamp

stortbui (stort-bur^ew^) c (pl ~en) downpour

storten (stor-tern) v *shed; deposit

storting (stor-tıng) c (pl ~en) remittance, deposit

*stoten (stōā-tern) v bump

stout (stout) *adj* naughty, bad

stoutmoedig (stout-*mōō*-derkh) *adj* bold

straal (straal) *c* (pl stralen) squirt, spout, jet; ray, beam; radius

straalvliegtuig (*straal*-vleekh-tur^{ew}kh) *nt* (pl ~en) turbojet, jet

straat (straat) *c* (pl straten) street; road

straatweg (*straat*-vehkh) *c* (pl ~en) causeway

straf (strahf) *c* (pl ~fen) punishment; penalty

straffen (*strah*-fern) *v* punish

strafrecht (*strahf*-rehkht) *nt* criminal law

strafschop (*strahf*-skhop) *c* (pl ~pen) penalty kick

strak (strahk) *adj* tight; **strakker maken** tighten

straks (strahks) *adv* in a moment

strand (strahnt) *nt* (pl ~en) beach

streek (strāyk) *c* (pl streken) region; district, country, area; trick

streep (strāyp) *c* (pl strepen) line; stripe

streng (strehng) *adj* strict, harsh; severe

stretcher (*streht*-sherr) *c* (pl ~s) camp-bed; cot *nAm*

streven (*strāy*-vern) *v* aspire

strijd (strayt) *c* fight, combat, battle; struggle, strife, contest

*strijden (*stray*-dern) *v* *fight; struggle

strijdkrachten (*strayt*-krahkh-tern) *pl* armed forces

*strijken (*stray*-kern) *v* iron; *strike, lower

strijkijzer (*strayk*-ay-zerr) *nt* (pl ~s) iron

strikje (*strik*-^Yer) *nt* (pl ~s) bow tie

strikt (strikt) *adj* strict

stripverhaal (*strip*-ferr-haal) *nt* (pl -ha-

len) comics *pl*

stro (strōa) *nt* straw

strodak (*strōa*-dahk) *nt* (pl ~en) thatched roof

stromen (*strōa*-mern) *v* stream, flow

stroming (*strōa*-ming) *c* (pl ~en) current

strook (strōak) *c* (pl stroken) strip

stroom (strōam) *c* (pl stromen) stream; current

stroomafwaarts (strōam-*ahf*-vaarts) *adv* downstream

stroomopwaarts (strōam-*op*-vaarts) *adv* upstream

stroomverdeler (*strōam*-verr-dāy-lerr) *c* distributor

stroomversnelling (*strōam*-verr-sneh-ling) *c* (pl ~en) rapids *pl*

stroop (strōap) *c* syrup

stropen (*strōa*-pern) *v* poach

structuur (sterk-*tewr*) *c* (pl -turen) structure; fabric, texture

struik (strur^{ew}k) *c* (pl ~en) scrub, bush, shrub

struikelen (*strur^{ew}*-ker-lern) *v* stumble

struisvogel (*strurss*-fōa-gerl) *c* (pl ~s) ostrich

studeerkamer (stew-*dāyr*-kaa-merr) *c* study

student (stew-*dehnt*) *c* (pl ~en) student

studente (stew-*dehn*-ter) *c* (pl ~s) student

studeren (stew-*dāy*-rern) *v* study

studie (*stew*-dee) *c* (pl ~s) study

studiebeurs (*stew*-dee-būrrs) *c* (pl -beurzen) scholarship

stuitend (*stur^{ew}*-ternt) *adj* revolting

stuk[1] (sterk) *adj* broken; ~ ***gaan** *break down

stuk[2] (sterk) *nt* (pl ~ken) part, piece; lump, chunk; fragment; stretch

sturen (*stew*-rern) *v* *send; navigate

stuurboord (*stewr*-bōart) *nt* starboard

stuurkolom (*stewr*-kōā-lom) *c*
steering-column

stuurman (*stewr*-mahn) *c* (pl -lieden,
-lui) steersman, helmsman

stuurwiel (*stewr*-veel) *nt* steering-
wheel

subsidie (serp-*see*-dee) *c* (pl ~s) subsidy

substantie (serp-*stahn*-see) *c* (pl ~s)
substance

subtiel (serp-*teel*) *adj* subtle

succes (serk-*sehss*) *nt* (pl ~sen) success

succesvol (serk-*sehss*-fol) *adj* successful

suède (sew-*vai*-der) *nt/c* suede

suf (serf) *adj* dumb

suiker (*sur*^{ew}-kerr) *c* sugar

suikerklontje (*sur*^{ew}-kerr-klon-t^yer) *nt*
(pl ~s) lump of sugar

suikerzieke (*sur*^{ew}-kerr-zee-ker) *c* (pl
~n) diabetic

suikerziekte (*sur*^{ew}-kerr-zeek-ter) *c*
diabetes

suite (*svee*-ter) *c* (pl ~s) suite

summier (ser-*meer*) *adj* concise

superieur (sew-per-ree-*y*ūrr) *adj* superior

superlatief (sew-perr-laa-*teef*) *c* (pl
-tieven) superlative

supermarkt (*sew*-perr-mahrkt) *c* (pl
~en) supermarket

supplement (ser-pler-*mehnt*) *nt* (pl
~en) supplement

suppoost (ser-*pōāst*) *c* (pl ~en) custodian, usher

surfplank (*serrf*-plahngk) *c* (pl ~en)
surf-board

surveilleren (serr-vay-*y*ai-rern) *v* patrol

Swahili (svaa-*hee*-lee) *nt* Swahili

symbool (sım-*bōāl*) *nt* (pl -bolen)
symbol

symfonie (sım-fōā-*nee*) *c* (pl ~ën)
symphony

sympathie (sım-paa-*tee*) *c* (pl ~ën)
sympathy

sympathiek (sım-paa-*teek*) *adj* nice

symptoom (sım-*tōām*) *nt* (pl -tomen)
symptom

synagoge (see-naa-*gōā*-ger) *c* (pl ~n)
synagogue

synoniem (see-nōā-*neem*) *nt* (pl ~en)
synonym

synthetisch (sın-*tāy*-teess) *adj* synthetic

Syrië (*see*-ree-^yer) Syria

Syriër (*see*-ree-^yerr) *c* (pl ~s) Syrian

Syrisch (*see*-reess) *adj* Syrian

systeem (seess-*tāym*) *nt* (pl -temen)
system

systematisch (seess-tāy-*maa*-teess) *adj*
systematic

T

taai (taa^{ee}) *adj* tough

taak (taak) *c* (pl taken) task; duty

taal (taal) *c* (pl talen) language;
speech

taalgids (*taal*-gıts) *c* (pl ~en) phrase-
book

taart (taart) *c* (pl ~en) cake

tabak (taa-*bahk*) *c* tobacco

tabakswinkel (taa-*bahks*-vıng-kerl) *c*
(pl ~s) tobacconist's

tabakszak (taa-*bahk*-sahk) *c* (pl ~ken)
tobacco pouch

tabel (taa-*behl*) *c* (pl ~len) chart,
table

tablet (taa-*bleht*) *nt* (pl ~ten) tablet

taboe (taa-*bōō*) *nt* (pl ~s) taboo

tachtig (*tahkh*-terkh) *num* eighty

tactiek (tahk-*teek*) *c* (pl ~en) tactics
pl

tafel (*taa*-ferl) *c* (pl ~s) table

tafellaken (taa-fer-laa-kern) nt (pl ~s) table-cloth

tafeltennis (taa-ferl-teh-nerss) nt table tennis, ping-pong

taille (tah-ʸer) c (pl ~s) waist

tak (tahk) c (pl ~ken) branch, bough

talenpracticum (taa-ler-prahk-tee-kerm) nt (pl -tica) language laboratory

talent (taa-lehnt) nt (pl ~en) faculty, talent

talkpoeder (tahlk-pōō-derr) nt/c talc powder

talrijk (tahl-rayk) adj numerous

tam (tahm) adj tame

tamelijk (taa-mer-lerk) adv pretty, fairly, quite, rather

tampon (tahm-pon) c (pl ~s) tampon

tand (tahnt) c (pl ~en) tooth

tandarts (tahn-dahrts) c (pl ~en) dentist

tandenborstel (tahn-der-bors-terl) c (pl ~s) toothbrush

tandestoker (tahn-der-stōa-kerr) c (pl ~s) toothpick

tandpasta (tahnt-pahss-taa) c/nt (pl ~'s) toothpaste

tandpijn (tahnt-payn) c toothache

tandpoeder (tahnt-pōō-derr) nt/c toothpowder

tandvlees (tahnt-flā̄yss) nt gum

tang (tahng) c (pl ~en) tongs pl, pliers pl

tank (tehngk) c (pl ~s) tank

tankschip (tehnk-skhip) nt (pl -schepen) tanker

tante (tahn-ter) c (pl ~s) aunt

tapijt (taa-payt) nt (pl ~en) carpet

tarief (taa-reef) nt (pl tarieven) rate, tariff; fare

tarwe (tahr-ver) c wheat

tas (tahss) c (pl ~sen) bag

tastbaar (tahst-baar) adj palpable; tangible

tastzin (tahst-sin) c touch

taxeren (tahk-sā̄y-rern) v estimate

taxi (tahk-see) c (pl ~'s) cab, taxi

taxichauffeur (tahk-see-shōa-fūrr) c (pl ~s) cab-driver, taxi-driver

taximeter (tahk-see-māy-terr) c taxi-meter

taxistandplaats (tahk-see-stahnt-plaats) c (pl ~en) taxi rank; taxi stand Am

te (ter) adv too

technicus (tehkh-nee-kerss) c (pl -ci) technician

techniek (tehkh-neek) c (pl ~en) technique

technisch (tehkh-neess) adj technical

technologie (tehkh-nōa-lōa-gee) c technology

teder (tā̄y-derr) adj delicate, tender

teef (tā̄yf) c (pl teven) bitch

teen (tā̄yn) c (pl tenen) toe

teer (tā̄yr) adj gentle, tender; c/nt tar

tegel (tā̄y-gerl) c (pl ~s) tile

tegelijk (ter-ger-layk) adv at the same time; at once

tegelijkertijd (ter-ger-lay-kerr-tayt) adv simultaneously

tegemoetkomend (ter-ger-mōōt-kōa-mernt) adj oncoming

tegemoetkoming (ter-ger-mōōt-kōa-ming) c (pl ~en) concession

tegen (tā̄y-gern) prep against

tegendeel (tā̄y-ger-dā̄yl) nt contrary, reverse

tegengesteld (tā̄y-ger-ger-stehlt) adj contrary, opposite

*tegenkomen (tā̄y-ger-kōa-mern) v *come across, *meet; run into

tegenover (tā̄y-ger-nōa-verr) prep opposite, facing

tegenslag (tā̄y-ger-slahkh) c (pl ~en) misfortune; reverse

*tegenspreken (tā̄y-ger-sprā̄y-kern) v contradict

tegenstander (táy-ger-stahn-derr) c (pl ~s) opponent

tegenstelling (táy-ger-steh-lıng) c (pl ~en) contrast

tegenstrijdig (táy-ger-stray-derkh) adj contradictory

***tegenvallen** (táy-ger-vah-lern) v *be disappointing

***tegenwerpen** (táy-ger-vehr-pern) v object

tegenwerping (táy-ger-vehr-pıng) c (pl ~en) objection

tegenwoordig (táy-ger-vóar-derkh) adj present; adv nowadays

tegenwoordigheid (táy-ger-vóar-derkh-hayt) c presence

tegenzin (táy-ger-zın) c aversion

tehuis (ter-hurᵉʷss) nt (pl tehuizen) home; asylum

teint (taint) c complexion

teken (táy-kern) nt (pl ~s, ~en) sign; indication, signal; token

tekenen (táy-ker-nern) v *draw, sketch; sign

tekenfilm (táy-ker-fılm) c (pl ~s) cartoon

tekening (táy-ker-nıng) c (pl ~en) drawing, sketch

tekort (ter-kort) nt (pl ~en) shortage; deficit; ~ *schieten fail

tekortkoming (ter-kort-kóa-mıng) c (pl ~en) shortcoming

tekst (tehkst) c (pl ~en) text

tel (tehl) c (pl ~len) second

telefoneren (táy-ler-fóa-náy-rern) v phone

telefoniste (táy-ler-fóa-nıss-ter) c (pl ~n, ~s) operator, telephonist

telefoon (táy-ler-fóan) c (pl ~s) phone, telephone

telefoonboek (táy-ler-fóan-bóök) nt (pl ~en) telephone directory; telephone book Am

telefooncel (táy-ler-fóan-sehl) c (pl ~len) telephone booth

telefooncentrale (táy-ler-fóan-sehn-traa-ler) c (pl ~s) telephone exchange

telefoongesprek (táy-ler-fóan-ger-sprehk) nt (pl ~ken) telephone call

telefoongids (táy-ler-fóan-gıts) c (pl ~en) telephone directory; telephone book Am

telefoonhoorn (táy-ler-fóan-hóa-rern) c (pl ~s) receiver

telefoontje (táy-ler-fóan-tᵞer) nt (pl ~s) call

telegraferen (táy-ler-graa-fáy-rern) v cable, telegraph

telegram (táy-ler-grahm) nt (pl ~men) cable, telegram

telelens (táy-ler-lehns) c (pl -lenzen) telephoto lens

telepathie (táy-láy-paa-tee) c telepathy

teleurstellen (ter-lúrr-steh-lern) v disappoint; *let down

teleurstelling (ter-lúrr-steh-lıng) c (pl ~en) disappointment

televisie (táy-ler-vee-zee) c television

televisietoestel (táy-ler-vee-zee-tóö-stehl) nt (pl ~len) television set

telex (táy-lehks) c telex

telkens (tehl-kerns) adv again and again

tellen (teh-lern) v count

telmachine (tehl-mah-shee-ner) c (pl ~s) adding-machine

telwoord (tehl-vóart) nt (pl ~en) numeral

temmen (teh-mern) v tame

tempel (tehm-perl) c (pl ~s) temple

temperatuur (tehm-per-raa-teᵂr) c (pl -turen) temperature

tempo (tehm-póa) nt pace

tendens (tehn-dehns) c (pl -denzen) tendency

tenminste (ter-mın-ster) adv at least

tennis (*teh*-nerss) *nt* tennis

tennisbaan (*teh*-nerss-baan) *c* (pl -banen) tennis-court

tennisschoenen (*teh*-ner-skhoo-nern) *pl* tennis shoes

tenslotte (tehn-*slo*-ter) *adv* at last

tent (tehnt) *c* (pl ~en) tent

tentdoek (*tehn*-dook) *nt* canvas

tentoonstellen (tehn-*tōan*-steh-lern) *v* exhibit; *show

tentoonstelling (tehn-*tōan*-steh-ling) *c* (pl ~en) exposition, exhibition; display, show

tenzij (tehn-*zay*) *conj* unless

teraardebestelling (tehr-*aar*-der-ber-steh-ling) *c* (pl ~en) burial

terecht (ter-*rehkht*) *adj* just; *adv* rightly

terechtstelling (ter-*rehkht*-steh-ling) *c* (pl ~en) execution

terloops (tehr-*lōaps*) *adj* casual

term (tehrm) *c* (pl ~en) term

termijn (tehr-*mayn*) *c* (pl ~en) term

terpentijn (tehr-pern-*tayn*) *c* turpentine

terras (teh-*rahss*) *nt* (pl ~sen) terrace

terrein (teh-*rayn*) *nt* (pl ~en) terrain; grounds

terreur (teh-*rūrr*) *c* terrorism

terrorisme (teh-ro-*riss*-mer) *nt* terrorism

terrorist (teh-rōa-*rist*) *c* (pl ~en) terrorist

terug (ter-*rerkh*) *adv* back

terugbetalen (ter-*rerkh*-ber-taa-lern) *v* *repay; reimburse, refund

terugbetaling (terrerkh-ber-taa-ling) *c* (pl ~en) repayment, refund

*terugbrengen (ter-*rerkh*-brehng-ern) *v* *bring back

*teruggaan (ter-*rer*-khaan) *v* *go back, *get back

teruggang (ter-*rer*-khahng) *c* depression, recession

terugkeer (ter-*rerkh*-kāyr) *c* return

terugkeren (ter-*rerkh*-kāy-rern) *v* return; turn back

*terugkomen (ter-*rerkh*-kōa-mern) *v* return

terugreis (ter-*rerkh*-rayss) *c* return journey

*terugroepen (ter-*rerkh*-rōo-pern) *v* recall

terugsturen (ter-*rerkh*-stew-rern) *v* *send back

*terugtrekken (ter-*rerkh*-treh-kern) *v* *withdraw

*terugvinden (ter-*rerkh*-fin-dern) *v* recover

terugweg (ter-*rerkh*-vehkh) *c* way back

*terugzenden (ter-*rerkh*-sehn-dern) *v* *send back

terwijl (terr-*vayl*) *conj* whilst, while

terylene (*teh*-ree-lāyn) *nt* terylene

terzijde (tehr-*zay*-der) *adv* aside

test (tehst) *c* (pl ~s) test

testament (tehss-taa-*mehnt*) *nt* (pl ~en) will

testen (*tehss*-tern) *v* test

tevens (*tāy*-verns) *adv* also

tevergeefs (ter-verr-*gāyfs*) *adv* in vain

tevoren (ter-*vōa*-rern) *adv* before; van ~ in advance

tevreden (ter-*vrāy*-dern) *adj* satisfied, content

tewaterlating (ter-vaa-terr-laa-ting) *c* launching

*teweegbrengen (ter-*vāykh*-brehngern) *v* effect

tewerkstellen (ter-*vehrk*-steh-lern) *v* employ

tewerkstelling (ter-*vehrk*-steh-ling) *c* (pl ~en) employment

textiel (tehks-*teel*) *c/nt* textile

Thailand (*tigh*-lahnt) Thailand

Thailander (*tigh*-lahn-derr) *c* (pl ~s) Thai

Thailands (*tigh*-lahnts) *adj* Thai

thans (tahns) *adv* now

theater (tāy-*Yaa*-terr) *nt* (pl ~s) theatre

thee (tāy) *c* tea

theedoek (*tāy*-dook) *c* (pl ~en) teacloth

theekopje (*tāy*-kop-*Yay*) *nt* (pl ~s) teacup

theelepel (*tāy*-lāy-perl) *c* (pl ~s) teaspoon

theepot (*tāy*-pot) *c* (pl ~ten) teapot

theeservies (*tāy*-sehr-veess) *nt* (pl -viezen) tea-set

thema (*tāy*-maa) *nt* (pl ~'s) theme; exercise

theologie (tāy-*Yōa*-lōa-*gee*) *c* theology

theoretisch (tāy-*Yōa*-*rāy*-teess) *adj* theoretical

theorie (tāy-*Yōa*-*ree*) *c* (pl ~ën) theory

therapie (tāy-raa-*pee*) *c* (pl ~ën) therapy

thermometer (tehr-mōa-māy-terr) *c* (pl ~s) thermometer

thermosfles (*tehr*-moss-flehss) *c* (pl ~sen) vacuum flask, thermos flask

thermostaat (tehr-moss-*taat*) *c* (pl -staten) thermostat

thuis (tur*ew*ss) *adv* home, at home

tien (teen) *num* ten

tiende (*teen*-der) *num* tenth

tiener (*tee*-nerr) *c* (pl ~s) teenager

tijd (tayt) *c* (pl ~en) time; **de laatste** ~ lately; **op** ~ in time; **vrije** ~ spare time, leisure

tijdbesparend (tayt-ber-*spaa*-rernt) *adj* time-saving

tijdelijk (*tay*-der-lerk) *adj* temporary

tijdens (*tay*-derns) *prep* during

tijdgenoot (*tayt*-kher-nōat) *c* (pl -noten) contemporary

tijdperk (*tayt*-pehrk) *nt* (pl ~en) period

tijdschrift (*tayt*-skhrɪft) *nt* (pl ~en) review, periodical, journal

tijger (*tay*-gerr) *c* (pl ~s) tiger

tijm (taym) *c* thyme

tikken (*tɪ*-kern) *v* type

timmerhout (*tɪ*-merr-hout) *nt* timber

timmerman (*tɪ*-merr-mahn) *c* (pl -lieden, -lui) carpenter

tin (tɪn) *nt* tin, pewter

tiran (tee-*rahn*) *c* (pl ~nen) tyrant

titel (*tee*-terl) *c* (pl ~s) title; heading; degree

toch (tokh) *adv* still; *conj* yet

tocht (tokht) *c* draught

toe (tōō) *adj* closed

toebehoren (*tōō*-ber-hōa-rern) *v* belong; *pl* accessories *pl*

toedienen (*tōō*-dee-nern) *v* administer

toegang (*tōō*-gahng) *c* admittance, admission, access; entry, entrance; approach

toegankelijk (tōō-*gahng*-ker-lerk) *adj* accessible

***toegeven** (*tōō*-gāy-vern) *v* admit, acknowledge; *give in, indulge

toehoorder (*tōō*-hōar-derr) *c* (pl ~s) auditor

toekennen (*tōō*-keh-nern) *v* award

toekomst (*tōō*-komst) *c* future

toekomstig (tōō-*kom*-sterkh) *adj* future

toelage (*tōō*-laa-ger) *c* (pl ~n) allowance, grant

***toelaten** (*tōō*-laa-tern) *v* admit

toelating (*tōō*-laa-tɪng) *c* (pl ~en) admission

toelichten (*tōō*-lɪkh-tern) *v* elucidate

toelichting (*tōō*-lɪkh-tɪng) *c* (pl ~en) explanation

toen (tōōn) *conj* when; *adv* then

toename (*tōō*-naa-mer) *c* increase

***toenemen** (*tōō*-nāy-mern) *v* increase; **toenemend** progressive

toenmalig (*tōōn*-maa-lerkh) *adj* contemporary

toepassen (*tōō*-pah-sern) *v* apply

toepassing (tōō-pah-sıng) c (pl ~en) application

toereikend (tōō-*ray*-kernt) adj adequate

toerisme (tōō-*rıss*-mer) nt tourism

toerist (tōō-*rıst*) c (pl ~en) tourist

toeristenklasse (tōō-*rıss*-ter-klah-ser) c tourist class

toernooi (tōōr-*nōā*ee) nt (pl ~en) tournament

toeschouwer (*tōō*-skhou-err) c (pl ~s) spectator

*****toeschrijven aan** (*tōō*-skhray-vern) assign to

*****toeslaan** (*tōō*-slaan) v *strike

toeslag (*tōō*-slahkh) c (pl ~en) surcharge

toespraak (*tōō*-spraak) c (pl -spraken) speech

*****toestaan** (*tōō*-staan) v allow, permit

toestand (*tōō*-stahnt) c (pl ~en) state; condition

toestel (*tōō*-stehl) nt (pl ~len) apparatus, appliance; aircraft; extension

toestemmen (*tōō*-steh-mern) v agree, consent

toestemming (*tōō*-steh-mıng) c authorization, permission; consent

toetje (*tōō*-tᵞer) nt (pl ~s) sweet

toeval (*tōō*-vahl) nt chance; luck

toevallig (tōō-*vah*-lerkh) adj accidental, casual, incidental; adv by chance

toevertrouwen (*tōō*-verr-trou-ern) v commit

toevoegen (*tōō*-vōō-gern) v add

toevoeging (*tōō*-vōō-gıng) c (pl ~en) addition

toewijden (*tōō*-vay-dern) v dedicate

*****toewijzen** (*tōō*-vay-zern) v allot

toezicht (*tōō*-zıkht) nt supervision; ~ *houden op** supervise

toffee (to-*fāy*) c (pl ~s) toffee

toilet (tvah-*leht*) nt (pl ~ten) toilet.

lavatory, bathroom; washroom nAm

toiletbenodigdheden (tvah-*leht*-ber-nōā-derkht-hāy-dern) pl toiletry

toiletpapier (tvah-*leht*-paa-peer) nt toilet-paper

toilettafel (tvah-*leh*-taa-ferl) c (pl ~s) dressing-table

toilettas (tvah-*leh*-tahss) c (pl ~sen) toilet case

tol (tol) c (pl ~len) toll

tolk (tolk) c (pl ~en) interpreter

tolken (*tol*-kern) v interpret

tolweg (*tol*-verkh) c (pl ~en) turnpike nAm

tomaat (tōā-*maat*) c (pl tomaten) tomato

ton (ton) c (pl ~nen) cask, barrel; ton

toneel (tōā-*nāyl*) nt drama; stage

toneelkijker (tōā-*nāyl*-kay-kerr) c (pl ~s) binoculars pl

toneelschrijver (tōā-*nāyl*-skhray-verr) c (pl ~s) dramatist, playwright

toneelspeelster (tōā-*nāyl*-spāy-sterr) c (pl ~s) actress

toneelspelen (tōā-*nāyl*-spāy-lern) v act

toneelspeler (tōā-*nāyl*-spāy-lerr) c (pl ~s) actor; comedian

toneelstuk (tōā-*nāyl*-sterk) nt (pl ~ken) play

tonen (*tōā*-nern) v *show; display

tong (tong) c (pl ~en) tongue; sole

tonicum (*tōā*-nee-kerm) nt (pl -ca, ~s) tonic

tonijn (tōā-*nayn*) c (pl ~en) tuna

toon (tōān) c (pl tonen) tone; note

toonbank (*tōām*-bahngk) c (pl ~en) counter

toonladder (*tōān*-lah-derr) c (pl ~s) scale

toonzaal (*tōān*-zaal) c (pl -zalen) showroom

toorn (*tōā*-rern) c anger

top (top) c (pl ~pen) peak; top, summit

toppunt (*to*-pernt) *nt* (pl ~en) height ;
zenith

toren (*tōā*-rern) *c* (pl ~s) tower

tot (tot) *prep* until, to, till ; *conj* till ;
~ **aan** till ; ~ **zover** so far

totaal[1] (tōā-*taal*) *adj* total, overall ; utter

totaal[2] (tōā-*taal*) *nt* (pl totalen) total ;
in ~ altogether

totalisator (tōā-taa-lee-*zaa*-tor) *c* (pl
~s) totalizator

totalitair (tōā-taa-lee-*tair*) *adj* totalitarian

totdat (to-*daht*) *conj* till

touw (tou) *nt* (pl ~en) twine, rope,
string

toverkunst (*tōā*-verr-kernst) *c* magic

traag (traakh) *adj* slow ; slack

traan (traan) *c* (pl tranen) tear

trachten (*trahkh*-tern) *v* try, attempt

tractor (*trahk*-tor) *c* (pl ~en, ~s) tractor

traditie (traa-*dee*-tsee) *c* (pl ~s) tradition

traditioneel (traa-dee-shōa-*nāyl*) *adj*
traditional

tragedie (traa-*gāy*-dee) *c* (pl ~s) tragedy

tragisch (*traa*-geess) *adj* tragic

trainen (*trāy*-nern) *v* drill, train

tralie (*traa*-lee) *c* (pl ~s) bar

tram (trehm) *c* (pl ~s) tram ; streetcar
nAm

transactie (trahn-*zahk*-see) *c* (pl ~s)
deal, transaction

transatlantisch (trahn-zaht-*lahn*-teess)
adj transatlantic

transformator (trahns-for-*maa*-tor) *c*
(pl ~en, ~s) transformer

transpiratie (trahn-spee-*raa*-tsee) *c*
perspiration

transpireren (trahn-spee-*rāy*-rern) *v*
perspire

transport (trahn-*sport*) *nt* (pl ~en)
transportation

transporteren (trahn-spor-*tāy*-rern) *v*
transport

trap (trahp) *c* (pl ~pen) stairs *pl*,
staircase ; kick

trapleuning (*trahp*-lūr-nıng) *c* (pl ~en)
banisters *pl*

trappen (*trah*-pern) *v* kick

trechter (*trehkh*-terr) *c* (pl ~s) funnel

trede (*trāy*-der) *c* (pl ~n) step

*****treffen** (*treh*-fern) *v* *hit ; *strike

trefpunt (*trehf*-pernt) *nt* (pl ~en)
meeting-place

trein (trayn) *c* (pl ~en) train ; **doorgaande** ~ through train

trek[1] (trehk) *c* (pl ~ken) trait

trek[2] (trehk) *c* appetite

*****trekken** (*treh*-kern) *v* pull ; *draw ;
extract ; hike

trekker (*treh*-kerr) *c* (pl ~s) trigger

trekking (*treh*-kıng) *c* (pl ~en) draw

treuren (*trūr*-rern) *v* grieve

treurig (*trūr*-rerkh) *adj* sad

treurspel (*trūrr*-spehl) *nt* (pl ~en) drama

tribune (tree-*bēw*-ner) *c* (pl ~s) stand

tricotgoederen (tree-*kōā*-gōō-der-rern)
pl hosiery

triest (treest) *adj* depressing

trillen (*trı*-lern) *v* tremble ; vibrate

triomf (tree-Yomf) *c* (pl ~en) triumph

triomfantelijk (tree-Yom-*fahn*-ter-lerk)
adj triumphant

troepen (*trōō*-pern) *pl* troops *pl*

trommel (*tro*-merl) *c* (pl ~s) canister ;
drum

trommelvlies (*tro*-merl-vleess) *nt* (pl
-vliezen) ear-drum

trompet (trom-*peht*) *c* (pl ~ten) trumpet

troon (trōan) *c* (pl tronen) throne

troost (trōāst) *c* comfort

troosten (*trōāss*-tern) *v* comfort

troostprijs (*trōast*-prayss) *c* (pl -prijzen) consolation prize

tropen (*trōa*-pern) *pl* tropics *pl*

tropisch (*trōa*-peess) *adj* tropical

trots (trots) *adj* proud; *c* pride

trottoir (tro-*tvaar*) *nt* (pl ~s) pavement; sidewalk *nAm*

trottoirband (tro-*tvaar*-bahnt) *c* (pl ~en) curb

trouw (trou) *adj* true, faithful

trouwen (*trou*-ern) *v* marry

trouwens (*trou*-erns) *adv* besides

trouwring (*trou*-rıng) *c* (pl ~en) wedding-ring

trui (trur^ew) *c* (pl ~en) jersey

Tsjech (ts^Yehkh) *c* (pl ~en) Czech

Tsjechisch (*ts^Yeh*-kheess) *adj* Czech

Tsjechoslowakije (ts^Yeh-khōa-slōa-vaa-kay-er) Czechoslovakia

tube (*tēw*-ber) *c* (pl ~s) tube

tuberculose (tēw-behr-kēw-*lōa*-zer) *c* tuberculosis

tuin (tur^ewn) *c* (pl ~en) garden

tuinbouw (*tur^ew*m-bou) *c* horticulture

tuinman (*tur^ew*n-mahn) *c* (pl -lieden, -lui) gardener

tuit (tur^ewt) *c* (pl ~en) nozzle

tulp (terlp) *c* (pl ~en) tulip

tumor (*tēw*-mor) *c* (pl ~s) tumour

Tunesië (tēw-*nāy*-zee-^Yer) Tunisia

Tunesiër (tēw-*nāy*-zee-^Yerr) *c* (pl ~s) Tunisian

Tunesisch (tēw-*nāy*-zeess) *adj* Tunisian

tuniek (tēw-*neek*) *c* (pl ~en) tunic

tunnel (*ter*-nerl) *c* (pl ~s) tunnel

turbine (terr-*bee*-ner) *c* (pl ~s) turbine

Turk (terrk) *c* (pl ~en) Turk

Turkije (terr-*kay*-er) Turkey

Turks (terrks) *adj* Turkish; ~ **bad** Turkish bath

tussen (*ter*-sern) *prep* between; among, amid

tussenbeide *komen (ter-serm-*bay*- der *kōa*-mern) interfere

tussenpersoon (*ter*-ser-pehr-sōan) *c* (pl -sonen) intermediary

tussenpoos (*ter*-ser-pōass) *c* (pl -pozen) interval

tussenruimte (*ter*-ser-rur^ewm-ter) *c* (pl ~n, ~s) space

tussenschot (*ter*-ser-skhot) *nt* (pl ~ten) partition; diaphragm

tussentijd (*ter*-ser-tayt) *c* interim

twaalf (tvaalf) *num* twelve

twaalfde (*tvaalf*-der) *num* twelfth

twee (tvāy) *num* two

tweede (*tvāy*-der) *num* second

tweedehands (tvāy-der-*hahnts*) *adj* second-hand

tweedelig (tvāy-*dāy*-lerkh) *adj* two-piece

tweeling (*tvāy*-lıng) *c* (pl ~en) twins *pl*

tweemaal (*tvāy*-maal) *adv* twice

tweesprong (*tvāy*-sprong) *c* (pl ~en) fork, road fork

tweetalig (tvāy-*taa*-lerkh) *adj* bilingual

twijfel (*tvay*-ferl) *c* (pl ~s) doubt

twijfelachtig (*tvay*-ferl-ahkh-terkh) *adj* doubtful

twijfelen (*tvay*-fer-lern) *v* doubt

twijg (tvaykh) *c* (pl ~en) twig

twintig (*tvın*-terkh) *num* twenty

twintigste (*tvın*-terkh-ster) *num* twentieth

twist (tvıst) *c* (pl ~en) quarrel

twisten (*tvıss*-tern) *v* quarrel, dispute

tyfus (*tee*-ferss) *c* typhoid

type (*tee*-per) *nt* (pl ~n, ~s) type

typen (*tee*-pern) *v* type

typisch (*tee*-peess) *adj* typical

typiste (tee-*pı*-ster) *c* (pl ~s, ~n) typist

U

u (ew) *pron* you

ui (ur^{ew}) *c* (pl ~en) onion

uil (ur^{ew}l) *c* (pl ~en) owl

uit (ur^{ew}t) *prep* from, out of; for; *adv* out

uitademen (ur^{ew}t-aa-der-mern) *v* expire, exhale

uitbarsting (ur^{ew}t-bahr-stern) *c* (pl ~en) outbreak

uitbenen (ur^{ew}t-bāy-nern) *v* bone

* **uitblinken** (ur^{ew}t-bling-kern) *v* excel

uitbreiden (ur^{ew}t-bray-dern) *v* extend, enlarge, expand

uitbreiding (ur^{ew}t-bray-ding) *c* (pl ~en) extension

uitbuiten (ur^{ew}t-bur^{ew}-tern) *v* exploit

uitbundig (ur^{ew}t-*bern*-derkh) *adj* exuberant

uitdagen (ur^{ew}-daa-gern) *v* dare, challenge

uitdaging (ur^{ew}-daa-ging) *c* (pl ~en) challenge

uitdelen (ur^{ew}-dāy-lern) *v* distribute; *deal

* **uitdoen** (ur^{ew}-dōon) *v* *put out

uitdrukkelijk (ur^{ew}-*drer*-ker-lerk) *adj* express, explicit

uitdrukken (-ur^{ew}-drer-kern) *v* express

uitdrukking (ur^{ew}-drer-king) *c* (pl ~en) expression; phrase

uiteindelijk (ur^{ew}t-*ayn*-der-lerk) *adj* eventual; *adv* at last

uiten (ur^{ew}-tern) *v* express; utter

uiteraard (ur^{ew}-ter-*raart*) *adv* of course, naturally

uiterlijk (ur^{ew}-terr-lerk) *adj* outward, external, exterior; *nt* outside; look

uiterst (ur^{ew}-terrst) *adj* extreme; utmost, very

uiterste (ur^{ew}-terr-ster) *nt* (pl ~n) extreme

* **uitgaan** (ur^{ew}t-khaan) *v* *go out

uitgang (ur^{ew}t-khahng) *c* (pl ~en) way out, exit; issue

uitgangspunt (ur^{ew}t-khahngs-pernt) *nt* (pl ~en) starting-point

uitgave (ur^{ew}t-khaa-ver) *c* (pl ~n) expense, expenditure; edition, issue

uitgebreid (ur^{ew}t-kher-brayt) *adj* comprehensive, extensive

uitgelezen (ur^{ew}t-kher-lāy-zern) *adj* select

uitgestrekt (ur^{ew}t-kher-strehkt) *adj* vast

* **uitgeven** (ur^{ew}t-khāy-vern) *v* *spend; publish, issue

uitgever (ur^{ew}t-khāy-verr) *c* (pl ~s) publisher

uitgezonderd (ur^{ew}t-kher-zon-derrt) *prep* except

uitgifte (ur^{ew}t-khif-ter) *c* (pl ~n) issue

* **uitglijden** (ur^{ew}t-khlay-dern) *v* slip

uithoudingsvermogen (ur^{ew}t-hou-dings-ferr-mōa-gern) *nt* stamina

uiting (ur^{ew}-ting) *c* (pl ~en) expression

* **uitkiezen** (ur^{ew}t-kee-zern) *v* select

* **uitkijken** (ur^{ew}t-kay-kern) *v* watch out, look out; ~ **naar** watch for

zich uitkleden (ur^{ew}t-klāy-dern) undress

* **uitkomen** (ur^{ew}t-kōa-mern) *v* *come out; *come true; *be convenient; ~ **op** open on

uitkomst (ur^{ew}t-komst) *c* (pl ~en) issue

uitlaat (ur^{ew}t-laat) *c* (pl -laten) exhaust

uitlaatgassen (ur^{ew}t-laat-khah-sern) *pl* exhaust gases

uitlaatpijp (ur^{ew}t-laat-payp) *c* (pl ~en) exhaust

* **uitladen** (ur^{ew}t-laa-dern) *v* unload, discharge

uitleg (*ur^ew t*-lehkh) c explanation
uitleggen (*ur^ew t*-leh-gern) v explain
uitlenen (*ur^ew t*-lāy-nern) v *lend
uitleveren (*ur^ew t*-lāy-ver-rern) v extradite
uitmaken (*ur^ew t*-maa-kern) v matter; determine; *put out
uitnodigen (*ur^ew t*-nōa-der-gern) v invite; ask
uitnodiging (*ur^ew t*-nōa-der-gıng) c (pl ~en) invitation
uitoefenen (*ur^ew t*-ōō-fer-nern) v exercise
uitpakken (*ur^ew t*-pah-kern) v unpack; unwrap
uitputten (*ur^ew t*-per-tern) v exhaust
uitrekenen (*ur^ew t*-rāy-ker-nern) v calculate
uitrit (*ur^ew t*-rıt) c (pl ~ten) exit
uitroep (*ur^ew t*-rōōp) c (pl ~en) exclamation
*****uitroepen** (*ur^ew t*-rōō-pern) v exclaim
uitrusten (*ur^ew t*-rerss-tern) v rest; equip
uitrusting (*ur^ew t*-rerss-tıng) c (pl ~en) equipment; gear, kit, outfit
uitschakelen (*ur^ew t*-skhaa-ker-lern) v switch off; disconnect
*****uitscheiden** (*ur^ew t*-skhay-dern) v quit
*****uitschelden** (*ur^ew t*-skhehl-dern) v call names
uitslag (*ur^ew t*-slahkh) c (pl ~en) result; rash
*****uitsluiten** (*ur^ew t*-slur^ew-tern) v exclude
uitsluitend (*ur^ew t*-*slur^ew*-ternt) adv solely, exclusively
uitspraak (*ur^ew t*-spraak) c (pl -spraken) pronunciation; verdict
uitspreiden (*ur^ew t*-spray-dern) v expand
*****uitspreken** (*ur^ew t*-sprāy-kern) v pronounce
uitstapje (*ur^ew t*-stahp-Yer) nt (pl ~s)

trip, excursion
uitstappen (*ur^ew t*-stah-pern) v *get off
uitstekend (*ur^ew t*-stāy-kernt) adj fine, excellent
uitstel (*ur^ew t*-stehl) nt delay; respite
uitstellen (*ur^ew t*-steh-lern) v delay, postpone; adjourn
*****uittrekken** (*ur^ew*-treh-kern) v extract
uitverkocht (*ur^ew t*-ferr-kokht) adj sold out
uitverkoop (*ur^ew t*-ferr-kōap) c sales
*****uitvinden** (*ur^ew t*-fın-dern) v invent
uitvinder (*ur^ew t*-fın-derr) c (pl ~s) inventor
uitvinding (*ur^ew t*-fın-dıng) c (pl ~en) invention
uitvoer (*ur^ew t*-fōōr) c exportation
uitvoerbaar (*ur^ew t*-fōōr-baar) adj feasible
uitvoeren (*ur^ew t*-fōō-rern) v carry out; implement, perform, execute; export
uitvoerend (*ur^ew t*-fōō-rernt) adj executive; **uitvoerende macht** executive
uitvoerig (*ur^ew t*-*fōō*-rerkh) adj detailed
uitwerken (*ur^ew t*-vehr-kern) v elaborate
*****uitwijzen** (*ur^ew t*-vay-zern) v expel
uitwisselen (*ur^ew t*-vi-ser-lern) v exchange
*****uitzenden** (*ur^ew t*-sehn-dern) v *broadcast, transmit
uitzending (*ur^ew t*-sehn-dıng) c (pl ~en) broadcast, transmission
uitzicht (*ur^ew t*-sıkht) nt (pl ~en) view
uitzondering (*ur^ew t*-son-der-rıng) c (pl ~en) exception
uitzonderlijk (*ur^ew t*-*son*-derr-lerk) adj exceptional
*****uitzuigen** (*ur^ew t*-sur^ew-gern) v *bleed
ultraviolet (erl-traa-vee-^Yōa-*leht*) adj ultraviolet
unaniem (ēw-naa-*neem*) adj unanimous

unie (ēw-nee) *c* (pl ~s) union
uniek (ēw-*neek*) *adj* unique
uniform[1] (ēw-nee-*form*) *adj* uniform
uniform[2] (ēw-nee-*form*) *nt/c* (pl ~en) uniform
universeel (ēw-nee-vehr-*zāyl*) *adj* universal
universiteit (ēw-nee-vehr-zee-*tayt*) *c* (pl ~en) university
urgent (err-*gehnt*) *adj* pressing
urgentie (err-*gehn*-see) *c* urgency
urine (ēw-*ree*-ner) *c* urine
Uruguay (ōō-rōō-gvigh) Uruguay
Uruguayaan (ōō-rōō-gvah-*yaan*) *c* (pl -yanen) Uruguayan
Uruguayaans (ōō-rōō-gvah-*yaans*) *adj* Uruguayan
uur (ēwr) *nt* (pl uren) hour; **om ... ~** at ... o'clock; **uur-** hourly
uw (ēw°°) *pron* your

V

vaag (vaakh) *adj* vague; faint; dim
vaak (vaak) *adv* often
vaandel (*vaan*-derl) *nt* (pl ~s) banner
vaardig (*vaar*-derkh) *adj* skilled, skilful
vaardigheid (*vaar*-derkh-hayt) *c* (pl -heden) skill; art
vaart (vaart) *c* speed
vaartuig (*vaar*-tur°kh) *nt* (pl ~en) vessel
vaarwater (*vaar*-vaa-terr) *nt* waterway
vaas (vaass) *c* (pl vazen) vase
vaatje (*vaa*-tᵞer) *nt* (pl ~s) keg
vaatwerk (*vaat*-vehrk) *nt* crockery
vacant (vaa-*kahnt*) *adj* vacant
vacature (vah-kah-*tēw*-rer) *c* (pl ~s) vacancy
vacuüm (*vaa*-kēw-erm) *nt* vacuum
vader (*vaa*-derr) *c* (pl ~s) father; dad
vaderland (*vaa*-derr-lahnt) *nt* native country, fatherland

vagebond (vaa-ger-bont) *c* (pl ~en) tramp
vak (vahk) *nt* (pl ~ken) profession, trade; section
vakantie (vaa-*kahn*-see) *c* (pl ~s) holiday, vacation; **met ~** on holiday
vakantiekamp (vaa-*kahn*-see-kahmp) *nt* (pl ~en) holiday camp
vakantieoord (vaa-*kahn*-see-ōart) *nt* (pl ~en) holiday resort
vakbond (*vahk*-bont) *c* (pl ~en) trade-union
vakkundig (vah-*kern*-derkh) *adj* skilled
vakman (*vahk*-mahn) *c* (pl -lieden) expert
val[1] (vahl) *c* fall
val[2] (vahl) *c* (pl ~len) trap
valk (vahlk) *c* (pl ~en) hawk
vallei (vah-*lay*) *c* (pl ~en) valley
***vallen** (*vah*-lern) *v* *fall; **laten ~** drop
vals (vahls) *adj* false
valuta (vaa-*lēw*-taa) *c* (pl ~'s) currency
van (vahn) *prep* of; from; off; with
vanaf (vah-*nahf*) *prep* from, as from
vanavond (vah-*naa*-vernt) *adv* tonight
vandaag (vahn-*daakh*) *adv* today
***vangen** (*vah*-ngern) *v* *catch; capture
vangrail (*vahng*-rāyl) *c* (pl ~s) crash barrier
vangst (vahngst) *c* (pl ~en) capture
vanille (vaa-*nee*-ᵞer) *c* vanilla
vanmiddag (vah-*mı*-dahkh) *adv* this afternoon
vanmorgen (vah-*mor*-gern) *adv* this morning
vannacht (vah-*nahkht*) *adv* tonight
vanwege (vahn-*vāy*-ger) *prep* on account of, for, owing to, because of
vanzelfsprekend (vahn-zehlf-*sprāy*-kernt) *adj* self-evident

* varen (*vaa*-rern) *v* sail, navigate

variëren (vaa-ree-*Yāy*-rern) *v* vary

variététheater (vaa-ree-*Yāy-tāy-*
Yaa-terr) *nt* (pl ~s) variety theatre;
music-hall

variétévoorstelling (vaa-ree-*Yāy-tāy-*
vōar-steh-lɪng) *c* (pl ~en) variety
show

varken (*vahr*-kern) *nt* (pl ~s) pig

varkensleer (*vahr*-kerss-lāyr) *nt* pigskin

varkensvlees (*vahr*-kerss-flāyss) *nt*
pork

vaseline (vaa-zer-*lee*-ner) *c* vaseline

vast (vahst) *adj* fixed, firm; steady,
permanent; *adv* tight; ~ **menu** set
menu

vastberaden (vahss-ber-*raa*-dern) *adj*
resolute

vastbesloten (vahss-ber-slōa-tern) *adj*
determined

vasteland (vahss-ter-*lahnt*) *nt* mainland; continent

* vasthouden (*vahst*-hou-dehn) *v*
* hold; **zich ~** * hold on

vastmaken (*vahst*-maa-kern) *v* fasten;
attach

vastomlijnd (vahss-tom-laynt) *adj* definite

vastspelden (*vahst*-spehl-dern) *v* pin

vaststellen (*vahst*-steh-lern) *v* establish, determine

vat (vaht) *nt* (pl ~en) cask, barrel;
vessel

* vechten (*vehkh*-tern) *v* * fight; combat, battle

vee (vāy) *nt* cattle *pl*

veearts (*vāy*-ahrts) *c* (pl ~en) veterinary surgeon

veel (vāyl) *adj* much, many; *adv*
much, far

veelbetekenend (vāyl-ber-tāy-ker-
nernt) *adj* significant

veelomvattend (vāyl-om-*vah*-ternt)

adj extensive

veelvuldig (vāyl-*verl*-derkh) *adj* frequent

veelzijdig (vāyl-*zay*-derkh) *adj* all-
round

veen (vāyn) *nt* moor

veer (vāyr) *c* (pl veren) feather;
spring

veerboot (*vāyr*-bōat) *c* (pl -boten)
ferry-boat

veertien (*vāyr*-teen) *num* fourteen; ~
dagen fortnight

veertiende (*vāyr*-teen-der) *num* fourteenth

veertig (*vāyr*-terkh) *num* forty

vegen (*vāy*-gern) *v* * sweep; wipe

vegetariër (vāy-ger-taa-ree-*Yerr*) *c* (pl
~s) vegetarian

veilig (*vay*-lerkh) *adj* safe; secure

veiligheid (*vay*-lerkh-hayt) *c* safety;
security

veiligheidsgordel (*vay*-lerkh-hayts-
khor-derl) *c* (pl ~s) safety-belt; seat-
belt

veiligheidsspeld (*vay*-lerkh-hayt-spehlt)
c (pl ~en) safety-pin

veiling (*vay*-lɪng) *c* (pl ~en) auction

vel (vehl) *nt* (pl ~len) skin

veld (vehlt) *nt* (pl ~en) field

veldbed (*vehlt*-beht) *nt* (pl ~den)
camp-bed

veldkijker (*vehlt*-kay-kerr) *c* (pl ~s)
field glasses

velg (vehlkh) *c* (pl ~en) rim

Venezolaan (vāy-nāy-zōa-*laan*) *c* (pl
-lanen) Venezuelan

Venezolaans (vāy-nāy-zōa-*laans*) *adj*
Venezuelan

Venezuela (vāy-nāy-zēw-*vāy*-laa) Venezuela

vennoot (ver-*nōat*) *c* (pl -noten) associate

vensterbank (*vehn*-sterr-bahngk) *c* (pl
~en) window-sill

vent (vehnt) *c* chap, guy

ventiel (vehn-*teel*) *nt* (pl ~en) valve

ventilatie (vehn-tee-*laa*-tsee) *c* (pl ~s) ventilation

ventilator (vehn-ti-*laa*-tor) *c* (pl ~s, ~en) ventilator, fan

ventilatorriem (vehn-tee-*laa*-to-reem) *c* (pl ~en) fan belt

ventileren (vehn-tee-*lāy*-rern) *v* ventilate

ver (vehr) *adj* far; remote, far-away, distant

verachten (verr-*ahkh*-tern) *v* scorn, despise

verachting (verr-*ahkh*-ting) *c* scorn, contempt

verademing (verr-*aa*-der-ming) *c* relief

veranda (ver-*rahn*-daa) *c* (pl ~'s) veranda

veranderen (verr-*ahn*-der-rern) *v* change; alter, transform; vary; ~ in turn into

verandering (verr-*ahn*-der-ring) *c* (pl ~en) change; alteration; variation

veranderlijk (verr-*ahn*-derr-lerk) *adj* variable

verantwoordelijk (verr-ahnt-*vōar*-der-lerk) *adj* responsible

verantwoordelijkheid (verr-ahnt-*vōar*-der-lerk-hayt) *c* (pl -heden) responsibility

verantwoorden (verr-*ahnt*-vōar-dern) *v* account for

verband (verr-*bahnt*) *nt* (pl ~en) connection, relation; bandage

verbandkist (verr-*bahnt*-kist) *c* (pl ~en) first-aid kit

verbazen (verr-*baa*-zern) *v* astonish, amaze, surprise; **zich** ~ marvel

verbazing (verr-*baa*-zing) *c* astonishment, amazement, surprise

zich verbeelden (verr-*bāyl*-dern) fancy, imagine

verbeelding (verr-*bāyl*-ding) *c* imagin-

ation

***verbergen** (verr-*behr*-gern) *v* *hide; conceal

verbeteren (verr-*bāy*-ter-rern) *v* improve; correct

verbetering (verr-*bāy*-ter-ring) *c* (pl ~en) improvement; correction

***verbieden** (verr-*bee*-dern) *v* prohibit, *forbid

***verbinden** (verr-*bin*-dern) *v* link, connect, join; dress; **zich** ~ engage

verbinding (verr-*bin*-ding) *c* (pl ~en) link; connection; **zich in** ~ **stellen met** contact

verblijf (verr-*blayf*) *nt* (pl -blijven) stay

verblijfsvergunning (verr-*blayfs*-ferr-ger-ning) *c* (pl ~en) residence permit

***verblijven** (verr-*blay*-vern) *v* stay

verblinden (verr-*blin*-dern) *v* blind; **verblindend** glaring

verbod (verr-*bot*) *nt* (pl ~en) prohibition

verboden (verr-*bōā*-dern) *adj* prohibited; ~ **te parkeren** no parking; ~ **te roken** no smoking; ~ **toegang** no entry, no admittance; ~ **voor voetgangers** no pedestrians

verbond (verr-*bont*) *nt* (pl ~en) union

verbouwen (verr-*bou*-ern) *v* cultivate, raise

verbranden (verr-*brahn*-dern) *v* *burn

verbruiken (verr-*brur*ew-kern) *v* use up

verbruiker (verr-*brur*ew-kerr) *c* (pl ~s) consumer

verdacht (verr-*dahkht*) *adj* suspicious

verdachte (verr-*dahkh*-teh) *c* (pl ~n) suspect; accused

verdampen (verr-*dahm*-pern) *v* evaporate

verdedigen (verr-*dāy*-der-gern) *v* defend

verdediging (verr-*dāy*-der-ging) *c* defence

verdelen (verr-*dāy*-lern) *v* divide

*__verdenken__ (verr-*dehng*-kern) *v* suspect

verdenking (verr-*dehng*-king) *c* (pl ~en) suspicion

verder (*vehr*-derr) *adj* further; *adv* beyond; ~ **dan** beyond

verdienen (verr-*dee*-nern) *v* earn; *make; deserve, merit

verdienste (verr-*deens*-ter) *c* (pl ~n) merit; **verdiensten** *pl* earnings *pl*

verdieping (verr-*dee*-ping) *c* (pl ~en) storey, floor

verdikken (verr-*di*-kern) *v* thicken

verdoving (verr-*dōā*-ving) *c* (pl ~en) anaesthesia

verdraaien (verr-*draa*ᵉᵉ-ern) *v* wrench

verdrag (verr-*drahkh*) *nt* (pl ~en) treaty

*__verdragen__ (verr-*draa*-gern) *v* endure, *bear; sustain

verdriet (verr-*dreet*) *nt* grief, sorrow

verdrietig (verr-*dree*-terkh) *adj* sad

*__verdrijven__ (verr-*dray*-vern) *v* chase

*__verdrinken__ (verr-*dring*-kern) *v* drown; *be drowned

verdrukken (verr-*drer*-kern) *v* oppress

verduidelijken (verr-*dur*ᵉʷ-der-ler-kern) *v* clarify

verduistering (verr-*dur*ᵉʷˢˢ-ter-rehn) *c* (pl ~en) eclipse

verdunnen (verr-*der* nern) *v* dilute

verdwaald (verr-*dvaalt*) *adj* lost

*__verdwijnen__ (verr-*dvay*-nern) *v* vanish, disappear

vereisen (verr-*ay*-sern) *v* demand, require; **vereist** requisite

vereiste (verr-*ayss*-ter) *c* (pl ~n) requirement

Verenigde Staten (verr-*āy*-nerkh-der-*staa*-tern) United States, the States

verenigen (verr-*āy*-ner-gern) *v* join; unite; **verenigd** joint

vereniging (verr-*āy*-ner-ging) *c* (pl ~en) association; union, society, club

verf (vehrf) *c* (pl verven) paint; dye

verfdoos (*vehrf*-dōass) *c* (pl -dozen) paint-box

verfrissen (verr-*fri*-sern) *v* refresh

verfrissing (verr-*fri*-sing) *c* (pl ~en) refreshment

vergadering (verr-*gaa*-der-ring) *c* (pl ~en) meeting; assembly

vergeefs (verr-*gāyfs*) *adj* vain; *adv* in vain

vergeetachtig (verr-*gāyt*-ahkh-terkh) *adj* forgetful

*__vergelijken__ (vehr-ger-*lay*-kern) *v* compare

vergelijking (vehr-ger-*lay*-king) *c* (pl ~en) comparison

*__vergeten__ (verr-*gāy*-tern) *v* *forget

*__vergeven__ (verr-*gāy*-vern) *v* *forgive

zich vergewissen van (verr-ger-*vi*-sern) ascertain

vergezellen (verr-ger-*zeh*-lern) *v* accompany

vergiet (verr-*geet*) *nt* (pl ~en) strainer

vergif (verr-*gif*) *nt* poison

vergiffenis (verr-*gi*-fer-niss) *c* pardon

vergiftig (verr-*gif*-terkh) *adj* toxic

vergiftigen (verr-*gif*-teh-gern) *v* poison

zich vergissen (verr-*gi*-sern) *be mistaken; err

vergissing (verr-*gi*-sing) *c* (pl ~en) oversight; error, mistake

vergoeden (verr-*gōō*-dern) *v* *make good, reimburse; remunerate

vergoeding (verr-*gōō*-ding) *c* (pl ~en) remuneration

vergrootglas (verr-*grōāt*-khlahss) *nt* (pl -glazen) magnifying glass

vergroten (verr-*grōā*-tern) *v* enlarge

vergroting (verr-*grōā*-ting) *c* (pl ~en) enlargement

verguld (verr-*gerlt*) *adj* gilt

vergunning (verr-*ger*-ning) *c* (pl ~en)

licence, permit, permission; **een ~ verlenen** license

verhaal (verr-*haal*) *nt* (pl -halen) story; tale

verhandeling (verr-*hahn*-der-ling) *c* (pl ~en) essay

verheugd (verr-*hūrkht*) *adj* glad

verhinderen (verr-*hin*-der-rern) *v* prevent

verhogen (verr-*hōā*-gern) *v* raise

verhoging (verr-*hōā*-ging) *c* (pl ~en) rise, increase

verhoor (verr-*hōār*) *nt* (pl -horen) examination, interrogation

verhouding (verr-*hou*-ding) *c* (pl ~en) affair

verhuizen (verr-*hurew*-zern) *v* move

verhuizing (verr-*hurew*-zing) *c* (pl ~en) move

verhuren (verr-*hēw*-rern) *v* *let; lease

verifiëren (vāy-ree-fee-*Yāy*-rern) *v* verify

vering (*vāy*-ring) *c* suspension

verjaardag (verr-*Yaar*-dahkh) *c* (pl ~en) birthday; anniversary

***verjagen** (verr-*Yaa*-gern) *v* chase

verkeer (verr-*kāyr*) *nt* traffic

verkeerd (verr-*kāyrt*) *adj* false, wrong

verkeersbureau (verr-*kāyrs*-bēw-rōā) *nt* (pl ~s) tourist office

verkeersopstopping (verr-*kāyrz*-op-sto-ping) *c* (pl ~en) traffic jam

verkennen (verr-*keh*-nern) *v* explore

***verkiezen** (verr-*kee*-zern) *v* elect

verkiezing (verr-*kee*-zing) *c* (pl ~en) election

verklaarbaar (verr-*klaar*-baar) *adj* accountable

verklaren (verr-*klaa*-rern) *v* state, declare; explain

verklaring (verr-*klaa*-ring) *c* (pl ~en) statement, declaration; explanation

zich verkleden (verr-*klāy*-dern) change

verkleuren (verr-*klūr*-rern) *v* fade; dis-

colour

verknoeien (verr-*knōōee*-ern) *v* muddle

verkoop (*vehr*-kōāp) *c* sale

verkoopbaar (verr-*kōā*-baar) *adj* saleable

verkoopster (verr-*kōāp*-sterr) *c* (pl ~s) salesgirl

***verkopen** (verr-*kōā*-pern) *v* *sell; **in het klein ~** retail

verkoper (verr-*kōā*-perr) *c* (pl ~s) salesman; shop assistant

verkorten (verr-*kor*-tern) *v* shorten

verkoudheid (verr-*kout*-hayt) *c* cold

verkrachten (verr-*krahkh*-tern) *v* rape

verkrijgbaar (verr-*kraykh*-baar) *adj* obtainable, available

***verkrijgen** (verr-*kray*-gern) *v* obtain

verlagen (verr-*laa*-gern) *v* lower, reduce; *cut

verlammen (verr-*lah*-mern) *v* paralise

verlangen¹ (verr-*lah*-ngern) *v* wish, desire; **~ naar** long for

verlangen² (verr-*lah*-ngern) *nt* (pl ~s) wish; longing

verlaten (verr-*laa*-tern) *adj* desert

***verlaten** (verr-*laa*-tern) *v* *leave; desert

verleden (verr-*lāy*-dern) *adj* previous; *nt* past

verlegen (verr-*lāy*-gern) *adj* shy, embarrassed

verlegenheid (verr-*lāy*-gern-hayt) *c* shyness, timidity; **in ~ brengen** embarrass

verleiden (verr-*lay*-dern) *v* seduce

verleiding (verr-*lay*-ding) *c* (pl ~en) temptation

verlenen (verr-*lāy*-nern) *v* grant; extend

verlengen (verr-*leh*-ngern) *v* lengthen; extend; renew

verlenging (verr-*leh*-nging) *c* (pl ~en) extension

verlengsnoer (verr-*lehng*-snoor) *nt* (pl ~en) extension cord

verlichten (verr-*lıkh*-tern) *v* illuminate; relieve

verlichting (verr-*lıkh*-ting) *c* lighting, illumination; relief

verliefd (verr-*leeft*) *adj* in love

verlies (verr-*leess*) *nt* (pl -liezen) loss

*****verliezen** (verr-*lee*-zern) *v* *lose

verlof (verr-*lof*) *nt* (pl -loven) leave; permission

verloofd (verr-*lōaft*) *adj* engaged

verloofde (verr-*lōaf*-der) *c* (pl ~n) fiancé; fiancée

verlossen (verr-*lo*-sern) *v* deliver; redeem

verlossing (verr-*lo*-sing) *c* (pl ~en) delivery

verloving (verr-*lōa*-ving) *c* (pl ~en) engagement

verlovingsring (verr-*lōa*-vings-ring) *c* (pl ~en) engagement ring

vermaak (verr-*maak*) *nt* entertainment, amusement

vermageren (verr-*maa*-ger-rern) *v* slim

vermakelijk (verr-*maa*-ker-lerk) *adj* entertaining

vermaken (verr-*maa*-kern) *v* entertain, amuse

vermeerderen (verr-*māyr*-der-rern) *v* increase

vermelden (verr-*mehl*-dern) *v* mention

vermelding (verr-*mehl*-ding) *c* (pl ~en) mention

vermenigvuldigen (verr-*māy*-nerkh-ferl-der-gern) *v* multiply

vermenigvuldiging (verr-*māy*-nerkh-ferl-der-ging) *c* (pl ~en) multiplication

*****vermijden** (verr-*may*-dern) *v* avoid

verminderen (verr-*mın*-der-rern) *v* decrease, lessen, reduce

vermindering (verr-*mın*-der-ring) *c* (pl ~en) decrease

vermiste (verr-*mıss*-ter) *c* (pl ~n) missing person

vermoedelijk (verr-*mōō*-der-lerk) *adj* presumable, probable

vermoeden (verr-*mōō*-dern) *v* suspect

vermoeien (verr-*mōō*ᵉᵉ-ern) *v* tire; **vermoeid** weary, tired

vermogen (verr-*mōa*-gern) *nt* (pl ~s) ability, faculty; capacity

zich vermommen (verr-*mo*-mern) disguise

vermomming (verr-*mo*-ming) *c* (pl ~en) disguise

vermoorden (verr-*mōar*-dern) *v* murder

vernielen (verr-*nee*-lern) *v* wreck, destroy

vernietigen (verr-*nee*-ter-gern) *v* destroy

vernietiging (verr-*nee*-ter-ging) *c* destruction

vernieuwen (verr-*nee*ᵒᵒ-ern) *v* renew

vernis (verr-*nıss*) *nt/c* varnish

veronderstellen (verr-on-derr-*steh*-lern) *v* assume, suppose

verontreiniging (verr-ont-*ray*-ner-ging) *c* (pl ~en) pollution

verontschuldigen (verr-ont-*skherl*-der-gern) *v* excuse; **zich** ~ apologize

verontschuldiging (verr-ont-*skherl*-der-ging) *c* (pl ~en) apology

verontwaardiging (verr-ont-*vaar*-der-ging) *c* indignation

veroordeelde (verr-*ōar*-dāyl-der) *c* (pl ~n) convict

veroordelen (verr-*ōar*-dāy-lern) *v* sentence

veroordeling (verr-*ōar*-dāy-ling) *c* (pl ~en) conviction

veroorloven (verr-*ōar*-lōa-vern) *v* allow, permit; **zich** ~ afford

veroorzaken (verr-*ōar*-zaa-kern) *v* cause

veroveraar (verr-*ōa*-ver-raar) *c* (pl ~s)

conqueror
veroveren (verr-*ōā*-ver-rern) *v* conquer
verovering (verr-*ōā*-ver-rıng) *c* (pl
~en) conquest
verpachten (verr-*pahkh*-tern) *v* lease
verpakking (verr-*pah*-kıng) *c* (pl ~en)
packing
verpanden (verr-*pahn*-dern) *v* pawn
verplaatsen (verr-*plaat*-sern) *v* move
verpleegster (verr-*plāykh*-sterr) *c* (pl
~s) nurse
verplegen (verr-*plāy*-gern) *v* nurse
verplicht (verr-*plıkht*) *adj* obligatory,
compulsory ; ~ **zijn om* *be obliged to
verplichten (verr-*plıkh*-tern) *v* oblige
verplichting (verr-*plıkh*-tıng) *c* (pl
~en) engagement
verraad (ver-*raat*) *nt* treason
***verraden** (ver-*raa*-dern) *v* betray
verrader (ver-*raa*-derr) *c* (pl ~s) traitor
verrassen (ver-*rah*-sern) *v* surprise
verrassing (ver-*rah*-sıng) *c* (pl ~en)
surprise
verrekijker (*veh*-rer-kay-kerr) *c* (pl ~s)
binoculars *pl*
verreweg (*veh*-rer-vehkh) *adv* by far
verrichten (ver-*rıkh*-tern) *v* perform
verrukkelijk (ver-*rer*-ker-lerk) *adj* delightful, wonderful
verrukking (ver-*rer*-kıng) *c* (pl ~en)
delight ; **in** ~ **brengen* delight
vers[1] (vehrs) *adj* fresh
vers[2] (vehrs) *nt* (pl verzen) verse
verschaffen (verr-*skhah*-fern) *v* furnish, provide
verscheidene (verr-*skhay*-der-ner)
num various ; several
verscheidenheid (verr-*skhay*-dern-
hayt) *c* (pl -heden) variety
verschepen (verr-*skhāy*-pern) *v* ship
***verschieten** (verr-*skhee*-tern) *v* fade
***verschijnen** (verr-*skhay*-nern) *v* ap-
pear

verschijning (verr-*skhay*-nıng) *c* (pl
~en) apparition
verschijnsel (verr-*skhayn*-serl) *nt* (pl
~en, ~s) phenomenon
verschil (verr-*skhıl*) *nt* (pl ~len) difference ; distinction, contrast
verschillen (verr-*skhı*-lern) *v* differ ;
vary
verschillend (verr-*skhı*-lernt) *adj* unlike, different ; distinct
verschrikkelijk (verr-*skhrı*-ker-lerk) *adj*
terrible ; horrible, frightful, awful
verschuldigd (verr-*skherl*-derkht) *adj*
due ; ~ **zijn* owe
versie (*vehr*-zee) *c* (pl ~s) version
versiering (verr-*see*-rıng) *c* (pl ~en)
decoration
versiersel (verr-*seer*-serl) *nt* (pl ~s,
~en) ornament
***verslaan** (verr-*slaan*) *v* defeat, *beat
verslag (verr-*slahkh*) *nt* (pl ~en) report, account
verslaggever (verr-*slah*-khāy-verr) *c* (pl
~s) reporter
zich *verslapen (verr-*slaa*-pern) *oversleep
versleten (verr-*slāy*-tern) *adj* worn-
out, worn, threadbare
***verslijten** (verr-*slay*-tern) *v* wear out
versnellen (verr-*sneh*-lern) *v* accelerate
versnelling (verr-*sneh*-lıng) *c* (pl ~en)
gear
versnellingsbak (verr-*sneh*-lıngs-bahk)
c (pl ~ken) gear-box
versnellingspook (verr-*sneh*-lıngs-pōā)
c gear lever
versperren (verr-*speh*-rern) *v* block
verspillen (verr-*spı*-lern) *v* waste
verspilling (verr-*spı*-lıng) *c* waste
verspreiden (verr-*spray*-dern) *v* scatter, *shed
***verstaan** (verr-*staan*) *v* *understand
verstand (verr-*stahnt*) *nt* brain ; wits

pl, reason ; **gezond** ~ sense

verstandig (verr-*stahn*-derkh) *adj* sensible

verstellen (verr-*steh*-lern) *v* patch

verstijfd (verr-*stayft*) *adj* numb

verstoppen (verr-*sto*-pern) *v* *hide

verstoren (verr-*stōā*-rern) *v* disturb ; upset

*verstrijken (verr-*stray*-kern) *v* expire

verstuiken (verr-*stur*ew-kern) *v* sprain

verstuiking (verr-*stur*ew-kıng) *c* (pl ~en) sprain

verstuiver (verr-*stur*ew-verr) *c* (pl ~s) atomizer

versturen (verr-*stēw*-rern) *v* *send off, dispatch

vertalen (verr-*taa*-lern) *v* translate

vertaler (verr-*taa*-lerr) *c* (pl ~s) translator

vertaling (verr-*taa*-lıng) *c* (pl ~en) translation ; version

verteerbaar (verr-*tāȳr*-baar) *adj* digestible

vertegenwoordigen (verr-tāy-ger-*vōār*-der-gern) *v* represent

vertegenwoordiger (verr-*tāy*-ger-*vōār*-der-gerr) *c* (pl ~s) agent

vertegenwoordiging (verr-tāy-ger-*vōār*-der-gıng) *c* (pl ~en) representation ; agency

vertellen (verr-*ter*-lern) *v* *tell ; relate

vertelling (verr-*teh*-lıng) *c* (pl ~en) tale

verteren (verr-*tāy*-rern) *v* digest

verticaal (vehr-tee-*kaal*) *adj* vertical

vertolken (verr-*tol*-kern) *v* interpret

vertonen (verr-*tōā*-nern) *v* exhibit ; display

vertragen (verr-*traa*-gern) *v* delay, slow down

vertraging (verr-*traa*-gıng) *c* (pl ~en) delay

vertrek[1] (verr-*trehk*) *nt* departure

vertrek[2] (verr-*trehk*) *nt* (pl ~ken)
room

*vertrekken (verr-*treh*-kern) *v* *leave ; depart, *set out, pull out

vertrektijd (verr-*trehk*-tayt) *c* (pl ~en) time of departure

vertrouwd (verr-*trout*) *adj* familiar

vertrouwelijk (verr-*trou*-er-lerk) *adj* confidential

vertrouwen (verr-*trou*-ern) *nt* confidence, trust, faith ; *v* trust ; ~ **op** rely on

vervaardigen (verr-*vaar*-der-gern) *v* manufacture

vervaldag (verr-*vahl*-dahkh) *c* expiry

vervallen (verr-*vah*-lern) *adj* expired ; due

*vervallen (verr-*vah*-lern) *v* expire

vervalsen (verr-*vahl*-sern) *v* forge, counterfeit

vervalsing (verr-*vahl*-sıng) *c* (pl ~en) fake

*vervangen (verr-*vah*-ngern) *v* replace, substitute

vervanging (verr-*vah*-ngıng) *c* substitute

vervelen (verr-*vāy*-lern) *v* bore ; bother

vervelend (verr-*vāy*-lernt) *adj* dull, boring, annoying ; unpleasant

verven (vehr-vern) *v* paint ; dye

vervloeken (verr-*vlōō*-kern) *v* curse

vervoer (verr-*vōōr*) *nt* transport

vervolg (verr-*volkh*) *nt* (pl ~en) sequel

vervolgen (verr-*vol*-gern) *v* continue ; pursue

vervolgens (verr-*vol*-gerss) *adv* then

vervuiling (verr-*vur*ew-lıng) *c* pollution

verwaand (verr-*vaant*) *adj* conceited, snooty

verwaarlozen (verr-*vaar*-lōā-zern) *v* neglect

verwaarlozing (verr-*vaar*-lōā-zıng) *c* neglect

verwachten (verr-*vahkh*-tern) *v* expect ; anticipate

verwachting (verr-*vahkh*-ting) *c* (pl ~en) expectation; outlook; **in ~** pregnant

verwant (verr-*vahnt*) *adj* related

verwante (verr-*vahn*-ter) *c* (pl ~n) relation

verward (verr-*vahrt*) *adj* confused

verwarmen (verr-*vahr*-mern) *v* heat, warm

verwarming (verr-*vahr*-ming) *c* heating

verwarren (verr-*vah*-rern) *v* confuse; *mistake

verwarring (verr-*vah*-ring) *c* confusion; disturbance; **in ~ brengen** embarrass

verwekken (verr-*veh*-kern) *v* generate

verwelkomen (verr-*vehl*-kōa-mern) *v* welcome

verwennen (verr-*veh*-nern) *v* *spoil

*verwerpen** (verr-*vehr*-pern) *v* turn down, reject

*verwerven** (verr-*vehr*-vern) *v* acquire

verwezenlijken (verr-*vāy*-zer-ler-kern) *v* realize

verwijden (verr-*vay*-dern) *v* widen

verwijderen (verr-*vay*-der-rern) *v* remove

verwijdering (verr-*vay*-der-ring) *c* removal

verwijt (verr-*vayt*) *nt* (pl ~en) reproach; blame

*verwijten** (verr-*vay*-tern) *v* reproach

*verwijzen naar** (verr-*vay*-zern) refer to

verwijzing (verr-*vay*-zing) *c* (pl ~en) reference

verwonden (verr-*von*-dern) *v* wound, injure

verwonderen (verr-*von*-der-rern) *v* amaze

verwondering (verr-*von*-der-ring) *c* wonder

verwonding (verr-*von*-ding) *c* (pl ~en) injury

verzachten (verr-*zahkh*-tern) *v* soften

verzamelaar (verr-*zaa*-mer-laar) *c* (pl ~s) collector

verzamelen (verr-*zaa*-mer-lern) *v* gather; collect

verzameling (verr-*zaa*-mer-ling) *c* (pl ~en) collection

verzekeren (verr-*zāy*-ker-rern) *v* assure; insure

verzekering (verr-*zāy*-ker-ring) *c* (pl ~en) insurance

verzekeringspolis (verr-*zāy*-ker-rings-pōā-lerss) *c* (pl ~sen) insurance policy

*verzenden** (verr-*zehn*-dern) *v* despatch, dispatch

verzending (verr-*zehn*-ding) *c* expedition

verzet (verr-*zeht*) *nt* resistance

zich verzetten (verr-*zeh*-tern) oppose

verzilveren (verr-*zil*-ver-rern) *v* cash

*verzinnen** (verr-*zi*-nern) *v* invent

verzinsel (verr-*zin*-serl) *nt* (pl ~s) fiction

verzoek (verr-*zōōk*) *nt* (pl ~en) request

*verzoeken** (verr-*zōō*-kern) *v* request, ask

verzoening (verr-*zōō*-ning) *c* (pl ~en) reconciliation

verzorgen (verr-*zor*-gern) *v* look after, *take care of; tend

verzorging (verr-*zor*-ging) *c* care

verzwikken (verr-*zvi*-kern) *v* sprain

vest (vehst) *nt* (pl ~en) cardigan; waistcoat, jacket; vest *nAm*

vestigen (*vehss*-ter-gern) *v* establish; **zich ~** settle down

vesting (*vehss*-ting) *c* (pl ~en) fortress

vet[1] (veht) *adj* fat; greasy

vet[2] (veht) *nt* (pl ~ten) fat; grease

veter (*vāy*-terr) *c* (pl ~s) lace

vettig (veh-terkh) adj greasy, fatty

vezel (vay-zerl) c (pl ~s) fibre

via (vee-Yaa) prep via

viaduct (vee-Yaa-derkt) c/nt (pl ~en) viaduct

vibratie (vee-braa-tsee) c (pl ~s) vibration

vice-president (vee-ser-pray-zee-dehnt) c (pl ~en) vice-president

vier (veer) num four

vierde (veer-der) num fourth

vieren (vee-rern) v celebrate

viering (vee-ring) c (pl ~en) celebration

vierkant (veer-kahnt) adj square; nt square

vies (veess) adj dirty

vijand (vay-ahnt) c (pl ~en) enemy

vijandig (vay-ahn-derkh) adj hostile

vijf (vayf) num five

vijfde (vayf-der) num fifth

vijftien (vayf-teen) num fifteen

vijftiende (vayf-teen-der) num fifteenth

vijftig (vayf-terkh) num fifty

vijg (vaykh) c (pl ~en) fig

vijl (vayl) c (pl ~en) file

vijver (vay-verr) c (pl ~s) pond

villa (vee-laa) c (pl ~'s) villa

vilt (vilt) nt felt

***vinden** (vin-dern) v *find; *come across; consider

vindingrijk (vin-ding-rayk) adj inventive

vinger (vi-ngerr) c (pl ~s) finger

vingerafdruk (vi-ngerr-ahf-drerk) c (pl ~ken) fingerprint

vingerhoed (vi-ngerr-hoot) c (pl ~en) thimble

vink (vingk) c (pl ~en) finch

violet (vee-Yoa-leht) adj violet

viool (vee-Yoal) c (pl violen) violin

viooltje (vee-Yoal-tYer) nt (pl ~s) violet

vis (viss) c (pl ~sen) fish

visakte (viss-ahk-ter) c (pl ~n, ~s) fishing licence

visgraat (viss-khraat) c (pl -graten) fishbone

vishaak (viss-haak) c (pl -haken) fishing hook

visie (vee-zee) c vision

visite (vee-zee-ter) c (pl ~s) visit; call

visitekaartje (vi-zee-ter-kaar-tYer) nt (pl ~s) visiting-card

viskuit (viss-kurewt) c roe

vislijn (viss-layn) c (pl ~en) fishing line

visnet (viss-neht) nt (pl ~ten) fishing net

vissen (vi-sern) v fish

visser (vi-serr) c (pl ~s) fisherman

visserij (vi-ser-ray) c fishing industry

vistuig (viss-turewkh) nt fishing tackle, fishing gear

visum (vee-zerm) nt (pl visa) visa

viswinkel (viss-ving-kerl) c (pl ~s) fish shop

vitamine (vee-taa-mee-ner) c (pl ~n, ~s) vitamin

vitrine (vee-tree-ner) c (pl ~s) showcase

vlag (vlahkh) c (pl ~gen) flag

vlak (vlahk) adj flat; smooth; level, plane

vlakgom (vlahk-khom) c/nt (pl ~men) rubber

vlakte (vlahk-ter) c (pl ~n, ~s) plain

vlam (vlahm) c (pl ~men) flame

vlees (vlayss) nt meat; flesh

vlek (vlehk) c (pl ~ken) stain, spot, blot

vlekkeloos (vleh-ker-loass) adj stainless, spotless

vlekken (vleh-kern) v stain

vlekkenwater (vleh-ker-vaa-terr) nt stain remover

vleugel (vlur-gerl) c (pl ~s) wing;

grand piano

vlieg (vleekh) c (pl ~en) fly

***vliegen** (vlee-gern) v *fly

vliegramp (vleekh-rahmp) c (pl ~en) plane crash

vliegtuig (vleekh-tur^(ew)kh) nt (pl ~en) aircraft, aeroplane, plane; airplane nAm

vliegveld (vleekh-fehlt) nt (pl ~en) airfield

vlijt (vlayt) c diligence

vlijtig (vlay-terkh) adj industrious; diligent

vlinder (vlin-derr) c (pl ~s) butterfly

vlinderdasje (vlin-derr-dah-sher) nt (pl ~s) bow tie

vlinderslag (vlin-derr-slahkh) c butterfly stroke

vloed (vloot) c flood

vloeibaar (vloo-ee-baar) adj liquid, fluid

vloeien (vloo-ee-ern) v flow; **vloeiend** fluent

vloeipapier (vloo-ee-paa-peer) nt blotting paper

vloeistof (vloo-ee-stof) c (pl ~fen) fluid

vloek (vlook) c (pl ~en) curse

vloeken (vloo-kern) v curse, *swear

vloer (vloor) c (pl ~en) floor

vloerkleed (vloor-klayt) nt (pl -kleden) carpet

vloot (vloat) c (pl vloten) fleet

vlot (vlot) nt (pl ~ten) raft

vlotter (vlo-terr) c (pl ~s) float

vlucht (vlerkht) c (pl ~en) flight

vluchten (vlerkh-tern) v escape

vlug (vlerkh) adj fast, quick, rapid; adv soon

vocaal (voa-kaal) adj vocal

vocabulaire (voa-kaa-bew-lair) nt vocabulary

vocht (vokht) nt damp

vochtig (vokh-terkh) adj humid, moist; damp, wet

vochtigheid (vokh-terkh-hayt) c humidity, moisture

vod (vot) nt (pl ~den) rag

voeden (voo-dern) v *feed

voedsel (voot-serl) nt food; fare

voedselvergiftiging (voot-serl-verr-gif-ter-ging) c food poisoning

voedzaam (voot-saam) adj nutritious, nourishing

zich voegen bij (voo-gern) join

voelen (voo-lern) v *feel; sense

voeren (voo-rern) v carry

voering (voo-ring) c (pl ~en) lining

voertuig (voor-tur^(ew)kh) nt (pl ~en) vehicle

voet (voot) c (pl ~en) foot; **te** ~ on foot, walking

voetbal (voot-bahl) nt soccer

voetbalwedstrijd (voot-bahl-veht-strayt) c (pl ~en) football match

voetganger (voot-khah-ngerr) c (pl ~s) pedestrian

voetpad (voot-paht) nt (pl ~en) footpath

voetpoeder (voot-poo-derr) nt/c foot powder

voetrem (voot-rehm) c foot-brake

vogel (voa-gerl) c (pl ~s) bird

vol (vol) adj full; full up

volbloed (vol-bloot) adj thoroughbred

***volbrengen** (vol-brah-ngern) v accomplish

voldaan (vol-daan) adj satisfied

voldoende (vol-doon-der) adj sufficient, enough; ~ *zijn *do, suffice

voldoening (vol-doo-ning) c satisfaction

volgen (vol-gern) v follow; **volgend** subsequent, next, following

volgens (vol-gerns) prep according to

volgorde (vol-gor-der) c order, sequence

***volhouden** (vol-hou-dern) v *keep up; insist

volk (volk) *nt* (pl ~en, ~eren) people; nation; folk; **volks-** national; popular; vulgar

volkomen (vol-*kō̄a*-mern) *adj* perfect; *adv* completely

volkorenbrood (vol-*kō̄a*-rerm-brō̄at) *nt* wholemeal bread

volksdans (*volks*-dahns) *c* (pl ~en) folk-dance

volkslied (*volks*-leet) *nt* (pl ~eren) folk song; national anthem

volledig (vo-*lāy*-derkh) *adj* complete

volmaakt (vol-*maakt*) *adj* perfect

volmaaktheid (vol-*maakt*-hayt) *c* perfection

volslagen (vol-*slaa*-gern) *adj* total, utter

volt (volt) *c* volt

voltage (vol-*taa*-zher) *c/nt* (pl ~s) voltage

voltooien (vol-*tō̄a*ᵉᵉ-ern) *v* complete

volume (vō̄a-*lēw*-mer) *nt* (pl ~n, ~s) volume

volwassen (vol-*vah*-sern) *adj* adult; grown-up

volwassene (vol-*vah*-ser-ner) *c* (pl ~n) adult; grown-up

vonk (vongk) *c* (pl ~en) spark

vonnis (*vo*-nerss) *nt* (pl ~sen) verdict, sentence

voogd (vō̄akht) *c* (pl ~en) tutor, guardian

voogdij (vō̄akh-*day*) *c* custody

voor (vō̄ar) *prep* before; ahead of, in front of; for; to

vooraanstaand (vō̄ar-*aan*-staant) *adj* leading, outstanding

***voorafgaan** (vō̄ar-*ahf*-khaan) *v* precede

vooral (vō̄a-*rahl*) *adv* essentially, especially, most of all

voorbarig (vō̄ar-*baa*-rerkh) *adj* premature

voorbeeld (*vō̄ar*-bāylt) *nt* (pl ~en) example, instance

voorbehoedmiddel (vō̄ar-ber-*hō̄ot*-mi-derl) *nt* (pl ~en) contraceptive

voorbehoud (vō̄ar-ber-hout) *nt* qualification

voorbereiden (vō̄ar-ber-ray-dern) *v* prepare

voorbereiding (vō̄ar-ber-ray-ding) *c* (pl ~en) preparation

voorbij (vō̄ar-*bay*) *adj* past, over; *prep* past, beyond

***voorbijgaan** (vō̄ar-*bay*-gaan) *v* pass

voorbijganger (vō̄ar-*bay*-gah-ngerr) *c* (pl ~s) passer-by

voordat (*vō̄ar*-daht) *conj* before

voordeel (vō̄ar-*dāyl*) *nt* (pl -delen) advantage; profit, benefit

voordelig (vō̄ar-*dāy*-lerkh) *adj* advantageous; cheap

zich *voordoen (vō̄ar-dō̄on) *v* occur

voorgaand (*vō̄ar*-khaant) *adj* previous, preceding

voorganger (*vō̄ar*-gah-ngerr) *c* (pl ~s) predecessor

voorgerecht (*vō̄ar*-ger-rehkht) *nt* (pl ~en) hors-d'œuvre

voorgrond (*vō̄ar*-gront) *c* foreground

voorhanden (vō̄ar-*hahn*-dern) *adj* available

voorheen (vō̄ar-*hāyn*) *adv* formerly

voorhoofd (*vō̄ar*-hō̄aft) *nt* (pl ~en) forehead

voorjaar (*vō̄ar*-ʸaar) *nt* springtime, spring

voorkant (*vō̄ar*-kahnt) *c* front

voorkeur (*vō̄ar*-kūrr) *c* preference; **de ~ *geven aan** prefer

voorkomen¹ (*vō̄ar*-kō̄a-mern) *nt* look, appearance

***voorkomen²** (vō̄ar-kō̄a-mern) *v* occur, happen

***voorkomen³** (vō̄ar-*kō̄a*-mern) *v* prevent; anticipate

voorkomend (vō̄ar-*kō̄a*-mernt) *adj* obliging

voorletter (*vōar*-leh-terr) *c* (pl ~s) initial

voorlopig (vōar-*lōō*-perkh) *adj* provisional, temporary; preliminary

voormalig (vōar-*maa*-lerkh) *adj* former

voorman (*vōar*-mahn) *c* (pl ~nen) foreman

voornaam[1] (vōar-*naam*) *adj* distinguished; **voornaamst** *adj* principal, main, leading, chief

voornaam[2] (*vōar*-naam) *c* (pl -namen) first name, Christian name

voornaamwoord (*vōar*-naam-vōart) *nt* (pl ~en) pronoun

voornamelijk (vōar-*naa*-mer-lerk) *adv* especially

vooroordeel (*vōar*-ōar-dāyl) *nt* (pl -delen) prejudice

vooroorlogs (vōar-*ōar*-lokhs) *adj* pre-war

voorraad (*vōa*-raat) *c* (pl -raden) stock, store, supply; provisions *pl*; in ~ *hebben stock

voorrang (*vōa*-rahng) *c* priority; right of way

voorrecht (*vōa*-rehkht) *nt* (pl ~en) privilege

vooruit (*vōa*-rur[ew]t) *c* (pl ~en) windscreen; windshield *nAm*

* **voorschieten** (vōar-skhee-tern) *v* advance

voorschot (*vōar*-skhot) *nt* (pl ~ten) advance

voorschrift (*vōar*-skhrɪft) *nt* (pl ~en) regulation

* **voorschrijven** (*vōar*-skhray-vern) *v* prescribe

voorspellen (vōar-*speh*-lern) *v* predict, forecast

voorspelling (vōar-*speh*-lɪng) *c* (pl ~en) forecast

voorspoed (*vōar*-spōōt) *c* prosperity

voorsprong (*vōar*-sprong) *c* lead

voorstad (*vōar*-staht) *c* (pl -steden) suburb

voorstander (*vōar*-stahn-derr) *c* (pl ~s) advocate

voorstel (*vōar*-stehl) *nt* (pl ~len) proposition, proposal; suggestion

voorstellen (*vōar*-steh-lern) *v* propose, suggest; present, introduce; represent; zich ~ conceive, fancy, imagine

voorstelling (*vōar*-steh-lɪng) *c* (pl ~en) show, performance

voortaan (*vōar*-taan) *adv* henceforth

voortduren (*vōar*-dēw-rern) *v* continue; **voortdurend** continuous, continual

* **voortgaan** (*vōart*-khaan) *v* continue; proceed

voortreffelijk (vōar-*treh*-fer-lerk) *adj* excellent; exquisite

voorts (vōarts) *adv* moreover

voortzetten (*vōart*-seh-tern) *v* carry on, continue

vooruit (vōa-*rur[ew]t*) *adv* ahead, forward; in advance

vooruitbetaald (vōa-*rur[ew]t*-ber-taalt) *adj* prepaid

* **vooruitgaan** (vōa-*rur[ew]t*-khaan) *v* advance

vooruitgang (vōa-*rur[ew]t*-khahng) *c* progress, advance

vooruitstrevend (vōa-rur[ew]t-*strāy*-vernt) *adj* progressive

vooruitzicht (vōa-*rur[ew]t*-sɪkht) *nt* (pl ~en) prospect

voorvader (*vōar*-vaa-derr) *c* (pl ~s, ~en) ancestor

voorvechter (*vōar*-vehkh-terr) *c* (pl ~s) champion

voorvoegsel (*vōar*-vōōkh-serl) *nt* (pl ~s) prefix

voorwaarde (vōar-vaar-der) *c* (pl ~n) condition; term

voorwaardelijk (vōar-*vaar*-der-lerk) *adj*

conditional

voorwaarts (*vōar*-vaarts) *adv* onwards, forward

voorwenden (*vōar*-vehn-dern) *v* pretend

voorwendsel (*vōar*-vehnt-serl) *nt* (pl ~s, ~en) pretext, pretence

voorwerp (*vōar*-vehrp) *nt* (pl ~en) object; **gevonden voorwerpen** lost and found

voorzetsel (*vōar*-zeht-serl) *nt* (pl ~s) preposition

voorzichtig (vōar-*zıkh*-terkh) *adj* careful; gentle

voorzichtigheid (vōar-*zıkh*-terkh-hayt) *c* caution

*voorzien** (vōar-*zeen*) *v* anticipate; ~ **van** furnish with

voorzitter (*vōar*-zı-terr) *c* (pl ~s) chairman, president

voorzorg (*vōar*-zorkh) *c* (pl ~en) precaution

voorzorgsmaatregel (*vōar*-zorkhs-maat-rāy-gerl) *c* (pl ~en) precaution

vorderen (*vor*-der-rern) *v* *get on; confiscate, claim

vorig (*vōa*-rerkh) *adj* last; past

vork (vork) *c* (pl ~en) fork

vorm (vorm) *c* (pl ~en) shape; form

vormen (*vor*-mern) *v* shape; form

vorming (*vor*-mıng) *c* background

vorst¹ (vorst) *c* (pl ~en) ruler, monarch, sovereign

vorst² (vorst) *c* frost

vos (voss) *c* (pl ~sen) fox

vouw (vou) *c* (pl ~en) fold; crease

*vouwen** (*vou*-ern) *v* fold

vraag (vraakh) *c* (pl vragen) question; inquiry, query

vraaggesprek (*vraa*-kher-sprehk) *nt* (pl ~ken) interview

vraagstuk (*vraakh*-sterk) *nt* (pl ~ken) problem, question

vraagteken (*vraakh*-tāy-kern) *nt* (pl

~s) question mark

vracht (vrahkht) *c* (pl ~en) freight, cargo

vrachtwagen (*vrahkht*-vaa-gern) *c* (pl ~s) lorry; truck *nAm*

*vragen** (*vraa*-gern) *v* ask; beg; **vragend** interrogative

vrede (*vrāy*-der) *c* peace

vreedzaam (*vrāyt*-saam) *adj* peaceful

vreemd (vrāymt) *adj* strange; odd, queer; foreign

vreemde (*vrāym*-der) *c* (pl ~n) stranger

vreemdeling (*vrāym*-der-lıng) *c* (pl ~en) foreigner; stranger, alien

vrees (vrāyss) *c* dread, fear

vreselijk (*vrāy*-ser-lerk) *adj* terrible; horrible, dreadful, frightful

vreugde (*vrūrkh*-der) *c* (pl ~n) gladness, joy

vrezen (*vrāy*-zern) *v* dread, fear

vriend (vreent) *c* (pl ~en) friend

vriendelijk (*vreen*-der-lerk) *adj* friendly; kind

vriendschap (*vreent*-skhahp) *c* (pl ~pen) friendship

vriendschappelijk (vreent-*skhah*-per-lerk) *adj* friendly

vriespunt (*vreess*-pernt) *nt* freezing-point

*vriezen** (*vree*-zern) *v* *freeze

vrij (vray) *adj* free; *adv* pretty, fairly, quite, rather

vrijdag (*vray*-dahkh) *c* Friday

vrijgevig (vray-*gāy*-verkh) *adj* liberal

vrijgezel (vray-ger-*zehl*) *c* (pl ~len) bachelor

vrijheid (*vray*-hayt) *c* (pl -heden) freedom, liberty

vrijkaart (*vray*-kaart) *c* (pl ~en) free ticket

vrijpostig (vray-*poss*-terkh) *adj* bold

vrijspraak (*vray*-spraak) *c* acquittal

vrijstellen (*vray*-steh-lern) *v* exempt;

vrijgesteld exempt

vrijstelling (*vray*-steh-lɪng) *c* (pl ~en) exemption

vrijwel (*vray*-vehl) *adv* practically

vrijwillig (vray-*vɪ*-lerkh) *adj* voluntary

vrijwilliger (vray-*vɪ*-ler-gerr) *c* (pl ~s) volunteer

vroedvrouw (*vrōōt*-frou) *c* (pl ~en) midwife

vroeg (vrōōkh) *adj* early

vroeger (*vrōō*-gerr) *adj* prior, previous, former; *adv* formerly

vrolijk (*vrōā*-lerk) *adj* gay, cheerful, merry, joyful

vrolijkheid (*vrōā*-lerk-hayt) *c* gaiety

vroom (vrōām) *adj* pious

vrouw (vrou) *c* (pl ~en) woman; wife

vrouwelijk (*vrou*-er-lerk) *adj* female; feminine

vrouwenarts (*vrou*-ern-ahrts) *c* (pl ~en) gynaecologist

vrucht (vrerkht) *c* (pl ~en) fruit

vruchtbaar (*vrerkht*-baar) *adj* fertile

vruchtensap (*vrerkh*-ter-sahp) *nt* (pl ~pen) squash

vuil (vur*ewl*) *adj* filthy, dirty; *nt* dirt

vuilnis (*vurewl*-nɪss) *nt* garbage

vuilnisbak (*vurewl*-nɪss-bahk) *c* (pl ~ken) rubbish-bin, dustbin; trash can *Am*

vuist (vur*ewl*st) *c* (pl ~en) fist

vuistslag (*vurewl*st-slahkh) *c* (pl ~en) punch

vulgair (verl-*gair*) *adj* vulgar

vulkaan (verl-*kaan*) *c* (pl -kanen) volcano

vullen (*ver*-lern) *v* fill

vulling (*ver*-lɪng) *c* (pl ~en) stuffing, filling; refill

vulpen (verl-pehn) *c* (pl ~nen) fountain-pen

vuur (vewr) *nt* (pl vuren) fire

vuurrood (*vēw*-rōāt) *adj* scarlet, crimson

vuursteen (*vewr*-stāyn) *c* (pl -stenen) flint

vuurtoren (*vewr*-tōā-rern) *c* (pl ~s) lighthouse

vuurvast (*vewr*-vahst) *adj* fireproof

W

*** waaien** (*vaaee*-ern) *v* *blow

waaier (*vaaee*-err) *c* (pl ~s) fan

waakzaam (*vaak*-saam) *adj* vigilant

waanzin (*vaan*-zɪn) *c* madness

waanzinnig (vaan-*zɪ*-nerkh) *adj* mad

waar[1] (vaar) *adj* true; very

waar[2] (vaar) *adv* where; *conj* where; ~ **dan ook** anywhere; ~ **ook** wherever

waarborg (*vaar*-borkh) *c* (pl ~en) guarantee

waard (vaart) *adj* worthy of; ~ *zijn *be worth

waarde (*vaar*-der) *c* (pl ~n) worth, value

waardeloos (*vaar*-der-lōāss) *adj* worthless

waarderen (vaar-*dāy*-rern) *v* appreciate

waardering (vaar-*dāy*-rɪng) *c* appreciation

waardevol (*vaar*-der-vol) *adj* valuable

waardig (*vaar*-derkh) *adj* dignified

waarheid (*vaar*-hayt) *c* (pl -heden) truth

waarheidsgetrouw (*vaar*-hayts-khertrou) *adj* truthful

*** waarnemen** (*vaar*-nāy-mern) *v* observe

waarneming (*vaar*-nāy-mɪng) *c* (pl ~en) observation

waarom (vaa-*rom*) *adv* why; what for

waarschijnlijk (vaar-*skhayn*-lerk) *adj* probable, likely; *adv* probably

waarschuwen (*vaar*-skhew͞oo-ern) *v* warn; caution; notify

waarschuwing (*vaar*-skhew͞oo-ing) *c* (pl ~en) warning

waas (vaass) *nt* haze

wachten (*vahkh*-tern) *v* wait; ~ **op** await

wachtkamer (*vahkht*-kaa-merr) *c* (pl ~s) waiting-room

wachtlijst (*vahkht*-layst) *c* (pl ~en) waiting-list

wachtwoord (*vahkht*-vōart) *nt* (pl ~en) password

waden (*vaa*-dern) *v* wade

wafel (*vaa*-ferl) *c* (pl ~s) waffle, wafer

wagen[1] (*vaa*-gern) *c* (pl ~s) cart

wagen[2] (*vaa*-gern) *v* dare, venture, risk

wagon (vaa-*gon*) *c* (pl ~s) carriage, waggon; passenger car *Am*

wakker (*vah*-kerr) *adj* awake; ~ *worden wake up

walgelijk (*vahl*-ger-lerk) *adj* revolting, disgusting

walnoot (*vahl*-nōat) *c* (pl -noten) walnut

wals (vahls) *c* (pl ~en) waltz

walvis (*vahl*-viss) *c* (pl ~sen) whale

wand (vahnt) *c* (pl ~en) wall

wandelaar (*vahn*-der-laar) *c* (pl ~s) walker

wandelen (*vahn*-der-lern) *v* stroll, walk

wandeling (*vahn*-der-ling) *c* (pl ~en) stroll, walk

wandelstok (*vahn*-derl-stok) *c* (pl ~ken) walking-stick

wandkleed (*vahnt*-klāyt) *nt* (pl -kleden) tapestry

wandluis (*vahnt*-lurew͏ss) *c* (pl -luizen) bug

wang (vahng) *c* (pl ~en) cheek

wanhoop (*vahn*-hōap) *c* despair

wanhopen (*vahn*-hōa-pern) *v* despair

wanhopig (vahn-*hōa*-perkh) *adj* desperate

wankel (*vahn*-kerl) *adj* unsteady

wankelen (*vahn*-ker-lern) *v* falter

wanneer (vah-*nāyr*) *adv* when; *conj* when; ~ **ook** whenever

wanorde (*vahn*-or-der) *c* disorder

want (vahnt) *conj* for

wanten (*vahn*-tern) *pl* mittens *pl*

wantrouwen (*vahn*-trou-ern) *nt* suspicion; *v* mistrust

wapen (*vaa*-pern) *nt* (pl ~s, ~en) weapon, arm

warboel (*vahr*-bōol) *c* muddle, mess

waren (*vaa*-rern) *pl* goods *pl*, wares *pl*

warenhuis (*vaa*-rer-hurew͏ss) *nt* (pl -huizen) department store

warm (vahrm) *adj* warm; hot; ~ *eten dine

warmte (*vahrm*-ter) *c* warmth; heat

warmwaterkruik (vahrm-*vaa*-terr-krurew͏k) *c* (pl ~en) hot-water bottle

was[1] (vahss) *c* laundry, washing

was[2] (vahss) *c* wax

wasbaar (*vahss*-baar) *adj* washable

wasbekken (*vahss*-beh-kern) *nt* (pl ~s) wash-basin

wasecht (vahss-*ehkht*) *adj* fast-dyed

wasgoed (*vahss*-khōot) *nt* washing

wasmachine (*vahss*-mah-shee-ner) *c* (pl ~s) washing-machine

wasmiddel (*vahss*-mi-derl) *nt* (pl ~en) detergent

waspoeder (*vahss*-pōo-derr) *c* (pl ~s) washing-powder

*wassen** (*vah*-sern) *v* wash

wassenbeeldenmuseum (vah-ser-*bāyl*-der-mew͏-zāy-yerm) *nt* (pl ~s, -musea) waxworks *pl*

wasserette (vah-ser-*reh*-ter) *c* (pl ~s) launderette

wasserij (vah-ser-*ray*) *c* (pl ~en) laundry

wastafel (*vahss*-taa-ferl) *c* (pl ~s)

wash-stand

wasverzachter (_vahss_-ferr-zahkh-terr) _c_ (pl ~s) water-softener

wat (vaht) _pron_ what; _adv_ how; ~ **dan ook** whatever; anything

water (_vaa_-terr) _nt_ water; **hoog ~** high tide; **laag ~** low tide; **stromend ~** running water; **zoet ~** fresh water

waterdicht (_vaa_-terr-dıkht) _adj_ rainproof, waterproof

waterkers (_vaa_-terr-kehrs) _c_ watercress

watermeloen (_vaa_-terr-mer-lōōn) _c_ (pl ~en) watermelon

waterpas (_vaa_-terr-pahss) _c_ (pl ~sen) level

waterpokken (_vaa_-terr-po-kern) _pl_ chickenpox

waterpomp (_vaa_-terr-pomp) _c_ (pl ~en) water pump

waterski (_vaa_-terr-skee) _c_ (pl ~'s) water ski

waterstof (_vaa_-terr-stof) _c_ hydrogen

waterstofperoxyde (_vaa_-terr-stof-pehr-ok-see-der) _nt_ peroxide

waterval (_vaa_-terr-vahl) _c_ (pl ~len) waterfall

waterverf (_vaa_-terr-vehrf) _c_ water-colour

watten (_vah_-torn) _pl_ cotton-wool

wazig (_vaa_-zerkh) _adj_ hazy

we (ver) _pron_ we

wedden (_veh_-dern) _v_ *bet

weddenschap (_veh_-der-skhahp) _c_ (pl ~pen) bet

wederverkoper (_vāy_-derr-verr-kōa-perr) _c_ (pl ~s) retailer

wederzijds (_vāy_-derr-zayts) _adj_ mutual

wedijveren (_veht_-ay-ver-rern) _v_ compete

wedloop (_veht_-lōap) _c_ (pl -lopen) race

wedstrijd (_veht_-strayt) _c_ (pl ~en) competition, contest; match

weduwe (_vāy_-dew̄ōō-er) _c_ (pl ~n) widow

weduwnaar (_vāy_-dew̄ōō-naar) _c_ (pl ~s) widower

weeën (_vāy_-ern) _pl_ labour

weefsel (_vāyf_-serl) _nt_ (pl ~s) tissue

weegschaal (_vāykh_-skhaal) _c_ (pl -schalen) weighing-machine, scales _pl_

week (vāyk) _c_ (pl weken) week

weekdag (_vāyk_-dahkh) _c_ (pl ~en) weekday

weekend (vee-kehnt) _nt_ (pl ~s) weekend

weemoed (_vāy_-mōōt) _c_ melancholy

weer[1] (vāyr) _nt_ weather

weer[2] (vāyr) _adv_ again

weerbericht (_vāyr_-ber-rıkht) _nt_ (pl ~en) weather forecast

***weerhouden** (vāyr-_hou_-dern) _v_ restrain

weerkaatsen (vāyr-_kaat_-sern) _v_ reflect

weerkaatsing (vāyr-_kaat_-sıng) _c_ reflection

weerklank (_vāyr_-klahngk) _c_ echo

weerzinwekkend (vāyr-zın-_veh_-kernt) _adj_ repulsive, repellent, revolting

wees (vāyss) _c_ (pl wezen) orphan

weg[1] (vehkh) _adv_ gone, away; lost; off

weg[2] (vehkh) _c_ (pl ~en) way; road, **doodlopende ~** cul-de-sac; **op ~ naar** bound for

***wegen** (_vāy_-gern) _v_ weigh

wegenkaart (_vāy_-ger-kaart) _c_ (pl ~en) road map

wegennet (_vāy_-ger-neht) _nt_ (pl ~ten) road system

wegens (_vāy_-gerns) _prep_ because of, for

***weggaan** (veh-_khaan_) _v_ *go away

wegkant (_vehkh_-kahnt) _c_ (pl ~en) roadside, wayside

***weglaten** (_vehkh_-laa-tern) _v_ omit, *leave out

*wegnemen (*vehkh*-nāȳ-mern) *v* *take out, *take away

wegomlegging (*vaykh*-om-leh-ging) *c* (pl ~en) diversion

wegrestaurant (*vehkh*-rehss-tōā-rahnt) *nt* (pl ~s) roadhouse; roadside restaurant

wegwerp- (*vehkh*-vehrp) disposable

wegwijzer (*vehkh*-vay-zerr) *c* (pl ~s) milepost, signpost

*wegzenden (*vehkh*-sehn-dern) *v* dismiss

wei (vay) *c* (pl ~den) meadow

weigeren (*vay*-ger-rern) *v* refuse; deny

weigering (*vay*-ger-ring) *c* (pl ~en) refusal

weiland (*vay*-lahnt) *nt* (pl ~en) pasture

weinig (*vay*-nerkh) *adj* little; few

wekelijks (*vāȳ*-ker-lerks) *adj* weekly

weken (*vāȳ*-kern) *v* soak

wekken (*veh*-kern) *v* *awake, *wake

wekker (*veh*-kerr) *c* (pl ~s) alarmclock

weldra (*vehl*-draa) *adv* soon, shortly

welk (vehlk) *pron* which; ~ **ook** whichever

welkom (*vehl*-kom) *adj* welcome; *nt* welcome

wellicht (veh-*likht*) *adv* perhaps

wellust (*veh*-lerst) *c* (pl ~en) lust

welnu! (vehl-*nēw*) well!

welvaart (*vehl*-vaart) *c* prosperity

welvarend (vehl-*vaa*-rernt) *adj* prosperous

welwillendheid (vehl-*vi*-lernt-hayt) *c* goodwill

welzijn (*vehl*-zayn) *nt* welfare

wending (*vehn*-ding) *c* (pl ~en) turn

wenk (vehngk) *c* (pl ~en) sign

wenkbrauw (*vehngk*-brou) *c* (pl ~en) eyebrow

wenkbrauwstift (*vehngk*-brou-stift) *c* (pl ~en) eye-pencil

wennen (*veh*-nern) *v* accustom

wens (vehns) *c* (pl ~en) wish, desire

wenselijk (*vehn*-ser-lerk) *adj* desirable

wensen (*vehn*-sern) *v* wish, desire; want

wereld (*vāȳ*-rerlt) *c* (pl ~en) world

wereldberoemd (*vāȳ*-rerlt-ber-rōōmt) *adj* world-famous

wereldbol (*vāȳ*-rerlt-bol) *c* globe

werelddeel (*vāȳ*-rerl-dāyl) *nt* (pl -delen) continent

wereldomvattend (*vāȳ*-rerlt-om-vah-ternt) *adj* global, world-wide

wereldoorlog (*vāȳ*-rerlt-ōar-lokh) *c* (pl ~en) world war

werk (vehrk) *nt* work; labour; occupation, employment; business; **te ~ *gaan** proceed; ~ **in uitvoering** road up

werkdag (*vehrk*-dahkh) *c* (pl ~en) working day

werkelijk (*vehr*-ker-lerk) *adj* actual, true; substantial, very; *adv* really

werkelijkheid (*vehr*-ker-lerk-hayt) *c* reality

werkeloos (*vehr*-ker-lōāss) *adj* unemployed; idle

werkeloosheid (vehr-ker-*lōāss*-hayt) *c* unemployment

werken (*vehr*-kern) *v* work; operate

werkgever (*vehrk*-khāy-verr) *c* (pl ~s) employer

werking (*vehr*-king) *c* operation, working; **buiten ~** out of order

werknemer (*vehrk*-nāy-merr) *c* (pl ~s) employee

werkplaats (*vehrk*-plaats) *c* (pl ~en) workshop

werktuig (*vehrk*-tur^(ew)kh) *nt* (pl ~en) tool; utensil, implement

werkvergunning (*vehrk*-ferr-ger-ning) *c* (pl ~en) work permit; labor permit *Am*

werkwoord (vehrk-vōārt) nt (pl ~en)
verb

*werpen (vehr-pern) v *cast, *throw

wesp (vehsp) c (pl ~en) wasp

west (vehst) c west

westelijk (vehss-ter-lerk) adj westerly

westen (vehss-tern) nt west

westers (vehss-terrs) adj western

wet (veht) c (pl ~ten) law

*weten (vāy-tern) v *know

wetenschap (vāy-ter-skhahp) c (pl
~pen) science

wetenschappelijk (vāy-ter-skhah-per-
lerk) adj scientific

wettelijk (veh-ter-lerk) adj legal

wettig (veh-terkh) adj legal, lawful;
legitimate

*weven (vāy-vern) v *weave

wever (vāy-verr) c (pl ~s) weaver

wezen¹ (vāy-zern) nt (pl ~s) creature,
being

wezen² (vāy-zern) nt essence

wezenlijk (vāy-zer-lerk) adj essential

wie (vee) pron who; whom; ~ dan
ook anybody; ~ ook whoever

wieg (veekh) c (pl ~en) cradle

wiel (veel) nt (pl ~en) wheel

wielrijder (veel-ray-derr) c (pl ~s) cyclist

wierook (vee-rōak) c incense

wig (vikh) c (pl ~gen) wedge

wijd (vayt) adj broad, wide

wijden (vay-dern) v devote

wijk (vayk) c (pl ~en) quarter, district

wijn (vayn) c (pl ~en) wine

wijngaard (vayn-gaart) c (pl ~en)
vineyard

wijnkaart (vayng-kaart) c (pl ~en)
wine-list

wijnkelder (vayng-kehl-derr) c (pl ~s)
wine-cellar

wijnkelner (vayng-kehl-nerr) c (pl ~s)
wine-waiter

wijnkoper (vayng-kōa-perr) c (pl ~s)

wine-merchant

wijnoogst (vayn-ōākhst) c (pl ~en)
vintage

wijnstok (vayn-stok) c (pl ~ken) vine

wijs¹ (vayss) adj wise

wijs² (vayss) c (pl wijzen) tune

wijsbegeerte (vayss-ber-gāyr-ter) c
philosophy

wijsgeer (vayss-khāyr) c (pl -geren)
philosopher

wijsheid (vayss-hayt) c (pl -heden)
wisdom

wijsvinger (vayss-fi-ngerr) c (pl ~s)
index finger

wijting (vay-ting) c (pl ~en) whiting

wijze (vay-zer) c (pl ~n) manner, way

*wijzen (vay-zern) v point; direct

wijzigen (vay-zer-gern) v change, alter,
modify

wijziging (vay-zer-ging) c (pl ~en)
change, alteration

wil (vil) c will

wild (vilt) adj wild; savage, fierce; nt
game

wildpark (vilt-pahrk) nt (pl ~en) game
reserve

willekeurig (vi-ler-kūr-rerkh) adj arbitrary

*willen (vi-lern) v want; *will

wilskracht (vils krahkht) c will-power

wimper (vim-perr) c (pl ~s) eyelash

wind (vint) c (pl ~en) wind

*winden (vin-dern) v *wind; twist

winderig (vin-der-rerkh) adj windy,
gusty

windmolen (vint-mōa-lern) c (pl ~s)
windmill

windstoot (vint-stōāt) c (pl -stoten)
gust

windvlaag (vint-flaakh) c (pl -vlagen)
blow

winkel (ving-kerl) c (pl ~s) store, shop

winkelcentrum (ving-kerl-sehn-trerm)
nt (pl -tra) shopping centre

winkelen (*ving*-ker-lern) *v* shop

winkelier (*ving*-ker-*leer*) *c* (pl ~s) shopkeeper

winnaar (*vı*-naar) *c* (pl ~s) winner

*****winnen** (*vı*-nern) *v* *win; gain

winst (vınst) *c* (pl ~en) profit; gain, winnings *pl*, benefit

winstgevend (vinst-*khāy*-vernt) *adj* profitable

winter (*vın*-terr) *c* (pl ~s) winter

wintersport (*vın*-terr-sport) *c* winter sports

wip (vıp) *c* (pl ~pen) seesaw

wirwar (*vır*-vahr) *c* muddle

wiskunde (*vıss*-kern-der) *c* mathematics

wiskundig (*vıss*-*kern*-derkh) *adj* mathematical

wissel (*vı*-serl) *c* (pl ~s) draft

wisselen (*vı*-ser-lern) *v* change; exchange

wisselgeld (*vı*-serl-gehlt) *nt* change

wisselkantoor (*vı*-serl-kahn-tōar) *nt* (pl -toren) money exchange, exchange office

wisselkoers (*vı*-serl-kōors) *c* (pl ~en) exchange rate

wisselstroom (*vı*-serl-strōam) *c* alternating current

wit (vıt) *adj* white

wittebroodsweken (*vı*-ter-brōats-vāy-kern) *pl* honeymoon

witvis (*vıt*-fıss) *c* (pl ~sen) whitebait

woede (*vōō*-der) *c* anger, rage

woeden (*vōō*-dern) *v* rage

woedend (*vōō*-dernt) *adj* furious

woensdag (*vōōns*-dahkh) *c* Wednesday

woest (vōost) *adj* wild, fierce; desert

woestijn (*vōōss*-*tayn*) *c* (pl ~en) desert

wol (vol) *c* wool

wolf (volf) *c* (pl wolven) wolf

wolk (volk) *c* (pl ~en) cloud

wolkbreuk (*volk*-brūrk) *c* (pl ~en) cloud-burst

wolkenkrabber (*vol*-ker-krah-berr) *c* (pl ~s) skyscraper

wollen (*vo*-lern) *adj* woollen

wond (vont) *c* (pl ~en) wound

wonder (*von*-derr) *nt* (pl ~en) wonder, miracle; marvel

wonderbaarlijk (von-derr-*baar*-lerk) *adj* miraculous

wonen (*vōā*-nern) *v* live; reside

woning (*vōā*-ning) *c* (pl ~en) house

woonachtig (vōan-*ahkh*-terkh) *adj* resident

woonboot (*vōān*-bōat) *c* (pl -boten) houseboat

woonkamer (*vōāng*-kaa-merr) *c* (pl ~s) living-room

woonplaats (*vōām*-plaats) *c* (pl ~en) domicile, residence

woonwagen (*vōān*-vaa-gern) *c* (pl ~s) caravan

woord (vōart) *nt* (pl ~en) word

woordenboek (*vōār*-der-bōōk) *nt* (pl ~en) dictionary

woordenlijst (*vōār*-der-layst) *c* (pl ~en) vocabulary

woordenschat (*vōār*-der-skhaht) *c* vocabulary

woordenwisseling (*vōār*-der-vı-ser-lıng) *c* (pl ~en) argument

*****worden** (*vor*-dern) *v* *become; *go, *get, *grow .

worm (vorm) *c* (pl ~en) worm

worp (vorp) *c* (pl ~en) cast

worst (vorst) *c* (pl ~en) sausage

worstelen (*vor*-ster-lern) *v* struggle

worsteling (*voar*-ster-lıng) *c* (pl ~en) struggle

wortel (*vor*-terl) *c* (pl ~s, ~en) root; carrot

woud (vout) *nt* (pl ~en) forest

wraak (vraak) *c* revenge

wrak (vrahk) *nt* (pl ~ken) wreck

wreed (vrāyt) *adj* harsh, cruel
***wrijven** (*vray*-vern) *v* rub
wrijving (*vray*-vɪng) *c* (pl ~en) friction
wurgen (*verr*-gern) *v* strangle, choke

Z

zaad (zaat) *nt* (pl zaden) seed
zaag (zaakh) *c* (pl zagen) saw
zaagsel (*zaakh*-serl) *nt* sawdust
zaaien (*zaa^ee*-ern) *v* *sow
zaak (zaak) *c* (pl zaken) cause; case, matter; business
zaal (zaal) *c* (pl zalen) hall
zacht (zahkht) *adj* soft; gentle, smooth, mild, mellow
zadel (*zaa*-derl) *nt* (pl ~s) saddle
zak (zahk) *c* (pl ~ken) pocket; sack, bag
zakdoek (*zahk*-dōok) *c* (pl ~en) handkerchief; **papieren** ~ tissue
zakelijk (*zaa*-ker-lerk) *adj* business-like
zaken (*zaa*-kern) *pl* business; **voor** ~ on business; ~ *doen met *deal with
zakenman (*zaa*-ker-mahn) *c* (pl -lieden, -lui) businessman
zakenreis (*zaa*-ker-rayss) *c* (pl -reizen) business trip
zakhorloge (*zahk*-hor-lōa-zher) *nt* (pl ~s) pocket-watch
zakkam (*zah*-kahm) *c* (pl ~men) pocket-comb
zakken (*zah*-kern) *v* fail
zaklantaarn (*zahk*-lahn-taa-rern) *c* (pl ~s) torch, flash-light
zakmes (*zahk*-mehss) *nt* (pl ~sen) pocket-knife, penknife
zalf (zahlf) *c* (pl zalven) ointment, salve
zalm (zahlm) *c* (pl ~en) salmon
zand (zahnt) *nt* sand

zanderig (*zahn*-der-rerkh) *adj* sandy
zanger (*zah*-ngerr) *c* (pl ~s) vocalist, singer
zangeres (zah-nger-*rehss*) *c* (pl ~sen) singer
zaterdag (*zaa*-terr-dahkh) *c* Saturday
ze (zer) *pron* she; they
zebra (*zāy*-braa) *c* (pl ~'s) zebra
zebrapad (*zāy*-braa-paht) *nt* (pl ~en) pedestrian crossing; crosswalk *nAm*
zedelijk (*zāy*-der-lerk) *adj* moral
zeden (*zāy*-dern) *pl* morals
zee (zāy) *c* (pl ~ën) sea
zeeëgel (*zāy*-āy-gerl) *c* (pl ~s) sea-urchin
zeef (zāyf) *c* (pl zeven) sieve
zeegezicht (*zāy*-ger-zɪkht) *nt* (pl ~en) seascape
zeehaven (*zāy*-haa-vern) *c* (pl ~s) seaport
zeehond (*zāy*-hont) *c* (pl ~en) seal
zeekaart (*zāy*-kaart) *c* (pl ~en) chart
zeekust (*zāy*-kerst) *c* (pl ~en) seacoast
zeeman (*zāy*-mahn) *c* (pl -lieden, -lui) seaman
zeemeermin (*zāy*-māyr-mɪn) *c* (pl ~nen) mermaid
zeemeeuw (*zāy*-māy^oo) *c* (pl ~en) seagull
zeep (zāyp) *c* soap
zeeppoeder (*zāy*-pōo-derr) *nt* soap powder
zeer (zāyr) *adj* sore; *adv* very, quite
zeeschelp (*zāy*-skhehlp) *c* (pl ~en) sea-shell
zeevogel (*zāy*-vōa-gerl) *c* (pl ~s) sea-bird
zeewater (*zāy*-vaa-terr) *nt* sea-water
zeeziek (*zāy*-zeek) *adj* seasick
zeeziekte (*zāy*-zeek-ter) *c* seasickness
zegel (*zāy*-gerl) *nt* (pl ~s) seal
zegen (*zāy*-gern) *c* blessing
zegenen (*zāy*-ger-nern) *v* bless

zegevieren (*zāy*-ger-vee-rern) *v* triumph

*****zeggen** (*zeh*-gern) *v* *say; *tell

zeil (zayl) *nt* (pl ~en) sail

zeilboot (*zayl*-bōat) *c* (pl -boten) sailing-boat

zeilclub (*zayl*-klerp) *c* (pl ~s) yacht-club

zeilsport (*zayl*-sport) *c* yachting

zeker (*zāy*-kerr) *adv* surely; *adj* certain, sure; ~ **niet** by no means

zekering (*zāy*-ker-rɪng) *c* (pl ~en) fuse

zelden (*zehl*-dern) *adv* seldom, rarely

zeldzaam (*zehlt*-saam) *adj* rare; uncommon, infrequent

zelf (zehlf) *pron* myself; yourself; himself; herself; oneself; ourselves; yourselves; themselves

zelfbediening (*zehlf*-ber-dee-nɪng) *c* self-service

zelfbedieningsrestaurant (*zehlf*-ber-dee-nɪngs-rehss-tōa-rahnt) *nt* (pl ~s) self-service restaurant

zelfbestuur (*zehlf*-ber-stēwr) *nt* self-government

zelfde (*zehlf*-der) *adj* same

zelfmoord (*zehlf*-mōart) *c* (pl ~en) suicide

zelfs (zehlfs) *adv* even

zelfstandig (zehlf-*stahn*-derkh) *adj* independent; self-employed; ~ **naamwoord** noun

zelfstrijkend (zehlf-*stray*-kernt) *adj* drip-dry, wash and wear

zelfzuchtig (zehlf-*serkh*-terkh) *adj* egoistic

*****zenden** (*zehn*-dern) *v* *send

zender (*zehn*-derr) *c* (pl ~s) transmitter

zending (*zehn*-dɪng) *c* (pl ~en) consignment

zenit (*zāy*-nɪt) *nt* zenith

zenuw (*zay*-nēw^oo) *c* (pl ~en) nerve

zenuwachtig (*zāy*-nēw^oo-ahkh-terkh) *adj* nervous

zenuwpijn (*zāy*-nēw^oo-payn) *c* (pl ~en) neuralgia

zes (zehss) *num* six

zesde (*zehss*-der) *num* sixth

zestien (*zehss*-teen) *num* sixteen

zestiende (*zehss*-teen-der) *num* sixteenth

zestig (*zehss*-terkh) *num* sixty

zet (zeht) *c* (pl ~ten) move; push

zetel (*zāy*-terl) *c* (pl ~s) chair; seat

zetpil (*zeht*-pɪl) *c* (pl ~len) suppository

zetten (*zeh*-tern) *v* place; *lay, *set, *put; **in elkaar** ~ assemble

zeurpiet (*zūrr*-peet) *c* (pl ~en) bore

zeven¹ (*zāy*-vern) *num* seven

zeven² (*zāy*-vern) *v* strain, sift, sieve

zevende (*zāy*-vern-der) *num* seventh

zeventien (*zāy*-vern-teen) *num* seventeen

zeventiende (*zāy*-vern-teen-der) *num* seventeenth

zeventig (*zāy*-vern-terkh) *num* seventy

zich (zɪkh) *pron* himself; herself; themselves

zicht (zɪkht) *nt* sight; visibility; **op** ~ on approval

zichtbaar (*zɪkht*-baar) *adj* visible

ziek (zeek) *adj* ill, sick

ziekenauto (*zee*-kern-ōa-tōa) *c* (pl ~'s) ambulance

ziekenhuis (*zee*-ker-hur^ewss) *nt* (pl -huizen) hospital

ziekenzaal (*zee*-ker-zaal) *c* (pl -zalen) infirmary

ziekte (*zeek*-ter) *c* (pl ~n, ~s) disease; ailment, illness, sickness

ziel (zeel) *c* (pl ~en) soul

*****zien** (zeen) *v* *see; notice; **er uit** ~ look; *laten ~ *show

zienswijze (*zeens*-vay-zer) *c* (pl ~n) outlook

zigeuner (zee-*gūr*-nerr) *c* (pl ~s) gipsy

zijbeuk (*zay*-būrk) *c* (pl ~en) aisle

zijde[1] (*zay*-der) *c* silk

zijde[2] (*zay*-der) *c* (pl ~n) side

zijden (*zay*-dern) *adj* silken

zijlicht (*zay*-lıkht) *nt* sidelight

zijn (zayn) *pron* his

*****zijn** (zayn) *v* *be

zijrivier (*zay*-ree-veer) *c* (pl ~en) tributary

zijstraat (*zay*-straat) *c* (pl -straten) side-street

zilver (*zıl*-verr) *nt* silver

zilveren (*zıl*-ver-rern) *adj* silver

zilverpapier (*zıl*-verr-paa-peer) *nt* tinfoil

zilversmid (*zıl*-verr-smıt) *c* (pl -smeden) silversmith

zilverwerk (*zıl*-verr-vehrk) *nt* silverware

zin[1] (zın) *c* sense; desire; ~ *hebben in *feel like, fancy

zin[2] (zın) *c* (pl ~nen) sentence

*****zingen** (*zı*-ngern) *v* *sing

zink (zıngk) *nt* zinc

*****zinken** (*zıng*-kern) *v* *sink

zinloos (*zın*-lōass) *adj* senseless

zintuig (*zın*-tur^ewkh) *nt* (pl ~en) sense

zitkamer (*zıt*-kaa-merr) *c* (pl ~s) sitting-room

zitplaats (*zıt*-plaats) *c* (pl ~en) seat

*****zitten** (*zı*-tern) *v* *sit; **gaan** ~ *sit down

zitting (*zı*-tıng) *c* (pl ~en) session

zitvlak (*zıt*-flahk) *nt* bottom

zo (zōā) *adv* so, thus; such; **zo'n** such a

zoals (zōā-*ahls*) *conj* like, as; such as

zodat (zōā-*daht*) *conj* so that

zodra (zōā-*draa*) *conj* as soon as

*****zoeken** (*zōō*-kern) *v* look for; *seek, search; hunt for

zoeker (*zōō*-kerr) *c* (pl ~s) view-finder

zoen (zōōn) *c* (pl ~en) kiss

zoet (zōōt) *adj* sweet; good; ~ **ma-**

ken sweeten

zoetzuur (*zōōt*-sewr) *nt* pickles *pl*

zogen (zōā-gern) *v* nurse

zogenaamd (zōā-ger-*naamt*) *adj* so-called

zolder (*zol*-derr) *c* (pl ~s) attic

zomer (zōā-merr) *c* (pl ~s) summer

zomertijd (zōā-merr-tayt) *c* summer time

zon (zon) *c* (pl ~nen) sun

zondag (*zon*-dahkh) *c* Sunday

zonde (*zon*-der) *c* (pl ~n) sin

zondebok (*zon*-der-bok) *c* (pl ~ken) scapegoat

zonder (*zon*-derr) *prep* without

zonderling (*zon*-derr-lıng) *adj* funny, queer

zone (*zaw*-ner) *c* (pl ~s) zone

zonlicht (*zon*-lıkht) *nt* sunlight

zonnebaden (*zo*-ner-baa-dern) *v* sunbathe

zonnebrand (*zo*-ner-brahnt) *c* sunburn

zonnebrandolie (*zo*-ner-brahnt-ōā-lee) *c* suntan oil

zonnebril (*zo*-ner-brıl) *c* (pl ~len) sunglasses *pl*

zonnescherm (*zo*-ner-skhehrm) *nt* (pl ~en) awning

zonneschijn (*zo*-ner-skhayn) *c* sunshine

zonnesteek (*zo*-ner-stāyk) *c* sunstroke

zonnig (*zo*-nerkh) *adj* sunny

zonsondergang (zons-*on*-derr-gahng) *c* (pl ~en) sunset

zonsopgang (zons-*op*-khahng) *c* (pl ~en) sunrise

zoogdier (*zōā*kh-deer) *nt* (pl ~en) mammal

zool (zōāl) *c* (pl zolen) sole

zoölogie (zōā-ōā-lōā-*gee*) *c* zoology

zoom (zōām) *c* (pl zomen) hem

zoon (zōān) *c* (pl zonen) son

zorg (zorkh) *c* (pl ~en) concern, worry, care; trouble

zorgen voor (*zor*-gern) look after, *take care of; see to

zorgvuldig (zorkh-*ferl*-derkh) *adj* careful

zorgwekkend (zorkh-*veh*-kernt) *adj* critical

zorgzaam (*zorkh*-saam) *adj* thoughtful

zout (zout) *nt* salt; *adj* salty

zoutvaatje (*zout*-faa-t^{y}er) *nt* (pl ~s) salt-cellar

zoveel (z$\bar{o}\bar{a}$-v$\bar{a}$yl) *adv* so much

zowel ... als (z$\bar{o}\bar{a}$-*veh*...ahls) both ... and

zuid (zur^{ew}t) *c* south

Zuid-Afrika (zur^{ew}t-*aa*-free-kaa) South Africa

zuidelijk (zur^{ew}-der-lerk) *adj* southern, southerly

zuiden (*zur^{ew}*-dern) *nt* south

zuidoosten (zur^{ew}t-$\bar{o}$ass-tern) *nt* south-east

zuidpool (*zur^{ew}t*-p$\bar{o}$al) *c* South Pole

zuidwesten (zur^{ew}t-*vehss*-tern) *nt* south-west

zuigeling (*zur^{ew}*-ger-ling) *c* (pl ~en) infant

zuigen (*zur^{ew}*-gern) *v* suck

zuiger (*zur^{ew}*-gerr) *c* (pl ~s) piston

zuigerring (*zur^{ew}*-ger-ring) *c* (pl ~en) piston ring

zuigerstang (*zur^{ew}*-gerr-stahng) *c* (pl ~en) piston-rod

zuil (zur^{ew}l) *c* (pl ~en) column, pillar

zuilengang (*zur^{ew}*-ler-gahng) *c* (pl ~en) arcade

zuinig (*zur^{ew}*-nerkh) *adj* economical, thrifty

zuivelwinkel (*zur^{ew}*-verl-ving-kerl) *c* (pl ~s) dairy

zuiver (*zur^{ew}*-verr) *adj* pure, clean

zulk (zerlk) *adj* such

zullen (*zer*-lern) *v* *will, *shall

zus (zerss) *c* (pl ~sen) sister

zuster (*zerss*-terr) *c* (pl ~s) sister; nurse

zuur^1 (z$\bar{e}$wr) *adj* sour

zuur^2 (z$\bar{e}$wr) *nt* (pl zuren) acid

zuurstof (*z$\bar{e}$wr*-stof) *c* oxygen

zwaaien (zvaa^{ee}-ern) *v* *swing; wave

zwaan (zvaan) *c* (pl zwanen) swan

zwaar (zvaar) *adj* heavy

zwaard (zvaart) *nt* (pl ~en) sword

zwaartekracht (*zvaar*-ter-krahkht) *c* gravity

zwager (*zvaa*-gerr) *c* (pl ~s) brother-in-law

zwak (zvahk) *adj* feeble, weak; faint; dim

zwakheid (*zvahk*-hayt) *c* (pl -heden) weakness

zwaluw (*zvaa*-l$\bar{e}$w^{oo}) *c* (pl ~en) swallow

zwanger (*zvah*-ngerr) *adj* pregnant

zwart (zvahrt) *adj* black

Zweden (*zv$\bar{a}$y*-dern) Sweden

Zweed (zv$\bar{a}$yt) *c* (pl Zweden) Swede

Zweeds (zv$\bar{a}$yts) *adj* Swedish

zweefvliegtuig (*zv$\bar{a}$y*-fleekh-tur^{ew}kh) *nt* (pl ~en) glider

zweep (zv$\bar{a}$yp) *c* (pl zwepen) whip

zweer (zv$\bar{a}$yr) *c* (pl zweren) ulcer, sore

zweet (zv$\bar{a}$yt) *nt* sweat, perspiration

zwellen (*zveh*-lern) *v* *swell

zwelling (*zveh*-ling) *c* (pl ~en) swelling

zwembad (*zvehm*-baht) *nt* (pl ~en) swimming pool

zwembroek (*zvehm*-br$\bar{o}$ok) *c* (pl ~en) swimming-trunks, bathing-trunks, bathing-suit

zwemmen (*zveh*-mern) *v* *swim

zwemmer (*zveh*-merr) *c* (pl ~s) swimmer

zwempak (*zvehm*-pahk) *nt* (pl ~ken) swim-suit

zwemsport (*zvehm*-sport) *c* swimming

zwendelarij (zvehn-der-laa-*ray*) *c* (pl ~en) swindle

*zweren (*zvāy*-rern) *v* *swear, vow
*zwerven (*zvehr*-vern) *v* roam, wander
zweten (*zvāy*-tern) *v* sweat, perspire
*zwijgen (*zvay*-gern) *v* *be silent, *keep quiet; **tot ~ *brengen** silence; **zwijgend** silent

zwijn (zvayn) *nt* (pl ~en) pig
Zwitser (*zvɪt*-serr) *c* (pl ~s) Swiss
Zwitserland (*zvɪt*-serr-lahnt) Switzerland
Zwitsers (*zvɪt*-serrs) *adj* Swiss
zwoegen (*zvoō*-gern) *v* labour

Menu Reader

Food

aalbes redcurrant
aardappel potato
  ~ **puree** mashed potatoes
aardbei strawberry
abrikoos apricot
amandel almond
  ~ **broodje** a sweet roll with al-
  mond-paste filling
ananas pineapple
andijvie endive (US chicory)
  ~ **stamppot** mashed potato and
  endive casserole
anijs aniseed
ansjovis anchovy
appel apple
  ~ **beignet** fritter
  ~ **bol** dumpling
  ~ **flap** puff-pastry containing
  an apple slice
  ~ **gebak** cake
  ~ **moes** sauce
Ardense pastei rich pork mixture
  cooked in a pastry crust, served
  cold in slices
artisjok artichoke
asperge asparagus
  ~ **punt** tip
aubergine aubergine (US eggplant)
augurk gherkin (US pickle)

avondeten dinner, supper
azijn vinegar
baars perch
babi pangang slices of roast suck-
  (l)ing pig, served with a sweet-
  and-sour sauce
bami goreng a casserole of
  noodles, vegetables, diced pork
  and shrimps
banaan banana
banketletter pastry with an al-
  mond-paste filling
basilicum basil
bediening service
belegd broodje roll with a variety
  of garnishes
belegen kaas pungent-flavoured
  cheese
biefstuk fillet of beef
  ~ **van de haas** small round fillet
  of beef
bieslook chive
bitterbal small, round breaded
  meatball served as an appetizer
blinde vink veal bird; thin slice of
  veal rolled around stuffing
bloedworst black pudding (US
  blood sausage)
  ~ **met appelen** with cooked ap-
  ples

bloemkool cauliflower

boerenkool met worst kale mixed with mashed potatoes and served with smoked sausage

boerenomelet omelet with diced vegetables and bacon

bokking bloater

boon bean

borrelhapje appetizer

borststuk breast, brisket

bosbes bilberry (US blueberry)

bot 1) flounder 2) bone

boter butter

boterham slice of buttered bread

bouillon broth

braadhaantje spring chicken

braadworst frying sausage

braam blackberry

brasem bream

brood bread

~ **maaltijd** bread served with cold meat, eggs, cheese, jam or other garnishes

~ **pudding** kind of bread pudding with eggs, cinnamon and rum flavouring

broodje roll

~ **halfom** buttered roll with liver and salted beef

~ **kaas** buttered roll with cheese

bruine bonen met spek red kidney beans served with bacon

Brussels lof chicory (US endive)

caramelpudding caramel mould

caramelvla caramel custard

champignon mushroom

chocola(de) chocolate

citroen lemon

cordon bleu veal scallop stuffed with ham and cheese

dadel date

dagschotel day's special

dame blanche vanilla ice-cream

with hot chocolate sauce

dille dill

doperwt green pea

dragon tarragon

drie-in-de-pan small, fluffy pancake filled with currants

druif grape

duif pigeon

Duitse biefstuk hamburger steak

Edam, Edammer kaas firm, mild-flavoured yellow cheese, coated with red wax

eend duck

ei egg

eierpannekoek egg pancake

erwt pea

erwtensoep met kluif pea soup with diced, smoked sausages, pork fat, pig's trotter (US feet), parsley, leeks and celery

exclusief not included

fazant pheasant

filet fillet

~ **américain** steak tartare

flensje small, thin pancake

foe yong hai omelet with leeks, onions, and shrimps served in a sweet-and-sour sauce

forel trout

framboos raspberry

Friese nagelkaas cheese made from skimmed milk, flavoured with cloves

frikadel meatball

frites, frieten chips (US french fries)

gaar well-done

gans goose

garnaal shrimp, prawn

gebak pastry, cake

gebakken fried

gebonden soep cream soup

gebraden roasted

gedroogde pruim prune

gehakt 1) minced 2) minced meat
~**bal** meatball
gekookt boiled
gekruid seasoned
gemarineerd marinated
gember ginger
~**koek** gingerbread
gemengd assorted, mixed
gepaneerd breaded
gepocheerd ei poached egg
geraspt grated
gerecht course, dish
gerookt smoked
geroosterd brood toast
gerst barley
gestoofd braised
gevogelte fowl
gevuld stuffed
gezouten salted
Goudakaas, Goudse kaas a re-
nowned Dutch cheese, similar
to *Edam*, large, flat and round;
it gains in flavour with maturity
griesmeel semolina
~**pudding** semolina pudding
griet brill
groente vegetable
Haagse bluf dessert of whipped
egg-whites, served with redcurrant sauce
haantje cockerel
haas hare
hachee hash of minced meat,
onions and spices
half, halve half
hardgekookt ei hard-boiled egg
haring herring
hart heart
havermoutpap (oatmeal) porridge
hazelnoot hazelnut
heilbot halibut
heldere soep consommé, clear
soup
hersenen brains

hete bliksem potatoes, bacon and
apples, seasoned with butter,
salt and sugar
Hollandse biefstuk loin section of
a porterhouse or T-bone steak
Hollandse nieuwe freshly caught,
filleted herring
honing honey
houtsnip 1) woodcock 2) cheese
sandwich on rye bread
hutspot met klapstuk hotch-potch
of mashed potatoes, carrots and
onions served with boiled beef
huzarensla salad of potatoes,
hard-boiled eggs, cold meat,
gherkins, beetroot and mayonnaise
ijs ice, ice-cream
inclusief included
Italiaanse salade mixed salad with
tomatoes, olives and tunny fish
jachtschotel a casserole of meat,
onions and potatoes, often
served with apple sauce
jonge kaas fresh cheese
jus gravy
kaas cheese
~**balletje** baked cheese ball
kabeljauw cod
kalfslapje, kalfsoester veal cutlet
kalfsrollade roast veal
kalfsvlees veal
kalkoen turkey
kapucijners met spek peas served
with fried bacon, boiled potatoes, onions and green salad
karbonade chop, cutlet
karper carp
kastanje chestnut
kaviaar caviar
kerrie curry
kers cherry
kievitsei plover's egg
kip chicken

kippeborst breast of chicken
kippebout leg, thigh of chicken
knakworst small frankfurter sausage
knoflook garlic
koek 1) cake 2) gingerbread
koekje biscuit (US cookie)
koffietafel light lunch consisting of bread and butter with a variety of garnishes, served with coffee
kokosnoot coconut
komijnekaas cheese flavoured with cumin seeds
komkommer cucumber
konijn rabbit
koninginnesoep cream of chicken
kool cabbage
~ **schotel met gehakt** casserole of meatballs and cabbage
kotelet chop, cutlet
koud cold
~ **vlees** cold meat (US cold cuts)
krab crab
krabbetje spare rib
krent currant
kroepoek large, deep-fried shrimp wafer
kroket croquette
kruiderij herb, seasoning
kruidnagel clove
kruisbes gooseberry
kwark fresh white cheese
kwartel quail
kweepeer quince
lamsbout leg of lamb
lamsvlees lamb
langoest spiny lobster
Leidse kaas cheese flavoured with cumin seeds
lekkerbekje fried, filleted haddock or plaice
lendestuk sirloin
lever liver

linze lentil
loempia spring roll (US egg roll)
maïskolf corn on the cob
makreel mackerel
mandarijntje tangerine
marsepein marzipan
meikaas a creamy cheese with high fat content
meloen melon
menu van de dag set menu
mossel mussel
mosterd mustard
nagerecht dessert
nasi goreng a casserole of rice, fried onions, meat, chicken, shrimps, vegetables and seasoning, usually topped with a fried egg
nier kidney
~ **broodje** roll filled with kidneys and chopped onions
noot nut
oester oyster
olie oil
~ **bol** fritter with raisins
olijf olive
omelet fines herbes herb omelet
omelet met kippelevertjes chicken liver omelet
omelet nature plain omelet
ongaar underdone (US rare)
ontbijt breakfast
~ **koek** honey cake
~ **spek** bacon, rasher
ossehaas fillet of beef
ossestaart oxtail
oude kaas any mature and strong cheese
paddestoel mushroom
paling eel
~ **in 't groen** braised in white sauce garnished with chopped parsley and other greens
pannekoek pancake

~ **met stroop** pancake served with treacle (US syrup)

pap porridge

paprika green or red (sweet) pepper

pastei pie, pasty

patrijs partridge

peer pear

pekeltong salt(ed) tongue

pekelvlees slices of salted meat

peper pepper

~ **koek** gingerbread

perzik peach

peterselie parsley

piccalilly pickle

pinda peanut

~ **kaas** peanut butter

pisang goreng fried banana

poffertje fritter served with sugar and butter

pommes frites chips (US french fries)

pompelmoes grapefruit

portie portion

postelein purslane (edible plant)

prei leek

prinsessenboon French bean (US green bean)

pruim plum

rabarber rhubarb

radijs radish

rauw raw

reebout, reerug venison

reine-claude greengage

rekening bill

ribstuk rib of beef

rijst rice

~ **tafel** an Indonesian preparation composed of some 30 dishes including stewed vegetables, spit-roasted meat and fowl, served with rice, various sauces, fruit, nuts and spices

rivierkreeft crayfish

rode biet beetroot

rode kool red cabbage

roerei scrambled egg

roggebrood rye bread

rolmops Bismarck herring

rolpens fried slices of spiced and pickled minced beef and tripe, topped with an apple slice

rookspek smoked bacon

rookworst smoked sausage

roomboter butter

roomijs ice-cream

rosbief roast beef

rozemarijn rosemary

runderlap beefsteak

rundvlees beef

Russische eieren Russian eggs; hard-boiled egg-halves garnished with mayonnaise, herring, shrimps, capers, anchovies and sometimes caviar; served on lettuce

salade salad

sambal kind of spicy paste consisting mainly of ground pimentos, usually served with *rijsttafel*, *bami* or *nasi goreng*

sardien sardine

saté, sateh skewered pieces of meat covered with a spicy peanut sauce

saucijzebroodje sausage roll

saus sauce, gravy

schaaldier shellfish

schapevlees mutton

scharretong lemon sole

schelvis haddock

schildpadsoep turtle soup

schnitzel cutlet

schol plaice

schuimomelet fluffy dessert omelet

selderij celery

sinaasappel orange

sjaslik skewered chunks of meat, grilled, then braised in a spicy sauce of tomatoes, onions and bacon

sla salad, lettuce

slaboon French bean (US green bean)

slagroom whipped cream

slak snail

sneeuwbal kind of cream puff, sometimes filled with currants and raisins

snijboon sliced French bean

soep soup
  ~ **van de dag** soup of the day

sorbet water ice (US sherbet)

speculaas spiced almond biscuit

spek bacon

sperzieboon French bean (US green bean)

spiegelei fried egg

spijskaart menu, bill of fare

spinazie spinach

sprits a kind of shortbread

spruitje brussels sprout

stamppot a stew of vegetables and mashed potatoes

steur sturgeon

stokvis stockfish (dried cod)

stroop treacle (US syrup)

suiker sugar

taart cake

tarbot turbot

tartaar steak tartare
  ~ **speciaal** extra-large portion, of prime quality

tijm thyme

tjap tjoy chop suey; a dish of fried meat and vegetables served with rice

toeristenmenu tourist menu

tomaat tomato

tong 1) tongue 2) sole

tonijn tunny (US tuna)

toost toast

tosti grilled cheese-and-ham sandwich

tournedos thick round fillet cut of prime beef (US rib or rib-eye steak)

truffel truffle

tuinboon broad bean

ui onion

uitsmijter two slices of bread garnished with ham or roast beef and topped with two fried eggs

vanille vanilla

varkenshaas pork tenderloin

varkenslapje pork fillet

varkensvlees pork

venkel fennel

vermicellisoep consommé with thin noodles

vers fresh

vijg fig

vis fish

vla custard

vlaai fruit tart

Vlaamse karbonade small slices of beef and onions braised in broth, with beer sometimes added

vlees meat

voorgerecht starter or first course

vrucht fruit

vruchtensalade fruit salad

wafel wafer

walnoot walnut

warm hot

waterkers watercress

waterzooi chicken poached in white wine and shredded vegetables, cream and egg-yolk

wentelteefje French toast; slice of white bread dipped in egg batter and fried, then sprinkled with cinnamon and sugar

wijnkaart wine list

wijting whiting
wild game
~ **zwijn** wild boar
wilde eend wild duck
witlof chicory (US endive)
~ **op zijn Brussels** chicory rolled in a slice of ham and oven-browned with cheese sauce

worst sausage
wortel carrot
zachtgekookt ei soft-boiled egg
zalm salmon
zeekreeft lobster
zeevis saltwater fish
zout salt
zuurkool sauerkraut
zwezerik sweetbread

Drinks

advocaat egg liqueur
ananassap pineapple juice
aperitief aperitif
bessenjenever blackcurrant gin
bier beer
bisschopswijn mulled wine
bittertje bitter-tasting aperitif
boerenjongens Dutch brandy with raisins
boerenmeisjes Dutch brandy with apricots
borrel shot
brandewijn brandy
cassis blackcurrant liqueur
chocolademelk, chocomel(k) chocolate drink
citroenbrandewijn lemon brandy
citroenjenever lemon-flavoured gin
citroentje met suiker brandy flavoured with lemon peel, with sugar added
cognac brandy, cognac
donker bier porter; dark sweet-tasting beer
druivesap grape juice

frisdrank soft drink
gekoeld iced
genever see *jenever*
Geuzelambiek a strong Flemish bitter beer brewed from wheat and barley
jenever Dutch gin
jonge jenever/klare young Dutch gin
karnemelk buttermilk
kersenbrandewijn kirsch; spirit distilled from cherries
koffie coffee
~ **met melk** with milk
~ **met room** with cream
~ **met slagroom** with whipped cream
~ **verkeerd** white coffee; equal quantity of coffee and hot milk
zwarte ~ black
Kriekenlambiek a strong Brussels bitter beer flavoured with morello cherries
kwast hot or cold lemon squash
licht bier lager; light beer
likeur liqueur

limonade lemonade
melk milk
mineraalwater mineral water
oude jenever/klare Dutch gin aged in wood casks, yellowish in colour and more mature than *jonge jenever*
oranjebitter orange-flavoured bitter
pils general name for beer
sap juice
sinas orangeade
spuitwater soda water
sterkedrank liquor, spirit
tafelwater mineral water

thee tea
  ~ met citroen with lemon
  ~ met suiker en melk with sugar and milk
trappistenbier malt beer brewed (originally) by Trappist monks
vieux brandy bottled in Holland
vruchtesap fruit juice
warme chocola hot chocolate
wijn wine
  droge ~ dry
  rode ~ red
  witte ~ white
  zoete ~ sweet
wodka vodka

Dutch Irregular Verbs

The following list contains the most common strong and irregular verbs. If a compound verb or a verb with a prefix (*be-, con-, dis-, im-, in-, mis-, om-, on-, ont-, ver-*, etc.) is not listed, its forms may be found by looking up the basic verb, e.g. *verbinden* is conjugated as *binden*.

Infinitive	*Past*	*Past participle*	
bakken	bakte	gebakken	*bake*
barsten	barstte	gebarsten	*burst, crack*
bederven	bedierf	bedorven	*spoil*
bedriegen	bedroog	bedrogen	*deceive*
beginnen	begon	begonnen	*begin*
bergen	borg	geborgen	*put*
bevelen	beval	bevolen	*order*
bewegen	bewoog	bewogen	*move*
bezwijken	bezweek	bezweken	*succumb*
bidden	bad	gebeden	*pray*
bieden	bood	geboden	*offer*
bijten	beet	gebeten	*bite*
binden	bond	gebonden	*tie*
blazen	blies	geblazen	*blow*
blijken	bleek	gebleken	*prove to be*
blijven	bleef	gebleven	*remain*
blinken	blonk	geblonken	*shine*
braden	braadde	gebraden	*fry*
breken	brak	gebroken	*break*
brengen	bracht	gebracht	*bring*
buigen	boog	gebogen	*bow*
delven	delfde/dolf	gedolven	*dig up*
denken	dacht	gedacht	*think*
dingen	dong	gedongen	*compete (for)*
doen	deed	gedaan	*do*
dragen	droeg	gedragen	*wear*
drijven	dreef	gedreven	*float*
dringen	drong	gedrongen	*push*
drinken	dronk	gedronken	*drink*
druipen	droop	gedropen	*drip*
duiken	dook	gedoken	*dive*
dwingen	dwong	gedwongen	*force*
eten	at	gegeten	*eat*
fluiten	floot	gefloten	*whistle*
gaan	ging	gegaan	*go*
gelden	gold	gegolden	*be valid*
genezen	genas	genezen	*heal*
genieten	genoot	genoten	*enjoy*
geven	gaf	gegeven	*give*
gieten	goot	gegoten	*pour*
glijden	gleed	gegleden	*slide*
glimmen	glom	geglommen	*shine*
graven	groef	gegraven	*dig*

grijpen	greep	gegrepen	catch
hangen	hing	gehangen	hang
hebben	had	gehad	have
heffen	hief	geheven	raise
helpen	hielp	geholpen	help
heten	heette	geheten	be called
hijsen	hees	gehesen	hoist
houden	hield	gehouden	keep
jagen	jaagde/joeg	gejaagd	chase
kiezen	koos	gekozen	choose
kijken	keek	gekeken	look
klimmen	klom	geklommen	climb
klinken	klonk	geklonken	sound
knijpen	kneep	geknepen	pinch
komen	kwam	gekomen	come
kopen	kocht	gekocht	buy
krijgen	kreeg	gekregen	get
krimpen	kromp	gekrompen	shrink
kruipen	kroop	gekropen	creep
kunnen	kon	gekund	can
lachen	lachte	gelachen	laugh
laden	laadde	geladen	load
laten	liet	gelaten	let
lezen	las	gelezen	read
liegen	loog	gelogen	tell lies
liggen	lag	gelegen	lie
lijden	leed	geleden	suffer
lijken	leek	geleken	seem
lopen	liep	gelopen	walk
malen	maalde	gemalen	grind
meten	mat	gemeten	measure
moeten	moest	gemoeten	must
mogen	mocht	gemogen/gemoogd	may
nemen	nam	genomen	take
prijzen	prees	geprezen	praise
raden	raadde/ried	geraden	guess
rijden	reed	gereden	ride
rijgen	reeg	geregen	thread
rijzen	rees	gerezen	rise
roepen	riep	geroepen	call
ruiken	rook	geroken	smell
scheiden	scheidde	gescheiden	separate
schelden	schold	gescholden	call names
schenken	schonk	geschonken	pour
scheppen	schiep	geschapen	create
scheren	schoor	geschoren	shave
schieten	schoot	geschoten	shoot
schijnen	scheen	geschenen	shine, seem to be
schrijden	schreed	geschreden	stride
schrijven	schreef	geschreven	write
schrikken	schrok	geschrokken	be frightened

schuiven	schoof	geschoven	*shove*
slaan	sloeg	geslagen	*hit*
slapen	sliep	geslapen	*sleep*
slijpen	sleep	geslepen	*sharpen*
slijten	sleet	gesleten	*wear down*
sluipen	sloop	geslopen	*sneak*
sluiten	sloot	gesloten	*close*
smelten	smolt	gesmolten	*melt*
snijden	sneed	gesneden	*cut*
spinnen	spon	gesponnen	*spin*
splijten	spleet	gespleten	*split*
spreken	sprak	gesproken	*speak*
springen	sprong	gesprongen	*jump*
spuiten	spoot	gespoten	*squirt*
staan	stond	gestaan	*stand*
steken	stak	gestoken	*sting*
stelen	stal	gestolen	*steal*
sterven	stierf	gestorven	*die*
stijgen	steeg	gestegen	*rise*
stijven	steef	gesteven	*starch*
stinken	stonk	gestonken	*stink*
stoten	stootte/stiet	gestoten	*push*
strijden	streed	gestreden	*fight*
strijken	streek	gestreken	*iron*
treden	trad	getreden	*tread*
treffen	trof	getroffen	*hit*
trekken	trok	getrokken	*pull*
vallen	viel	gevallen	*fall*
vangen	ving	gevangen	*catch*
varen	voer	gevaren	*sail*
vechten	vocht	gevochten	*fight*
verbergen	verborg	verborgen	*hide*
verdwijnen	verdween	verdwenen	*disappear*
vergeten	vergat	vergeten	*forget*
verliezen	verloor	verloren	*lose*
vermijden	vermeed	vermeden	*avoid*
verslinden	verslond	verslonden	*devour*
vinden	vond	gevonden	*find*
vliegen	vloog	gevlogen	*fly*
voortspruiten	sproot voort	voortgesproten	*result*
vouwen	vouwde	gevouwen	*fold*
vragen	vroeg	gevraagd	*ask*
vriezen	vroor	gevroren	*freeze*
waaien	waaide/woei	gewaaid	*blow*
wassen	waste	gewassen	*wash*
wegen	woog	gewogen	*weigh*
werpen	wierp	geworpen	*throw*
werven	wierf	geworven	*recruit*
weten	wist	geweten	*know*
weven	weefde	geweven	*weave*
wijken	week	geweken	*yield*

wijten	weet	geweten	*impute*
wijzen	wees	gewezen	*show*
willen	wilde/wou	gewild	*want*
winden	wond	gewonden	*wind*
winnen	won	gewonnen	*win*
worden	werd	geworden	*become*
wreken	wreekte	gewroken	*revenge*
wrijven	wreef	gewreven	*rub*
zeggen	zei	gezegd	*say*
zenden	zond	gezonden	*send*
zien	zag	gezien	*see*
zijn	was	geweest	*be*
zingen	zong	gezongen	*sing*
zinken	zonk	gezonken	*sink*
zinnen	zon	gezonnen	*brood*
zitten	zat	gezeten	*sit*
zoeken	zocht	gezocht	*seek*
zuigen	zoog	gezogen	*suck*
zullen	zou	—	*shall, will*
zwellen	zwol	gezwollen	*swell*
zwemmen	zwom	gezwommen	*swim*
1) zweren	zwoer	gezworen	*swear*
2) zweren	zweerde/zwoor	gezworen	*ulcerate*
zwerven	zwierf	gezworven	*wander*
zwijgen	zweeg	gezwegen	*be silent*

Dutch Abbreviations

A°	*anno*	(built) in the year
afd.	*afdeling*	department
alg.	*algemeen*	general
A.N.W.B.	*Algemene Nederlandse Wielrijdersbond*	Dutch Touring Association
a.s.	*aanstaande*	next
a.u.b.	*alstublieft*	please
Bfr.	*Belgische frank*	Belgian franc
b.g.	*begane grond*	ground floor
b.g.g.	*bij geen gehoor*	if no answer
blz.	*bladzijde*	page
B.R.T.	*Belgische Radio en Televisie*	Belgian Broadcasting Company
B.T.W.	*Belasting Toegevoegde Waarde*	VAT, value added tax
b.v.	*bijvoorbeeld*	e.g.
B.V.	*besloten vennootschap*	limited liability company
C.S.	*Centraal Station*	main railway station
ct.	*cent*	1/100 of the guilder
dhr.	*de heer*	Mr.
drs.	*doctorandus*	Master of Arts
d.w.z.	*dat wil zeggen*	i.e.
EEG	*Europese Economische Gemeenschap*	EEC, European Economic Community (Common Market)
E.H.B.O.	*Eerste Hulp bij Ongelukken*	first aid
enz.	*enzovoort*	etc.
excl.	*exclusief*	exclusive, not included
fl/f	*gulden*	guilder
geb.	*geboren*	born
H.K.H.	*Hare Koninklijke Hoogheid*	Her Royal Highness
H.M.	*Hare Majesteit*	His/Her Majesty
hs	*huis*	ground floor
incl.	*inclusief*	inclusive, included
i.p(l).v.	*in plaats van*	in the place of
ir.	*ingenieur*	engineer
jl.	*jongstleden*	last
K.A.C.B.	*Koninklijke Automobiel- club van België*	Royal Automobile Association of Belgium
km/u	*kilometer per uur*	kilometres per hour
K.N.A.C.	*Koninklijke Nederlandse Automobielclub*	Royal Dutch Automobile Association

K.N.M.I.	*Koninklijk Nederlands Meteorologisch Instituut*	Royal Dutch Meteorological Institute
m.a.w.	*met andere woorden*	in other words
Mej.	*mejuffrouw*	Miss
Mevr.	*mevrouw*	Mrs.
Mij.	*maatschappij*	company
Mr.	*meester in de rechten; mijnheer*	barrister, lawyer; Mr.
N.A.V.O.	*Noordatlantische Verdragsorganisatie*	NATO
N.B.T.	*Nederlands Bureau voor het Toerisme*	Dutch National Tourist Office
n.Chr.	*na Christus*	A.D.
nl.	*namelijk*	namely
n.m.	*namiddag*	afternoon
N.M.B.S.	*Nationale Maatschappij der Belgische Spoorwegen*	Belgian National Railways
N.P.	*niet parkeren*	no parking
N.S.	*Nederlandse Spoorwegen*	Dutch National Railways
N.V.	*naamloze vennootschap*	Ltd. or Inc.
p.a.	*per adres*	in care of
pk	*paardekracht*	horsepower
r.-k./R.-K.	*rooms-katholiek*	Roman Catholic
t.e.m.	*tot en met*	up to and including
t.o.v.	*ten opzichte van*	with regard to
v.a.	*volgens anderen, vanaf*	from
V.A.B.	*Vlaamse Automobilisten-bond*	Flemish Automobile Association
v.Chr.	*voor Christus*	B.C.
v.m.	*voormiddag*	morning
V.N.	*Verenigde Naties*	UN
V.S.	*Verenigde Staten*	USA
V.T.B.	*Vlaamse Toeristenbond*	Flemish Tourist Association
V.V.V.	*Vereniging voor Vreemdelingenverkeer*	tourist-information office
zgn.	*zogenaamd*	so-called
Z.K.H.	*Zijne Koninklijke Hoogheid*	His Royal Highness
z.o.z.	*zie ommezijde*	pto, please turn over

Numerals

Cardinal numbers		Ordinal numbers	
0	nul	1e	eerste
1	een	2e	tweede
2	twee	3e	derde
3	drie	4e	vierde
4	vier	5e	vijfde
5	vijf	6e	zesde
6	zes	7e	zevende
7	zeven	8e	achtste
8	acht	9e	negende
9	negen	10e	tiende
10	tien	11e	elfde
11	elf	12e	twaalfde
12	twaalf	13e	dertiende
13	dertien	14e	veertiende
14	veertien	15e	vijftiende
15	vijftien	16e	zestiende
16	zestien	17e	zeventiende
17	zeventien	18e	achttiende
18	achttien	19e	negentiende
19	negentien	20e	twintigste
20	twintig	21e	eenentwintigste
21	eenentwintig	22e	tweeëntwintigste
22	tweeëntwintig	23e	drieëntwintigste
23	drieëntwintig	24e	vierentwintigste
24	vierentwintig	25e	vijfentwintigste
30	dertig	26e	zesentwintigste
40	veertig	30e	dertigste
50	vijftig	40e	veertigste
60	zestig	50e	vijftigste
70	zeventig	60e	zestigste
80	tachtig	70e	zeventigste
90	negentig	80e	tachtigste
100	honderd	90e	negentigste
101	honderdeen	100e	honderdste
230	tweehonderddertig	101e	honderdeerste
1000	duizend	230e	tweehonderddertigste
1001	duizendeen	1000e	duizendste
1100	elfhonderd	1001e	duizendeerste
2000	tweeduizend	1100e	elfhonderdste
1 000 000	een miljoen	2000e	tweeduizendste

Time

Although official time in Holland and Belgium is based on the 24-hour clock, the 12-hour system is used in conversation.

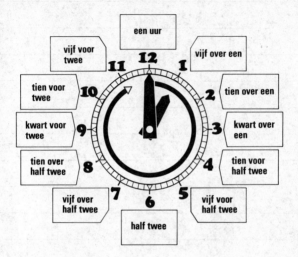

To avoid confusion, you can make use of the terms *'s morgens* (morning), and *'s middags* (afternoon) or *'s avonds* (evening).

Ik kom om vier uur 's morgens.	I'll come at 4 a.m.
Ik kom om vier uur 's middags.	I'll come at 4 p.m.
Ik kom om acht uur 's avonds.	I'll come at 8 p.m.

Days of the Week

zondag	Sunday	*donderdag*	Thursday
maandag	Monday	*vrijdag*	Friday
dinsdag	Tuesday	*zaterdag*	Saturday
woensdag	Wednesday		

Aantekeningen